Accounting
An Introduction

second edition

Accounting
An Introduction

Eddie McLaney
and
Peter Atrill

FT Prentice Hall
FINANCIAL TIMES

An imprint of **Pearson Education**
Harlow, England • London • New York • Boston • San Francisco • Toronto
Sydney • Tokyo • Singapore • Hong Kong • Seoul • Taipei • New Delhi
Cape Town • Madrid • Mexico City • Amsterdam • Munich • Paris • Milan

Pearson Education Limited
Edinburgh Gate
Harlow
Essex CM20 2JE
England

and Associated Companies throughout the world

Visit us on the World Wide Web at:
www.pearsoned.co.uk

───────────────

First published 1999 by Prentice Hall Europe
Second edition published 2002

© Prentice Hall Europe 1999
© Pearson Education Limited 2002

ISBN 0 273 65550 7

British Library Cataloguing-in-Publication Data
A catalogue record for this book is available from the British Library.

Library of Congress Cataloging-in-Publication Data

McLaney, E. J.
    Accounting : an introduction / Eddie McLaney & Peter Atrill.--2nd ed.
       p. cm.
    Includes bibliographical references and index.
    ISBN 0-273-65550-
       1. Accounting. I. Atrill, Peter. II. Title.

  HF5635 .M48833 2002
  657--dc21   2001033281

10 9 8 7 6 5 4
07 06 05 04 03

Typeset by 25 in Stone Serif.
Printed and bound in Great Britain by Ashford Colour Press Ltd., Gosport.

Brief contents

Brief Contents

Detailed contents

Part 2 Management accounting

Part 3   Financial management

Part 4 Supplementary information

Preface

This text provides a comprehensive introduction to financial accounting, management accounting and core elements of financial management. It is aimed primarily at students who are not majoring in accounting or finance but who are, nevertheless, studying introductory-level accounting and/or financial management as part of their course in business, economics, hospitality management, tourism, engineering or some other area. Students who are majoring in either accounting or finance should, however, find the book useful as an introduction to the main principles, which can serve as a foundation for further study. The text does not focus on the technical aspects, but rather examines the basic principles and underlying concepts, and the ways in which accounting statements and financial information can be used to improve the quality of management decision-making. To reinforce further this practical emphasis, there are, throughout the text, numerous illustrative extracts with commentary from company reports, survey data and other sources.

The text is written in an 'open-learning' style. This means that there are numerous integrated activities, worked examples and questions throughout the text to help you to understand the subject fully. You are expected to interact with the material and to check your progress continually. Irrespective of whether you are using the book as part of a taught course or for personal study, we have found that this approach is more 'user-friendly' and makes it easier for you to learn.

We recognise that most of you will not have studied accounting or finance before, and we have therefore tried to write in a concise and accessible style, minimising the use of technical jargon. We have also tried to introduce topics gradually, explaining everything as we go. Where technical terminology is unavoidable we try to provide clear explanations. In addition, you will find all the key terms highlighted in the text, and then listed at the end of each chapter with a page reference to help you rapidly revise the main techniques and concepts. All these key terms are also listed alphabetically with a concise definition in the glossary given in Appendix B towards the end of the book, thereby providing a convenient and single point of reference from which to revise.

A further important consideration in helping you to understand and absorb the topics covered is the design of the text itself. The page layout and colour scheme have been carefully considered to allow for the easy navigation and digestion of material. The layout features a large page format, an open design, and clear signposting of the various features and assessment material.

More detail about the nature and use of these features is given in the 'How to use this book' section below; and the main points are also summarised, using example pages from the text, in the Guided tour on pages xxii–xxiii hereafter.

How to use this book

We have organised the chapters to reflect what we consider to be a logical sequence and, for this reason, we suggest that you work through the text in the order in which it is presented. We have tried to ensure that earlier chapters do not refer to concepts or terms that are not explained until a later chapter. If you work through the chapters in the 'wrong' order, you will probably encounter concepts and terms that were explained previously.

Irrespective of whether you are using the book as part of a lecture/tutorial-based course or as the basis for a more independent mode of study, we advocate following broadly the same approach.

Integrated assessment material

Interspersed throughout each chapter are numerous **Activities**. You are strongly advised to attempt all these questions. They are designed to simulate the sort of quick-fire questions that your lecturer might throw at you during a lecture or tutorial. Activities serve two purposes:

- To give you the opportunity to check that you understand what has been covered so far.
- To encourage you to think about the topic just covered, either to see a link between that topic and others with which you are already familiar, or to link the topic just covered to the next.

The answer to each Activity is provided immediately after the question. This answer should be covered up until you have deduced your solution, which can then be compared with the one given.

Towards the middle/end of each chapter there is a **Self-assessment question**. This is more comprehensive and demanding than any of the Activities, and is designed to give you an opportunity to check and apply your understanding of the core coverage of the chapter. The solution to each of these questions is provided in Appendix C at the end of the book. As with the activities, it is important that you attempt each question thoroughly before referring to the solution. If you have difficulty with a self-assessment question, you should go over the relevant chapter again.

End-of-chapter assessment material

At the end of each chapter there are four **Review questions**. These are short questions requiring a narrative answer or discussion within a tutorial group. They are intended to help you assess how well you can recall and critically evaluate the core terms and concepts covered in each chapter. Answers to these questions are provided in a separate Instructors' Manual.

At the end of each chapter, except for Chapter 1, there are eight **Exercises**. These are mostly computational and are designed to reinforce your knowledge and understanding. Exercises are graded as 'more advanced' according to their level of difficulty. The basic-level questions are fairly straightforward; the more advanced ones can be quite demanding but are capable of being successfully completed if you have worked conscientiously through the chapter and have attempted the basic exercises. Solutions to five of the exercises in each chapter are provided in Appendix D at the end of the book; these five are identified by a coloured exercise number. Here, too, a thorough attempt should be made to answer each exercise before referring to the solution. Solutions to the other three exercises and to the review questions in each chapter are provided in a separate Instructors' Manual.

To familiarise yourself with the main features and how they will benefit your study from this text, an illustrated Guided tour is provided on pages xxii–xxiii.

● ● ● ● Content and structure

The text comprises 16 chapters organised into three core parts: financial accounting, management accounting and financial management. The market research for this text revealed a divergence of opinions, given the target market, on whether or not to include material on double-entry bookkeeping techniques. So as to not interrupt the flow and approach of the financial accounting chapters, Appendix A on recording financial transactions (including activities and exercise questions) has been placed in Part 4. A brief introductory outline of the coverage of each part and its component chapters is given in the opening double-page spread which precedes each part.

Guided tour

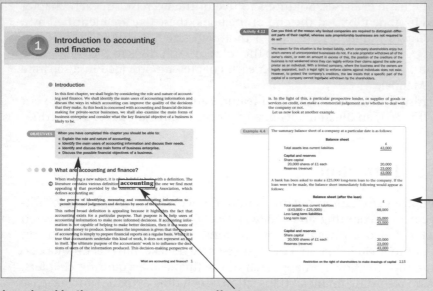

Activities
These short questions, integrated throughout each chapter, allow you to check your understanding as you progress through the text. They comprise either a narrative question requiring you to review or critically consider topics, or a numerical problem requiring you to deduce a solution. A suggested answer is given immediately after each activity.

Examples
At frequent intervals throughout most chapters, there are numerical examples that give you step-by-step workings to follow through to the solution.

Learning objectives
Bullet points at the start of each chapter highlight the core coverage in terms of the expected learning outcomes after completing each chapter.

Key terms
The key concepts and techniques in each chapter are colour-highlighted with an adjacent icon in the margin where they are first introduced, assisting you in navigating through the material.

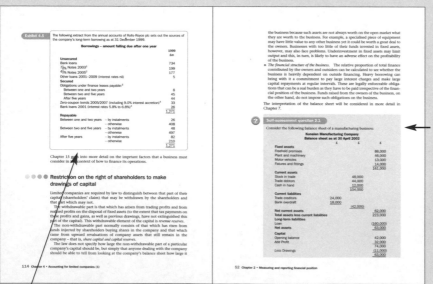

Self-assessment questions
Towards the end of most chapters you will encounter one of these questions, allowing you to attempt a comprehensive question before tackling the end-of-chapter assessment material. To check your understanding and progress, solutions are provided in Appendix C.

Exhibits
Integrated throughout the text, these illustrative examples highlight the practical application of accounting concepts and techniques by real companies, including extracts from company reports and accounts, survey data and other interesting insights from business.

Key terms summary

Each chapter ends with a chronological listing and page reference of all the key terms, enabling you to revise rapidly the key concepts and techniques covered.

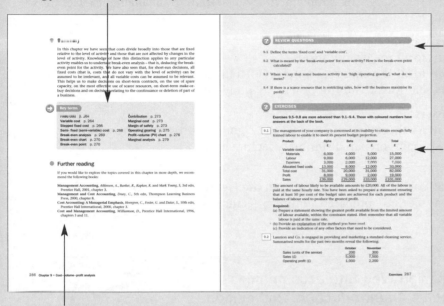

Review questions

These short questions encourage you to review and/or critically discuss your understanding of the main topics covered in each chapter, either individually or in a group.

Exercises

There are eight of these comprehensive questions at the end of most chapters. The more advanced questions are separately identified. Solutions to five of the questions are provided in Appendix D, enabling you to assess your progress.

Further reading

This section comprises a listing of relevant chapters in other textbooks that you might refer to in order to pursue a topic in more depth or gain an alternative perspective.

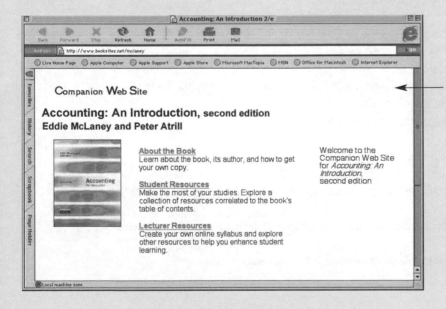

Companion Web Site

A Companion Web Site accompanies *Accounting: An Introduction*, offering valuable teaching and learning material for both lecturers and students.

● ● ● ● Supplements and website

A comprehensive range of supplementary materials is available to lecturers adopting this text.

- **Solutions Manual**
  - Solutions to all review questions.
  - Solutions to all the exercises not provided in the text.
  - Debriefs/solutions to all the case study problems.

- **OHP masters**
  - Over 150 A4 sheets comprising all the Figures and Exhibits from the text, as well as specially prepared summary lecture notes.

- **PowerPoint**
  - Over 150 colour slides comprising all the Figures and Exhibits from the text, as well as specially prepared summary lecture notes.

A Companion Web Site accompanies *Accounting: An Introduction*, 2nd edition by Eddie McLaney and Peter Atrill

Visit the *Accounting: An Introduction* Companion Web Site at www.booksites.net/atrillmclaney to find valuable teaching and learning material including:

For Students:
- Study material designed to help you improve your results
- Comprehensive learning objectives detailing what you need to know
- Multiple choice and short form questions to test your learning
- Links to relevant sites on the World Wide Web
- Extra case studies and questions.

For Lecturers:
- A secure, password protected site with teaching material
- A downloadable version of the full Instructors' Manual including solutions to questions
- A syllabus manager that will build and host your very own course web page.

Also: This regularly maintained site has search functions.

Acknowledgements

We should like to thank those lecturers who reviewed the first edition of the text and who made numerous useful comments. We believe that this second edition has benefited significantly from their help and advice.

We should also like to thank the Association of Chartered Certified Accountants for permission to include questions from the Certified Diploma in Finance and Accounting as well as those organisations that have allowed us to use extracts from accounts, news items and other material to help illustrate issues dealt with in the book.

Finally, we should like to thank Vera Iordanova Atrill for her help in developing the graphs and diagrams contained within the book.

Publisher's acknowledgements

We are grateful to the following for permission to reproduce copyright material:

Exhibit 2.3 from the 2000 annual report, Manchester United plc; Exhibit 3.4 from Ong, A. 'The problems of accounting for intangible assets in the food and drink industry' in Atrill, P. and Lindley, L. (Eds.), *Issues in Accounting and Finance*, 1997, Ashgate Publishing Ltd; Exhibit 4.4 from the balance sheet, 31 December 1999, Nichols plc; Exhibit 4.5 from the 1999 annual report Rolls Royce plc; Exhibit 5.2 from the balance sheet 31 December 1999, GlaxoSmithkline plc; Question 5.1 from the 2000 annual report, J. Sainsbury plc; Exhibit 7.4 from the 2000 annual report, Tate & Lyle plc; Exhibit 11.8 from 'Using the balanced scorecard as a strategic management system' by Robert Kaplan & David Norton, Vol. 76, January–February 1996, *Harvard Business Review*, © 1996 by the President and Fellows of Harvard College, all rights reserved; Exhibit 12.4 from *Financial Management and Working Capital Practices in UK SMEs*, by Chittenden, F., Poutziouris, P. and Michaelis, N., 1998, reprinted by permission of Manchester Business School.

Chartered Institute of Management Accountants for an extract from 'Beyond Budgeting' by J. Hope and R. Fraser, published in *Management Accounting*, January 1999; Harvard Business School Publishing for an extract from *The Balanced Scorecard* by Robert S. Kaplan and David P. Norton, Boston: Harvard Business School Press, 1996, p. 1, © 1996 by the Harvard Business School Publishing Corporation, all rights reserved; Kingfisher plc for an extract from their 2000 *Annual Report*; Monsoon plc for extracts from their 2000 *Annual Report*; and National Express Group plc for an extract from their 1999 *Annual Report*.

Whilst every effort has been made to trace the owners of copyright material, in a few cases this has proved impossible and we take this opportunity to offer our apologies to any copyright holders whose rights we may have unwittingly infringed.

1 Introduction to accounting and finance

Introduction

In this first chapter, we shall begin by considering the role and nature of accounting and finance. We shall identify the main users of accounting information and discuss the ways in which accounting can improve the quality of the decisions that they make. As this book is concerned with accounting and financial decision-making for private-sector businesses, we shall also examine the main forms of business enterprise and consider what the key financial objective of a business is likely to be.

OBJECTIVES When you have completed this chapter you should be able to:

- Explain the role and nature of accounting.
- Identify the main users of accounting information and discuss their needs.
- Identify and discuss the main forms of business enterprise.
- Discuss the possible financial objectives of a business.

What are accounting and finance?

When studying a new subject, it is often helpful to begin with a definition. The literature contains various definitions of **accounting**, but the one we find most appealing is that provided by the American Accounting Association, which defines accounting as:

> the process of identifying, measuring and communicating information to permit informed judgements and decisions by users of the information.

This rather broad definition is appealing because it highlights the fact that accounting exists for a particular purpose. That purpose is to help users of accounting information to make more informed decisions. If accounting information is not capable of helping to make better decisions, then it is a waste of time and money to produce. Sometimes the impression is given that the purpose of accounting is simply to prepare financial reports on a regular basis. Whilst it is true that accountants undertake this kind of work, it does not represent an end in itself. The ultimate purpose of the accountants' work is to influence the decisions of users of the information produced. This decision-making perspective of accounting is a major theme of this book and will shape the way in which we deal with each topic.

Finance, like accounting, exists to help decision makers. It is concerned with the way in which funds for a business are raised and invested. A business is basically an organisation that raises funds from investors (owners and lenders) and then uses these funds to make investments (equipment, premises, stocks and so on) in order to make the business, and its owners, more wealthy. Raising and investing funds are import decision-making areas, as they often involve large amounts of money and require relatively long-term commitments. Finance should help decision makers to evaluate the different forms in which funds may be raised. It is important that funds are raised in a way that is appropriate to the particular needs of the business. Finance should also help decision makers to ensure that funds are properly managed, and that they are invested in a way that will provide the business with a worthwhile return.

Who are the users?

For accounting information to be useful, an accountant must be clear about *for whom* the information is being prepared and *for what purpose* the information will be used. There are likely to be various user groups with an interest in a particular organisation, in the sense of needing to make decisions about that organisation. The most important groups that use accounting information about private-sector businesses are shown in Figure 1.1.

Figure 1.1

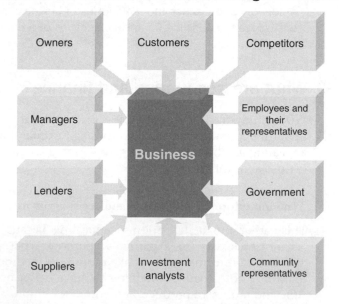

Main users of financial information relating to a business

Owners | Customers | Competitors

Managers | **Business** | Employees and their representatives

Lenders | | Government

Suppliers | Investment analysts | Community representatives

The figure shows that there are several user groups with an interest in the accounting information relating to a business. The majority of these are outside the business but nevertheless they have a stake in the business. This is not meant to be an exhaustive list of potential users, however, the user groups identified are normally the most important.

Why do each of the user groups identified in Figure 1.1 need accounting information relating to a business?

Your answer may be as follows:

User group	Use
Customers	To assess the ability of the business to continue in business and to supply the needs of the customers.
Competitors	To assess the threat to sales and profits posed by those businesses. To provide a benchmark against which the competitor's performance can be measured.
Employees (non-management)	To assess the ability of the business to continue to provide employment and to reward employees for their labour.
Government	To assess how much tax the business should pay, whether it complies with agreed pricing policies and whether financial support is needed.
Community representatives	To assess the ability of the business to continue to provide employment for the community and to purchase community resources. To assess whether the business could help fund environmental improvements.
Investment analysts	To assess the likely risks and returns associated with the business in order to determine its investment potential and to advise clients accordingly.
Suppliers	To assess the ability of the business to pay for the goods and services supplied.
Lenders	To assess the ability of the business to meet its obligations and to pay interest and to repay the amount borrowed.
Managers	To help make decisions and plans for the business and to exercise control so that the plans come to fruition.
Owners	To assess how effectively the managers are running the business and to make judgements about likely levels of risk and return in the future.

You may have thought of other reasons why each group would find accounting information useful.

The conflicting interests of users

There may be conflicts of interest arising between the various user groups over the ways in which the wealth of the business is generated and/or distributed. For example, a conflict of interest may arise between the managers and the owners of the business. Although managers are appointed to act on behalf of the owners, there is always a risk that they will put their own interests first. They may use the wealth of the business to furnish large offices, buy expensive cars or whatever. Accounting information has an important role to play in reporting the extent to which various groups have benefited from the business. Thus, owners may rely on accounting information to check whether the pay and benefits of managers are in line with agreed policy. A further example of potential conflict is between lenders and owners. There is a risk that the funds loaned to a business will be used for purposes that have not been agreed. Lenders may, therefore, rely on accounting information to check that the funds have been applied in an appropriate manner and that the terms of the loan agreement are being adhered to.

Not-for-profit organisations

Although the focus of this book is accounting as it relates to private sector-businesses, there are many organisations that exist with their prime purpose not being the pursuit of profit yet they produce accounting information for decision-making purposes. Examples of such organisations include charities, clubs and associations, universities, local government authorities, churches and trade unions. Accounting information about these types of organisation is needed by user groups. These groups are often the same as, or similar to, those identified for private-sector businesses. These groups may have a stake in the future viability of an organisation and may use accounting information to check that its wealth is being properly controlled and used in a way that is consistent with the objectives of the organisation.

How useful is accounting information?

No one would seriously claim that accounting information fully meets the needs of the various user groups identified. Accounting is a developing subject and we still have much to learn about user needs and the ways in which these needs should be met. Nevertheless, the information contained within accounting reports should reduce uncertainty in the minds of users over the financial position and performance of the business. It should help to answer questions concerning the availability of cash to pay owners a return for their investment or to repay loans, and so on. Often, there is no close substitute for the information contained within accounting reports and so the reports are usually regarded as more useful than other sources of information that are available regarding the financial health of a business.

What other sources of information might users employ to gain an impression of the financial position and performance of a business? What kind of information might be gleaned from these sources?

Other sources of information available include:

- Meetings with managers of the business
- Public announcements made by the business
- Newspaper and magazine articles
- Radio and TV reports
- Information-gathering agencies (for example, Dun and Bradstreet)
- Industry reports
- Economy-wide reports.

These sources can provide information on various aspects of the business, such as new products or services being offered, management changes, new contracts offered or awarded, the competitive environment within which the business operates, the impact of new technology, changes in legislation, changes in interest rates and future levels of inflation. It should be said that the various sources of information identified are not really substitutes for accounting reports. Rather, they should be used in conjunction with the reports in order to obtain a clearer picture of the financial health of a business.

There is convincing evidence and arguments that accounting information is at least *perceived* as being useful to users. There has been a number of studies that ask users to rank the importance of accounting information in relation to other sources of information for decision-making purposes. Generally speaking, these studies have found that users rank accounting information more highly than other sources of information. There is also considerable evidence that businesses choose to produce accounting information for users that exceeds the minimum requirements imposed by accounting regulations (for example, businesses often produce a considerable amount of management accounting information, which is not required by any regulations). Presumably, the cost of producing this additional information is justified on the grounds that users believe that it is useful to them. Such evidence and arguments, however, leave unanswered the question as to whether the information produced is actually being used for decision-making purposes – that is, whether accounting information has a direct effect on *behaviour*.

It is normally very difficult to assess the impact of accounting on human behaviour, however, one situation arises where the impact of accounting information can be observed and measured. This is where the **shares** (that is, portions of ownership of a business) are traded on a stock exchange. The evidence reveals that, following an announcement concerning a business's accounting profits, the price and volume of its shares traded often change significantly. This suggests that investors change their views about the future prospects of the business as a result of this new information and that this, in turn, leads them either to buy or sell shares in the business.

Thus, we can see that there is evidence that accounting reports are perceived as being useful and are used for decision-making purposes. However, it is impossible to measure just how useful accounting reports really are to users. Accounting information will usually represent only one input to a particular decision and the precise weight attached to the accounting information by the decision maker and the benefits that flow as a result cannot be accurately assessed. We shall see below, however, that it is at least possible to identify the kinds of qualities that accounting information must possess in order to be useful. Where these qualities are lacking, the usefulness of the information will be diminished.

Accounting as a service function

One way of viewing accounting is as a form of service. Accountants provide economic information to their 'clients', who are the various users identified in Figure 1.1. The quality of the service provided will be determined by the extent to which the information needs of the various user groups have been met. It can be argued that, to be useful, accounting information should possess certain key 'qualitative' characteristics. These are:

- **Relevance**. Accounting information must have the ability to influence decisions. Unless this characteristic is present, there is really no point in producing the information. The information may be relevant to the prediction of future events (for example, in predicting how much profit is likely to be earned next year) or relevant in helping confirm past events (for example, in establishing how much profit was earned last year). The role of accounting in confirming past events is improtant because users often wish to check on the accuracy of earlier predictions that they have made.

- **Reliability**. Accounting should be free from significant errors or bias. It should be capable of being relied upon by users to represent what it is supposed to represent. Although both relevance and reliability are very important, the problem that we often face in accounting is that information that is highly relevant may not be very reliable, and that which is reliable may not be very relevant.

Activity 1.4

To illustrate this last point, let us assume that a manager is charged with selling a custom-built machine owned by the business and has recently received a bid for it. What information would be relevant to the manager when deciding whether to accept the bid? How reliable would that information be?

....

The manager would probably like to know the current market value of the machine in order to decide whether or not to accept the bid. The current market value would be highly relevant to the final decision, but it might not be very reliable because the machine is unique and there is likely to be little information concerning market values.

Where a choice has to be made between providing information that has either more relevance *or* more reliability, the maximisation of relevance should be the guiding rule.

- **Comparabilty**. This quality will enable users to identify changes in the business over time (for example, the trend in sales over the past five years), also to evaluate the performance of the business in relation to other similar businesses. Comparability is achieved by treating items that are basically the same in the same manner for measurement and presentation purposes, and by making clear the policies that have been adopted in measuring and presenting the information.

→ ● **Understandability**. Accounting reports should be expressed as clearly as possible and should be understood by those at whom the information is aimed.

Do you think that accounting reports should be understandable to those who have not studied accounting?

....

This may prove to be an impossible challenge for those preparing accounting reports. The complexity of financial events and transactions cannot normally be so easily reported. It is probably best that we regard accounting reports in the same way as we regard a piece of modern art (an interesting thought!). To understand both, we really have to do a bit of homework. Generally speaking, accounting reports assume that the user not only has a reasonable knowledge of business and accounting but is also prepared to invest some time in studying the reports.

→ ● **Materiality**. When preparing accounting reports, we should make sure that all material information is provided. Information will be regarded as material if it is likely to have an influence on the decisions made by users. If information is not regarded as material, it is best to exclude it from the reports as it will merely clutter up the reports and, perhaps, interfere with the users ability to interpret the financial results.

● ● ● ● Costs and benefits of accounting information

In the previous section, the five key characteristics of relevance, reliability, comparability, understandability and materiality were identified. However, there is a further key characteristic that is also very important. It is raised in Activity 1.6.

Suppose an item of information is capable of being provided. It is relevant to a particular decision; it is also reliable, comparable, understandable and material. Can you think of any good reason why, in practice, you might choose not to produce the information?

....

The reason that you may decide not to produce, or discover, the information is that you judge the cost of doing so to be greater than the potential benefit of having the information.

For example, suppose that you wish to buy a particular audio-cassette player, which you have seen in a local shop for sale at £20. You believe that other local shops may have the same model on offer for as little as £19. The only ways in which you can find out the prices at other shops are either to telephone them or visit them. Telephone calls cost money and involve some of your time. Visiting the shops may not involve the outlay of money, but more of your time will be involved. Is it worth the cost of finding out the price of the cassette player at various shops? The answer is, of course, that if the cost of discovering the price is less than the potential benefit, it is worth having that information. Supplying accounting information to users is similar.

Figure 1.2

Relationship between costs and the value of providing additional financial information

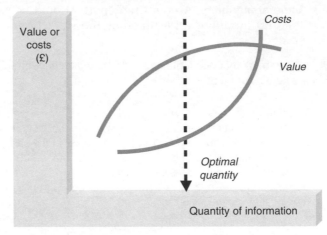

The figure shows how the benefits of financial information will eventually decline. The cost of providing information, however, will rise with each additional piece of information. The optimal level of information provision is where the gap between the value of the information and the costs of providing it is at its greatest.

In theory, financial information should be produced only if the cost of providing that piece of information is less than the benefit, or value, to be derived from its use. Figure 1.2 shows the relationship between the cost and value of providing additional financial information. The figure shows how the value of information received by the decision maker eventually begins to decline, perhaps because additional information becomes less relevant or because of the problems that a decision maker may have in processing the sheer quantity of information provided. The cost of providing the information, however, will increase with each additional piece of information. The point at which the gap between the value of information and the cost of providing that information is at its greatest (indicated in the figure by the dotted line) represents the optimal amount of information that can be provided. This theoretical model, however, poses a number of problems in practice, as discussed below.

The provision of accounting information can be very costly. However, the cost is often difficult to quantify. The direct, out-of-pocket costs such as the salaries of accounting staff are not really a problem, but these are only part of the total cost involved. There are also less-direct costs such as the cost of managers' time spent on analysing and interpreting the information contained within the reports. In addition, costs will also be incurred if the accounting information is used to the disadvantage of the business. For example, if suppliers were to discover from the accounting reports that the business is in a poor financial state, they may refuse to supply further goods or may impose strict conditions.

The economic benefit of having accounting information is even harder to assess. It is possible to apply some 'science' to the problem of weighing the costs and benefits (see Figure 1.3), but a lot of subjective judgement is likely to be involved. Although no one would seriously advocate that the typical business

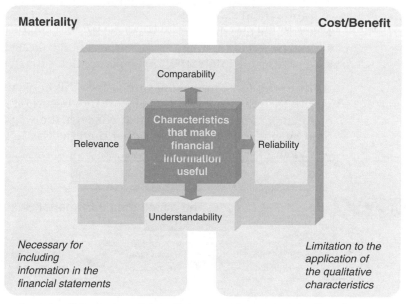

Figure 1.3

The characteristics that influence the usefulness of accounting information

Materiality

Cost/Benefit

Comparability

Characteristics that make financial information useful

Relevance

Reliability

Understandability

Necessary for including information in the financial statements

Limitation to the application of the qualitative characteristics

The figure shows that there are four main qualitative characteristics that influence the usefulness of accounting information. In addition, however, accounting information should be material and the benefits of providing the information should outweigh the costs.

should produce no accounting information, at the same time no one would advocate that every item of information that could be seen as possessing one or more of the key characteristics should be produced, irrespective of the cost of producing it.

When weighing the cost of providing additional financial information against the benefit, there is also the problem that those who bear the burden of the cost may not be the ones who benefit from the additional information. The cost of providing accounting information is usually borne by the owners, but other user groups may be the beneficiaries.

Accounting as an information system

We have already seen that accounting can be viewed as the provision of a service to 'clients'. Another way of viewing accounting is as part of the total information system within a business. Users, both inside and outside the business, have to make decisions concerning the allocation of scarce economic resources. To ensure that these resources are allocated in an efficient and effective manner, users require economic information on which to base decisions. It is the role of the accounting system to provide that information, and this will involve both information-gathering and communication.

The **accounting information system** is depicted in Figure 1.4. It has certain features that are common to all information systems within a business. These are:

- Identifying and capturing relevant information (in this case economic information).
- Recording the information collected in a systematic manner.
- Analysing and interpreting the information collected.
- Reporting the information in a manner that suits the needs of users.

Given the decision-making emphasis of this book, we shall be concerned primarily with the final two elements of the process – the analysis and reporting of financial information. We shall consider the way in which information is used by, and is useful to, users rather than the way in which it is identified and recorded.

Figure 1.4

The accounting information system

Information identification → Information recording → Information analysis → Information reporting

The figure shows the four sequential stages of an accounting information system. The first two stages are concerned with preparation, whereas the last two stages are concerned with using the information collected.

Financial and management accounting

Accounting is usually seen as having two distinct strands:

- **Management accounting**, which seeks to meet the needs of a business's managers.
- **Financial accounting**, which seeks to meet the accounting needs of all of the other users identified in Figure 1.1.

The differences between the two types of accounting reflect the different user groups that they address. Briefly, the major differences are as follows:

- *Nature of the reports produced.* Financial accounting reports tend to be general-purpose reports. That is, they contain financial information that will be useful for a broad range of users and decisions rather than being specifically designed for the needs of a particular group or set of decisions. Management accounting reports, on the other hand, are often specific-purpose reports. They are designed either with a particular decision in mind or for a particular manager.
- *Level of detail.* Financial accounting reports provide users with a broad overview of the position and performance of a business for a period. As a result, information is aggregated and detail is often lost. Management accounting reports, however, often provide managers with considerable detail to help them with a particular operational decision.

- *Regulations.* Financial reports, for many businesses, are subject to accounting regulations that exist to try to ensure that they are produced according to a standardised format. These regulations are imposed by law and the accounting profession. Because management accounting reports are for internal use only, there is no regulation from external sources concerning their form and content; they can be designed to meet the needs of particular managers.
- *Reporting interval.* For most businesses, financial accounting reports are produced on an annual basis. However, large companies may produce semi-annual reports and a few produce quarterly reports. Management accounting reports may be produced as frequently as required by managers. In many businesses, managers are provided with certain reports on a daily, weekly or monthly basis, which allows them to check progress frequently.
- *Time horizon.* Financial accounting reports reflect the performance and position of the business for the past period. In essence, they are backward-looking. Management accounting reports, on the other hand, often provide information concerning future performance as well as past performance. It is an over-simplification, however, to suggest that financial accounting reports never incorporate expectations concerning the future; occasionally, businesses will release forecast information to other users in order to raise capital or to fight off unwanted takeover bids.
- *Range and quality of information.* Financial accounting reports concentrate on information that can be quantified in monetary terms. Management accounting also produces such reports, but is also more likely to produce reports that contain information of a non-financial nature, such as measures of physical quantities of stocks and output. Financial accounting places greater emphasis on the use of objective, verifiable evidence when preparing reports. Management accounting reports may use information that is less objective and verifiable in order to provide managers with the information that they require.

We can see from the above that management accounting is less constrained than financial accounting. It may draw from a variety of sources and use information that has varying degrees of reliability. The only real test to be applied when assessing the value of the information produced for managers is whether or not it improves the quality of decisions made.

Activity 1.7

Do you think a distinction between management accounting and financial accounting may be misleading? Is there any overlap between the information needs of managers and the needs of other users?

....

The distinction between management and financial accounting suggests that there are differences between the information needs of managers and those of other users. Although differences undoubtedly exist, there is also a good deal of overlap between these needs. For example, managers will, at times, be interested in receiving an historic overview of business operations of the sort provided to other users. Equally, the other users would be interested in receiving information relating to the future, such as the forecast level of profits, and non-financial information such as the state of the order book and product innovations.

The distinction between the two areas reflects, to some extent, the differences in access to financial information. Managers have much more control than other users over the form and content of information they receive. Other users have to rely on what managers are prepared to provide or what the financial reporting regulations state must be provided. Although the scope of financial accounting reports has increased over time, fears concerning loss of competitive advantage and of user ignorance concerning the reliability of forecast data have led businesses to resist providing other users with the detailed and wide-ranging information that is available to managers.

The changing nature of accounting

We are currently witnessing radical changes to both financial and management accounting. In the past, financial accounting has been criticised for lacking rules based on a clear theoretical framework. In addition, the accounting rules developed have been criticised for being too loose, for lacking consistency and for failing to portray economic reality. These weaknesses have been highlighted by a number of financial scandals over the years. The accounting profession has responded by trying to develop a framework that provides a clearer rationale for the subject and for the way in which accounting information is prepared and presented. This framework tries to address fundamental questions such as: 'What is the nature and purpose of accounting?', 'Who are the users of financial reports?', and 'What kinds of financial report should be prepared and what should they contain?' Although much work has still to be done, by answering these questions we shall have the foundations necessary to develop accounting rules and practices in a more logical and consistent manner. This framework is considered in more detail in Chapter 5.

Management accounting has also been confronted with radical change. The environment in which businesses operate has become increasingly turbulent and competitive, and there have been rapid advances in production technology. These developments have, in turn, resulted in radical changes to the way in which businesses are organised and to the marketing and manufacturing strategies employed. Increasingly, successful businesses are distinguished by their ability to secure and maintain competitive advantage. In the face of such changes, management accounting has had to develop new approaches. In order to provide relevant information to managers, it has had to become more outward looking. In the past, information supplied to managers has been largely restricted to that collected within the business. Increasingly, however, information relating to market share, innovations, customer evaluation of services provided, and costs of production compared with those of competitors is supplied to managers in many businesses. Changes in the environment have also created a need to develop more sophisticated methods of measuring and controlling costs. Businesses can no longer risk the damage to competitive advantage that might occur where decisions are based on inaccurate and misleading information, particularly when information technology can now help to provide sophisticated costing systems at relatively low cost.

Nowadays, we have a more questioning attitude to conventional rules and methods, and the result is that the boundaries of accounting are being redrawn.

The changes that have taken place in recent years, and those that are currently taking place, are largely in response to changes in the external environment in which accounting exists. Given the increasing rate of change in the external environment, accounting is likely to change at an even faster pace in the future.

Why do I need to study accounting and finance?

At this point you may be asking yourself 'Why do I need to study accounting and finance? I don't intend to become an accountant!' Well, from the explanation of what accounting and finance is about, which was given earlier in the chapter, it should be clear that the accounting/finance function within an organisation is a central part of its management-information system. On the basis of information provided by the system, managers make decisions concerning the allocation of resources. Such decisions can have a profound effect on all those connected with the organisation. It is important, therefore, that *all* those who intend to work in organisations should have a fairly clear idea of certain important aspects of accounting and finance. These aspects include:

- How financial reports should be read and interpreted.
- How financial plans are made.
- How investment decisions are made.
- How businesses are financed.

Many, perhaps most, students have a career goal of being a manager within an organisation – perhaps a personnel manager, a marketing manager or an IT manager. If you are one of these students, an understanding of accounting and finance is very important. When you become a manager, even a junior one, it is almost certain that you will have to use financial reports to help you to carry out your management tasks. It is equally certain that it is largely on the basis of financial information and reports that your performance as a manager will be judged.

As a manager, it is likely that you will be expected to help in forward planning for the organisation. This will often involve the preparation of forecast financial statements and the setting of financial targets.

If you do not understand what the financial statements really mean and the extent to which the financial information is reliable, you will find yourself at a distinct disadvantage to others who know their way round the system. As a manager, you will also be expected to help decide how the limited resources available to your organisation should be allocated between competing options. This will require an ability to evaluate the costs and benefits of the different options available. Once again, an understanding of accounting and finance is important to carrying out this management task.

This is not to say that you cannot be an effective and successful personnel, marketing or computing manager unless you are a qualified accountant as well. It does mean, however, that you need to be a bit 'streetwise' in accounting and finance in order to succeed. This book is aimed at giving you just that.

Scope of this book

This book covers both financial accounting and management accounting topics. Broadly speaking, the next six chapters (Part 1, Chapters 2 to 7) are concerned with financial accounting topics, and the six thereafter (Part 2, Chapters 8 to 13) with management accounting topics. Part 3 of this book, comprising Chapters 14 to 16, is concerned with the **financial management** of the business. That is, the chapters examine issues relating to the financing and investing activities of the business. Accounting information is usually vitally important for these kinds of decisions.

Forms of business unit

Businesses may be classified according to their form of ownership. The particular classification has important implications when accounting for businesses – as we shall see in later chapters – and so it is useful to be clear about the main forms of ownership that can arise.

There are basically three arrangements:

- Sole proprietorship
- Partnership
- Limited company.

Sole proprietorship

Sole proprietorship, as the name suggests, is where an individual is the sole owner of a business. This type of business is often quite small in terms of size (as measured, for example, by sales generated or number of staff employed), however, the number of such businesses is very large indeed. Examples of sole-proprietor businesses can be found in most industrial sectors but particularly within the service sector. Hence, services such as electrical repairs, picture framing, photography, driving instruction, retail shops and hotels have a large proportion of sole-proprietor businesses. The sole-proprietor business is easy to set up. No formal procedures are required and operations can often commence immediately (unless special permission is required because of the nature of the trade or service, such as running licensed premises). The owner can decide the way in which the business is to be conducted and has the flexibility to restructure or dissolve the business whenever it suits. The law does not recognise the sole-proprietor business as being separate from the owner, and so the business will cease on the death of the owner. Although the owner must produce accounting information to satisfy the taxation authorities, there is no legal requirement to produce accounting information relating to the business for other user groups. However, some user groups may demand accounting information about the business and may be in a position to have their demands met (for example, lenders requiring accounting information on a regular basis as a condition of a loan.) The sole proprietor will have unlimited liability which means that no distinction will be made between the proprietor's personal wealth and that of the business if there are business debts that must be paid.

Partnership

A **partnership** exists where there are at least two individuals – but usually no more than 20 – carrying on a business together with the intention of making a profit. Partnerships have much in common with sole-proprietor businesses. They are often quite small in size (although partnerships of accountants and solicitors can be large as they are permitted to have more than 20 partners). Partnerships are also easy to set up as no formal procedures are required (and it is not even necessary to have a written agreement between the partners). The partners can agree whatever arrangements suit them concerning the financial and management aspects of the business, and the partnership can be restructured or dissolved by agreement between the partners.

Partnerships are not recognised in law as separate entities and so contracts with third parties must be entered into in the name of individual partners. The partners of a business usually have unlimited liability, although it is possible to grant limited liability to partners who have no say in the running of the business.

Activity 1.8

What are the main advantages and disadvantages that should be considered when deciding between a sole proprietorship and a partnership?

The main advantages of a partnership over a sole-proprietor business are:

- Sharing the burden of ownership.
- The opportunity to specialise rather than cover the whole range of services (for example, a doctors' practice).
- The ability to raise capital where this is beyond the capacity of a single individual.
- The ability to limit the liability of owners who are not engaged in running the business.

The main disadvantages of a partnership compared with a sole proprietorship are:

- The risks of sharing ownership of a business with unsuitable individuals.
- The limits placed on individual decision making that a partnership will impose.

Limited company

Limited companies can range in size from quite small to very large. The number of individuals who subscribe capital and become the owners may be unlimited, which provides the opportunity to create a very large-scale business. The liability of owners, however, is limited (hence 'limited' company), which means that those individuals subscribing capital to the company are liable only for debts incurred by the company up to the amount that they have agreed to invest. This cap on the liability of the owners is designed to limit risk and to produce greater confidence to invest. Without such limits on owner liability, it is difficult to see how a modern capitalist economy could operate. In many cases, the owners of a limited company are not involved in the day-to-day running of the business and will only invest in a business if there is a clear limit set on the level of investment risk.

The benefit of limited liability, however, imposes certain obligations on such a company. To start up a limited company, documents of incorporation must be prepared that set out, amongst other things, the objectives of the business. Furthermore, a framework of regulations exists that places obligations on the way in which such a company conducts its affairs. Part of this regulatory framework requires annual financial reports to be made available to owners and lenders and an annual general meeting of the owners to be held to approve the reports. In addition, a copy of the annual financial reports must be lodged with the Registrar of Companies for public inspection. In this way, the financial affairs of a limited company enter the public domain. With the exception of small companies, there is also a requirement for the annual financial reports to be subject to an audit. This involves an independent firm of accountants examining the annual reports and underlying records to see whether the reports provide a true and fair view of the financial health of the company and whether they comply with the relevant accounting rules established by law and by the accounting profession.

The features of limited companies will be considered in more detail in Chapter 4.

| Activity 1.9 | What are the main advantages and disadvantages that should be considered when deciding between a partnership business and a limited liability company? |

The main advantages of a partnership over a limited company are:

- The ease of setting up the business.
- The degree of flexibility concerning the way in which the business is conducted.
- The degree of flexibility concerning restructuring and dissolution of the business.
- Freedom from administrative burdens imposed by law (for example, the annual general meeting and the need for an independent audit).

The main disadvantages of a partnership compared with a limited company are:

- Restrictions placed on the number of partners, which can limit the ability to raise capital.
- The fact that it is not possible to limit the liability of owners who play an active part in running the business.

In this book we shall be concentrating on the accounting aspects of limited liability companies, because this type of business is by far the most important in economic terms. However, the accounts of limited companies are more complex than those of partnerships and sole proprietorships and so it is not really a good idea to introduce the basic principles of accounting using examples based on this form of business unit. The early chapters will, therefore, introduce accounting concepts through examples based on sole-proprietor businesses, this being the simplest form of business unit. Once we have dealt with the basic accounting principles, which are the same for all three types of business, we can then go on to see how they are applied to limited companies.

● ● ● ● Business objectives

Throughout this book we shall assume that increasing the wealth of the owners is the principal financial objective of a business. In order to justify this assumption, we shall briefly consider other financial objectives that have been identified by various commentators as likely practical targets for businesses. We shall then expand on the wealth enhancement objective a little more.

Popular suggested objectives include the following:

1. *Maximisation of sales revenue.* Most businesses seek to sell as many of their goods or services as possible. As a business objective, however, it is far from adequate. Almost any business could sell enormous quantities of goods and/or services if it were to lower its prices to gain market share. This may, however, lead to the business collapsing as a result of the sales revenues being insufficient to cover the costs of running the business.

2. *Maximisation of profit.* This is probably an improvement on sales maximisation because it takes account both of sales revenues and of expenses. It is probably also too limited as a business goal.

Activity 1.10

Can you think of any reasons why making the maximum possible profit this year may not be in the best interests of the business and those who are involved with it?

....

The reasons that we thought of are:

- *Risk.* The profit may be achieved by taking large risks, like not having expensive quality-control mechanisms. This may make the business profitable, but it could lead to disaster sooner or later.
- *Short termism.* Concentrating on the short term and ignoring the long term may lead to immediate profits. For example, cutting out spending on things that are likely to pay off in the longer term, such as research and development, and training, can have immediate short-term benefits at the expense of longer-term ones.
- *Size of the investment required.* Expanding the business, through increased investment, could lead to higher profit, but the benefits of the investment may diminish with each additional amount invested.

---

3. *Maximisation of return on investment.* This suggestion overcomes the last of the three objections to the profit-maximisation suggestion raised in Activity 1.10, since it takes account both of the level of profit and of the investment made to achieve it. It still suffers, however, from the risk and short-termist weaknesses of profit maximisation.

4. *Survival.* Businesses obviously aim to survive, however, this is unlikely to be enough, except in exceptional short-term circumstances. Businesses must normally have a more challenging reason for their existence.

5. *Long-term stability.* Though businesses may pursue this goal to some extent, it is not a primary objective for most businesses in that, like survival, it is insufficiently challenging.

6. *Growth.* This is probably fairly close to what most businesses seek to do. This objective seeks to strike a balance between long-term and short-term benefits. It also encompasses survival and, probably, long-term stability. 'Growth' in itself is probably not specific enough to act as a suitable target. Is any level of growth acceptable or is it to be a specific level of growth? Is it growth of profits, growth of assets or, perhaps, growth of something else?

7. *'Satisficing'.* It has been argued that all of the other suggested objectives are too much concerned with profits and the welfare of the owners of the business. The business can be seen as an alliance of various 'stakeholders', which includes not only owners but also employees, suppliers, customers and the community in which the business operates. Thus, it is suggested, the objective should be not to maximise the returns of any one of these stakeholders, but to try to give all of them a satisfactory return (known as 'satisficing'). It is difficult to argue with this general principle, but it is not clear how this can be stated as a practical touchstone for making business decisions.

8. *Enhancement/maximisation of the wealth of the owners.* This means that the business would take decisions such that the owners would be worth more as a result of the decision. When valuing businesses, people logically tend to take account of future profitability, both long-term and short-term, and of the risk attaching to future profits. Thus, all of the valuable features of suggestions 1 to 6 above are taken into account by this wealth-enhancement objective.

It can also be argued that this objective has the maximum potential to satisfy all the stakeholders (suggestion 7) as it can be said that any decision that fails to consider the position of the various stakeholders could be a bad one from a wealth-enhancement point of view. For example, a decision that led to customers being exploited and not getting a satisfactory deal would pretty certainly not be one that would have a wealth-enhancing effect for the owners. This is because disenchanted customers would avoid dealing with the business in future and would, possibly, influence others to do the same.

Although wealth enhancement of owners may not be a perfect description of what businesses seek to achieve, it is certainly something that businesses cannot ignore. Unless the owners feel that their wealth is being enhanced, there would be little reason for them to continue the business.

For the remainder of this book we shall treat enhancement/maximisation of owner wealth as the key objective against which decisions will be assessed. There will usually be other non-financial or non-economic factors that also tend to bear on decisions. The final decision may well involve some compromise.

● Summary

This chapter has identified the main users of accounting and examined their information needs. We have seen that accounting exists in order to improve the quality of economic decisions made by users. Unless accounting information fulfils this purpose, it has no real value. We have considered two views of accounting that help us to understand its essential features. The first view is that accounting is a form of service and that the information provided should contain certain key characteristics or qualities to ensure its usefulness. The second view is that accounting can be seen as part of the total information system of a business, which is concerned with identifying, recording, analysing and reporting economic information. These two views are not competing views of the subject; by embracing both views we can achieve a better understanding of the nature and role of accounting.

We have seen that accounting has two distinct strands, management accounting and financial accounting. Closely linked to accounting is financial management. This deals with decision making in the areas of investment and funding.

Finally, we considered the three main forms of business enterprise and discussed the kinds of financial objective that have been suggested for businesses. We have argued that enhancement/maximisation of owner wealth is the key objective against which managers' actions and decisions will be assessed.

Key terms

Accounting p. 1	Accounting information system p. 10
Finance p. 2	Management accounting p. 10
Share p. 5	Financial accounting p. 10
Relevance p. 6	Financial management p. 14
Reliability p. 6	Sole proprietorship p. 14
Comparability p. 6	Partnership p. 15
Understandability p. 7	Limited company p. 15
Materiality p. 7	

Further reading

If you would like to explore the topics covered in this chapter in more depth, we recommend the following books:

Financial Accounting, *Bebbington J., Gray R. and Laughlin R.*, 3rd edn, Thomson Learning, 2001, chapter 1.

Management Accounting, *Atkinson, A., Banker, R., Kaplan, R. and Mark Young, S.*, 3rd edn, Prentice Hall International, 2001, chapter 1.

Fundamentals of Corporate Finance, *Brealey, R., Myers, S. and Marcus, A.*, 2nd edn, McGraw Hill, 1999, chapter 1.

Financial Accounting and Reporting, *Elliott, B. and Elliott, J.*, 5th edn, Financial Times Prentice Hall, 2001, chapter 1.

Accounting Theory: Text and readings, *Schroeder, R. and Clark, M.*, 5th edn, Wiley, 1995, chapter 1.

1.1 Identify the main users of accounting information for a university. Do these users, or the way in which they use accounting information, differ very much from the users of accounting information for private-sector businesses?

1.2 Management accounting has been described as 'the eyes and ears of management'. What do you think this expression means?

1.3 Financial accounting statements tend to reflect past events. In view of this, how can they be of any help to a user in making a decision when decisions, by their very nature, can only be made about future actions?

1.4 'Accounting information should be understandable. As some users of accounting information have a poor knowledge of accounting, we should produce simplified financial reports to help them.' To what extent do you agree with this view?

PART 1

Financial accounting

Part 1 of this book deals with the area of accounting and finance usually referred to as 'financial accounting'. Here we shall introduce the three principal financial statements:

- Balance sheet
- Profit and loss account
- Cash flow statement.

In Chapter 2, these three statements are briefly reviewed to explain their nature and purpose, before we go on to consider the balance sheet in more detail. Included in our consideration of the balance sheet will be an introduction to the conventions of accounting – 'conventions' are the rules that accountants tend to follow when preparing financial statements. Chapter 3 introduces the second of the major financial statements, the profit and loss account. Here we shall be looking at such issues as how profit is measured and the point in time at which we recognise that a profit has been made. We shall also consider some accounting conventions that are used when preparing the profit and loss account.

The most important business form in the UK is the limited company, and in Chapters 4 and 5 we focus on accounting specifically for companies. There is nothing in essence that makes companies different from other types of private-sector business in the accounting area, but there some points of detail that we need to consider. Chapter 5 deals specifically with companies reporting to their shareholders and with public accountability. Here we shall consider the framework of principles that has been proposed to guide the preparation of financial reports. We shall also review the current set of regulations surrounding the preparation of company accounts.

Chapter 6 deals with the last of the three principal financial statements, the cash flow statement. This document is viewed as an important supplement to the other two statements because it identifies from where the business obtained cash and how the cash was used during an accounting period.

Reading the three statements will provide information about the businesses performance for the period concerned. It is possible, however, to gain even more helpful insights to the business by analysing the statements, using financial ratios and other techniques. Combining two figures from the accounts in a ratio, and comparing this with a similar ratio for, say, another business, can often tell us much more than just reading the figures themselves. Chapter 7 is concerned with techniques for analysing financial statements.

Measuring and reporting financial position

Introduction

We begin this chapter by providing an overview of the major financial statements. We shall see how each of these statements contributes towards providing users with a picture of the financial position and performance of a business. We shall then turn our attention towards a detailed examination of one of these financial statements – the balance sheet. We shall examine the principles underpinning this statement and see how it is prepared. We shall also consider its value for decision-making purposes.

OBJECTIVES   When you have completed this chapter you should be able to:

- Explain the nature and purpose of the major financial statements.
- Prepare a balance sheet and interpret the information contained within it.
- Discuss the accounting conventions underpinning the balance sheet.
- Identify the limitations of the balance sheet in portraying financial position.

The major financial statements – an overview

The major financial statements are designed to provide a picture of the overall financial position and performance of the business. To provide this overall picture, the accounting system will normally produce three major financial statements on a regular basis. These are concerned with answering the following:

- What cash movements took place over a particular period?
- How much wealth (that is, profit) was generated by the business over a particular period?
- What is the accumulated wealth of the business at the end of a particular period?

These questions are addressed by the three financial statements, each of which deals with one of them. The financial statements produced are:

- **The cash flow statement**
- **The profit and loss account**
- **The balance sheet.**

When taken together, they provide an overall picture of the financial health of a business.

Perhaps the best way to introduce the financial statements is to look at an example of a very simple business. From this we shall be able to see the sort of information that each of the statements can usefully provide. We can see from the financial statements in the example that each provides part of a picture which sets out the financial performance and position of the business. We begin

Example 2.1

Paul was unemployed and was unable to find a job. He therefore decided to embark on a business venture. Christmas was approaching and so he decided to buy gift-wrapping paper from a local supplier and sell it on the corner of his local high street. He felt that the price of wrapping paper in the high street shops was excessive and that this provided him with a useful business opportunity.

He began the venture with £40 in cash. On the first day of trading he purchased wrapping paper for £40 and sold three-quarters of his stock for £45 cash.

● **What cash movements took place in the first day of trading?**
On the first day of trading a cash flow statement, showing the cash movements for the day, can be prepared as follows:

Cash flow statement for day 1

	£
Opening balance (cash introduced)	40
Proceeds from sale of wrapping paper	45
	85
Cash paid to purchase wrapping paper	(40)
Closing balance	45

(Note that a bracket round a figure as shown with the second £40 here, means that it is to be deducted. This is common in accounting statements, and we shall tend to use it throughout the book.)

● **How much wealth (profit) was generated by the business in the first day of trading?**
A profit and loss account can be prepared to show the wealth (profit) generated on the first day. The wealth generated will represent the difference between the value of the sales made and the cost of the goods (the wrapping paper) sold:

Profit and loss account for day 1

	£
Sales	45
Cost of goods sold ($\frac{3}{4}$ of £40)	(30)
Profit	15

Note that it is only the *cost* of the wrapping sold that is matched against the sales in order to find the profit, and not the whole of the cost of wrapping paper acquired. Any unsold stock (in this case $\frac{1}{4}$ of £40 = £10) will be charged against future sales of that stock.

● **What is the accumulated wealth at the end of the first day?**
To establish the accumulated wealth at the end of the first day, we can draw up a balance sheet. This will list the resources held at the end of the day:

Balance sheet at the end of day 1

	£
Cash (closing balance)	45
Stock of goods for resale ($\frac{1}{4}$ of £40)	10
Total business wealth	55

by showing the cash movements. Cash is a vital resource that is necessary for any business to function effectively. Cash is required to meet maturing obligations and to acquire other resources (such as stock). Cash has been described as the lifeblood of a business and movements in cash usually attract scrutiny by users of financial statements.

It is clear, however, that reporting cash movements alone would not be enough to portray the financial health of the business. The changes in cash over time do not give an insight into the profit generated. The profit and loss account provides information on this aspect of performance. For day 1 in Example 2.1, we saw that the cash balance increased by £5, but the profit generated, as shown in the profit and loss account, was £15. The cash balance did not increase by the amount of the profit made because part of the wealth generated (£10) was held in the form of stock.

To gain an insight to the total wealth of the business, a balance sheet is drawn up at the end of the day. Cash is only one form in which wealth can be held. In the case of this business, wealth is also held in the form of a stock of goods for resale. Hence, when drawing up the balance sheet for our example, both forms of wealth held will be listed. In the case of a large business, there will be many other forms in which wealth will be held, such as land and buildings, equipment and motor vehicles.

Let us now continue with our example.

Example 2.2

On the second day of trading, Paul purchased more wrapping paper for £20 cash. He managed to sell all of the new stock and half of the earlier stock for a total of £38.

The cash flow statement on day 2 will be as follows:

Cash flow statement for day 2

	£
Opening balance (from day 1)	45
Cash proceeds from sale of wrapping paper	38
	83
Cash paid to purchase wrapping paper	(20)
Closing balance	63

The profit and loss account for day 2 will be as follows:

Profit and loss account for day 2

	£
Sales	38
Cost of goods sold (£20 + $\frac{1}{2}$ of £10)	(25)
Profit	13

The balance sheet at the end of day 2 will be thus:

Balance sheet at the end of day 2

	£
Cash	63
Stock of goods for resale ($\frac{1}{2}$ of £10)	5
Total business wealth	68

We can see that the total business wealth had increased to £68 by the end of day 2. This represents an increase of £13 (that is, £68 – £55) over the previous day – which, of course, is the amount of profit made during day 2 as shown on the profit and loss account.

Activity 2.1

On the third day of his business venture, Paul purchased more stock for £46 cash. However, it was raining hard for much of the day and sales were slow. After Paul had sold for £32 stock that had cost £23, he decided to stop trading until the following day.

Have a try at drawing up the three financial statements for day 3 of Paul's business venture.

Cash flow statement for day 3

	£
Opening balance (from day 2)	63
Cash proceeds from sale of wrapping paper	32
	95
Cash paid to purchase wrapping paper	(46)
Closing balance	49

The profit and loss account for day 3 will be as follows:

Profit and loss account for day 3

	£
Sales	32
Cost of goods sold	(23)
Profit	9

The balance sheet at the end of day 3 will be thus:

Balance sheet at the end of day 3

	£
Cash	49
Stock of goods for resale £(5 + 46 – 23)	28
Total business wealth	77

Note that at the end of day 3 the total business wealth had increased by £9 (that is, the amount of the day's profit) even though the cash balance declined. This is owing to the fact that the business is now holding more of its wealth in the form of stock rather than cash compared with the end of day 2.

Note also that the profit and loss account and cash flow statement are both concerned with measuring flows (of wealth and cash respectively) over time. The period of time may be one day, one month, one year, or whatever. The balance sheet, however, is concerned with the financial position at a particular moment in time (the end of one day, one week, etc.). Figure 2.1 illustrates this point.

The profit and loss account, cash flow statement and balance sheet, when taken together, are often referred to as the **final accounts** of the business.

For external (that is, non-managerial) users of the accounts, these statements are normally backward-looking and are based on information concerning past events and transactions. This can be useful in providing feedback on past performance and in identifying trends that provide clues to future performance. However, the statements can also be prepared using projected data in order to help assess likely future profits, cash flows and so on. The financial statements are normally prepared on a projected basis for internal decision-making purposes only. Managers are usually reluctant to publish these projected statements for external users, as they may reveal valuable information to competitors.

Nevertheless, as external users also have to make decisions about the future, projected financial statements prepared by managers are likely to be useful for this purpose. Managers are, after all, in a good position to assess future performance and so their assessments are likely to provide a valuable source of information. In certain circumstances, such as raising new capital or resisting a hostile takeover bid, managers are prepared to depart from normal practice and issue projected financial statements to external users. Where publication occurs, some independent verification of the assumptions underlying the forecast statements is often provided by a firm of accountants to help lend credibility to the figures produced.

Figure 2.1

Relationship between the balance sheet, profit and loss account, and cash flow statement

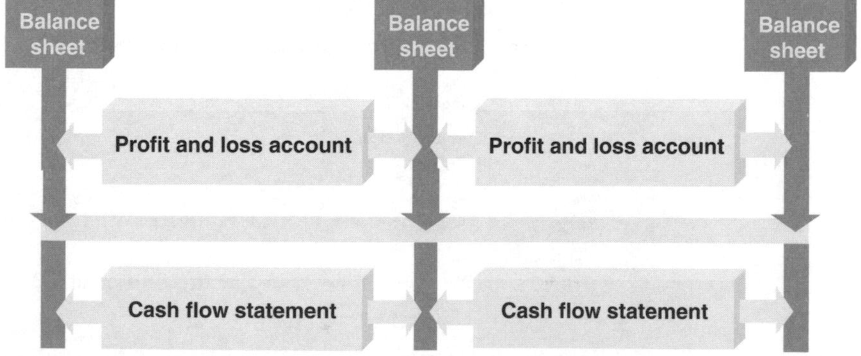

This figure shows how the profit and loss account and cash flow statement are concerned with measuring flows of wealth over time. The balance sheet, however, is concerned with measuring the stock of wealth at a particular moment in time.

Now that we have considered an overview of the financial statements, we shall consider each statement in more detail. In Chapter 3 we shall look at the profit and loss account, and in Chapter 6 we shall go into more detail on the cash flow statement.

The balance sheet

The purpose of the balance sheet is simply to set out the financial position of a business at a particular moment in time. (The balance sheet is sometimes referred to as the 'position statement' because it seeks to provide the user with a picture of financial position.) We saw earlier that the balance sheet will reveal the forms in which the wealth of the business is held and how much wealth is held in each form. We can, however, be more specific about the nature of the balance sheet by saying that it sets out the **assets** of the business, on the one hand, and the **claims** against the business on the other. Before looking at the balance sheet in more detail, we need to be clear about what these terms mean.

Assets

In everyday language, the term 'asset' is used to denote something that is of value. Thus, for example, you may hear someone say 'She is a tremendous asset to the organisation', meaning that the individual is making a valuable contribution to the work of the organisation. In accounting, however, the term is used in a much more narrow sense than this. For accounting purposes, the term is used to describe a resource held by a business that has certain characteristics. The major characteristics of an accounting asset are set out next:

- *A probable future economic benefit exists.* This simply means that the item is expected to have some future monetary value. This value can arise through its use within the business or through its hire or sale. Thus, an obsolete piece of equipment that can be sold for scrap would still be considered an asset, whereas an obsolete piece of equipment that could not be sold for scrap would not be regarded as an asset.
- *The business has an exclusive right to control the benefit.* Unless the business has exclusive rights over the resource, it cannot be regarded as an asset. Thus, for a business offering holidays on barges, the canal system may be a very valuable resource, however, as the business will not be able to control the access of others to the system, it cannot be regarded as an accounting asset of the business. (The barges owned by the business would be regarded as assets.)
- *The benefit must arise from some past transaction or event.* This means the transaction (or other event) giving rise to the business's right to the benefit must have already occurred and will not arise at some future date. Thus, an agreement by a business to purchase a piece of machinery at some future date would not mean that the item is currently an asset of the business.
- *The asset must be capable of measurement in monetary terms.* Unless the item can be measured in monetary terms with a reasonable degree of reliability, the item will not be regarded as an asset for inclusion on the balance sheet. Thus

the loyalty of customers may be extremely valuable to a business, but is usually impossible to quantify and so will be excluded from the balance sheet.

We can see that these conditions will strictly limit the kinds of item that may be referred to as assets for accounting purposes. Certainly, not all resources exploited by a business will be accounting assets of the business. This is viewed by many as a weakness of accounting as it means that valuable resources are being excluded from the financial statements of businesses. (We shall return to this point later in the chapter.) Once an asset has been acquired by a business, it will continue to be considered an asset until the benefits are exhausted or the business disposes of it in some way.

Activity 2.2

State which of the following items could appear on the balance sheet of business A as an asset. Explain your reasoning in each case.

(a) £1,000 owing to business A by a customer who will never be able to pay.
(b) The purchase of a patent from an inventor that gives business A the right to produce a product designed by that business. Production of the new product is expected to increase profits over the period in which the patent is held.
(c) The hiring of a new marketing director by business A who is confidently expected to increase profits by over 30 per cent over the next three years.
(d) Purchase of a machine that will save business A £10,000 per annum. It is currently being used by the business but has been acquired on credit and is not yet paid for.

....

(a) Under normal circumstances a business would expect a customer to pay the amount owed. Such an amount is, therefore, typically shown as an asset under the heading 'debtors'. However, in this particular case, the debtor is unable to pay. Hence, the item is incapable of providing future benefits, and the £1,000 owing would not be regarded as an asset. Debts that are not paid are referred to as 'bad debts'.
(b) The purchase of the patent would meet all of the conditions set out above and would, therefore, be regarded as an asset.
(c) The hiring of a new marketing director would not be considered the acquisition of an asset. One argument against its classification as an asset is that the business does not have exclusive rights of control over the director. Nevertheless, it may have an exclusive right to the services that the director provides. Perhaps a stronger argument is that the value of the director cannot be measured in monetary terms with any degree of reliability.
(d) The machine would be considered an asset even though it is not yet paid for. Once the business has agreed to purchase the machine and has accepted it, the business has exclusive rights over the machine even though payment is still outstanding. (The amount outstanding would be shown as a claim, as we shall see below.)

The sorts of item that often appear as assets in the balance sheet of a business include:

- Freehold premises
- Machinery and equipment
- Fixtures and fittings
- Patents and trademarks

- Debtors
- Investments.

Activity 2.3

Can you think of three additional items that might appear as assets in the balance sheet of a business?

....

Some items that you might have identified are:

- Motor vehicles
- Copyright
- Stock of goods
- Computer equipment
- Cash at bank
- Cash in hand.

Note that an asset does not have to be a physical item – it may also be a non-physical right to certain benefits (for example, patents and copyright). Assets that have a physical substance and that can be touched are referred to as **tangible assets**. Assets that have no physical substance but, nevertheless, provide expected future benefits are referred to as **intangible assets**.

Claims

A claim is an obligation on the part of a business to provide cash, or some other form of benefit, to an outside party. A claim will normally arise as a result of the outside party providing funds in the form of assets for use by the business. There are essentially two types of claim against a business. These are:

- **Capital**. This represents the claim of the owner(s) against the business. This claim is sometimes referred to as the owners' equity. Some find it hard to understand how the owner can have a claim against the business, particularly when we consider the example of a sole-proprietor business where the owner *is*, in effect, the business. However, for accounting purposes, a clear distinction is made between the business (whatever its size) and the owner(s). The business is viewed as being quite separate from the owner, irrespective of the form of business. This means that when financial statements are prepared, they are prepared from the perspective of the business rather than that of the owner(s). Viewed from this perspective, therefore, any funds contributed by the owner to help finance the business will be regarded as a claim against the business in its balance sheet.
- **Liabilities**. Liabilities represent the claims of individuals and organisations, apart from the owner, that have arisen from past transactions or events, such as supplying goods or lending money to the business.

Once a claim has been incurred by a business, it will remain as an obligation until it is settled.

Now that the meaning of the terms **assets** and **claims** has been established, we can go on to discuss the relationship between the two. This relationship is quite simple and straightforward. If a business wishes to acquire assets, it will have to raise the necessary funds from somewhere. It may raise the funds from the owner(s) or from other outside parties or from both. To illustrate the relationship, let us take the example of a new business as set out in Example 2.3.

Jerry and Co. deposits £20,000 in a bank account on 1 March in order to commence business. Let us assume that the cash is supplied by the owner (£6,000) and an outside party (£14,000). The raising of the funds in this way gives rise to a claim on the business by both the owner (capital) and the outside party (liability). If a balance sheet of Jerry and Co. is prepared following the above transactions, the assets and claims of the business would appear as follows:

Balance sheet as at 1 March

	£			£
Assets			**Claims**	
Cash at bank	20,000		Capital	6,000
			Liability – loan	14,000
	20,000			20,000

We can see from the balance sheet that the total claims are the same as the total assets. Thus:

$$\text{Assets} = \text{Capital} + \text{Liabilities}$$

This equation – which is often referred to as the **balance sheet equation** – will always hold true. Whatever changes may occur to the assets of the business or the claims against the business, there will be compensating changes elsewhere that will ensure that the balance sheet always 'balances'. By way of illustration, consider some further possible transactions for Jerry and Co. Assume that, after the £20,000 had been deposited in the bank, the following transactions took place:

2 March	Purchased a motor van for £5,000, paying by cheque
3 March	Purchased stock in trade (that is, goods to be sold) on one month's credit for £3,000
4 March	Repaid £2,000 of the loan from outside party
6 March	Owner introduced £4,000 into the business bank account

A balance sheet may be drawn up after each day in which transactions have taken place. In this way, the effect can be seen of each transaction on the assets and claims of the business. The balance sheet as at 2 March will be as follows:

Balance sheet as at 2 March

	£			£
Assets			**Claims**	
Cash at bank	15,000		Capital	6,000
Motor van	5,000		Liabilities – loan	14,000
	20,000			20,000

As can be seen, the effect of purchasing a motor van is to decrease the balance at the bank by £5,000 and to introduce a new asset – a motor van – to the balance sheet. The total assets remain unchanged. It is only the 'mix' of assets that will change. The claims against the business will remain the same because there has been no change in the funding arrangements for the business.

The balance sheet as at 3 March, following the purchase of stock, will be as follows:

Balance sheet as at 3 March

Assets	£	Claims	£
Cash at bank	15,000	Capital	6,000
Motor van	5,000	Liabilities – loan	14,000
Stock	3,000	– trade creditor	3,000
	23,000		23,000

The effect of purchasing stock has been to introduce another new asset (stock) to the balance sheet. In addition, the fact that the goods have not yet been paid for means that the claims against the business will be increased by the £3,000 owed to the supplier who is referred to as a 'trade creditor' on the balance sheet.

Activity 2.4

Try drawing up a balance sheet for Jerry and Co. as at 4 March.

The balance sheet as at 4 March, following the repayment of part of the loan, will be as follows:

Balance sheet as at 4 March

Assets	£	Claims	£
Cash at bank	13,000	Capital	6,000
Motor van	5,000	Liabilities – loan	12,000
Stock	3,000	– trade creditor	3,000
	21,000		21,000

The repayment of £2,000 of the loan will result in a decrease in the balance at the bank of £2,000 and a decrease in the loan claim against the business by the same amount.

Activity 2.5

Try drawing up a balance sheet as at 6 March for Jerry and Co.

The balance sheet as at 6 March, following the introduction of more funds, will be as follows:

Balance sheet as at 6 March

Assets	£	Claims	£
Cash at bank	17,000	Capital	10,000
Motor van	5,000	Liabilities – loan	12,000
Stock	3,000	– trade creditor	3,000
	25,000		25,000

The introduction of more funds by the owner will result in an increase in the capital of £4,000 and and increase in the cash at the bank by the same amount.

Example 2.3 illustrates the point that the balance sheet equation (Assets = Capital + Liabilities) will always hold true. This is because the equation is based on the fact that, if a business wishes to acquire assets, it must raise funds equal to the cost of those assets. These funds must be provided by the owners (capital), or other outside parties (liabilities), or both. Hence, the total cost of assets acquired should always equal the total capital plus liabilities.

It is worth pointing out that a business would not draw up a balance sheet after each day of transactions as shown in the example above. Such an approach is likely to be impractical given even a relatively small number of transactions each day. A balance sheet for the business is usually prepared at the end of a defined reporting period. Determining the length of the reporting interval will involve weighing up the costs of producing the information against the perceived bene-fits of the information for decision-making purposes. In practice, the reporting interval will vary between businesses and could be monthly, quarterly, half-yearly or annually. For external reporting purposes, an annual reporting cycle is the norm (although certain businesses, typically larger ones, report more fre-quently than this). However, for internal reporting purposes, many businesses produce monthly financial statements.

The effect of trading operations on the balance sheet

In Example 2.3 we dealt with the effect on the balance sheet of a number of dif-ferent types of transactions that a business might undertake. These transactions covered the purchase of assets for cash and on credit, the repayment of a loan, and the injection of capital. However, one form of transaction – trading – has not yet been considered. In order to deal with the effect of trading transactions on the balance sheet, let us look at Example 2.4.

Example 2.4

Let us return to the balance sheet that we drew up for Jerry and Co. as at 6 March. The balance sheet at that date was as follows:

Balance sheet as at 6 March

Assets	£	Claims	£
Cash at bank	17,000	Capital	10,000
Motor van	5,000	Liabilities – loan	12,000
Stock	3,000	– trade creditor	3,000
	25,000		25,000

Let us assume that, on 7 March, the business managed to sell all of the stock for £5,000 and received a cheque immediately from the customer for this amount. The balance sheet on 7 March, after this transaction has taken place, will be as follows:

Balance sheet as at 7 March

Assets	£	Claims	£
Cash at bank	22,000	Capital [10,000 + (5,000 – 3,000)]	12,000
Motor van	5,000	Liabilities – loan	12,000
		– trade creditor	3,000
	27,000		27,000

We can see that the stock (£3,000) has now disappeared from the balance sheet but the cash at bank has increased by the selling price of the stock (£5,000). The net effect has therefore been to increase assets by £2,000 (£5,000 – £3,000). This increase represents the net increase in wealth (the profit) that has arisen from trading. Also note that the capital of the business has increased by £2,000 in line with the increase in assets. This increase in capital reflects the fact that increases in wealth as a result of trading or other operations will be to the benefit of the owner and will increase his/her stake in the business.

Activity 2.6

What would have been the effect on Jerry and Co.'s balance sheet if the stock had been sold on 7 March for £1,000 rather that £5,000?

The balance sheet on 7 March would be as follows:

Balance sheet as at 7 March

	£		£
Assets		**Claims**	
Cash at bank	18,000	Capital [10,000	
		+ (1,000 – 3,000)]	8,000
Motor van	5,000	Liabilities – loan	12,000
		– trade creditor	3,000
	23,000		23,000

As we can see, the stock (£3,000) will disappear from the balance sheet but the cash at bank will rise by only £1,000. This will mean a net reduction in assets of £2,000. This reduction represents a loss arising from trading and will be reflected in a reduction in the capital of the owner.

Thus, we can see from Activity 2.6 that any decrease in wealth (loss) arising from trading or other transactions will lead to a reduction in the owner's stake in the business. If the business wished to maintain the level of assets as at 6 March, it would be necessary to obtain further funds from the owner or outside parties, or both.

What we have just seen means that the balance sheet equation can be extended as follows:

$$\text{Assets} = \text{Capital} +(-)\ \text{Profit(Loss)} + \text{Liabilties}$$

The profit for the period is usually shown separately in the balance sheet as an addition to capital. Any funds introduced or withdrawn by the owner for living expenses or other reasons are also shown separately. Thus, if we assume that the above business sold the stock for £5,000, as in the earlier example, and further assume that the owner withdrew £1,500 of the profit for his or her own use, the capital of the owner would appear as follows on the balance sheet:

	£
Capital	
Opening balance	10,000
Add Profit	2,000
	12,000
Less Drawings	(1,500)
Closing balance	10,500

If the drawings were in cash, then the balance of cash would decrease by £1,500 and this would be reflected in the balance sheet.

Note that, like all balance sheet items, the amount of capital is cumulative. This means that any profit made that is not taken out as drawings by the owner(s) remains in the business. These 'retained earnings' have the effect of expanding the business.

The classification of assets

To help users of financial information to locate easily items of interest on the balance sheet, it is customary to group assets and claims into categories. Assets are normally categorised as being either fixed or current.

Fixed assets are defined primarily according to the purpose for which they are held. Fixed assets are held with the intention of being used to generate wealth rather than being held for resale (although they may be sold by the business when there is no further use for the asset). They can be seen as the tools of the business. Fixed assets are normally held by the business on a continuing basis. The minimum period for which a fixed asset is expected to be held is not precisely defined, although one year is sometimes quoted.

Activity 2.7

Can you think of two examples of assets that may be classified as fixed assets within a particular business?

Examples of assets that often meet the definition of fixed assets include:

● Freehold premises
● Plant and machinery
● Motor vehicles
● Patents
● Copyrights.

This is not an exhaustive list. You may have thought of others.

Current assets are assets that are not held on a continuing basis. They include cash itself and other assets that are expected to be converted to cash at some future point in time in the normal course of trading. Current assets are normally held as part of the day-to-day trading activity of the business. The most common current assets are stock, trade debtors (that is, customers who owe money for goods or services supplied on credit) and cash itself. The current assets mentioned are interrelated and circulate within a business, as shown in Figure 2.2. We can see that the cash can be used to purchase stock, which is then sold on credit. When the debtors pay, the business receives an injection of cash, and so on.

Figure 2.2

The circulating nature of current assets

The figure shows how stock may be sold on credit to customers. When the customers pay, the trade debtors will be converted into cash which can then be used to purchase more stocks, and so the cycle begins again.

It is important to appreciate that the classification of an asset as fixed or current may vary according to the nature of the business being carried out. This is because the *purpose* for which a particular type of business holds a certain asset may vary. For example, a motor-vehicle manufacturer will normally hold the motor vehicles produced for resale and would therefore classify them as stock in trade (a current asset). On the other hand, a business that uses motor vehicles for transportation purposes would classify them as fixed assets.

Activity 2.8

The assets of Poplilova and Co., a large metalworking business, are shown below:

- Cash at bank
- Fixtures and fittings
- Office equipment
- Motor vehicles
- Freehold factory premises
- Goodwill purchased from business taken over
- Plant and machinery
- Computer equipment
- Stock of work in progress (that is, partly completed products)
- Short-term investments.

Which of the above do you think should be defined as fixed assets and which should be defined as current assets?

The item 'goodwill purchased' in the list of fixed assets in Activity 2.8 requires some explanation. When a business takes over another business, the amount that is paid for the business taken over will often exceed the total value of the individual assets that have been acquired. This additional amount represents a payment for goodwill that arises from such factors as the quality of products sold, the skill of the workforce and the relationship with customers.

We saw earlier that these qualitative items are normally excluded from the balance sheet as they are difficult to measure. However, when they have been acquired by a business at an agreed price, the amount paid provides an objective basis for measurement. Hence, goodwill purchased can be regarded as an asset and included on the balance sheet. Goodwill is regarded as a fixed asset as it is not held primarily for resale and will be held on a continuing basis. We shall discuss some of the issues surrounding goodwill later in this chapter and also in Chapter 3.

The classification of claims

As we have already seen, claims are normally classified into capital (owners' claims) and liabilities (claims of outsiders). Liabilities are further classified into two groups:

- **Long-term liabilities** represent those amounts due to other parties that are not liable for repayment within the twelve-month period following the balance sheet date.
- **Current liabilities** represent amounts due for repayment to outside parties within 12 months of the balance sheet date.

Unlike assets, the purpose for which the liabilities are held is not an issue. It is only the period for which the liability is outstanding that is important. Thus, a long-term liability will turn into a current liability when the settlement date comes within 12 months of the balance sheet date.

| *Activity 2.9* | Can you think of an example of a long-term liability and a current liability? |

One example of a long-term liability would be a long-term loan. Two examples of a current liability would be trade creditors (that is, amounts owing to suppliers for goods supplied on credit) and a bank overdraft (a form of bank borrowing that is repayable on demand).

Balance sheet formats

Now that we have considered the classification of assets and liabilities, it is possible to consider the format of the balance sheet. Although there is an almost infinite number of ways in which the same balance sheet information could be presented, there are, in practice, two basic formats. The first of these follows the style we adopted with Jerry and Co. earlier. A more comprehensive example of this style is shown in Example 2.5.

Brie Manufacturing
Balance sheet as at 31 December 2001

	£	£		£
Fixed assets			**Capital**	
Freehold premises		45,000	Opening balance	50,000
Plant and machinery		30,000	*Add* Profit	14,000
Motor vans		19,000		64,000
		94,000	*Less* Drawings	4,000
				60,000
			Long-term liabilities	
			Loan	50,000
Current assets			**Current liabilities**	
Stock in trade	23,000		Trade creditors	37,000
Trade debtors	18,000			
Cash at bank	12,000			
		53,000		
		147,000		147,000

Note that, within each category of asset (fixed and current) shown in Example 2.5, the items are listed with the least liquid (furthest from cash) first, going down to the most liquid last. This is a standard practice that is followed irrespective of the format used. Note also that the current assets are listed individually in the first column and a subtotal of current assets (£53,000) is carried out to the second column to be added to the subtotal of fixed assets (£94,000). This convention is designed to make the balance sheet easier to read.

An obvious change in the format shown in Example 2.5 from the format of Example 2.4, is to show claims on the left and assets on the right. Some people prefer this approach because the claims can be seen as the source of finance for the business and the assets show how that finance has been deployed. It could be seen as more logical to show sources first and uses second.

The format shown above is sometimes referred to as the **horizontal layout**. However, in recent years, a more common form of layout for the balance sheet is the **narrative** or **vertical form** of layout. This format is based on a rearrangement of the balance sheet equation. With the horizontal format above, the balance sheet equation is set out as:

$$FA + CA = C + LTL + CL$$

where   FA = fixed assets
         CA = current assets
          C = capital
        LTL = long-term loans
         CL = current liabilities

The vertical format merely rearranges this to:

$$FA + (CA - CL) - LTL = C$$

This rearranged equation is expressed in the format depicted in Figure 2.3.

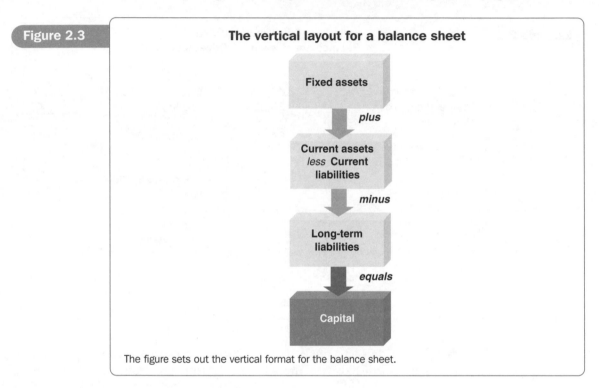

Figure 2.3

The vertical layout for a balance sheet

The figure sets out the vertical format for the balance sheet.

We can now rearrange the balance sheet layout of Brie Manufacturing as shown in Example 2.6.

Example 2.6

Brie Manufacturing
Balance sheet as at 31 December 2001

	£	£
Fixed assets		
Freehold premises		45,000
Plant and machinery		30,000
Motor vans		19,000
		94,000
Current assets		
Stock in trade	23,000	
Trade debtors	18,000	
Cash at bank	12,000	
	53,000	

Current liabilities		
Trade creditors	(37,000)	
		16,000
Total assets less current liabilities		110,000
Long-term liabilities		
Loan		(50,000)
Net assets		60,000
Capital		
Opening balance		50,000
Add Profit		14,000
		64,000
Less Drawings		(4,000)
		60,000

Some people find the vertical format of Example 2.6 easier to read than the horizontal format. It usefully highlights the relationship between current assets and current liabilities. We shall consider shortly why this relationship is an important one. The figure derived from deducting current liabilities from current assets (a net amount of £16,000 for Brie Manufacturing) is sometimes referred to as **net current assets** or **working capital**.

Activity 2.10

The following information relates to the Simonson Engineering Company as at 30 September 2001:

	£
Plant and machinery	25,000
Trade creditors	18,000
Bank overdraft	26,000
Stock in trade	45,000
Freehold premises	72,000
Long-term loans	51,000
Trade debtors	48,000
Capital at 1 October 2000	117,500
Cash in hand	1,500
Motor vehicles	15,000
Fixtures and fittings	9,000
Profit for the year to 30 September 2001	18,000
Drawings for the year to 30 September 2001	15,000

Prepare a balance sheet in narrative form.

The balance sheet you prepare should be set out as follows:

Simonson Engineering Company
Balance sheet as at 30 September 2001

Fixed assets	£	£	£
Freehold premises			72,000
Plant and machinery			25,000
Motor vehicles			15,000
Fixtures and fittings			9,000
			121,000

Current assets		
Stock in trade		45,000
Trade debtors		48,000
Cash in hand		1,500
		94,500
Current liabilities		
Trade creditors	18,000	
Bank overdraft	26,000	
		(44,000)
		50,500
Total assets less current liabilities		171,500
Long-term liabilities		
Loan		(51,000)
Net assets		120,500
Capital		
Opening balance		117,500
Add Profit		18,000
		135,500
Less Drawings		(15,000)
		120,500

● ● ● ● The balance sheet as a position at a point in time

The balance sheet is a statement of the financial position of a business at a specified point in time. The balance sheet has been compared with a photograph. A photograph 'freezes' a particular moment in time and will only represent the position at that moment; events may be quite different immediately before and immediately after. So it is with a balance sheet. When examining a balance sheet, therefore, it is important to establish the date at which it was drawn up. This information should be prominently displayed in the balance sheet heading, as is shown in the above examples. The more current the balance sheet date, the better when you are trying to assess a current financial position.

A business will normally prepare a balance sheet as at the close of business on the last day of its accounting year. In the UK, businesses are free to choose their accounting year. When making a decision on which year-end date to choose, commercial convenience can often be a deciding factor. Thus a business operating in the retail trade may choose to have a year-end date early in the calendar year (for example 31 January) because trade tends to be slack during that period and more staff time is available to help with the tasks involved with the preparation of the annual accounting statements (such as checking the amount of stock held). Since trade is slack, it is also a time when the amount of stock held by the business is likely to be low as compared with other times of the year. Thus the balance sheet, though showing a fair view of what it purports to show, may not show a picture of what is more typically the position of the business over the year.

Accounting conventions and the balance sheet

Accounting is based on a number of rules, or conventions, that have evolved over time. They have evolved in order to deal with practical problems experienced by preparers and users rather than to reflect some theoretical ideal. When preparing balance sheets in this book, we have adhered to various accounting conventions though these have not been explicitly mentioned. Here we identify and discuss the major conventions that have been employed.

Money measurement convention

Accounting normally deals with only those items that are capable of being expressed in monetary terms. Money has the advantage that it is a useful common denominator with which to express the wide variety of resources held by a business. However, not all such resources are capable of being measured in monetary terms and so will be excluded from a balance sheet. The **money measurement convention**, therefore, limits the scope of accounting reports.

Activity 2.11

Can you think of resources held by a business that are not normally included on the balance sheet because they cannot be quantified in monetary terms?

You may have thought of the following:

- The quality of the workforce
- The reputation of the business's products
- The location of the business
- The relationship with customers
- The quality of management.

Although normally excluded from the balance sheet, the items listed in Activity 2.11 may be seen as forming part of the goodwill of a business. As explained earlier, a business that purchases goodwill, by taking over another business, can show the amount paid on the balance sheet. Whilst the valuation process may be highly subjective, the amount actually paid represents an amount that can be objectively measured.

Accounting is a developing subject and the boundaries of financial measurement can change. In recent years, attempts have been made to measure particular resources of a business that have been previously excluded from the balance sheet. For example, we have seen the development of human resource accounting, which attempts to measure the value of the employees of a business. It is often claimed that employees are the most valuable 'assets' to a business. By measuring these assets and putting the amount on the balance sheet, it is sometimes argued that we have a more complete picture of financial position. For similar reasons, we have also seen attempts by certain large businesses to measure the value of product brand names that they hold (to be discussed later in the chapter). However, some of the measurement methods proposed have been controversial and often conflict with other accounting conventions. There are mixed views as to whether extending the boundaries of financial measurement will succeed in making the balance sheet a more useful representation of the financial position of a business.

Another approach to overcoming some of the limitations of money measurement is to publish a narrative financial statement. Rather than trying to 'quantify the unquantifiable', a narrative financial statement could be published to help users to assess financial health. Thus, in order to give a more complete picture of a financial position, a narrative statement might incorporate a discussion of such matters as investment policy, financial structure, liquidity and of valuable resources that have not been quantified. Many large businesses now produce such a statement, which is referred to as a 'financial review'. We shall consider this statement in more detail in Chapter 7.

Historic cost convention

Assets are shown on the balance sheet at a value that is based on their **historic cost** (that is, acquisition cost). This method of measuring asset value has been adopted by accountants in preference to methods based on some form of current value. Many commentators find this particular convention difficult to support as outdated historic costs are unlikely to help in the assessment of current financial position. It is often argued that recording assets at their current value would provide a more realistic view of financial position and would be relevant for a wide range of decisions. However, a system of measurement based on current values can present a number of problems.

Activity 2.12	**Can you think of reasons why current value accounting may pose problems for both preparers and users of financial statements?**

The term 'current value' can be defined in a number of ways. For example, it can be defined broadly as either the current replacement cost or the current realisable value (selling price) of an item. These two types of valuation may result in quite different figures being produced to represent the current value of an item. (Think, for example, of second-hand car values; there is often quite a difference between buying and selling prices.) In addition, the broad terms 'replacement cost' and 'realisable value' can be defined in different ways. We must therefore be clear about what kind of current value accounting we wish to use. There are also practical problems associated with attempts to implement any system of current value accounting. For example, current values, however defined, are often difficult to establish with any real degree of objectivity. This may mean that the figures produced are heavily dependent on the opinion of managers. Unless the current value figures are capable of some form of independent verification, there is a danger that the financial statements will lose their credibility among users.

By reporting assets at their historic cost, it is argued that more reliable information is produced. Reporting in this way reduces the need for subjective opinion as the amount paid for a particular asset is usually a matter of demonstrable fact. However, information based on past costs may not always be relevant to the needs of users.

Later in the chapter we will consider the valuation of assets in the balance sheet in more detail. We will see that the historic cost convention is not always rigidly adhered to and that departures from this convention often occur.

Going concern convention

The **going concern convention** holds that a business will continue operations for the foreseeable future. In other words, there is no intention or need to sell off the assets of the business. Such a sale may arise where the business is in financial difficulties and it needs cash to pay the creditors. This convention is important because the value of fixed assets on sale is often low in relation to the recorded values, and an expectation of having to sell off the assets would mean that anticipated losses on sale should be fully recorded. However, where there is no expectation of the need to sell off the assets, the value of fixed assets can continue to be shown at their recorded values (that is, based on historic cost). This convention, therefore, provides support for the historic cost convention under normal circumstances.

Business entity convention

For accounting purposes, the business and its owner(s) are treated as quite separate and distinct. This is why owners are treated as being claimants against their own business in respect of their investment in the business. The **business entity convention** must be distinguished from the legal position that may exist between businesses and their owners. For sole proprietorships and partnerships, the law does not make any distinction between the business and its owner(s). For limited companies, on the other hand, there is a clear legal distinction between the business and its owners. (Indeed, as Chapter 4 explains, the limited company is regarded as having a separate legal existence.) For accounting purposes, these legal distinctions are irrelevant and the business entity convention applies to all businesses.

Dual aspect convention

Each transaction has two aspects, both of which will affect the balance sheet. Thus, the purchase of a motor car for cash results in an increase in one asset (motor car) and a decrease in another (cash). The repayment of a loan results in the decrease in a liability (loan) and the decrease in an asset (cash/bank).

Activity 2.13

What are the two aspects of each of the following transactions?

- Purchase £1,000 stock on credit
- Owner withdraws £2,000 in cash
- Sale of stock (purchased for £1,000) for £2,000 cash.

Your answer should be as follows:

- Stock increases by £1,000; creditors increase by £1,000
- Capital reduces by £2,000; cash reduces by £2,000
- Assets show net increase of £1,000 (cash + £2,000; stock – £1,000); profit increases by £1,000.

Recording the **dual aspect** of each transaction ensures that the balance sheet will continue to balance.

Prudence convention

➡ The **prudence convention** holds that financial statements should err on the side of caution. The convention evolved to counteract the excessive optimism of some managers and owners, which, in the past, resulted in an overstatement of financial position. Operation of the prudence convention results in the recording of both actual and anticipated losses in full, whereas profits are not recognised until they are realised (that is, there is reasonable certainty that the profit will be received). When the prudence convention conflicts with another convention, it is prudence that will normally prevail. We shall see an example of this when we consider the valuation of current assets later in the chapter.

Activity 2.14

Can you think of a situation where certain users might find a cautious view of the financial position of a business can work to their disadvantage?

Applying the prudence convention can result in an understatement of financial position, because unrealised profits are not recognised, whereas anticipated losses are recognised in full. This may result in owners selling their stake in the business at a price that is lower than they would have done had a more realistic approach to valuation been employed. The amount of this bias towards understatement may be difficult to judge. It is likely to vary according to the views of the individual carrying out the valuation.

Stable monetary unit convention

➡ The **stable monetary unit convention** holds that money, which is the unit of measurement in accounting, will not change in value over time. However, in the UK and throughout much of the world, inflation has been a persistent problem over the years and this has meant that the value of money has declined in relation to other assets. In past years, high rates of inflation have resulted in balance sheets, which are drawn up on a cost basis, reflecting figures for assets that were much lower than if current values were employed. The value of freehold land and buildings, in particular, increased rapidly during much of the 1970s, 1980s and 1990s, at least partly as a result of a reduction in the value of each £1. Where land and buildings were held for some time by a business, there was often a significant difference between their original cost and their current market value. This led to the criticism that balance sheet values were seriously understated and, as a result, some businesses broke away from the use of historic cost as the basis for valuing this particular asset. Instead, freehold land is periodically revalued in order to provide a more realistic statement of financial position. Although this represents a departure from accounting convention, it is a practice that has become increasingly common.

Activity 2.15

Refer to the balance sheet for the Simonson Engineering Company shown in the answer to Activity 2.10. What would be the effect on the balance sheet of revaluing the freehold land to a figure of £110,000?

The effect on the balance sheet would be to increase the freehold land to £110,000 and the gain on revaluation (£110,000 – £72,000 = £38,000) would be added to the capital of the owner as it is the owner who will benefit from the gain. The revised balance sheet would therefore be as follows:

Balance sheet as at 30 September 2001

Fixed assets	£	£	£
Freehold premises (at valuation)			110,000
Plant and machinery			25,000
Motor vehicles			15,000
Fixtures and fittings			9,000
			159,000
Current assets			
Stock in trade		45,000	
Trade debtors		48,000	
Cash in hand		1,500	
		94,500	
Current liabilities			
Trade creditors	18,000		
Bank overdraft	26,000		
		(44,000)	
			50,500
Total assets less current liabilities			209,500
Long-term liabilities			
Loan			(51,000)
Net assets			158,500
Capital			
Opening balance			117,500
Add Revaluation gain			38,000
Profit			18,000
			173,500
Less Drawings			15,000
			158,500

In practice, the revaluation of land and buildings often has a significant effect on the size of the balance sheet figures for tangible fixed assets. In past years, this effect has usually been beneficial as property has risen in value throughout much of the past four decades. However, during the early 1990s there was not only a fall in property values but also some reluctance among those businesses that revalued their land and buildings upwards in earlier years to make downward revaluations in recessionary years. A common reason cited was that the fall in value was considered to be only temporary.

Objectivity convention

➡ The **objectivity convention** seeks to reduce personal bias in financial statements. As far as possible, financial statements should be based on objective, verifiable evidence rather than matters of opinion.

Activity 2.16

Which of the above conventions does the objectivity convention support and with which does it conflict?

The objectivity convention provides further support (along with the going concern convention) for the use of historic cost as a basis of valuation. It can conflict, however, with the prudence convention which requires the use of judgement in determining values.

The basis of valuation of assets on the balance sheet

It was mentioned earlier that, when preparing a balance sheet, the historic cost convention is normally applied for the reporting of assets. However, this point requires further elaboration as, in practice, it is not simply a matter of recording each asset on the balance sheet at its original cost. Below, we consider the valuation procedures used for both current assets and fixed assets.

Current assets

Where the net realisable value (that is, selling price less any selling costs) of current assets falls below the cost of the assets, the former will be used as the basis of valuation instead. This reflects the influence of the prudence convention on the balance sheet. Current assets are short-term assets that are expected to be liquidated in the near future, and so any loss arising from a fall in value below their original cost is reflected in the balance sheet. The accounting policies of companies regarding their current assets will normally be shown as a note to the annual accounts that are published for external users (see Exhibit 2.1).

Exhibit 2.1

The published accounts for 2000 of J.D. Wetherspoon plc, which manages a large number of public houses throughout the UK, contains the following note:

Stocks
Stocks are held for resale and are stated at the lower of invoiced cost and net realisable value.

Tangible fixed assets

Many tangible fixed assets, such as plant and machinery, motor vehicles, computer equipment and buildings, have a limited useful life. Ultimately, these assets will be used up as a result of wear and tear, obsolescence and so on. The amount of a particular asset that has been used up over time by a business is referred to as *depreciation*. Depreciation is an expense of running the business and the amount involved each year appears in the profit and loss account. The total depreciation relating to a fixed asset, since the business first acquired it, will normally be deducted from the cost of the asset on the balance sheet. This procedure is not really a contravention of the historic cost convention; it is simply recognition of the fact that a proportion of the fixed asset has been consumed in the process of generating benefits for the business. There are, however, examples where the cost convention is contravened. We shall look at depreciation in more detail in Chapter 3.

We saw earlier that some assets *appreciate* in value over time. Freehold property was mentioned as an example. As a result of this appreciation, it has become widespread practice to revalue freehold property by using current market values rather than historic cost. This practice not only contravenes the cost convention but it also contravenes the objectivity convention. This is because an opinion of what is the current market value is substituted for a cost figure (which is usually a matter of verifiable fact).

Once assets are revalued, the frequency of revaluation then becomes an important issue as assets recorded at out-of-date values can mislead users. It has been argued that using out-of-date revaluations on the balance sheet is the worst of both worlds as it lacks the objectivity and verifiability of historic cost and also lacks the realism of current values. Ideally revaluations should take place on an annual basis particularly if it is likley that a significant change in value has occurred. However, in practice, revaluations tend to be less frequent.

Exhibit 2.2

The revaluation policies of House of Fraser plc, which owns and manages a number of department stores throughout the UK, are shown in its accounts for the year ended 29 January 2000 as follows:

Properties
Freehold and long leasehold properties are stated at cost or valuation on the basis of existing use. Independent professsional valuations are performed on a regular basis with directors' valuation in the intervening years. New store developments are carried at cost for a maximum of five years until the trading pattern is sufficiently established for a valuation to be carried out. Short leasehold properties and all other fixed assets are stated at cost.

This note reveals who carries out the revaluations. The fact that external valuers are involved periodically in the revaluations should give greater credibility to the values derived.

Intangible fixed assets

Some intangible assets are similar to tangible assets in so far as they have a separate identity, the rights to the assets can be clearly established and the cost of the assets can be determined. Patents, trademarks, copyright and licences would normally fall into this category. For such assets, the balance sheet treatment used for tangible fixed assets can be applied. That is, they can be recorded at their purchase cost and depreciated (or 'amortised' as it is usually termed in this context) over their useful life.

Exhibit 2.3

The following is an extract from the annual report of Manchester United plc for 2000.

Intangible fixed assets

Group	£'000
Cost of players' registrations	
At 1 August 1999	54,608
Additions	19,697
Disposals	(6,013)

At 31 July 2000	68,292

Amortisation of players' registrations	
At 1 August 1999	24,483
Charge for year	13,092
Disposals	(1,598)
At 31 July 2000	35,977

Net Book Value of players' registrations	
At 31 July 2000	32,315

The figures show how the club depreciated (or amortised) the value of the transfer fees paid for players over the life of each player's contract with the club. This provides a relatively rare example of a business's human assets being reflected on the balance sheet. The treatment is typical of how football clubs deal with transfer fees.

The logic of football clubs treating their human assets in this way is that when they pay a transfer fee for a player there is a 'part transaction', 'capable of measurement in monetary terms' – features that are normal requirements of the accounting definition of an asset (earlier in this chapter). Players brought on by the club and not, therefore, the subject of a transfer fee (David Beckham and Paul Scholes, for example) are not reflected in the Manchester United balance sheet.

At the beginning of the financial year (1 August 1999) the club had players for whom it had paid a total of £54,608,000. During the year it bought further players for £19,697,000 and players for whom the club had paid, at some stage, £6,013,000 left the club.

Of the £54,608,000, £24,483,000 had been treated as an expense by the start of the year. During the year a further £13,092,000 was treated as an expense as players' contract periods shortened by a year. Players who left the club during the year had already had £1,598,000 of their transfer value treated as an expense (depreciation or amortisation).

Some intangible assets, however, are quite different in nature from tangible fixed assets. They lack a clear and separate identity as they are really a hotch-potch of attributes that form part of the essence of the business. We saw earlier, for example, that 'goodwill' is a term used to cover the benefits arising from such factors as the quality of the products, the skill of the workforce and the relationship with customers. We also saw that goodwill is normally excluded from the balance sheet unless it has been acquired at an agreed price. The amount paid to purchase the goodwill would then provide the appropriate balance sheet value. However, the issue as to whether purchased goodwill should be shown at cost, or at cost *less* some measure of depreciation (or 'amortised' as it is usually termed in this context) is not straightforward. As we shall see in Chapter 3, there are different ways in which purchased goodwill can be treated.

The value of product brands is often regarded as part of the goodwill of a business. It can be argued that product brands are also a hotch-potch of attributes, which include the brand image, the quality of the product, the trademark and so on. In recent years, however, some large businesses (for example, Cadbury Schweppes plc) have attempted to give their brands a separate identity and place a value on them. There is no doubt that product brands may be very valuable to a business because they can generate customer loyalty that, in turn, can lead to increased sales. This brand loyalty is often built up through many years of promotional and advertising expenditure. However, such expenditure may be difficult to trace and so some form of current valuation is often used as the basis for including brand names on the balance sheet. (It should be said that including internally generated brands on the balance sheet remains a controversial issue in accounting because of the measurement issues mentioned earlier in the chapter.)

The table below shows how assets may be categorised according to whether they are tangible or intangible.

Tangible fixed assets	Intangible fixed assets	
	Separable	Non-separable
Plant and machinery	Patents	Goodwill
Computer equipment	Trademarks	Product brands
Fixtures and fittings	Copyright	
Freehold buildings	Licences	
Motor vehicles	Magazine titles	

Furthermore, intangible assets can be categorised according to our ability to separate them from other assets. Although tangible assets are usually separable we can see that not all intangible assets are. We can also see that there are exceptions to the rule that assets are recorded at their historic cost. Moreover, the list of exceptions appears to be growing. In recent years, the balance sheets of many businesses have increasingly reflected a mixture of valuation approaches. This trend is a matter of concern for the accountancy profession as users are unlikely to find a variety of valuation methods very helpful when trying to assess financial position.

Interpreting the balance sheet

We have seen that the conventional balance sheet has a number of limitations. This has led some users of financial information to conclude that the balance sheet has little to offer in the way of useful information. However, this is not necessarily the case. The balance sheet can provide useful insights to the financing and investing activities of a business. In particular, the following aspects of financial position can be examined:

- *The liquidity of the business.* This is the ability of the business to meet its short-term obligations (current liabilities) from its liquid (cash and near-cash) assets. One of the reasons that the vertical format for the balance sheet is preferred by many users of accounts is the fact that it highlights the liquidity of the business: the current assets are directly compared to the current liabilities. Liquidity is particularly important because business failures occur when the business cannot meet its maturing obligations, whatever the root cause of that inability may be.
- *The mix of assets held by the business.* The relationship between fixed assets and current assets is important. Businesses with too much of their funds tied up in fixed assets could be vulnerable to financial failure. This is because fixed assets are typically not easy to turn into cash in order to meet short-term obligations. Converting many fixed assets into cash may well lead to substantial losses for

the business because such assets are not always worth on the open market what they are worth to the business. For example, a specialised piece of equipment may have little value to any other business yet it could be worth a great deal to the owners. Businesses with too little of their funds invested in fixed assets, however, may also face problems. Underinvestment in fixed assets may limit output and this, in turn, is likely to have an adverse effect on the profitability of the business.

- *The financial structure of the business.* The relative proportion of total finance contributed by the owners and outsiders can be calculated to see whether the business is heavily dependent on outside financing. Heavy borrowing can bring with it a commitment to pay large interest charges and make large capital repayments at regular intervals. These are legally enforceable obligations that can be a real burden as they have to be paid irrespective of the financial position of the business. Funds raised from the owners of the business, on the other hand, do not impose such obligations on the business.

The interpretation of the balance sheet will be considered in more detail in Chapter 7.

Self-assessment question 2.1

Consider the following balance sheet of a manufacturing business:

Kunalan Manufacturing Company
Balance sheet as at 30 April 2002

	£	£	£
Fixed assets			
Freehold premises			88,000
Plant and machinery			46,000
Motor vehicles			13,000
Fixtures and fittings			14,000
			161,000
Current assets			
Stock in trade		48,000	
Trade debtors		44,000	
Cash in hand		12,000	
		104,000	
Current liabilities			
Trade creditors	24,000		
Bank overdraft	18,000		
		(42,000)	
Net current assets			62,000
Total assets less current liabilities			223,000
Long-term liabilities			
Loan			(160,000)
Net assets			63,000
Capital			
Opening balance			42,000
Add Profit			32,000
			74,000
Less Drawings			(11,000)
			63,000

Required:
What can you deduce about the financial position of the business from the information contained in its balance sheet?

● Summary

This chapter began with an overview of the three major financial statements. We saw how each statement has a part to play in providing a picture of the financial position and performance of the business. We then went on to examine one of these financial statements – the balance sheet – in some detail. We saw that this statement shows the assets of the business and the claims against those assets at a particular moment in time. It is a statement of financial position, although it can be argued that it is not a complete statement of financial position; there are certain valuable resources held by the business that cannot be accommodated easily within conventional accounting definitions and measurement methods. We examined the conventions of accounting that underpin the balance sheet and saw how these place limits on the usefulness of the balance sheet in assessing current financial position.

Key terms

Cash flow statement   p. 24
Profit and loss account   p. 24
Balance sheet   p. 24
Final accounts   p. 28
Asset   pp. 29, 31
Claim   pp. 29, 31
Tangible assets   p. 31
Intangible assets   p. 31
Capital   p. 31
Liabilities   p. 31
Fixed asset   p. 36

Current asset   p. 36
Long-term liabilities   p. 38
Current liabilities   p. 38
Money measurement convention   p. 43
Historic cost convention   p. 44
Going concern convention   p. 45
Business entity convention   p. 45
Dual aspect convention   p. 45
Prudence convention   p. 46
Stable monetary unit convention   p. 46
Objectivity convention   p. 47

● Further reading

If you would like to explore the topics covered in this chapter in more depth, we recommend the following books:

Financial Reporting, *Alexander, D. and Britton, A.*, 6th edn, International Thompson Business Press, 2001, chapter 3.
Accounting Principles, *Anthony, R. and Reece, J.*, 7th edn, Richard D. Irwin, 1995, chapters 2 and 3.
Accounting Theory: Text and readings, *Schroeder, R. and Clark, M.*, 5th edn, Wiley, 1995, chapter 5.
Accounting Theory and Practice, *Glautier, M. and Underdown, B.*, 7th edn, Financial Times Prentice Hall, 2001, chapter 12.

2.1 An accountant prepared a balance sheet for a business using the horizontal layout. In the balance sheet, the capital of Mr Dimitrov, the owner, was shown next to the liabilities. This confused Mr Dimitrov, who argued, 'My capital is my major asset and so should be shown as an asset on the balance sheet.' How would you explain this misunderstanding to Mr Dimitrov?

2.2 'The balance sheet shows how much a business is worth.' Do you agree with this statement? Discuss.

2.3 Can you think of a more appropriate name for the balance sheet?

2.4 In recent years there have been attempts to place a value on the 'human assets' of a business in order to derive a figure that can be included on the balance sheet. Do you think humans should be treated as assets? Would 'human assets' meet the conventional definition of an asset for inclusion on the balance sheet?

? **EXERCISES**

Exercises 2.5–2.8 are more advanced than 2.1–2.4. Those with coloured numbers have answers at the back of the book.

2.1 On the fourth day of his business venture, Paul, the street trader in wrapping-paper (see earlier in the chapter), purchased more stock for £53 cash. During the day he sold stock that had cost £33 for a total of £47.

Required:
Draw up the three financial statements for day 4 of Paul's business venture.

2.2 The 'total business wealth' belongs to Paul because he is the sole owner of the business. Can you explain how the figure for total business wealth at the end of day 4 has arisen? You will need to look back at the events of days 1, 2 and 3 (in this chapter) to do this.

2.3 Whilst on holiday in Bridlington, Helen had her credit cards and purse stolen from the beach while she was swimming. She was left with only £40, which she had kept in her hotel room, but she had three days of her holiday remaining. She was determined to continue her holiday and decided to make some money in order to be able to do so. She decided to sell orange juice to holidaymakers using the local beach. On day 1 she purchased 80 cartons of orange juice at £0.50 each for cash and sold 70 of these at £0.80 each. On the following day she purchased 60 cartons for cash and sold 65 at £0.80 each. On the third and final day she purchased another 60 cartons for cash. However, it rained and, as a result, business was poor. She managed to sell 20 at £0.80 each but sold off the rest of her stock at £0.40 each.

Required:
Prepare a profit and loss account and cash flow statement for each day's trading and prepare a balance sheet at the end of each day's trading.

2.4 On 1 March, Joe Conday started a new business. During March he carried out the following transactions:

1 March   Deposited £20,000 in a bank account
2 March   Purchased fixtures and fittings for £6,000 cash, and stock £8,000 on credit
3 March   Borrowed £5,000 from a relative and deposited it in the bank
4 March   Purchased a motor car for £7,000 cash and withdrew £200 for own use
5 March   A further motor car costing £9,000 was purchased. The motor car purchased on 4 March was given in part exchange at a value of £6,500. The balance of purchase price for the new car was paid in cash
6 March   Conday won £2,000 in a lottery and paid the amount into the business bank account. He also repaid £1,000 of the loan

Required:
Draw up a balance sheet for the business at the end of each day.

2.5 The following is a list of the assets and claims of Crafty Engineering Ltd at 30 June 2001:

	£000
Creditors	86
Motor vehicles	38
Loan from Industrial Finance Co.	260
Machinery and tools	207
Bank overdraft	116
Stock in trade	153
Freehold premises	320
Debtors	185

Required:
(a) Prepare the balance sheet of the business as at 30 June 2001 from the above information using the vertical format. *Hint*: There is a missing item that needs to be deduced and inserted.
(b) Discuss the significant features revealed by this financial statement.

2.6 The balance sheet of a business at the start of the week is as follows:

Assets	£	Claims	£
Freehold premises	145,000	Capital	203,000
Furniture and fittings	63,000	Bank overdraft	43,000
Stock in trade	28,000	Trade creditors	23,000
Trade debtors	33,000		
	269,000		269,000

During the week the following transactions take place:

(a) Stock sold for £11,000 cash; this stock had cost £8,000.
(b) Sold stock for £23,000 on credit; this stock had cost £17,000.
(c) Received cash from trade debtors totalling £18,000.
(d) The owners of the business introduced £100,000 of their own money, which was placed in the business bank account.
(e) The owners brought a motor van, valued at £10,000, into the business.
(f) Bought stock in trade on credit for £14,000.
(g) Paid trade creditors £13,000.

Required:
Show the balance sheet after all of these transactions have been reflected.

2.7 The following is a list of assets and claims of a manufacturing business at a particular point in time:

	£
Bank overdraft	22,000
Freehold land and buildings	245,000
Stock of raw materials	18,000
Trade creditors	23,000
Plant and machinery	127,000
Loan from Industrial Finance Co.	100,000
Stock of finished goods	28,000
Delivery vans	54,000
Trade debtors	34,000

Required:
Write out a balance sheet in the standard vertical form incorporating these figures. *Hint*: There is a missing item that needs to be deduced and inserted.

2.8 You have been talking to someone who had read the first chapter of an accounting text some years ago. During your conversation the person made the following statements:

(a) The profit and loss account shows how much cash has come into and left the business during the accounting period and the resulting balance at the end of the period.
(b) In order to be included in the balance sheet as an asset, an item needs to be worth something in the market, that is all.
(c) The balance sheet equation is:

$$\text{Assets} + \text{Capital} = \text{Liabilities}$$

(d) An expense is an event that reduces capital, so when the owner of the business withdraws some capital, the business has incurred an expense.
(e) Fixed assets are things that cannot be moved.
(f) Current assets are things that stay in the business for less than 12 months.
(g) Working capital is the name given to the sum of the current assets.

Required:
Comment critically on each of the above statements, going into as much detail as you can.

3

Measuring and reporting financial performance

Introduction

In this chapter the profit and loss account will be examined. We shall see how this statement is prepared and what insights it provides concerning financial performance. We shall also consider some of the key measurement problems to be faced when preparing this statement.

The profit and loss account (income statement)

In the previous chapter, we examined the nature and purpose of the balance sheet. We saw that this statement was concerned with setting out the financial position of a business at a particular moment in time. However, it is not usually enough for users to have information relating only to the amount of wealth held by the business at one moment in time; businesses exist for the primary purpose of generating wealth, or profit, and it is the profit generated *during a period* that is the primary concern of many users. Although the amount of profit generated is of particular interest to owners of the business, other groups such as managers, employees and suppliers will also have an interest in the profit-making ability of the business. The purpose of the profit and loss (P and L) account – or income statement, as it is sometimes called – is to measure and report how much **profit** (wealth) the business has generated over a period.

The measurement of profit requires that the total revenues of the business, generated during a particular period, be calculated. **Revenue** is simply a measure of the inflow of assets (for example, cash or amounts owed to a business by debtors) that arise as a result of trading operations. Different forms of business enterprise will generate different forms of revenue. Some examples of the different forms which revenue can take are:

- Sales of goods (for example, of a manufacturer)
- Fees for services (for example, of a solicitor)
- Subscriptions (for example, of a club)
- Interest received (for example, of an investment fund).

The following represent different forms of business enterprise:

(a) Accountancy practice
(b) Squash club
(c) Bus company
(d) Newspaper
(e) Finance company
(f) Songwriter
(g) Retailer
(h) Magazine publisher.

Can you identify the major source(s) of revenue for each type of business enterprise?

Your answer to this activity should be along the following lines:

Type of business	Main source(s) of revenue
(a) Accountancy practice	Fees for services
(b) Squash club	Subscriptions, court fees
(c) Bus company	Ticket sales, advertising
(d) Newspaper	Newspaper sales, advertising
(e) Finance company	Interest received on loans
(f) Songwriter	Royalties, commission fees
(g) Retailer	Sale of goods
(h) Magazine publisher	Magazine sales and advertising

As you can see, it is possible for a business to have more than one form of revenue.

The total expenses relating to each accounting period must also be calculated. An **expense** represents the outflow of assets incurred as a result of generating, or attempting to generate, revenues. The nature of the business will again determine the types of expense that will be incurred. Examples of some of the more common types of expense are:

- The cost of buying goods that are subsequently sold – known as 'cost of sales' or 'cost of goods sold'.
- Salaries and wages.
- Rent and rates.
- Motor-vehicle running expenses.
- Insurances.
- Printing and stationery.
- Heat and light.
- Telephone and postage.

The P and L account for a period simply shows the total revenue generated during a particular period and deducts from this the total expenses incurred in generating that revenue. The difference between the total revenue and total expenses will represent either profit (if revenues exceed expenses) or loss (if expenses exceed revenues). Thus, we have:

Profit(loss) for the period = Total revenue – Total expenses
incurred in generating the revenue

Relationship between the P and L account and the balance sheet

The P and L account and the balance sheet should not be viewed as substitutes for one another. Rather, they should be seen as performing different functions. The balance sheet is, as stated earlier, a statement of the financial position of a business at a single moment in time – a 'snapshot' of the stock of wealth held by the business. The P and L account, on the other hand, is concerned with the *flow* of wealth over a period of time. The two statements are closely related. The profit and loss account can be viewed as linking the balance sheet at the beginning of a period with the balance sheet at the end of that period. Thus, at the commencement of business, a balance sheet could be produced to reveal the opening financial position. After an appropriate period, a P and L account will be prepared to show the wealth generated over the period. A balance sheet will also be prepared to reveal the new financial position at the end of the period covered by the P and L account. This balance sheet will incorporate the changes in wealth that have occurred since the previous balance sheet was drawn up.

We saw in the previous chapter that the effect, on the balance sheet, of making a profit (or loss) means that the balance sheet equation can be extended as follows:

Assets = Capital + (–) Profit(loss) + Liabilities

The amount of profit or loss for the period is shown separately in the balance sheet as an adjustment to capital. The above equation can then be further extended to:

Assets = Capital + (Revenues – Expenses) + Liabilities

In theory, it would be possible to calculate profit and loss for the period by making all adjustments for revenues and expenses through the capital account. However, this would be rather cumbersome. A better solution is to have an 'appendix' to the capital account in the form of a P and L account. By deducting expenses from the revenues for the period, the P and L account derives the profit (loss) for adjustment in the capital account. This figure represents the net effect of operations for the period. Providing this appendix means that a detailed and more informative view of performance is presented to users.

The format of the P and L account

The format of the P and L account will vary according to the type of business to which it relates. In order to illustrate a P and L account, let us consider the case of a retail business (that is, a business that purchases goods in their completed state and resells them). This type of business usually has straightforward operations and, as a result, the P and L account is easy to understand. Example 3.1 sets out a typical format for the P and L account of a retail business.

Hi-Price Stores
Trading and P and L account for the year ended 31 October 2001

	£	£
Sales		232,000
Less Cost of sales		154,000
Gross profit		78,000
Interest received from investments		2,000
		80,000
Less		
Salaries and wages	24,500	
Rent and rates	14,200	
Heat and light	7,500	
Telephone and postage	1,200	
Insurance	1,000	
Motor-vehicle running expenses	3,400	
Loan interest	1,100	
Depreciation – fixtures and fittings	1,000	
motor van	600	
		(54,500)
Net profit		25,500

The first part of the statement in Example 3.1 is concerned with calculating the **gross profit** for the period. The trading revenue, which arises from selling the goods, is the first item that appears. Deducted from this item is the trading expense, which is the cost of acquiring the goods sold during the period. The difference between the trading revenue and trading expense is referred to as 'gross profit'. This represents the profit from simply buying and selling goods without taking into account any other expenses or revenues associated with the business. This first part of the statement, which is concerned with the calculation of gross profit, is referred to as the **trading account** or **trading section**. The remainder of the statement is referred to as the P and L account. Hence, the heading of **trading and P and L account**, which is shown in Example 3.1. (You may often find, however, that the term 'P and L account' is used to describe the whole of this income statement.)

Having calculated the gross profit, any additional revenues of the business are then added to this figure. In Example 3.1, interest from investments represents an additional revenue. (Presumably, the business has some cash on deposit or similar.) From this subtotal of gross profit and additional revenues, the other expenses (overheads) that have to be incurred in order to operate the business (salaries, wages, rent, rates and so on) are deducted. The final figure derived is the **net profit** for the period. This figure represents the wealth generated during the period that is attributable to the owner(s) of the business and that will be added to their capital in the balance sheet. As can be seen, net profit is a residual – that is, the amount left over after deducting all expenses incurred in generating the sales for the period.

The P and L account – some further aspects

Having set out the main principles involved in preparing a profit and loss account, some further points need to be considered.

Cost of sales

The approach taken to identifying the **cost of sales** figure can vary between businesses. In some businesses, the cost of sales is identified at the time each sale is made. For example, the more sophisticated supermarkets tend to have point-of-sale (checkout) devices that not only record each sale but that simultaneously pick up the cost of the particular sale. Businesses that sell a relatively small number of high value items (for example an engineering business that produces custom-made equipment) also tend to match each sale with the cost of the goods sold at the time of the sale. However, some businesses (for example, small retailers) do not usually find it practical to match each sale to a particular cost-of-sale figure as the accounting period progresses; they find it easier to identify the figure at the end of the accounting period.

To understand how this is done, it is important to recognise that the cost of sales figure represents the cost of goods that were *sold* during the period rather than the cost of goods that were *purchased* in the period. Goods purchased during a period may be held in stock to be sold during a later period. In order to derive the cost of sales for a period, it is necessary to know the amounts of opening and closing stocks for the period and the cost of goods purchased during the period.

The opening stocks for the period *plus* the goods purchased during the period will represent the total goods available for resale. The closing stocks will represent that portion of the total goods available for resale that remains unsold at the end of the period. Thus, the cost of goods sold during the period must be the cost associated with the total goods available for resale *less* the stocks remaining at the end of the period. Example 3.2 sets out how this calculation is sometimes shown on the face of the trading account. (The trading account in Example 3.2 is simply an expanded version of the earlier trading account for Hi-Price Stores (Example 3.1) using additional information concerning stock balances and purchases for the year.)

Example 3.2

	£	£
Sales		232,000
Less Cost of sales		
Opening stock	40,000	
Add Goods purchased	189,000	
	229,000	
Less Closing stock	75,000	154,000
Gross profit		78,000

Classification of expenses

The classifications for the revenue and expense items, as with the classification of various assets and claims in the balance sheet, is often a matter of judgement by those who design the accounting system. In the P and L account in Example 3.1, for instance, the insurance expense could have been included with telephone and postage under a single heading of, say, general expenses. Such decisions are normally based on how useful a particular classification will be to users. However, for businesses that trade as limited companies, there are statutory rules dictating the classification of various items appearing in the accounts for external reporting purposes. These rules will be discussed in Chapter 4.

Activity 3.2

The following information relates to the activities of H&S Retailers for the year ended 30 April 2001:

	£
Motor-vehicle running expenses	1,200
Rent received from subletting	2,000
Closing stock	3,000
Rent and rates payable	5,000
Motor vans	6,300
Annual depreciation – motor vans	1,500
Heat and light	900
Telephone and postage	450
Sales	97,400
Goods purchased	68,350
Insurance	750
Loan interest payable	620
Balance at bank	4,780
Salaries and wages	10,400
Opening stock	4,000

Prepare a trading and P and L account for the year ended 30 April 2001.
Hint: Not all items shown above should appear on this statement.

Your answer to this activity should be as follows:

Trading and P and L account for the year ended 30 April 2001

	£	£
Sales		97,400
Less Cost of sales		
Opening stock	4,000	
Purchases	68,350	
	72,350	
Closing stock	(3,000)	(69,350)
Gross profit		28,050
Rent received		2,000
		30,050
Less		
Salaries and wages	10,400	
Rent and rates	5,000	
Heat and light	900	
Telephone and postage	450	
Insurance	750	
Motor-vehicle running expenses	1,200	

	£	£
Loan interest	620	
Depreciation – motor van	1,500	
		(20,820)
Net profit		9,230

In the case of the balance sheet, we saw that the information could be presented in either a horizontal format or a vertical format. This is also true of the trading and P and L account. Where a horizontal format is used, expenses are listed on the left-hand side and revenues on the right, the difference being either net profit or net loss. The vertical format has been used in Activity 3.2 as it is easier to understand and is now almost always used.

The reporting period

We have seen already that, for reporting to those outside the business, a financial reporting cycle of one year is the norm. However, some large businesses will provide a half-yearly, or 'interim', financial statement to give more frequent feedback on progress. For those who manage a business, it is important to have much more frequent feedback on performance. Thus, it is quite common for P and L accounts to be prepared on a quarterly or monthly basis to show the progress (or otherwise) being made during the year.

● ● ● ● Profit measurement and the recognition of revenue

A key issue in the measurement of profit concerns the point at which revenue is recognised. It is possible to recognise revenue at different points in the production/selling cycle and the particular point chosen could have a significant effect on the total revenues reported for the period.

Activity 3.3

A manufacturing business sells goods on credit (that is, the customer is allowed to pay some time after the goods have been received). Below are four points in the production/selling cycle at which revenue might be recognised by the business:

(1) When the goods are produced.
(2) When an order is received from a customer.
(3) When the goods are delivered to, and accepted by, the customer.
(4) When the cash is received from the customer.

A substantial amount of time may elapse between these different points. At what point do you think the business should recognise revenue?

Although you may have come to a different conclusion, the point at which we normally recognise revenue is (3) above. The reasons for this are explained in the text.

The **realisation convention** in accounting is designed to solve the revenue recognition problem (or at least to provide some consistency). This convention states that revenue should only be recognised when it has been 'realised'. Normally, realisation is considered to have occurred when:

- The activities necessary to generate the revenue (for example, delivery of goods, carrying out of repairs) are substantially complete.
- The amount of revenue generated can be objectively determined.
- There is reasonable certainty that the amounts owing from the activities will be received.

These criteria will probably be fulfilled when the goods are passed to the customers and are accepted by them. This is the normal point of recognition when goods are sold on credit. It is also the point at which there is a legally enforceable contract between the parties.

The realisation convention in accounting means that a sale on credit is usually recognised *before* the cash is received. Thus, the total sales figure shown in the profit and loss account may include sales transactions for which the cash has yet to be received. The total sales figure in the P and L account will, therefore, be different from the total cash received from sales.

Not all businesses will wait to recognise revenue until all of the work necessary to generate the revenue is complete. A construction business, for example, which is engaged in a long-term project such as building a dam, will not usually wait until the contract is complete; doing so could mean that no revenue would be recognised by the business until several years after the work commenced. Instead, the business will normally recognise a proportion of the total value of such a contract when an agreed stage of the contract has been completed. This approach to revenue recognition is really a more practical interpretation of the realisation convention rather than a deviation from it.

Profit measurement and the recognition of expenses

Having decided on the point at which revenue is recognised, we must now turn to the issue of the recognition of expenses. The **matching convention** in accounting is designed to provide guidance concerning the recognition of expenses. This convention states that expenses should be matched to the revenues that they helped to generate. In other words, expenses must be taken into account in the same P and L account in which the associated sale is recognised.

Applying this convention may mean that a particular expense reported in the P and L account for a period may not be the same as the cash paid in respect of that item during the period – indeed, the expense reported may be either more or less than the cash paid during the period. Examples 3.3 to 3.5 illustrate this point.

When the expense for the period is more than the cash paid during the period

Example 3.3

Suppose that sales staff are paid a commission of 2 per cent of sales generated and that total sales during the period amounted to £300,000. This will mean that the commission to be paid in respect of the sales for the period will be £6,000. Let us say, however, that by the end of the period the sales commission paid to staff was £5,000. If the business included only the amount paid in the P and L account, it will mean that this statement will not reflect the full expense for the year. This will contravene the matching convention because not all of the expenses associated with the revenues of the period will have been matched in the P and L account. This will be remedied as follows:

- Sales commission expense in the P and L account will include the amount paid *plus* the amount outstanding (£6,000 = £5,000 + £1,000).
- The cash paid (£5,000) will appear in the cash flow statement and will reduce the cash balance.
- The amount outstanding (£1,000) represents an outstanding liability at the balance sheet date and will be included under the heading 'Accruals' or **Accrued expenses** in the balance sheet. As this item will probably have to be paid within 12 months of the balance sheet date, it will be treated as a current liability.

These point are illustrated in Figure 3.1 below.

Figure 3.1

Accounting for sales commission

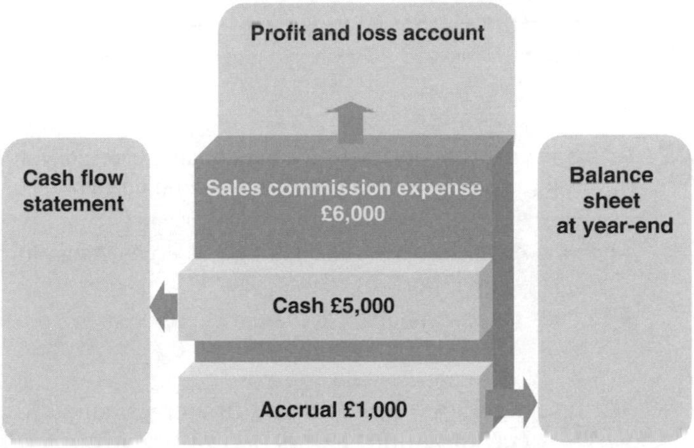

Profit and loss account

Cash flow statement

Sales commission expense £6,000

Balance sheet at year-end

Cash £5,000

Accrual £1,000

The figure illustrates the main points of Example 3.3. We can see that the sales commission expense of £6,000 (which appears in the profit and loss account) is made up of a cash element £5,000 and an accrued element £1,000. The cash element appears in the cash flow statement and the accruals element will appear as a year-end liability in the balance sheet.

Ideally, all expenses should be matched to the period in which the sales to which they relate are reported. However, it is often difficult to match closely certain expenses to sales in the same way that we have matched sales commission to sales. It is unlikely, for example, that electricity charges incurred can be linked directly to particular sales in this way. Thus, as an expedient, the electricity charges incurred will normally be matched to the *period* to which they relate, as Example 3.4 illustrates.

Example 3.4

Suppose a business has reached the end of its accounting year and it has only been charged electricity for the first three quarters of the year (amounting to £1,900), simply because the electricity company has yet to send out bills for the quarter that ends on the same date as the business's year-end. Where this situation exists, an estimate should be made of the electricity expense outstanding (that is, the bill for the last three months of the year is estimated). This figure (let us say the estimate is £500) is dealt with as follows:

- Electricity expense in the P and L account will include the amount paid *plus* the amount of the estimate (£1,900 + £500 = £2,400) to cover the whole year.
- The cash paid (£1,900) will appear in the cash flow statement and will reduce the cash balance.
- The amount of the estimate (£500) represents an outstanding liability at the balance sheet date and will be included under the heading 'Accruals' or 'Accrued expenses' in the balance sheet. As this item will have to be paid within 12 months of the balance sheet date, it will be treated as a current liability.

The above treatment will have the desired effect of increasing the electricity expense to the 'correct' figure for the year in the profit and loss account, assuming that the estimate is reasonably accurate. It will also have the effect of showing that, at the end of the accounting year, the business owed the amount of the last quarter's electricity bill. Dealing with the outstanding amount in this way reflects the dual aspect of the item and will ensure that the balance sheet equation is maintained.

Activity 3.4

Let us say that the estimate for outstanding electricity in Example 3.4 was correct. How will the payment of the electricity bill be dealt with?

When the electricity bill is eventually paid, it will be dealt with as follows:

- Reduce cash by the amount of the bill.
- Reduce the amount of the accrued expense as shown on the balance sheet.

If there is a slight error in the estimate, a small adjustment (either negative or positive, depending on the direction of the error) can be made to the following year's expense. Dealing with the estimation error in this way is not strictly correct, but the amount is likely to be insignificant.

Activity 3.5

Can you think of other expenses that cannot be linked directly to sales and where matching will, therefore, normally be done on a time basis?

You may have thought of the following examples:

- Rent and rates
- Insurance
- Interest payments
- Licences.

This is not an exhaustive list. You may have thought of others.

When the amount paid during the year is more than the full expense for the period

Example 3.5

Suppose a business pays rent for its premises quarterly in advance (on 1 January, 1 March, 1 June and 1 September) and that, on the last day of the accounting year (31 December), it pays the next quarter's rent to the following 31 March (£400) which is a day earlier than required. This would mean that a total of five quarters' rent was paid during the year. If the business reports the cash paid in the P and L account, this would be more than the full expense for the year. This treatment would also contravene the matching convention because a higher figure than the expenses associated with the revenues of the year appears in the profit and loss account.

The problem is overcome by dealing with the rental payment as follows:

- Show the rent for four quarters as the appropriate expense in the P and L account (4 × £400 = £1,600).
- Reduce the cash balance to reflect the full amount of the rent paid during the year (5 × £400 = £2,000).
- Show the quarter's rent paid in advance (£400) as a **prepaid expense** on the asset side of the balance sheet. (The prepaid expense will appear as a current asset in the balance sheet, under the heading 'Prepayments'.)

In the next period, this prepayment will cease to be an asset and become an expense in the profit and loss account of that period. This is because the rent prepaid relates to the next period and will be 'used up' during it.

In practice, the treatment of accruals and prepayments will be subject to the **materiality convention** in accounting. This convention states that, where the amounts involved are immaterial, we should consider only what is expedient. This may mean that an item will be treated as an expense in the period in which it is paid rather than being strictly matched to the revenues to which it relates. For example, a business may find that, at the end of an accounting period, there is a bill of £5 owing for stationery that has been used during the year. The time and effort involved in recording this as an accrual would have little effect on the measurement of profit or financial position for a business of any size, and so it would be ignored when preparing the P and L account for the period. The bill would, presumably, be paid in the following period and, therefore, treated as an expense of that period.

● ● ● ● Profit and cash

The foregoing sections on revenues and expenses reveal that revenues do not usually represent cash received, and expenses are not the same as cash paid. As a result, the net profit figure (that is, total revenue minus total expenses) will not normally represent the net cash generated during a period. It is therefore important to distingish between profit and liquidity. Profit is a measure of achievement, or productive effort, rather than a measure of cash generated. Although making a profit will increase wealth, we have already seen in the previous chapter that cash is only one form in which that wealth may be held.

●●●● Profit measurement and the calculation of depreciation

➡ The expense of **depreciation** that appeared in the P and L account in Example 3.1 requires further explanation. Fixed assets (with the exception of freehold land) do not have a perpetual existence. They are eventually used up in the process of generating revenues for the business. In essence, depreciation is an attempt to measure that portion of the cost of a fixed asset that has been 'used up' in generating the revenues recognised during a particular period. The depreciation charge is considered to be an expense of the period to which it relates.

To calculate a depreciation charge for a period, four factors have to be considered. These are:

- The cost of the asset
- The useful life of the asset
- Residual value
- Depreciation method.

The cost of an asset

This will include all costs incurred by the business to bring the asset to its required location and to make it ready for use. Thus, in addition to the costs of acquiring the asset, any delivery costs, installation costs (for example, for plant) and legal costs incurred in the transfer of legal title (for example, for freehold property) will be included as part of the total cost of the asset. Similarly, any costs incurred in improving or altering an asset in order to make it suitable for its intended use within the business will also be included as part of the total cost.

Activity 3.6

Andrew Wu (Engineering) Ltd purchased a new motor car for its marketing director. The invoice received from the motor-car supplier revealed the following:

	£	£
New BMW 325i		26,350
Delivery charge	80	
Alloy wheels	660	
Sun-roof	200	
Petrol	30	
Number plates	130	
Road fund licence	155	1,255
		27,605
Part exchange – Reliant Robin		(1,000)
Amount outstanding		26,605

What is the total cost of the new car?

....

The cost of the new car will be as follows:

	£	£
New BMW 325i		26,350
Delivery charge	80	
Alloy wheels	660	

	£	£
Sun-roof	200	
Number plates	130	1,070
		27,420

These costs include delivery costs and number plates as they are a necessary and integral part of the asset. Improvements (alloy wheels and sun roof) are also regarded as part of the total cost of the motor car. The petrol costs and road fund licence represent a cost of operating the asset rather than a part of the total cost of acquiring the asset and making it ready for use, hence these amounts will be charged as an expense in the period incurred (though part of the cost of the licence may be regarded as a prepaid expense) in the period incurred.

The part-exchange figure shown is part payment of the total amount outstanding and is not relevant to a consideration of the total cost.

There has been an increasing tendency for businesses to add to the cost of fixed assets being produced any interest charges incurred in financing the production of the asset. For example, some supermarket chains have used this approach when funds have been borrowed to build new stores. This practice is referred to as 'capitalising' interest payments. The argument in favour of this approach is that interest payments incurred before a particular store opens represent part of the total cost of development and should, therefore, be included as part of the cost of the asset. The interest capitalised will then normally be written off (that is, treated as an expense) over the asset's useful life. Exhibit 3.1 describes how one business capitalises its interest charges.

Exhibit 3.1

The following extract has been taken from the 2000 annual report of J. Sainsbury plc, a large supermarket business.

Capitalisation of interest
Interest incurred on borrowings for the financing of specific property developments is capitalised.

The amount of interest capitalised by the business for the year to 1 April 2000 was £10 million. As the profit for the financial year was £349 million, the capitalisation of interest (rather than charging it to the profit and loss account for 2000) did not have a significant effect on the reported profit.

The useful life of an asset

An asset has both a physical life and an economic life. The physical life of an asset will be exhausted through the effects of wear and tear and/or the passage of time, although it is possible for the physical life to be extended considerably through careful maintenance, improvements and so on. The economic life of an asset is determined by the effects of technological progress and changes in demand. After a while, the benefits of using the asset may be less than the costs involved. This may be because the asset is unable to compete with newer assets or because it is no longer relevant to the needs of the business. The economic life of an asset may be much shorter than its physical life. For example, a computer may have a physical life of eight years and an economic life of three years.

It is the economic life of an asset that will determine the expected useful life for the purpose of calculating depreciation. Forecasting the economic life of an asset, however, may be extremely difficult in practice. Both the rate at which technology progresses and shifts in consumer tastes can be swift and unpredictable.

Residual value (disposal value)

When a business disposes of a fixed asset that may still be of value to others, some payment may be received. This payment will represent the **residual value** or 'disposal value' of the asset. To calculate the total amount to be depreciated with regard to an asset, the residual value must be deducted from the cost of the asset. The likely amount to be received on disposal is, once again, often difficult to predict.

Depreciation method

Once the amount to be depreciated (that is, the cost less any residual value) has been estimated, the business must select a method of allocating this depreciable amount over the useful life of the fixed asset. Although there are various ways in which the total depreciation may be allocated and a depreciation charge for a period derived, there are really only two methods that are commonly used in practice.

The first of these is known as the **straight-line method** (see Example 3.6). This method simply allocates the amount to be depreciated evenly over the useful life of the asset. In other words, an equal amount of depreciation will be charged for each year the asset is held.

Example 3.6

To illustrate the straight-line method, consider the following information:

Cost of machine	£40,000
Estimated residual value at the end of its useful life	£1,024
Estimated useful life	4 years

To calculate the depreciation charge for each year, the total amount to be depreciated must be calculated. This will be the total cost *less* the estimated residual value, that is £40,000 – £1,024 = £38,976. Having done this, the annual depreciation charge can be derived by dividing the amount to be depreciated by the estimated useful life of the asset of four years. The calculation is therefore:

$$\frac{£38,976}{4} = £9,744$$

Thus, the annual depreciation charge that appears in the P and L account in relation to this asset will be £9,744 for each of the four years of the asset's life.

The amount of depreciation relating to the asset will be accumulated for as long as the asset continues to be owned by the business. This accumulated depreciation

---

figure will increase each year as a result of the annual depreciation amount charged to the P and L account, the accumulated amount being deducted from the cost of the asset on the balance sheet. Thus, for example, at the end of the second year, the accumulated depreciation will be £9,744 × 2 = £19,488 and the asset details will appear on the balance sheet as follows:

	£	£
Machine at cost	40,000	
Less Accumulated depreciation	(19,488)	
		20,512

The balance of £20,512 is referred to as the **written-down value** or **net book value** of the asset. It represents that portion of the cost of the asset that has not been treated as an expense. It must be emphasised that this figure does *not* represent the current market value, which may be quite different.

The straight-line method derives its name from the fact that the written-down value of the asset at the end of each year, when plotted on a graph against time, will result in a straight line, as shown in Figure 3.2.

Figure 3.2

Graph of written-down value against time using the straight-line method

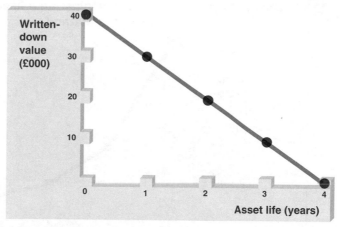

The figure shows that the written-down value of the asset declines by a constant amount each year. This is because the straight-line method provides a constant depreciation charge each year. The result, when plotted on a graph, is a straight line.

The second popular approach to calculating depreciation for a period is referred to as the **reducing-balance method**. This method applies a fixed percentage rate of depreciation to the written-down value of an asset each year. The effect of this will be high annual depreciation charges in the early years and lower charges in the later years. To illustrate this method, let us take the same information used in Example 3.6 and use a fixed percentage (60 per cent) of the written-down value to determine the annual depreciation charge. The calculations will be:

	£
Cost of machine	40,000
Year 1 Depreciation charge (60% of cost – see formula below)	(24,000)
Written-down value (WDV)	16,000
Year 2 Depreciation charge (60% WDV)	(9,600)
Written-down value	6,400
Year 3 Depreciation charge (60% WDV)	(3,840)
Written-down value	2,560
Year 4 Depreciation charge (60% WDV)	(1,536)
Residual value	1,024

Deriving the fixed percentage to be applied requires the use of the following formula:

$$P = (1 - \sqrt[n]{R/C}) \times 100\%$$

where

P = the depreciation percentage
n = the useful life of the asset (in years)
R = the residual value of the asset
C = the cost of the asset.

We can see that the pattern of depreciation is quite different for the two methods. Figure 3.3 plots the written-down value of the asset, which has been derived using the reducing balance method, against time.

Figure 3.3

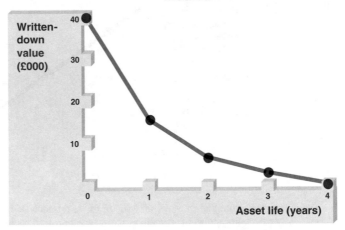

Graph of written-down value against time using the reducing-balance method

The figure shows that, under the reducing-balance method, the written-down value of an asset falls by a larger amount in the earlier years than in the later years. This is because the depreciation charge is based on a fixed percentage of the written-down value.

Activity 3.7

Assume that the machine used in Example 3.6 was owned by a business that made a profit *before* depreciation of £20,000 for each of the four years in which the asset was held. Calculate the net profit for the business for each year under each depreciation method and comment on your findings.

Your answer should be as follows:

Straight-line method

	Profit before depr'n £	Depr'n £	Net profit £
Year 1	20,000	9,744	10,256
Year 2	20,000	9,744	10,256
Year 3	20,000	9,744	10,256
Year 4	20,000	9,744	10,256

Reducing-balance method

	Profit before depr'n £	Depr'n £	Net profit (loss) £
Year 1	20,000	24,000	(4,000)
Year 2	20,000	9,600	10,400
Year 3	20,000	3,840	16,160
Year 4	20,000	1,536	18,464

The above calculations reveal that the straight line method of depreciation results in a constant net profit figure over the four-year period. This is because both the profit before depreciation and the depreciation charge are constant over the period.

The reducing-balance method, however, results in a changing profit figure over time. In the first year a net loss is reported, and thereafter a rising net profit.

Although the *pattern* of net profit over the period will be quite different, depending on the depreciation method used, the *total* net profit for the period will remain the same. This is because both methods of depreciating will allocate the same amount of total depreciation (£38,976) over the whole period. It is only the amount allocated between years that will differ.

In practice, the effects of using different depreciation methods may not have such a dramatic effect on profits as suggested by Activity 3.7. Where a business replaces some of its assets each year, the total depreciation charge calculated under the reducing-balance method will reflect a range of charges (from high through to low) as assets will be at different points in the replacement cycle. This could mean that the total depreciation charge may not be significantly different from the total depreciation charge that would be derived under the straight-line method.

Activity 3.8

Assume that a business purchases a machine (as described in Example 3.6) each year and that each machine is replaced at the end of its useful life of four years. Assume that this policy has been operating for several years and that the business owns four machines. What is the total depreciation charge for a year under:

(a) the straight-line method?
(b) the reducing-balance method?

Your answer should be as follows:

(a) Depreciation charges under the straight-line method will be:

£9,744 × 4 = £38,976 (At any point in time, four machines are held)

(b) Depreciation charges under the reducing-balance method will be:

		£	
Machine	1	24,000	(Depr'n yr 1)
	2	9,600	(Depr'n yr 2)
	3	3,840	(Depr'n yr 3)
	4	1,536	(Depr'n yr 4)
		38,976	

In this case, the total depreciation charges under each method will be identical. (In practice, however, it would be unusual for both methods to give exactly the same total depreciation charge for a group of machines at different points in the replacement cycle.)

Figure 3.4

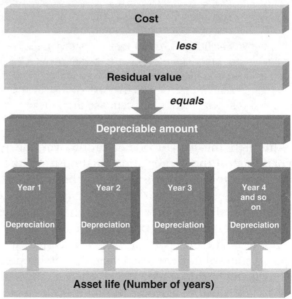

Calculating an annual depreciation charge

The figure shows how the annual depreciation charge is calculated. The depreciable amount (cost less residual value) is allocated over the life of the fixed asset using an appropriate depreciation method.

Selecting a depreciation method

How does a business choose which depreciation method to use for a particular asset? The most appropriate method should be the one that best matches the depreciation expense to the revenues that it helped generate. The business may, therefore, decide to undertake an examination of the pattern of benefits flowing from the asset. Where the benefits are likely to remain fairly constant over time (for example, from buildings), the straight-line method may be considered appropriate. Where assets lose their efficiency over time and the benefits decline as a result (for example, with certain types of machinery), the reducing-balance method may be considered more appropriate. However, other approaches to selecting a depreciation method are also used.

The accountancy profession has developed an accounting standard to deal with the problem of depreciation. As we shall see in Chapter 5, the purpose of accounting standards is to narrow the areas of difference in accounting between businesses by producing statements on best accounting practice. The standard for handling depreciation endorses the view that the depreciation method chosen should reflect the economic benefits flowing from the asset. The standard also requires that limited companies disclose, in their financial statements, the methods of depreciation used, the total depreciation for the period, and either the depreciation rates applied or the useful lives of the assets. An example of the type of disclosure required concerning depreciation policies is provided in Exhibit 3.2.

Exhibit 3.2

This extract from the 1999 published accounts of Rolls-Royce plc, a business that builds engines for aircraft, ships and other purposes, describes how the business calculates its depreciation charge.

Depreciation
(i) Land and buildings. Depreciation is provided on the original cost of purchases since 1996 and on the valuation of properties adopted at December 31, 1996 and is calculated on the straight-line basis at rates sufficient to reduce them to their estimated residual value. Estimated lives, as advised by the Group's professional valuers, are:

    (a) Freehold buildings – five to 45 years (average 23 years).
    (b) Leashold land and buildings – lower valuer's esitmates or period of lease.

    No depreciation is provided in respect of freehold land.

(ii) Plant and equipment. Depreciation is provided on the original cost of plant and equipment and is calculated on a straight-line basis at rates sufficient to reduce them to their estimated residual value. Estimated lives are in the range five to 25 years (average 17 years).

(iii) Aircraft and engines. Depreciation is provided on the original cost of aircraft and engines and is calculated on a straight-line basis at rates sufficient to reduce them to their estimated residual value. Estimated lives are in the range 10 to 25 years (average 18 years).

(iv) In course of construction. No depreciation is provided on assets in the course of construction.

It is clear from what we have considered that making different judgements on depreciation can lead to vastly different profit figures being recorded by businesses. Exhibit 3.3 provides an example of this and how it could have led to a particular business decision being made.

Exhibit 3.3

BMW, the German car manufacturer, had owned Rover, one of the UK's car manufacturers since 1994. Early in 2000, BMW announced its decision to close the UK business because it was losing BMW £2 million a day. It transpired that this was true using German accounting standards when deriving Rover's annual depreciation expense, but when UK standards were applied, the depreciation charge was £0.44 million a day less. This still left a very large loss, but significantly less than was stated by BMW.

Source: Based on an article appearing in *Accounting Age*, 4 May 2000.

In the case of certain intangible fixed assets, such as purchased goodwill and research and development expenditure, determining the period over which the benefits extend may be extremely difficult to judge. In practice, different approaches to dealing with this problem arise. Some businesses adopt a prudent view and write off such assets immediately, whereas others may write off the assets over time (see Exhibit 3.4).

In a study of the accounting treatment of intangible assets of companies operating in the food and drink industry, it was found that where intangible assets were capitalised a wide variety of depreciation (amortisation) policies were being applied. The table below sets out the various write-off periods that are applied to different types of intangible assets in the industry.

	Patents	Brands	Goodwill	Devel. cost	Other	No. of occurrences
10 yrs only		1	2	1		4
10–25 yrs	1		2	1		4
25–40 yrs			1			1
40 yrs	1		2			3
Not stated	3			1		4
No amortisation	1	5	1		1	8
						24

Source: Ong (see reference at the end of the chapter), p. 184.

It is possible to avoid making a depreciation charge for a fixed asset on the grounds that it has an infinite economic life (for example, freehold land) or that the estimated residual value of the fixed asset will be more or less the same as the cost or valuation figure shown in the balance sheet and, therefore, any depreciation charge would be insignificant. This latter situation will usually arise where the business provides a high standard of maintenance for its assets. Large retail chains and breweries, in particular, often argue that any depreciation charge for the freehold properties they own, such as stores and public houses, would be immaterial (see Exhibit 3.5).

The 2000 accounts of Next plc, a large fashion-clothing retail chain, show that the company considers that the depreciation charge to its freehold properties is immaterial. In its statement of accounting policies, the company argues:

> Freehold and long leashold properties for use in the high street retailing business are maintained to a standard whereby the estimated residual values (based on prices prevailing at the date of acquisition or revaluation) and lives of these properties are such that any depreciation would not be significant. For all other fixed assets, depreciation is provided to write down the cost less residual value of the asset over its remaining useful life by equal annual instalments.

The non-depreciation of fixed assets can be justified for the reasons stated above. However, it is not usually possible for a business to maintain the value of its fixed assets for an infinite period simply through regular maintenance and refurbishment.

Depreciation and the replacement of fixed assets

These seems to be a misunderstanding in the mind of some people that the purpose of depreciation is to provide for the replacement of an asset when it reaches the end of its useful life. However, this is *not* the purpose of depreciation as conventionally defined. It was mentioned earlier that depreciation represents an attempt to allocate the cost (less any residual value) of an asset over its expected useful life. The resulting depreciation charge in each period represents an expense, which is then used in the calculation of net profit for the period. Calculating the depreciation charge for a period is, therefore, necessary for the proper measurement of financial performance and must be calculated whether or not the business intends to replace the asset in the future.

If there is an intention to replace the asset, the depreciation charge in the profit and loss account will not ensure that liquid funds are set aside by the business specifically for this purpose. Although the effect of a depreciation charge is to reduce net profit and, therefore, to reduce the amount available for distribution to owners, the amounts retained within the business as a result may be invested in ways that are unrelated to the replacement of the specific assets.

Activity 3.9	Suppose that a business sets aside liquid funds, equivalent to the depreciation charge each year, with the intention of using this to replace the asset at the end of its useful life. Will this ensure that there will be sufficient funds available for this purpose?

No. Even if funds are set aside each year that are equal to the depreciation charge for the year, the total amount accumulated at the end of the asset's useful life may be insufficient for replacement purposes. This may be because inflation or technological advances have resulted in an increase in the replacement cost.

Depreciation – some further issues

It is possible for certain fixed assets to appreciate in value over the short term and yet still be used up over time in the process of generating revenue. An example of such an asset is leasehold buildings. Leasehold buildings have a fixed life and will eventually be worthless to the leaseholder even though the value of the leasehold may rise at certain points during the period of the lease.

It was mentioned in the previous chapter that some businesses depart from the historic cost convention and revalue such assets periodically in order to reflect their current value on the balance sheet. When revaluation occurs, it is still appropriate to depreciate the asset, because the benefits flowing from the asset will eventually be exhausted. However, the depreciation charge should be based on the revalued amount rather than on the original cost of the asset. This will usually result in a higher depreciation charge for the asset, but it will represent a more realistic measure of the economic cost of using the asset.

When reading this section on depreciation it may have struck you that accounting is not so precise and objective as is sometimes suggested. There are areas where subjective judgement is required and depreciation provides a good illustration of this.

Activity 3.10

What kinds of judgement must be made to calculate a depreciation charge for a period?

....

In answering this activity, you may have thought of the following:

- The cost of the asset (for example, deciding whether to include interest charges or not)
- The expected residual or disposal value of the asset
- The expected useful life of the asset
- The choice of depreciation method.

The effect of making different judgements on these matters would result in a different pattern of depreciation charges over the life of the asset and, therefore, a different pattern of reported profits. However, under- or overestimations will be adjusted for in the final year of an asset's life so that the total depreciation charge (and total profit) over the asset's life will not be affected by estimation errors.

Activity 3.11

Sally Dalton (Packaging) Ltd purchased a machine for £40,000. At the end of its useful life of four years, the amount received on sale was £4,000. When the asset was purchased the business received two estimates of the likely residual value of the asset, which were: (a) £8,000, and (b) zero.

Show the pattern of annual depreciation charges over the four years and the total depreciation charges for the asset under each of the two estimates. The straight-line method should be used to calculate the annual depreciation charges.

....

The depreciation charge, assuming estimate (a), will be £8,000 per year ((£40,000 – £8,000)/4). The depreciation charge, assuming estimate (b), will be £10,000 per year (£40,000/4). As the actual residual value is £4,000, estimate (a) will lead to under-depreciation of £4,000 (£8,000 – £4,000) over the life of the asset, and estimate (b) will lead to overdepreciation of £4,000 (£0 – £4,000). These under- and overestimations will be dealt with in year 4.

The pattern of depreciation and total depreciation charges will therefore be:

		Estimate	
		(a)	(b)
Year		£	£
1	Annual depreciation	8,000	10,000
2	Annual depreciation	8,000	10,000
3	Annual depreciation	8,000	10,000
4	Annual depreciation	8,000	10,000
		32,000	40,000
4	Under/(over)depreciation	4,000	(4,000)
	Total depreciation	36,000	36,000

The final adjustment for underdepreciation of an asset is often referred to as 'loss on sale of fixed asset', as the amount actually received is less than the resid-ual value. Similarly, the adjustment for overdepreciation is often referred to as 'profit on sale of fixed asset'.

Profit measurement and the valuation of stocks

The way in which we measure the value of stock is important, because the amount of stock sold during a period will affect the calculation of net profit and the remaining stock held at the end of the period will affect the portrayal of the financial position. In Chapter 2 we saw that historical cost is the basis for valuing assets, and so you may think that stock valuation should not be a difficult issue. However, where there is a period of changing prices, the valuation of stock can be a problem.

A business must determine the cost of the stock sold during the period and the cost of the stock remaining at the end of the period. To do this the cost, of both the stock sold during the period and that remining at the end of the period, is calculated as if it had been physically handled in a particular assumed manner. The assumptiion made has nothing to do with how the stock is *actually* handled; it is concerned only with which assumption is likely to lead to the most useful accounting information.

The two most common assumptions used are:

- **First in, first out (FIFO)** – the earlier stocks held are the first to be sold.
- **Last in, first out (LIFO)** – the latest stocks held are the first to be sold.

Another approach to deriving the cost of stocks is to assume that stocks entering the business lose their separate identity and any issues of stock reflect the average cost of the stocks that are held. This is the **weighted average cost (AVCO)** method, where the weights used – in deriving the average cost figure are the quantities of each batch of stock purchased.

Let us now use the information contained in Example 3.7 to calculate the cost of goods sold and closing stock figures for the business using these three methods.

Example 3.7

A business that supplies coal to factories has the following transactions during a period:

		Tonnes	*Cost/tonne*
1 May	Opening stock	1,000	£10
2 May	Purchased	5,000	£11
3 May	Purchased	8,000	£12
		14,000	
6 May	Sold	(9,000)	
	Closing stock	5,000	

First in, first out (FIFO)

Using the first in, first out approach, the first 9,000 tonnes of coal are assumed to be those that are sold and the remainder will comprise the closing stock. Thus we have:

	Cost of sales			Closing stock		
	Tonnes	Cost/tonne £	Total £000	Tonnes	Cost/tonne £	Total £000
1 May	1,000	10	10.0			
2 May	5,000	11	55.0			
3 May	3,000	12	36.0	5,000	12	60.0
Cost of sales			101.0	Closing stock		60.0

Last in, first out (LIFO)

Using the last in, first out approach, the later purchases will be the first to be sold and the earlier purchases will comprise the closing stock. Thus we have:

	Cost of sales			Closing stock		
	Tonnes	Cost/tonne £	Total £000	Tonnes	Cost/tonne £	Total £000
3 May	8,000	12	96.0			
2 May	1,000	11	11.0	4,000	11	44.0
1 May				1,000	10	10.0
Cost of sales			107.0	Closing stock		54.0

Weighted average cost (AVCO)

Using this approach, a weighted average cost will be determined that will be used to derive both the cost of goods sold and the cost of the remaining stocks held. Thus we have:

	Purchases		
	Tonnes	Cost/tonne £	Total £000
1 May	1,000	10	10.0
2 May	5,000	11	55.0
3 May	8,000	12	96.0
	14,000		161.0

Average cost = £161,000/14,000 = £11.5 per tonne.

Cost of sales			Closing stock		
Tonnes	Cost/tonne £	Total £000	Tonnes	Cost/tonne £000	Total £000
9,000	11.5	103.5	5,000	11.5	57.5

Activity 3.12

Suppose the 9,000 tonnes of stock in the Example 3.7 were sold for £15 per tonne.

(a) Calculate the gross profit for the period under each of the three methods.
(b) What observations concerning the portrayal of financial position and performance can you make about each method when prices are rising?

Your answer should be along the following lines:

(a) Gross profit calculation:

	FIFO £000	LIFO £000	AVCO £000
Sales	135.0	135.0	135.0
Cost of sales	101.0	107.0	103.5
Gross profit	34.0	28.0	31.5
	£000	£000	£000
Closing stock figure	60.0	54.0	57.5

(b) The above figures reveal that FIFO will give the highest gross profit during a period of rising prices. This is because sales are matched with the earlier (and cheaper) purchases. LIFO will give the lowest gross profit because sales are matched against the more recent (and dearer) purchases. The AVCO method will normally give a figure that is between these two extremes.

The closing stock figure in the balance sheet will be highest with the FIFO method. This is because the cost of goods still held will be based on the more recent (and dearer) purchases. LIFO will give the lowest closing stock figure as the goods held in stock will be based on the earlier (and cheaper) stocks purchased. Once again, the AVCO method will normally give a figure that is between these two extremes.

Activity 3.13

Assume that prices in Activity 3.12 are falling rather than rising. How would your observations concerning the portrayal of financial performance and position be different for the various stock valuation methods?

When prices are falling, the position of FIFO and LIFO is reversed. FIFO will give the lowest gross profit as sales are matched against the earlier (and dearer) goods purchased. LIFO will give the highest gross profit as sales are matched against the more recent (and cheaper) goods purchased. AVCO will give a cost of sales figure between these two extremes. The closing stock figure in the balance sheet will be lowest under FIFO as the cost of stock will be based on the more recent (and cheaper) stocks purchased. LIFO will provide the highest closing stock figure and AVCO will provide a figure between the two extremes.

It is important to recognise that the different stock valuation methods will only have an effect on the reported profit *from one year to the next*. The figure derived for closing stock will be carried forward and matched with sales in a later period. Thus, if the cheaper purchases of stocks are matched to sales in the current period, it will mean that the dearer purchases will be matched to sales in a later period. Over the life of the business, therefore, the total profit will be the same whichever valuation method has been used.

Stock valuation – some further issues

Determining the cost of stock held by a manufacturing business can be more of a problem than for other types of business. This is because manufacturing businesses will normally hold three different categories of stock:

- Raw materials
- Work in progress (that is, partly finished goods)
- Finished goods.

The general principle to be applied when determining the cost of the stocks held is that any amounts incurred in bringing the goods to their current condition and location should be included. This will mean that, for raw materials, the cost of purchasing will include amounts incurred for transportation, handling and import duties. For work in progress and finished goods, the costs of converting the raw materials to products should be included. These costs of conversion will typically include such things as labour costs, production overheads and subcontractors' costs. However, in practice, there may be various items of expenditure that are really a matter of judgement as to whether or not they are included in the cost figure.

We saw in Chapter 2 that the closing stock figure will appear as part of the current assets of the business and that the convention of prudence requires current assets to be valued at the lower of cost and net realisable value. (The net realisable value of stocks is the estimated selling price less any further costs that may be necessary to complete the goods and any costs involved in selling and distributing the goods.) This rule may mean that the valuation method applied to stock will switch each year depending on which of cost and net realisable value is the lower. In practice, however, the cost of the stock held is usually below the current net realisable value – particularly during a period of rising prices. It is, therefore, the cost figure that will normally appear in the balance sheet.

| **Activity 3.14** | Can you think of any circumstances where the net realisable value will be lower than the cost of stocks held, even during a period of generally rising prices? |

The net realisable value may be lower where:

- Goods have deteriorated or become obsolete.
- There has been a fall in the market price of the goods.
- The goods are being used as a 'loss leader'.
- Bad purchasing decisions have been made.

The accountancy profession has produced an accounting standard to deal with the issue of stock valuation. This standard supports the lower of cost and net realisable value rule and states that, when comparing the cost with the net realisable value, each item of stock should be compared separately. If this is not practical, categories of similar stock should be grouped together. The standard also identifies a number of methods of arriving at the cost of stock that are acceptable.

Although FIFO and AVCO are regarded as acceptable, the LIFO approach is not. The LIFO approach is also unacceptable to the Inland Revenue for taxation purposes. As a result, LIFO is rarely used in the UK, although it is in widespread use in the United States. The policies of one company with respect to its stock holdings are set out in Exhibit 3.6.

Exhibit 3.6

The following extract has been taken from the 2000 published accounts of Tate and Lyle plc, the sugar and other starch-based food processor, which sets out the accounting policy adopted with respect to stocks:

> Stock is valued at the lower of direct cost together with attributable overheads and net realisable value and is transferred to the profit and loss account on a 'first in, first out' basis.

Stock valuation and depreciation provide two examples where the **consistency convention** must be applied. This convention holds that when a particular method of accounting is selected to deal with a transaction, this method should be applied consistently over time. Thus, it would not be acceptable to switch from, say, FIFO to AVCO between periods (unless there are exceptional circumstances that make this appropriate). The purpose of this convention is to try to ensure that users are able to make valid comparisons between periods.

Activity 3.15

Stock valuation provides a further example of where subjective judgement is required to derive the figures for inclusion in the financial statements. Can you identify the main areas where judgement is required?

....

The main areas are:

● The choice of cost method (FIFO, LIFO, AVCO).
● Deciding which items should be included in the cost of stocks (particularly for work in progress and the finished goods of a manufacturing business).
● Deriving the net realisable value figure for stocks held.

Profit measurement and the problem of bad and doubtful debts

Many businesses sell goods on credit. When credit sales are made, the revenue is usually recognised as soon as the goods are passed to, and accepted by, the customer. Recording the dual aspect of a credit sale will involve:

● increasing the sales;
● increasing debtors by the amount of the credit sale.

However, with this type of sale there is always the risk that the customer will not pay the amount due, however reliable the customer might have appeared to be at the time of the sale. When it becomes reasonably certain that the customer will never pay, the debt is considered to be 'bad' and this must be taken into account when preparing the financial statements.

To provide a more realistic picture of financial performance and position, the **bad debt** must be 'written off'. This will involve:

- reducing the debtors;
- increasing expenses (by creating an expense known as 'bad debts written off') by the amount of the bad debt.

The matching convention requires that the bad debt is written off in the same period as the sale, that gave rise to the debt, is recognised.

Note that, when a debt is bad, the accounting response is not simply to cancel the original sale. If this were done, the P and L account would not be so inform-ative. Reporting the bad debts as an expense can be extremely useful in the eval-uation of management performance.

At the end of the accounting period, it may not be possible to identify with rea-sonable certainty all the bad debts that have been incurred during the period. It may be that some debts appear doubtful, but only at some later point in time will the true position become clear. The uncertainty that exists does not mean that, when preparing the financial statements, we should ignore the possibility that some of the debtors outstanding will eventually prove to be bad. It would not be prudent to do so, nor would it comply with the need to match expenses to the period in which the associated sale is recognised. As a result, the business will normally try to identify all those debts that, at the end of the period, can be clas-sified as doubtful (that is, there is a possibility that they may eventually prove to be bad). This can be done by examining individual accounts of debtors or by taking a proportion of the total debtors outstanding based on past experience.

Once a figure has been derived, a **provision for doubtful debts** can be created. This provision will be:

- shown as an expense in the profit and loss account, and
- deducted from the total debtors figure in the balance sheet.

By doing this, full account is taken, in the appropriate accounting period, of those debts where there is a risk of non-payment. This accounting treatment of doubtful debts will be in addition to the treatment of bad debts described above.

Example 3.8 illustrates the reporting of bad and doubtful debts.

Example 3.8

Desai Enterprises has debtors of £350,000 at the end of the accounting year to 30 June 2001. Investigation of these debtors revealed that £10,000 was likely to prove irrecoverable and that a further £30,000 was doubtful.

Extracts from the P and L account would have been as follows:

Profit and loss account (extracts) for the year ended 30 June 2001

	£
Bad debts written off	10,000
Provision for doubtful debts	30,000

Balance sheet (extracts) as at 30 June 2001

	£
Debtors	340,000[a]
Less Provision for doubtful debts	30,000
	310,000

[a] (that is, £350,000 − £10,000 irrecoverable debts)

The provision for doubtful debts is, of course, an estimate, and it is quite likely that the actual amount of debts that prove to be bad will be different from the estimate. Let us say that, during the next accounting period, it was discovered that £26,000 of the doubtful debts in fact proved to be irrecoverable. These debts must now be written off as follows:

- Reduce debtors by £26,000, and
- Reduce provision for doubtful debts by £26,000.

However, a provision for doubtful debts of £4,000 will remain. This amount represents an overestimate made when creating the provision in the P and L account for the year to 30 June 2001. As the provision is no longer needed, it should be eliminated. Remember that the provision was made by creating an expense in the P and L account for the year to 30 June 2001. As the expense was too high, the amount of the overestimate should be 'written back' in the next accounting period. In other words, it will be treated as revenue for the year to 30 June 2002. This will mean:

- Reducing the provision for doubtful debts by £4,000, and
- Increasing revenues by £4,000.

Ideally, of course, the amount should be written back to the 2001 P and L account, however, it is too late to do this. At the end of 2002, not only will 2001's over-provision be written back but a new provision should be created to allow for the debts, arising from 2002's sales, that seem doubtful.

Activity 3.17

Clayton Conglomerates had debts of £870,000 outstanding at the end of the accounting year to 31 March 2002. The chief accountant believed that £40,000 of those debts were irrecoverable and that a further £60,000 were doubtful. In the subsequent year, it was found that an overoptimistic estimate had been made and that a further £45,000 of debts had actually proved to be bad.

Show the relevant extracts in the profit and loss account for both 2002 and 2003 to report the bad debts written off and the provision for doubtful debts. Also show the relevant balance sheet extract as at 31 March 2002.

Your answer should be as follows:

P and L account (extracts) for the year ended 31 March 2002

	£
Bad debts written off	40,000
Provision for doubtful debts	60,000

P and L account (extracts) for the year ended 31 March 2003

	£
Provision for doubtful debts written back (revenue)	15,000

Note: This figure will usually be netted off against any provision created for doubtful debts in respect of 2003.

Balance sheet (extracts) as at 31 March 2002

	£
Debtors	830,000
Less Provision for doubtful debts	(60,000)
	770,000

Activity 3.18

Bad and doubtful debts represent further areas where judgement is required in deriving expenses figures for a particular period. What will be the effect of different judgements concerning the amount of bad and doubtful debts on the profit for a particular period and on the total profit reported over the life of the business?

Judgement is often required in order to derive a figure for bad debts incurred during a period. There may be situations where views will differ concerning whether or not a debt is irrecoverable. The decision concerning whether or not to write off a bad debt will have an effect on the expenses for the period and, hence, the reported profit. However, over the life of the business, the total reported profit will not be affected as incorrect judgements in one period will be adjusted for in a later period.

Suppose, for example, that a debt of £100 was written off in a period and that, in a later period, the amount owing was actually received. The increase in expenses of £100 in the period in which the bad debt was written off would be compensated for by an increase in revenues of £100 when the amount outstanding was finally received (bad debt recoverable). If, on the other hand, the amount owing of £100 was never written off in the first place, the profit for the two periods would not be affected by the bad debt adjustment and would, therefore, be different – but the total profit for the two periods would be the same.

A similar situation would apply where there are differences in judgements concerning doubtful debts.

Self-assessment question 3.1 brings together some of the points that have been raised in this chapter.

Self-assessment question 3.1

TT Limited is a new business that started trading on 1 January 2000. The following is a summary of transactions that occurred during the first year of trading:

1. The owners introduced £50,000 of capital, which was paid into a bank account opened in the name of the business.
2. Premises were rented from 1 January 2000 at an annual rental of £20,000. During the year, rent of £25,000 was paid to the owner of the premises.
3. Rates on the premises were paid during the year as follows:

   - For the period 1 January 2000 to 31 March 2000: £500
   - For the period 1 April 2000 to 31 March 2001: £1,200

4. A delivery van was bought on 1 January 2000 for £12,000. This is expected to be used in the business for four years and then to be sold for £2,000.
5. Wages totalling £33,500 were paid during the year. At the end of the year, the business owed £630 of wages for the last week of the year.
6. Electricity bills for the first three quarters of the year were paid, totalling £1,650. After 31 December 2000 but before the accounts had been finalised for the year, the bill for the last quarter arrived showing a charge of £620.
7. Stock in trade totalling £143,000 was bought on credit.
8. Stock in trade totalling £12,000 was bought for cash.
9. Sales on credit totalled £152,000 (cost £74,000).
10. Cash sales totalled £35,000 (cost £16,000).
11. Receipts from trade debtors totalled £132,000.
12. Payments to trade creditors totalled £121,000.
13. Van running expenses paid totalled £9,400.
14. At the end of the year it was clear that a trade debtor who owed £400 would not be able to pay any part of the debt.

The business uses the straight-line method for depreciating fixed asets.

Required:
Prepare a balance sheet as at 31 December 2000 and a P and L account for the year to that date.

Interpreting the P and L account

When a P and L account is presented to users, it is sometimes the case that the only item that will concern them will be the final net profit figure or 'bottom line'. Although the net profit figure is a primary measure of performance and its importance is difficult to overstate, the P and L account contains other information which should be of interest. In order to evaluate business performance effectively, it is important to find out how the final net profit figure was derived. Thus, the level of sales, the nature and amount of expenses incurred and the profit in relation to sales are important factors in understanding the performance of the business over a period. The analysis and interpretation of financial statements is considered in detail in Chapter 7, however, it may be useful at this point to consider some of the ways in which the information contained within the P and L account will be used. We shall take the profit and loss account set out in Example 3.9 as our basis.

Example 3.9

Patel Wholesalers
Trading and P and L account for the year ended 31 March 2001

	£	£
Sales		460,500
Less Cost of sales		345,800
Gross profit		114,700
Less		
Salaries and wages	45,900	
Rent and rates	15,300	
Telephone and postage	1,400	
Motor vehicle expenses	3,900	
Loan interest	4,800	
Depreciation – Motor van	2,300	
– Fixtures and fittings	2,200	
		(75,800)
Net profit		38,900

To evaluate performance the following points might be considered:

● The sales figure represents an important measure of output and can be compared with the sales figure of earlier periods and the planned sales figure for the current period in order to assess the achievement of the business.

● The gross profit figure can be related to the sales figure in order to find out the profitability of the goods being sold. In the statement shown above, we can see that the gross profit is about 25 per cent of the sales figure or, to put it another way, for every £1 of sales generated the gross profit is 25p. This level of profitability may be compared with that of past periods, with planned levels of profitability or with comparable figures of similar businesses.

● The expenses of the businesses may be examined and compared with those of past periods (and so on) in order to evaluate operating efficiency. Individual expenses can be related to sales to assess whether the level of expenses is appropriate. Thus, in Example 3.9 the salaries and wages represent almost 10 per cent of sales or, for every £1 of sales generated, 10p is absorbed by employee costs.

● Net profit can also be related to sales. In the statement shown above, net profit is about 8 per cent of sales. Thus, for every £1 of sales, the owners of the business benefit by 8p. Whether or not this is acceptable will again depend on making the kinds of comparison referred to above. Net profit as a percentage of sales can vary substantially between different types of business. There is usually a trade-off to be made between profitability and sales volume. Some businesses are prepared to accept a low net profit percentage in return for generating a high volume of sales. At the other extreme, some businesses may prefer to have a high net profit percentage but accept a relatively low volume of sales. For example, a supermarket may fall into the former category and a trader in luxury cars may fall into the latter.

Chan Exporters
Trading and P and L account for the year ended 31 May 2002

	£	£
Sales		840,000
Less Cost of sales		620,000
Gross profit		220,000
Less		
Salaries and wages	92,000	
Selling and distribution costs	44,000	
Rent and rates	30,000	
Bad debts written off	86,000	
Telephone and postage	4,000	
Insurance	2,000	
Motor vehicle expenses	8,000	
Loan interest	5,000	
Depreciation – Motor van	3,000	
– Fixtures and fittings	4,000	
		(278,000)
Net profit (loss)		(58,000)

In the previous year to 31 May 2001, sales were £710,000. The gross profit was £200,000 and the net profit was £37,000.

Analyse the performance of the business for the year to 31 May 2002 in so far as the information allows.

....

Sales increased by nearly 18 per cent over the previous year but the 'bottom line' fell from a net profit of £37,000 to a loss of £58,000. The rapid expansion of the business has clearly brought problems in its wake. In the previous period, the business was making a gross profit of more than 28p for every £1 of sales made. This reduced in the year to 31 May 2002 to around 26p for every £1 of sales made. This seems to suggest that the rapid expansion was partly fuelled by a reduction in prices.

The gross profit increased in absolute terms by £20,000, however, there was a drastic decline in net profits during the period. In the previous period, the business was making a net profit of nearly 5p for every £1 of sales whereas, for the year to 31 May 2002, this reduced to a loss of nearly 7p for every £1 of sales made. This means that overhead expenses have increased considerably. Some increase in overhead expenses may be expected in order to service the increased level of activity. However, the increase appears to be exceptional. If we look at the list of overhead expenses, we can see that the bad debts written off seem very high (more than 10 per cent of total sales). This may be a further effect of the rapid expansion that has taken place. In order to generate sales, insufficient regard may have been paid to the creditworthiness of customers. A comparison of overhead expenses with those of the previous period would be useful.

● Summary

In this chapter we have considered the P and L account. We have examined the main principles underpinning this statement and we have looked at various measurement issues connected with the determination of profit. We have seen that the profit and loss account seeks to measure *accomplishment* during a period rather than the cash generated. Thus, revenues and expenses are not the same as cash received and cash paid, and net profit does not normally reflect the net cash flows for the period. Although cash flows are important to the assessment of business performance, these are dealt with in a separate financial statement.

Although accountants try to be objective when measuring profit, there are certain areas where they have to rely on subjective judgement. Three of these areas – depreciation, stock valuation and bad debts – were examined in some detail. We saw that different judgements can lead to quite different calculations of profit between years.

In this chapter and in the previous chapter, we have considered a number of accounting conventions. These have been summarised as an Appendix to this chapter to help consolidate your knowledge.

Key terms

Profit p. 57	Depreciation p. 68
Revenue p. 57	Residual value p. 70
Expense p. 58	Straight-line method p. 70
Gross profit p. 60	Written-down value p. 71
Trading and P and L account p. 60	Reducing-balance method p. 71
Net profit p. 60	First in, first out (FIFO) p. 79
Cost of sales p. 61	Last in, first out (LIFO) p. 79
Realisation convention p. 63	Weighted average cost (AVCO) p. 79
Matching convention p. 64	Consistency convention p. 83
Accrued expense p. 65	Bad debt p. 84
Prepaid expense p. 67	Provision for doubtful debts p. 84
Materiality convention p. 67	

Further reading

If you would like to explore the topics covered in this chapter in more depth, we recommend the following books:

Financial Reporting, *Alexander, D. and Britton*, A., 6th edn, International Thomson Business Press, 2001, chapter 4.

Accounting Principles, *Anthony, R. and Reece, J.*, 7th edn, Irwin, 1995, chapters 5, 6 and 7.

Accounting Theory and Practice, *Glautier, M. and Underdown, B.*, 7th edn, Financial Times Prentice Hall, 2001, chapters 10 and 16.

Financial Accounting and Reporting, *Elliott, B. and Elliott, J.*, 5th edn, Financial Times Prentice Hall, 2001, chapters 14 and 17.

Reference

'The problems of accounting for intangible assets in the food and drink industry', Ong, A., in **Accounting and Finance**, Atrill, P. and Lindley, L. (eds), Ashgate, 1997.

3.1 'Although the P and L account is a record of past achievement, the calculations required for certain expenses involve estimates of the future.' What is meant by this statement? Can you think of examples where estimates of the future are used?

3.2 'Depreciation is a process of allocation and not valuation.' What do you think is meant by this statement?

3.3 What is the convention of consistency? Does this convention help users in making more valid comparisons *between* businesses?

3.4 Explain the relationship between an asset and an expense. Use the two possible treatments of interest charges dealt with in the chapter to illustrate this relationship.

? **EXERCISES**

Exercises 3.6–3.8 are more advanced than 3.1–3.5. Those with coloured numbers have answers at the back of the book.

3.1 You have heard the following statements made. Comment critically on them.

(a) 'Capital only increases or decreases as a result of the owners putting more cash into the business or taking some out.'
(b) 'An accrued expense is one that relates to next year.'
(c) 'Unless we depreciate this asset we will be unable to provide for its replacement.'
(d) 'There is no point in depreciating the factory building. It is appreciating in value each year.'

3.2 Singh Enterprises has an accounting year to 31 December. On 1 January 1999 the business purchased a machine for £10,000. The machine had an expected life of four years and an estimated residual value of £2,000. On 1 January 2000 the business purchased another machine for £15,000. This machine had an expected useful life of five years and an estimated residual value of £2,500. On 31 December 2001, the business sold the first machine purchased for £3,000.

The business employs the straight-line method of depreciation for machinery.

Required:
Show the relevant P and L account extracts and balance sheet extracts for 1999, 2000 and 2001.

3.3 The owner of a business is confused and comes to you for help. The financial statements for his business, prepared by an accountant, for the last accounting period reveal an increase in profit of £50,000. However, during the accounting period the bank balance declined by £30,000. What reasons might explain this apparent discrepancy?

3.4 Spratley Ltd is a builders merchant. On 1 September the business had 20 tonnes of sand in stock at a cost of £18 per tonne and thus at a total cost of £360. During the first week in September, the business purchased the following amounts of sand:

	Tonnes	Cost/tonne
2 September	48	20
4 September	15	24
6 September	10	25

On 7 September, the business sold 60 tonnes of sand to a local builder.

Required:
Calculate the cost of goods sold and the closing stock figures from the above information using the following stock costing methods:

(a) First in first out
(b) Last in, first out
(c) Weighted average cost.

3.5 Fill in the values (a) to (f) in the following table on the assumption that there were no opening balances involved:

	Relating to period		At end of period	
	Paid/ received	Expense/ revenue for period	Prepaid	Accruals/ deferred revenues
	£	£	£	£
Rent payable	10,000	a	1,000	
Rates and insurance	5,000	b		1,000
General expenses	c	6,000	1,000	
Loan interest payable	3,000	2,500	d	
Salaries	e	9,000		3,000
Rent receivable	f	1,500		1,500

3.6 The following is the balance sheet of TT Limited at the end of its first year of trading (from Self-assessment question 3.1):

Balance sheet as at 31 December 2000

	£	£	£
Fixed assets			
Motor van – Cost			12,000
– Depreciation			2,500
			9,500
Current assets			
Stock in trade	65,000		
Trade debtors	19,600		
Prepaid expenses[a]	5,300		
Cash	750		
		90,650	

(Continued)

Balance sheet as at 31 December 2000 *continued*

Less **Current liabilities**

Trade creditors	22,000	
Accrued expenses[b]	1,250	
		23,250
		67,400
		76,900

Capital

Original	50,000
Retained profit	26,900
	76,900

Notes:
[a] The prepaid expenses consisted of rates (£300) and rent (£5,000).
[b] The accrued expenses consisted of wages (£630) and electricity (£620).

During 2001, the following transactions took place:

1. The owners withdrew capital in the form of cash of £20,000.
2. Premises continued to be rented at an annual rental of £20,000. During the year, rent of £15,000 was paid to the owner of the premises.
3. Rates on the premises were paid during the year for the period 1 April 2001 to 31 March 2002 and amounted to £1,300.
4. A second delivery van was bought on 1 January for £13,000. This is expected to be used in the business for four years and then to be sold for £3,000.
5. Wages totalling £36,700 were paid during the year. At the end of the year, the business owed £860 of wages for the last week of the year.
6. Electricity bills for the first three quarters of the year and £620 for the last quarter of the previous year were paid, totalling £1,820. After 31 December 2001 but before the accounts had been finalised for the year, the bill for the last quarter arrived showing a charge of £690.
7. Stock in trade totalling £67,000 was bought on credit.
8. Stock in trade totalling £8,000 was bought for cash.
9. Sales on credit totalled £179,000 (cost £89,000).
10. Cash sales totalled £54,000 (cost £25,000).
11. Receipts from trade debtors totalled £178,000.
12. Payments to trade creditors totalled £71,000.
13. Van running expenses paid totalled £16,200.

The business uses the straight-line method for depreciating fixed assets.

Required:
Prepare a balance sheet as at 31 December 2001 and a P and L account for the year to that date.

3.7 The following is the balance sheet of WW Limited as at 31 December 2000:

Balance sheet as at 31 December 2000

	£	£	£
Fixed assets			
Machinery			25,300

(Continued)

Balance sheet as at 31 December 2000 *continued*

	£	£	£
Current assets			
Stock in trade	12,200		
Trade debtors	21,300		
Prepaid expenses (rates)	400		
Cash	8,300		
		42,200	
Less **Current liabilities**			
Trade creditors	16,900		
Accrued expenses (wages)	1,700		
		18,600	
			23,600
			48,900
Capital			
Original			25,000
Retained profit			23,900
			48,900

During 2001 the following transactions took place:

1. The owners withdrew capital in the form of cash of £23,000.
2. Premises were rented at an annual rental of £20,000. During the year, rent of £25,000 was paid to the owner of the premises.
3. Rates on the premises were paid during the year for the period 1 April 2001 to 31 March 2002 and amounted to £2,000.
4. Some machinery, which was bought on 1 January 2000 for £13,000, has proved to be unsatisfactory. It was part-exchanged for some new machinery on 1 January 2001, and WW Limited paid a cash amount of £6,000. The new machinery would have cost £15,000 had the business bought it without the trade-in.
5. Wages totalling £23,800 were paid during the year. At the end of the year, the business owed £860 of wages.
6. Electricity bills for the four quarters of the year were paid totalling £2,700.
7. Stock in trade totalling £143,000 was bought on credit.
8. Stock in trade totalling £12,000 was bought for cash.
9. Sales on credit totalled £211,000 (cost £127,000).
10. Cash sales totalled £42,000 (cost £25,000).
11. Receipts from trade debtors totalled £198,000.
12. Payments to trade creditors totalled £156,000.
13. Van running expenses paid totalled £17,500.

The business uses the reducing-balance method of depreciation for fixed assets at the rate of 30 per cent each year.

Required:
Prepare a balance sheet as at 31 December 2001 and a P and L account for the year to that date.

3.8 The following is the trading and profit and loss account for Nikov and Co. for the year ended 31 December 2001 along with information relating to the preceding year.

Trading and profit and loss account for the year ended 31 December

	2000		2001	
	£000	£000	£000	£000
Sales		382.5		420.2
Less Cost of sales		114.8		126.1
Gross profit		267.7		294.1
Less				
Salaries and wages	86.4		92.6	
Selling and distribution costs	75.4		98.9	
Rent and rates	22.0		22.0	
Bad debts written off	4.0		19.7	
Telephone and postage	4.4		4.8	
Insurance	2.8		2.9	
Motor vehicle expenses	8.6		10.3	
Loan interest	5.4		4.6	
Depreciation – Motor van	3.3		3.1	
– Fixtures and fittings	4.5		4.3	
		216.8		263.2
Net profit (loss)		50.9		30.9

Required:

Analyse the performance of the business for the year to 31 December 2001 in so far as the information allows.

Summary of the major accounting conventions

The major accounting conventions that have been covered in Chapters 2 and 3 may be summarised as follows:

- **Money measurement.** Accounting only deals with those items that are capable of being expressed in monetary terms.

- **Historical cost.** Items should be recorded at their historical (acquisition) cost.

- **Going concern.** The business will continue in operation for the foreseeable future; there is no intention to liquidate the business.

- **Business entity.** For accounting purposes, the business and its owner(s) are treated as separate and distinct.

- **Dual aspect.** Each transaction has two aspects and each aspect must be reflected in the financial statements.

- **Prudence.** Financial statements should err on the side of caution.

- **Stable monetary unit.** Money, which is the unit of measurement, is assumed to have the same purchasing power over time.

- **Objectivity.** As far as possible, financial statements should be prepared on the basis of objective, verifiable evidence.

- **Realisation.** Revenue should only be recognised when it is realised.

- **Matching.** When measuring income, expenses should be matched to the revenues they helped to generate. In other words, they should appear in the same accounting period as that in which those revenues were realised.

- **Materiality.** Where the amounts involved are immaterial, only what is expedient should be considered.

- **Consistency.** Where a particular method is selected to deal with a transaction, this method should be applied consistently over time.

4

Accounting for limited companies (1)

● Introduction

In the UK, most businesses, except the very smallest, trade in the form of limited companies. In this chapter we shall examine the nature of limited companies and see how they differ in practical terms from sole proprietorships. This will involve our considering the ways in which finance is provided by the owners. It will also require us to consider the ways in which companies' financial statements (the balance sheet and the profit and loss account) differ from those of sole proprietors.

OBJECTIVES

When you have completed this chapter you should be able to:

- Discuss the nature of the limited company.
- Explain the role of directors of limited companies.
- Outline and explain the particular features and restrictions of the owners' claim, in the context of limited companies.
- Outline the nature and preparation of group accounts.

●●●●● Generating wealth through limited companies

The nature of limited companies

A limited company is an artificial legal person. This means that a company has many of the rights and obligations that 'real' people have. With the rare exceptions of those that are created by Act of Parliament or by royal charter, all UK companies are created as a result of the Registrar of Companies entering the name of the new company on the Registry of Companies (if the necessary formalities have been met). The Registrar of Companies is an officer of the Department of Trade and Industry. The necessary formalities are the simple matters of filling in a few forms and paying a modest registration fee. Thus, in the UK, companies can be formed easily and cheaply (for about £100).

Normally, companies are owned by at least two people. The owners of a limited company are usually known as 'members' or 'shareholders'. The ownership of a company is normally divided into a number – frequently a large number – of shares each of equal size. Each shareholder owns one or more shares in the company.

A limited company is legally separate from those who own and manage it. This fact leads to the important features of the limited company: perpetual life and limited liability, as described next.

Perpetual life

The life of the company is not related to the life of the individuals who own or manage it. Shares may be sold by an existing shareholder to another person who wishes to become a shareholder. When an owner of part of the shares of the company dies, that person's shares pass to the beneficiary of his or her estate.

Limited liability

Since the company is a legal person in its own right, it must take responsibility for its own debts and losses. This means that once the shareholders have paid what they have agreed to pay for the shares, their obligation to the company, and to the company's creditors, is satisfied. Thus shareholders can limit their losses to the amount that they have paid or agreed to pay for their shares. This is of great practical importance to potential shareholders, since they know that what they can lose, as part-owners of the business, is limited.

Contrast this with the position of sole proprietors or partners (that is, the owners or part-owners of unincorporated businesses). Here, there is not the opportunity that shareholders have to 'ring-fence' the assets that they choose not to put into the business. If a sole proprietorship business finds itself in a position where liabilities exceed the business assets, the law gives unsatisfied creditors the right to demand payment out of what the sole proprietor had regarded as 'non-business' assets. Thus the sole proprietor could lose everything – house, car, the lot. This is because the law sees Jill, the sole proprietor, as being the same as Jill the private individual. The shareholder, by contrast, can lose only the amount invested in that company. Legally, a business operating as a limited company, in which Jack owns shares, is not the same as Jack himself. This is true even where Jack owns all of the shares in the company.

| Activity 4.1 | We have just said that the fact that shareholders can limit their losses to the amount that they have paid or have agreed to pay for their shares is of great practical importance to potential shareholders. Can you think of any practical benefit to a private-sector economy, in general, of this ability of shareholders to limit losses? |

Business is a risky venture, and in some cases a very risky one. People with money to invest will tend to be more content to do so where they know the limit of their liability. This means that more businesses will tend to be formed and that existing ones will find it easier to raise additional finance from existing and/or additional part-owners. This is good for the private-sector economy, since businesses will tend to form and expand more readily. Thus the wants of society are more likely to be met, and choice offered, where limited liability exists.

Though **limited liability** has this advantage to the providers of capital, namely the shareholders, it is not necessarily to the advantage of all others who have a stake in a business. Limited liability is attractive to shareholders because they can, in effect, walk away from the unpaid debts of the company if the contribution of the shareholders has not been sufficient to meet those debts. This is likely to make any individual or another business, contemplating advancing credit, wary of dealing with the limited company. This can be a real problem for smaller, less-established companies. For example, suppliers may insist on cash payment before delivery. Alternatively, the bank may require a personal guarantee from a major shareholder that debts will be paid, before allowing a company trade credit. In the latter case the supplier of credit will circumvent the company's limited liability status by establishing the personal liability of an individual. Larger, more established companies, on the other hand, tend to have built up the confidence of suppliers.

It is mainly to warn those contemplating dealing with a limited company that the liability of the owners is limited, and that this fact must be indicated in the name of the company. As we shall see later in this chapter, there are other safeguards for those dealing with a limited company, in that the extent to which shareholders may withdraw their investment from the company is restricted.

Another important safeguard for those dealing with a limited company is that all limited companies must produce annual accounts (including a profit and loss account and a balance sheet) and, in effect, make these available to the public. The rules surrounding the accounts of limited companies will be discussed in Chapter 5.

Public and private companies

When a company is registered with the Registrar of Companies, it must be registered either as a public or as a private company. The main practical difference between these is that a **public company** can offer its shares for sale to the general public, but a **private company** is restricted from doing so. A public limited company must signal its status to all interested parties by having the words 'public limited company', or its abbreviation 'plc' in its name. For a private limited company, the word 'limited' or 'Ltd' must appear as part of its name.

Private limited companies tend to be smaller businesses where the ownership is divided among relatively few shareholders who are usually fairly close to one another – for example, a family company. Numerically, there are vastly more private limited companies in the UK than there are public ones. Since the public ones tend to be individually larger, they probably represent a much more important group economically. Many private limited companies are no more than the vehicle through which businesses, which are little more than sole proprietorships, operate.

Regarding accounting requirements, there is no distinction made between private and public companies.

Transferring share ownership – the role of the Stock Exchange

Shares in a company may be transferred from one owner to another without this change of share ownership having any direct impact on that company's business, or on the shareholders not involved with the particular transfer. With major companies, the desire of some existing shareholders to sell their shares, coupled with the desire of others to buy those shares, has led to the existence of a formal market in which the shares can be bought and sold. The Stock Exchange (of the UK and the Republic of Ireland), and similar organisations around the world, are simply marketplaces in which shares in major companies are bought and sold. Prices are determined by the law of supply and demand. Supply and demand are themselves determined by investors' perceptions of the future economic prospects of the companies concerned.

Activity 4.2

If, as has been pointed out, the change in ownership of the shares of a particular company does not directly affect that company, why would a particular company welcome the fact that the shares are traded in a recognised market?

The main reason is that investors are generally reluctant to pledge their money unless they can see some way in which they can turn their investment back into cash. In theory, the shares of a particular company may be very valuable as a result of the company having a very bright economic future, but unless this value is capable of being realised in cash, the benefit to the shareholders is doubtful. After all, you cannot spend shares; you generally need cash.

This means that potential shareholders are much more likely to be prepared to buy new shares from a company (thus providing the company with new finance) when they can see a way of liquidating their investment (turning it into cash) as and when they need to. The stock exchanges provide such a means of liquidation.

Though the buying and selling of 'second-hand' shares does not provide a company with cash, the fact that the buying and selling facility exists will make it easier for the company to raise new share capital as and when it wishes to do so.

Taxation

Another consequence of the legal separation of the limited company from its owners is the fact that companies must be accountable to the Inland Revenue for tax on their profits and gains. This introduces the effects of tax into the accounting statements of limited companies. The charge for tax is shown in the profit and loss account. Since only 50 per cent of a company's tax liability is due for payment during the year concerned, the other 50 per cent will appear on the end-of-year balance sheet as a short-term liability. This will be illustrated a little later in the chapter. The tax position of companies contrasts with that of the sole proprietorship or partnership, where tax is levied not on the business but on the owner(s). Thus tax does not impact on the accounts of unincorporated businesses, but is an individual matter between the owner(s) and the Inland Revenue.

Companies are charged **corporation tax** on their profits and gains. The percentage rates of tax tend to vary from year to year, but have recently been in the low thirties for larger companies and in the low twenties for smaller companies. These rates of tax are levied on the company's taxable profit, which is not necessarily the same as the profit shown on the profit and loss account. This is because tax law does not, in every respect, follow the normal accounting rules. Generally, however, the taxable profit and the company's accounting profit are pretty close to one another.

Managing a company – corporate governance and the role of directors

A limited company may have legal personality but it is not a human being capable of making decisions and plans about the business and exercising control over it. These management tasks must be undertaken by people. The most senior level of management of a company is the board of directors.

➡ The shareholders elect **directors** (by law there must be at least one director) to manage the company on a day-to-day basis on behalf of those shareholders. In a small company, the board may be the only level of management and consist of all of the shareholders. In larger companies, the board may consist of 10 or so directors out of many thousands of shareholders. Indeed, directors are not required even to be shareholders. Below the board of directors could be several layers of management comprising thousands of people.

➡ In recent years, the issue of **corporate governance** has generated much debate. The term is used to describe the ways in which companies are directed and controlled. The issue of corporate governance is important because, in companies of any size, those who own the company (that is, the shareholders) are usually divorced from the day-to-day control of the business. The directors are employed by the shareholders to manage the company on behalf of the shareholders. Given this position, it may seem safe to assume that the directors' decisions will be guided by the interests of shareholders. However, in practice this does not always occur. The directors may be more concerned with pursuing their own interests, such as increasing their pay and 'perks' (such as expensive motor cars, overseas visits and so on) and improving their job security and status. As a result, a conflict can occur between the interests of shareholders and the interests of directors.

Where directors pursue their own interests at the expense of the shareholders, it is clearly a problem for the shareholders. However, it may also be a problem for society as a whole. If shareholders feel their funds are likely to be mismanaged, they will be reluctant to invest. A shortage of funds will mean fewer investments can be made and the costs of funds will increase as businesses compete for what funds are available. Thus, a lack of concern for shareholders can have a profound effect on the performance of the economy. To avoid these problems, most competitive market economies have a framework of rules to help monitor and control the behaviour of directors.

These rules are usually based around three guiding principles:

- *Disclosure.* This lies at the heart of good corporate governance. An OECD report (see reference at end of chapter for details) summed up the benefits of disclosure as follows:

  Adequate and timely information about corporate performance enables investors to make informed buy-and-sell decisions and thereby helps the market reflect the value of a corporation under present management. If the market determines that present management is not performing, a decrease in stock (share) price will sanction management's failure and open the way to management change.

- *Accountability.* This involves defining the roles and duties of the directors and establishing an adequate monitoring process. In the United Kingdom, company law requires that directors of a business act in the best interests of shareholders. This means, among other things, that they must not try to use their position and knowledge to make gains at the expense of the shareholders. The law also requires larger companies to have their annual accounts independently audited. The purpose of an independent audit is to lend credibility to the accounts prepared by the directors.

- *Fairness*. Directors should not be able to benefit from access to 'inside' information that is not available to shareholders. As a result, both the law and the Stock Exchange place restrictions on the ability of directors to deal in the shares of the business. One example of these restrictions is that the directors cannot buy or sell shares immediately before the announcement of the final results of the business or before the announcement of a significant event such as a planned merger or the loss of the chief executive.

Strengthening the framework of rules

The number of rules designed to safeguard shareholders has increased considerably over the years. This has been in response to weaknesses in corporate governance procedures, which have been exposed through well-publicised business failures and frauds, large pay increases to directors of privatised businesses, and evidence that some financial reports were being 'massaged' so as to mislead shareholders. However, some believe that the shareholders must shoulder some of the blame for any weaknesses. It is often argued that large institutional shareholders (which own around 80 per cent, by market value, of the shares quoted on the UK Stock Exchange) are not very active in corporate governance matters, and so there has been little monitoring of directors. However, things are changing.

During the 1990s there was a real effort by the accountancy profession and the London Stock Exchange to address the problems mentioned above. The Cadbury Committee was formed in 1991 to consider the problems relating to fnancial reporting and accountability, and in 1992 the committee produced a code of Best Practice on Corporate Governance. Following that Committee, the Greenbury Committee was set up to consider the issue of directors' pay in more detail. In 1995, this committee also issued a code of practice. Soon after, the Hampel Committee was formed and, in 1998, produced a report that sought to 'fine-tune' the recommendations of the two earlier committees. The Hampel Committee also set out the principles of good practice that embraced the work of all three committees. The **Combined Code** was thereby created which has received the backing of the London Stock Exchange. This means that companies listed on the London Stock Exchange are expected to comply with the requirements of the Code or must give their shareholders good reason why they do not.

The Combined Code sets out a number principles relating to such matters as the role of the directors, their relations with shareholders, and their accountability. Exhibit 4.1 outlines some of the more important of these.

Exhibit 4.1

The Combined Code
Some of the key elements of the Combined Code are as follows:

- Every listed company should have a board of directors to lead and control the company.
- There should be a clear division of responsibilities between the chairman and the chief

---

executive officer of the company to ensure that a single person does not have unbridled power.

- There should be a balance between executive and non-executive (who are often part-time and independent) members of the board, to ensure that small groups of individuals cannot dominate proceedings.
- The board should receive timely information that is of sufficient quality to enable them to carry out their duties.
- Appointments to the board should be the subject of formal and transparent procedures. All directors should submit themselves for re-election by the shareholders within a maximum period of three years.
- Boards should use the Annual General Meeting to communicate with private investors and to encourage their participation.
- The board should publish a balanced and understandable assessment of the company's position and performance.
- Internal controls should be in place to protect the shareholders' wealth.
- The board should set up an audit committee of non-executive directors to oversee the internal controls and financial reporting principles that are being applied, and to liaise with the external auditors.

Strengthening the framework of rules has improved the quality of information available to shareholders, resulted in better checks on the powers of directors, and provided greater transparency in corporate affairs. However, rules can only be a partial answer. A balance must be struck between the need to protect shareholders and the need to encourage the entrepreneurial spirit of directors – which could be stifled under a welter of rules. This implies that rules should not be too tight and so unscrupulous directors may still find ways around them.

Activity 4.3

Can you think of ways in which the shareholders themselves may try to ensure that the directors act on their behalf?

Two ways are commonly used in practice:

- The shareholders may insist on monitoring closely the actions of the directors and the way in which they use the resources of the company.
- The shareholders may introduce incentive plans for managers that link their pay to the share performance of the company. In this way, the interests of the directors and shareholders will become more closely aligned.

Exhibit 4.2 shows an extract from the statement on corporate governance made by the directors of Kingfisher plc, the retail business that owns Woolworths, Superdrug, B & Q, Comet and a number of other chains, including some in France.

Exhibit 4.2

The following extract from the 2000 annual accounts of Kingfisher plc starts with a general statement that the directors have complied with the Combined Code during the year in question. It then goes on to detail how they complied in the specific context of board meetings and the establishment of committees to deal with sensitive issues.

Corporate governance – combined code statement

Kingfisher recognises the importance of, and is committed to, high standards of corporate governance. The principles of good governance adopted by the Group have been applied in the following way:

Directors

The Kingfisher Board currently comprises the Chairman, the Chief Executive, five other executive directors and six non-executive directors. Their biographies appear on pages 30 and 31 and illustrate the directors' range of experience, which ensures an effective board to lead and control the Group. All directors have access to the Company Secretary and may take independent professional advice at the Group's expense. Non-executive directors are appointed for an initial term of three years and each director receives appropriate training on appointment and subsequently as necessary.

The Board meets not less than 11 times a year and has adopted a schedule of matters reserved for its decision. It is primarily responsible for the strategic direction of the Group. All directors have full and timely access to information. Continuing the process started last year, the Board has again undertaken a review of its effectiveness, under the leadership of the Chairman.

The Board has established five standing committees with defined terms of reference as follows:

- The Audit Committee, chaired by John Bullock comprises not less than three independent non-executive directors and currently has five non-executive directors. This committee is responsible for providing an independent oversight of the Group's systems of internal control and financial reporting processes. Each of our UK major operating businesses is a substantial size and each has its own audit committee, which is attended by both Kingfisher's internal auditor and the external auditors.
- The Nomination Committee comprises the Chairman, Chief Executive and three other non-executive directors and is responsible for the consideration of and recommendation for the appointment of new directors.
- The Remuneration Committee comprises the Chairman and three other independent non-executive directors and advises the Board on the Company's executive remuneration policy and its costs and, on behalf of the Board, the application of this policy to the remuneration and benefits of executive directors and certain senior executives. The Remuneration Report on pages 37 to 42 contains a more detailed description of the Group's policy and procedures in relation to directors' and officers' remuneration.
- The Finance Committee comprises the Chief Executive and three executive directors and is responsible for the approval and authorisation of financing documents within its terms of reference and the authority limits laid down by the Board. On behalf of the Board, it reviews borrowing arrangements and other financial transactions, and makes appropriate recommendations. It also allots new shares in the Company to Group employees following the exercise of share options.
- The Social Responsibility Committee comprises representatives of the operating companies and at least one executive director and one non-executive director. This committee is responsible for discussing and developing a general policy relating to environmental, community and equal opportunities matters. Sir Geoffrey Mulcahy is chairman of this committee and the main board director with overall responsibility for environmental matters.

● ● ● ● ● Financing a limited company

Capital (owners' claim) of limited companies

The owner's claim of a sole proprietorship is normally encompassed in one figure on the balance sheet, usually labelled 'capital'. With companies, this is usually a little more complicated, though in essence the same broad principles apply. With a company, the owners' claim is divided between shares – for example, the original investment – on the one hand and reserves – that is, profits and gains subsequently made – on the other. There is also the possibility that there will be shares of more than one type and reserves of more than one type. Thus, within the basic divisions of share capital and reserves, there might well be further subdivisions. This might seem quite complicated, but later we shall consider the reasons for these subdivisions and try to make things clear.

The basic division

When a company is first formed, those who take steps to form it, usually known as the promoters of the company, will decide how much needs to be raised by the potential shareholders to set up the company with the necessary assets to operate. Example 4.1 acts as a basis for illustration.

Example 4.1

Let us imagine that several people get together and decide to form a company to operate a particular business. They estimate that the company will need £50,000 to obtain the necessary assets to operate. Between them, they raise the cash which they use to buy shares in the company, on 31 March 2001, with a **nominal (or par) value** of £1 each.

At this point the balance sheet of the company would be thus:

Balance sheet as at 31 March 2001

	£
Net assets (all in cash)	50,000
Capital and reserves	
Share capital	
50,000 shares of £1 each	50,000

The company now buys the necessary fixed assets and stock in trade and starts to trade. During the first year, the company makes a profit of £10,000. This, by definition, means that the owners' claim expands by £10,000. During the year, the shareholders (owners) make no drawings of their capital, so at the end of the year the summarised balance sheet looks like this:

Balance sheet as at 31 March 2002

	£
Net assets (various assets less liabilities)	60,000
Capital and reserves	
Share capital	
50,000 shares of £1 each	50,000
Reserves (revenue reserve)	10,000
	60,000

➡ The profit is shown in a reserve, known as a **revenue reserve**, because it arises from generating revenues through sales. Note that we do not simply add the profit to the share capital: we must keep the two amounts separate (to satisfy company law). The reason for this is that there is a legal restriction on the
➡ maximum drawings of capital (or payment of a **dividend**) that the owners can make. This is defined by the amount of revenue reserves, and so it is helpful to show these separately. We shall look at why there is this restriction, and how it works, later in this chapter.

Share capital

Shares represent the basic units of ownership of a business. All companies issue
➡ **ordinary shares**. The ordinary shares of a company often referred to collectively
➡ as the **equity** of the company. The nominal value of such shares is at the discretion of the people that start up the company. For example, if the initial capital is to be £50,000, this could be two shares of £25,000 each, 5 million shares of one penny each or any other combination that gives a total of £50,000. Each share must have the same value.

Activity 4.4	The initial capital requirement for a new company is £50,000. There are to be two equal shareholders. Would you advise them to issue two shares of £25,000? Why?

Such large denomination shares tend to be unwieldy. Suppose that one of the shareholders wanted to sell his or her shares. S/he would have to find one buyer. If there were shares of smaller denomination, it would be possible to sell part of the shareholding to various potential buyers. Similarly, it would be possible to sell just part of the holding and retain a part.

In practice, £1 is the normal maximum nominal value for shares. Shares of 25 pence each and 50 pence each are probably the most common.
➡ Some companies also issue other classes of shares, **preference shares** being the most common. Preference shares guarantee that *if a dividend is paid*, the preference shareholders will be entitled to the first part of it up to a maximum value. This maximum is normally defined as a fixed percentage of the nominal value of the preference shares. If, for example, a company issues 10,000 preference shares of £1 each with a dividend rate of 6 per cent, this means that the preference shareholders are entitled to receive the first £600 (that is, 6 per cent of £10,000) of any dividend that is paid by the company for a year. The excess over £600 goes to the ordinary shareholders. Normally, any undistributed profits and gains accrue to the ordinary shareholders. Thus the ordinary shareholders are the primary risk-takers, and their potential rewards reflect this risk. Power normally resides in the hands of the ordinary shareholders. Usually, only the ordinary shareholders are able to vote on issues that affect the company, such as who the directors should be.

It is open to the company to issue shares of various classes – perhaps with some having unusual and exotic conditions – but in practice it is rare to find other than straightforward ordinary and preference shares.

Though a company may have different classes of shares whose holders have different rights, within each class all shares must be treated equally. The rights of the various classes of shareholders, as well as other matters relating to a particular company, are contained in that company's set of rules, known as the 'articles and memorandum of association'. A copy of these rules is, in effect, available to the public because one must be lodged with the Registrar of Companies so as to be available for access by the general public.

Reserves

Reserves are profits and gains that have been made by a company and that still form part of the shareholders' (owners') claim because they have not been paid out to the shareholders. Profits and gains tend to lead to cash flowing into the company.

It is worth mentioning that retained profits represent overwhelmingly the largest source of new finance for UK companies – amounting for most companies to more than share issues and borrowings combined. These ploughed-back profits create most of a typical company's reserves. As well as reserves, the shareholders' claim consists of share capital.

Activity 4.5

Are reserves amounts of cash? Can you think of a reason why this is an odd question?

To deal with the second point first, it is an odd question because reserves are a claim, or part of one, on the assets of the company, whereas cash is an asset. So reserves cannot be cash.

Reserves are classified as either revenue reserves or capital reserves. As we have already seen, revenue reserves arise from trading profit. They also arise from gains made on the disposal of fixed assets.

Capital reserves arise for two main reasons: issuing shares at above their nominal value (for example, issuing £1 shares at £1.50) and revaluing (upwards) fixed assets. Where a company issues shares at above their nominal value, UK law requires that the excess of the issue price over the nominal value is shown separately.

Activity 4.6

Can you think why shares might be issued at above their nominal value? *Hint*: this would not usually happen when a company is first formed and the initial shares are being issued.

Once a company has traded and has been successful, the shares would normally be worth more than the nominal value at which they were issued. If additional shares are to be issued to new shareholders to raise finance for further expansion, unless they are issued at a value higher than the nominal value, the new shareholders will be gaining at the expense of the original ones.

Now let us consider another example.

Based on future prospects, the net assets of a company are worth £1.5 million. There are currently 1 million ordinary shares in the company. The company wishes to raise an additional £0.6 million of cash for expansion and has decided to raise it by issuing new shares. If the shares are issued for £1 each, that is 600,000 shares, the number of shares will increase to 1.6 million and their total value will be £2.1 million (£1.5 million + £0.6 million). This means that the value of the shares after the new issue will be £1.3125 each (£2.1 ÷ 1.6). So the original shareholders will have lost £0.1875 per share (£1.5 – £1.3125) and the new shareholders will have gained £0.3125 per share. The new shareholders will, no doubt, be delighted with this; the original ones will be less ecstatic.

Things could be made fair between the two sets of shareholders described in Example 4.2 by issuing the new shares at £1.50 each. In this case the £1 per share nominal value will be included with share capital in the balance sheet. The £0.50 per share premium will be shown as a capital reserve known as the **share premium account**. It is not clear why UK company law insists on the distinction between nominal share values and the premium. Certainly, other countries with a similar set of laws governing the corporate sector (for example, the United States) do not see the necessity to distinguish between share capital and share premium, but instead show the total value at which shares are issued as one comprehensive figure on the company balance sheet.

Altering the nominal value of shares

The point has already been made that the people who start up a new company may make their own choice of the nominal or par value of the shares. This value need not be permanent. At a later date the shareholders can decide to change it.

For example, a company has at issue 1 million ordinary shares of £1 each. A decision is made to change the nominal value of the shares from £1 to £0.50, in other words to halve the value. As a result, the company would issue each shareholder with a new share certificate (the shareholders' evidence of ownership of their shareholding) for exactly twice as many shares, each with half the nominal value. This would leave each shareholder with a holding of the same total nominal value. This process is known, not unnaturally, as splitting the shares. The opposite, reducing the number of shares by increasing their nominal value, is known as **consolidating**.

Since each shareholder would be left, after a split or consolidation, with exactly the same proportion of ownership of the company's assets as before, the process should not increase the value of the shares.

Why might the shareholders want to split their shares in the manner described above?

The answer is probably to avoid individual shares becoming too valuable and making them a bit unwieldy, in the way discussed in the answer to Activity 4.4. If a company trades successfully, the value of each share is likely to rise, and in time could increase to a level that is considered unwieldy. Splitting would solve this problem.

Exhibit 4.3

Photo-Me has a share split

In October 1999, Photo-Me International plc split its ordinary shares' nominal value of 2.5p per share to 0.5p per share. This meant that each ordinary shareholder became the owner of five times as many new shares, with each share having a market value of one fifth of each of the old ones. In the business's report and accounts for 2000, the chairman (Dan David) said that the split 'was undertaken to improve the liquidity of the company's shares'.

Photo-Me provides many of the coin-operated photobooths that are found in bus and train stations and elsewhere.

Bonus shares

It is always open to a company to take reserves of any kind (capital or revenue) and turn them into share capital. The new shares arising from such a conversion are known as **bonus shares**. Issues of bonus shares are quite frequently encountered in practice. Example 4.3 illustrates this aspect of share issues.

Example 4.3

The summary balance sheet of a company is as follows:

Balance sheet as at 31 March 2002

	£
Net assets (various assets less liabilities)	128,000

Capital and reserves
Share capital

50,000 shares of £1 each	50,000
Reserves	78,000
	128,000

The company decides that it will issue to existing shareholders one new share for every share owned by each shareholder. The balance sheet immediately following this will appear as follows:

Balance sheet as at 31 March 2002

	£
Net assets (various assets less liabilities)	128,000

Capital and reserves
Share capital

100,000 shares of £1 each (50,000 + 50,000)	100,000
Reserves (78,000 − 50,000)	28,000
	128,000

A shareholder of the company in Example 4.3 owned 100 shares before the bonus issue. How will things change for this shareholder as regards the number of shares owned and the value of the shareholding?

The answer should be that the number of shares will double from 100 to 200. Now the shareholder owns 1/500 of the company (200/100,000). Before the bonus issue, the shareholder also owned 1/500 of the company (100/50,000). The company's assets and liabilities have not changed as a result of the bonus issue and so, logically, 1/500 of the value of the company should be identical to what it was before. Thus each share is worth half as much.

A bonus issue simply takes one part of the owners' claim (part of a reserve) and puts it into another part of the owners' claim (share capital). Note that this is not the same as a share split, where the reserves are not affected.

Can you think of any reasons why a company might want to make a bonus issue if it has no economic consequence?

We think that there are three possible reasons:

- To lower the value of each share without reducing the shareholders' collective or individual wealth. This is the same effect as splitting and may be seen as an alternative to splitting.
- To provide the shareholders with a 'feel-good factor'. It is believed that shareholders like bonus issues because it seems to make them better off, though in practice it should not affect their wealth.
- Where reserves arising from operating profits and/or realised gains on the sale of fixed assets are used to make the bonus issue, it has the effect of taking part of that portion of the owners' claim that could be drawn by the shareholders, as drawings (or dividends), and locking it up. We shall see, a little later in this chapter, that there are severe restrictions on the extent to which shareholders may make drawings from their capital. An individual or organisation contemplating lending money to the company may insist that the dividend payment possibilities are restricted as a condition of making the loan. This point will be explained later.

Rights issues

Rights issues are made when companies that have been established for some time seek to raise additional share capital for expansion, or even to solve a liquidity problem (cash shortage) by issuing additional shares for cash. Company law gives existing shareholders the first right of refusal on these new shares. So the new shares would be offered to shareholders in proportion to their existing holding. Thus existing shareholders are each given the right to buy some new shares. Only where the existing shareholders agree to waive their right would the shares be offered to the investing public generally.

The company (that is, the existing shareholders) would typically prefer that the shares are bought by existing shareholders, irrespective of the legal position. This is for two reasons:

- The ownership (and, therefore, control) of the company remains in the same hands.
- The costs of making the issue (advertising, complying with various company law requirements) tend to be less if the shares are to be offered to existing shareholders.

To encourage existing shareholders to take up their 'rights' to buy some new shares, those shares are virtually always offered at a price below the current market price of the existing ones.

Activity 4.10

Earlier, in Example 4.2, the point was illustrated that issuing new shares at below their current worth was to the advantage of the new shareholders at the expense of the old ones. In view of this, does it matter that rights issues are almost always made at below the current value of the shares?

....

The answer is that it does not matter *in these particular circumstances*. This is because, in a rights issue, the existing shareholders and the new shareholders are exactly the same people. Not only this, but the new shares will be held by the shareholders in the same proportion as they held the existing shares. Thus, a particular shareholder will be gaining on the new shares exactly as much as he or she is losing on the existing ones: in the end, no one is better or worse off as a result of the rights issue being made at a discount.

You should be clear that a rights issue is a totally different notion from a bonus issue. Rights issues result in an asset (cash) being transferred from shareholders to the company. Bonus issues involve no transfer of assets in either direction.

Share capital – some expressions used in company law

Before leaving our detailed discussion of share capital, it might be helpful to clarify some of the jargon used in company accounts.

When a company is first formed, the shareholders give the directors an upper limit on the amount of nominal value of the shares that can be issued. This is known as the **authorised share capital**. This value can easily be revised upwards, but only if the shareholders agree.

That part of the authorised share capital that has been issued to shareholders is the **issued** (or **allotted**) **share capital**.

Sometimes, but not very commonly, a company may not require shareholders to pay all of the price of the shares issued at the time of issue. This would normally be where the company does not need the money all at once. Some money would normally be paid at the time of issue and the company would 'call' for further instalments until the shares were **fully paid**. That part of the total issue price that has been 'called' is known as the **called-up share capital**. That part that has been called and paid is known as the **paid-up share capital**.

Exhibit 4.4 shows equity capital and reserves of Nichols plc, the business that manufactures a range of foods and drinks, including the Vimto soft drink.

Exhibit 4.4

The following extract shows the equity capital and reserves section of the balance sheet of Nichols plc as at 31 December 1999. Note that the company has just one class of shares and three types of reserve.

	1999 £'000
Share capital	
Authorised 52,000,000 (1988 – 52,000,000) ordinary 10p shares	**5,200**
Allotted, issued and fully paid 36,968,772 (1998 – 36,960,645)	
ordinary 10p shares	**3,697**

During the year the company purchased and cancelled 1,900,000 shares at an average price, including cost of 134p per share. 1,908,127 shares were issued for part consideration of the purchase of Balmoral Trading Limited.

Reserves

	Share premium account (Group) £000	Capital redemption reserve (Group) £000	Profit and loss account (Group) £000
At 1 January 1999	746	1,019	24,557
Retained profit for the year	—	—	3,004
Ordinary shares issued	2,509	—	—
Ordinary shares cancelled	—	190	(2,548)
At 31 December 1999	**3,255**	**1,209**	**25,013**

Long-term loans and other sources of finance

While we are looking at the role of the company's owners in financing the company, it is worth briefly considering other sources of finance used by companies. Many companies borrow money on a long-term basis, perhaps on a ten-year contract. Lenders may be banks and other professional providers of loan finance. Many companies raise loan finance in such a way that small investors, including private individuals, are able to lend small amounts. This method is particularly favoured by the larger, Stock Exchange-listed, companies and involves their making a **loan stock** or **debenture** issue, which, though large in total, can be taken up in small slices by individual investors, both private individuals and investing institutions, such as pension funds and insurance companies. In some cases, these slices of loans can be bought and sold through the Stock Exchange. This means that investors do not have to wait the full term of the loan to obtain repayment, but can sell their slice of the loan to another would-be lender at intermediate points in the term of the loan.

Some of the features of loan financing, particularly the possibility that loan stock may be marketable on the Stock Exchange, can lead to a confusion that loan stock are shares by another name. You should be clear that this is not the case. It is the shareholders who own the company and therefore who share in its losses and profits. Loan stock holders lend money to the company under a legally binding contract that normally specifies the rate of interest, the interest payment dates and the date of repayment of the loan itself. Usually, long-term loans are secured on assets of the company.

Long-term financing of companies can be depicted as in Figure 4.1.

Figure 4.1

Sources of long-term finance for a typical limited company

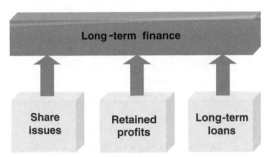

Companies derive their long-term financing needs from three sources: new share issues, retained profit and long-term borrowings. For a typical company, the sum of the first two (jointly known as 'equity finance') exceeds the third. Retained profit usually exceeds either of the other two in terms of the amount of finance raised in most years.

Companies may also borrow finance on a short-term basis, perhaps from a bank as an overdraft. Most companies buy goods and services on a month or two's credit, as is normal in business-to-business transactions. This is, in effect, an interest-free loan.

It is important to the prosperity and stability of a company that it strikes a suitable balance between finance provided by the shareholders (equity) and loan financing. This topic will be explored in Chapter 7.

Exhibit 4.5 shows the long-term borrowings of Rolls-Royce plc, the engine-building business, at 31 December 2000. Note the large number of sources from which the company borrows. This is typical of most large companies and probably reflects a desire to exploit all available means of raising finance, each of which may have some advantages and disadvantages. 'Secured' in this context means that the lender would have the right, should Rolls-Royce fail to meet its interest and/or capital repayment obligations, to seize a specified asset of the business (probably some land) and use it to raise the sums involved. Normally, a lender would accept a lower rate of interest where the loan is secured in this way as there is less risk involved. It should be said that whether a loan to a company like Rolls-Royce is secured or unsecured is usually pretty academic. It is unlikely that such a large and profitable company would fail to meet its obligations.

'Finance leases' are, in effect, arrangements where Rolls-Royce needs the use of a fixed asset and, instead of buying the asset itself, it arranges for a financier to buy the asset and then to lease it to the business, probably for the entire economic life of the asset. Though legally it is the financier who owns the asset, from an accounting point of view the essence of the arrangement is that, in effect, Rolls-Royce has borrowed cash from the financier to buy the asset. Thus, the asset appears among the business's fixed assets and the financial obligation to the financier is shown here as a long-term loan. This is a good example of how accounting tries to report the economic *substance* of a transaction, rather than its strict legal *form*. Finance leasing is a fairly popular means of raising long-term funds.

The following extract from the annual accounts of Rolls-Royce plc sets out the sources of the company's long-term borrowing as at 31 December 1999.

Borrowings – amount falling due after one year

	1999 £m
Unsecured	
Bank loans	734
$7\frac{1}{8}$% Notes 2003[1]	199
$4\frac{1}{2}$% Notes 2005[2]	177
Other loans 2001–2009 (interest rates nil)	5
Secured	
Obligations under finance leases payable:[3]	
Between one and two years	8
Between two and five years	45
After five years	44
Zero-coupon bonds 2005/2007 (including 9.0% interest accretion)[4]	33
Bank loans 2001 (interest rates 5.8% to 6.8%)[4]	26
	1,271
Repayable	
Between one and two years – by instalments	26
– otherwise	408
Between two and five years – by instalments	48
– otherwise	497
After five years – by instalments	82
– otherwise	210
	1,271

Chapter 15 goes into more detail on the imprtant factors that a business must consider in the context of how to finance its operations.

● ● ● ● Restriction on the right of shareholders to make drawings of capital

Limited companies are required by law to distinguish between that part of their capital (shareholders' claim) that may be withdrawn by the shareholders and that part which may not.

The withdrawable part is that which has arisen from trading profits and from realised profits on the disposal of fixed assets (to the extent that tax payments on these profits and gains, as well as previous drawings, have not extinguished this part of the capital). This withdrawable element of the capital is *revenue reserves*.

The non-withdrawable part normally consists of that which has risen from funds injected by shareholders buying shares in the company and that which came from upward revaluations of company assets that still remain in the company – that is, *share capital and capital reserves*.

The law does not specify how large the non-withdrawable part of a particular company's capital should be, but simply that anyone dealing with the company should be able to tell from looking at the company's balance sheet how large it

Can you think of the reason why limited companies are required to distinguish different parts of their capital, whereas sole proprietorship businesses are not required to do so?

The reason for this situation is the limited liability, which company shareholders enjoy but which owners of unincorporated businesses do not. If a sole proprietor withdraws all of the owner's claim, or even an amount in excess of this, the position of the creditors of the business is not weakened since they can legally enforce their claims against the sole proprietor as an individual. With a limited company, where the business and the owners are legally separated, such a legal right to enforce claims against individuals does not exist. However, to protect the company's creditors, the law insists that a specific part of the capital of a company cannot legally be withdrawn by the shareholders.

is. In the light of this, a particular prospective lender, or supplier of goods or services on credit, can make a commercial judgement as to whether to deal with the company or not.

Let us now look at another example.

Example 4.4

The summary balance sheet of a company at a particular date is as follows:

Balance sheet

	£
Total assets less current liabilities	43,000
Capital and reserves	
Share capital	
20,000 shares of £1 each	20,000
Reserves (revenue)	23,000
	43,000

A bank has been asked to make a £25,000 long-term loan to the company. If the loan were to be made, the balance sheet immediately following would appear as follows:

Balance sheet (after the loan)

	£
Total assets less current liabilities	
(£43,000 + £25,000))	68,000
Less **Long-term liabilities**	
Long-term loan	25,000
	43,000
Capital and reserves	
Share capital	
20,000 shares of £1 each	20,000
Reserves (revenue)	23,000
	43,000

As things stand in our company in Example 4.4, there are total assets less current liabilities to a total balance sheet value of £68,000 to meet the bank's claim of £25,000. It would be possible, however, for the company to pay perfectly legally a dividend (which is a cash return to shareholders) of £23,000. The balance sheet would then appear as follows:

Balance sheet (after dividend)	£
Total assets less current liabilities	
(£68,000 − £23,000))	45,000
Less **Long-term liabilities**	
Long-term loan	25,000
	20,000
Capital and reserves	
Share capital	
20,000 shares of £1 each	20,000
Reserves (revenue (£23,000 − £23,000))	–
	20,000

This leaves the bank in a very much weaker position, in that there are now total assets less current liabilities with a balance sheet value of £45,000 to meet a claim of £25,000. Note that the difference between the amount of the bank loan and the total assets less current liabilities always equals the capital and reserves total. Thus, the capital and reserves represent a **margin of safety** for creditors. The larger the amount of the owners' claim withdrawable by the shareholders, the smaller is the potential margin of safety for creditors.

It is important to recognise that company law says nothing about how large the margin of safety must be. It is left as a matter of commercial judgement of the company concerned as to what is desirable. The larger it is, the easier will the company find it to persuade potential lenders to lend and suppliers to supply goods and services on credit. Put another way, a large margin of safety would normally enhance creditor confidence and increase the abilty of the business to borrow, if required.

Activity 4.12

Would you expect a company to pay all of its revenue reserves as a dividend? What factors might be involved with a dividend decision?

It would be rare for a company to pay all of its revenue reserves as a dividend: a legal right to do so does not necessarily make it a good idea. Most companies see ploughed-back profits as a major – usually *the* major – source of new finance.

The factors, that influence the dividend decision are likely to include:

- The availability of cash to pay a dividend. It would not be illegal to borrow to pay a dividend, but it would be unusual and, possibly, imprudent.
- The needs of the business for finance for investment.
- Possibly a need for the directors to create good relations with investors, who may regard a dividend as a positive feature.

You might have thought of others.

The law is adamant, however, that it is illegal, under normal circumstances, for shareholders to withdraw that part of their claim that is represented by shares and capital reserves. This means that potential creditors of the company know the maximum amount of the shareholders' claim that can be drawn by the shareholders. Figure 4.2 shows the important division between that part of the shareholders' claim that can be withdrawn as a dividend and that part that cannot.

Figure 4.2

Availability for dividends of various parts of the shareholders' claim

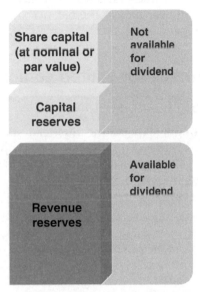

Total equity finance of limited companies consists of share capital, capital reserves and revenue reserves. Only the revenue reserves (which arise from realised profits and gains) can be used to fund a dividend. In other words, the maximum legal dividend is the amount of the revenue reserves.

Earlier in this chapter, the point was made that a potential creditor may insist that some revenue reserves are converted to bonus shares (or capitalised) in order to increase the margin of safety, as a condition of granting the loan.

Perhaps it is worth pointing out, as a practical footnote to Example 4.4, that most potential long-term lenders would seek to have their loan secured against a particular asset of the company – particularly an asset like freehold property. This would give them the right to seize the asset concerned, sell it and satisfy their claim, should the company default. Lenders often place restrictions or *covenants* on the borrowing company's freedom of action, as a condition of granting the loan. The covenants typically restrict the level of risk to which the company, and the lender's asset, is exposed.

Activity 4.13

Can you think of any circumstances where the non-withdrawable part of a company's capital could be reduced, without contravening the law?

It can be reduced, but only as a result of the company sustaining trading losses, or losses on disposal of fixed assets, that exceed the amount of the withdrawable portion of the company's capital. It cannot be reduced by shareholders making drawings.

Drawings are usually made in the form of a dividend paid by the company to the shareholders, in proportion to the number of shares owned by each one.

If we refer back to Exhibit 4.4, we can see that Nichols plc could legally have paid a dividend of £25.013 million on 31 December 1999, which is the amount of its revenue reserves. For several reasons, including the fact that this would represent well over half of the balance sheet value of the company's net assets, no such dividend was paid.

Accounting for limited companies

The main financial statements

As we might expect, the financial statements of a limited company are, in essence, identical to those of a sole proprietor. There are, however, some differences of detail, and we shall now consider these.

Set out in Example 4.5 are the profit and loss account and balance sheet of a limited company:

Example 4.5

Da Silva plc
Profit and loss account for the year ended 31 December 2001

	£m	£m
Sales		840
Less Cost of sales		520
Gross profit		320
Less Operating expenses		
Wages and salaries	98	
Heat and light	18	
Rent and rates	24	
Motor-vehicle expenses	20	
Insurance	4	
Printing and stationery	12	
Depreciation	45	
Audit fee	4	
		225
Operating profit		95
Less Interest payable		10
Profit before tax		85
Tax on profit		24
Profit after tax		61
Less Transfer to general reserve	20	
Proposed dividend	25	
		45
Unappropriated profit carried forward		16

Balance sheet as at 31 December 2001

	£m	£m
Fixed assets		
Land and buildings		132
Plant and machinery		171
		303
Current assets		
Stock	65	
Debtors	112	
Cash	36	
	213	
Less Creditors: amounts falling due within 12 months		
Creditors	74	
Corporation tax	12	
Proposed dividend	25	
	111	
Net current assets (working capital)		102
Total assets less current liabilities		405
Less Creditors: amounts falling due in more than 12 months		
10% debentures		100
Net assets		305
Share capital		
Ordinary shares of £0.50 each		200
Reserves		
Share premium account	30	
General reserve	50	
Profit and loss account	25	
		105
		305

You may well feel that the most striking thing about these statements is the extent to which they look exactly the same as those that you have been used to with sole proprietors. This is correct; the differences are small. Let us go through and pick up these differences.

The profit and loss account

There is a number of features in the P and L account that need consideration:

- *Layout.* The profit from trading activities, before interest payable (or receivable), is separately identified as **operating profit**, interest is then deducted to find the profit for the year. The statement does not end there as it would were this the profit and loss account of a sole proprietor. The statement goes on to show how the profit has been appropriated between funds set aside to meet the tax on the profit, to pay a dividend to shareholders, and to make a transfer to a general (revenue) reserve. This last part of the statement is known as the **appropriation account**.

- *Audit fees.* As we shall see later in this chapter, companies are normally required to have their financial statements audited by an independent firm of auditors, for which they are charged a fee. Though it is open to all sole proprietors to have their accounts audited, very few do so. This is therefore an expense that will normally be present in the P and L account of a company but not that of a sole proprietor.

- *Tax.* As separate legal entities, companies are required to be responsible for their own tax on profit. The calculation of the tax known as **corporation tax** would be based on the profit for the year.

- *Dividend.* This is the amount of dividend that will be paid to the shareholders. This is in the nature of drawings of capital by the owners of the company. The fact that the dividend is 'proposed' means that the cash had not yet been paid at 31 December 2001 (the year-end). Sometimes shareholders receive a dividend before the end of the year. With many companies, they receive an 'interim' dividend part-way through the year, and a 'final' one shortly after the year-end.

- *Transfer to general reserve.* What is left over of the year's profit, after tax and dividends have been accounted for, is retained, normally to be reinvested ('ploughed back') into the operations of the company. For this company, the amount left is £36 million (that is, £61 million – £25 million). This could all have gone to increasing the profit and loss balance in the balance sheet. As is quite common in practice, however, an amount (£20 million for this company) has been transferred to a general reserve.

It is not totally clear why directors decide to make transfers to general reserve, since the funds concerned remain part of the revenue reserves, still available for dividend. The most plausible explanation seems to be that directors feel that taking funds out of the profit and loss account and placing them in a 'reserve' indicates an intention to retain the funds permanently in the company and not to use them to pay a dividend. Of course, the balance on the profit and loss account is also a reserve, but that fact is not indicated in its title.

The balance sheet

For the balance sheet, certain items need special consideration:

- *Terminology.* Two terms used in the balance sheet are 'Creditors: amounts falling due within 12 months' and 'Creditors: amounts falling due in more than 12 months'. These terms refer to current liabilities and long-term liabilities respectively. As we shall see in the next chapter, the law requires that these new terms be used when reporting to external users.

- *Corporation tax.* The amount that appears in short-term liabilities represents 50 per cent of the tax on the profit of the year [2001]. It is half of the tax charge that appears in the profit and loss account; the other 50 per cent will already have been paid. The unpaid 50 per cent will be paid shortly following the balance sheet date. These payment dates are set down by law.

- *Dividend.* The dividend that was proposed in the profit and loss account also appears under short-term liabilities, once more to be paid early in the new accounting year.

- *Share capital and reserves.* We have aleady discussed this area at length earlier in the chapter. Before the year end, the general reserve balance must have stood at £30 million, to be enhanced to its final level by the transferred appropriation of the year [2001] profit. Similarly, the P and L account balance must have been £9 million, just before the year end. As was mentioned above, the general reserve and the profit and loss account balance are identical in all respects; they both arise from retained profits, and are both available for dividend.

Accounting for groups of companies

Most large businesses, including nearly all of the well known ones, operate not as a single company but as a group of companies. In these circumstances, one company (the **parent** or **holding company**) owns sufficient of the shares of various subsidiary companies to control them. In the case of many larger businesses, there is a number of subsidiary companies. Each of the subsidiaries operates some aspect of the group's activities. The reasons why many businesses operate in the form of groups include:

- A desire for each part of the business to have its own limited liability, so that financial problems in one part of a business cannot have an adverse effect on other parts.
- An attempt to make each part of the business have some sense of independence and autonomy and, perhaps, to create or perpetuate a market image of a smaller independent business.

From an accounting point of view, each company prepares its own independent annual final accounts. Company law also requires that the parent company of the group prepares **consolidated** or **group accounts**. These group accounts amalgamate the accounts of all of the group members. Thus, for example, the group profit and loss account includes the total sales figure for all group companies and the balance sheet includes the stock in trade figure for all group members added together. As we might expect, the group final accounts would look exactly like the accounts of the parent company had it owned and operated all of the assets of the business directly, instead of through subsidiary companies.

From what has just been said, if we look at a set of group final accounts, we might not be able to say whether the business operates through a single company or through a large number of subsidiaries. Only by referring to the heading at the top of each statement, which would mention the word 'consolidated' or 'group', might we know. In some cases, however, there might be one or two items in the group accounts that tend to occur only there. These items are:

- *Goodwill arising on consolidation.* This occurs when a parent acquires a subsidiary from previous owners and pays more for the subsidiary than the values of the individual assets, net of liabilities, of the new subsidiary than they appear to be worth. This excess might represent such things as the value of a good reputation that the new subsidiary already has in the market, or the value of it having a loyal and skilled workforce.

  Goodwill arising on consolidation will appear as an intangible fixed asset on the group balance sheet. Any amount of the goodwill that is depreciated will appear, as an expense, in the group profit and loss account.

● *Minority or outsiders' interests.* One of the principles followed when preparing group accounts is that all of the revenues, expenses, assets, claims and cash flows of each subsidiary are reflected to their full extent in the group accounts. This is true whether or not the parent owns all of the shares in each subsidiary, provided that the parent has control. Control normally means owning more than 50 per cent of the subsidiary's ordinary shares. Where not all of the shares are owned by the parent, this fact is reflected in the group balance sheet in that the investment of those shareholders in the subsidiary other than the parent company appears as part of the owners' claim (share capital and reserves). This indicates that the net assets of the group are being financed mainly by the parent company's shareholders, but that 'outside' shareholders finance a part of them. Similarly, the group profit and loss account reflects the fact that not all of the net profit of the group is attributable to the shareholders of the parent company; a part of them is attributable to the 'outside' shareholders.

Example 4.6 shows how the balance sheet of Major plc and its subsidiary is drawn up. Note that the group balance sheet closely resembles that of individual companies.

Example 4.6

Major plc has just bought, from the previous shareholders, 45 million (out of 60 million) ordinary shares in Minor plc, paying £75 million for them. The other 15 million Minor plc shares are owned by other shareholders. These shareholders are now referred to by Major plc as the 'minority'. Minor plc is thus now a subsidiary of Major plc and, as is clear from Major plc's balance sheet, the latter's only subsiduary company.

 The balance sheets of the two companies immediately following the **takeover** of Minor plc by Major plc were as follows:

	Major plc £m	Major plc £m	Minor plc £m	Minor plc £m
Fixed assets				
Tangible – plant and machinery		63		67
Intangible – 45 million shares in Minor plc		75		–
		138		67
Current assets				
Stocks	37		21	
Debtors	22		12	
Cash	16		2	
	75		35	
Creditors: amounts falling due within one year				
Creditors	(18)		(9)	
		57		26
		195		93
Creditors: amounts falling due after more than one year				
Loan stocks		(35)		(13)
		160		80
Share capital and reserves				
Ordinary shares of £1 each		100		60
Reserves		60		20
		160		80

If a balance sheet were to be drawn up immediately following the takeover, it would be as follows:

	Major plc and its subsidiary	
	£m	£m
Fixed assets		
Tangible – plant and machinery (63 + 67)		130
Intangible – goodwill (75 − ($\frac{45}{60}$ × 80)		15
		145
Current assets		
Stock (37 + 21)	58	
Debtors (22 + 12)	34	
Cash (16 + 2)	18	
	110	
Creditors: amounts falling due within one year		
Creditors (18 + 9)	(27)	
		83
		228
Creditors: amounts falling due after more than one year		
Loan stocks (35 + 13)		(48)
		180
Share capital and reserves		
Ordinary shares of £1 each		100
Reserves		60
		160
Minority interests ($\frac{15}{60}$ × 80)		20
		180

Note that all of the items, except two, in the group balance sheet are simply the two figures for the item concerned added together. This is despite the fact that Major plc only owns three-quarters of the shares of Minor plc. The logic of group accounts is that if the parent owns enough shares to control its subsidiary, all of the subsidiary's assets and claims should be reflected on the group balance sheet.

The two exceptions to this approach are goodwill and minority interests. Goodwill is simply the excess of what Major paid for the shares over their balance sheet value. Major plc bought 45 million of 60 million shares, paying £75 million. According to Minor plc's balance sheet, this was net assets (fixed and current assets, less current and long-term liabilities) of £80 million. So Major plc paid £75 million for £60 million (that is, $\frac{45}{60}$ × £80 million) of net assets – an excess of £15 million usually referred to as 'goodwill arising on consolidation'. Minority interests take account of the fact that although Major plc may control all of the assets and liabilities of Minor plc, it only provides the equity finance for three-quarters of them. The other quarter, £20 million (that is, $\frac{15}{60}$ × £80 million), is still provided by shareholders in Minor plc, other than Major plc.

Example 4.7 shows the profit and loss account of Major plc and its subsidiary (Minor plc) for the first year following the takeover. As with the balance sheet, the various revenue and expense figures are simply the individual figures for each company added together. The minority interest figure (£2 million) represents $\frac{15}{60}$ of the after-tax profit of Minor plc.

Example 4.7

Profit and loss account of Major plc and its subsidiary

	£m	£m
Turnover		123
Cost of sales		(56)
Gross profit		67
Administration expenses	(28)	
Distribution expenses	(9)	(37)
Profit before tax		30
Taxation		(12)
Profit after tax		18
Attributable to minorities		(2)
Profit after tax attributable to Major plc shareholders		16
Profit and loss account balance brought forward from previous year		37
		53
Dividend on ordinary shares		(6)
Profit and loss account balance carried forward to following year		47

Self-assessment question 4.1

The summarised balance sheet of Dev Ltd is as follows:

Balance sheet as at 31 December 2001

	£
Net assets (various assets less liabilities)	235,000
Capital and reserves	
Share capital: 100,000 shares @ £1	100,000
Share premium account	30,000
Revaluation reserve	37,000
Profit and loss account balance	68,000
	235,000

Required:

(a) Without any other transactions occurring at the same time, the company made a one-for-five rights share issue at £2 per share payable in cash (all shareholders taking up their rights) and, immediately afterwards, made a one-for-two bonus issue. Show the balance sheet immediately following the bonus issue, assuming that the directors wanted to retain the maximum dividend payment potential for the future.

(b) Explain what external influence might cause the directors to choose not to retain the maximum dividend payment possibilities.

(c) Show the balance sheet immediately following the bonus issue, assuming that the directors wanted to retain the *minimum* dividend payment potential for the future.

(d) What is the maximum dividend that could be paid before and after the events described in (a) if the minimum dividend payment potential is achieved?

(e) Lee owns 100 shares in Dev Ltd before the events described in (a). Assuming that the net assets of the company have a value equal to their balance sheet value, show how these events will affect Lee's wealth.

(f) Looking at the original balance sheet of Dev Ltd, shown above, what four things do we know about the company's status and history that are not specifically stated on the balance sheet?

Summary

This chapter has reviewed the position of limited companies, particularly in the context of accounting. Limited companies have their own legal status as 'people', which leads to many of their peculiarities, including the close attention that the law pays to company accounting. The owners' claim on limited companies is made up of share capital and reserves. Each share represents a part of the ownership of the company. There are strict limits on the extent to which companies are allowed to make payments to their owners (the shareholders) as 'drawings' of capital.

The accounts of companies are, in essence, very similar to those of sole-proprietorship businesses, but there are some important differences. Where companies are in a group, the parent company must prepare accounts for the group as a whole.

Key terms

Limited liability p. 99	Capital reserves p. 107
Public company p. 99	Share premium account p. 108
Private company p. 99	Consolidating p. 108
Corporation tax pp. 100, 120	Bonus shares p. 109
Director p. 101	Rights issues p. 110
Corporate governance p. 101	Authorised share capital p. 111
Combined Code p. 102	Issued share capital p. 111
Nominal value p. 105	Fully paid shares p. 111
Revenue reserve p. 106	Called-up share capital p. 111
Dividend p. 106	Paid-up share capital p. 111
Ordinary shares p. 106	Debenture p. 112
Equity p. 106	Group accounts p. 121
Preference shares p. 106	Takeover p. 122
Reserves p. 107	

Further reading

If you would like to explore the topics covered in this chapter in more depth, we recommend the following books:

Financial Reporting, *Alexander, D. and Britton, A.*, 6th edn, International Thomson Business Press, 2001, chapter 12.

Financial Accounting and Reporting, *Elliott, B. and Elliott, J.*, 5th edn, Financial Times Prentice Hall, 2001, chapters 10 and 19.

Accounting Theory and Practice, *Glautier, M. and Underdown, B.*, 7th edn, Financial Times Prentice Hall, 2001, chapter 13.

Reference

'Corporate Governance: Improving competitiveness and access to capital in global markets', an OECD report by Business Sector Advisory Group on Corporate Governance, Organisation for Economic Co-operation and Development, 1988, p. 14.

4.1 How does the liability of a limited company differ from the liability of a real person in respect of amounts owed to others?

4.2 Some people are about to form a company as a vehicle through which to run a new business. What are the advantages to them of forming a private limited company rather than a public one?

4.3 What is a reserve, in the context of the owners' claim on a limited company?

4.4 What is called-up share capital?

? EXERCISES

Exercises 4.6–4.8 are more advanced than 4.1–4.5. Those with coloured numbers have answers at the back of the book.

4.1 Comment on the following quotation:

> Limited companies can set a limit on the amount of debts which they will meet. They tend to have reserves of cash, as well as share capital and they can use these reserves to pay dividends to the shareholders. Many companies have preference as well as ordinary shares. The preference shares give a guaranteed dividend. The shares of many companies can be bought and sold on the Stock Exchange, and a shareholder selling his or her shares can represent a useful source of new capital to the company.

4.2 Comment on the following quotes:

(a) 'Bonus shares increase the shareholders' wealth because, after the issue, they have more shares, but each one of the same nominal value as they had before. Share splits, on the other hand, do not make the shareholders richer, because the total nominal value of their shareholding is the same before the issue as after it.'

(b) 'By law, once shares have been issued at a particular nominal value, they must always be issued at that value in any future share issues.'

(c) 'By law, companies can pay as much as they like by way of dividends on their shares, provided that they have sufficient cash to do so.'

(d) 'Companies do not have to pay tax on their profits because the shareholders have to pay tax on their dividends.'

4.3 Briefly explain each of the following expressions that you have seen in the accounts of a limited company:

(a) Dividend
(b) Debenture
(c) Share premium account.

4.4 Iqbal Ltd started trading on 1 January 1998. During the first five years of trading, the following occurred:

Year ended 31 December	Trading profit (loss)	Profit (loss) on sale of fixed assets	Upward revaluation of fixed assets
	£	£	£
1998	(15,000)	–	–
1999	8,000	–	10,000
2000	15,000	5,000	–
2001	20,000	(6,000)	–
2002	22,000	–	–

Required

Assuming that the company paid the maximum legal dividend each year, how much would each year's dividend be?

4.5 Da Silva plc's outline balance sheet as at a particular date was as follows:

	£m
Sundry net assets	72
£1 ordinary shares	40
General reserve	32
	72

The directors made a one-for-four bonus issue, immediately followed by a one-for-four rights issue at a price of £1.80 per share.

Required:

Show the balance sheet of Da Silva plc immediately following the two share issues.

4.6 Presented below is a draft set of simplified accounts for Pear Limited for the year ended 30 September 2001.

Profit and loss account for the year ended 30 September 2001

	£000	£000
Turnover		1,456
Costs of sales		(768)
Gross profit		688
Less Expenses:		
Salaries	220	
Depreciation	249	
Other operating costs	131	(600)
Operating profit		88
Interest payable		(15)
Profit before taxation		73
Taxation at 30%		(22)
Profit after taxation		51

Balance sheet as at 30 September 2001

	£000	£000
Fixed assets		
Cost	1,570	
Depreciation	(690)	880
Current assets		
Stocks	207	
Debtors	182	
Cash at bank	21	
	410	
Less **Creditors: amounts due within one year**		
Trade creditors	88	
Other creditors	20	
Taxation	22	
Bank overdraft	105	
	235	
Net current assets		175
Less **Creditors: amounts due after more than**		
one year 10% debenture – repayable 2008		(300)
		755
Capital and reserves		
Share capital		300
Share premium account	300	
Retained profit at beginning of year	104	
Profit for year	51	455
		755

The following information is available:

(i)   Depreciation has not been charged on office equipment with a written-down value of £100,000. This class of assets is depreciated at 12 per cent per annum using the reducing-balance method.

(ii)   A new machine was purchased, on credit, for £30,000 and delivered on 29 September but has not been included in the financial statements.

(iii)   A sales invoice to the value of £18,000 for September has been omitted from the accounts. (The cost of sales is stated correctly.)

(iv)   A dividend has been proposed of £25,000.

(v)   The interest payable on the debenture for the second half-year has not been included in the accounts.

(vi)   A general provision against bad debts is to be made at the level of 2 per cent of debtors.

(vii)   An invoice for electricity to the value of £2,000 for the quarter ended 30 September 2001 arrived on 4 October and has not been included in the accounts.

(viii) The charge for taxation will have to be amended to take account of the above information. Make the simplifying assumption that tax is payable shortly after the end of the year, at the rate of 30 per cent.

Required:
Prepare a revised set of financial statements for the year ended 30 September 2001 incorporating the additional information in (i)–(viii) above. Note: work to the nearest £1,000.

4.7 Presented below is a draft set of financial statements for Chips Limited.

Chips Limited
Profit and loss account for the year ended 30 June 2001

	£000	£000
Turnover		1,850
Cost of sales		(1,040)
Gross profit		810
Less Depreciation	(220)	
Other operating costs	(375)	(595)
Operating profit		215
Interest payable		(35)
Profit before taxation		180
Taxation		(60)
Profit after taxation		120

Balance sheet as at 30 June 2001

Fixed assets	Cost	Depreciation	
	£000	£000	£000
Buildings	800	112	688
Plant and equipment	650	367	283
Motor vehicles	102	53	49
	1,552	532	1,020

Current assets		
Stock		950
Debtors		420
Cash at bank		16
		1,386

Less Creditors due within one year		
Trade creditors		(361)
Other creditors		(117)
Taxation		(60)
		(538)

Net current assets		848
Less Creditors due after more than one year		
Secured 10% loan		(700)
		1,168

Capital and reserves		
Ordinary shares of £1, fully paid		500
6% preference shares of £1		300
Reserves at 1 July 2000	248	
Profit for year	120	368
		1,168

The following additional information is available:

(i) Purchase invoices for goods received on 29 June 2001 amounting to £23,000 have not been included.

(ii) A motor vehicle costing £8,000 with depreciation amounting to £5,000 was sold on 30 June 2001 for £2,100, paid by cheque. This transaction has not been included in the company's records.

(iii) No depreciation on motor vehicles has been charged. The annual rate is 20 per cent of cost at the year end.

(iv) A sale on credit for £16,000 made on 1 July 2001 has been included in the accounts in error.

(v) A half-yearly payment of interest on the secured loan due on 30 June 2001 has not been paid.

(vi) The tax charge should be 30 per cent of the reported profit before taxation. Assume that it is payable, in full, shortly after the year-end.

(vii) A dividend will be proposed by the directors of 2p per ordinary share; the preference dividend has not been incorporated.

Required:

Prepare a revised set of financial statements incorporating the additional information in (i)–(vii) above. Note: work to the nearest £1,000.

4.8 Rose Limited operates a small chain of retail shops that sell high-quality teas and coffees. Approximately half of sales are on credit. Abbreviated and unaudited accounts are given below:

Profit and loss account for the year ended 31 March 2001

	£000	£000
Sales		12,080
Cost of sales		6,282
Gross profit		5,798
Labour costs	2,658	
Depreciation	625	
Other operating costs	1,003	
		4,286
Net profit before interest		1,512
Interest payable		66
Net profit before tax		1,446
Tax payable		434
Net profit after tax		1,012
Dividend payable		300
Retained profit for year		712
Retained profit brought forward		756
Retained profit carried forward		1,468

Balance sheet as at 31 March 2001

	£000	£000
Fixed assets		2,728
Current assets		
Stocks	1,583	
Debtors	996	
Cash	26	
	2,605	

Creditors: amounts due within one year

Trade creditors	1,118	
Other creditors	417	
Tax	434	
Dividends	300	
Overdraft	296	
	2,565	

Net current assets		40

Creditors: amounts due after more than one year

Secured loan (2010)		(300)
		2,468

Share capital		
(50p shares, fully paid)		750
Share premium		250
Retained profit		1,468
		2,468

Since the unaudited accounts for Rose Limited were prepared, the following information has become available:

(i) An additional £74,000 of depreciation should have been charged on fixtures and fittings.

(ii) Invoices for credit sales on 31 March 2001 amounting to £34,000 have not been included; costs of sales is not affected.

(iii) Bad debts should be provided at a level of 2 per cent of debtors at the year-end.

(iv) Stocks, which had been purchased for £2,000, have been damaged and are unsaleable.

(v) Fixtures and fittings to the value of £16,000 were delivered just before 31 March 2001, but these assets were not included in the accounts and the purchase invoice had not been processed.

(vi) Wages for Saturday-only staff, amounting to £1,000, have not been paid for the final Saturday of the year.

(vii) Tax is payable at 30 per cent of net profit after tax. Assume that it is payable shortly after the year-end.

Required:

Prepare a balance sheet and profit and loss account for Rose Limited for the year ended 31 March 2001, incorporating the information in (i)–(vii) above. Note: work to the nearest £1,000.

5 Accounting for limited companies (2)

Introduction

In this chapter we continue our examination of the accounts of limited companies. We begin by considering the regulatory framework of limited company accounts. We identify the legal responsibilities of directors and auditors and discuss the main sources of accounting rules that govern the published accounts of limited companies. Although a detailed consideration of these accounting rules is beyond the scope of this text, we discuss the ways in which accounting regulations shape the form and content of the profit and loss account and balance sheet that are published for external use.

The degree of accounting regulation affecting limited companies has increased significantly over the past two decades and this has inevitably produced a reaction. It has been argued that such regulation is costly and unnecessary. In this chapter we review the case for and against accounting regulation. One important criticism of the accounting rules that have been developed is that they lack a clear framework of principles. In this chapter we consider the attempts that have been made by the accounting profession to deal with this problem.

The increasing complexity of business and the increasing demands for information by users have led to the publication of a number of additional financial statements. In this chapter we consider two of the more important, namely the segmental financial report and the operating and financial review. The aim of both these reports is to provide users with a more complete picture of financial performance and position.

OBJECTIVES

When you have completed this chapter, you should be able to:

- Describe the legal responsibilities of directors and auditors concerning the annual accounts provided to external users.
- Identify the main sources of regulation affecting the accounts of limited companies and discuss the case for and against regulation.
- Discuss the progress made in developing a framework of principles for accounting.
- Prepare a profit and loss account and balance sheet for a limited company in accordance with an acceptable legal format.
- Explain the purpose of segmental reports and the operating and financial review and discuss the contents of these reports.

The directors' duty to account – the role of company law

It is not usually possible for all of the shareholders to be involved in the general management of the company, nor do most of them wish to be involved, and so they elect directors to act on their behalf. It is both logical and required by company law that directors are accountable for their actions in respect of their stewardship (management) of the company's assets. In this context, directors are required by law:

- To maintain appropriate accounting records.
- To prepare an annual profit and loss account, a balance sheet that shows a 'true and fair' view of events, as well as a directors' report, and to make these available to all shareholders and to the public at large.

Exhibit 5.1 is an extract from the 2000 annual accounts of Pizza Express plc, the high street restaurant chain. This statement sets out what the directors regard as their responsibilities for the annual accounts.

Exhibit 5.1

The following extract is from the 2000 annual report of Pizza Express plc:

Statement of Directors' Responsibilities

Company law requires the directors to prepare financial statements for each financial year which give a true and fair view of the state of affairs of the Company and the Group and of the profit or loss of the Group for that period. In preparing those financial statements, the directors are required to:

- select suitable accounting policies and then apply them consistently;
- make judgements and estimates that are reasonable and prudent;
- state whether applicable accounting standards have been followed, subject to any material departures disclosed and explained in the financial statements;
- prepare the financial statements on the going concern basis unless it is inappropriate to presume that the Group will continue in business.

The directors confirm that the financial statements comply with the above requirements.

The directors are responsible for keeping proper accounting records which disclose with reasonable accuracy at any time the financial position of the Company and the Group and which enable them to ensure that the financial statements comply with the Companies Act 1985. They are also responsible for safeguarding the assets of the Group and hence for taking reasonable steps for the prevention and detection of fraud and other irregularities.

The relevant rules on director's duties are embodied in the Companies Acts 1985 and 1989. Company law goes quite a long way in prescribing the form and content of the accounting statements that directors must publish. A copy of each year's accounts must be made available to all of the company's shareholders and debenture holders. The accounts must also be made available to the general public. This is achieved by the company submitting a copy to the Registrar of Companies (Department of Trade and Industry), which allows anyone who wishes to do so to inspect these accounts.

Activity 5.1

Can you think of any reasons why various parliaments have decreed that companies must account, and have set up rules as to how they should do this?
We think there are broadly three reasons.

We thought of the following:

- *To inform and protect shareholders.* If shareholders feel that they are not getting a reasonable supply of reliable information from their company, they have no means of assessing their investment and how well it is being managed. In these circumstances, they would be reluctant to provide risk (equity) finance. As a result, the corporate sector could not function effectively, if at all. Any society with a significant private sector needs to encourage equity investment.
- *To inform and protect suppliers of labour, goods, services and finance, particularly those supplying credit (loans) or goods and services on credit.* People and organisations may be reluctant to engage in commercial relationships with a company, including being employed by it and lending it money, where they have no information about the company's likely future viability. This is likely to be more so when the company has limited liability, so that unsatisfied claims against the company cannot be pursued against the shareholders' other assets. Again, if people are reluctant to deal commercially with companies, the private sector cannot flourish.
- *To inform and protect society more generally.* Some companies exercise enormous power and influence in society generally, particularly on a geographically local basis. For example, a particular company may be the dominant employer and purchaser of commercial goods and services in a particular town or city. The legislators have tended to take the view that society generally has the right to information about the company and its activities.

True and fair

The legislation uses the expression 'true and fair view' in stating what the published accounts of companies should show, although the expression is not defined in the legislation. It is probably reasonable to say that accounts show a true and fair view when they seem unlikely to mislead a user into gaining a false impression of the company. The requirement for accounts to show a true and fair view tends to override any other requirements.

Activity 5.2	Why, in your opinion, does the legislation not require that accounts show a 'correct' or an 'accurate' view? Hint: think of depreciation of fixed assets.

Financial accounting can never really be said to be 'correct' or 'accurate' in that these words imply that there is just one value that any asset, claim, revenue or expense could have. This is simply not true in many, if not most, cases. Depreciation provides a good example. The annual depreciation expense, and in turn the balance sheet values of depreciating fixed assets, are based on judgements about the future.

How long is the economic life of an asset? What will its residual value be at the end of that life? How should the depreciation, over the economic life of the asset, best be matched against the revenues that it helps to generate? All these are matters of judgement. Someone who has a reasonable understanding of business and accounting could probably say whether or not the judgements are reasonable, given all the circumstances. If the judgements are reasonable, then they are likely to lead to accounts that show a true and fair view.

The profit and loss account

Company law offers companies the choice of four formats in which they may publish their profit and loss account. Each company must choose just one and is encouraged to continue to use that format. The objective of allowing companies to use one of only four formats is an attempt to standardise presentation, so as to make comparison of one company's accounts with those of another one somewhat easier.

Format 1 seems to be the most popular in practice. We shall concern ourselves only with this one. Not surprisingly, the four formats are quite similar in principle and provide more or less identical information. Example 5.1 shows a profit and loss account that has been set out according to Format 1.

<table>
<tr><td>**Example 5.1**</td><td colspan="3">**Jhamna plc**
Profit and loss account for the year ended 31 December 2001</td></tr>
<tr><td></td><td></td><td>£000</td><td>£000</td></tr>
<tr><td></td><td>Turnover</td><td></td><td>576</td></tr>
<tr><td></td><td>Cost of sales</td><td></td><td>307</td></tr>
<tr><td></td><td>Gross profit</td><td></td><td>269</td></tr>
<tr><td></td><td>Distribution costs</td><td>65</td><td></td></tr>
<tr><td></td><td>Administrative expenses</td><td>26</td><td>91</td></tr>
<tr><td></td><td></td><td></td><td>178</td></tr>
<tr><td></td><td>Other operating income</td><td></td><td>21</td></tr>
<tr><td></td><td></td><td></td><td>199</td></tr>
<tr><td></td><td>Income from other fixed-asset investments</td><td>5</td><td></td></tr>
<tr><td></td><td>Other interest receivable and similar income</td><td>12</td><td>17</td></tr>
<tr><td></td><td></td><td></td><td>216</td></tr>
<tr><td></td><td>Interest payable and similar charges</td><td></td><td>23</td></tr>
<tr><td></td><td></td><td></td><td>193</td></tr>
<tr><td></td><td>Tax on profit or loss on ordinary activities</td><td></td><td>46</td></tr>
<tr><td></td><td>Profit on ordinary activities after taxation</td><td></td><td>147</td></tr>
<tr><td></td><td>Retained profit brought forward from last year</td><td></td><td>56</td></tr>
<tr><td></td><td></td><td></td><td>203</td></tr>
<tr><td></td><td>Transfer to general reserve</td><td>60</td><td></td></tr>
<tr><td></td><td>Proposed dividend on ordinary shares</td><td>50</td><td>110</td></tr>
<tr><td></td><td>Retained profit carried forward</td><td></td><td>93</td></tr>
</table>

The legislation requires that comparative figures for the previous year are also given for each entry in the profit and loss account. Note that tax is included in the format. This is because companies, as independent legal entities, are responsible for their own tax. As we saw in the last chapter, companies are subject to corporation tax on their profits. This fact will tend to be reflected in both the profit and loss account and the balance sheet.

Though not mentioned in any of the formats, there is also a requirement to include the last part shown in Example 5.1 – the part that starts after 'Profit on ordinary activities after taxation'. This section shows how the sum of the current year's after-tax profit and any unappropriated (retained) profit accumulated from previous years has been appropriated. In the example, the current year's after-tax profit is £147,000. To this is added £56,000 that was unappropriated from previous years, giving £203,000 that could be appropriated. Of this, £60,000 has been transferred to general reserve and £50,000 earmarked for the payment of a dividend, probably within a few weeks of the accounting year-end. The remaining £93,000 is carried forward until next year, when it will be entered as 'retained profit brought forward from last year'. This figure is a reserve; it is part of the shareholders' claim, but it is not share capital. The transfer of the £60,000 to general reserve has no legal significance. It tends to be seen as a statement by the directors that they do not see this amount as available for payment of a dividend. This does not preclude the directors from reversing this transfer at a later date.

Most of the items in the profit and loss account are self-explanatory, but there are four that are not defined in the legislation. They are generally interpreted as follows:

- *Cost of sales.* This includes all of the expenses of producing the goods or services that were sold during the period. This would include materials, production labour, depreciation of production facilities and so on. For a company that does not manufacture – for example, a retailer – the cost of sales would simply be the cost of the stock that was sold during the year.
- *Distribution costs.* The expenses concerned with selling and delivering goods or services sold during the year.
- *Administrative expenses.* Virtually any other expenses of running the company during the year that are not included in cost of sales, distribution costs or any other expense categories appearing in Format 1.
- *Other operating income.* All income (revenues) of the company for the year that are not specified elsewhere in Format 1.

The balance sheet

There are two formats available for the balance sheet. Format 1 is the one most used in practice, and so we shall concentrate on it here. As with the profit and loss account, the other format gives exactly the same basic information but is set out differently. Again, as with the profit and loss account, comparative figures from the previous year are required and a category of asset or claim need not be mentioned if it does not exist as far as a particular company is concerned.

Jhamna plc's balance sheet, set out in Format 1 style, is shown in Example 5.2.

Example 5.2

Jhamna plc
Balance sheet as at 31 December 2001

	£000	£000	£000
Fixed assets:			
Intangible assets:			
Patents and trademarks		37	
Tangible assets:			
Land and buildings	310		
Plant and machinery	125		
Fixtures, fittings, tools and equipment	<u>163</u>	<u>598</u>	635

Current assets:

Stocks:			
Raw materials and consumables	8		
Work in progress	11		
Finished goods and goods for resale	22	41	
Debtors:			
Trade debtors	123		
Prepayments and accrued income	16	139	
Cash at bank and in hand		17	
		197	
Creditors: amounts falling due within one year			
Trade creditors	36		
Other creditors including taxation and social security	101		
Accruals and deferred income	15	152	
Net current assets			45
Total assets less current liabilities			680
Creditors: amounts falling due after more than one year			
Debenture loans		250	
Provisions for liabilities and charges			
Pensions		33	283
			397
Capital and reserves			
Called-up share capital			150
Share premium account			50
Revaluation reserve			34
General reserves			70
Profit and loss account			93
			397

'Creditors: amounts falling due within one year' are usually known as **current liabilities**. 'Creditors: amounts falling due after more than one year' are usually known as **long-term liabilities**. It is not obvious why the legislators introduced these new expressions, except to make clear to readers of the accounts the time periods involved. 'Current' and 'long-term' remain the adjectives used by most people when referring to liabilities.

Notes to the accounts

As well as providing the information set out in the profit and loss account and balance sheet, additional information must also be made public. This information is usually contained in the notes to the accounts and is mainly concerned with directors' and highly-paid employees' salaries and with fixed-asset movements.

Directors' report

Company law requires the directors to prepare an annual report to shareholders and other interested parties. This report contains information of both a financial and a non-financial nature and goes beyond that which is contained in the profit and loss account and balance sheet. The information disclosed falls under the following categories:

- *Business activities.* This covers such matters as the main activities carried out by the company during the year and any significant changes that may have occurred. It will also include the disclosure of any events affecting the company since the end of the financial year and a discussion of any likely future developments.
- *Share ownership.* This includes disclosure of the purchase by the company of its own shares and details of shareholders that hold more than 3 per cent of the nominal share capital of the company.
- *Dividend policy.* This deals with the dividend that the directors' propose for the year.
- *Asset values.* Any significant difference between the market value of land and buildings held and the current market value must be stated.
- *Details of directors.* The names of the directors of the company must be disclosed. In addition, details of any directors' interest in shares or debentures of the company or any contract in which a director has a significant interest must be disclosed.
- *Social and employee matters.* This rather broad category deals with a variety of matters, including disclosure of charitable and political donations made by the company. It also deals with the disclosure of the creditor payment policy and employment policies relating to such matters as employment of diasabled persons, health and safety at work, and the involvement of employees in the management of the company.

The auditors do not carry out an audit of the **directors' report**. However, they will check to see that the information in the report is consistent with that contained within the audited accounts.

Smaller companies

The reduced economic impact and the rather more close-knit structure of share ownership of smaller companies, plus the proportionately higher costs of complying with the requirements, has led to the legislators reducing the amount of information disclosure required of smaller companies. The criteria for being classified as a small company are concerned with size of turnover, total assets and workforce. Relaxation of information disclosure requirements is allowed to companies that can meet two of the following three criteria:

- Total assets (balance sheet figures) less than £5.6 million.
- Annual turnover (sales) less than £11.2 million.
- Number of employees fewer than 250.

Further relaxations in the rules are available for even smaller companies.

Summary financial statements

Though directors of all companies are required to make a set of the company accounts available to each shareholder, these accounts can be a summarised version of the full version that follows the complete legal requirements. The reasons for not requiring that the full version be sent to all shareholders are broadly that:

- Many shareholders do not wish to receive the full version, because they may not have the time, interest or skill necessary to be able to gain much from it.
- Directors could improve their communication with their shareholders by providing something closer to the needs of many shareholders.
- Reproducing and posting copies of the full version is expensive and a waste of resources where particular shareholders do not wish to receive it.

Many companies send all of their private shareholders a copy of the **summary financial statements**, with a clear message that the full versions are available on request. Each full version is, however, required for filing with the Registrar of Companies.

Exhibit 5.2 is the summarised group balance sheet for 1999 of Glaxo Wellcome plc, the UK-based pharmaceutical business that now forms part of GlaxcoSmith Kline plc. This is much briefer than the full balance sheet that the company would make available on request.

Exhibit 5.2

The following extract is the summarised group balance sheet of Glaxco Wellcome plc as at 31 December 1999.

Summary Accounts for the year to 31st December 1999

	1999 £m	1998 £m
Summary Group balance sheet		
Net operating assets	4,306	3,934
Long-term investments	58	87
Own shares	425	11
Net debt	(1,596)	(1,264)
Net assets	3,193	2,768
Shareholders' funds	3,142	2,702
Minority interests	51	66
Financing of net assets	3,193	2,768
Fixed assets	4,347	3,837
Current assets	6,080	5,509
Current liabilities: due within one year	(5,263)	(4,145)
Current assets less current liabilities	817	1,364
Total assets less current liabilities	5,164	5,201
Liabilities: due after one year	(1,376)	(1,965)
Provisions for liabilities and charges	(595)	(468)
Net assets	3,193	2,768

Role of accounting standards in company accounting

→ **Accounting standards** (sometimes called **financial reporting standards**) are rules established by the UK accounting profession that should be followed by preparers of the annual accounts of companies. Though they do not have the same status as company law, the standards define what is meant by a true and fair view, in various contexts and circumstances. Since company law requires that accounting statements show a true and fair view, this gives accounting standards an important place in company accounts preparation.

When UK accounting standards were introduced in the 1970s, the committee responsible for developing them saw the role of the standards as being to 'narrow the difference and variety of accounting practice by publishing authoritative statements on best practice – which will, whenever possible, be definitive'. This continues to reflect the role of accounting standards.

Exhibit 5.3

The following list of the accounting standards currently in force in the UK will give an idea of the range of topics involved:

SSAP 4	Accounting for government grants	1992
SSAP 5	Accounting for value added tax	1974
SSAP 8	The treatment of taxation under the imputation system in the accounts of companies	1992
SSAP 9	Stocks and long-term contracts	1988
SSAP 13	Accounting for research and development	1989
SSAP 17	Accounting for post balance sheet events	1980
SSAP 19	Accounting for investment properties	1994
SSAP 20	Foreign currency translation	1983
SSAP 21	Accounting for leases and hire purchase contracts	1997
SSAP 24	Accounting for pension costs	1992
SSAP 25	Segmental reporting	1990
FRS 1	Cash flow statements	1996
FRS 2	Accounting for subsidiary undertakings	1992
FRS 3	Reporting financial performance	1993
FRS 4	Capital instruments	1993
FRS 5	Reporting the substance of transactions	1998
FRS 6	Acquisitions and mergers	1994
FRS 7	Fair values in acquisition accounting	1994
FRS 8	Related party disclosures	1995
FRS 9	Associates and joint ventures	1997
FRS 10	Goodwill and intangible assets	1997
FRS 11	Impairment of fixed assets and goodwill	1998
FRS 12	Provisions, contingent liabilities and contingent assets	1998
FRS 13	Derivatives and other financial instruments	1998
FRS 14	Earnings per share	1998
FRS 15	Tangible fixed assets	1999
FRS 16	Current tax	1999
FRS 17	Retirement benefits	2000
FRS 18	Accounting policies	2000
FRS 19	Deferred tax	2000

Key:
SSAP = Statement of Standard Accounting Practice
FRS = Financial Reporting Standard

Several standards have been issued and subsequently withdrawn, which explains the gaps in the numerical sequence. In addition, many of them have been revised and reissued. The dates given are the reissue dates, where relevant. This explains why they are not listed in chronological order.

Accounting standards can be seen as being of four types:

- Those that deal with *describing* how a particular item has been treated in the accounts, without seeking to prescribe how it should be treated. For example, FRS 15 requires that relevant assets should be depreciated and that the accounts should reveal how assets have been depreciated.
- Those that are concerned with *presenting* information in accounts. SSAP 5 is of this type in that it sets out how the incidence of value added tax should be reflected in the accounts of companies.
- Those that set out rules on *disclosing* information in the accounts above and beyond that which is prescribed by company law. FRS 1, which requires most companies to produce a cash flow statement, in addition to the other statements required by law, is of this type.
- Those that give guidance on *valuing* assets and *measuring* profit. SSAP 9 is of this type in that it sets out rules on how to value stocks, which has a direct effect on the profit figure.

We have already met some of the rules set out in accounting standards. For example, the rules that we use to value stocks and to charge depreciation were discussed in Chapter 3. Another of them we shall meet in the next chapter (FRS 1 in Chapter 6). Some of the others are rather specialised and, for most companies, of no great importance. This leaves a couple that we shall look at now.

FRS 18: Accounting policies

This standard is concerned with the way in which a company should approach the selection, application and disclosure of its accounting policies. The purpose of the standard is threefold. First, it seeks to ensure that each company selects accounting policies that are most suitable to its particular circumstances. When selecting a policy, the standard requires that the key characteristics of relevance, reliability, comparability and understandability (which we considered in Chapter 1) should be used as the appropriate benchmarks. Second, it seeks to ensure that the accounting policies that have been adopted are reviewed on a regular basis. Where existing policies are no longer considered to be appropriate, they should be replaced by new policies. Finally, the standard seeks to ensure that users of financial reports are properly informed about the particular accounting policies that have been adopted, as well as any changes to those policies. This means that there must be adequate disclosure in the accounts.

FRS 3: Reporting financial performance

This standard is concerned with trying to give users of the accounts greater insights to the company's performance for the period to which the accounts relate and, through this, enable them to make more informed judgements about the future prospects for the company. To achieve this objective, the standard requires that all companies should provide the following items as part of their accounts:

- *An analysis of the turnover, cost of sales, operating expenses and resultant profit (before interest).* These amounts should be analysed between continuing operations and discountinued operations:

– *continuing operations*, that is, those parts of the company's business that will continue to exist in the year following the one being reported on in the accounts. Continuing operations should further be analysed between those that were acquired during the year (for example, as a result of a takeover of another company) and those that were existing operations of the company at the start of the year being reported on;

– *discontinued operations*, that is, those operations of the company that were sold or terminated during the year being reported on.

This analysis should aid users of the accounts in assessing the extent to which a company's reported performance has been affected by acquiring new operations and/or abandoning others.

● *Information on exceptional items.* An exceptional item is a revenue or expense that, though part of the company's normal operations, is large or remarkable enough to require special mention if users of the accounts are to gain a true and fair view of the company's operations. An example of an exceptional item could be a particularly large loss suffered by a civil engineering company on a major contract. It is part of normal operations, but unless users of the accounts are provided with information about the loss, they are lacking information that might help them to gain a true and fair impression of the company's operations.

Information on exceptional items should be disclosed by way of a note. The items should be included in the accounts as if they were unexceptional.

● *Information on extraordinary items.* These are items that are material in size and that fall outside the ordinary activities of the company. Like exceptional items, failure to give information on them could mislead a user of the accounts. An example of an extraordinary item might be the sales proceeds, less the book value, of a painting on the wall of an office that was subsequently discovered to have been by well-known artist and was, therefore, very valuable. The company is not in the business of selling its fixed assets at a profit, and so this transaction is deemed extraordinary.

Extraordinary items should be disclosed by showing them separately in the profit and loss account. They should be shown after 'profit or loss on ordinary activities after tax'. The tax on the extraordinary item should be shown as deducted from the item itself. The item should be described, either on the face of the profit and loss account or in a separate note, in enough detail to enable users of the accounts to understand its nature. The objective of this treatment is to enable users to see the results of trading operations, ignoring the extraordinary item, but also to see the effect of the item.

● *A* **statement of recognised gains and losses**. This is a statement that summarises all of the profits (and losses) that have been recognised in the year being reported on. This statement is deemed to be necessary because not all of the profits and losses will appear in the profit and loss account. For example, it is common practice for companies to revalue (upwards) certain of their fixed assets, particularly land and buildings. These increases in value are not shown on the profit and loss account – reasonably enough, because they are not revenues arising from trading operations. The amount of the revaluation is added to a revaluation reserve.

Company law permits companies to charge the administrative costs of making a share issue direct to the share premium account, where one exists, and to the extent that there is a sufficiently large balance, as an alternative to charging these costs to the profit and loss account. The net effect on the shareholder is the same whichever way it is done. If the amount is charged to the share premium account, that balance diminishes; if it is charged to the profit and loss account, the retained profit (the balance on the profit and loss account) diminishes by the same amount.

The objective of the statement of recognised gains and losses is to give users of the accounts a summary of the overall change in the shareholders funds, other than as a result of injections (new share issues) and withdrawals (dividends) of capital by the shareholders.

Note that the statement of recognised gains and losses is now regarded as a 'primary financial statement' and so takes its place alongside the balance sheet, the profit and loss account and the cash flow statement.

Exhibit 5.4 is the statement of recognised gains and losses for Anglia Water plc, the water utility business.

<table>
<tr><td>Exhibit 5.4</td><td colspan="3">The following extract from the annual accounts of Anglia Water plc, shows the statement of total recognised gains and losses for the year ended 31 March 2000. Note that, apart from the normal trading profit (which also appears in the company's profit and loss account), the only other gains (losses) arose from a difference, on translating the value of some overseas assets, between the start of the year and the end.</td></tr>
</table>

**Statement of total recognised gains and losses
for the year ended 31 March**

	Group	
	2000	1999
	£m	£m
Profit for the financial year	164.8	223.7
Currency translation differences on foreign currency net investments	(5.0)	(0.1)
Total recognised gains and losses	159.8	223.6

<table>
<tr><td>Activity 5.3</td><td>Why does company law not deal with all of the detailed rules? Why do we also need accounting standards?</td></tr>
</table>

Probably the main reason is that circumstance and commercial practices alter at a faster rate than Parliament is prepared to legislate on accounting rules for companies. The law, therefore, sets out the broad framework and leaves it, in effect, to the accounting profession to flesh it out. The accounting standard setters are able to respond relatively quickly to fresh needs and, perhaps as important, have a more direct interest in doing so.

International accounting standards

The internationalisation of business has led to a need for some degree of international harmonisation of accounting rules. It can no longer be assumed that the potential users of the accounts of a company whose head office is in the UK are familiar with UK accounting standards. Whichever user group we care to think of – employees, suppliers, customers, shareholders – some members of that group are likely to be residents of another country. It seems likely, too, that the trend towards internationalisation of business will increase.

These facts have led to the need for international accounting standards and the creation of the International Accounting Standards Committee (IASC). The IASC has issued a number of standards, but there is a problem: it is difficult to reconcile international differences on accounting procedures, which has tended to mean that the international standards have been slow to emerge. They have also tended to be fairly permissive of variations in practice. Nevertheless, international accounting standards are likely to become increasingly important.

Role of the London Stock Exchange in company accounting

The London Stock Exchange extends the accounting rules for those companies that are listed as being eligible to have their shares traded there. These extensions include the following requirements:

- Summarised interim (half-year) accounts in addition to the annual accounts required by statute law.
- A geographical analysis of turnover.
- Details of holdings of more than 20 per cent of the shares of other companies.

Figure 5.1 illustrates the sources of accounting rules with which larger UK companies must comply.

Figure 5.1

Sources of external accounting rules for a UK limited company listed on the London Stock Exchange

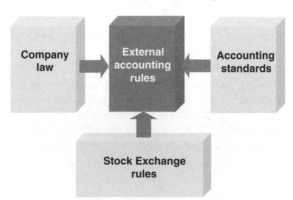

Company law provides the basic framework of company accounting regulation. This is augmented by the accounting standards, which have virtually the force of law. The London Stock Exchange has its own additional rules for companies listed by it.

Auditors

Shareholders are required to elect a qualified and independent person or, more usually, a firm to act as **auditor**. The auditor's main duty is to make a report as to whether, in his or her opinion, the statements do what they are supposed to do, namely show a true and fair view and comply with statutory and accounting-standard requirements. To be in a position to make such a statement, auditors must scrutinise both the annual accounting statements prepared by the directors and the evidence on which they are based. The auditors' opinion must be included with the accounting statements that are sent to the shareholders and to the Registrar of Companies.

The relationship between the shareholders, the directors and the auditors is illustrated in Figure 5.2. This shows that the shareholders elect the directors to act on their behalf, in the day-to-day running of the company. The directors are required to 'account' to the shareholders on the performance, position and cash flows of the company, on an annual basis. The shareholders also elect auditors, whose role it is to give the shareholders an impression of the extent to which they can regard as reliable the accounting statements prepared by the directors.

Exhibit 5.5 is the auditors' report for National Express Group plc, the business that operates various bus and train services in the UK, the US and Australia. The statement appeared with the annual accounts of the business for the year ended 31 December 1999. Note how the auditors, in their report, try to tell the reader exactly what they have done and the standards that they applied in doing so.

National Express Group's auditors are Ernst & Young, one of the world's

| Figure 5.2 | The relationship between the shareholders, the directors and the auditors |

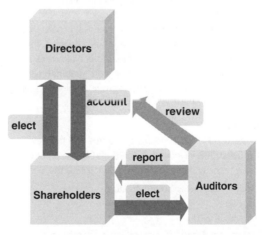

The directors are appointed by the shareholders to manage the company on the shareholders' behalf. The directors are required to report each year to the shareholders, principally by means of accounting statements, on the company's performance and position. To give greater confidence in the reports, the shareholders also appoint auditors to investigate the reports and express an opinion on their reliability.

Exhibit 5.5

Report of the Auditors

To the shareholders of National Express Group plc

We have audited the accounts on pages 46 to 74 which have been prepared under the historical cost convention, as modified by the revaluation of certain fixed assets and the accounting policies set out on pages 50 to 52.

Respective responsibilities of Directors and Auditors

The Directors are responsible for preparing the Annual Report. As described on page 44, this includes responsibility for preparing the accounts in accordance with applicable United Kingdom law and accounting standards. Our responsibilities, as independent auditors, are established in the United Kingdom by statute, the Auditing Practices Board, the Listing Rules of the London Stock Exchange and by our profession's ethical guidance.

We report to you our opinion as to whether the accounts give a true and fair view and are properly prepared in accordance with the Companies Act. We also report to you if, in our opinion, the Directors' report is not consistent with the accounts, if the Company has not kept proper accounting records, if we have not received all the information and explanations we require for our audit, or if the information specified by law or the Listing Rules regarding Directors' remuneration and transactions with the Company is not disclosed.

We review whether the corporate governance statement on pages 39 to 40 reflects the Company's compliance with the seven provisions of the Combined Code specified for our review by the Stock Exchange, and we report if they do not. We are not required to consider whether the Board's statements on internal control cover all risks and controls, or form an opinion on the effectiveness of either the Group's corporate governance procedures or its risk and control procedures.

We read the other information contained in the Annual Report, including the corporate governance statement, and consider whether it is consistent with the audited accounts. We consider the implications for our report if we become aware of any apparent misstatements or material inconsistencies with the accounts.

Basis of audit opinion

We conducted our audit in accordance with Auditing Standards issued by the Auditing Practices Board. An audit includes examination, on a test basis, of evidence relevant to the amounts and disclosures in the accounts. It also includes an assessment of the significant estimates and judgements made by the Directors in the preparation of the accounts, and of whether the accounting policies are appropriate to the Group's circumstances, consistently applied and adequately disclosed.

We planned and performed our audit so as to obtain all the information and explanations which we considered necessary in order to provide us with sufficient evidence to give reasonable assurance that the accounts are free from material misstatement, whether caused by fraud or other irregularity or error. In forming our opinion we also evaluated the overall adequacy of the presentation of information in the accounts.

Opinion

In our opinion the accounts give a true and fair view of the state of affairs of the Company and the Group as at 31 December 1999 and of the profit of the Group for the year then ended and have been properly prepared in accordance with the Companies Act 1985.

Ernst & Young *Registered Auditor*
London
14 March 2000

leading firms of accountants. According to the 1999 accounts of National Express Group, it was charged a fee of £600,000 for this audit work, but to put that into perspective, the National Express Group made a pre-tax profit of £89.6 million during that year.

The case for and against accounting regulation

So far in this chapter we have treated the existence of a body of company law and accounting standards as being a good thing. However, not everyone accepts that the development of accounting rules is really a form of progress. It is, therefore, worth reciting the main arguments for and against accounting regulation.

Let us begin with the case for regulation. It seems that there are really four major arguments in favour of regulation:

● *To protect investors.* A lack of regulation increases the risk that unscrupulous directors will introduce 'unacceptable' accounting practices that will portray a different view of company performance than is actually warranted. This, it is argued, may mislead investors and, in turn, may result in them making losses.

Activity 5.4

Is there any way that we could test whether or not a lack of regulation will result in unacceptable accounting practices?

....

One way of examining this argument is to look back at the state of affairs that existed when the regulatory framework was in its infancy.

There is evidence from both the UK and the US to support the view that manipulation and concealment have been a real problem in the past. Indeed, the development of accounting standards is really a response to various financial scandals that have been unearthed over the years.

● *To improve the functioning of financial markets.* Where there is no accounting regulation, investors are likely to find it difficult to judge the relative performance of different businesses. The introduction of regulation, so it is argued, will help bring greater uniformity of practice – which, in turn, should help investors distinguish between the efficient and less-efficient businesses and so ensure that funds are allocated in the most profitable way.

● *To maintain the credibility of the accounts.* Where there is no accounting regulation, there will be greater flexibility in accounting practice. Thus, it is argued, it would be possible for two accountants, each using the same basic financial information relating to a business, to prepare accounts showing quite different profits earned during a period and quite different financial positions at the end of that period. The differences between each set of accounts prepared would simply reflect the particular accounting practices adopted (for example, the use of FIFO rather than LIFO for stock valuation). Through regulation we can reduce the areas of difference and bring about greater uniformity, and this should lend greater credibility to the accounts among readers.

Activity 5.5

Could the use of rules to provide greater uniformity 'backfire' on accountants? Is there a risk that attempts to achieve greater uniformity will not satisfy the readers of accounts?

....

Some argue that we run the risk that the expectations of readers concerning the accuracy and comparability of the accounts will be increased beyond what can be achieved.

Accounting is not a precise science, as we have already seen, and it will always be necessary for judgements and estimates to be made. In addition, there may be valid reasons for different companies to adopt different accounting methods in certain circumstances (for example, the use of the straight-line method and reducing-balance methods of depreciation are appropriate to different circumstances). Thus, readers must recognise that comparing the performance of different companies can only yield limited benefits.

- *To reduce pressures on auditors and preparers of accounts.* Company directors may put their auditors and accounting staff under considerable pressure to agree to particular accounting practices that will provide the particular story that the directors wish to tell the readers of accounts rather than what is, in the accountants' and auditors' opinion, a true and fair view of performance and position. It is argued that where there are accounting rules in place, there is a source of external support to resist this kind of pressure.

Although the arguments above have some force, let us now consider the case against regulation. There are five main arguments against accounting regulation:

- *Ossifying accounting practice.* There is a danger that regulation tends to discourage the natural development of better approaches to financial reporting. Accountants may be discouraged from finding a better approach because it is recognised that any new approach would not be permitted under the rules. Although changes to the rules can occur, it may be difficult to persuade the regulators that a particular new approach is an improvement. They may feel that the matter was resolved when the existing rules were developed, and so dissent may not be tolerated.
- *Slowness of reaction.* Even when the need for change is accepted, policy makers are often slow to react. The development of new law tends to be very slow because of the length of the law-making process and the competing pressures on legislators' time. Accounting standards, which are developed by the accounting profession, can change more quickly although even these can lag behind events. As a result, there is a danger that the accounting rules become increasingly irrelevant to the changing environment.
- *False uniformity.* There is a risk that accounting regulations may be imposed on businesses in such a rigid manner that a false uniformity will result that obscures the real differences between businesses. However, this risk may not be as great as is sometimes suggested. It is worth remembering that company law requires that the accounts must show a *true and fair view* of performance and position. This requirement overrides any requirement for particular accounting rules to be followed, and so there is always room to exercise judgement and thereby avoid this problem.
- *The myth of 'best practice'.* Accounting rules are designed to reflect 'best practice'. However, some would argue that there is often wide disagreement about what constitutes best practice. There has been much criticism over the years that accounting rules lack any underpinning body of theory or principles to guide accounting rule-makers. The accounting profession has recognised this problem and in recent years there have been efforts to develop a body of accounting principles to underpin the development of rules. This topic will be considered in more detail in the following section.

- *The political nature of accounting rules.* Some argue (see, for instance, reference (1) at the end of the chapter) that setting regulations is, in essence, a political process and that the rules developed will often reflect the requirements of particular interest groups (such as large companies that must implement the rules) that have lobbied for a particular solution rather than the technically 'correct' solution. The effect of successful lobbying can result in bad accounting practices being imposed and can undermine the credibility of accounting rules. Although there have been suggestions that, in both the US and the UK, accounting policy makers have yielded to lobbying pressure, there is no real evidence that this is a major problem.

The debate for and against regulation rumbles on and is unlikely to be resolved in the near future. A major problem preventing early resolution is that the costs of developing, monitoring and complying with the rules have not been properly identified or measured, and the benefits of accounting rules are even more vague. Until the costs of regulation can be weighed against the benefits, the debate will remain inconclusive. In the meantime, however, the number of accounting rules continues to increase.

In search of principles

In the early chapters of this book, we came across various accounting conventions such as prudence, historic cost, going concern, and so on. These conventions were developed as a practical response to particular problems that were confronted when preparing accounts. Nowadays, they help to guide the preparers of accounting information when deciding which items should be reported and *how* they should be reported. These conventions have stood the test of time and are still of value to preparers today. However, they do not provide, and were never designed to provide, accounting with a framework for the development of accounting reports. As we grapple with increasingly complex financial reporting problems, it becomes very clear indeed that we need to have a sound understanding of *why* we account for things in a particular way. Knowing *why* we account rather than simply *how* we account is very important if we are to identify best practice and move the discipline of accounting forward.

In recent years, much effort has been expended in various countries, including the UK, to develop a clear framework of principles that will guide us in the development of accounting. Such a framework should provide clear answers to such fundamental questions as:

- What is the purpose of financial reports?
- Who are the main users of accounting information?
- What qualities should accounting information possess?
- What kind of accounting reports should be prepared?
- What should accounting reports include?
- How should items be included in the accounting reports?

If we can answer these questions, accounting rule-makers will be in a stronger position to identify best practice and to develop rules based on rigorous logic, which should increase the credibility of financial reports in the eyes of users. It may even help reduce the possible number of rules, because some issues may be resolved by reference to the application of general principles rather than the generation of further rules.

The Statement of Principles

The quest for accounting principles began in earnest in the 1970s when the Financial Accounting Standards Board (FASB) in the United States devoted a very large amount of time and resources to developing a framework of principles for financial reports. In the UK, this development was watched with considerable interest and in the 1990s a draft Statement of Principles (see reference (2) at the end of the chapter) was developed by the Accounting Standards Board (ASB) that draws upon much of the early work of the FASB. This draft Statement begins by identifying the objectives of financial statements as being:

> to provide information about the reporting entity's financial performance and financial position that is useful to a wide range of users for assessing the stewardship of management and for making economic decisions.

This objective is consistent with other recent attempts to define the purpose of accounting or the purpose of financial statements. For this reason, perhaps, it has not generated any real debate.

The draft Statement of Principles then goes on to identify those groups potentially interested in financial statements and these are:

- Investors
- Lenders
- Suppliers and other trade creditors
- Employees
- Customers
- Government and its agencies
- The public.

This again is uncontentious ground: it reflects mainstream opinion and is similar to other lists that have been compiled over recent years. Interestingly, the draft, Statement assumes that financial statements should focus on the interests of investors as all other users are likely to share the investors' concern for such matters as cash generation and financial adaptability. This implies that information that is not needed by investors will not need to be included in the financial reports. Where the assumption of 'what is good for investors is good for everyone' is not valid, there is no reason in principle why the needs of others should not be accommodated.

| Activity 5.6 | **Can you think of situations where this assumption may not be valid?** |

There is likely to be a number of situations where the needs of investors and those of other groups do not coincide. For example, employees may require more information concerning the profitability of particular manufacturing plants in order to establish the future prospects within those plants. However, investors may not be concerned with this issue, provided that the impact on overall profitability is not significant.

The draft Statement of Principles continues by setting out:

- How the entities that should prepare and publish financial statements are identified.
- The qualitative characteristics of financial information (relevance, reliability, comparability, understandability, materiality).

These aspects of the draft Statement have also created little debate. The qualitative characteristics identified are those set out in the first chapter and have achieved a wide degree of acceptance.

So far, so good. However, the draft Statement then ventures into more dangerous territory by considering:

- The main elements of financial statements (including the definition of assets, liabilities, owners' interests and contributions, gains and losses).
- The way in which transactions or events are recognised in the main elements of financial statements.
- The measurement process and how a choice is made between measurement bases that are available.
- The presentation of financial information (including what constitutes good presentation).
- Accounting for interest in other entities (including consolidated financial statements).

The first three topics in the above list, in particular, have proved to be very contentious. The first draft of the Statement of Principles, published in 1995, generated heated debate and the ASB received much criticism for it. It is beyond the scope of this text to consider the criticisms in detail, however, the main charges against the draft Statement are that it favours the balance sheet at the expense of the profit and loss account; it favours current values rather than historic cost; and the importance of the matching convention is not recognised. Ernest & Young, a major international firm of accountants, is a strong critic and has argued in a paper (reference (3) at the end of chapter) that the draft Statement of Principles is 'fundamentally misguided. It strives for a model that we do not believe is desirable based on principles that we do not considerable workable'. This provoked a response from the chairman of the ASB (reference (4)) that the paper in question 'had all the vision of a mole and the elequence of a whoopee cushion'.

It seems safe to conclude from this exchange, that it will be some time before a consensus will emerge! Developing a single framework of principles that will satisfy the views of users, preparers, and assorted commentators on accounting is a difficult task. However, it is also difficult to see what other choices exist for the ASB. If we accept the need for accounting rules, we must also accept the need for a clear framework of principles that will give these rules coherence. The goal of an agreed framework of principles will, therefore, continue to be pursued.

Segmental financial reports

Most large businesses do not undertake a single type of activity; they are usually diverse entities that are engaged in a number of different business activities. Each type of activity undertaken will involve the supply of different products or services and will have different levels of risk, growth and profitability. The problem for users of financial statements is that the profit and loss account, balance sheet and so on will normally aggregate the information relating to each type of business activity in order to provide an overall picture of financial performance and position. For the purposes of analysis and interpretation, however, these aggregate figures are not particularly useful. It is very difficult to evaluate the performance of a business that has diverse interests from the aggregated financial information, because comparisons cannot easily be made. The various activities undertaken by the business are likely to differ in range and/or scale by comparison with other businesses.

Where a business operates in different geographical markets, the same kind of arguments apply. The markets of different countries may well have different levels of risk, profitability and growth associated with them, and aggregation will obscure these differences. It will not be possible, for example, to assess the impact on a business of political changes, or changes in inflation or exchange rates occurring in relation to a particular country or geographical region unless the degree of exposure to the country/region is known.

To undertake any meaningful analysis of financial performance and position, it is usually necessary to disaggregate the information contained within the conventional financial statements. By breaking down the financial information according to business activities and/or geographical markets, we can evaluate the relative risks and profitability of each segment and make useful comparisons with other businesses or other business segments. We can also see the trend of performance for each segment over time and so determine more accurately the likely growth prospects for the business as a whole. We should also be able to assess more easily the impact on the overall business of changes in market conditions relating to particular activities.

Disclosure of the performance of each segment should also be useful in improving the efficiency of the business and of its managers. Information concerning business segments that are performing poorly will be revealed to shareholders, and this may in turn put pressure on managers to take corrective action. Where a particular business segment has been sold, the shareholders will be better placed to assess the wisdom of the managers' decision from the segmental information provided.

Activity 5.7	Shareholders are unlikely to be the only user group interested in the disclosure of segmental information. How might the following groups find segmental information useful?

(a) Employees
(b) Consumers
(c) Government.

....

(a) Employees may find the information relating to profitability and turnover in the area in which they work useful when they are assessing pay and job prospects.
(b) Consumers may be interested to find out the profits arising from particular business activities in order to assess whether the business is making excessive returns.
(c) A government may wish to assess the level of investment, profitability and market presence of a large business operating within the economy. This may be useful when making a range of policy decisions relating to industry grants, subsidies and pricing regulations.

Segmental reporting: regulations and practice

In the UK, an accounting standard (SSAP 25) requires that large companies normally disclose segmental information according to each class of business *and* to each geographical region. Both forms of segmentation are regarded as important to users. A 'class of business', for the purposes of the standard, is a part of the overall business that can be identified as providing a separate product or service, or group of related products or services. A geographical segment may comprise an individual country or a group of countries in which the business operates.

Where a business is involved in two or more classes of business activity or two or more geographical segments, there should normally be separate disclosure for each segment. Each segment should normally include the following key items:

- Turnover, distinguishing between turnover from external customers and turnover from other segments of the business.
- Profit (loss) before taxation, minority interests and extraordinary items.
- Net assets.

Turnover for each geographical segment is according to origin. However, if the destination of the goods or services is substantially different from the geographical region from which they were supplied, the geographical segmentation of turnover according to the *destination* of the goods and services should also be shown.

Example 5.3 shows a simple **segmental financial report** for a company with two classes of business. A similar layout can be used to show geographical segments.

Example 5.3

	Segment X £m	Segment Y £m	Total £m
Turnover			
Total sales	150	200	350
Intersegment sales	(20)	–	(20)
Sales to third parties	130	200	330
Profit before taxation			
Segment profit	15	19	34
Less Common costs			16
			18
Net assets			
Segment net assets	74	86	160
Unallocated assets			32
			192

Note: common costs are those costs that relate to more than one business segment. They may include such items as head office costs, research and development costs, and marketing and advertising costs. You will note that they have not been apportioned between the two segments but have been deducted from the total profit. The treatment of common costs is discussed further below.

Unallocated assets are those assets that are not used in the operations of a particular segment (for example, the head office buildings).

Problems of segmental reporting

A number of problems arise concerning the publication of segmental reports. Some directors are reluctant to disclose this type of information for fear that it may damage the competitive position of the business. This may be a particularly sensitive issue where the main competitors of the business are based abroad and do not have to disclose segmental information. The accounting standard on segmental reporting recognises this problem and states that companies do not have to comply with the disclosure requirements if the directors feel that publication would seriously prejudice the interests of the business.

Activity 5.8

Can you think of any reasons why it may not be a good idea to allow directors discretion regarding disclosure of segmental information?

There is a risk that directors of a company will use the opt-out clause for reasons for which it was not designed. For example, disclosure of segmental information might be opposed by directors because it would expose managerial inefficiency in certain areas or because it would reveal that excessive profits are being made in particular areas of activity.

An interesting point to note is that a diverse company can keep its various activities obscured from close scrutiny if it so wishes. However, a business operating a single class of business is not able to do this. Information concerning turnover, profits and so on relating to that particular class of business must be disclosed whatever the effect on competitive position.

Some have questioned the usefulness of segmental data. It is sometimes argued that shareholders invest in the business as a whole, and therefore it is the overall results that are relevant to this end. It is also argued that unsophisticated shareholders may be confused by the segmental reports and may not be able 'to see the wood for the trees'. Both of these arguments, however, may be challenged.

Activity 5.9

Can you think what counterarguments may be used in order to defend segmental reporting?

It can be argued that segmental reports help in arriving at a better understanding of the overall performance and position of a business. By breaking down the business into its constituent parts, it is possible to see more readily the various sources of profit, turnover, growth and so on, and therefore obtain a better understanding of the overall results. It should also be borne in mind that the segmental information is a supplement to the overall results, and so shareholders are not denied the aggregated results. We should also remember that shareholders are not the only users of financial information. We saw earlier that other users may have good reason to examine the segmental information provided by a business.

The point concerning unsophisticated users raises the question as to who the financial reports are really for. Many would argue that it is the sophisticated users who need to understand company results, because their decisions will enable a fair price to be set for the shares of the company. If the unsophisticated user cannot understand the accounts, then he/she should either obtain expert advice or study accountancy.

In addition to issues of principle, there are certain technical problems that relate to segmental reports. To begin with, there is the problem of what exactly constitutes a segment for reporting purposes. Unfortunately, the relevant standard does not identify the particular characteristics that determine a class of business or a geographical region. Identifying a set of characteristics that could be applied to each type of business is probably an impossible task. As a result, the issue of what constitutes a segment for reporting purposes is left largely to the judgement of the directors of companies. Although this may be the only sensible course of action, it does mean that comparisons between businesses may be difficult owing to different definitions of a class of business or geographical segment being applied.

Having established a segment for reporting purposes, the next problem is how to deal with common transactions and costs. It is unlikely that each segment will operate in a completely independent manner. There may be, for example, a significant amount of sales of goods or services between segments. If this is the case, the **transfer price** of the goods or services between segments can have a substantial impact on the reported profits of each segment. Indeed, it may be possible to manipulate profit figures for each segment through the use of particular transfer pricing policies. Although the standard requires that turnover be divided between external sales and intersegment sales, the effect of the latter on the results will be difficult to determine because details of transfer pricing policies are not required by the standard and so are not normally disclosed.

There is also the problem of **common costs** – that is, costs that relate to more than one of the business segments. These may include such items as head office costs, research and development costs and marketing costs. Common costs may be apportioned between the segments in some way or simply deducted from the total of the segment results, as shown in Example 5.3 (above). There are no clear-cut rules concerning how such costs should be treated and so, once again, the solution to this problem is left to the directors of companies to determine. This can lead to variations in practice, which will therefore hinder comparisons.

Self-assessment question 5.1

Segmental information relating to J. Sainsbury plc (a retailer with four separate store chains, a bank and a property development activity) for the year to 1 April 2000 is shown below, together with the equivalent information for the preceding year.

	Turnover (excluding taxes)		Profit (before exceptional items)		Net assets	
	2000 £m	1999 £m	2000 £m	1999 £m	2000 £m	1999 £m
Food retailing (UK)	12,353	13,074	509	731	4,750	4,554
Food retailing (USA)	2,376	1,970	79	55	796	505
Do it yourself retailing (UK)	1,217	1,187	55	65	522	442
Banking (UK)	136	158	3	(6)(loss)	113	101
Property development (UK)	165	32	16	9	123	130

> **Required:**
> Analyse the performance of each of the business segments over the two-year period and comment on your results.

Operating and financial review

Businesses have become more complex over time and, as a result, their financial statements have become more difficult to understand. The way in which businesses organise, the nature of their financing and investing activities and the types of trading relationships entered into can make it difficult for users to analyse and interpret the figures set out in annual reports. This has led to growing support for the inclusion of a narrative report from the directors, within the annual reports, that discusses the main points concerning the performance and position of the company.

To some extent, information in narrative form is already available to users through the chairman's report and the directors' report, and various studies have shown that private investors find these reports very useful. However, there are wide variations in practice. In particular, the content of the chairman's report (which is a voluntary form of disclosure) can vary considerably between companies. As a result, many believe there is a need for a separate report that sets out, in a systematic fashion, the key points and issues that affect the business.

The Accounting Standards Board (ASB) has recognised the need for such a report and has recommended that large companies prepare an **operating and financial review** (OFR) each year, which will contain a discussion and interpretation of the business activities and the main factors that affect it. Although the report is meant to be a review of the past year rather than a forecast of the future, it should help users to identify those factors that are useful in assessing future trends and prospects.

The review should be clear and succinct in its style and therefore easy for users to understand. It should also be balanced and objective. There is always a risk with such reports that the directors will seek to emphasise positive aspects of performance and play down or ignore negative ones. It is recommended that the OFR should also try to distinguish between those factors that have affected the results of the business during the current year but are not expected to continue and those that are likely to affect performance in future years. This distinction should help users to form a view of the future, particularly as the business will not normally publish a profit forecast. Where individual aspects of a business are discussed within the review, they should be placed within the context of the overall business.

The operating review

The recommended format of the OFR consists of two elements: the operating review and the financial review. The operating review is designed to help explain to the user the main influences on the various lines of the business. It also discusses the main factors that underlie the business and any changes that have occurred, or are likely to occur, to these factors. The following areas have been identified by the ASB as providing a framework for the operating review.

Operating results for the period

This section should discuss the significant features of the operating performance of the various business segments, as well as the business as a whole (see Exhibit 5.6). It should also discuss any significant changes within the industry or in the environment, such as changes in market conditions, new products, fluctuations in exchange rates, and so on.

Monsoon plc operates a high-street women's fashion business. The company's operating review for the year ended 27 May 2000 includes a trading summary from which the following extracts have been taken:

During the year to 27 May 2000, profit before tax was up 13% to £23.0m. The group increased operating profit before exceptionals from £20.8m to £22.9m, an increase of 10%. Turnover increased by 17%, from £132.0m to £154.5m.

UK operating profits rose as a result of an increase in total UK sales of 18%, including a like-for-like sales increase of 6% and an improvement in gross margin of 0.34 percentage points.

Dynamics of the business

This section should include a discussion of the main factors that are likely to influence future results. It will also consider the main risks and uncertainties relating to the various lines of business and how they are managed (see Exhibit 5.7). These risks and uncertainties may cover a wide range of matters and could include inflation, skills shortages, product liability, scarcity of raw materials, and so on.

Monsoon plc includes in its operating review for 2000 a section concerning its assessment of the best strategy for overseas operations. The following extracts have been taken from this section:

Over the medium and long term we believe that significant opportunities exist to expand overseas. We currently have operations in fifteen countries, of which ten are franchise partnerships or distributorships. We are convinced that franchise partnerships with good local operators are the best strategy. The risks to the group are minimised, as we have no property or employee obligations and no funding requirements for capital expenditure. Our return from these franchise partnerships, although not as high as from our own UK stores, is still good. We believe that the key to the success of these ventures lies in choosing the right partners and in aligning our interests closely together.

As a result of this strategy we are looking to convert our existing wholly owned overseas stores to partnership arrangements.

Investment in the future

This section should include a discussion of current and planned levels of capital expenditure. In addition, other forms of investment, such as marketing and advertising campaigns, training programmes and research and development programmes, should be discussed (see Exhibit 5.8). The likely future benefits from the various forms of investment should also be considered.

The issue of investment can be dealt with in various ways by a business. In its operating review for 2000, Monsoon plc includes sections that discuss the enhancement of its brand and its stores:

We continued to invest in the brand through the restructuring of the Design and Buying teams and have recruited additional specialist resource.

We introduced our new store design into three of five existing stores that we re-sited into larger and more prominent locations during the year. We have continued to enhance this new design and with our latest opening we believe we have created a store environment that reflects the core values of the brand and also makes the shopping experience more pleasurable.

Profit for the year

The OFR should discuss the returns to shareholders in terms of dividends, earnings per share, and changes in shareholders' funds. It should also comment on any significant gains and losses that are shown in the statement of total gains and losses.

Accounting policies

The directors are often required to make judgements concerning accounting policies (for example, the choice of depreciation method). Where the financial results are sensitive to the particular policies adopted, the directors should explain and discuss the choices made.

The financial review

The second part of the OFR, the financial review, is concerned with explaining the capital structure of the business, its treasury policy and the influences on its financial position. The following areas have been identified as providing a framework for the review.

Capital structure and treasury policy

This should involve a discussion of the capital structure (that is, the mix of share capital, reserves and long-term borrowing) of the business along with any relevant ratios. **Treasury policy** is concerned with such matters as managing cash and credit, obtaining finance, managing relationships with financial institutions, and dividend payments to shareholders. Possible areas for discussion in the financial review are interest and foreign-exchange risk, and the maturity of loans (see Exhibit 5.9).

Monsoon plc included the following statement on foreign exchange risk in its 2000 operating and financial review:

A substantial proportion of the group's product offering is imported and the group currently holds deposits in key trading currencies. In addition, from time to time, when there is clear justification for so doing, the group uses forward currency contracts to give greater certainty to future costs, although no such contracts were used during the period under review.

The group has several overseas subsidiaries, whose revenues and expenses are denominated in local currencies. None of these operations is sufficiently substantial in group terms for adverse exchange rate fluctuations to affect materially the outcome of group results, therefore, no hedging of these exchange rates is made.

Taxation

The OFR should contain a discussion of any difference between the normal tax rate applied to corporate profits and the actual rate applied.

Funds from operating activities and other sources of cash

This section should include a discussion of the cash flows either from operations or other sources and the special factors, if any, that influenced these (see Exhibit 5.10).

Exhibit 5.10

Monsoon plc included the following statement on cash flows and financing in its 2000 operating and financial review:

The group has not, to date, borrowed funds to fund the expansion of the business. The cash requirements of the business are carefully monitored and there are no current plans to arrange bank facilities. The cash flows for the period are shown in the consolidated cash flow statement on page 16. At the end of the period net funds totalled £16.2m compared with £9.2m the previous year.

Current liquidity

The liquidity at the end of the accounting period should be discussed, along with comment on the level of borrowing at the end of the period. Any loan conditions or restrictions on the ability to transfer funds within the business should be mentioned.

Going concern and balance sheet values

The OFR should contain a confirmation, if appropriate, that the business is a going concern and should comment on the strengths and resources of the business where the value of these items are not reflected in the balance sheet.

Activity 5.10

What resources might not be reflected in the balance sheet?

These may include, among others:

- Brand names
- Goodwill
- Quality of employees.

We can see from the list of headings above that the OFR can be quite a long report – often between five and ten pages in length. However, for many companies, the OFR is really an incremental rather than a radical change in reporting practice. The OFR builds on best practice, as many of the topics identified are already contained within the chairman's report or directors' report of progressive companies.

It should be emphasised that the headings above might not always be relevant to particular companies. The OFR of a particular company may therefore contain different, but nevertheless valid, information for users. There is some survey evidence to suggest there are wide variations in the content of OFRs, which may hinder comparisons between businesses. The fact that the OFR is a voluntary report is likely to increase the degree of variation in content. It may also increase the risk that a business will emphasise the positive aspects of performance and obscure the shortcomings.

● Summary

In this chapter we discussed the legal aspects of limited company accounts. We began by considering the responsibilities of the directors and auditors of a company. We saw that it is the responsibility of the directors of the company to prepare the annual accounts for external users and to ensure that these accounts show a true and fair view of the company's performance and position: it is the responsibility of the auditors to report on whether the directors have fulfilled their statutory duty. We also saw that company law sets out fairly precise rules that must be followed concerning the form and content of the annual accounts. These statutory rules are augmented by accounting standards and Stock Exchange rules.

We reviewed the case for and against accounting regulation. We saw that accounting rules are not universally regarded as a valuable step towards better accounting practice. However, there are powerful arguments in favour of accounting regulation that, so far and throughout the world, have won the day. We also reviewed the progress that has been made to date in providing a framework of principles for accounting rules. We saw that, although some progress has been made, there is likely to be much more heated debate before an agreed framework is developed.

Finally, we considered two additional financial statements that companies often prepare. It was argued that as companies grow larger and more diverse, the basic financial statements become less useful to users. This is because the aggregated information they contain tends to obscure the results of the various activities or geographical markets in which the company is engaged. As a result, large companies produce segmental reports that disaggregate the financial data so that the risk, profitability and growth of the separate aspects of the business can be more readily understood. The second additional financial statement examined was the operating and financial review (OFR). The complexity of modern business has led to a need for a report that discusses and intereprets the performance and position of a business. The OFR is designed to do just this. We considered the various elements that an OFR might include and that could provide the basis for a report to users. A further important financial statement, the cash flow statement, will be considered in detail in the following chapter.

Key terms

Directors' report   p. 138
Summary financial statement   p. 139
Accounting (financial reporting)
standards   p. 140
Statement of recognised gains and
losses   p. 142

Auditor   p. 145
Segmental financial report   p. 153
Transfer price   p. 155
Common costs   p. 155
Operating and financial review (OFR)
   p. 156

Further reading

If you would like to explore the topics covered in this chapter in more depth, we recommend the following books:

Statement of Principles for Financial Reporting, Revised Exposure Draft, Accounting Standards Board, 1999.
Students' Guide to Accounting and Financial Reporting Standards, *Black, G.*, 7th edn, Financial Times Prentice Hall, 2000, chapters 1, 2 and 10.
Financial Accounting and Reporting, *Elliott, B. and Elliott, J.*, 5th edn, Financial Times Prentice Hall, 2001, chapters 6–8.
Accountants without Standards, *Myddleton, D.*, Institute of Economic Affairs, 1995.
Advanced Financial Accounting, *Lewis, R. and Pendrill, D.*, 6th edn, Financial Times Prentice Hall, 2000, chapters 1, 2 and 11.

References

1. **Accountants without Standards**, *Myddleton, D.*, Institute of Ecomomic Affairs, 1995.
2. **Statement of Principles for Financial Reporting: Revised Exposure Draft**, Accounting Standards Board, 1999.
3. **The ASB's Framework – Time to Decide**, Ernst & Young, 1996. Quoted in 'The ASB's statement of principles – blueprint or blind alley?', Sir Julian Hodge Lecture by R. Paterson, The University of Wales, February 1998, p. 3.
4. *Financial Times*, 26 February 1996. Quoted in Paterson, 1998 (see ref. (3)).

5.1 'Searching for an agreed framework of principles for accounting rules is likely to be a journey without an ending'. Discuss

5.2 The size of annual financial reports published by limited companies has increased steadily over the years. Can you think of any reasons, apart from the increasing volume of accounting regulation, why this has occurred?

5.3 What problems does a user of segmental financial statements face when seeking to make comparisons between businesses?

5.4 'An OFR should not be prepared by accountants but should be prepared by the board of directors.' Why should this be the case?

? **EXERCISES**

Exercises 5.6–5.8 are more advanced than 5.1–5.5. Those with coloured numbers have answers at the back of the book.

5.1 It has been suggested that too much information might be as bad as too little information for users of annual reports. Explain.

5.2 What problems are likely to be encountered when preparing summary financial statements for shareholders?

5.3 The following information was extracted from the accounts of I. Ching (Booksellers) plc for the year to 31 December:

	£m
Interest payable	40
Retained profit brought forward from previous year	285
Cost of sales	460
Distribution costs	110
Income from fixed asset investments	42
Turnover	943
Other operating income	86
Administration expenses	314
Other interest receivable	25

Note:
1. Corporation tax is calculated at 25 per cent of the profit on ordinary activities.
2. The directors wish to transfer £100m to general reserve at the end of the year.
3. Dividends proposed on ordinary shares for the year will be 30 per cent of the profit on ordinary activities after tax (to nearest £m)

Required:
Prepare a profit and loss account for the year ended 31 December that is set out in accordance with the requirements of Format 1 of the UK's Companies Acts.

5.4 The following items appeared in the accounts of G. Stavros and Co. plc at the end of the current financial period:

	£m
Raw materials and consumables stock	120
Land and buildings at written down values	165
Trade creditors	75
Debenture loans	230
Pension liabilities	54
Share premium account	30
Taxation and social security creditors	23
General reserve	163
Motor vehicles at written down values	22
Trade debtors	86
Plant and machinery at written down values	143
Retained profit carried forward	75
Accruals and deferred income	47
Work in progress	18
Cash at bank and in hand	12
Revaluation reserve	100
Finished goods	96
Patents and trademarks	170
Prepayments	15

Required:

Prepare a balance sheet for the business as at the end of the current financial period in accordance with the requirements of Format 1 of the UK's Companies Acts. (One figure is missing from the list of balances and must be deduced.)

5.5 Professor Myddleton argues that accounting standards should be limited to disclosure requirements and should not impose rules on companies as to how to measure particular items in the financial statements. He states: 'The volume of accounting instructions is already high. If things go on like this, where will we be in 20 or 30 years time? On balance I conclude we would be better off without any standards on accounting measurement. There could still be some disclosure requirements for listed companies, though probably less than now.' Do you agree with this idea? Discuss.

5.6 The following information has been extracted from the accounts of a major retailer.

	Current year £m	Previous year £m
Turnover		
United Kingdom and Europe		
Retailing		
Books	390.3	368.3
Music	333.1	310.8
News	182.5	171.5
Greeting cards and stationery	175.7	168.7
Video	126.4	109.8
Other	140.3	157.9
	1,348.3	1,287.0

	Current year £m	Previous year £m
Distribution		
News and books	863.4	825.9
Office supplies	153.9	135.1
	1,017.3	961.0
Do-it-yourself	192.2	194.4
	2,557.8	2,442.4
USA		
Retailing		
Books	16.6	12.4
Music	104.4	91.5
News	17.2	15.7
Gifts and other	85.1	81.0
	223.3	200.6
Total turnover	2,781.1	2,643.0
Analysed as:		
Group companies	2,441.6	2,311.8
Intragroup	89.6	82.6
Share of associated undertakings	249.9	248.6
	2,781.1	2,643.0

Note: Turnover by destination is not significantly different from turnover by origin.

Operating profit including associated undertakings

	Before exceptional items £m	Exceptional items £m	Total Current year £m	Total Previous year £m
Retailing				
UK and Europe	93.8	(6.0)	87.8	86.0
USA	11.8	–	11.8	11.0
Distribution	37.7	–	37.7	33.2
Do-it-yourself	(10.5)	(36.6)	(47.1)	(14.3)
Operating profit inc. associated undertakings	132.8	(42.6)	90.2	115.9
Analysed as:				
Group companies	141.1	(6.0)	135.1	130.3
Share of results of associated undertakings	(8.3)	(36.6)	(44.9)	(14.4)
	132.8	(42.6)	90.2	115.9

	Total Current year £m	Total Previous year £m
Total net assets		
Retailing		
UK and Europe	496.6	490.7
USA	65.3	51.1
Distribution	41.3	20.7
Do-it-yourself	34.9	64.7
Net operating assets	638.1	627.2
Net unallocated liabilities	(66.8)	(65.2)
Net borrowings	(95.1)	(86.0)
Total net assets	476.?	476.0

Required:

(a) Compare the turnover of the UK and European operations with those of the USA operations of the retailer in the following retailing areas:

  (i)   Books
  (ii) Music
  (iii) News.

(b) Compare the profitability of the UK and European operations with those of the USA operations in the area of retailing.

5.7 Obtain a copy of an operating and financial review of two companies within the same industry. Compare the usefulness of each. In answering this question, you should consider the extent to which the OFRs incorporate the recommendations made by the Accounting Standards Board.

5.8 Segmental information for an electricity distribution business is as follows:

Notes to the accounts for the year ended 31 March 2002

Segmental information
(a) Turnover and operating profit

	Turnover		Operating profit	
	2002 £m	2001 £m	2002 £m	2001 £m
Distribution	**363.8**	337.7	**149.4**	138.7
Supply	**1,215.6**	1,210.7	**16.1**	13.5
Retail	**187.0**	139.1	**7.1**	6.0
Other	**48.6**	33.5	**0.9**	(2.8)
Inter-business adjustments	**(344.4)**	(307.5)	–	–
	1,470.6	1,413.5	**173.5**	155.4

(b) Net assets by class of business

	2002 £m	2001 £m
Distribution	**496.1**	451.5
Supply	**(88.3)**	20.8
Retail	**141.6**	88.0
Other	**255.2**	197.2
Inter-business adjustments	**(18.6)**	(63.6)
	786.0	693.9
Unsecured bonds	**(153.0)**	(153.0)
	633.0	540.9

Operating assets and liabilities are allocated or apportioned to the business to which they relate. All cash, investments, borrowings, dividends receivable and payable and taxation items have not been allocated and are included in 'Other'.

Required:

(a) Analyse the performance of each of the *three* major business segments over the two-year period for which information is available.

(b) Do you think the information contained in the segmental reports could be presented in a more informative way? Discuss.

6

Measuring and reporting cash flows

Introduction

Despite the undoubted value of the P and L account as a means of assessing the effect on a business's wealth of its trading activities, it has increasingly been recognised that the approach taken in preparing the P and L account can mask problems, or potential problems, of cash shortages. This is because in the P and L account we concern ourselves not with cash receipts and payments, but with revenues and expenses. This is principally because large expenditures on such things as fixed assets and stocks do not necessarily have an immediate effect on the P and L account. You may recall from Chapter 2, when we were considering the business of Paul, the wrapping-paper seller, that the P and L account and the cash flow statement showed quite different information.

Cash is important because, in practice, without it no business can operate. Companies are required to produce a cash flow statement as well as the more traditional P and L account and balance sheet. In this chapter we consider the deficiencies of these traditional statements, in the context of assessing cash flow issues. We go on to consider how the cash flow statement is prepared and how it may be interpreted.

OBJECTIVES

When you have completed this chapter you should be able to:

- Discuss the crucial importance of cash to a business.
- Explain the nature of the cash flow statement and discuss how it can be helpful in identifying cash flow problems.
- Prepare a cash flow statement.
- Interpret a cash flow statement.

The importance of cash and cash flow

Some simple organisations, such as small clubs and other not-for-profit associations, limit their accounting activities to a record of cash receipts and cash payments. Periodically (normally annually), a summary of all cash transactions – the **cash flow** – for the period is produced for the members. The summary would show one single figure for each category of payment or receipt, for example membership subscriptions. This summary is usually the basis of decision making for a club and the main means of its management committee fulfilling its moral duty to account to the club members. This is usually found to be sufficient for such organisations.

Most organisations, including most businesses and many not-for-profit organisations, do not simply rely on a summary of cash receipts and payments but also produce a profit-and-loss type of statement. Can you remember the difference between a cash receipts and payments statement and an 'accruals-based' profit and loss account? Can you think why simple organisations do not feel the need for a profit-and-loss type of statement?

The difference between the two is that while a receipts and payments summary confines itself to cash movements, an accruals-based (that is, profit-and-loss type of statement) is concerned with movements in wealth.

Increases and decreases in wealth do not necessarily involve cash. A business making a sale (generating revenue) increases its wealth, but if the sale is made on credit, no cash changes hands – not at the time of the sale, at least. Here the increase in wealth is reflected in another asset: an increase in trade debtors. If an item of stock is the subject of the sale, the business incurs an expense in order to make the sale – wealth is lost to the business through the reduction in stock. Here an expense has been incurred but no cash has changed hands. There is also the important distinction for profit-seeking organisations that the participants are going to be very concerned with *wealth* generation, not just with cash generation.

For an organisation with any real level of complexity, a cash receipts and payments summary would not tell the participants all that they would want to know. An 'accruals-based' statement is necessary.

A simple organisation may just collect subscriptions from its members, perhaps raise further cash from activities, and spend cash on pursuing the purposes of the club, for example making payments to charity. Here everything which accounting is capable of reflecting is reflected in a simple cash receipts and payments statement. The club has no stock. There are no fixed assets. All transactions are for cash, rather than on credit.

Clearly, organisations that are more complicated than simple clubs need to produce a P and L account that reflects movements in wealth, and the net increase (profit) or decrease (loss) for the period concerned. Until the mid-1970s, in the UK, there was not generally felt to be any need for businesses to produce more than a P and L account and balance sheet. It seemed to be believed that all that shareholders and other interested parties needed to know, in accounting terms, about a business could be taken more or less directly from those two statements. This view seemed to be based partly on the implicit belief that if a business was profitable, then automatically it would have plenty of cash. Though in the very long run this is likely to be true, it is not necessarily true in the short-to-medium term.

The following is a list of business/accounting events. In each case, state the effect (increase, decrease or no effect) on both cash and profit:

		Effect	
		on profit	on cash
1.	Repayment of a loan	....	....
2.	Making a sale on credit	....	....
3.	Buying a fixed asset for cash	....	....
4.	Receiving cash from a trade debtor	....	....
5.	Depreciating a fixed asset	....	....
6.	Buying some stock for cash	....	....
7.	Making a share issue for cash	....	....

You should have come up with the following:

		Effect	
		on profit	on cash
1.	Repayment of a loan	none	decrease
2.	Making a sale on credit	increase	none
3.	Buying a fixed asset for cash	none	decrease
4.	Receiving cash from a trade debtor	none	increase
5.	Depreciating a fixed asset	decrease	none
6.	Buying some stock for cash	none	decrease
7.	Making a share issue for cash	none	increase

The reasons for this are as follows:

1. Repaying the loan requires that cash is paid to creditors. Thus, two figures in the balance sheet will be affected, but not the P and L account.
2. Making a sale on credit will increase the sales figure and probably profit (unless the sale was made for a price that precisely equalled the expenses involved). No cash will change hands, however, at this point.
3. Buying a fixed asset for cash obviously reduces the cash balance of the business, but its profit figure is not affected.
4. Receiving cash from a debtor increases the cash balance and reduces the debtors' balance. Both of these figures are on the balance sheet. The P and L account is unaffected.
5. Depreciating a fixed asset means that an expense is recognised. This causes the value of the asset, as it is recorded on the balance sheet, to fall by an amount equal to the amount of the expense.
6. Buying some stock for cash means that the value of the stock will increase and the cash balance will decrease by a similar amount. Profit is not affected.
7. Making a share issue for cash increases the owners' claim and increases the cash balance; profit is unaffected.

In 1991, a financial reporting standard, FRS 1, emerged that requires all but the smallest companies to produce and publish, in addition to the P and L account and balance sheet, a statement that reflects movements in cash. The reason for this requirement was the increasing belief that, despite their usefulness, the P and L account and balance sheet do not concentrate sufficiently on liquidity. It was believed that the accruals-based nature of the P and L account tends to obscure the question of how and where the business is generating the cash that it needs to continue its operations. Why liquidity is viewed as being so important we shall consider next.

Why is cash so important?

To businesses that are pursuing a goal that is concerned with profit/wealth, why is cash so important? Activity 6.1 illustrated the fact that cash and profit do not go hand in hand, so why the current preoccupation with cash? After all, cash is just an asset that a business needs in order to help it to function. The same could be said of stock or fixed assets.

The reason for the importance of cash is that people and organisations will not normally accept other than cash in settlement of their claims against a business. If a business wants to employ people, it must pay them in cash. If it wants to buy a new fixed asset to exploit a business opportunity, the seller of the asset will normally insist on being paid in cash, probably after a short period of credit. When businesses fail, it is their inability to find the cash to pay claimants that really drives them under. These factors lead to cash being the pre-eminent business asset and, therefore, the one that analysts and others watch most carefully in trying to assess the ability of businesses to survive and/or to take advantage of commercial opportunities as they arise.

The cash flow statement

The cash flow statement is, in essence, a summary of the cash receipts and payments over the period concerned. All payments of a particular type – for example, cash payments to acquire additional fixed assets – are added together to give just one figure that appears in the statement. The net total of the statement is the net increase or decrease of the cash of the business over the period. The statement is basically an analysis of the business's cash movements for the period. The cash flow statement is now accepted, along with the P and L account, balance sheet and statement of recognised gains and losses as a primary financial statement.

The relationship between the cash flow statement, P and L account and balance sheet is shown in Figure 6.1. The balance sheet reflects the combination of assets (including cash) and claims (including the owners' capital) of the business *at a particular point in time*. Both the cash flow statement and the P and L account explain the *changes over a period* to two of the items in the balance sheet, namely cash and owners' claim respectively. In practice, this period is typically the business's accounting year.

The standard layout of the cash flow statement is summarised in Figure 6.2. An explanation of the terms used in the figure is as follows:

- **Net cash flow from operating activities**. This is the net inflow or outflow from trading operations. It is equal to the sum of cash receipts from trade debtors (and cash sales where relevant) less the sums paid to buy stock, to pay rent, to pay wages and so on. Note that it is the amounts of cash received and paid, not the revenue and expense, that feature in the cash flow statement. It is, of course, the P and L account that deals with the expenses and revenues.

- **Returns from investment and servicing of finance**. This category deals with payments made to suppliers of fixed-return finance to reward them for the use of their money. Fixed-return finance includes preference shares and interest-bearing loans and the rewards are preference dividends and interest, respectively. Similarly, this part of the statement deals with cash that the business receives as interest and dividends from investments (in loans and shares) that

Figure 6.1

The relationship between the balance sheet, the profit and loss account, and the cash flow statement

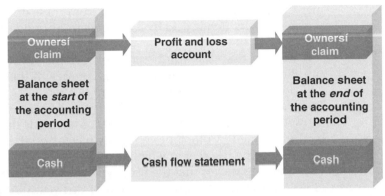

The balance sheet shows the position, at a particular point in time, of the business's assets and claims. The profit and loss account explains how, over a period between two balance sheets, the owners' claim figure in the first balance sheet has altered, as a result of trading operations, to become the figure in the second balance sheet. The cash flow statement also looks at changes over the accounting period, but this statement explains the alteration in the cash balances shown in the two consecutive balance sheets.

Figure 6.2

Standard layout of the cash flow statement

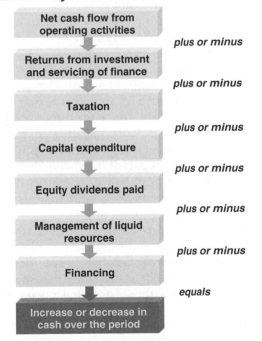

The figure sets out in diagrammatic form the standard layout for the cash flow statement as required by FRS 1, *Cash Flow Statements*.

it has made. The object of distinguishing between payments and receipts arising from financing and investment outside of the business and money deriving from normal operating activities is to enable the reader of the statement to separate the cash flow arising from these different types of activity.

Note that dividends paid by a business to its ordinary shareholders are dealt with later in the statement.

Note also that the word 'servicing' in this context refers to rewarding suppliers of finance for the use of their money. If they are not rewarded, they will not normally allow their money to be used.

- **Taxation.** This is fairly obvious, but you should be clear that the amounts shown here are payments and receipts of tax made during the period covered by the statement. Companies normally pay tax on their profits in two parts: 50 per cent during the year in which it is earned, and 50 per cent shortly after the year-end. This means that the tax payment that is made this year is 50 per cent of last year's liability, *plus* 50 per cent of this year's. At the end of any year, 50 per cent of that year's tax liability remains unpaid and will appear as a creditor (current libility) in the balance sheet.

- **Capital expenditure.** This part of the statement is concerned with cash payments made to acquire additional fixed assets and cash receipts from the disposal of fixed assets. These fixed assets could be loans made by the business, or shares in another business bought by the business, as well as the more usual fixed assets such as buildings, machinery and so on.

- **Equity dividends paid.** This is cash dividends paid to the business's ordinary shareholders (equity holders) during the period covered by the statement. Businesses frequently declare a dividend that is shown in one year's P and L account but that is not paid until the following year, being treated as a current liability until it is paid. This means that the dividend 'for the year' is often not paid until the following year.

- **Management of liquid resources.** This part of the statement deals with cash receipts and payments arising from the acquisition and disposal of readily disposable investments. These are investments that the business did not or does not intend to hold for any other reason than to find a profitable depository for what will probably be a short-term cash surplus. Readily disposable investments of this type will typically be investments in shares of businesses listed on a stock exchange, and government bills (short-term loans to the government).

- **Financing.** This part of the statement is concerned with the long-term financing of the business. So we are considering borrowings (other than in the very short term) and finance from share issues. This category is concerned with repayment/redemption of finance as well as the raising of it.

- **Increase or decrease in cash over the period.** Naturally, the total of the statement must be the net increase or decrease in cash over the period covered by the statement. Cash here means notes and coins in hand and deposits in banks and similar institutions that are accessible to the business within 24 hours' notice without incurring a penalty for premature withdrawal.

Example 6.1 sets out a cash flow statement according to the requirements of FRS 1. The headings printed in bold type are specifically required, and are the primary categories into which cash payments and receipts for the period must be analysed.

Example 6.1

Propulsion plc
Cash flow statement for the year ended 31 December 2001

	£m	£m
Net cash inflows from operating activities		55
Returns from investment and servicing of finance		
Interest received	1	
Interest paid	(2)	
Net cash outflow from returns on investment and servicing of finance		(1)
Taxation		
Corporation tax paid	(4)	
Net cash outflow for taxation		(4)
Capital expenditure		
Payments to acquire intangible fixed assets	(6)	
Payments to acquire tangible fixed assets	(23)	
Receipts from sales of tangible fixed assets	4	
Net cash outflow for capital expenditure		(25)
		25
Equity dividends		
Dividend on ordinary shares	(10)	
Net cash outflow for equity dividends		(10)
		15
Management of liquid resources		
Disposal of treasury bills	3	
Net cash inflow from management of liquid resources		3
Financing		
Repayments of debenture stock	(6)	
Net cash outflow for financing		(6)
Increase in cash		12

Note in Example 6.1 that there is a subtotal in the statement after 'Capital expenditure'. This is to highlight the extent to which the cash flows of the period, arising from the 'normal' activities of the business (operations, servicing loans, tax and capital investment), cover the dividend on ordinary shares paid during the period.

Similarly there is a subtotal after the ordinary share dividend paid. The reason for drawing this subtotal is to highlight the extent to which the business has relied on additional external finance to support its trading and other normally-recurring operations. It is claimed that, before the requirement for businesses to produce the cash flow statement, some businesses were able to obscure the fact that they were only able to continue their operations as a result of a series of borrowings and/or share issues. It is no longer possible to obscure such actions.

The effect on a business's cash balance of its various activities is shown in Figure 6.3. The activities that affect cash are analysed in the same way as is

Figure 6.3

Diagrammatical representation of the cash flow statement

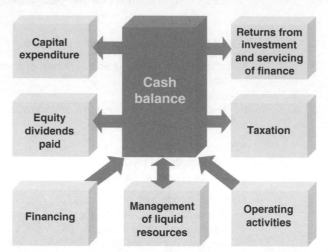

Various activities of the business each have their own effect on its cash balance, either positive (increasing the cash balance) or negative (decreasing the cash balance). The increase or reduction in the cash balance over a period will be the sum of these individual effects, taking account of the direction (cash in or cash out) of each activity's effect on cash.

Note that the direction of an arrow shows the *normal* direction of the cash flow in respect of each activity. In certain circumstances each of these arrows could be reversed in direction; for example, in some circumstances the business might be eligible to claim a repayment of tax instead of having to pay it. Only with 'management of liquid resources' will there not be a 'normal' direction of the cash flow.

required by FRS 1. As explained above, the arrows in the figure show the *normal* direction of cash flow for the typical healthy, profitable business in a typical year.

Normally 'operating activities' provide positive cash flow – that is, they help to increase a business's cash resources. In fact, for UK businesses, cash generated from normal trading, even after deducting tax, interest and dividends, is overwhelmingly the most important source of new finance for most businesses.

Activity 6.3

Last year's cash flow statement for Angus plc showed a negative cash flow from operating activities. What could be the reason for this and should the business's management be alarmed by it? *Hint*: we think that there are two broad possible reasons for a negative cash flow.

....

The two reasons are:

● *The business is unprofitable.* This leads to more cash being paid out to employees, suppliers of goods and services, and so on than is received from debtors in respect of sales. This would be particularly alarming because a major expense for most businesses is depreciation of fixed assets. Since depreciation does not lead to a cash flow, it is not considered in cash flow from operating activities. Neither would interest paid on any money borrowed by the business be included here, because it is taken into account under 'servicing of finance'. Thus, a negative operating cash flow might well indicate a very much larger negative trading profit, and a significant loss of the business's wealth.

- *The business is expanding.* This reason might be less alarming. A business that is expanding its activities (its levels of sales) would tend to spend quite a lot of cash, relative to the amount of cash coming in from sales. This is because it will probably be expanding its stockholdings to accommodate the increased demand. In the first instance, it would not necessarily benefit, in cash flow terms, from all of the additional sales. Normally, a business may well have to have the stock in place before additional sales could be made. Even when the additional sales *are* made, the sales would normally be made on credit, with the cash inflow lagging behind the sale. This is likely to be particularly true of a new business, which would be expanding stocks and other assets from zero.

  Expansion typically causes cash flow strains for the reasons just explained. This can be a particular problem because a business's increased profitability might encourage a feeling of optimism, which could lead in turn to a lack of concern for the cash flow problem.

To continue with our consideration of the 'normal' direction of cash flow, a business would, in general, pay out more to service its loan finance than it receives from the financial investments (loans made and shares owned) that it has itself made.

Companies pay tax on profits, and so the cash flow would be from the company to the Inland Revenue when the company is profitable. When a company makes a trading loss, there would be no cash flow. However, if the loss followed a period where tax was paid on profits, the company would be entitled to set the current loss against past profits and obtain a refund of past tax paid as a result. Thus, there might be positive cash flow from taxation.

Investing activities can give rise to positive cash flows when a business sells some fixed assets. Because most types of fixed asset wear out and because businesses tend to seek to expand their asset base, the normal direction of cash in this area is out of the business, that is negative.

Financing can go in either direction, depending on the financing strategy at the time. Since businesses seek to expand, there is a general tendency for this area to lead to cash coming into the business rather than leaving it.

Deducing net cash inflows from operating activities

The first category of cash flow that appears in the cash flow statement, and the one that is typically the most important for most businesses, is the cash flow from operations. There are two methods that can be used to derive the figure for inclusion in the statement: the direct method and the indirect method.

The direct method

The **direct method** involves an analysis of the cash records of the business for the period, picking out all payments and receipts relating to operating activities. These are summarised to give the net figure for inclusion in the cash flow statement. This could be a time-consuming and laborious activity, although it could be done by computer. Not many businesses adopt this approach.

The indirect method

The **indirect method** is the more popular method. It relies on the fact that, broadly, sales give rise to cash inflows, and expenses give rise to outflows. Broadly, therefore, net profit will be equal in amount to the net cash inflow from operating activities. Since businesses have to produce a profit and loss account in any case, information from it can be used to deduce the cash from operating activities.

Within a particular accounting period, however, it is not strictly true that the net profit equals the net cash inflow from operating activities. We have already seen in Chapter 3 that sales revenues are not the same as cash received from sales during a particular period and expenses are not the same as cash paid for expenses during a period. Thus profit (which is the difference between revenues and expenses) will not equal operating cash flows (which is the difference between cash received from sales and cash paid for expenses).

Activity 6.4

How can we deduce the cash inflow from sales using the P and L account and balance sheet for the business?

....

The balance sheet will tell us how much was owed in respect of credit sales at the beginning and end of the year (trade debtors). The P and L account tells us the sales figure. If we adjust the sales figure by the increase or decrease in trade debtors over the year, we deduce the cash from sales for the year.

When sales are made on credit, the cash receipt occurs some time after the sale. This means that sales made towards the end of an accounting year will be included in that year's profit and loss account, but most of the cash from those sales will flow into the business, and should be included in the cash flow statement, in the following year. Fortunately, it is easy to deduce the cash received from sales if we have the relevant profit and loss account (see Examples 6.2 and 6.3 following).

Example 6.2

The sales figure for a business for the year is £34 million. The trade debtors were £4 million at the beginning of the year, but had increased to £5 million by the end of the year.

Basically, the debtors figure is affected by sales and cash receipts. It is increased when a sale is made and decreased when cash is received from a debtor. If, over a year, the sales and the cash receipts had been equal, the beginning-of-year and end-of-year debtors figures would have been equal. Since the debtors figure increased, it must mean that less cash was received than sales were made. Thus, the cash receipts from sales must be £33 million (34 − (5 − 4)).

Put slightly differently, we can say that, as a result of sales, assets of £34 million flowed into the business during the year. If £1 million of this went to increasing the asset of trade debtors, this leaves only £33 million that went to increase cash.

A similar approach to that applied in respect of sales can be applied to most expense items. However, in the case of depreciation, the charge in the P and L account may not be associated with any movement in cash during the accounting period. (This is because the cash movement will usually occur when the fixed asset is acquired.)

All of this means that if we take the operating profit (that is, the profit before interest and tax) for the year, add back the depreciation charged in arriving at

Example 6.3

The relevant information from the accounts of Dido plc for last year is as follows:

	£m
Net operating profit	122
Depreciation charged in arriving at net operating profit	34
At the beginning of the year:	
Stock	15
Debtors	24
Creditors	18
At the end of the year:	
Stock	17
Debtors	21
Creditors	19

The cash flow from operating activities is derived as follows:

		£m
Net operating profit		122
Add Depreciation		34
Net inflow of working capital from operations		156
Less Increase in stock		(2)
		154
Add Decrease in debtors	3	
Increase in creditors	1	4
Net cash inflow from operating activities		158

Thus, the net increase in working capital was £156 million. Of this, £2 million went into increased stocks. More cash was received from debtors than sales were made, and less cash was paid to creditors than purchases were of goods and services on credit. Both of these had a favourable effect on cash, which increased by £158 million.

that profit and adjust this total by movements in stock, debtors and creditors, we have the effect on cash.

The indirect method of deducing the net cash flow from operating activities is summarised in Figure 6.4.

The relevant information from the accounts of Pluto plc for last year is as follows:

	£m
Net operating profit	165
Depreciation charged in arriving at net operating profit	41
At the beginning of the year:	
Stock	22
Debtors	18
Creditors	15
At the end of the year:	
Stock	23
Debtors	21
Creditors	17

What figure should appear in the cash flow statement for 'net cash inflow from operating activities'?

Net cash flow from operating activities:

	£m	£m
Net operating profit		165
Add Depreciation		41
Net increase in working capital from operations		206
Less Increase in stock	1	
Increase in debtors	3	(4)
		202
Add Increase in creditors		2
Net cash inflow from operating activities		204

Figure 6.4

The indirect method of deducing the net cash flow from the operating activities

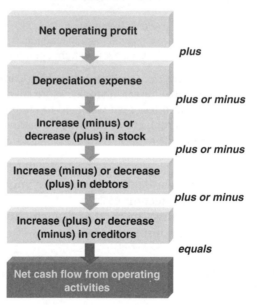

The figure sets out the indirect method of determining the net cash flows from operating activities. This involves adding back the depreciation charge to the net profit for the period and then adjusting for increases or decreases in stock, debtors and creditors.

We can now go on to take a look at the preparation of a complete cash flow statement – see Example 6.4.

Torbryan plc's profit and loss account for the year ended 31 December 2001 and the balance sheets as at 31 December 2000 and 2001 are as follows:

Profit and loss account for the year ended 31 December 2001

	£m	£m
Turnover		576
Cost of sales		307
Gross profit		269
Distribution costs	65	
Administrative expenses	26	91
		178
Other operating income		21
		199
Interest receivable and similar income		17
		216
Interest payable and similar charges		23
		193
Tax on profit or loss on ordinary activities		46
Profit on ordinary activities after taxation		147
Retained profit brought forward from last year		26
		173
Proposed dividend on ordinary shares		(50)
Retained profit carried forward		123

Balance sheet as at 31 December 2000 and 2001

	2000 £m	2001 £m
Fixed assets		
Tangible assets:		
Land and buildings	241	241
Plant and machinery	309	325
	550	566
Current assets		
Stocks	44	41
Trade debtors	121	139
	165	180
Creditors: amounts falling due within one year		
Bank overdraft	28	6
Trade creditors	55	54
Corporation tax	16	23
Dividend proposed	40	50
	139	133
Net current assets	26	47
Total assets less current liabilities	576	613

Creditors: amounts falling due after more than one year

Debenture loans	400	250
	176	363

Capital and reserves

Called-up ordinary share capital	150	200
Share premium account	–	40
Profit and loss account	26	123
	176	363

During 2001, the business spent £95 million on additional plant and machinery. There were no other fixed-asset acquisitions or disposals. The cash flow statement would be as follows:

Torbryan plc
Cash flow statement for the year ended 31 December 2001

	£m	£m
Net cash inflows from operating activities (note 1)		262
Returns from investment and servicing of finance		
Interest received	17	
Interest paid	(23)	
Net cash outflow from returns on investment and servicing of finance		(6)
Taxation		
Corporation tax paid (note 2)	(39)	
Net cash outflow for taxation		(39)
Capital expenditure		
Payments to acquire tangible fixed assets	(95)	
Net cash outflow for capital expenditure		(95)
		122
Equity dividends paid		
Dividends paid (note 3)	(40)	
Net cash outflow for dividends		(40)
		82
Management of liquid resources		–
Financing		
Repayments of debenture stock (note 4)	(150)	
Issue of ordinary shares (note 5)	90	
Net cash outflow for financing		(60)
Net increase in cash		22

To see how this relates to the cash of the business at the beginning and end of the year it is useful to show a reconciliation as follows:

Reconciliation of cash movements during the year ended 31 December 2001

	£m
Balance at 1 January 2000	(28)
Net cash inflow	22
Balance at 31 December 2001	(6)

Notes

1. **Calculation of net cash inflow from operating activities**

	£m	£m
Net operating profit (from the profit and loss account)		199
Add Depreciation of plant and machinery[a]		79
		278
Less Increase in debtors (139 – 121)	18	
Decrease in creditors (55 – 54)	1	19
		259
Add Decrease in stocks (44 – 41)		3
		262

[a] Since there were no disposals, the depreciation charges must be the difference between the start and end of the year's fixed asset values, adjusted by the cost of any additions.

	£m
Book value, at 1 January 2001	309
Add Additions	95
	404
Less Depreciation (balancing figure)	79
Book value, at 31 December 2001	325

2. **Taxation**

50 per cent of the tax due from companies is paid during the accounting year and 50 per cent in the following year. Thus the 2001 payment would have been half of the tax on the 2000 profit plus half of the 2001 tax charge; put another way, it is the figure that would have appeared in the current liabilities at the end of 2000, plus half of the 2001 tax charge, that is, $16 + (\frac{1}{2} \times 46) = 39$.

Probably the easiest way to deduce the amount paid during the year to 31 December 2001 is by following this approach:

	£m
Tax owed by the business at start of year (1.1.00)	16
Add: Tax charge for the year	46
	62
Less: Tax owed by the business at the end of the year	(23)
Tax paid during the year	39

This follows the logic that if we start with what the business owed at the beginning of the year, add on the increase in what was owed as a result of the current year's tax and then deduct what was still owed at the end, the resulting figure must be what was paid during the year. A similar approach can be taken with equity dividend payments, if the situation is at all complicated.

3. **Dividend**

   Since all of the dividend for 2001 was unpaid at the end of 2001, it seems that the business pays just one final dividend each year, some time after the year-end. Thus it is the 2000 dividend that will have led to a cash outflow in 2001.

4. **Debentures**

   It has been assumed that the debentures were redeemed for their balance sheet value. This is not always the case, however.

5. **Shares**

   The share issue raised £90 million, of which £50 million went into the share capital total on the balance sheet and £40 million into share premium.

Exhibit 6.1 shows the cash flow statement of Monsoon plc, the high-street fashion retail business, for the year ended 27 May 2000.

Exhibit 6.1	**Monsoon plc's cash flow statement for the year ended 27 May 2000**		
For the 52 weeks ended 27 May 2000		2000 £000	1999 £000
Net cash inflow from operating activities		29,917	25,874
Returns on investments and servicing of finance		567	488
Taxation		(7,457)	(6,723)
Capital expenditure and financial investment		(8,616)	(10,104)
Equity dividends paid		(7,998)	(7,998)
Net cash inflow before management of liquid resources		6,413	1,537
Management of liquid resources		(2,720)	(6,262)
Increase/(decrease) in net cash in the period		3,693	(4,725)

●●●● What the cash flow statement tells us

The cash flow statement tells us how the business has generated cash during the period and where that cash has gone. Since cash is properly regarded as the life-blood of just about any business, this is potentially very useful information. Tracking the sources and uses of cash over several years could show financing trends that a reader of the statements could use to help to make predictions about the likely future behaviour of the business.

Looking specifically at the cash flow statement for Torbryan plc in Example 6.4, we can see the following:

- Net cash flow from operations was strong – much larger than the profit figure. This would be expected because depreciation is deducted in arriving at profit. There was a general tendency for working capital to absorb some cash. This would not be surprising had there been an expansion of activity (sales output) over the year. However, from the information supplied, we do not know whether there was an expansion or not.
- There were net outflows of cash in servicing of finance, payment of tax and increasing fixed assets.
- There seems to be a healthy figure of net cash flow after equity dividends.
- There was a fairly major outflow of cash to redeem some debt finance, partly offset by the proceeds of a share issue.
- The net effect was a rather healthier-looking cash position in 2001 than was the case in 2000.

Chapter 7 deals, in a more analytical manner, with the interpretation of cash flow statements.

Self-assessment question 6.1

Touchstone plc's P and L accounts for the years ended 31 December 2000 and 2001, and the balance sheets as at 31 December 2000 and 2001, are as follows:

Profit and loss accounts for the years ended 2000 and 2001

	2000 £m	2001 £m
Turnover	173	207
Cost of sales	(96)	(101)
Gross profit	77	106
Distribution costs	(18)	(22)
Administrative expenses	(25)	(26)
	34	58
Other operating income	3	4
	37	62
Interest receivable and similar income	1	2
	38	64
Interest payable and similar charges	(2)	(4)
	36	60
Tax on profit or loss on ordinary activities	(8)	(16)
Profit on ordinary activities after taxation	28	44
Retained profit brought forward from last year	16	30
	44	74
Dividend (proposed and paid) on ordinary shares	(14)	(18)
Retained profit carried forward	30	56

Balance sheet as at 31 December 2000 and 2001

	2000 £m	2001 £m
Fixed assets		
Tangible assets:		
Land and buildings	94	110
Plant and machinery	53	62
	147	172
Current assets		
Stocks	25	24
Debtors	16	26
Cash at bank and in hand	4	19
	45	69
Creditors: amounts falling due within one year		
Trade creditors	26	23
Corporation tax	4	8
Dividend proposed	12	14
	42	45
Net current assets	3	24
Total assets less current liabilities	150	196
Creditors: amounts falling due after more than one year		
Debenture loans (10%)	20	40
	130	156
Capital and reserves		
Called-up ordinary share capital	100	100
Profit and loss account	30	56
	130	156

Included in 'cost of sales', 'distribution costs' and 'administration expenses', depreciation was as follows:

	2000 £m	2001 £m
Land and buildings	5	6
Plant and machinery	6	10

There were no fixed-asset disposals in either year. In both years an interim dividend was paid in the year in whose profit and loss account it was shown, and a final dividend just after the end of the year concerned.

Required:
Prepare a cash flow statement for the business for 2001.

● Summary

In this chapter we have seen that users of accounting information find it of considerable benefit to have a statement that highlights how a business has generated cash, how it has used its cash, and the resultant effect on its cash resources over a period (typically one year). The cash flow statement does this. The cash flow statement contrasts with the P and L account to the extent that the former shows cash movements, whereas the latter shows changes in business wealth (not just that which is represented by cash) as a result just of trading activities. The statement used by UK businesses is of the form and content laid down by FRS 1. This standard requires that cash flows are analysed into various types of cash flows.

Key terms

Cash flow   p. 167
Net cash flow from operating activities p. 170
Returns from investment and servicing of finance   p. 170
Taxation   p. 172

Capital expenditure   p. 172
Equity dividends paid   p. 172
Management of liquid resources   p. 172
Financing   p. 172
Direct method   p. 175
Indirect method   p. 175

● Further reading

If you would like to explore the topics covered in this chapter in more depth, we recommend the following books:

Financial Reporting, *Alexander, D. and Britton, A.*, 6th edn, International Thompson Business Press, 2001, chapter 27.
Students' Guide to Accounting and Financial Reporting Standards, *Black, G.*, 7th edn, Financial Times Prentice Hall, 2000, chapter 12.
Financial Accounting and Reporting, *Elliott, B. and Elliott, J.*, 5th edn, Financial Times Prentice Hall, 2001, chapter 24.
Students' Manual of Accounting, *PriceWaterhouseCoopers*, International Thomson Business Press, 1999, chapter 30.

6.1 The typical business outside of the service sector has about 50 per cent more of its resources tied up in stock than in cash, yet there is no call for a 'stock flow statement' to be prepared. Why is cash regarded as more important than stock?

6.2 What is the difference between the direct and indirect methods of deducing cash flow from operating activities?

6.3 Taking each of the categories of the cash flow statement in turn, in which direction would you normally expect the cash flow to be?

(a) Cash flow from operations
(b) Cash flow from returns from investments and servicing of finance
(c) Cash flow from taxation
(d) Cash flow from capital expenditure
(e) Cash flow from equity dividends
(f) Cash flow from management of liquid resources
(g) Cash flow from financing.

6.4 What causes the net profit for the year not to equal the net cash inflow?

? **EXERCISES**

Exercises 6.3–6.8 are more advanced than 6.1 and 6.2. Those with coloured numbers have answers at the back of the book.

6.1 How will each of the following events ultimately affect the amount of cash in a business?

(a) An increase in the level of stock in trade
(b) A rights issue of ordinary shares
(c) A bonus issue of ordinary shares
(d) Writing off the value of some stock in trade
(e) The disposal of a large number of the business's shares by a major shareholder
(f) Depreciating a fixed asset.

6.2 The following information has been taken from the accounts of Juno plc for 2000 and 2001:

	2001	2000
	£m	£m
Net operating profit	187	156
Depreciation charged in arriving at net operating profit	55	47
Stock held at end of year	31	27
Debtors at end of year	23	24
Creditors at end of year	17	15

Required:
What is the cash flow from operations figure for Juno plc for 2001?

6.3 Torrent plc's profit and loss account for the year ended 31 December 2001 and the balance sheets as at 31 December 2000 and 2001 are as follows:

Profit and loss account	£m	£m
Turnover		623
Cost of sales		(353)
Gross profit		270
Distribution costs	(71)	
Administrative expenses	(30)	(101)
		169
Other operating income		13
		182
Interest receivable and similar income		14
		196
Interest payable and similar charges		(26)
		170
Tax on profit on ordinary activities		(36)
Profit on ordinary activities after taxation		134
Retained profit brought forward from last year		123
		257
Proposed dividend on ordinary shares		(60)
Retained profit carried forward		197

Balance sheet as at 31 December 2000 and 2001

	2000 £m	2001 £m
Fixed assets		
Land and buildings	310	310
Plant and machinery	325	314
	635	624
Current assets		
Stocks	41	35
Trade debtors	139	145
	180	180
Creditors: amounts falling due within one year		
Bank overdraft	6	29
Trade creditors	54	41
Corporation tax	23	18
Dividend proposed	50	60
	133	148
Net current assets	47	32
Total assets less current liabilities	682	656
Creditors: amounts falling due after more than one year		
Debenture loans	250	150
	432	506
Capital and reserves		
Called-up ordinary share capital	200	300
Share premium account	40	–
Revaluation reserve	69	9
Profit and loss account	123	197
	432	506

During 2001, the business spent £67 million on additional plant and machinery. There were no other fixed asset acquisitions or disposals. There was no share issue for cash during the year.

Required:

Prepare the cash flow statement for Torrent plc for the year ended 31 December 2001.

6.4 Cheng plc's profit and loss accounts for the years ended 31 December 2000 and 2001 and balance sheets as at 31 December 2000 and 2001 are as follows:

Profit and loss account

	2000	2001
	£m	£m
Turnover	207	153
Cost of sales	(101)	(76)
Gross profit	106	77
Distribution costs	(22)	(20)
Administrative expenses	(26)	(28)
	58	29
Other operating income	4	–
	62	29
Interest receivable and similar income	2	–
	64	29
Interest payable and similar charges	(4)	(4)
	60	25
Tax on profit or loss on ordinary activities	(16)	(6)
Profit on ordinary activities after taxation	44	19
Retained profit brought forward from last year	30	56
	74	75
Dividends on ordinary shares (paid and proposed)	(18)	(18)
Retained profit carried forward	56	57

Balance sheet as at 31 December 2000 and 2001

	2000	2001
	£m	£m
Fixed assets		
Tangible assets:		
Land and buildings	110	130
Plant and machinery	62	56
	172	186
Current assets		
Stocks	24	25
Debtors	26	25
Cash at bank and in hand	19	–
	69	50
Creditors: amounts falling due within one year		
Bank overdraft	–	2
Trade creditors	23	20
Corporation tax	8	3
Dividend proposed	14	14
	45	39

	£m	£m
Net current assets	24	11
Total assets less current liabilities	196	197
Creditors: amounts falling due after more than one year		
Debenture loans (10%)	40	40
	156	157
Capital and reserves		
Called-up ordinary share capital	100	100
Profit and loss account	56	57
	156	157

Included in 'cost of sales', 'distribution costs' and 'administration expenses', depreciation was as follows:

	2000	2001
	£m	£m
Land and buildings	6	10
Plant and machinery	10	12

There were no fixed-asset disposals in either year. In both years, an interim dividend was paid in the year in whose profit and loss account it was shown, and a final dividend was paid just after the end of the year concerned.

Required:
Prepare a cash flow statement for the business for 2001.

6.5 The following are the accounts for Nailsea Limited for the year ended 30 June 2001 and 2002.

Profit and loss accounts for year ended 30 June

	2001	2002
	£000	£000
Sales	1,230	2,280
Operating costs	(722)	(1,618)
Depreciation	(270)	(320)
Operating profit	238	342
Interest	–	(27)
Profit before tax	238	315
Tax	(110)	(140)
Profit after tax	128	175
Dividend	(80)	(85)
Retained profit for year	48	90

Balance sheets as at 30 June

	2001		2002	
	£000	£000	£000	£000
Fixed assets (see note below)		2,310		2,640
Current assets				
Stock	275		450	
Debtors	100		250	
Bank	–		83	
	375		783	

Less **Creditors due within one year**

Creditors	130	190
Taxation	55	70
Dividend	80	85
Bank overdraft	32	–
	297	345

Net current assets

	78	438
	2,388	3,078

Less **Creditors falling due after more than one year**

9% debentures	–	300
	2,388	2,778

Capital and reserves

Share capital (fully paid £1 shares)	1,400	1,600
Share premium account	200	300
Retained profits	788	878
	2,388	2,778

Note: **Schedule of fixed assets**

	Land and buildings £m	Plant and machinery £m	Total £m
Cost			
At 1 July 2001	1,500	1,350	2,850
Additions	400	250	650
At 30 June 2002	1,900	1,600	3,500
Depreciation			
At 1 July 2001	–	540	540
Charge for year at 20%	–	320	320
At 30 June 2002	–	860	860
Net book value at 30 June 2002	1,900	740	2,640

Required:

Prepare a cash flow statement for Nailsea Limited for the year ended 30 June 2002.

6.6 The following financial statements for Blackstone plc are a slightly simplified set of published accounts. Blackstone plc is an engineering firm that developed a new range of products in 2000; these now account for 60 per cent of its turnover.

Profit and loss account for the years ended 31 March

	notes	2001 £m	2002 £m
Turnover		7,003	11,205
Cost of sales		(3,748)	(5,809)
Gross profit		3,255	5,396
Operating costs	1	(2,205)	(3,087)
Operating Profit		1,050	2,309
Interest payable		(216)	(456)
Profit before taxation		834	1,853
Taxation		(210)	(390)

		£m	£m
Profit after taxation		624	1,463
Dividends		(300)	(400)
Retained profit for the year		324	1,063
Retained profit brought forward		361	685
Retained profit carried forward		685	1,748

Balance sheets as at 31 March

	notes	2001 £m	£m	2002 £m	£m
Fixed assets					
Intangible assets	2	–		700	
Tangible assets	3	4,300		7,535	
			4,300		8,235
Current assets					
Stocks		1,209		2,410	
Trade debtors		941		1,573	
		2,150		3,983	
Creditors: amounts falling due within one year					
Trade creditors		731		1,507	
Taxation		105		195	
Dividends		300		400	
Overdraft		77		1,816	
		1,213		3,918	
Net current assets			937		65
Creditors: amounts falling due after more than one year					
Bank loan (repayable 2007)			(1,800)		(3,800)
			3,437		4,500
Capital and reserves					
Share capital			1,800		1,800
Share premium			600		600
Capital reserves			352		352
Retained profits			685		1,748
			3,437		4,500

Notes to the accounts
1. Operating costs include the following items:

	£m
Exceptional items	503
Depreciation	1,251
Administrative expenses	527
Marketing expenses	785

2. Intangible assets represent the amounts paid for the goodwill of another engineering business acquired during the year.

3. The movements in tangible fixed assets during the year are set out below.

	Land and buildings £m	Plant and machinery £m	Fixtures and fittings £m	Total £m
Cost				
At 1 April 2001	4,500	3,850	2,120	10,470
Additions	–	2,970	1,608	4,578
Disposals	–	(365)	(216)	(581)
At 31 March 2002	4,500	6,455	3,512	14,467
Depreciation				
At 1 April 2001	1,275	3,080	1,815	6,170
Charge for year	225	745	281	1,251
Disposals	–	(305)	(184)	(489)
At 31 March 2002	1,500	3,520	1,912	6,932
Net book value				
At 31 March 2002	3,000	2,935	1,600	7,535

Proceeds from the sale of fixed assets in the year ended 31 March 2002 amounted to £54 million.

Required:
Prepare a cash flow statement for Blackstone plc for the year ended 31 March 2002. *Hint*: a loss (deficit) on disposal of fixed assets is simply an additional amount of depreciation and should be dealt with as such in preparing the cash flow statement.

6.7 Simplified financial statements for York plc are set out below.

York plc
Profit and loss account for the year ended 30 September 2001

	£m
Turnover	290.0
Cost of sales	(215.0)
Gross profit	75.0
Less Operating expenses (note 1)	(62.0)
Operating profit	13.0
Interest paid	(3.0)
Profit before taxation	10.0
Taxation	(2.6)
Profit after taxation	7.4
Dividends	(3.5)
Retained profit	3.9

Balance sheet at 30 September

	2000 £m	2000 £m	2001 £m	2001 £m
Fixed assets (note 2)		80.0		85.0
Current assets				
Stock and debtors	110.8		122.1	
Cash at bank	9.2		16.6	
	129.0		138.7	
Current liabilities				
Trade creditors	(78.2)		(80.5)	
Dividends	(1.8)		(2.0)	
Taxation	(1.0)		(1.3)	
	(81.0)		(83.8)	
Net current assets		48.0		54.9
Long-term liabilities		(32.0)		(35.0)
		96.0		104.9
Share capital		35.0		40.0
Share premium account		30.0		30.0
Reserves		31.0		34.9
		96.0		104.9

Notes to the accounts

1. Operating expenses include depreciation of £13 million and a profit of £3.2 million on the sale of fixed assets.
2. Fixed assets costs and depreciation:

	Cost £m	Accumulated depreciation £m	Net book value £m
At 1 October 2000	120.0	40.0	80.0
Disposals	(10.0)	(8.0)	(2.0)
Additions	20.0		20.0
Depreciation		13.0	(13.0)
At 30 September 2001	130.0	45.0	85.0

Required:

Prepare a cash flow statement for York plc for the year ended 30 September 2001 using the data above.

6.8 The balance sheets of Axis plc as at 31 December 2000 and 2001 and the summary profit and loss account for the year ended 31 December 2001 were as follows:

Balance sheet as at 31 December

	2000 £m	2000 £m	2001 £m	2001 £m
Fixed assets				
Land and building at cost	130		130	
Less Accumulated depreciation	30	100	32	98
Plant and machinery at cost	70		80	
Less Accumulated depreciation	17	53	23	57
		153		155

Current assets

Stock	25	24
Debtors	16	26
Short-term investments	–	12
Cash at bank and in hand	–	7
	41	69

Creditors: amounts due in less than one year

Trade creditors	19	22
Taxation	7	8
Proposed dividends	12	14
	38	44

Net current assets	3	25
	156	180

Creditors: amounts due beyond one year

10% debentures	20	40
	136	140

Financed by:

Share capital	100	100
Revenue reserves	36	40
	136	140

Profit and loss account for the year ended 31 December 2001

	£m	£m
Sales		173
Less Cost of sales		(96)
Gross profit		77
Interest receivable		2
		79
Less		
Sundry expenses	24	
Interest payable	2	
Loss on sale of fixed asset	1	
Depreciation – buildings	2	
– plant	16	(45)
Net profit before tax		34
Corporation tax		(16)
Net profit after tax		18
Proposed dividend		(14)
Unappropriated profit added to revenue reserves		4

During the year, plant costing £15 million and with accumulated depreciation of £10 million was sold for £4 million.

Required:

Prepare a cash flow statement for Axis plc for the year ended 31 December 2001.

7 Analysing and interpreting financial statements

Introduction

In this chapter we will see how financial ratios can help in the analysis and interpretation of financial statements. We shall also consider problems that are encountered when applying this technique. Financial ratios can be used to examine various aspects of financial position and performance and are widely used for planning and control purposes. They can be used to evaluate the financial health of a business and can be utilised by management in a wide variety of decisions involving such areas as profit planning, pricing, working-capital management, financial structure and dividend policy.

Financial ratios

Financial ratios provide a quick and relatively simple means of examining the financial condition of a business. A ratio simply expresses the relation of one figure appearing in the financial statements to some other figure appearing there (for example, net profit in relation to capital employed) or perhaps to some resource of the business (for example, net profit per employee, sales per square metre of counter space).

Ratios can be very helpful when comparing the financial health of different businesses. Differences may exist between businesses in the scale of operations, and so a direct comparison of, say, the profits generated by each business may be misleading. By expressing profit in relation to some other measure (for example, sales), the problem of scale is eliminated. A business with a profit of, say, £10,000 and a sales turnover of £100,000 can be compared with a much larger business with a profit of, say, £80,000 and a sales turnover of £1,000,000 by the use of a simple ratio. The net profit to sales turnover ratio for the smaller company is 10 per cent [(10,000/100,000) × 100%] and the same ratio for the larger company is 8 per cent [(80,000/1,000,000) × 100%]. These ratios can then be directly compared, whereas comparison of the absolute profit figures would be less meaningful. The need to eliminate differences in scale through the use of ratios can also apply when comparing the performance of the same business over time.

By calculating a relatively small number of ratios, it is often possible to build up a reasonably good picture of the position and performance of a business. Thus, it is not surprising that ratios are widely used by those who have an interest in businesses and business performance. Although ratios are not difficult to calculate, they can be difficult to interpret. For example, a change in the net profit per employee of a business may be for a number of possible reasons such as:

- A change in the number of employees without a corresponding change in the level of output.
- A change in the level of output without a corresponding change in the number of employees.
- A change in the mix of goods/services being offered which, in turn, changes the level of profit.

It is important to appreciate that ratios are really only the starting point for further analysis. They help to highlight the financial strengths and weaknesses of a business but they cannot, by themselves, explain why certain strengths or weaknesses exist or why certain changes have occurred. Only a detailed investigation will reveal these underlying reasons.

Ratios can be expressed in various forms, for example as a percentage, as a fraction or as a proportion. The way in which a particular ratio is presented will depend on the needs of those who will use the information. Although it is possible to calculate a large number of ratios, only a few, based on key relationships, are likely to be helpful to a user. Many ratios that could be calculated from the financial statements (for example, rent payable in relation to current assets) may not be considered because there is no clear or meaningful relationship between the items.

There is no generally accepted list of ratios that can be applied to financial statements, nor is there a standard method of calculating many of them. Variations in both the choice of ratios and their precise definition will be found in the literature and in practice. However, it is important to be *consistent* in the way in which ratios are calculated for comparison purposes. The ratios discussed below are those that are widely used because many consider them to be among the more important for decision-making purposes.

Financial ratio classification

Ratios can be grouped into certain categories, each of which reflects a particular aspect of financial performance or position. The following broad categories provide a useful basis for explaining the nature of the financial ratios to be dealt with:

- *Profitability*.   Businesses come into being with the primary purpose of creating wealth for the owners. Profitability ratios provide an insight to the degree of success in achieving this purpose. They express the profits made (or figures bearing on profit, such as overheads) in relation to other key figures in the financial statements or to some business resource.

- *Efficiency.* Ratios may be used to measure the efficiency with which certain resources have been utilised within the business. These ratios are also referred to as **activity ratios**.
- *Liquidity.* We have seen in Chapter 2 that it is vital to the survival of a business that there be sufficient liquid resources available to meet maturing obligations. Certain ratios may be calculated that examine the relationship between liquid resources held and creditors due for payment in the near future.
- *Gearing.* This is the relationship between the amount financed by the owners of the business and the amount contributed by outsiders, which has an important effect on the degree of risk associated with a business. Gearing is thus something that managers must consider when making financing decisions.
- *Investment.* Certain ratios are concerned with assessing the returns and performance of shares held in a particular business.

We shall consider ratios falling into each of these categories later in this chapter.

●●●● The need for comparison

Calculating a ratio will not by itself tell you very much about the position or performance of a business. For example, if a ratio reveals that a business was generating £100 in sales per square metre of counter space, it would not be possible to deduce from this information alone whether this particular level of performance was good, bad or indifferent. It is only when you compare this ratio with some 'benchmark' that the information can be interpreted and evaluated.

| Activity 7.1 | Can you think of any bases that could be used to compare a ratio you have calculated from the financial statements of a particular period? |

In answering this activity you may have thought of the following bases:

- *Past periods.* By comparing the ratio you have calculated with the ratio of a previous period, it is possible to detect whether there has been an improvement or deterioration in performance. Indeed, it is often useful to track particular ratios over time (say, five or 10 years) in order to see whether it is possible to detect trends. However, the comparison of ratios from different time periods brings certain problems. In particular, there is always the possibility that trading conditions may have been quite different in the periods being compared. There is a further problem that when comparing the performance of a single business over time, operating inefficiencies may not be clearly exposed. For example, the fact that net profit per employee has risen by 10 per cent over the previous period may at first sight appear to be satisfactory, however, this may not be the case if similar businesses have shown an improvement of 50 per cent for the same period. Finally, there is the problem that inflation may have distorted the figures on which the ratios are based. As we shall see later, inflation can lead to an overstatement of profit and an understatement of asset values.

- *Planned performance.* Ratios may be compared with the targets that management developed before the commencement of the period under review. The comparison of planned performance with actual performance may therefore be a useful way of revealing the level of achievement attained. However, the planned levels of performance must be based on realistic assumptions if they are to be useful for comparison purposes.

- *Similar businesses.* In a competitive environment, a business must consider its performance in relation to those of other businesses operating in the same industry. Survival may depend on the ability to achieve comparable levels of performance. Thus, a useful basis for comparing a particular ratio is the ratio achieved by similar businesses during the same period. This basis is not, however, without its problems. Competitors may have different year-ends, and therefore trading conditions might not be identical. They may also have different accounting policies, which have a significant effect on reported profits and asset values (for example, different methods of calculating depreciation, different methods of valuing stock). Finally, it may be difficult to obtain the accounts of competitor businesses. Sole proprietorships and partnerships, for example, are not obliged to publish their financial statements. In the case of limited companies, there is a legal obligation to publish accounts, however, a diversified company may not provide a detailed breakdown of activities sufficient for analysts to compare with the activities of other businesses.

Key steps in financial ratio analysis

When employing financial ratios, a sequence of steps is carried out by an analyst. The first step involves identifying the key indicators and relationships that require examination. In order to carry out this step, the analyst must be clear *who* the target users are and *why* they need the information. Different types of users of financial information are likely to have different information needs that will, in turn, determine the ratios that they find useful. For example, shareholders are likely to be interested in their returns in relation to the level of risk associated with their investment. Thus, profitability, investment and gearing ratios will be of particular interest. Long-term lenders are concerned with the long-term viability of the business. In order to help them to assess this, the profitability ratios and gearing ratios of the business are also likely to be of particular interest. Short-term lenders, such as suppliers, may be interested in the ability of the business to repay the amounts owing in the short term. As a result, the liquidity ratios should be of interest.

The next step in the process is to calculate ratios that are considered appropriate for the particular users and the purpose for which they require the information.

The final step is interpretation and evaluation of the ratios. Interpretation involves examining the ratios in conjunction with an appropriate basis for comparison and any other information that may be relevant. The significance of the ratios calculated can then be established. Evaluation involves forming a judgement concerning the value of the information uncovered in the calculation and interpretation of the ratios. Whilst calculation is usually straightforward, and can be easily carried out by computer, the interpretation and evaluation are more difficult and often require high levels of skill. This skill can only really be acquired through much practice. The three steps described are shown in Figure 7.1.

Figure 7.1

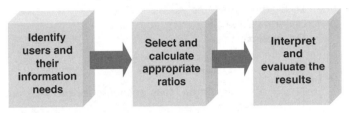

The key steps of financial ratio analysis

Identify users and their information needs → Select and calculate appropriate ratios → Interpret and evaluate the results

The three steps involve: firstly, identifying for whom and for what purpose the analysis and interpretation is required; secondly, selecting appropriate ratios and calculating them; and, finally, forming a judgement on the information produced.

The ratios calculated

Probably the best way to explain financial ratios is to work through an example. Example 7.1 provides a set of financial statements from which we can calculate important ratios in the subsequent sections.

Example 7.1

The following financial statements relate to Alexis plc, which owns a small chain of wholesale/retail carpet stores.

Balance sheets as at 31 March

	2001		2002	
	£000	£000	£000	£000
Fixed assets				
Freehold land and buildings at cost	451.2		451.2	
Less Accumulated depreciation	70.0	381.2	75.0	376.2
Fixtures and fittings at cost	129.0		160.4	
Less Accumulated depreciation	64.4	64.6	97.2	63.2
		445.8		439.4
Current assets				
Stock at cost	300.0		370.8	
Trade debtors	240.8		210.2	
Bank	3.4		3.0	
	544.2		584.0	
Creditors due within one year				
Trade creditors	(221.4)		(228.8)	
Dividends proposed	(40.2)		(60.0)	
Corporation tax due	(30.1)		(38.0)	
	(291.7)	252.5	(326.8)	257.2
		698.3		696.6

	2001 £000	2002 £000
Creditors due beyond one year		
12% debentures (secured)	200.0	60.0
	498.3	636.6
Capital and reserves		
£0.50 ordinary shares	300.0	334.1
General reserve	26.5	40.0
Retained profit	171.8	262.5
	498.3	636.6

Profit and loss accounts for the year ended 31 March

		2001		2002
	£000	£000	£000	£000
Sales		2,240.8		2,681.2
Less Cost of sales				
Opening stock	241.0		300.0	
Purchases	1,804.4		2,142.8	
	2,045.4		2,442.8	
Less closing stock	300.0	1,745.4	370.8	2,072.0
Gross profit		495.4		609.2
Wages and salaries	137.8		195.0	
Directors' salaries	48.0		80.6	
Rates	12.2		12.4	
Heat and light	8.4		13.6	
Insurance	4.6		7.0	
Postage and telephone	3.4		7.4	
Audit fees	5.6		9.0	
Depreciation:				
Freehold buildings	5.0		5.0	
Fixtures and fittings	27.0	252.0	32.8	362.8
Net profit before interest and tax		243.4		246.4
Less Interest payable		24.0		6.2
Net profit before tax		219.4		240.2
Less Corporation tax		60.2		76.0
Net profit after tax		159.2		164.2
Add Retained profit brought forward		52.8		171.8
		212.0		336.0
Less Transfer to general reserve		–		(13.5)
Dividends proposed		(40.2)		(60.0)
Retained profit carried forward		171.8		262.5

Cash flow statement for the year ended 31 March

		2001		2002
	£000	£000	£000	£000
Net cash inflow from operating activities		231.0		251.4
Returns on investments and servicing of finance				
Interest paid	(24.0)		(6.2)	
Net cash inflow (outflow) from returns on investments and servicing of finance		(24.0)		(6.2)

Taxation				
Corporation tax paid	(46.4)		(68.1)	
Tax paid		(46.4)		(68.1)
Capital expenditure				
Purchase of fixed assets	(121.2)		(31.4)	
Net cash inflow (outflow) from capital expenditure		(121.2)		(31.4)
Equity dividends				
Dividend on ordinary shares	(32.0)		(40.2)	
Net cash outflow for equity dividends		(32.0)		(40.2)
Management of liquid resources		–		–
Financing				
Issue of ordinary shares	20.0		34.1	
Repayment of loan capital	–	20.0	(140.0)	(105.9)
Increase (decrease) in cash and cash equivalents		27.4		(0.4)

The company has employed 14 staff in 2001 and 18 in 2002. All sales and purchases are made on credit. The market value of the shares of the company at the end of each year was £2.50 and £3.50 respectively. The issue of equity shares during the year ended 31 March 2002 occurred at the beginning of the year.

Profitability ratios

Ratio used to evaluate the profitability of a business include the following: return on ordinary shareholders' funds, return on capital employed, net profit margin, and gross profit margin. We shall look at all of these in turn.

Return on ordinary shareholders' funds (ROSF)

The **return on ordinary shareholders' funds** compares the amount of profit for the period available to the ordinary shareholders with the ordinary shareholders' stake in the business. For a limited company, the ratio (which is normally expressed in percentage terms) is as follows:

$$ROSF = \frac{\text{Net profit after taxation and preference dividend (if any)}}{\text{Ordinary share capital plus reserves}} \times 100\%$$

The net profit after taxation and any preference dividend is used in calculating the ratio, because this figure represents the amount of profit available to the ordinary shareholders.

In the case of Alexis plc, the ratio for the year ended 31 March 2001 is:

$$ROSF = \frac{159.2}{498.3} \times 100\%$$
$$= 31.9\%$$

Calculate the return on ordinary shareholders' funds for Alexis plc for the year to 31 March 2002.

The return on ordinary shareholders' funds for the year to 31 March 2002 will be:

$$\text{ROSF} = \frac{164.2}{636.6} \times 100\%$$

$$= 25.8\%$$

Note that in calculating the ROSF, the figure for ordinary shareholders' funds as at the end of the year has been used. However, it can be argued that it is preferable to use an average figure for the year as this would be more representative of the amount invested by ordinary shareholders during the period. The easiest approach to calculating the average ordinary shareholder investment would be to take a simple average based on the opening and closing figures for the year. However, where these figures are not available, it is usually acceptable to use the year-end figures, provided that this approach is consistently applied.

Return on capital employed (ROCE)

The **return on capital employed** is a fundamental measure of business performance. This ratio expresses the relationship between the net profit generated by the business and the long-term capital invested in the business. The ratio is expressed in percentage terms and is as follows:

$$\text{ROCE} = \frac{\text{Net profit before interest and taxation}}{\text{Share capital} + \text{Reserves} + \text{Long-term loans}} \times 100\%$$

Note, in this case, that the profit figure used in the ratio is the net profit *before* interest and taxation. This figure is used because the ratio attempts to measure the returns to all suppliers of long-term finance before any deductions for interest payable to lenders or payments of dividends to shareholders are made.

For the year to 31 March 2001, the ratio for Alexis plc is:

$$\text{ROCE} = \frac{243.4}{698.3} \times 100\%$$

$$= 34.9\%$$

Calculate the return on capital employed for Alexis plc for the year to 31 March 2002.

For the year ended 31 March 2002, the ratio is:

$$\text{ROCE} = \frac{246.4}{696.6} \times 100\%$$

$$= 35.4\%$$

ROCE is considered by many to be a primary measure of profitability. It compares inputs (capital invested) with outputs (profit). This comparison is of vital importance in assessing the effectiveness with which funds have been deployed.

Once again, an average figure for capital employed may be used where the information is available.

It is important to be clear about the distinction between ROSF and ROCE. Although both ROSF and ROCE measure returns on capital invested, ROSF is concerned with measuring the returns achieved by ordinary shareholders, whereas ROCE is concerned with measuring returns achieved from all the long-term capital invested.

Net profit margin

The **net profit margin** ratio relates the net profit for a period to the sales during that period. The ratio is expressed as:

$$\text{Net profit margin} = \frac{\text{Net profit before interest and taxation}}{\text{Sales}} \times 100\%$$

The net profit before interest and taxation is used in this ratio as it represents the profit from trading operations before any costs of servicing long-term finance are taken into account. This is often regarded as the most appropriate measure of operational performance for comparison purposes, because differences arising from the way in which a particular business is financed will not influence this measure. However, this is not the only way in which this ratio may be calculated in practice. The net profit after taxation is also used, on occasions, as the numerator (the top part of the fraction). The purpose for which the ratio is required will determine which form of calculation is appropriate.

For the year ended 31 March 2001, the net profit margin of Alexis plc (based on the net profit before interest and taxation) is:

$$\text{Net profit margin} = \frac{243.4}{2,240.8} \times 100\%$$

$$= 10.9\%$$

This ratio compares one output of the business (profit) with another output (sales). The ratio can vary considerably between types of business. For example, a supermarket will often operate on low prices and, therefore, low profit margins in order to stimulate sales and thereby increase the total amount of profit generated. A jeweller, on the other hand, may have a high net profit margin but have a much lower level of sales volume. Factors such as the degree of competition, the type of customer, the economic climate and industry characteristics (such as the level of risk) will influence the net profit margin of a business.

Activity 7.4

Calculate the net profit margin for Alexis plc for the year to 31 March 2002.

....

The net profit margin for the year to 31 March 2002 will be:

$$\text{Net profit margin} = \frac{246.4}{2,681.2} \times 100\%$$

$$= 9.2\%$$

Gross profit margin

→ The **gross profit margin** ratio relates the gross profit of the business to the sales generated for the same period. Gross profit represents the difference between sales value and the cost of sales. The ratio is therefore a measure of profitability in buying (or producing) and selling goods before any other expenses are taken into account. As cost of sales represents a major expense for retailing, wholesaling and manufacturing businesses, a change in this ratio can have a significant effect on the **bottom line** (that is, the net profit for the year). The gross profit ratio is calculated as follows:

$$\text{Gross profit margin} = \frac{\text{Gross profit}}{\text{Sales}} \times 100\%$$

For the year to 31 March 2001, the ratio for Alexis plc is:

$$\text{Gross profit margin} = \frac{495.4}{2,240.8} \times 100\%$$

$$= 22.1\%$$

Activity 7.5

Calculate the gross profit margin for Alexis plc for the year to 31 March 2002.

The gross profit margin for the year to 31 March 2002 is:

$$\text{Gross profit margin} = \frac{609.2}{2,681.2} \times 100\%$$

$$= 22.7\%$$

Thus the profitability ratios for Alexis plc over the two years can be set out as follows:

	2001	2002
ROSF	31.9%	25.8%
ROCE	34.9%	35.4%
Net profit margin	10.9%	9.2%
Gross profit margin	22.1%	22.7%

Activity 7.6

What do you deduce from a comparison of the profitability ratios of Alexis plc over the two years?

The gross profit margin shows a slight increase in 2002 over the previous year. This may be for a number of reasons, such as an increase in selling prices or a decrease in the cost of sales. However, the net profit margin has shown a slight decline over the period. This means that operating expenses (wages, rates, insurance and so on) are absorbing a greater proportion of sales income in 2002 than in the previous year.

The net profit available to ordinary shareholders has risen only slightly over the period, whereas the share capital and reserves of the company have increased considerably (see the financial statements). The effect of this has been to reduce the return on ordinary shareholders' funds. The return on capital employed has improved slightly in 2002. The slight decrease in long-term capital over the period and increase in net profit before interest and tax has resulted in a better return.

● ● ● ● Efficiency ratios

Ratios used to examine the efficiency with which various resources of the business are managed include the following: average stock turnover period, average settlement period for debtors, average settlement period for creditors, sales to capital employed, and sales per employee. We shall look at all of these in turn.

Average stock turnover period

Stocks often represent a significant investment for a business. For some types of business (for example, manufacturers), stocks may account for a substantial proportion of the total assets held. The **average stock turnover period** measures the average number of days for which stocks are being held. The ratio is calculated thus:

$$\text{Stock turnover period} = \frac{\text{Average stock held}}{\text{Cost of sales}} \times 365 \text{ days}$$

The average stock for the period can be calculated as a simple average of the opening and closing stock levels for the year. However, in the case of a highly seasonal business, where stock levels may vary considerably over the year, a monthly average may be more appropriate.

In the case of Alexis plc, the stock turnover period for the year ended 31 March 2001 is:

$$\text{Stock turnover period} = \frac{(241 + 300)/2}{1,745.4} \times 365 \text{ days}$$

$$= 57 \text{ days} \quad \text{(to nearest day)}$$

This means that, on average, the stock held is being 'turned over' every 57 days.

A business will normally prefer a low stock turnover period to a high period as funds tied up in stocks cannot be used for other profitable purposes. In judging the amount of stocks to carry, a business must consider such things as the likely future demand, the possibility of future shortages, the likelihood of future price rises, the amount of storage space available, and the perishability of the product. The management of stocks will be considered in more detail in Chapter 16.

The stock turnover period is sometimes expressed in terms of months rather than days. Multiplying by 12 rather than 365 will achieve this.

Activity 7.7

Calculate the average stock turnover period for Alexis plc for the year ended 31 March 2002.

....

The stock turnover period for the year to 31 March 2002 will be:

$$\text{Stock turnover period} = \frac{(300 + 370.8)/2}{2,072} \times 365 \text{ days}$$

$$= 59 \text{ days}$$

Average settlement period for debtors

A business will usually be concerned with how long it takes for customers to pay the amounts owing. The speed of payment can have a significant effect on the cash flows of the business. The **average settlement period for debtors** calculates how long, on average, credit customers take to pay the amounts they owe to the business. The ratio is as follows:

$$\text{Average settlement period} = \frac{\text{Trade debtors}}{\text{Credit sales}} \times 365 \text{ days}$$

We are told that all sales made by Alexis plc are on credit and so the average settlement period for debtors for the year ended 31 March 2001 is:

$$\text{Average settlement period} = \frac{240.8}{2,240.8} \times 365 \text{ days}$$

$$= 39 \text{ days}$$

As no figures for opening debtors are available, the year-end debtors figure only is used. This is common practice.

Activity 7.8	Calculate the average settlement period for debtors for Alexis plc for the year ended 31 March 2002. (For the sake of consistency, use the year-end debtors figure rather than an average figure.)

The average settlement period for the year to 2002 is:

$$\text{Average settlement period} = \frac{210.2}{2,681.2} \times 365 \text{ days}$$

$$= 29 \text{ days}$$

A business will normally prefer a shorter average settlement period to a longer one as, once again, funds are being tied up that may be used for more profitable purposes. Although this ratio can be useful, it is important to remember that it produces an *average* figure for the number of days that debts are outstanding. This average may be badly distorted by, for example, a few large customers who are very slow payers.

Average settlement period for creditors

The **average settlement period for creditors** tells us how long, on average, the business takes to pay its trade creditors. The ratio is calculated as follows:

$$\text{Average settlement period} = \frac{\text{Trade creditors}}{\text{Credit purchases}} \times 365 \text{ days}$$

For the year ended 31 March 2001, the average settlement period for Alexis plc is:

$$\text{Average settlement period} = \frac{221.4}{1,804.4} \times 365 \text{ days}$$

$$= 45 \text{ days}$$

Once again, the year-end figure rather than an average figure for creditors has been employed in the calculations.

Calculate the average settlement period for creditors for Alexis plc for the year ended 31 March 2002. (For the sake of consistency, use a year-end figure for creditors.)

The average settlement period for creditors is:

$$\text{Average settlement period} = \frac{228.8}{2,142.8} \times 365 \text{ days}$$

$$= 39 \text{ days}$$

This ratio provides an average figure, which, like the average settlement period for debtors ratio, can be distorted by the time taken to pay one or two large suppliers.

As trade creditors provide a free source of finance for the business, it is perhaps not surprising that some businesses attempt to increase their average settlement period for trade creditors. However, such a policy can be taken too far and can result in a loss of goodwill by suppliers. We shall return to the issues concerning the management of trade debtors and trade creditors in Chapter 16.

Sales to capital employed

The **sales to capital employed** ratio examines how effective the long-term capital employed of the business has been in generating sales revenue. It is calculated as follows:

Sales to capital employed ratio =

$$\frac{\text{Sales}}{\text{Long-term capital employed (that is, Shareholders' funds + Long-term loans)}}$$

For the year ended 31 March 2001, this ratio for Alexis plc is as follows:

$$\text{Sales to capital employed} = \frac{2,240.8}{(498.3 + 200.0)}$$

$$= 3.2 \text{ times}$$

Once again, year-end figures have been used, although an average figure for long-term capital employed could also be used if sufficient information was available.

Calculate the sales to long-term capital employed ratio for Alexis plc for the year ended 31 March 2002. (For the sake of consistency, use a year-end figure for capital employed.)

The sales to long-term capital employed ratio for the year ended 31 March 2002 will be:

$$\text{Sales to capital employed} = \frac{2,681.2}{(636.6 + 60.0)}$$

$$= 3.8 \text{ times}$$

Generally speaking, a higher ratio for sales to capital employed is preferred to a lower one. A higher ratio will normally suggest that the capital (as represented by the total assets less current liabilities) is being used more productively in the generation of revenue. However, a *very* high ratio may suggest that the business is undercapitalised – that is, it has insufficient long-term capital to support the level of sales achieved. When comparing this ratio between businesses, such factors as the age and condition of assets held, the valuation bases for assets, and whether assets are rented or purchased outright can affect the calculation of the capital employed figure (as represented by total assets less current liabilities) and can complicate interpretation.

A variation of this formula is to use the total assets less current liabilities (which is equivalent to long-term capital employed) in the denominator (the lower part of the fraction) – the identical result is obtained. This variation is sometimes referred to as the **net asset turnover ratio**.

Sales per employee

The **sales per employee** ratio relates sales generated to a particular business resource. It provides a measure of the productivity of the workforce. The ratio is:

$$\text{Sales per employee} = \frac{\text{Sales}}{\text{Number of employees}}$$

For the year ended 31 March 2001, the ratio for Alexis plc is:

$$\text{Sales per employee} = \frac{£2,240,800}{14}$$

$$= £160,057$$

It would also be possible to use other ratios, such as sales per square metre of floorspace or sales per member of the sales staff, in order to help assess productivity.

Activity 7.11

Calculate the sales per employee for Alexis plc for the year ended 31 March 2002.

The ratio for the year ended 31 March 2002 is:

$$\text{Sales per employee} = \frac{£2,681,200}{18}$$

$$= £148,956$$

Thus the activity ratios for Alexis plc may be summarised as follows:

	2001	2002
Stock turnover period	57 days	59 days
Average settlement period for debtors	39 days	29 days
Average settlement period for creditors	45 days	39 days
Sales to capital employed	3.2 times	3.8 times
Sales per employee	£160,057	£148,956

Activity 7.12

What do you deduce from a comparison of the efficiency ratios of Alexis plc over the two years?

A comparison of the efficiency ratios between years provides a mixed picture. The average settlement period for both debtors and creditors has reduced. The reduction may have been the result of deliberate policy decisions – for example, tighter credit control for debtors, or paying creditors promptly in order to maintain goodwill or to take advantage of discounts. However, it must always be remembered that these ratios are *average* figures and therefore may be distorted by a few exceptional amounts owed to, or owed by, a company.

The stock turnover period has shown a slight increase over the period but this may not be significant. Overall, there has been an increase in the sales to capital employed ratio, which means that the sales have increased by a greater proportion than the capital employed by the company. Sales per employee, however, have declined and the reasons for this should be investigated.

Relationship between profitability and efficiency

In our earlier discussions concerning profitability ratios, you will recall that return on capital employed (ROCE) is regarded as a key ratio by many businesses. The ratio is:

$$\text{ROCE} = \frac{\text{Net profit before interest and taxation}}{\text{Long-term capital employed}} \times 100\%$$

(where long-term capital employed comprises share capital plus reserves plus

Figure 7.2

The main elements comprising the ROCE ratio

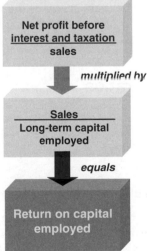

The ROCE ratio can be divided into two main elements: net profit to sales and sales to capital employed. By analysing ROCE in this way, we can see the influence of both profitability and efficiency on this important ratio.

long-term loans). This ratio can be broken down into two elements, as shown in Figure 7.2.

The first ratio is, of course the net profit margin ratio and the second ratio is the sales to capital employed ratio that we discussed earlier. By breaking down the ROCE ratio in this manner, we highlight the fact that the overall return on funds employed within the business will be determined both by the profitability of sales and by the efficiency in the use of capital.

Example 7.2

Consider the following information concerning two different businesses, A and B, operating in the same industry:

	Business	
	A	B
Profit before interest and tax	£20m	£15m
Long-term capital employed	£100m	£75m
Sales	£200m	£300m

The ROCE for each business is identical (20 per cent). However, the manner in which the return was achieved by each business was quite different. In the case of business A, the net profit margin is 10 per cent and the sales to capital employed is two times (hence ROCE = [10% × 2] = 20%). In the case of business B, the net profit margin is 5 per cent and the sales to capital employed ratio is four times (hence ROCE = [5% × 4] = 20%).

Example 7.2 demonstrates that a relatively low net-profit margin can be compensated for by a relatively high sales to capital employed ratio, and a relatively low sales to capital employed ratio can be compensated for by a relatively high net profit margin. In many areas of retail and distribution (for example, supermarkets and delivery services) the net profit margins are quite low but the ROCE can be high, provided that the capital employed is used productively.

Liquidity ratios

There is a number of liquidity ratios, each of which is described further below: the current ratio, the acid test ratio, and the operating cash flows to maturing obligations ratio.

Current ratio

The **current ratio** compares the 'liquid' assets (cash and those assets held that will soon be turned into cash) of a business with the current liabilities (creditors due within one year). The ratio is calculated as follows:

$$\text{Current ratio} = \frac{\text{Current assets}}{\text{Current liabilities (creditors due within one year)}}$$

For the year ended 31 March 2001, the current ratio of Alexis plc is:

$$\text{Current ratio} = \frac{544.2}{291.7}$$

$$= 1.9 \text{ times}$$

The ratio reveals that the current assets cover the current liabilities by 1.9 times.

In some texts the notion of an 'ideal' current ratio (usually two times) is suggested for businesses. However, this fails to take into account the fact that different types of business require different current ratios. For example, a manufacturing business will often have a relatively high current ratio because it is necessary to hold stocks of finished goods, raw materials and work in progress. It will also normally sell goods on credit, thereby incurring debtors. A supermarket chain, on the other hand, will have a relatively low current ratio as it will hold only fast-moving stocks of finished goods and will generate mostly cash sales (see Exhibit 7.1).

The higher the ratio, the more liquid the business is considered to be. As liquidity is vital to the survival of a business, a higher current ratio is normally preferred to a lower one. However, if a business has a *very* high ratio, this might suggest that funds are being tied up in cash or other liquid assets and are not being used as productively as they might otherwise be.

Activity 7.13

Calculate the current ratio for Alexis plc for the year ended 31 March 2002.

The current ratio for the year ended 31 March 2002 is:

$$\text{Current ratio} = \frac{584.0}{326.8}$$

$$= 1.8 \text{ times}$$

Acid test ratio

The **acid test ratio** represents a more stringent test of liquidity. It can be argued that, for many businesses, the stock in hand cannot be converted into cash quickly. (Note that, in the case of Alexis plc, the stock turnover period was more than 50 days in both years). As a result, it may be better to exclude this particular asset from any measure of liquidity. The acid test ratio is based on this idea and is calculated as follows:

$$\text{Acid test ratio} = \frac{\text{Current assets (excluding stock)}}{\text{Current liabilities (creditors due within one year)}}$$

The acid test ratio for Alexis plc for the year ended 31 March 2001 is:

$$\text{Acid test ratio} = \frac{(544.2 - 300)}{291.7}$$

$$= 0.8 \text{ times}$$

We can see that the 'liquid' current assets do not quite cover the current liabilities, and so the business may be experiencing some liquidity problems. In some types of business, however, where a pattern of strong positive cash flows exists, it is not unusual for the acid test ratio to be below 1.0 without causing liquidity problems (see Exhibit 7.1).

The current and acid test ratios of Alexis plc for 2001 can be expressed as 1.9 : 1 and 0.8 : 1 respectively, rather than as a number of times. This form can be found in some texts. The interpretation of the ratios, however, will not be affected by this difference in form.

Exhibit 7.1

The average current ratio and average acid test ratio for UK listed companies operating in various industrial sectors is given below.

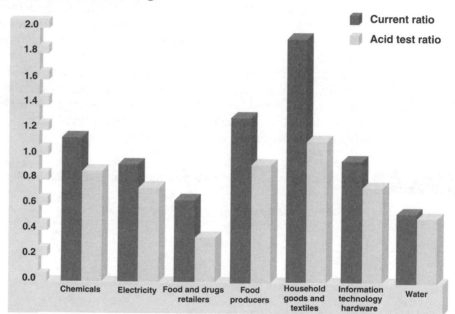

It is interesting to note that nearly all of the sectors reveal an average acid test ratio of less than 1.0 and that some sectors reveal an average current ratio of less than 1.0.

Source: Adapted from Datastream data, February 2001.

Activity 7.14

Calculate the acid test ratio for Alexis plc for the year ended 31 March 2002.

The acid test ratio for the year ended 31 March 2002 is:

$$\text{Acid test ratio} = \frac{(584.0 - 370.8)}{326.8}$$

$$= 0.7 \text{ times}$$

Both the current ratio and acid test ratio derive the relevant figures from the balance sheet. As the balance sheet is simply a 'snapshot' of the financial position of the business at a single moment in time, care must be taken when interpreting the ratios. It is possible that the balance sheet figures are not representative of the liquidity position during the year. This may be owing to exceptional factors or simply to the fact that the business is seasonal in nature and the balance sheet figures represent the cash position at just one particular point in the cycle.

Operating cash flows to maturing obligations

→ The **operating cash flows to maturing obligations** ratio compares the operating cash flows to the current liabilities of the business. It provides a further indication of the ability of the business to meet its maturing obligations. The ratio is expressed as:

$$\text{Operating cash flows to maturing obligations} = \frac{\text{Operating cash flows}}{\text{Current liabilities}}$$

The higher this ratio, the better the liquidity of the business. This ratio has the advantage that the operating cash flows for a period usually provide a more reliable guide to the liquidity of a business than the current assets held at the balance sheet date. The ratio for the year ended 31 March 2001 of Alexis plc is:

$$\text{Operating cash flows to maturing obligations} = \frac{231.0}{291.7}$$

$$= 0.8 \text{ times}$$

This ratio indicates that the operating cash flows for the period are not sufficient to cover the current liabilities at the end of the period.

Activity 7.15	Calculate the operating cash flows to maturing obligations ratio for Alexis plc for the year ended 31 March 2002.

The ratio is:

$$\text{Operating cash flow to maturing obligations} = \frac{251.4}{326.8}$$

$$= 0.8 \text{ times}$$

Thus, the liquidity ratios for Alexis plc for the two-year period may be summarised as follows:

	2001	2002
Current ratio	1.9	1.8
Acid test ratio	0.8	0.7
Operating cash flows to maturing obligations	0.8	0.8

Activity 7.16	What do you deduce from a comparison of the liquidity ratios of Alexis plc over the two years?

The table above reveals a decrease in both the current ratio and the acid test ratio. These changes suggest a worsening liquidity position for the business. The company must monitor its liquidity carefully and be alert to any further deterioration in these ratios. The operating cash flows to maturing obligations ratio has not changed over the period. This ratio is quite low and reveals that the cash flows for the period do not cover the maturing obligations. This ratio should give some cause for concern.

Gearing ratios

Financial gearing occurs when a business is financed, at least in part, by contributions from outside parties. The level of gearing (that is, the extent to which a business is financed by outside parties) is often an important factor in assessing risk. Where a business borrows heavily, it takes on a commitment to pay interest charges and make capital repayments. This can be a significant financial burden and can increase the risk of a business becoming insolvent. Nevertheless, it is the case that most businesses are geared to a greater or lesser extent.

Given the risks involved, you may wonder why a business would want to take on gearing. One reason may be that the owners have insufficient funds and, therefore, the only way to finance the business adequately is to borrow from others. Another reason may be that loan interest is an allowable charge against tax (whereas dividends paid to shareholders are not), and this can reduce the costs of financing the business. A third reason may be that gearing can be used to increase the returns to owners. This is possible provided that the returns generated from borrowed funds exceed the cost of paying interest. Example 7.3 can be used to illustrate this point.

| Example 7.3 | Two companies X Ltd and Y Ltd commence business with the following long-term capital structures: |

	X Ltd	Y Ltd
	£	£
£1 ordinary shares	100,000	200,000
10% loan	200,000	100,000
	300,000	300,000

In the first year of operations they both make a profit before interest and taxation of £50,000.

Although both companies have the same total long-term capital employed, the mix of funding is quite different. X Ltd would be considered highly geared as it has a high proportion of borrowed funds in its long-term capital structure; Y Ltd is much lower geared. The profit available to the shareholders of each company in the first year of operations will be:

	X Ltd	Y Ltd
	£	£
Profit before interest and taxation	50,000	50,000
Interest payable	(20,000)	(10,000)
Profit before taxation	30,000	40,000
Taxation (30%)	(9,000)	(12,000)
Profit available to ordinary shareholders	21,000	28,000

The return on ordinary shareholders' funds for each company will be:

$$\text{X Ltd: } \frac{£21,000}{£100,000} \times 100\% = 21.0\%$$

$$\text{Y Ltd: } \frac{£28,000}{£200,000} \times 100\% = 14.0\%$$

We can see that X Ltd, the more highly geared company, has generated a better return on ordinary shareholders' funds than Y Ltd.

One particular effect of gearing is that returns to ordinary shareholders become more sensitive to changes in profits. For a highly geared company, a change in profits can lead to a proportionately greater change in the returns to ordinary shareholders.

Activity 7.17

Assume that the profit before interest and tax was 20 per cent higher for each company than stated above. What would be the effect of this on the return on ordinary shareholders' funds?

The revised profit available to the shareholders of each company in the first year of operations will be:

	X Ltd £	Y Ltd £
Profit before interest and taxation	60,000	60,000
Interest payable	(20,000)	(10,000)
Profit before taxation	40,000	50,000
Taxation (30%)	(12,000)	(15,000)
Profit available to ordinary shareholders	28,000	35,000

The return on ordinary shareholders' funds for each company will now be:

$$\text{X Ltd: } \frac{£28,000}{£100,000} \times 100\% = 28.0\%$$

$$\text{Y Ltd: } \frac{£35,000}{£200,000} \times 100\% = 17.5\%$$

We can see in Activity 7.17 that, for X Ltd, the higher-geared company, the returns to ordinary shareholders have increased by 33 per cent, whereas for the lower geared company the benefit of gearing is less pronounced; the increase in the returns to equity for Y Ltd has only been 25 per cent. The effect of gearing can, of course, work in both directions. Thus, for a highly geared company a small decline in profits may bring about a much greater decline in the returns to ordinary shareholders. This means that gearing increases the potential for greater returns to ordinary shareholders but also increases the level of risk that they must bear.

The effect of gearing is like that of two intermeshing cogs of unequal size (see Figure 7.3). The movement in the larger cog (profit before interest and tax) causes a more than proportionate movement in the smaller cog (returns to ordinary shareholders).

Gearing ratio

The **gearing ratio** measures the contribution of long-term lenders to the long-term capital structure of a business. It is calculated as follows:

$$\text{Gearing ratio} = \frac{\text{Long-term liabilities}}{\text{Share capital} + \text{Reserves} + \text{Long-term liabilities}} \times 100\%$$

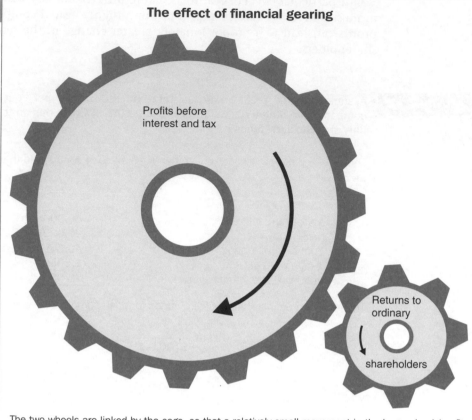

Figure 7.3

The effect of financial gearing

Profits before interest and tax

Returns to ordinary shareholders

The two wheels are linked by the cogs, so that a relatively small movement in the large wheel (profit before interest and tax) leads to a relatively large circular movement in the small wheel (returns to ordinary shareholders).

The gearing ratio for Alexis plc for the year ended 31 March 2001 is:

$$\text{Gearing ratio} = \frac{200}{(498.3 + 200)} \times 100\%$$

$$= 28.6\%$$

This ratio reveals a level of gearing that would not normally be considered to be very high. However, in deciding what an acceptable level of gearing might be, we should consider the likely future pattern and growth of profits and cash flows. A business that has profits and cash flows that are stable or growing is likely to feel more comfortable about taking on higher levels of gearing than a business that has a volatile pattern of cash flows and profit. This is because the consequences of defaulting on payments of interest, or repayments of capital, are likely to be very serious for the business.

Activity 7.18

Calculate the gearing ratio of Alexis plc for the year ended 31 March 2002.

The gearing ratio will be:

$$\text{Gearing ratio} = \frac{60}{(636.6 + 60)} \times 100\%$$

$$= 8.6\%$$

This ratio reveals (by comparison with the 2001 result above) a substantial fall in the level of gearing over the year for the company.

Interest cover ratio

➔ The **interest cover ratio** measures the amount of profit available to cover the interest payable. The ratio may be calculated as follows:

$$\text{Interest cover ratio} = \frac{\text{Profit before interest and taxation}}{\text{Interest payable}}$$

The ratio for Alexis plc for the year ended 31 March 2001 is:

$$\text{Interest cover ratio} = \frac{(219.4 + 24)}{24}$$

$$= 10.1 \text{ times}$$

This ratio shows that the level of profit is considerably higher than the level of interest payable. Thus, a significant fall in profits could occur before profit levels failed to cover interest payable. The lower the level of profit coverage, the greater the risk to lenders that interest payments will not be met.

Activity 7.19

Calculate the interest cover ratio of Alexis plc for the year ended 31 March 2002.

....

The interest cover ratio for the year ended 31 March 2002 is:

$$\text{Interest cover ratio} = \frac{(240.2 + 6.2)}{6.2}$$

$$= 39.7 \text{ times}$$

Activity 7.20

What do you deduce from a comparison of the gearing ratios over the two years?

....

The gearing ratios are:

	2001	2002
Gearing ratio	28.6%	8.6%
Interest cover ratio	10.1 times	39.7 times

Both the gearing ratio and interest cover ratio have improved significantly in 2002. This is owing mainly to the fact that a substantial part of the long-term loan was repaid during 2002. This repayment has had the effect of reducing the relative contribution of long-term lenders to the financing of the company and reducing the amount of interest payable.

The gearing ratio at the end of 2002 would normally be considered to be very low and may indicate that the business has some debt capacity (that is, it is capable of borrowing more if required). However, other factors such as the availability of adequate security and profitability must also be taken into account before the debt capacity of a business can be properly assessed.

●●●● Investment ratios

There are various ratios available that are designed to help investors who hold shares in a company to assess the returns on their investment. We consider some of these ratios next.

Dividend per share

→ The **dividend per share** ratio relates the dividends announced during a period to the number of shares in issue during that period. The ratio is calculated as follows:

$$\text{Dividend per share} = \frac{\text{Dividends announced during the period}}{\text{Number of shares in issue}}$$

In essence, the ratio provides an indication of the cash return that a shareholder receives from holding shares in a company. Although it is a useful measure, it must always be remembered that the dividends received will usually only represent a partial measure of return to investors. Dividends are usually only a proportion of the total earnings generated by a company and available to shareholders. A company may decide to plough back some of its earnings into the business in order to achieve future growth. These ploughed-back profits also belong to the shareholders and should, in principle, increase the value of the shares held.

When assessing the total returns to investors, we must take account of both the cash returns received *plus* any change in the market value of the shares held.

The dividend per share for Alexis plc for the year ended 31 March 2001 is:

$$\text{Dividend per share} = \frac{40.2}{600} \text{ (that is, £0.50 shares and £300 share capital)}$$
$$= 6.7\text{p}$$

This ratio can be calculated for each class of share issued by a company. Alexis plc has only ordinary shares in issue and therefore only one dividend per share ratio can be calculated.

Activity 7.21

Calculate the dividend per share of Alexis plc for the year ended 31 March 2002.

....

The dividend per share for the year ended 31 March 2002 is:

$$\text{Dividend per share} = \frac{60.0}{668.2}$$
$$= 9.0\text{p}$$

Dividends per share can vary considerably between companies. A number of factors will influence the amount that a company is willing or able to issue in the form of dividends to shareholders. These factors include:

- The profit available for distribution to investors.
- The future expenditure commitments of the company.
- The expectations of shareholders concerning the level of dividend payment.
- The cash available for dividend distribution.

Comparing dividend per share between companies is not always useful as there may be differences between the nominal value of shares issued. However, it is often useful to monitor the trend of dividends per share for a company over a period of time.

Dividend payout ratio

The **dividend payout ratio** measures the proportion of earnings that a company pays out to shareholders in the form of dividends. The ratio is calculated as follows:

$$\text{Dividend payout ratio} = \frac{\text{Dividends announced for the year}}{\text{Earnings for the year available for dividends}} \times 100\%$$

In the case of ordinary (equity) shares, the earnings available for dividend will normally be the net profit after taxation and after any preference dividends announced during the period. This ratio is normally expressed as a percentage.

The dividend payout ratio for Alexis plc for the year ended 31 March 2001 is:

$$\text{Dividend payout ratio} = \frac{40.2}{159.2} \times 100\%$$
$$= 25.3\%$$

The information provided by this ratio is often expressed slightly differently as the **dividend cover ratio**. Here, the calculation is the inverse of the dividend payout ratio:

$$\text{Dividend cover ratio} = \frac{\text{Earnings for the year available for dividend}}{\text{Dividend announced for the year}}$$

In the case of Alexis plc, it would be (159.2/40.2) = 3.96 times. That is to say, the earnings available for dividend cover the amount announced by nearly four times.

Activity 7.22

Calculate the dividend payout ratio of Alexis plc for the year ended 31 March 2002.

....

The dividend payout ratio for the year ended 31 March 2002 is:

$$\text{Dividend payout ratio} = \frac{60.0}{164.2} \times 100\%$$
$$= 36.5\%$$

Dividend yield ratio

⊙ The **dividend yield ratio** relates the cash return from a share to its current market value. This can help investors to assess the cash return on their investment in the company. The ratio is calculated as:

$$\text{Dividend yield} = \frac{\text{Dividend per share}/(1-t)}{\text{Market value per share}} \times 100\%$$

where t is the 'lower' rate of income tax. The numerator (the top part) of this ratio requires some explanation. In the UK, investors who receive a dividend from a company also receive a tax credit. This tax credit is equal to the amount of tax that would be payable on the dividends received by a lower-rate income-tax payer. As this tax credit can be offset against any tax liability arising from the dividends received, this means that the dividends are in effect issued net of tax to lower-rate income-tax payers.

Investors may wish to compare the returns from shares with the returns from other forms of investment. As these other forms of investment are often quoted on a 'gross' (pre-tax) basis, it is useful to 'gross up' the dividend in order to make comparison easier. This can be done by dividing the dividend per share by $(1 - t)$.

Assuming a lower rate of income tax of 10 per cent, the dividend yield for Alexis plc for the year ended 31 March 2001 is:

$$\text{Dividend yield} = \frac{£0.067^*/(1-0.10)}{£2.50} \times 100\%$$

$$= 3.0\%$$

$$* \; \frac{\text{Dividend proposed}}{\text{Number of shares}} = \frac{£40.2}{300.0 \times 2} = £0.067 \text{ dividend per share}$$

(The 300.0 is multiplied by 2 because they are £0.50 shares.)

| Activity 7.23 | **Calculate the dividend yield for Alexis plc for the year ended 31 March 2002.** |

The dividend yield for the year ended 31 March 2002 is:

$$\text{Dividend yield} = \frac{£0.09^*/(1-0.10)}{£3.50} \times 100\%$$

$$= 2.9\%$$

$$* \; \frac{£60.0}{334.1 \times 2} = £0.09$$

Earnings per share (EPS)

⊙ The **earnings per share** (EPS) relates the earnings generated by the company during a period and available to shareholders to the number of shares in issue. For ordinary shareholders, the amount available will be represented by the net profit after tax (less any preference dividend where applicable). The ratio for ordinary shareholders is calculated as follows:

$$\text{Earnings per share} = \frac{\text{Earnings available to ordinary shareholders}}{\text{Number of ordinary shares in issue}}$$

In the case of Alexis plc, the earnings per share for the year ended 31 March 2001 will be as follows:

$$\text{Earnings per share} = \frac{£159.2}{600}$$

$$= 26.5\text{p}$$

The EPS is regarded by many investment analysts as a fundamental measure of share performance. The trend in earnings per share over time is used to help assess the investment potential of a company's shares.

Although it is possible to make total profits rise through ordinary shareholders investing more in a company, this will not necessarily mean that the profitability *per share* will rise as a result.

Activity 7.24

Calculate the earnings per share of Alexis plc for the year ended 31 March 2002.

......

The earnings per share for the year ended 31 March 2002 will be:

$$\text{Earnings per share} = \frac{£164.2}{668.2}$$

$$= 24.6\text{p}$$

In the case of Alexis plc, the new issue of shares occurred at the beginning of the financial year. Where an issue is made part-way through the year, a weighted average of the shares in issue will be taken based on the date at which the new share issue took place.

It is not usually very helpful to compare the earnings per share from one company to another. Differences in capital structures can render any such comparison meaningless. However, like dividend per share, it can be very useful to monitor the changes that occur in this ratio for a particular company over time.

Operating cash flow per share

It can be argued that, in the short run at least, operating cash flows provide a better guide to the ability of a company to pay dividends and to undertake planned expenditures than the earnings per share figure. The **operating cash flow (OCF) per ordinary share** is calculated as follows:

$$\text{OCF per ordinary share} = \frac{\text{Operating cash flows} - \text{Preference dividends (if any)}}{\text{Number of ordinary shares in issue}}$$

The ratio for Alexis plc for the year ended 31 March 2001 is as follows:

$$\text{OCF per share} = \frac{£231.0}{600.0}$$

$$= 38.5\text{p}$$

Calculate the OCF per ordinary share for Alexis plc for the year ended 31 March 2002.

The OCF per share for the year ended 31 March 2002 is:

$$\text{OCF per share} = \frac{£251.4}{668.2}$$

$$= 37.6p$$

There has been a slight decline in this ratio over the two-year period.

Note that, for both years, the operating cash flow per share for Alexis plc is higher than the earnings per share. This is not unusual. The effect of adding back depreciation in order to derive operating cash flows will often ensure that a higher figure is derived.

Price/earnings (P/E) ratio

The **price/earnings ratio** relates the market value of a share to the earnings per share. This ratio can be calculated as follows:

$$\text{P/E ratio} = \frac{\text{Market value per share}}{\text{Earnings per share}}$$

The EPS figure for Alexis plc was calculated earlier in this chapter for the year to 31 March 2001 as 26.5p. The P/E ratio for Alexis plc for that year can be calculated thus:

$$\text{P/E ratio} = \frac{£2.50}{£0.265}$$

$$= 9.4 \text{ times}$$

This ratio reveals that the capital value of the share is 9.4 times higher than its current level of earnings.

The ratio is, in essence, a measure of market confidence in the future of a company. The higher the P/E ratio, the greater the confidence in the future earning power of the company and, consequently, the more that investors are prepared to pay in relation to the earnings stream of the company.

Price/earnings ratios provide a useful guide to market confidence concerning the future, and therefore they can be helpful when comparing different companies. However, differences in accounting conventions between businesses can lead to different profit and earnings-per-share figures, and this can distort comparisons.

Calculate the P/E ratio of Alexis plc for the year ended 31 March 2002.

The P/E ratio for the year ended 31 March 2002 is:

$$\text{P/E ratio} = \frac{£3.50}{£0.246}$$

$$= 14.2 \text{ times}$$

Thus, the investment ratios for Alexis plc over the two-year period are as follows:

	2001	2002
Dividend per share	6.7p	9.0p
Dividend payout ratio	25.3%	36.5%
Dividend yield ratio	3.0%	2.9%
Earnings per share	26.5p	24.6p
Operating cash flow per share	38.5p	37.6p
Price/earnings ratio	9.4 times	14.2 times

Activity 7.27

What do you deduce from the investment ratios set out above?

There has been a significant increase in the dividend per share in 2002 when compared with the previous year. The dividend payout ratio reveals that this can be attributed, at least in part, to an increase in the proportion of earnings distributed to ordinary shareholders. However, the payout ratio for the year ended 31 March 2002 is still fairly low. Only about one third of earnings available for dividend is being distributed. The dividend yield has changed very little over the period and remains fairly low.

Earnings per share show a slight fall in 2002 when compared with the previous year. A slight fall also occurs in the operating cash flows per share. However, the price/earnings ratio shows a significant improvement. The market is clearly much more confident about the future prospects of the business at 31 March 2002 than it had been 12 months earlier.

Exhibit 7.2 gives some information about the shares of several large food retailers and Exhibit 7.3 shows how investment ratios can vary between different industry sectors.

Exhibit 7.2

The following shares were extracted from the *Financial Times* of 8 December 2000, relating to the previous day's trading on the London Stock Exchange:

Retail food Share	Price	(+/−)	52 week High	52 week Low	Volume 000s	Y'ld Gr's	P/E
Iceland	334	+3	$345\frac{1}{2}$	228	7,828	2.0	15.0
Safeway	300	−6	335	147	6,221	2.9	16.3
Sainsbury	394	$+11\frac{1}{4}$	438	237	6,815	3.6	22.5
Somerfield	$85\frac{1}{2}$	$-\frac{1}{2}$	$97\frac{1}{2}$	45	3,121	1.8	7.4
Tesco	$270\frac{1}{4}$	$+7\frac{1}{4}$	$292\frac{1}{2}$	$153\frac{1}{2}$	30,001	1.7	25.2

The column headings are as follows:

Price	Mid-market price (that is, the price midway between buying and selling price) of the stock at the end of 7 December 2000.
(+/−)	Gain or loss (usually stated in pence) from the previous day's mid-market price.
High/Low	Highest and lowest prices reached by the share during the year (stated in pence).
Volume	The number of shares (in thousands) that were bought and sold on 7 December 2000.

Exhibit 7.3

Investment ratios can vary significantly between industries. To give you some indication of the variation that occurs, the average dividend yield ratio and the P/E ratio for Stock Exchange listed companies falling within 12 different industries are shown below in the charts. The relevant financial information was derived from that available in the *Financial Times* of 8 December 2000.

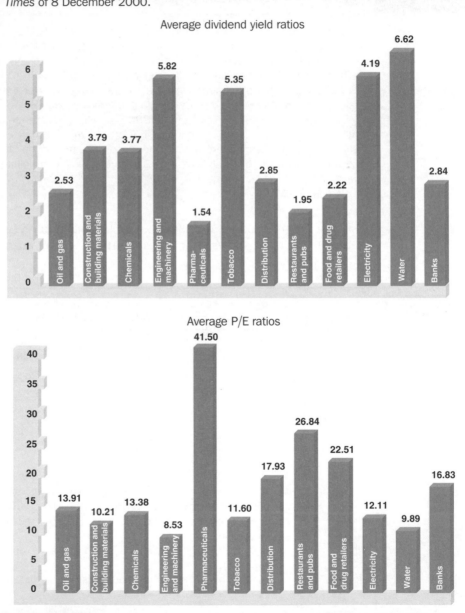

Average dividend yield ratios

Average P/E ratios

A plc and B plc operate electrical wholesale stores in the south of England. The accounts of each company for the year ended 30 June 2001 are as follows:

Balance sheets as at 30 June 2001

	A plc		B plc	
	£000	£000	£000	£000
Fixed assets				
Freehold land and buildings at cost	436.0		615.0	
Less Accumulated depreciation	76.0	360.0	105.0	510.0
Fixtures and fittings at cost	173.4		194.6	
Less Accumulated depreciation	86.4	87.0	103.4	91.2
		447.0		601.2
Current assets				
Stock at cost	592.0		403.0	
Debtors	176.4		321.9	
Cash at bank	84.6		91.6	
	853.0		816.5	
Creditors due within one year				
Trade creditors	(271.4)		(180.7)	
Dividends	(135.0)		(95.0)	
Corporation tax	(16.0)		(17.4)	
	(422.4)	430.6	(293.1)	523.4
		877.6		1,124.6
Creditors due beyond one year				
Debentures		(190.0)		(250.0)
		687.6		874.6
Capital and reserves				
£1 ordinary shares		320.0		250.0
General reserves		355.9		289.4
Retained profit		11.7		335.2
		687.6		874.6

Trading and profit and loss accounts for the year ended 30 June 2001

	A plc		B plc	
	£000	£000	£000	£000
Sales		1,478.1		1,790.4
Less Cost of sales				
Opening stock	480.8		372.6	
Purchases	1,129.5		1,245.3	
	1,610.3		1,617.9	
Less closing stock	592.0	1,018.3	403.0	1,214.9
Gross profit		459.8		575.5
Wages and salaries	150.4		189.2	
Directors salaries	45.4		96.2	
Rates	28.5		15.3	
Heat and light	15.8		17.2	
Insurance	18.5		26.8	
Postage and telephone	12.4		15.9	

	£000	£000	£000	£000
Audit fees	11.0		12.3	
Depreciation:				
Freehold buildings	8.8		12.9	
Fixtures and fittings	17.7	308.5	22.8	408.6
Net profit before interest and tax		151.3		166.9
Less Interest charges		19.4		27.5
Net profit before tax		131.9		139.4
Corporation tax		(32.0)		(34.8)
Net profit after taxation		99.9		104.6
Add Retained profit brought forward		46.8		325.6
		146.7		430.2
Dividends proposed		(135.0)		(95.0)
Retained profit carried forward		11.7		335.2

All purchases and sales are on credit. The market values of the shares in each company at the end of the year were £6.50 and £8.20 respectively.

Required:
For each company, calculate two ratios that are concerned with each of liquidity, gearing and investment (six ratios in total). What can you conclude from the ratios you have calculated?

●●●● Financial ratios and the problem of overtrading

➔ **Overtrading** occurs where a business is operating at a level of activity that cannot be supported by the amount of finance that has been committed. This situation usually reflects a poor level of financial control over the business. The reasons for overtrading are varied. It may occur in young, expanding businesses that fail to prepare adequately for the rapid increase in demand for its goods or services. It may also occur in businesses where the managers may have miscalculated the level of expected sales demand or have failed to control escalating project costs. It may occur as a result of a fall in the value of money (inflation), causing more finance to be committed to stock in trade and debtors, even where there is no expansion in the real volume of trade. It may occur where the owners are unable both to inject further funds into the business and to persuade others to invest in the business. Whatever the reason for overtrading, the problems that it brings must be dealt with if the business is to survive over the longer term.

Overtrading results in liquidity problems such as exceeding borrowing limits, or slow repayment of lenders and creditors. It can also result in suppliers withholding supplies, thereby making it difficult to meet customer needs. The managers of the business might be forced to direct all their efforts to dealing with immediate and pressing problems, such as finding cash to meet interest charges due or paying wages. Longer-term planning becomes difficult and managers may spend their time going from crisis to crisis. At the extreme, a business may collapse because it cannot meet its maturing obligations.

In order to deal with the overtrading problem, a business must ensure that the finance available is commensurate with the level of operations. Thus, if a business that is overtrading is unable to raise new finance, it should cut back its level of operations in line with the finance available. Although this may mean lost sales and lost profits in the short term, it may be necessary to ensure survival over the longer term.

Activity 7.28

If a business is overtrading, do you think the following ratios would be higher or lower than normally expected?

(a) Current ratio
(b) Average stock turnover period
(c) Average settlement period for debtors
(d) Average settlement period for creditors.

....

Your answer should be as follows:

(a) The current ratio would be lower than normally expected. This is a measure of liquidity, and lack of liquidity is an important symptom of overtrading.
(b) The average stock turnover period would be lower than normally expected. Where a business is overtrading, the level of stocks held will be low because of the problems of financing stocks. In the short term, sales may not be badly affected by the low stock levels and therefore stocks will be turned over more quickly.
(c) The average settlement period for debtors may be lower than normally expected. Where a business is suffering from liquidity problems it may chase debtors more vigorously so as to improve cash flows.
(d) The average settlement period for creditors may be higher than normally expected. The business may try to delay payments to creditors because of the liquidity problems arising.

Trend analysis

It is important to see whether there are trends occurring that can be detected from the use of ratios. Thus, key ratios can be plotted on a graph to provide users with a simple visual display of changes occurring over time. The trends occurring within a company may be plotted against those occurring within the industry as a whole for comparison purposes. An example of trend analysis is shown in Figure 7.4.

Some companies publish key financial ratios as part of their annual accounts in order to help users identify important trends. Exhibit 7.4 shows ratios for a 10-year period for Tate & Lyle plc, as taken from its 2000 annual accounts.

Exhibit 7.4

The following ratios, covering the period 1991–2000 are included in the annual accounts of Tate & Lyle plc, the food ingredients business.

Business Ratios

	1991	1992	1993	1994	1995	1996	1997	1998	1999	2000
Interest cover – times	6.5	5.0	5.5	6.7	7.9	6.6	3.5	4.2	3.5	**3.9**

	1991	1992	1993	1994	1995	1996	1997	1998	1999	2000
Profit before interest less share of joint ventures' and associates' interest divided by net interest charge – excluding exceptional items	5.9	5.0	5.5	6.7	8.2	6.9	5.0	4.3	3.6	**4.5**
Gearing	81%	96%	92%	84%	75%	75%	84%	92%	84%	**64%**
Net borrowing as a percentage of net assets										
Net margin	8.8%	9.0%	7.6%	7.9%	8.7%	8.3%	5.6%	6.4%	5.9%	**7.0%**
Profit before interest and exceptional items as a percentage of turnover										
Return on net operating assets	20.5%	20.7%	16.2%	17.7%	20.4%	20.3%	13.3%	13.7%	11.9%	**13.5%**
Profit before interest and exceptional items as a percentage of average net operating assets										
Dividend cover – times	3.6	2.6	2.7	3.1	3.3	3.1	1.0	1.8	1.8	**1.1**
Earnings per share divided by dividends per share – excluding exceptional items	3.3	2.6	2.4	2.9	3.0	3.3	2.2	2.1	1.7	**1.4**

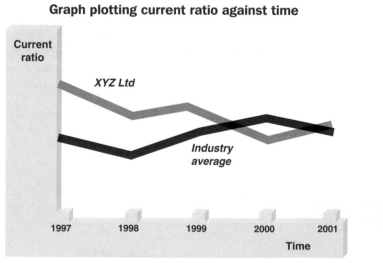

Figure 7.4

Graph plotting current ratio against time

Plotting key ratios for a company over time, along with the relevant industry ratios, can be a useful way of detecting trends for a particular business and for comparing the extent to which these trends are in line with those of the industry as a whole.

The use of ratios in predicting financial distress

Financial ratios, based on current or past performance, are often used to help predict the future. However, both the choice of ratios and the interpretation of results are normally dependent on the judgement of the analyst. In recent years, however, attempts have been made to develop a more rigorous and systematic approach to the use of ratios for prediction purposes. In particular, researchers have shown an interest in the ability of ratios to predict financial distress in a business. This, of course, is an area with which all those connected with the business are likely to be concerned.

A number of methods and models employing ratios have now been developed that claim to predict future financial distress. Early research focused on the examination of ratios on an individual basis to see whether they were good or bad predictors of financial distress. The first research in this area was carried out by Beaver (see reference (1) at the end of the chapter) which compared the mean ratios of 79 businesses that failed over a ten-year period with a sample of 79 businesses that did not fail over this period. (The research used a matched-pair design, where each failed business was matched with a non-failed business of similar size and industry type.) Beaver found that certain mean ratios exhibited a marked difference between the failed and non-failed businesses for up to five years prior to failure (see Figure 7.5).

Research by Zmijewski (see reference (2) at the end of the chapter) using a sample of 72 failed and 3,573 non-failed businesses over a six year period found that failed businesses were characterised by lower rates of return, higher levels of gearing, lower levels of coverage for their fixed interest payments and more variable returns on shares. Whilst you may not find these results very surprising, it is interesting to note that Zmijewski, like a number of other researchers in this area, did not find liquidity ratios particularly useful in identifying financial distress.

The approach adopted by Beaver and Zmijewski is referred to as **univariate analysis** because it looks at one ratio at a time. Although this approach can produce interesting results, there are practical problems associated with its use. Let us say, for example, that past research has identified two ratios as being good predictors in identifying financial distress. When applied to a particular business, however, it may be found that one ratio predicts financial distress whereas the other does not. Given these conflicting signals, how should the decision maker interpret the results?

The weaknesses of univariate analysis have led researchers to develop models that combine ratios in such a way as to produce a single index that can be interpreted more clearly. One approach to model development, much favoured by researchers, employs **multiple discriminate analysis (MDA).** This is, in essence, a statistical technique that can be used to draw a boundary between those businesses that fail and those businesses that do not. This boundary is referred to as the **discriminate function**. MDA attempts to identify those factors likely to influence a particular event (such as financial failure). However, unlike regression analysis, MDA assumes that the observations come from two different populations (for example, failed and non-failed businesses) rather than from a single population.

To illustrate this approach, let us assume that we wish to test whether two

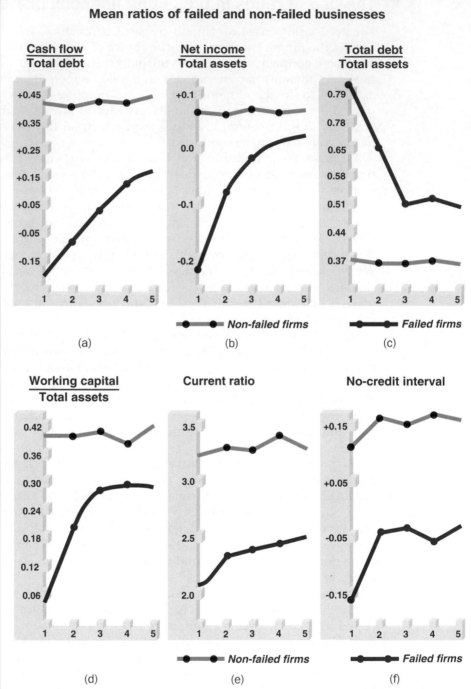

Figure 7.5

Mean ratios of failed and non-failed businesses

(a) Cash flow / Total debt

(b) Net income / Total assets

(c) Total debt / Total assets

(d) Working capital / Total assets

(e) Current ratio

(f) No-credit interval

Non-failed firms — *Failed firms*

Each of the ratios (a)–(f) above indicates a marked difference in the average ratio between the sample of failed businesses and a matched sample of non-failed businesses. The difference between each of the average ratios can be detected five years prior to the failure of those businesses within the failed sample. (From Beaver – see reference (1) at the end of chapter.)

Note: The no-credit interval is the same as the operating cash flows to maturing obligations ratio discussed earlier in the chapter.

ratios (say, the current ratio and the return on capital employed) can help to predict distress. In order to do this, we can calculate these ratios first for a sample of failed businesses and then for a matched sample of non-failed businesses. From these two sets of data we can produce a scatter diagram that plots each business according to these two ratios to produce a single co-ordinate. Figure 7.6 illustrates this approach. Using the observations plotted on the diagram, we try to identify the boundary between the failed and the non-failed businesses.

We can see in Figure 7.6 that those businesses that fall to the left of the line are predominantly failed companies and those that fall to the right are predominantly non-failed companies. Note that there is some overlap between the two populations. The boundary produced is unlikely, in practice, to eliminate all errors, and so some businesses that fail may fall on the side of the boundary with non-failed companies, and vice versa. However, it will *minimise* the misclassification errors.

The boundary shown in Figure 7.6 can be expressed in the form:

$$Z = a + b \times (\text{Current ratio}) + c \times (\text{ROCE})$$

where a is a constant and b and c are weights to be attached to each ratio. A weighted average or total score (Z) is then derived. The weights given to the two ratios will depend on the slope of the line and its absolute position.

Edward Altman (see reference (3) at the end of the chapter) in the USA was the first to develop a model using financial ratios in order to predict financial distress. His model, the Z score model, is based on five financial ratios and is as

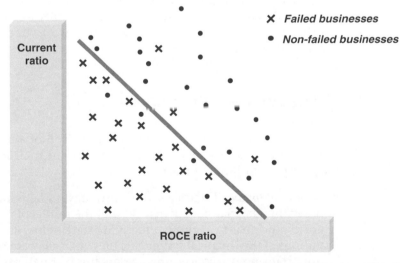

Figure 7.6

Scatter diagram showing the distribution of failed and non-failed businesses

The figure shows the distribution of failed and non-failed businesses based on two ratios. The line represents a boundary between the samples of failed and non-failed businesses. Although there is some crossing of the boundary, the boundary represents the line that minimises the problem of misclassifying particular businesses.

follows:

$$Z = 1.2a + 1.4b + 3.3c + 0.6d + 1.0e$$

where a = Working capital/Total assets

b = Accumulated retained profits/Total assets

c = Profit before interest and taxation/Total assets

d = Market value of ordinary and preference shares/Total liabilities at book value

e = Sales/Total assets

In order to develop this model, Altman carried out experiments using a paired sample of failed businesses and non-failed businesses and collected relevant data for each business for five years prior to failure. He found that the model shown through the formula above was able to predict failure for up to two years prior to bankruptcy. However, the predictive accuracy of the model became weaker the further the period from failure.

The ratios used in this model were identified by Altman through a process of trial and error as there is no underlying theory of financial distress to help guide researchers in their selection of appropriate ratios. According to Altman, those companies with a Z score of less than 1.81 failed, and the lower the score the greater the probability of failure. Those with a Z score greater than 2.99 did not fail. Those businesses with a Z score between 1.81 and 2.99 occupied a 'zone of ignorance' and were difficult to classify. However, the model was able overall to classify 95 per cent of the businesses correctly.

In recent years, this model has been updated and other models, using a similar approach, have been developed throughout the world. In the UK, Taffler (see reference (4) at the end of the chapter) has developed separate Z score models for different types of business.

The prediction of financial distress is not the only area where research into the predictive ability of ratios has taken place. Researchers have also developed ratio-based models that claim to assess the vulnerability of a company to takeover by another company. This is another area that is of vital importance to all those connected with the business.

●●●● Limitations of ratio analysis

Although ratios offer a quick and useful method of analysing the position and performance of a business, they are not without their limitations. Some of the more important limitations are considered below.

● *Quality of financial statements.* It must always be remembered that ratios are based on financial statements and that the results of ratio analysis are dependent on the quality of those underlying statements. Ratios will inherit the limitations of the financial statements on which they are based. Some of the more important points concerning the quality of financial statements are considered next.

One important issue when making comparisons between businesses is the degree of conservatism that each business adopts in the reporting of profit. Any review of the financial statements should, therefore, include an examination of the accounting policies that are being adopted. Some businesses adopt a very conservative approach, which would be reflected in particular accounting policies such as the immediate writing off of intangible assets (for example, research and development and goodwill), the use of the reducing balance method of depreciation (which favours high depreciation charges in the early years), and so on. The effect of these policies is to report profit later rather than sooner, and so when profits are reported they are often referred to as being 'of high quality'. Businesses that do not adopt conservative accounting policies would report profits more quickly. The writing off of intangible assets over a long period (or perhaps, not writing off intangible assets at all), the use of the straight-line method of depreciation, and so on will mean that profits are reported more quickly.

In addition, there are some businesses that may adopt particular accounting policies or structure particular transactions in such a way that portrays a picture of financial health that is in line with what those who prepared the financial statements would like to see rather than what is a true and fair view of financial performance and position. This practice is referred to as **creative accounting** and has been a major problem for accounting rule-makers.

Exhibit 7.5

The thoughts of Warren Buffet

Warren Buffet is regarded by many as the world's most successful investor and is one of the world's richest individuals. He has expressed concern about the problem of creative accounting as follows:

> A growing number of otherwise high-grade managers – CEOs [chief executive officers] you would be happy to have as spouses for your children or as trustee under your will – have come to the view that it's okay to manipulate earnings to safisfy what they believe are Wall Street's desires. Indeed, many CEOs think this kind of manipulation is not only okay, but actually their duty.

Activity 7.29

Why might the managers of a business engage in creative accounting?

....

There are many reasons and these include:

– To get around restrictions (for example, to report sufficient profit to pay a dividend)
– To avoid government action (for example, the taxation of excessive profits)
– To hide poor management decisions
– To achieve sales or profit targets, thereby ensuring that management bonuses are paid
– To attract new share capital or loan capital by showing a healthy financial position
– To satisfy the demands of major investors concerning levels of return.

When examining the financial statements of a business, a number of checks may be carried out on the financial statements to help gain a 'feel' for their reliability. These will include checks to see whether:

- the reported profits are significantly higher than the operating cash flows for the period (which may suggest profits have been overstated);
- the corporation tax charge is low in relation to reported profits (which may, again, suggest that profits are overstated, although there may be other, more innocent, explanations);
- the valuation methods used for assets held are based on historic cost or current values (and if the latter approach is used, it is important to find out why and what particular valuation approach has been adopted);
- there have been any changes in accounting policies over the period, particularly in key areas such as depreciation, stock valuation, and the reporting of doubtful debts that can have a significant impact on reported profit;
- the accounting policies adopted are in line with those adopted by the rest of the industry;
- the auditors' report gives a 'clean bill of health' to the financial statements;
- the 'small print' (that is, the notes to the accounts) is not being used to hide significant events or changes.

Although such checks are useful, they are not guaranteed to identify creative accounting practices, some which may be very deeply seated.

Exhibit 7.6

Look out for what is hidden under the carpet

The following is an extract from *The Times* (29 April 1999):

> Allied Carpets admitted last summer that its store managers had been marketing a carpet as 'sold' as soon as an order was placed. The practice, known as 'pre-dispatching', is not illegal but violated company policy that sales should not be marked as completed until delivery. The scam flattered trading figures and led to a £3m charge against profits last year.

One consequence of this 'scam' was the firing of the managing director.

- *Inflation.* A persistent problem in most Western countries is that the financial results of a business are distorted as a result of inflation. One effect of inflation is that the values of assets held for any length of time may bear little relation to current values. Generally speaking, the value of assets will be understated in current terms during a period of inflation as they are usually recorded at their original cost (less any amounts written off for depreciation). This means that comparisons, either between businesses or between periods, will be hindered. A difference in, say, return on capital employed may simply be owing to the fact that assets in one of the balance sheets being compared were acquired more recently (ignoring the effect of depreciation on the asset values). Another effect of inflation is to distort the measurement of profit. Sales revenue for a period is often matched against costs from an earlier period. This is because there is often a time lag between acquiring a particular resource and using it in the business. For example, stocks may be acquired in one period and sold in a later period. During a period of inflation, this will mean that the costs do not reflect current prices. As a result, costs will be understated in the current profit and loss account and this, in turn, means that profit will be overstated. One effect of this will be to distort the profitability ratios discussed earlier.

- *The restricted vision of ratios.* It is important not to rely on ratios exclusively and thereby lose sight of information contained in the underlying financial statements. Some items reported in these statements can be vital in assessing position and performance. For example, the total sales, capital employed and profit figures may be useful in assessing changes in absolute size that occur over time, or differences in scale between businesses. Ratios do not provide such information. In comparing one figure with another, ratios measure *relative* performance and position and therefore provide only part of the picture. Thus, when comparing two businesses, it will often be useful to assess the absolute size of profits as well as the relative profitability of each business. For example, company A may generate £1 million profit and have a ROCE of 15 per cent and company B may generate £100,000 profit and have a ROCE of 20 per cent. Although company B has a higher level of *profitability*, as measured by ROCE, it generates lower total profits.
- *The basis for comparison.* We saw earlier that ratios require a basis for comparison in order to be useful. Moreover, it is important that the analyst compares like with like. When comparing businesses, however, no two businesses will be identical, and the greater the differences between the businesses being compared, the greater the limitations of ratio analysis. Furthermore, when comparing businesses, differences in such matters as accounting policies, financing policies and financial year-ends will add to the problems of evaluation.
- *Balance sheet ratios.* Because the balance sheet is only a 'snapshot' of the business at a particular moment in time, any ratios based on balance sheet figures, such as the liquidity ratios, may not be representative of the financial position of the business for the year as a whole. For example, it is common for a seasonal business to have a financial year-end that coincides with a low point in business activity. Thus, stocks and debtors may be low at the balance sheet date and the liquidity ratios may also be low as a result. A more representative

| Exhibit 7.7 | **Remember it's people that really count ...** |

Lord Weinstock was an influential industrialist whose management style and philosophy helped to shape management practice in many UK businesses. During his long reign at GEC plc, a major engineering business, Lord Weinstock relied heavily on financial ratios to assess performance and to exercise control. In particular, he relied on ratios relating to sales, costs, debtors, profit margins and stock turnover. However, he was keenly aware of the limitations of ratios and recognised that, ultimately, profits are produced by people.

In a memo written to GEC managers he pointed out that ratios are an aid to, rather than a substitute for, good management. He wrote:

The operating ratios are of great value as measures of efficiency but they are only the measures and not efficiency itself. Statistics will not design a product better, make it for a lower cost or increase sales. If ill-used, they may so guide action as to diminish resources for the sake of apparent but false signs of improvement ...

Management remains a matter of judgement, of knowledge of products and processes and of understanding and skill in dealing with people. The ratios will indicate how well all these things are being done and will show comparison with how they are done elsewhere. But they will tell us nothing about how to do them. That is what you are meant to do.

Source: *Aris* (see reference (5) at the end of the chapter).

picture of liquidity can only be gained by taking additional measurements at other points in the year.

● Summary

In this chapter, we have seen that ratios can be used to analyse various aspects of the position and performance of a business. Used properly, they help provide a quick thumbnail sketch of a business. However, they require a sound basis for comparison and will only be as useful as the quality of the underlying financial statements permit. Though they can highlight certain strengths and weaknesses concerning financial performance and position, ratios do not identify underlying causes. This can only be done through a more detailed investigation of business practices and records.

We have also seen that ratios are being used increasingly to predict the future. Indeed, we saw how certain ratios, when combined into a single index, can be used to predict financial distress.

Key terms

Return on ordinary shareholders' funds (ROSF) p. 201
Return on capital employed (ROCE) p. 202
Net profit margin p. 203
Gross profit margin p. 204
Average stock turnover period p. 205
Average settlement period for debtors p. 206
Average settlement period for creditors p. 206
Sales to capital employed p. 207
Sales per employee p. 208
Current ratio p. 210
Acid test ratio p. 211

Operating cash flows to maturing obligations p. 213
Financial gearing p. 214
Gearing ratio p. 215
Interest cover ratio p. 217
Dividend per share p. 218
Dividend payout ratio p. 219
Dividend cover ratio p. 219
Dividend yield ratio p. 220
Earnings per share p. 220
Operating cash flow per ordinary share p. 221
Price/earnings ratio p. 222
Overtrading p. 226
Creative accounting p. 233

● Further reading

If you would like to explore the topics covered in this chapter in more depth, we recommend the following books:

Financial Accounting and Reporting, *Elliott, B. and Elliott, J.*, 5th edn, Financial Times Prentice Hall, 2001, chapters 25 and 26.

Financial Reporting and Analysis, *Revsine, L., Collins, D. and Bruce Johnson, W.*, Prentice Hall, 1999, chapter 4.

Financial Analysis, *Rees, B.*, 2nd edn, Prentice Hall International, 1995, chapters 1–3.

The Analysis and Use of Financial Statements, *White, G. and Sondhi, A.*, 2nd edn, Wiley, 1997, chapter 4.

References

1. 'Financial ratios as predictors of failure', *Beaver, W. H.*, in **Empirical Research in Accounting: Selected studies**, 1966, pp. 71–111.
2. **Predicting Corporate Bankruptcy: An empirical comparison of the extent of financial distress models**, *Zmijewski, M. E.*, Research Paper, State University of New York, 1983.
3. 'Financial ratios, discriminant analysis and the prediction of corporate bankruptcy', *Altman, E. I.*, in **Journal of Finance**, September 1968, pp. 589–609.
4. 'The assessement of company solvency and performance using a statistical model: a comparative UK-based study', *Taffler, R.*, in **Accounting and Business Research**, Autumn 1983, pp. 295–307.
5. **Arnold Weinstock and the Making of GEC**, *Aris, S.*, Arum Press, 1998, published in *Sunday Times*, 22 February 1998, p. 3.

7.1 Some businesses operate on a low net-profit margin (for example, a supermarket chain). Does this mean that the return on capital employed from the business will also be low?

7.2 What potential problems arise from the use of balance sheet figures in the calculation of financial ratios?

7.3 Is it responsible to publish the *Z*-scores of companies that are in financial difficulties? What are the potential problems of doing this?

7.4 Identify and discuss three reasons why the P/E ratio of two companies operating within the same industry may differ.

? **EXERCISES**

Exercises 7.5–7.8 are more advanced than 7.1–7.4. Those with coloured numbers have answers at the back of the book.

7.1 Jiang (Western) Ltd has recently produced its accounts for the current year. The board of directors met to consider the accounts and, at this meeting, concern was expressed that the return on capital employed had decreased from 14 per cent last year to 12 per cent for the current year.

The following reasons were suggested as to why this reduction in ROCE had occurred:

(a) Increase in the gross profit margin
(b) Reduction in sales
(c) Increase in overhead expenses
(d) Increase in amount of stock held
(e) Repayment of a loan at the year-end
(f) Increase in the time taken by debtors to pay.

Required:
State, with reasons, which of the above might lead to a reduction in ROCE.

7.2 Business A and Business B are both engaged in retailing, but seem to take a different approach to this trade according to the information available. This information consists of a table of ratios, shown below.

Ratio	Business A	Business B
Return on capital employed (ROCE)	20%	17%
Return on ordinary shareholders' funds (ROSF)	30%	18%
Average settlement period for debtors	63 days	21 days
Average settlement period for creditors	50 days	45 days
Gross profit percentage	40%	15%
Net profit percentage	10%	10%
Stock turnover period	52 days	25 days

Required:
(a) Explain how each ratio is calculated.

(b) Describe what this information indicates about the differences in approach between the two businesses. If one of them prides itself on personal service and one of them on competitive prices, which do you think is which and why?

7.3 Conday and Co. Ltd has been in operation for three years and produces reproduction antique furniture for the export market. The most recent set of accounts for the company is set out below:

Balance sheet as at 30 November 2001

	£000	£000	£000
Fixed assets			
Freehold land and buildings at cost			228
Plant and machinery at cost		942	
Less Accumulated depreciation		180	762
			990
Current assets			
Stocks		600	
Trade debtors		820	
		1,420	
Less Creditors: amounts falling due within one year			
Trade creditors	665		
Taxation	48		
Bank overdraft	432	1,145	275
			1,265
Less Creditors: amounts falling due in more than one year			
12% debentures (note 1)			200
			1,065
Capital and reserves			
Ordinary shares of £1 each			700
Retained profits			365
			1,065

Profit and loss account for the year ended 30 November 2001

	£000	£000
Sales		2,600
Less Cost of sales		1,620
Gross profit		980
Less Selling and distribution expenses (note 2)	408	
Administration expenses	174	
Finance expenses	78	660
Net profit before taxation		320
Less Corporation tax		95
Net profit after taxation		225
Less Proposed dividend		160
Retained profit for the year		65

Notes:
1. The debentures are secured on the freehold land and buildings.
2. Selling and distribution expenses include £170,000 in respect of bad debts.

An investor has been approached by the company to invest £200,000 by purchasing ordinary shares in the company at £6.40 each. The company wishes to use the funds to finance a programme of further expansion.

Required:

(a) Analyse the financial position and performance of the company and comment on any features you consider to be significant.

(b) State, with reasons, whether or not the investor should invest in the company on the terms outlined.

7.4 The directors of Helena Beauty Products Ltd have been presented with the following abridged accounts for the current year and the preceding year:

Helena Beauty Products Ltd

Profit and loss account for the year ended 30 September

	2000		2001	
	£000	£000	£000	£000
Sales		3,600		3,840
Less Cost of sales				
Opening stock	320		400	
Purchases	2,240		2,350	
	2,560		2,750	
Less Closing stock	400	2,160	500	2,250
Gross profit		1,440		1,590
Less Expenses		1,360		1,500
Net profit		80		90

Balance sheets as at 30 September

	2000		2001	
	£000	£000	£000	£000
Fixed assets		1,900		1,860
Current assets				
Stock	400		500	
Debtors	750		960	
Bank	8		4	
	1,158		1,464	
Less Creditors: amounts due within one year	390	768	450	1,014
		2,668		2,874
Financed by				
£1 ordinary shares		1,650		1,766
Reserves		1,018		1,108
		2,668		2,874

Required:

Using six ratios, comment on the profitability and efficiency of the business as revealed by the accounts shown above.

| | 7.5 | Threads Limited manufactures nuts and bolts, which are sold to industrial users. The abbreviated accounts for 2000 and 2001 are given below. |

Profit and loss account for the year ended 30 June

	2000		2001	
	£000	£000	£000	£000
Sales		1,180		1,200
Cost of sales		(680)		(750)
Gross profit		500		450
Operating expenses	(200)		(208)	
Depreciation	(66)		(75)	
Interest	(–)		(8)	
		(266)		(291)
Profit before tax		234		159
Tax		(80)		(48)
Profit after tax		154		111
Dividend proposed		(70)		(72)
Retained profit for year		84		39

Balance sheets as at 30 June

	2000		2001	
	£000	£000	£000	£000
Fixed assets		702		687
Current assets				
Stocks	148		236	
Debtors	102		156	
Cash	3		4	
	253		396	
Creditors: amounts due within one year				
Trade creditors	(60)		(76)	
Other creditors and accruals	(18)		(16)	
Dividend	(70)		(72)	
Tax	(40)		(24)	
Bank overdraft	(11)		(50)	
	(199)		(238)	
Net current assets		54		158
		756		845
Creditors: amounts due beyond one year				
Bank loan		–		(50)
		756		795
Capital and reserves				
Ordinary share capital of £1 (fully paid)		500		500
Retained profits		256		295
		756		795

Required:

(a) Calculate the following financial statistics for both 2000 and 2001, using end-of-year figures where appropriate:

(i)   return on capital employed
(ii) net profit margin
(iii) gross profit margin
(iv) current ratio
(v)   liquidity ratio (acid test ratio)
(vi) days debtors (settlement period)
(vii) days creditors (settlement period)
(viii) stock turnover period.

(b) Comment on the performance of Threads Limited from the viewpoint of a company considering supplying a substantial amount of goods to Threads Limited on usual credit terms.

(c) What action could a supplier take to lessen the risk of not being paid should Threads Limited be in financial difficulty?

7.6 Bradbury Ltd is a family-owned clothes manufacturer based in the south-west of England. For a number of years the chairman and managing director was David Bradbury. During his period of office the company's sales turnover had grown steadily at a rate of 2 to 3 per cent each year. David Bradbury retired on 30 November 2000 and was succeeded by his son Simon. Soon after taking office, Simon decided to expand the business. Within weeks he had successfully negotiated a five-year contract with a large clothes retailer to make a range of sports and leisurewear items. The contract will result in an additional £2 million in sales during each year of the contract. In order to fulfil the contract, new equipment and premises were acquired by Bradbury Ltd.

Financial information concerning the company is given below.

Profit and loss account for the year ended 30 November

	2000 £000	2001 £000
Turnover	9,482	11,365
Profit before interest and tax	914	1,042
Interest charges	22	81
Profit before tax	892	961
Taxation	358	386
Profit after tax	534	575
Dividend	120	120
Retained profit	414	455

Balance sheet as at 30 November

	2000 £000	2000 £000	2001 £000	2001 £000
Fixed assets				
Freehold premises at cost		5,240		7,360
Plant and equipment (net)		2,375		4,057
		7,615		11,417
Current assets				
Stock	2,386		3,420	
Trade debtors	2,540		4,280	
	4,926		7,700	

Creditors: amounts due within one year	£000	£000	£000	£000
Trade creditors	(1,157)		(2,245)	
Taxation	(179)		(193)	
Dividends payable	(120)		(120)	
Bank overdraft	(52)		(2,616)	
	(1,508)		(5,174)	
Net current assets		3,418		2,526
		11,033		13,943
Creditors: amounts due beyond one year				
Loans		(1,220)		(3,674)
Total net assets		9,813		10,269
Capital and reserves				
Share capital		2,000		2,000
Reserves		7,813		8,269
Net worth		9,813		10,269

Required:

(a) Calculate for each year the following ratios:
   - (i) net profit margin
   - (ii) return on capital employed
   - (iii) current ratio
   - (iv) gearing ratio
   - (v) days debtors (settlement period)
   - (vi) sales to capital employed.

(b) Using the above ratios, and any other ratios or information you consider relevant, comment on the results of the expansion programme.

7.7 The financial statements for Harridges Limited are given below for the two years ended 30 June 2001 and 2002. Harridges Limited operates a department store in the centre of a small town.

Harridges Limited

Profit and loss account for the years ended 30 June

		2001		2002
	£000	£000	£000	£000
Sales		2,600		3,500
Cost of sales		(1,560)		(2,350)
Gross profit		1,040		1,150
Expenses: Wages and salaries	(320)		(350)	
Overheads	(260)		(200)	
Depreciation	(150)		(250)	
		(730)		(800)
Operating profit		310		350
Interest payable		(50)		(50)
Profit before taxation		260		300
Taxation		(105)		(125)
Profit after taxation		155		175
Dividend proposed		(65)		(75)
Profit retained for the year		90		100

Balance sheet as at 30 June

	2001 £000	2001 £000	2002 £000	2002 £000
Fixed assets		1,265		1,525
Current assets				
Stocks	250		400	
Debtors	105		145	
Cash at bank	380		115	
	735		660	
Creditors: amounts falling due within one year				
Trade creditors	(235)		(300)	
Dividend	(65)		(75)	
Other	(100)		(110)	
	(400)		(485)	
Net current assets		335		175
Total assets less current liabilities		1,600		1,700
Creditors: amounts falling due after more than one year				
10% loan stock		(500)		(500)
		1,100		1,200
Capital and reserves				
Share capital: £1 shares fully paid		490		490
Share premium		260		260
Profit and loss account		350		450
		1,100		1,200

Required:

(a) Choose and calculate eight ratios that would be helpful in assessing the performance of Harridges Limited. Use end-of-year values and calculate ratios for both 2002 and 2001.

(b) Using the ratios calculated in (a) and any others you consider helpful, comment on the company's performance from the viewpoint of a prospective purchaser of a majority of shares.

7.8 Genesis Ltd was incorporated in 1998 and has grown rapidly over the past three years. The rapid rate of growth has created problems for the business, which the directors of the company have found difficult to deal with. Recently, a firm of management consultants has been asked to help the directors of the company overcome these problems.

In a preliminary report to the board of directors of the company, the management consultants state: 'Most of the difficulties faced by the company are symptoms of an underlying problem of overtrading.'

The most recent accounts of the business are set out below:

Balance sheet as at 31 October 2001

	£000	£000	£000
Fixed assets			
Freehold land and buildings at cost		530	
Less Accumulated depreciation		88	442
Fixtures and fittings at cost		168	
Less Accumulated depreciation		52	116

	£000	£000	£000
Motor vans at cost		118	
Less Accumulated depreciation		54	64
			622
Current assets			
Stock in trade		128	
Trade debtors		104	
		232	
Less Creditors: amount falling			
due within one year			
Trade creditors	184		
Proposed dividend	4		
Taxation	8		
Bank overdraft	354	550	(318)
			304
Less Creditors: amounts falling			
due beyond one year			
10% debentures (secured)			(120)
			184
Capital and reserves			
Ordinary £0.50 shares			60
General reserve			50
Retained profit			74
			184

Profit and loss account for the year ended 31 October 2001

	£000	£000
Sales		1,640
Less Cost of sales		
Opening stock	116	
Purchases	1,260	
	1,376	
Less Closing stock	128	(1,248)
Gross profit		392
Less Selling and distribution expenses	204	
Administration expenses	92	
Interest expenses	44	(340)
Net profit before taxation		52
Corporation tax		(16)
Net profit after taxation		36
Proposed dividend		(4)
Retained profit for the year		32

All purchases and sales were on credit.

Required:
(a) Explain the term 'overtrading' and state how overtrading might arise for a business.
(b) Discuss the kinds of problem that overtrading can create for a business.
(c) Calculate and discuss *five* financial ratios that might be used to establish whether or not the business is overtrading.
(d) State the ways in which a business may overcome the problem of overtrading.

PART 2

Management accounting

Part 2 deals with the area of accounting usually known as 'management' or 'managerial accounting'. This area of accounting is concerned with providing information to managers that is intended to help them to make decisions, to plan and to ensure that plans are in fact achieved.

Part 2 starts with a consideration of the basics of financial decision-making. Chapter 8 deals with how we identify those items of information that are relevant to a particular decision and those that may be ignored. Chapter 9 continues this theme by considering how financial costs and benefits alter as the volume of activity alters. In this chapter we include an examination of break-even analysis. This is concerned with deducing the level of activity at which the sales revenues, from some business activity, exactly cover the costs so that neither profit nor loss is made by the activity. Knowledge of this figure can be useful in assessing the risk exposure of a business operating in the activity concerned.

In Chapter 10 we look at how businesses can determine the full cost of each unit of their output. By 'full cost' we mean that the figure takes account of all of the costs of producing a product or service. This includes not just those costs that are directly caused by the unit of output, but those, like rent and administrative costs, that are indirectly involved. This subject is continued in Chapter 11, when we consider some recent developments in cost determination and how the business can set prices for its output.

Chapter 12 deals with the way in which businesses convert their general objectives and long-term plans into workable short-term plans or budgets. Here we shall be looking at the budgeting process and the likely effect of involving junior managers in the derivation of their own budgets. We shall also see how budgets need to be produced for each department, or area of the business, and that the budget of each department needs to fit in with the budgets of other departments to which its work is related. In Chapter 13 we shall consider how, after the period of the budget, the actual performance can be compared with the budgeted performance. This can be done in such a way as to enable managers to see, fairly precisely, the activity that led to any failure to meet the budget. They can then try to find out what has gone wrong and put things right for the future.

8   Relevant costs

Introduction

In this chapter we shall consider the identification and use of costs in making management decisions. We shall see that not all costs surrounding an area are relevant to a particular decision. It is important to distinguish carefully between costs (and revenues) that are relevant and those that are not, since failure to do so could well lead to bad decisions being made.

OBJECTIVES When you have completed this chapter, you should be able to:

- Define and distinguish between relevant costs, outlay costs and opportunity costs.
- Identify and quantify the costs that are relevant to a particular decision.
- Use the relevant costs to make decisions.
- Set out the analysis in a logical form so that the conclusion may be communicated to managers.

What is meant by 'cost'?

The answer to this question is, at first sight, very obvious. Most people would say that **cost** is how much was paid for an item of goods being supplied or a service being provided.

Activity 8.1 You own a motor car, for which you paid a purchase price of £5,000 – much below list price – at a recent car auction. You have just been offered £6,000 for this car. What is the cost to you of keeping the car for your own use? *Note:* ignore running costs and so on; just consider the 'capital' cost of the car.

The real economic cost of retaining the car is £6,000, since this is what you are being deprived of to retain the car. Any decision that you make with respect to the car's future should logically take account of this figure. This cost is known as the 'opportunity cost' since it is the value of the opportunity forgone in order to pursue the other course of action. In this case, the other course of action is to retain the car.

In one sense, the cost of the car in Activity 8.1 is £5,000 because that is how much you paid for it. However, this cost, which for obvious reasons is known as the **historic cost**, is only of academic interest. It cannot logically ever be used to make a decision on the car's future. If you disagree with this point, ask yourself how you would assess an offer of £5,500, from another person, for the car. You would obviously compare the offer price of £5,500 with the **opportunity cost** of £6,000. You would not accept the £5,500 on the basis that it was bigger than the £5,000 you paid in the first place; you would reject it on the basis that it was less than the £6,000 offered. The only other figure that should concern you is the value to you, in terms of pleasure, usefulness and so on, that retaining the car would provide. If you valued this more highly than the £6,000 opportunity cost, you would reject both offers.

It may occur to you that the £5,000 is to some degree relevant here because, if you sold the car, either you would make a profit of £500 (£5,500 – £5,000) or £1,000 (£6,000 – £5,000). Since you would choose to make the higher profit, you would sell the car for £6,000 and make the right decision as a result. But ask yourself, what decision you would make if the car cost you £4,000 to buy? Clearly you would still sell the car for £6,000 rather than for £5,500. What is more, you would reach the same conclusion whatever the historic cost was. Thus the historic cost can never be relevant to a future decision.

You should note particularly that even if the car cost, say, £10,000, the historic cost would still be irrelevant. If you had just bought a car for £10,000 and find that shortly after it is only worth £6,000, you may well be fuming at your mistake, but this does not make the £10,000 a **relevant cost**. The only relevant factors, in a decision on whether to sell the car or to keep it, are the £6,000 and the value of the benefits of keeping it.

Historic cost is normally used in accounting statements, like the balance sheet and the profit and loss account. This is logical, however, since these statements are intended to be accounts of what has actually happened and are drawn up after the event. In the context of decision making, which is always related to the future, historic cost is always irrelevant.

To say that historic cost is an **irrelevant cost** is not to say that the effects of having incurred that cost are always irrelevant. The fact that you own the car and you are thus in a position to exercise choice as to how you use it is not irrelevant.

It might be useful to formalise what we have discussed so far.

A definition of cost

Cost may be defined as the amount of resources, usually measured in monetary terms, sacrificed to achieve a particular objective. The objective might be to retain a car, to buy a particular house, to make a particular product or to render a particular service. If we are talking about a **past cost**, we are talking about historic costs. If we are considering the future, we are interested in future opportunity costs and future **outlay costs**.

● ● ● ● Relevant costs: opportunity and outlay costs

An opportunity cost can be defined as the value in monetary terms of being deprived of the next-best opportunity in order to pursue the particular objective.

An outlay cost is an amount of money that will have to be spent to achieve that objective. We shall shortly meet plenty of examples of both of these types of future cost.

To be relevant to a particular decision, a cost must satisfy both of the following criteria:

- *It must relate to the objectives of the business.* Most businesses have some wealth-enhancement objective, that is, they are seeking to become richer (see Chapter 1). Thus, to be relevant to a particular decision, a cost must have an effect on the wealth of the business, assuming a wealth-enhancement objective.
- *It must differ from one possible decision outcome to the next.* Only items that are different between outcomes can be used to distinguish between them. Thus the reason that the historic cost of the car that we discussed earlier, is irrelevant, is that it is the same whichever decision is taken about the future of the car. This means that all past costs are irrelevant because what has happened in the past must be the same for all possible future outcomes.

It is not only past costs that are the same from one decision outcome to the next; future costs may also be the same. Take for example, a road haulage business that has decided that it will buy a new lorry and the decision lies between two different models. The load capacity, the fuel and maintenance costs are different for each lorry. The potential costs and revenues associated with these are relevant items. The lorry will require a driver, so the business will need to employ one, but a qualified driver could drive either lorry equally well, for the same wage. The cost of employing the driver is thus irrelevant to the decision as to which lorry to buy. This is despite the fact that this cost is a future one.

If, however, the decision were whether to operate an additional lorry or not, the cost of employing the driver would be relevant because here it would be a cost that would vary with the outcome.

| Activity 8.2 | A garage has an old car standing around that it bought several months ago for £3,000. The car needs a replacement engine before it can be sold. It is possible to buy a reconditioned engine for £300. This would take seven hours to fit by a mechanic who is paid £8 an hour. At present the garage is short of work, but the owners are reluctant to lay off any mechanics or even to cut down their basic working week because skilled labour is difficult to find and an upturn in repair work is expected soon. |

Without the engine the car could be sold for an estimated £3,500. What is the minimum price at which the garage would have to sell the car, with a reconditioned engine fitted, to justify doing the work?

....

The minimum price is:

	£
Opportunity cost of the car	3,500
Cost of the reconditioned engine	300
Total	3,800

The original cost of the car is irrelevant. It is the opportunity cost that concerns us. The cost of the new engine is relevant because, if the work is done, the garage will have to pay out the £300; if the job is not done, nothing will have to be paid. This is known as an outlay cost.

The labour cost is irrelevant because the same cost will be incurred whether the mechanic undertakes the work or not. This is because the mechanic is being paid to do nothing if this job is not undertaken; thus the additional cost arising from this job is zero.

It should be emphasised that the garage will not seek to sell the car with its reconditioned engine for £3,800; it will seek to charge as much as possible for it. On the other hand, any price above the £3,800 will make the garage better off financially than not undertaking the job.

Activity 8.3

Assume exactly the same circumstances as in Activity 8.2, except that the garage is quite busy at the moment. If a mechanic is to be put on the engine replacement job, it will mean that other work that the mechanic could have done during the seven hours, all of which could be charged to a customer, will not be undertaken. The garage's labour charge is £12 an hour.

What is the minimum price at which the garage would have to sell the car, with a reconditioned engine fitted, to justify doing the work under these altered circumstances?

....

The minimum price is:

	£
Opportunity cost of the car	3,500
Cost of the reconditioned engine	300
Labour cost (7 × £12)	84
Total	3,884

The relevant labour cost here is that which the garage will have to sacrifice in making the time available to undertake the engine replacement job. While the mechanic is working on this job, the garage is losing the opportunity to do work for which a customer would pay £84. Note that the £8/hour mechanic's wage is still not relevant. This is because the mechanic will be paid the £8 irrespective of whether it is the engine replacement work or some other job that is undertaken.

Activity 8.4

A business is considering offering a tender to undertake a contract. Fulfilment of the contract will require the use of two types of raw material, a quantity of both of which are held in stock by the business. All of the stock of these two raw materials will need to be used on the contract. Information on the stock required is as follows:

Stock item	Quantity (units)	Historic cost (£/unit)	Sales value (£/unit)	Replacement cost (£/unit)
A1	500	5	3	6
B2	800	7	8	10

Stock item A1 is in frequent use in the business on a variety of work. The stock of item B2 was bought a year ago for a contract that was abandoned. It has recently become obvious that there is no likelihood of ever using this stock if the contract currently being considered does not proceed.

Management wishes to deduce the minimum price at which it could undertake the contract without reducing its wealth as a result. This can be used as the baseline in deducing the tender price.

How much should be included in the minimum price in respect of the two stock items detailed above?

....

$$
\begin{aligned}
\text{Stock item:} \quad &\text{A1} \quad £6 \times 500 = £3,000 \\
&\text{B2} \quad £8 \times 800 = £6,400
\end{aligned}
$$

Since A1 is frequently used, if the stock is used on the contract it will need to be replaced. Sooner or later, if this stock is used on the contract, the business will have to buy 500 units (currently costed at £6 per unit) of it additional to that which would have been required had the contract not been undertaken.

Under the circumstances, the only reasonable behaviour of the business, if the contract is not undertaken, is to sell the stock of B2. Thus, using this stock has an opportunity cost equal to the potential proceeds from disposal, reckoned at £8 per unit.

Activity 8.5

HLA Ltd is in the process of preparing a quotation for a special job for a customer. The job will have the following material requirements:

		Units currently held in stock			
		Quantity	Cost	Saleable value	Replacement cost
Material	Units req'd		(£/unit)	(£/unit)	(£/unit)
P	400	0	–	–	40
Q	230	100	62	50	64
R	350	200	48	23	59
S	170	140	33	12	49
T	120	120	40	0	68

Material Q is used consistently by the company on various jobs. Materials R, S and T are in stock as the result of previous overbuying. No other use can be found for R, but the 140 units of S could be used in another job as a substitute for 225 units of material V that are about to be purchased at a price of £10 per unit. Material T has no other use and the company has been informed that it will cost £160 to dispose of the material currently in stock.

What is the relevant cost of the materials for the job specified above?

....

	£
Material P will have to be purchased at £40 per unit (400 × £40)	16,000
Material Q will have to be replaced, therefore, the relevant price is (230 × £64)	14,720
200 units of Material R are in stock and could be sold. The relevant price of these is the sales revenue forgone (200 × £23)	4,600
The remaining 150 units of R would have to be purchased (150 × £59)	8,850

Material S could be sold or used as a substitute for material V. The existing stock could be sold for £1,680 (140 × £12), however, the saving on material V is higher and therefore should be taken as the relevant amount (225 × £10)	2,250
The remaining units of material S must be purchased (30 × £40)	1,470
A saving on disposal will be made if material T is used	(160)
Total relevant cost	£47,730

Sunk costs and committed costs

Sunk cost is simply another way of saying past cost and the two expressions can be used interchangeably. A **committed cost** is also, in effect, a past cost to the extent that an irrevocable decision has been made to incur the cost because, for example, the business has entered into a binding contract. As a result, it is more or less a past cost despite the fact that the cash may not be paid in respect of it until some point in the future. Since the business has no choice as to whether it incurs the cost or not, a committed cost cannot be a relevant cost.

It is important to remember that, to be relevant, a cost must be capable of varying according to the decision made. If the business is already committed by legally binding contract to a cost, that cost cannot vary with the decision.

Activity 8.6	**Past costs are irrelevant costs. Does this mean that what happened in the past is irrelevant?**

No, it does not mean this. The fact that the business has an asset that it can deploy in the future is highly relevant. What is not relevant is how much it cost to acquire that asset. This point was examined in the discussion which followed Activity 8.1.

Another reason why the past is not irrelevant is that it generally – though not always – provides us with our best guide to the future. Suppose that we need to estimate the cost of doing something in the future to help us to decide whether or not it is worth doing. In these circumstances our own experience, or that of others, on how much it has cost to do the thing in the past may provide us with a valuable guide to how much it is likely to cost in the future.

Figure 8.1 summarises the relationship between relevant, irrelevant, opportunity, outlay and past costs.

Qualitative factors of decisions

Though businesses must look closely at the obvious financial effects when making decisions, they must also consider factors that are not directly economic. These are likely to be factors that have a broader but less immediate impact on the business. Ultimately, however, these factors are likely to have economic effect – that is, to affect the wealth of the business.

Figure 8.1

Summary of the relationship between relevant and irrelevant costs

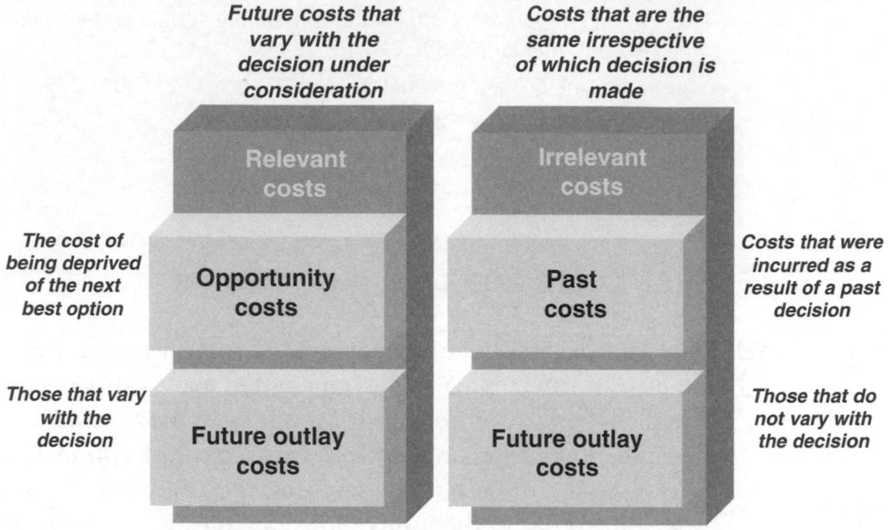

This figure summarises the main points relating to the identfication of relevant and irrelevant costs. Note in particular that future outlay costs may be either relevant or irrelevant costs depending on whether they vary with the decision. Future opportunity costs and outlay costs, that vary with the decision, are relevant; future outlay costs, that do not vary with the decisions and all past costs are irrelevant.

Activity 8.7

Activity 8.3 was concerned with the cost of putting a car into a marketable condition. Apart from whether the car could be sold for more than the relevant cost of doing this, are there any other factors that should be taken into account in making a decision as to whether or not to do the work?

We can think of three points:

● Turning away another job in order to do the engine replacement may lead to customer dissatisfaction.
● On the other hand, having the car available for sale may be useful commercially for the garage, beyond the profit that can be earned from that particular car sale. For example, having a good stock of second-hand cars may attract potential customers.
● There is also the more immediate economic point that it has been assumed that the only labour opportunity cost is the charge-out rate for the seven hours concerned. In practice, most car repairs involve the use of some materials and spare parts. These are usually charged to customers at a profit to the garage. Any such profit from a job turned away would be lost to the garage, and this lost profit would be an opportunity cost of the engine replacement and should, therefore, be included in the calculation of the minimum price to be charged for the sale of the car.

You may have thought of additional points.

It is important to consider 'qualitative' factors carefully. They can seem unimportant because they are virtually impossible to assess in terms of their ultimate economic effect. This effect can nevertheless be very significant.

JB Limited is a small specialist manufacturer of electronic components and much of its output is used by makers of aircraft, for both civil and military purposes. One of the aircraft manufacturers has offered a contract to JB Limited for the supply, over the next 12 months, of 400 identical components. The data relating to the production of each component are as follows:

(i)   *Material requirements*:
       3 kg of material M1 (see note 1 below)
       2 kg of material P2 (see note 2 below)
       1 part no. 678 (see note 3 below)

Note 1: Material M1 is in continuous use by the company, 1,000 kg are currently held in stock. Their original cost was £4.70/kg, but it is known that future purchases will cost £5.50/kg.

Note 2: 1,200 kg of material P2 are held in stock. The original cost of this material was £4.30/kg. The material has not been required for the last two years. Its scrap value is £1.50/kg. The only foreseeable alternative use is as a substitute for material P4 (in current use) but this would involve further processing costs of £1.60/kg. The current cost of material P4 is £3.60/kg.

Note 3: It is estimated that part no. 678 could be bought in for £50 each.

(ii)   *Labour requirements*:   Each component would require five hours of skilled labour and five hours of semi-skilled. A skilled employee is available and is currently paid £7/hour. A replacement would, however, have to be obtained at a rate of £6/hour for the work, which would otherwise be done by the skilled employee. The current rate for semi-skilled work is £5/hour and an additional employee could be appointed for this work.

(iii) *General manufacturing costs*:   It is JB Limited's policy to charge a share of the general costs (rent, heating and so on) to each contract undertaken at the rate of £20 for each machine hour used. If the contract is undertaken, the general costs are expected to increase over the duration of the contract by £3,200.

Spare machine capacity is available and each component would require four machine hours. A price of £150 per component has been offered by the potential customer.

Required:

(a) Should the contract be accepted? Support your conclusion with appropriate figures to present to management.

(b) What other factors ought management to consider that might influence the decision?

● Summary

In this chapter we have seen that 'cost' can have several meanings. Relevant costs are those that relate to the objectives of the decision-making business and that will vary with the decision. Relevant costs include not only outlay costs, but opportunity costs as well. Past costs are always irrelevant because they will be the same irrespective of the course of action taken in the future. Some future costs will also be irrelevant – where they are the same, irrespective of the decision. We saw that financial/economic decisions almost inevitably have qualitative aspects, which the financial analysis probably cannot really handle, and that these aspects are typically very important.

Key terms

Cost   p. 248
Historic cost   p. 249
Opportunity cost   p. 249
Relevant cost   p. 249
Irrelevant cost   p. 249

Past cost   p. 249
Outlay cost   p. 249
Sunk cost   p. 253
Committed cost   p. 253

Further reading

If you would like to explore the topics covered in this chapter in more depth, we recommend the following books:

Accounting for Management Decisions, *Arnold, J. and Turley, S.*, 3rd edn, Prentice Hall International, 1996, chapter 10.

Management and Cost Accounting, *Drury, C.*, 5th edn, Thompson Learning Business Press, 2000, chapter 9.

Cost Accounting: A managerial emphasis, *Horngren, C., Foster, G. and Datar, S.*, 10th edn, Prentice Hall International, 2000, chapter 11.

Cost and Management Accounting, *Williamson, D.*, Prentice Hall International, 1996, chapter 12.

8.1 To be relevant to a particular decision, a cost must have two attributes. What are they?

8.2 Distinguish between a sunk cost and an opportunity cost.

8.3 Define the word 'cost' in the context of management accounting.

8.4 What is meant by the expression 'committed cost'?

EXERCISES

Exercises 8.7 and 8.8 are more advanced than 8.1–8.6. Those with coloured numbers have answers at the back of the book.

8.1 Lombard Ltd has been offered a contract for which there is available production capacity. The contract is for 20,000 items, manufactured by an intricate assembly operation, to be produced and delivered in the next financial year at a price of £80 each. The specification per item is as follows:

Assembly labour	4 hours
Component X	4 units
Component Y	3 units

There would also be the need to hire equipment at an outlay cost of £200,000.

The assembly is a highly skilled operation and the workforce is currently underutilised. It is the business's policy to retain this workforce on full pay in anticipation of high demand in a few years' time, for a new product currently being developed. Skilled workers are paid £10 per hour.

Component X is used in a number of other subassemblies produced by the business; it is readily available, and a small stock is held and replenished regularly. Component Y was a special purchase in anticipation of an order that did not in the end materialise. It is, therefore, surplus to requirements and 100,000 units that are in stock may have to be sold at a loss. An estimate of alternative values for components X and Y provided by the materials planning department is as follows:

	X £/unit	Y £/unit
Historic cost	4	10
Replacement cost	5	11
Net realisable value	3	8

It is estimated that any additional costs associated with the contract will amount to £8 per item.

Required:
Analyse the information in order to advise Lombard on the desirability of the contract.

8.2 The local authority of a small town maintains a theatre and arts centre for the use of a local repertory company, other visiting groups and exhibitions. Management decisions are taken by a committee that meets regularly to review the accounts and plan the use of the facilities.

The theatre employs a full-time staff and a number of artistes at costs of £4,800 and £17,600 per month, respectively. They mount a new production every month for 20 performances. Other monthly expenditure of the theatre is as follows:

	£
Costumes	2,800
Scenery	1,650
Heat and light	5,150
A share of the administration costs of local authority	8,000
Casual staff	1,760
Refreshments	1,180

On average the theatre is half full for the performances of the repertory company. The capacity and seat prices in the theatre are:

200 seats at £6 each
500 seats at £4 each
300 seats at £3 each

In addition, the theatre sells refreshments during the performances for £3,880 per month. Programme sales cover their costs but advertising in the programme generates £3,360.

The management committee has been approached by a popular touring group to take over the theatre for one month (25 performances). The group is prepared to pay half of its ticket income for the booking. It expects to fill the theatre for 10 nights and achieve two-thirds capacity on the remaining 15 nights. The prices charged are 50p less than normally applies in the theatre.

The local authority will pay for heat and light costs and will still honour the contracts of all artistes and pay the full-time employees who will sell refreshments, programmes and so on. The committee does not expect any change in the level of refreshments or programme sales if they agree to this booking.

Note: The committee includes the share of the local authority administration costs when making profit calculations. It assumes occupancy applies equally across all seat prices.

Required:

(a) On financial grounds should the management committee agree to the approach from the touring group? Support your answer with appropriate workings.
(b) Assume the group will fill the theatre for 10 nights as predicted. What occupancy is required for the remaining 15 nights for the committee to:
   (i)   exactly cover all of its costs for the month?
   (ii) be financially indifferent to the booking?
(c) What other factors may have a bearing on the decision by the committee?

8.3 Andrews and Co. Ltd has been invited to tender for a contract. It is to produce 10,000 metres of a cable in which the business specialises. The estimating department of the business has produced the following information relating to the contract:

● *Materials.*   The cable will require a steel core, which the business buys in. The steel core is to be coated with a special plastic, also bought in, using a special process.

Plastic for the covering will be required at the rate of 0.10 kg/metre of completed cable.

- *Direct labour.*   Skilled: 10 minutes/metre
                      Unskilled: 5 minutes/metre

The business already has sufficient stock of each of the materials required, to complete the contract. Information on the cost of the stock is as follows:

	Steel core £/metre	Plastic £/kg
Historic cost	1.50	0.60
Current buying-in cost	2.10	0.70
Scrap value	1.40	0.10

The steel core is in constant use by the business for a variety of work that it regularly undertakes. The plastic is a surplus from a previous contract where a mistake was made and an excess quantity ordered. If the current contract does not go ahead, this plastic will be scrapped.

Unskilled labour, which is paid at the rate of £5 an hour, will need to be taken on specifically to undertake the contract. The business is fairly quiet at the moment which means that a pool of skilled labour exists that will still be employed at full pay of £7 an hour to do nothing if the contract does not proceed. The pool of skilled labour is sufficient to complete the contract.

Required:
Indicate the minimum price at which the contract could be undertaken, such that the business would neither be better or worse off as a result of doing it.

8.4 SJ Ltd has been asked to quote a price for a special contract that will take the business one week to complete. Information relating to labour for the contract is as follows:

Grade of labour	Hours required	Basic rate/hour
Skilled	27	£9
Semi-skilled	14	£7
Unskilled	20	£5

A shortage of skilled labour means that the necessary staff to undertake the contract would have to be moved from other work that is currently yielding an excess of sales revenue over labour and material cost of £8 per hour.

Semi-skilled labour is currently being paid at semi-skilled rates to undertake unskilled work. If the relevant staff are moved to work on the contract, unskilled labour will have to be employed for the week to replace them.

The unskilled labour actually needed to work on the contract will be employed for the week.

All labour is charged to contracts at 50 per cent above the rate paid to the employees, so as to cover the contract's fair share of the various production overheads of the company. It is estimated that the cost of overheads will increase by £50 as a result of undertaking the contract.

Undertaking the contract will require the use of a specialised machine for the week. The business owns such a machine, which it depreciates at the rate of £120 per week. This machine is currently being hired out to another business at a weekly rental of £175 on a week-by-week contract.

To derive the above estimates, the business has had to spend £300 on specialised drawings. If the contract does not proceed, the drawings can be sold for £250.

An estimate of the contract's fair share of the business rent and rates is £150 per week.

Required:
Deduce the minimum price at which SJ Ltd could undertake the contract such that it would be neither better nor worse off as a result of undertaking it.

8.5 A business in the food industry is currently holding 2,000 tonnes of material in bulk storage. This material deteriorates with time, and so in the near future it needs to be repackaged for sale or sold in its present form.

The stock was aquired in two batches: 800 tonnes at a price of £40 per tonne and 1,200 tonnes at a price of £44 per tonne. The current market price of any additional purchases is £48 per tonne. If the business were to dispose of the material, it could sell any quantity but only for £36 per tonne; it does not have the contacts or reputation to command a higher price.

Repackaging of this bulk material may be undertaken to develop either Product A or Product X. No weight loss occurs with repackaging, that is, one tonne of material will make one tonne of A or X. For Product A, there is an additional cost of £60 per tonne, after which it will sell for £105 per tonne. The marketing department estimates that 500 tonnes could be sold in this way.

In the development of Product X, the business incurs additional costs of £80 per tonne for repackaging. A market price for X is not known and no minimum price has been agreed. The management is currently engaged in discussions over the minimum price that may be charged for Product X in the current circumstances.

Required:
Identify the relevant unit cost for pricing the increments of Product X, given sales volumes of X of:

(a) up to 1,500 tonnes
(b) over 1,500 tonnes, up to 2,000 tonnes
(c) over 2,000 tonnes.

Explain your answer.

8.6 A local education authority is faced with a predicted decline in the demand for school places in its area. It is believed that some schools will have to close in order to remove up to 800 places from current capacity levels. The schools that may face closure are referenced as A, B, C or D. Their details are as follows:

● *School A.* (capacity 200) was built 15 years ago at a cost of £1.2 million. It is situated in a 'socially disadvantaged' community area. The authority has been offered £14 million for the site by a property developer.
● *School B.* (capacity 500) was built 20 years ago and cost £1 million. It was renovated only two years ago at a cost of £3 million to improve its facilities. An offer of £8 million has been made for the site by a company planning a shopping complex in this affluent part of the town.
● *School C.* (capacity 600). The land for this school is rented from a local company for an annual cost of £30,000. The school cost £5 million to build five years ago.
● *School D.* (800 capacity) cost £7 million to build eight years ago; last year £1.5 million was spent on an extension. It offers considerable space, which is

currently used for sporting events. This factor makes it popular with developers, who have recently offered £9 million for the site.

In the accounting system, the local authority depreciates fixed assets based on 2 per cent per year on the original cost. It also differentiates between one-off, large items of capital expenditure or revenue, and annually recurring items.

The land rented for School C is based on a 100-year lease. If the school closes, the property reverts immediately to the owner. If School C is not closed, it will require a £3 million investment to improve safety at the school.

If School D is closed, it will be necessary to pay £1.8 million to adapt facilities at other schools to accommodate the change.

The local authority has a central staff, which includes an administrator for each school costing £20,000 per year each, and a chief education officer costing £40,000 per year in total.

Required:

(a) Prepare a summary of the relevant cash flows (costs/revenues) under the following options:
   (i)   no closures
   (ii) closure of D only
   (iii) closure of A and B
   (iv) closure of A and C.
   Show separately the one-off effects and annually recurring items, rank the options open to the local authority, and briefly interpret your answer. *Note*: various approaches are acceptable providing they are logical.
(b) Identify and comment on any two different types of irrelevant cost contained in the information given.
(c) Discuss other factors that might have a bearing on the decision.

8.7 Rob Otics Ltd, a small business that specialises in building electronic-control equipment, has just received an order from a customer for eight identical robotic units. These will be completed using Rob Otic's own labour force and factory capacity. The product specification prepared by the estimating department shows the following:

- Material and labour requirements per robotic unit:
  Component X   2 per unit
  Component Y   1 per unit
  Component Z   4 per unit.
- Other miscellaneous items:
  Assembly labour   25 hours per unit (but see below)
  Inspection labour   6 hours per unit.

As part of the costing exercise, the business has collected the following information:

- *Component X.* This is a stock item normally held by the business as it is in constant demand. The 10 units currently in stock were invoiced to Rob Otics at £150 per unit, but the sole supplier has announced a price rise of 20 per cent effective immediately. Rob Otics has not yet paid for the items in stock.
- *Component Y.* 25 units are in stock. This component is not normally used by Rob Otics but is in stock because of a cancelled order following the bankruptcy of a customer. The stock originally cost the company £4,000 in total, although Rob Otics has recouped £1,500 from the liquidator. As Rob Otics can see no use for it, the finance director proposes to scrap the 25 units.

- *Component Z.* This is in regular use by Rob Otics. There is none in stock but an order is about to be sent to a supplier for 75 units, irrespective of this new proposal. The supplier charges £25 per unit on small orders but will reduce the price by 20 per cent to £20 per unit for all units on any order over 100 units.
- *Other miscellaneous items.* These are expected to cost £250 in total.

Assembly labour is currently in short supply in the area and is paid at £10 per hour. If the order is accepted, all necessary labour will have to be transferred from existing work, and other orders will be lost. It is estimated that for each hour transferred to this contract £38 will be lost (calculated as lost sales revenue £60, less materials £12 and labour £10). The production director suggests that, owing to a learning process, the time taken to make each unit will reduce, from 25 hours to make the first one, by 1 hour per unit made.

Inspection labour can be provided by paying existing personnel overtime which is at a premium of 50 per cent over the standard rate of £12 per hour.

When the company is working out its contract prices, it normally adds an amount equal to £20 per assembly hour to cover overheads. To the resulting total, 40 per cent is normally added as a profit mark-up.

Required:
(a) Prepare an estimate of the minimum price that you would recommend Rob Otics to charge for the proposed contract, and provide explanations for any items included.
(b) Identify any other factors that you would consider before fixing the final price.

8.8 A business places substantial emphasis on customer satisfaction and to this end delivers its product in special protective containers. These containers have been developed in a separate department, which has been assessed recently to be too expensive to continue. As a result, tenders have been issued for the provision of these containers by an outside supplier. A quote of £250,000 a year has been received for a volume that compares with current internal provision.

An investigation into the internal costs of container manufacture is undertaken and the following emerges:

(a) The annual cost of material is £120,000 according to the stores records maintained at actual historic cost. Three-quarters of this represents material that is regularly stocked and replenished. The remaining 25 per cent of the material cost is a special foaming chemical that is not used for any other purpose, and there are 40 tonnes still in stock. It was bought in bulk for £750 per tonne. Today's replacement price for this material is £1,050 per tonne but it is unlikely that the business could realise more than £600 per tonne if it had to be disposed of owing to the high handling costs and special transport facilities required.
(b) The annual labour cost is £80,000 for this department, however, most are casual employees or recent starters, and so, if an outside quote was accepted, little redundancy would be payable. There are two long-serving employees who would each accept as a salary £15,000 per annum until they reached retirement age in two years' time.
(c) The department manager has a salary of £30,000. The closure of this department would release him to take over another department for which a vacancy is about to be advertised. The status and prospects are similar.
(d) A rental charge of £9,750 based on floor area is allocated to the containers department. If the department was closed, the floorspace released would be used for

warehousing and, as a result, the company would give up the tenancy of an existing warehouse for which it is paying £15,750 a year.

(e) The plant cost £162,000 and was expected to be exhausted in nine years. Its market value now is £28,000 and it could continue for another two years.

(f) Annual plant maintenance costs are £9,900 and allocated general administrative costs £33,750 for the coming year.

Required:

Calculate the annual cost of manufacturing containers for comparison with the quote using relevant figures for establishing the cost or benefit of accepting the quote. Indicate any assumptions or qualifications you wish to make.

9 Cost–volume–profit analysis

Introduction

This chapter is concerned with the relationship between volume of activity, costs and profit. Broadly, costs can be analysed between costs that are fixed, relative to the volume of activity, and those that vary with it. We shall consider how we can use knowledge of this relationship to make decisions and assess risk, particularly in the context of short-term decisions.

When you have completed this chapter you should be able to:

- Distinguish between fixed costs and variable costs.
- Use knowledge of this distinction to deduce the break-even point for some activity.
- Make decisions on the use of spare capacity using knowledge of the relationship between fixed and variable costs.
- Make decisions about the acceptance (or continuance) or rejection of a particular contract or activity, based on knowledge of the relationship between fixed and variable costs.

The behaviour of costs

It is an observable fact that, for many commercial/business activities, costs may be broadly classified as follows:

- Those that stay fixed (the same) when changes occur to the volume of activity.
- Those that vary according to the volume of activity.

These are known as **fixed costs** and **variable costs** respectively.

We shall see in this chapter that knowledge of how much of each type of cost is involved with some particular activity can be of great value to a decision maker.

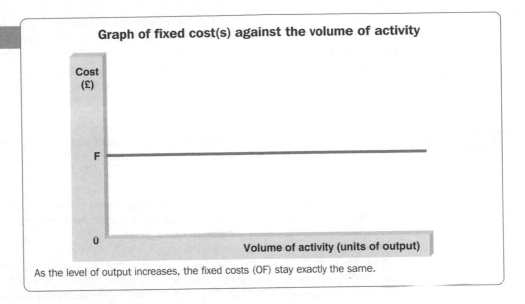

Figure 9.1

Graph of fixed cost(s) against the volume of activity

Cost (£)

F

0

Volume of activity (units of output)

As the level of output increases, the fixed costs (OF) stay exactly the same.

Fixed costs

The way in which fixed costs behave is depicted in Figure 9.1 The distance OF represents the amount of fixed costs in an activity, and this stays the same irrespective of the level of activity.

Activity 9.1

A business operates a small chain of hairdressing salons. Can you give some examples of costs that are likely to be fixed for this business?

We came up with the following:

- Rent
- Insurance
- Cleaning costs
- Staff salaries.

These costs seem likely to be the same irrespective of alterations in the number of customers having their hair cut or styled.

Staff salaries and wages sometimes tend to be referred to as always being variable costs. In fact, they tend to be fixed. People are generally not paid according to the level of output and it is not normal to sack staff when there is a short-term downturn in activity. If there is a long-term downturn in activity, or at least if it looks that way to management, redundancies may occur, with fixed-cost savings. This, however, is true of all costs. If there is seen to be a likely reduction in demand, the business may decide to close some branches and make rental-cost savings. Thus 'fixed' does not mean set in stone for all time; it usually means fixed over the short to medium term.

Nevertheless, in some circumstances, labour costs are variable, but probably in a minority of cases.

It is important to be clear that 'fixed', in this context, only means that the cost is not altered by changes in the **level of activity**.

Fixed costs are likely to be affected by inflation. If rent (a typical fixed cost) goes up owing to inflation, a fixed cost will have increased, but not owing to a change in the level of activity.

More generally, the level of fixed costs does not stay the same irrespective of the time period involved. Fixed costs are almost always 'time based', that is, they vary with the length of time concerned. The rental charge for two months is normally twice that for one month. You should note that when we talk of fixed costs being, say, £1,000, we must add the period concerned, say, £1,000 a month.

Activity 9.2

Do fixed costs stay the same irrespective of the level of output, even where there is a massive rise in that level? Think in terms of the rent cost for the hairdressing business.

In fact, the rent is only fixed over a particular range (known as the 'relevant' range). If the number of people wanting to have their hair cut by the business increases, and the business wishes to meet this increased demand, it would have to expand its physical size eventually. This might be by opening additional branches, or perhaps by moving existing branches to larger premises in the same vicinity. It may be possible to cope with minor increases in activity by using existing space more efficiently, or having longer opening hours. If activity continued to expand, increased rental charges would seem inevitable.

Figure 9.2

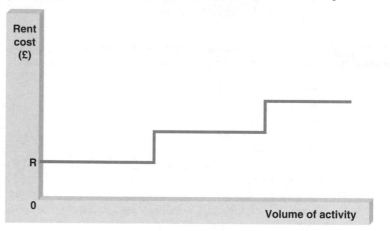

Graph of rent cost against the volume of activity

As the volume of activity increases from zero, the rent (a fixed cost) is unaffected. At a particular point, the volume of activity cannot increase without additional space being rented. The cost of renting the additional space will cause a 'step' in the rent cost. The higher rent cost will continue unaffected if volume were to rise further until, eventually, another step point would be reached.

Thus, in practice, the situation described in Activity 9.2 would look something like Figure 9.2. At lower levels of activity the rent cost shown in Figure 9.2 would be OR. As the level of activity expands, the accommodation becomes inadequate and further expansion requires an increase in premises and, therefore, cost. This higher level of accommodation provision will enable further expansion to take place. Eventually, further costs will need to be incurred if further expansion is to occur. Fixed costs that behave like this are often referred to as **stepped fixed costs**.

Variable costs

Variable costs are costs that vary with the level of activity. In a manufacturing business, for example, these would include raw materials used.

Can you think of some examples of variable costs in the hairdressing business?

We can think of a couple:

- Lotions and other materials used
- Laundry costs to wash towels used to dry the hair of customers.

As with many types of business activity, variable costs of hairdressers tend to be relatively light in comparison with fixed costs, in other words fixed costs tend to make up the bulk of total costs.

Debenhams's fixed costs

Debenhams plc, the department store chain, has a level of fixed costs that amount to less that 10 per cent of its total sales revenue for 2000, according to that year's annual report and accounts.

The fact that this information is reported indicates that businesses actually analyse their costs between fixed and variable. It is unusual, however, for a business to report its level of fixed costs as Debenhams has done. The retail trade is relatively unusual in having such a small fixed cost element.

Variable costs can be represented graphically as in Figure 9.3, which shows that, at zero level of activity, the variable cost is zero. This cost increases in a straight line as activity increases. The straight line for variable cost on this graph implies that the cost of materials will normally be the same per unit of activity irrespective of the level of activity concerned. We shall consider the practicality of this assumption a little later in this chapter.

Graph of the cost of hairdresser's materials against the volume of activity

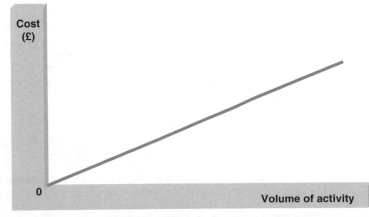

At zero activity, there are no variable costs. As the level of activity increases, so does the variable cost.

Semi-fixed (semi-variable) costs

In some cases, costs have both an element of fixed and of variable cost about them. They can be described as **semi-fixed (semi-variable) costs**.

Usually it is not obvious how much of each element a particular cost contains. It is normally necessary to look at past experience. If we have data on what the electricity cost has been for various levels of activity – say, the relevant data over several three-month periods (electricity is usually billed by the quarter) – we can estimate the fixed and variable portions. This may be done graphically, as shown in Figure 9.4. We tend to use past data here purely because it provides us

Figure 9.4

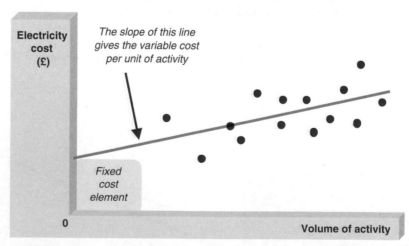

Graph of electricity cost against the volume of activity

Here the electricity bill for a time period (for example, three months) is plotted against the volume of activity for that same period. This is done for a series of periods. A line is then drawn which best 'fits' the various points on the graph. From this line we can then deduce both the cost at zero activity (the fixed element) and the slope of the line (indicating the variable element).

with an estimate of future costs; past costs are not, of course, relevant for their own sake.

Each dot in Figure 9.4 is a reading of the electricity charge for a particular level of activity (probably measured in terms of sales revenue). The diagonal line is the 'line of best fit'. This means that, to us, it looked like the line that best represents the data. A better estimate can usually be made using a statistical technique (least-squares regression), which does not involve drawing graphs and making estimates. In practice though, it usually makes little difference which approach is taken.

From the graph we can say that the fixed element of the electricity cost is the amount represented by the vertical distance from the origin at zero (bottom left-hand corner) to the point where the line of best fit crosses the vertical axis. The variable cost per unit is the amount that the line of best fit rises for each unit increase in the volume of activity.

By analysing semi-fixed costs into their fixed and variable elements in this way, we are left with only two types of cost. This means that we can use the information for further analysis.

Now that we have considered the nature of fixed and variable costs, we can go on to do something useful with that knowledge – carry out a **break-even analysis**.

Break-even analysis

If, in respect of a particular activity, we know the total fixed costs for a period and the total variable cost per unit, we can produce a graph like Figure 9.5.

The bottom part of the figure shows the fixed-cost area. Added to this is the

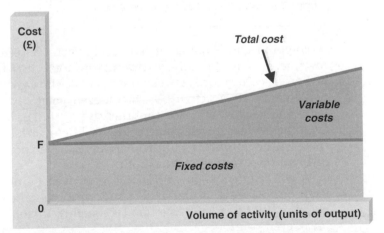

Figure 9.5

Graph of total cost against volume of activity

The bottom part of the graph represents the fixed-cost element. To this is added the wedge-shaped top portion, which represents the variable costs. The two parts together represent total cost. At zero activity, the variable costs are zero, and so total cost equals fixed costs. As activity increases, so does total cost, but only because variable costs increase. We are assuming that there are no steps in the fixed costs.

variable cost, the wedge-shaped portion at the top of the graph. The uppermost line represents the **total cost** at any particular level of activity. This total is the vertical distance between the horizontal axis and the uppermost line, for the particular level of activity concerned. Logically enough, the total cost at zero activity is the amount of the fixed costs. This is because, even where there is nothing going on, the business will still be paying rent, salaries and so on, at least in the short term. The fixed cost is augmented by the amount of the relevant variable costs, as the volume of activity increases.

If we superimpose onto this total-cost graph a line representing total revenue for each level of activity, we obtain the **break-even chart** shown in Figure 9.6.

Figure 9.6

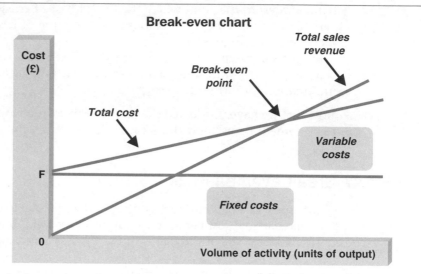

Break-even chart

The sloping line starting at 0 represents the sales revenue at various levels of activity. The point at which this finally catches up with the sloping total-cost line, which starts at F, is the break-even point. Below this point a loss will be made, above it a profit.

Note, in Figure 9.6, that at zero level of activity (zero sales) there is zero sales revenue. The profit (total sales revenue less total cost) at various levels of activity is the vertical distance between the total sales line and the total cost line, at that particular level of activity. At **break-even point**, there is no vertical distance between these two lines and thus there is no profit or loss, and the activity breaks even. Below break-even point, a loss will be incurred; above break-even point, there will be a profit. The further below break-even point, the greater the loss; the further above, the greater the profit.

As you might imagine, deducing break-even points by graphical means is a laborious business. It may have struck you that since the relationships in the graph are all linear (the lines are all straight), it would be easy to calculate the break-even point.

We know that at break-even point (but not at any other point):

$$\text{Total revenues} = \text{Total costs}$$

That is,

$$\text{Total revenues} = \text{Fixed costs} + \text{Total variable costs}$$

If we call the number of units of output at break-even point b, then

$$b \times \text{Sales revenue per unit} = \text{Fixed costs} + (b \times \text{Variable costs per unit})$$

thus,

$$(b \times \text{Sales revenue per unit}) - (b \times \text{Variable costs per unit}) = \text{Fixed costs}$$

and,

$$b \times (\text{Sales revenue per unit} - \text{Variable costs per unit}) = \text{Fixed costs}$$

giving

$$b = \frac{\text{Fixed costs}}{\text{Sales revenue per unit} - \text{Variable costs per unit}}$$

If you look back at the break-even chart, this looks logical. The total-cost line starts with an 'advantage' over the sales revenue line equal to the amount of the fixed costs. Because the sales revenue per unit is greater than the variable cost per unit, the sales revenue line will gradually catch up with the total cost line. The rate at which it will catch it up is dependent on the relative steepnesses of the two lines, and the amount that it has to catch up is the amount of the fixed costs. Bearing in mind that the slopes of the two lines are the variable cost per unit and the selling price per unit, the above equation for calculating b looks perfectly logical.

Though the break-even point can be calculated quickly and simply, as shown, it does not mean that the break-even chart is without value. The chart shows the relationship between cost, volume and profit in a form that can readily be understood by non-financial managers. The break-even chart can therefore be a useful device for explaining this relationship.

Example 9.1

Cottage Industries Ltd makes baskets. The fixed costs of operating the workshop for a month total £500. Each basket requires materials that cost £2. Each basket takes two hours to make and the business pays the basketmakers £5 an hour. The basketmakers are all on contracts such that if they do not work for any reason, they are not paid. The baskets are sold to a wholesaler for £14 each.

What is the break-even point for basketmaking for the business?

The break-even point (in number of baskets) is:

$$\frac{\text{Fixed costs}}{\text{Sales revenue per unit} - \text{Variable costs per unit}}$$

$$= \frac{£500}{£14 - (2 + 10)} = 250 \text{ baskets per month}$$

Note that the break-even point must be expressed with respect to a period of time.

Exhibit 9.2

Break-even point at British Airways plc (BA)

In its annual report and accounts for 2000, BA reported that it breaks even at a level of about 66 per cent. In general terms, if BA's planes fly at about two-thirds full, the business will break even, During the late 1990s the break-even point was, on average, a percentage point or two below the 2000 level.

The fact that BA has mentioned this implies that, in practice, businesses consider cost–volume relationships when assessing their financial performance.

Activity 9.5

Can you think of reasons why the managers of a business might find it useful to know the break-even point of some activity that they are planning to undertake?

The usefulness of being able to deduce a break-even point is to compare the planned or expected level of activity with the break-even point and so make a judgement about risk. Operating only just above the level of activity necessary in order to break even may indicate that it is a risky venture, since only a small fall from the planned level of activity could lead to a loss.

Activity 9.6

Cottage Industries Ltd (see Example 9.1) expects to sell 500 baskets a month. The business has the opportunity to rent a basketmaking machine. Doing so would increase the total fixed costs of operating the workshop for a month to £3,000. Using the machine would reduce the labour time to one hour per basket. The basketmakers would still be paid £5 an hour.

(a) How much profit would the business make each month from selling baskets, assuming first that the basketmaking machine is not rented and then assuming that it is rented?
(b) What is the break-even point if the machine is rented?

What do you notice about the figures that you calculate?

(a) Estimated profit, per month, from basketmaking:

			Without the machine		With the machine	
			£	£	£	£
Sales (500 × £14)				7,000		7,000
Less	Materials	(500 × £2)	1,000		1,000	
	Labour	(500 × 2 × £5)	5,000			
		(500 × 1 × £5)			2,500	
	Fixed costs		500		3,000	
				6,500		6,500
Profit				500		500

(b) The break-even point (in number of baskets) with the machine is:

$$\frac{\text{Fixed costs}}{\text{Sales revenue per unit} - \text{Variable costs per unit}}$$

$$= \frac{£3,000}{£14 - (2 + 5)} = 429 \text{ baskets per month}$$

The break-even point without the machine is 250 baskets per month (see Example 9.1, above).

There seems to be nothing to choose between the two manufacturing strategies regarding profit, at the estimated sales volume. There is, however, a distinct difference between the two strategies regarding the break-even point. Without the machine, the actual level of sales could fall by a half of that which is expected (from 500 to 250) before the business would fail to make a profit. With the machine, a 14 per cent fall (from 500 to 429) would be enough to cause the business to fail to make a profit. On the other hand, for each additional basket sold, above the estimated 500, an additional profit of only £2 (£14 – (2 + 10)) would be made without the machine, whereas £7 (£14 – (2 + 5)) would be made with the machine.

(Note that knowledge of the break-even point and the planned level of activity gives some basis of assessing the riskiness of the activity.)

We shall take a closer look at the relationship between fixed costs, variable costs and breaking even, together with any advice that we might give the management of Cottage Industries Ltd, after we have briefly considered the notion of contribution.

Contribution

The bottom part of the break-even formula (sales revenue per unit less variable costs per unit), is known as the **contribution** per unit. Thus, for the basketmaking activity, without the machine the contribution per unit is £2 and with the machine it is £7. This can be a useful figure to know in a decision-making context. It is referred to as 'contribution' because it contributes to meeting the fixed costs and, if there is any excess, it also contributes to profit.

The variable cost per unit will usually be equal to the **marginal cost** – that is, the additional cost of making one more basket. Where making one more will involve a step in the fixed costs, the marginal cost is not just the variable cost but will include the increment, or step, in the fixed costs.

Margin of safety and operating gearing

The **margin of safety** is the extent to which the planned level of output or sales lies above the break-even point. Going back to Activity 9.6, we saw that the following situation exists:

	Without the machine	With the machine
Expected level of sales	500	500
Break-even point	250	429
Difference (margin of safety):		
Number of baskets	250	71
Percentage of estimated level of sales	50%	14%

Activity 9.7

What advice would you give Cottage Industries Ltd about renting the machine on the basis of the figures for margin of safety?

It is a matter of personal judgement, which in turn is related to individual attitudes to risk, as to which strategy to adopt. Most people, however, would prefer the strategy of not renting the machine since the margin of safety between the expected level of activity and the break-even point is much greater.

The relative margins of safety are directly linked to the relationship between the selling price per basket, the variable costs per basket and the fixed costs per month. Without the machine, the contribution (selling price less variable costs) per basket is £2; with the machine, it is £7. On the other hand, without the machine the fixed costs are £500 a month and with the machine they are £3,000. This means that, with the machine, the contributions have more fixed costs to 'overcome' before the activity becomes profitable. However, the rate at which the

Figure 9.7

Break-even charts for Cottage Industries' basketmaking activities (a) without the machine and (b) with the machine

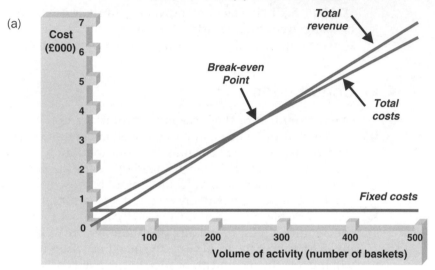

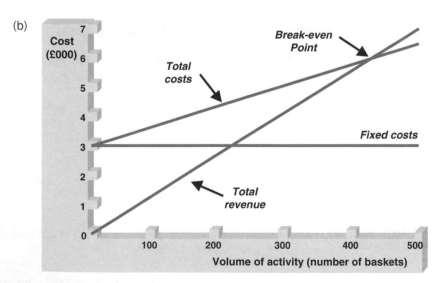

Without the machine the contribution per unit is low. Thus, each additional basket sold does not make a dramatic difference to the profit or loss. With the machine, however, the opposite is true, and small increases or decreases in the sales volume will have a marked effect on the profit or loss.

contributions can overcome fixed costs is higher with the machine, because variable costs are lower. This means that one more, or one less, basket sold has a greater impact on profit than it does if the machine is not rented. The contrast between the two scenarios is shown graphically in Figure 9.7

The relationship between contribution and fixed costs is known as **operating gearing**. An activity with relatively high fixed costs compared with its variable costs is said to have high operating gearing. Thus, Cottage Industries Ltd is more highly operating geared with the machine than without it. Renting the machine quite dramatically increases the level of operating gearing because it causes an increase in fixed costs, but at the same time it leads to a reduction in variable costs per basket.

The reason why the word 'gearing' is used in this context is that, as with intermeshing gear wheels of different circumferences, a movement in one of the factors (volume of output) causes a disproportionately greater movement in the other (profit), as illustrated by Figure 9.8.

We can demonstrate operating gearing with Cottage Industries Ltd's basket-making activities, as follows:

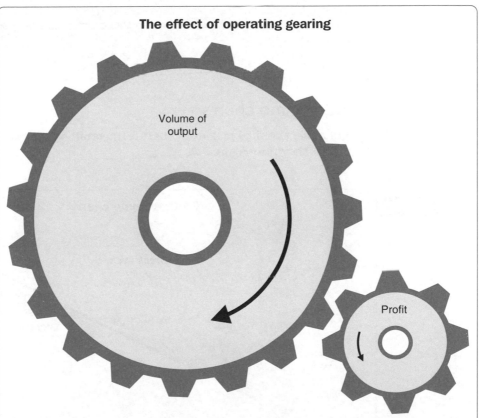

Figure 9.8

The effect of operating gearing

Volume of output

Profit

Where operating gearing is relatively high, as in the diagram, an amount of circular motion in the volume wheel causes a greater amount of circular motion in the profit wheel. An increase in volume would cause a disproportionally greater increase in profit. The equivalent would be true of a decrease in activity, however.

	Without the machine			With the machine		
Volume	500	1,000	1,500	500	1,000	1,500
	£	£	£	£	£	£
Contributions	1,000	2,000	3,000	3,500	7,000	10,500
Less Fixed costs	500	500	500	3,000	3,000	3,000
Profit	500	1,500	2,500	500	4,000	7,500

where contributions are calculated as £2 per basket without the machine and £7 per basket with it.

Note that without the machine (low operating gearing), a doubling of the output from 500 to 1,000 brings a trebling of the profit. With the machine (high operating gearing), doubling output causes profit to rise by eight times.

Operating gearing is quite similar in nature and effect to the financial gearing that we met in Chapter 6.

●●●● Profit–volume charts

➔ A slight variant of the break-even chart is the **profit–volume (PV) chart**. A typical PV chart is shown in Figure 9.9.

Figure 9.9

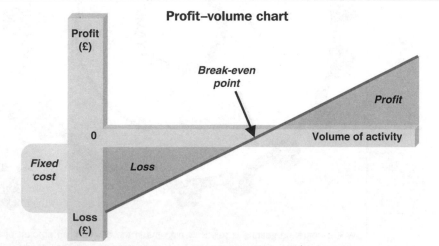

The sloping line is profit plotted against volume of activity. As activity increases, so does total contribution (sales revenue less variable costs). At zero activity there are no contributions, and so there will be a loss equal in amount to the total fixed costs.

The PV chart is obtained by plotting loss or profit against volume of activity. The slope of the graph is equal to the contribution per unit, since each additional unit sold decreases the loss, or increases the profit, by the sales revenue per unit less the variable cost per unit. At zero level of activity, there are no contributions and so there is a loss equal to the amount of the fixed costs. As the level of activity increases, the amount of the loss gradually decreases until break-even point is reached. Beyond break-even point, profits increase as activity increases.

It may have occurred to you that the PV chart does not tell us anything not shown by the break-even chart. Though this is true, information is perhaps more easily absorbed from the PV chart. This is particularly true of the profit at any level of volume. This information is provided by the break-even chart as the vertical distance between the total cost and total sales revenue lines. The PV chart, in effect, combines the total sales revenue and total variable cost lines, which means that profit (or loss) is plotted directly.

● ● ● ● ● The economist's view of the break-even chart

So far in this chapter we have treated all the relationships as linear – that is, all of the lines in the graphs have been straight. This is typically the approach taken in accounting, though it may not be strictly valid.

Consider, for example, the variable cost line in the break-even chart; accountants would normally treat this as being a straight line. Strictly, however, the line perhaps should not be straight because at high levels of output **economies of scale** may be available to an extent not available at lower levels. For example, a raw material (a typical variable cost) may be able to be used more efficiently with higher volumes of activity. Similarly, the relatively large quantities of material and services bought may enable the business to benefit from bulk discounts and general power in the marketplace to negotiate lower prices.

There is also a general tendency for sales revenue per unit to reduce as volume is expanded, since to sell more units of the product or service, it will probably be necessary to lower the selling price.

Economists tend to recognise that, in real life, the relationships portrayed in the break-even chart are usually non-linear. The typical economist's view of the chart is shown in Figure 9.10.

Note, in that diagram, that the variable costs start to increase quite steeply with volume, but around point A economies of scale start to take effect and further increases in volume do not cause such a large increase, per unit of output, in variable costs. These economies of scale continue to have a benign effect on costs until a point is reached where the business will be operating towards the end of its efficient range. Here the business may have problems with finding supplies of the variable-cost elements, which will normally adversely affect their price. Also, the business may find it more difficult to produce, there may be machine breakdowns, and so on.

At low levels of output, sales may be made at a relatively high price per unit. To increase sales output beyond point B it may be necessary to lower the average sales price per unit.

Note how this 'curvilinear' representation of the break-even chart can easily lead to the existence of two break-even points.

Figure 9.10

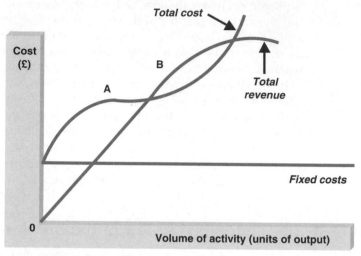

The economist's view of the break-even chart

Cost (£)

Total cost

B

A

Total revenue

Fixed costs

0

Volume of activity (units of output)

As volume increases, economies of scale have a favourable effect on variable costs, but this effect is reversed at still higher levels of output. At the same time, sales revenue per unit will tend to decrease at higher levels to encourage additional buyers.

Accountants justify their approach to this topic by the fact that, although the line may not in practice be perfectly straight, this defect is probably not worth taking into account in most cases. This is partly because all of the information used in the analysis is based on estimates of the future. Since this will inevitably be flawed, it seems pointless to be pedantic about minor approximations, such as treating the total cost and revenue lines as straight ones when strictly this is invalid. Only where significant economies or diseconomies of scale are involved should the non-linearity of the variable costs be taken into account. Also, in practice, for most businesses the range of possible volumes of activity at which they might operate (the **relevant range**) is pretty narrow. Over very short distances, it is perfectly reasonable to treat a curved line as being straight.

●●●● Weaknesses of break-even analysis

As we have seen, break-even analysis can provide some useful insights to the important relationship between fixed costs, variable costs and the volume of activity. It does, however, have its weaknesses. There are probably three general points:

● *Non-linear relationships.* The normal approach to break-even analysis, in practice, assumes that the relationships between sales revenues, variable costs and volume are strictly straight-line ones. In real life this is unlikely to be true. This is probably not a major problem, since break-even analysis is normally conducted in advance of the activity actually taking place. Our ability to predict future costs, revenues and so on is somewhat limited, hence, what are probably minor variations from strict linearity are unlikely to be significant compared with other forecasting errors.

- *Stepped fixed costs.* Most fixed costs are not fixed over all volumes of activity. They tend to be 'stepped' in the way depicted in Figure 9.2. This means that, in practical circumstances, great care must be taken in making assumptions about fixed costs. The problem is particularly heightened because most activities will probably involve fixed costs of various types (rent, supervisory salaries, administration costs), all of which are likely to have their steps at different points.

- *Multi-product businesses.* Most businesses do not offer just one product or service. This is a problem for break-even analysis since it raises the question of the effect of additional sales of one product or service on sales of another of the business's products or services. There is also the problem of identifying the fixed costs of one particular activity. Fixed costs tend to relate to more than one activity, for example, two activities may be carried out in the same rented premises. There are ways of dividing fixed costs between activities, but these tend to be arbitrary, which calls the value of the break-even analysis into question.

Marginal analysis

If you cast your mind back to Chapter 8, when we were discussing relevant costs for decision making, you will recall that we concluded that only costs varying with the decision should be included in the decision analysis. For many decisions that involve relatively small variations from existing practice and/or are for relatively limited periods of time, fixed costs are not relevant to the decision. This is because either:

- Fixed costs tend to be impossible to alter in the short term, or
- Managers are reluctant to alter them in the short term.

Suppose that a business occupies premises that it owns in order to carry out its activities. There is a downturn in demand for the service that the business provides and it would be possible to carry on the business from smaller, cheaper premises. Does this mean that the business will sell its old premises and move to new ones overnight? Clearly, it cannot mean this. This is partly because it is not usually possible to find a buyer for premises at very short notice, and it may be difficult to move premises quickly where there is, say, delicate equipment to be moved. Apart from external constraints on the speed of any such move, management may feel that the downturn is not permanent and would thus be reluctant to take such a dramatic step as to deny itself the opportunity to benefit from a possible revival of trade.

A business's premises may provide an example of an area of one of the more inflexible types of cost, but most fixed costs tend to be broadly similar in this context.

We shall now consider some decision-making areas where fixed costs can be regarded as irrelevant, and we shall then analyse decisions in those areas. The fact that the decisions that we are considering here are short term means that the objective of wealth enhancement will be promoted by seeking to generate as much net cash inflow as possible. In **marginal analysis**, we concern ourselves just with costs and revenues that vary with the decision. This often means that fixed costs are ignored.

Accepting/rejecting special contracts

Activity 9.9

Cottage Industries Ltd (see Example 9.1), has spare capacity in that it has spare basketmakers. An overseas retail chain has offered the business an order for 300 baskets at a price of £13 each. Without considering any wider issues, should the business accept the order? *Note*: assume that the business does not rent the machine.

Since the fixed costs will be incurred in any case, they are not relevant to this decision. All we need to do is to see whether the price offered will yield a contribution. If it will, then the business will be better off by accepting the contract than by refusing it.

	£
Additional revenue per unit	13
Less Additional cost per unit	12
Additional contribution per unit	1

For 300 units, the additional contribution will be £300. Since no fixed cost increase is involved, irrespective of whatever else may be happening to the business, it will be £300 better off by taking this contract than by refusing it.

As ever with decision making, there are other factors that are either difficult or impossible to quantify. These should be taken into account before reaching a final decision. In the case of Cottage Industries Ltd's decision on the overseas customer these could include:

- The possibility that spare capacity will be 'sold off' cheaply when there is another potential customer who will offer a higher price, but by which time the capacity will be fully committed. It is a matter of commercial judgement as to how likely this will be.
- The problem that selling the same product, but at different prices, could lead to a loss of customer goodwill. The fact that a different price will be set for customers in different countries (that is, in different markets) may be sufficient to avoid this potential problem.
- If the business is going to suffer continually from being unable to sell its full production potential at the 'regular' price, it might be better in the long run to reduce capacity and make fixed-cost savings. Using the spare capacity to produce marginal benefits may lead to the business failing to address this issue.
- On a more positive note, the business may see this as a way of breaking into the overseas market. This is something that might be impossible to achieve if the business charges its regular price.

The most efficient use of scarce resources

We tend to think in terms of the size of the market being the brake on output. That is to say, the ability of a business to sell is likely to limit production, rather than the ability to produce being likely to limit sales. In some cases, however, it is a limit on what can be produced that limits sales. Limited production might stem from a shortage of any factor of production – labour, raw materials, space, machinery, and so on.

The most profitable combination of products will occur where the **contribution per unit of the scarce factor** is maximised. Let us look at Example 9.2 to illustrate this point.

A business provides three different services, the details of which are as follows:

Service (codename)	AX107	AX109	AX220
	£	£	£
Selling price per unit	50	40	65
Variable cost per unit	25	20	35
Contribution per unit	25	20	30
Labour time per unit	5 hours	3 hours	6 hours

Within reason, the market will take as many units of each service as can be provided, but the ability to provide the service is limited by the availability of labour, all of which needs to be skilled. Fixed costs are not affected by the choice of service provided because provision of all three services uses the same production facilities.

The most profitable service is AX109 because it generates a contribution of £6.67 (£20/3) per hour. The other two generate only £5.00 each per hour (£25/5 and £30/6).

Your first reaction to Example 9.2 may have been that the business should provide only service AX220, because this is the one that yields the highest contribution per unit sold. If so, you are making the mistake of thinking of the ability to sell as being the limiting factor. If you are not convinced by the analysis, take an imaginary number of available labour hours and ask yourself what is the maximum contribution (and, therefore, profit) that could be made by providing each service exclusively. Bear in mind that there is no shortage of anything else, including market demand – just a shortage of labour.

A business makes three different products, the details of which are as follows:

Product (codename)	B14	B17	B22
Selling price per unit (£)	25	20	23
Variable cost per unit (£)	10	8	12
Weekly demand (units)	25	20	30
Machine time per unit	4 hours	3 hours	4 hours

Fixed costs are not affected by the choice of product because all three products use the same machine. Machine time is limited to 148 hours a week.

Which combination of products should be manufactured if the business is to produce the highest profit?

Product (codename)	B14	B17	B22
	£	£	£
Selling price per unit	25	20	23
Variable cost per unit	10	8	12
Contribution per unit	15	12	11
Machine time per unit	4 hours	3 hours	4 hours
Contribution per machine hour	3.75	4.00	2.75
Order of priority	2nd	1st	3rd

Therefore

produce	20 units of product B17 using	60	hours
	22 units of product B14 using	88	hours
		148	hours

This leaves unsatisfied the market demand for a further three units of product B14 and 30 units of product B22.

Activity 9.11

What steps could be contemplated that could lead to a higher level of contribution for the business in Activity 9.10?

....

The possibilities for improving matters might include:

- Contemplate obtaining additional machine time. This could mean obtaining a new machine, subcontracting the machining to another business or, perhaps, squeezing a few more hours per week out of the business's own machine. Perhaps a combination of two or more of these is a possibility.
- Redesign the products in a way that requires less time per unit on the machine.
- Increase the price per unit of the three products. This may well have the effect of dampening demand, but the existing demand cannot be met at present and it may be more profitable, in the long run, to make a greater contribution on each unit sold than to take one of the other courses of action to overcome the problem.

Activity 9.12

Going back to Activity 9.10, what is the maximum price that the business concerned would logically be prepared to pay to have the remaining B14s machined by a subcontractor, assuming that no fixed or variable costs would be saved as a result of not doing the machining 'in-house'? Would there be a different maximum if we were considering the B22s?

....

If the remaining three B14s were subcontracted at no cost, the business would be able to earn a contribution of £15 that it would not otherwise be able to gain. Any price up to £15 per unit would be worth paying a subcontractor to undertake the machining, therefore. Naturally, the business would prefer to pay as little as possible, but anything up to £15 would still make it worthwhile subcontracting the machining.

This would not be true of the B22s because they have a different contribution per unit. £11 would be the relevant figure in their case.

Make-or-buy decisions

Businesses are frequently confronted by the need to decide whether to produce their product or service themselves or to buy it in from some other business. Thus, a producer of electrical appliances might decide to subcontract the manufacture of one of its products to another business, perhaps because there is a shortage of production capacity in the producer's own factory, or because it believes it to be cheaper to subcontract than to make the appliance itself.

It might be just part of a product that is subcontracted. For example, the producer may have a component for the appliance made by another manufacturer. In principle, there is hardly any limit to the scope of make-or-buy decisions. Virtually any part, component or service, that is required in production of the main product or service, or the main product or service itself, could be the subject of a make-or-buy decision. So, for example, the personnel function of a business, which is normally performed 'in-house', could be subcontracted. At the same time, electrical power, which is typically provided by an outside electrical utility business, could be generated 'in-house'.

Example 9.3

Shah Ltd needs a component for one of its products. It can subcontract production of the component to a subcontractor, who will provide the component for £20 each. The business can produce the components internally for total variable costs of £15 per component. Shah Ltd has spare capacity. Should the component be subcontracted or produced internally?

The answer is that Shah Ltd should produce the component internally since the variable cost of subcontracting is greater by £5 than the variable cost of internal manufacture.

Activity 9.13

Now assume that Shah Ltd (Example 9.3) has no spare capacity, so it can only produce the component internally by reducing its output of another of its products. While it is making each component, it will lose contributions of £12 from the other product. Should the component be subcontracted or produced internally?

....

The answer is to subcontract. The relevant cost of internal production of each component is:

	£
Variable cost of production of the component	15
Opportunity cost of lost production of the other product	12
	27

This is clearly more costly than the £20 per component that will have to be paid to the subcontractor.

What factors, other than those immediately financially quantifiable, would you consider when making a make-or-buy decision?

....

We suggest the following factors:

● *The general problems of subcontracting*, namely loss of control of quality, and the potential unreliability of supply.
● *Expertise and specialisation*. It is possible for most businesses, with sufficient determination, to do virtually everything 'in-house'. This may, however, require a level of skill and facilities that most businesses neither have or do not feel inclined to acquire. Though it is true that most businesses could generate their own electricity, their managements tend to take the view that this is better done by a specialist generator business.

Closing or continuation decisions

It is quite common for businesses to account separately for each department or section to try to assess the relative effectiveness of each one.

Example 9.4

Goodsports Ltd is a retail shop that operates through three departments, all in the same premises. The three departments occupy roughly equal areas of the shop. The trading results for the year just ended showed the following:

	Total	Sports equipment	Sports clothes	General clothes
	£000	£000	£000	£000
Sales	534	254	183	97
Costs	482	213	163	106
Profit(loss)	52	41	20	(9)

It would appear that if the general clothes department were to close, the business would be more profitable, by £9,000 a year, assuming last year's performance to be a reasonable indication of future performance.

When the costs are analysed between those that are variable and those that are fixed, however, the following results were obtained:

	Total	Sports equipment	Sports clothes	General clothes
	£000	£000	£000	£000
Sales	534	254	183	97
Variable costs	344	167	117	60
Contribution	190	87	66	37
Fixed costs (rent, etc.)	138	46	46	46
Profit (loss)	52	41	20	(9)

Now it is clear that closing the general clothes department, without any other developments, would make the business worse off by £37,000 (the department's contribution). The department should not be closed, because it makes a positive contribution. The fixed costs would continue whether the department closed or not. As can be seen from analysis, distinguishing between variable and fixed costs can make the picture a great deal clearer.

Activity 9.15

In considering Goodsports Ltd in Example 9.4, we said that the general clothes department should not be closed 'without any other developments'. What 'other developments' could affect this decision, making continuation either more attractive or less attractive?

....

The things that we thought of include:

- Expansion of the other departments or replacing the general clothes department with a completely new activity. This would make sense only if the space currently occupied by the general clothes department could generate contributions totalling at least £37,000 a year.
- Subletting the space occupied by the general clothes department. Once again, this would need to generate a net rent of more than £37,000 a year to make it more financially beneficial than keeping the department open.
- There may be advantages in keeping the department open even if it generated no contribution whatsoever (assuming no other use for the space). This is because customers may be attracted into the shop because it has general clothing and they may then buy something from one of the other departments. By the same token, the activity of a sub-tenant may attract customers into the shop. On the other hand, it may drive them away!

Self-assessment question 9.1

Khan Ltd can make three products (A, B and C) using the same machines. Various estimates for next year have been made as follows:

	A £/unit	B £/unit	C £/unit
Selling price	30	45	20
Variable material cost	15	18	10
Other variable production costs	6	16	5
Share of fixed overheads	8	12	4
Time required on machines (hr/unit)	2	3	1

Fixed overhead costs for next year are expected to total £40,000.

Required:

(a) If the business were to make only product A next year, how many units would it need to make in order to break even? (Assume for this part of the question that there is no effective limit to market size and production capacity.)

(b) If the business has maximum machine capacity for next year of 10,000 hours, in which order of preference would the three products come?

(c) The maximum market for next year for the three products is as follows:

    Product A   3,000 units
    Product B   2,000 units
    Product C   5,000 units.

If we continue to assume a maximum machine capacity of 10,000 hours for the year, what quantities of which product should the business make next year and how much profit would this be expected to yield?

● Summary

In this chapter we have seen that costs divide broadly into those that are fixed relative to the level of activity and those that are not affected by changes in the level of activity. Knowledge of how this distinction applies to any particular activity enables us to undertake break-even analysis – that is, deducing the break-even point for the activity. We have also seen that, for short-run decisions, all fixed costs (that is, costs that do not vary with the level of activity) can be assumed to be irrelevant, and all variable costs can be assumed to be relevant. This helps us to make decisions on short-term contracts, on the use of spare capacity, on the most effective use of scarce resources, on short-term make-or-buy decisions and on decisions relating to the continuance or deletion of part of a business.

Key terms

Fixed cost p. 264	Break-even point p. 270
Variable cost p. 264	Contribution p. 273
Stepped fixed cost p. 266	Marginal cost p. 273
Semi-fixed (semi-variable) cost p. 268	Margin of safety p. 273
Break-even analysis p. 269	Operating gearing p. 275
Total cost p. 270	Profit–volume (PV) chart p. 276
Break-even chart p. 270	Marginal analysis p. 279

● Further reading

If you would like to explore the topics covered in this chapter in more depth, we recommend the following books:

Management Accounting, *Atkinson, A., Banker, R., Kaplan, R. and Mark Young, S.*, 3rd edn, Prentice Hall, 2001, chapter 3.
Management and Cost Accounting, *Drury, C.*, 5th edn, Thompson Learning Business Press, 2000, chapter 8.
Cost Accounting: A managerial emphasis, *Horngren, C., Foster, G. and Datar, S.*, 10th edn, Prentice Hall International, 2000, chapter 3.
Cost and Management Accounting, *Williamson, D.*, Prentice Hall International, 1996, chapters 3 and 11.

REVIEW QUESTIONS

9.1 Define the terms 'fixed cost' and 'variable cost'.

9.2 What is meant by the 'break-even point' for some activity? How is the break-even point calculated?

9.3 When we say that some business activity has 'high operating gearing', what do we mean?

9.4 If there is a scarce resource that is restricting sales, how will the business maximise its profit?

EXERCISES

Exercises 9.5–9.8 are more advanced than 9.1–9.4. Those with coloured numbers have answers at the back of the book.

9.1 The management of your company is concerned at its inability to obtain enough fully trained labour to enable it to meet its present budget projection.

Product:	Alpha	Beta	Gamma	Total
	£	£	£	£
Variable costs:				
Materials	6,000	4,000	5,000	15,000
Labour	9,000	6,000	12,000	27,000
Expenses	3,000	2,000	2,000	7,000
Allocated fixed costs	13,000	8,000	12,000	33,000
Total cost	31,000	20,000	31,000	82,000
Profit	8,000	9,000	2,000	19,000
Sales	£39,000	£29,000	£33,000	£101,000

The amount of labour likely to be available amounts to £20,000. All of the labour is paid at the same hourly rate. You have been asked to prepare a statement ensuring that at least 50 per cent of the budget sales are achieved for each product and the balance of labour used to produce the greatest profit.

Required:
(a) Prepare a statement showing the greatest profit available from the limited amount of labour available, within the constraint stated. *Hint*: remember that all variable labour is paid at the same rate.
(b) Provide an explanation of the method you have used.
(c) Provide an indication of any other factors that need to be considered.

9.2 Lannion and Co. is engaged in providing and marketing a standard cleaning service. Summarised results for the past two months reveal the following:

	October	November
Sales (units of the service)	200	300
Sales (£)	5,000	7,500
Operating profit (£)	1,000	2,200

There were no price changes of any description during these two months.

Required:
(a) Deduce the break-even point (in units of the service) for Lannion.
(b) State why the company might find it useful to know its break-even point.

9.3 A hotel group prepares accounts on a quarterly basis. The senior managers are reviewing the performance of one hotel and making plans for next year. They have in front of them the results for this year (based on some actual results and some forecasts to the end of this year):

Quarter	Sales £000	Profit(loss) £000
1	400	(280)
2	1,200	360
3	1,600	680
4	800	40
Total	4,000	800

The total estimated number of visitors (guest nights) for this year is 50,000. The results follow a regular pattern, there being no unexpected cost fluctuations beyond the seasonal trading pattern exhibited. The managers intend to incorporate into their plans for next year an anticipated increase in unit variable costs of 10 per cent and a profit target for the hotel of £1m.

Required:
(a) Determine the total variable and total fixed costs of the hotel for this year, by the use of a PV chart or by calculation. Tabulate the provisional annual results for this year in total, showing variable and fixed costs separately; show also the revenue and costs per visitor.
(b) (i)   If there is no increase in visitors next year, what will be the required revenue rate per hotel visitor to meet the profit target?
   (ii) If the required revenue rate per visitor is not raised above this year's level, how many visitors will be required to meet the profit target?
(c) Outline and briefly discuss the assumptions that are contained within the accountants' typical PV or break-even analysis, and assess whether they limit its usefulness.

9.4 Motormusic Ltd makes a standard model of car radio, which it sells to car manufacturers for £60 each. Next year the company plans to make and sell 20,000 radios. The company's costs are as follows:

Manufacturing	
Variable materials	£20 per radio
Variable labour	£14 per radio
Other variable costs	£12 per radio
Fixed costs	£80,000 per year
Administration and selling	
Variable	£3 per radio
Fixed	£60,000 per year

Required:
(a) Calculate the break-even point for next year, expressed both in radios and sales value.

(b) Calculate the margin of safety for next year, expressed both in radios and sales value.

9.5 A company makes three products, A, B and C. All three products require the use of two types of machine: cutting machines and assembling machines. Estimates for next year include the following:

	A	B	C
Selling price (per unit)	£25.00	£30.00	£18.00
Sales demand (units)	2,500	3,400	5,100
Variable material cost (per unit)	£12.00	£13.00	£10.00
Variable production cost (per unit)	£7.00	£4.00	£3.00
Time required per unit on cutting machines	1.0 hours	1.0 hours	0.5 hours
Time required per unit on assembling machines	0.5 hours	1.0 hours	0.5 hours

Fixed overhead costs for next year are expected to total £42,000. It is the company's policy for each unit of production to absorb these in proportion to its total variable costs. The company has cutting machine capacity of 5,000 hours a year and assembling machine capacity of 8,000 hours a year.

Required:
(a) State, with supporting workings, which products in which quantities the company should plan to make next year on the basis of the above information. *Hint*: first determine which machines will be a limiting factor (scarce resource).
(b) State the maximum price per product that it would be worth the company paying a subcontractor to carry out that part of the work which could not be done internally.

9.6 Darmor Ltd has three products, A, B and C, which require the same production facilities. Information about their per-unit production costs is as follows:

	A	B	C
	£	£	£
Labour – skilled	6	9	3
– unskilled	2	4	10
Materials	12	25	14
Other variable costs	3	7	7
Fixed costs	5	10	10

All labour and materials are variable costs. Skilled labour is paid a basic rate of £6 an hour and unskilled labour is paid a basic rate of £4 an hour. The labour costs per unit, shown above, are based on basic rates of pay. Skilled labour is scarce, which means that the business could sell more than the maximum that it is able to make of any of the three products.

Product A is sold in a regulated market and the regulators have set a price of £30 per unit for it.

Required:
(a) State, with supporting workings, the price that must be charged for Products B and C, such that the business would find it equally profitable to make and sell any of the three products.

(b) State, with supporting workings, the maximum rate of overtime premium that the business would logically be prepared to pay its skilled workers to work beyond the basic time.

9.7 Intermediate Products Ltd produces four types of water pump. Two of these (A and B) are sold by the business. The other two (C and D) are incorporated, as components, into other of the business's products. Neither C nor D is incorporated into A or B. Costings (per unit) for the products are as follows:

	A £	B £	C £	D £
Variable materials	15	20	16	17
Variable labour	25	10	10	15
Other variable costs	5	3	2	2
Other fixed costs	20	8	8	12
	£65	£41	£36	£46
Selling price (per unit)	£70	£45		

There is an outside supplier who is prepared to supply unlimited quantities of products C and D to the business, charging £40 per unit for type C and £55 per unit for type D.

Next year's estimated demand for the products, from the market (in the case of A and B) and from other production requirements (in the case of C and D) is as follows:

	Units
A	5,000
B	6,000
C	4,000
D	3,000

For strategic reasons, the business wishes to supply a minimum of 50 per cent of the above demand for products A and B.

Manufacture of all four products requires the use of a special machine. The products require time on this machine as follows:

	Hours per unit
A	0.5
B	0.4
C	0.5
D	0.3

Next year there are expected to be a maximum of 6,000 special machine hours available. There will be no shortage of any other factor of production.

Required:
(a) State, with supporting workings and assumptions, which products the business should plan to make next year.
(b) Explain the maximum amount that it would be worth the business paying per hour to rent a second special machine.
(c) Suggest ways, other than renting an additional special machine, that could solve the problem of the shortage of special machine time.

9.8 Gandhi Ltd renders a promotional service to small retailing businesses. There are three levels of service: the 'basic', the 'standard' and the 'comprehensive'. On the basis of past experience, the business plans next year to work at absolute full capacity as follows:

Service	Number of units of the service	Selling price £	Variable cost per unit
	£	£	
Basic	11,000	50	25
Standard	6,000	80	65
Comprehensive	16,000	120	90

The business's fixed costs total £660,000 a year. Each service takes about the same length of time, irrespective of the level.

One of the accounts staff has just produced a report that seems to show that the standard service is unprofitable. The relevant extract from the report is as follows:

Standard service cost analysis

	£	
Selling price per unit	80	
Variable cost per unit	(65)	
Fixed cost per unit	(20)	(£660,000/(11,000 + 6,000 + 16,000))
Net loss	(5)	

The producer of the report suggests that the business should not offer the standard service next year. In contrast, the marketing manager believes that the market for the basic service could be expanded by dropping its price to all customers.

Required:
(a) Should the standard service be offered next year, assuming that the quantity of the other services could not be expanded to use the spare capacity?
(b) Should the standard service be offered next year, assuming that the released capacity could be used to render a new service, the 'nova', for which customers would be charged £75, and which would have variable costs of £50 and take twice as long as the other three services?
(c) What is the minimum price that could be accepted for the basic service, assuming that the necessary capacity to expand it will come only from not offering the standard service?

10 Full costing

Introduction

In this chapter we are going to look at a widely-used approach for deducing the cost of a unit of output, which takes account of all of the costs. The precise approach taken tends to depend on whether each unit of output is identical to the next or whether each job has its own individual characteristics. It also tends to depend on whether or not the business draws up its accounts for overheads on a departmental basis. We shall look at how full costing is achieved and then we shall consider its usefulness for management purposes.

OBJECTIVES When you have completed this chapter you should be able to:

- Deduce the full cost of a unit of output in a single-product environment.
- Distinguish between direct and indirect costs and use this distinction to deduce the full cost of a job in a multi-product environment.
- Discuss the problem of charging overheads to jobs in a multi-product environment.
- Deduce the overheads to be charged to a job in a departmental-costing environment.

The nature of full costing

With **full costing**, we are not concerned with relevant or with variable costs, but with all costs involved with achieving some objective. The logic of full costing is that all of the costs of running a particular facility, say a factory, are part of the cost of the output of that factory. For example, the rent may be a cost that will not alter merely because we make one more unit of production, but if the factory were not rented there would be nowhere for production to take place and so rent is an important element of the cost of each unit of output.

Full cost is the total amount of resources, usually measured in monetary terms, sacrificed to achieve a particular objective. It takes account of *all* resources sacrificed to achieve the objective.

Uses of full cost information

Why do we need to deduce full cost information? There are probably two reasons:

- *For pricing purposes.* In some industries and circumstances, full costs are used as the basis of pricing. Here, the full cost is deduced and a percentage is added on for profit. This is known as **cost-plus pricing**. Garages carrying out vehicle repairs typically operate this way.

  In many circumstances, suppliers are not in a position to set prices on a cost-plus basis. Where there is a competitive market, a supplier will usually have to accept the price that the market offers, that is, most suppliers are 'price takers' not 'price makers'. We shall take a closer look at the subject of pricing, and the place of full costs in it, in Chapter 11.

- *For income measurement purposes.* You may recall from Chapter 3 that to provide a valid means of measuring a business's income it is necessary to match expenses with the revenues realised in the same accounting period. Where manufactured stock is made or partially made in one period but sold in the next, or where a service is partially rendered in one accounting period but the revenue is realised in the next, the full cost (including an appropriate share of overheads) must be carried from one accounting period to the next. Unless we are able to identify the full cost of work done in one period, which is the subject of a sale in the next, the profit figures of the periods concerned will become meaningless. This will mean that users of accounting information will not have a reliable means of assessing the effectiveness of the business or its parts.

This second reason for needing full cost information is illustrated by Example 10.1.

Example 10.1

During the accounting year that ended on 31 December last year, Engineers Ltd made a special machine for a customer. At the beginning of this year, after having a series of tests successfully completed by a subcontractor, the machine was delivered to the customer. The business's normal practice (typical of most businesses) is to take account of sales when the product passes to the customer. The sale price of the machine was £25,000.

During last year, the total cost of making the machine was £17,000. Testing the machine cost £1,000.

With these facts in mind:

(a) How much profit or loss did the business make on the machine last year?
(b) How much profit or loss did the business make on the machine this year?
(c) At what value must the business carry the machine in its balance sheet at the end of last year so that the correct profit will be recorded for each of the two years?

(a) No profit or loss was made last year, following the business's (and the generally accepted) approach to recognising sales revenues (the realisation convention). If the sale were not to be recognised until this year, it would be illogical (and contravene the matching convention) to treat the costs of making the machine as expenses until that time.

(b) During this year the sale would be recognised and all of the costs, including a reasonable share of overheads, would be set against it in this year's profit and loss account, as follows:

	£000	£000
Sales price		25,000
Costs – total incurred last year	17,000	
– testing cost	1,000	
Total cost		18,000
This year's profit from the machine		£7,000

(c) The machine would have been shown as an asset of the business at £17,000 at the end of last year.

Unless all production costs are charged in the same accounting period as the sale is recognised in the profit and loss account, distortions will occur that will render the profit and loss account much less useful. Thus, it is necessary to deduce the full cost of any production undertaken completely or partially in one accounting period, but sold in a subsequent one.

Much of this chapter will be devoted to how the cost of doing something, like the £17,000 cost of making the machine in Example 10.1, is deduced in practice.

Criticisms of full costing

Full costing is widely criticised because, in practice, it tends to use past costs and to restrict its consideration of future costs to outlay costs. In Chapter 8 we argued that past costs are irrelevant, irrespective of the purpose for which the information is to be used, and that opportunity costs can be very important. Advocates of full costing would argue that it provides a long-run relevant cost and that so-called relevant costing gives information that relates only to the narrow circumstances of the moment.

Despite the criticisms that are made of full costing, it is, according to the survey evidence that we shall consider later in this chapter, very widely practised.

Full costs in single-product operations

The simplest case for which to deduce the full cost per unit is where the business has only one product line or service, that is, each unit of its product or service is identical. Here it is simply a question of adding up all the costs of production incurred in the period (materials, labour, rent, fuel, power and so on) and dividing this total by the total number of units of output for the period.

Rustic Breweries Ltd has just one product, a bitter beer that is marketed as 'Old Rustic'. During last month the business produced 7,300 pints of the beer. The costs incurred were as follows:

	£
Ingredients	390
Labour	880
Fuel	85
Rental of brewery premises	350
Depreciation of brewery equipment	75

What is the full cost per pint of producing 'Old Rustic'?

This is found simply by taking all of the costs and dividing by the number of pints brewed, as follows:

$$\frac{£(390 + 880 + 85 + 350 + 75)}{7,300} = £0.24 \text{ per pint}$$

There can be problems of deciding exactly how much cost was incurred. In the case of Rustic Breweries Ltd, for example, how is the cost of depreciation deduced? It is certainly an estimate and so its reliability is open to question. Should we use the 'relevant' cost of the raw materials (almost certainly the replacement cost) or the actual price paid for the stock used? If it is worth calculating the cost per pint, then it must be because this information will be used for some decision-making purpose and so the replacement cost is probably more logical. In practice, however, it seems that historic costs are more often used to deduce full costs.

There can also be problems in deciding precisely how many units of output there were. Brewing beer is not a very fast process. This means that there is likely to be some beer that is in the process of being brewed at any given moment. This in turn means that part of the costs incurred last month were in respect of some beer that was work in progress at the end of the month and is not therefore included in the output quantity of 7,300 pints. Similarly, part of the 7,300 pints was started and incurred costs in the previous month, yet all of those pints were included in the 7,300 pints that we used in our calculation of the cost per pint. Work in progress is not a serious problem, but account does need to be taken of it if reliable full-cost information is to be obtained.

This approach to full costing, which can be taken with identical or near-identical units of output, is usually referred to as **process costing**.

Full costs in multi-product operations

Where the units of output of the product or service are not identical, for the purposes for which full costing is used it will not be acceptable to adopt the approach that we used with pints of 'Old Rustic' in Activity 10.1. It is clearly reasonable to ascribe an identical cost to units of output that are identical; it is *not* reasonable where the units of output are obviously different. Every pint of 'Old

Rustic' will be more or less identical, but every case handled by a solicitor for a client, for example, is not identical to every other. Whether full costs are being used as a basis for pricing, as a basis for income measurement or for both purposes, treating each client's case the same will not normally be acceptable.

Direct and indirect costs

Where the units of output are not identical, we normally separate costs into two categories. These are:

- **Direct costs**. These are costs that can be identified with specific cost units. That is to say, the effect of the cost can be measured in respect of each particular unit of output. The main examples of these are direct materials and direct labour. Collecting direct costs is a simple matter of having a cost-recording system that is capable of capturing the cost of direct material used on each job and the cost, based on the hours worked and the rate of pay, of direct workers.
- **Indirect costs** (or **overheads**). These are all other costs – that is, those that cannot be directly measured in respect of each particular unit of output.

We shall use the terms 'indirect costs' and 'overheads' interchangeably for the remainder of this book. Overheads are sometimes known as **'common costs'** because they are common to all production of the production unit (for example, factory) for the period.

Exhibit 10.1	**Direct and indirect costs in practice** A survey of 176 fairly large UK businesses conducted during 1999 revealed that, on average, total costs of businesses are in the following proportions: ● Direct costs 70 per cent ● Indirect costs 30 per cent. Perhaps surprisingly, these proportions did not vary greatly between manufacturers, retailers and service businesses. The only significant variation from the 70/30 proportions was with financial and commercial businesses, which had an average 52/48 split. Source: Based on information taken from Drury and Tayles (see reference (1) at the end of the chapter).

Job costing

The term **job costing** is used to describe the way in which we identify the full cost per unit of output (job) where the units of output differ. To cost (that is, deduce the full cost of) a particular unit of output (job), we usually ascribe the direct costs to the job, which, by the definition of direct costs, is capable of being done. We then seek to 'charge' each unit of output with a fair share of indirect costs. This is shown graphically in Figure 10.1.

Activity 10.2	Sparky Ltd is a business that employs a number of electricians. The business undertakes a range of work for its customers, from repairing fuses, to installing complete wiring systems in new houses.

In respect of a particular job done by Sparky Ltd, into which category, direct or indirect, would each of the following costs fall?

(a) The wages of the electrician who did the job.
(b) Depreciation (wear and tear) of the tools used by the electrician.
(c) The salary of Sparky Ltd's accountant.
(d) The cost of cable and other materials used on the job.
(e) Rental of the premises where Sparky Ltd stores its stock of cable and other materials.

Only (a) and (d) are direct costs. This is because it is possible to measure how much time (and, therefore, the labour cost) was spent on the particular job and how much material was used in the job.

All of the other costs are general costs of running the business. As such, they must form part of the full cost of doing the job, but they cannot be directly measured in respect of the particular job.

It is important to note that whether a cost is direct or indirect depends on the item being costed (the cost objective). People tend to refer to overheads without stating what the cost objective is; this is incorrect.

Activity 10.3

Into which category, direct or indirect, would each of the costs listed in Activity 10.2 fall if we were seeking to find the cost of operating the entire business of Sparky Ltd for a month?

The answer is that all of them will be direct costs, since they can all be related to, and measured in respect of, running the business for a month.

Figure 10.1

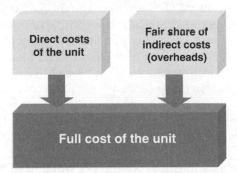

The relationship between direct costs and indirect costs

The full cost of any particular job is the sum of those costs that can be measured specifically in respect of the job (direct costs) and a share of those costs that create the environment in which production (of an object or service) can take place, but that do not relate specifically to any particular job (overheads).

Naturally, broader-reaching cost units, like operating Sparky Ltd for a month, tend to include a higher proportion of direct costs than do more limited ones, such as a particular job done by Sparky Ltd. As we shall see shortly, this makes costing broader cost units rather more straightforward than costing narrower ones, since direct costs are easier to deal with.

Full costing and the behaviour of costs

We saw in Chapter 9 that the relationship between fixed and variable costs is that, between them, they make up the full cost (or total cost, as it is usually known in the context of marginal analysis). This is illustrated in Figure 10.2.

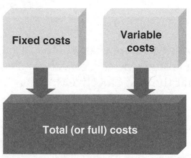

| Figure 10.2 | **The relationship between fixed costs, variable costs and total costs** |

The total cost of a job is the sum of those costs that remain the same irrespective of the level of activity (fixed costs) and those that vary according to the level of activity (variable costs).

The similarity of what is shown in Figure 10.2 to that depicted in Figure 10.1, might lead us to believe that there might be some relationship between fixed, variable, direct and indirect costs. More specifically, some people seem to believe – mistakenly – that variable costs and direct costs are the same and that fixed costs and overheads are the same. This is incorrect.

The notions of 'fixed' and 'variable' are concerned entirely with **cost behaviour** in the face of changes to the volume of output. *Directness* of costs is simply concerned with collecting together the elements that make up the full cost, that is, with the extent to which costs can be measured directly in respect of particular units of output or jobs. These are entirely different concepts. Though it may be true that there is a tendency for fixed costs to be overheads and for variable costs to be direct costs, there is no direct link and there are many exceptions to this tendency. For example, most operations have variable overheads. Labour, a major element of direct cost in most business contexts, is usually a fixed cost, certainly over the short term.

The relationship between the reaction of costs to volume changes, on the one hand, and how costs need to be gathered to deduce the full cost, on the other, in respect of a particular job is shown in Figure 10.3.

Total cost is the sum of direct and indirect costs. It is also the sum of fixed and variable costs. These two facts are independent of one another. Thus, a particular

Figure 10.3

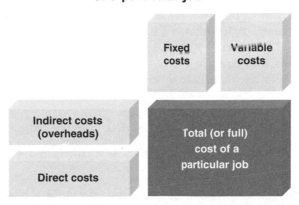

The relationship between direct, indirect, variable and fixed costs of a particular job

A particular job's full (or total) cost will be made up of some variable and some fixed element. It will also be made up of some direct and some indirect (overhead) element.

cost may be fixed relative to the level of output, on the one hand, and be either direct or indirect on the other.

The problem of indirect costs

The notion of distinguishing between direct and indirect costs is only related to deducing full cost in a job-costing environment. You may recall that when we were considering costing a pint of 'Old Rustic' beer in Activity 10.1, whether particular elements of cost were direct or indirect was of absolutely no consequence. This was because all costs were shared equally between the pints of beer. Where we have units of output that are not identical, we have to look more closely at the make-up of the costs to achieve a fair measure of the total cost of a particular job.

Indirect costs of any activity must form part of the cost of each unit of output. By definition, however, indirect costs cannot be directly related to individual **cost units**. This raises a major practical issue; how are indirect costs to be apportioned to individual cost units?

It is reasonable to view the overheads as rendering a service to the cost units. A manufactured product can be seen as being rendered a service by the factory in which the product is made. In this sense, it is reasonable to charge each cost unit with a share of the costs of running the factory (rent, lighting, heating, cleaning, building maintenance and so on). It also seems reasonable to relate the charge for the 'use' of the factory to the level of service that the product received from the factory.

The next step is the difficult one. How might the cost of running the factory, which is a cost of all production, be divided among individual products that are not similar in size and complexity of manufacture? One possibility is sharing this overhead cost equally among each cost unit produced in the period. Most of us would not propose this method unless the cost units were close to being identical in terms of the extent to which they had 'benefited' from the overheads. If we are not to propose equal shares, we must identify something observable and measurable about the cost units that we feel provides a reasonable basis for distinguishing between one cost unit and the next in this context.

In practice, time spent working on the cost unit by direct labour is the basis that is most popular. (Later in the chapter we shall consider survey evidence of what happens in practice.) It must be stressed that this is not the 'correct' way and it certainly is not the *only* way. We could, for example, use relative size of products as measured by weight or by relative material cost. Possibly, we could use the relative lengths of time that each unit of output was worked on by machines.

Job costing: a worked example

To see how job costing (as is is usually called) works, let us consider Example 10.2.

Example 10.2

Johnson Ltd, a business that provides a television repair service to its customers, has overheads of £10,000 each month. Each month also 2,500 direct labour hours are worked and charged to units of output (repairs carried out by the business). A particular repair job undertaken by the business used direct materials costing £15. Direct labour worked on the job was 15 hours and the wage rate is £5 an hour. Overheads are charged to jobs on a direct-labour-hour basis. We need to establish what the full cost of the job is.

First let us establish the **overhead absorption (recovery) rate** – that is, the rate at which jobs will be charged with overheads. This is £4 (£10,000/2,500) per direct labour hour. Thus, the full cost of the job is:

	£
Direct materials	15
Direct labour (15 × £5)	75
	90
Overheads (15 × £4)	60
Full cost of the job	150

Note that in Example 10.2, the number of labour hours (15) appears twice in deducing the full cost: once to deduce the direct labour cost and a second time to deduce the overheads to be charged to the job. These are really two separate issues, though they are both based on the same number of labour hours.

Note also that if all of the jobs that are undertaken during the month are assigned overheads in a similar manner, all £10,000 of overheads will be charged to the jobs between them. Jobs that involve a lot of direct labour will be assigned a large share of overhead costs and those that involve little direct labour will be assigned a small share of overheads.

Activity 10.4

Can you think of reasons why direct labour hours are regarded as the most logical basis for sharing overheads among cost units?

The reasons that occurred to us are:

- Large jobs should logically attract large amounts of overheads because they are likely to have been rendered more 'service' by the overheads than small ones. The length of time that they are worked on by direct labour may be seen as a rough-and-ready way of measuring relative size, even though other means of doing this may be found (for example, relative physical size, where the cost unit is a physical object, like a manufactured product).

- Most overheads are related to time. Rent, heating, lighting, fixed-asset depreciation, supervisors' and managers' salaries and loan interest, which are all typical overheads, are all more or less time-based. That is to say, the overhead cost for one week tends to be about half of that for a similar two-week period. Thus, a basis of apportioning overheads to jobs that takes account of the length of time that the units of output benefited from the 'service' rendered by the overheads seems logical.
- Direct labour hours are capable of being measured in respect of each job. They will normally be measured to deduce the direct labour element of cost in any case. Thus, a direct-labour-hour basis of dealing with overheads is practical to apply in the real world.

It cannot be emphasised enough that there is no 'correct' way to apportion overheads to jobs. Overheads (indirect costs), by definition, do not naturally relate to individual jobs. If, nevertheless, we wish to take account of the fact that overheads are part of the cost of all jobs, we must find some acceptable way of including a share of the total overheads in each job. If a particular means of doing this is accepted by those who are affected by the full cost deduced, then the method is as good as any other method. Accounting is concerned only with providing useful information to decision makers. In practice, the method that gains the most acceptability as being useful is the direct-labour-hour method.

Activity 10.5

Marine Suppliers Ltd undertakes a range of work, including making sails for small sailing boats on a made-to-measure basis. The following costs are expected to be incurred by the business during next month:

Indirect labour cost	£9,000
Direct labour time	6,000 hours
Depreciation (wear and tear) of machinery, etc.	£3,000
Rent and rates	£5,000
Direct labour costs	£30,000
Heating, lighting and power	£2,000
Machine time	2,000 hours
Indirect materials	£500
Other miscellaneous indirect costs	£200
Direct materials cost	£3,000

The business has received an enquiry about a sail and it is estimated that the sail will take 12 direct labour hours to make and will require 20 square metres of sailcloth (which costs £2 per square metre). The business normally uses a direct-labour-hour basis of charging overheads to individual jobs.

What is the full cost of making the sail?

....

Firstly it is necessary to identify which are the indirect costs and total them as follows:

	£
Indirect labour	9,000
Depreciation	3,000

Rent and rates	5,000
Heating, lighting and power	2,000
Indirect materials	500
Other miscellaneous indirect costs	200
Total indirect costs	19,700

(Note that this list does not include the direct costs. We shall deal with these separately.)

Since the business uses a direct-labour-hour basis of charging overheads to jobs, we need to deduce the indirect cost or overhead recovery rate per direct labour hour. This is simply:

$$\frac{£19,700}{6,000} = £3.28 \text{ per direct labour hour}$$

Thus, the full cost of the sail would be expected to be:

	£
Direct materials (20 × £2)	40.00
Direct labour (12 × (£30,000/6,000))	60.00
Indirect costs (12 × £3.28)	39.36
Total cost	£139.36

Activity 10.6

Suppose that Marine Suppliers Ltd (Activity 10.5) used a machine-hour basis of charging overheads to jobs. What would be the cost of the job detailed, if it is expected to take five machine hours (as well as 12 direct labour hours)?

The total overheads will, of course, be the same irrespective of the method of charging them to jobs. Thus the overhead recovery rate, on a machine-hour basis, will be:

$$\frac{£19,700}{2,000} = £9.85 \text{ per machine hour}$$

Thus the full cost of the sail would be expected to be:

	£
Direct materials (20 × £2)	40.00
Direct labour (12 × (£30,000/6,000))	60.00
Indirect costs (5× £9.85)	49.25
Total cost	149.25

●●●● Selecting the basis for charging overheads

A question now presents itself as to which of the two costs for this sail – that in Activity 10.5 or that in Activity 10.6 – is the correct one, or simply the better one? The answer is that neither is the correct one, as was pointed out earlier. Which is the better is a matter of judgement. This judgement is concerned entirely with usefulness of information, which in this context is probably concerned with the attitudes of those who will be affected by the figure used. Thus fairness, as it is perceived by those people, is likely to be the important issue.

Probably, most people would feel that the nature of the overheads should influence the choice of the basis of charging the overhead to jobs. Where, because the operation is a capital-intensive one, the overheads are dominated by those relating to machinery (depreciation, machine maintenance, power and so on), machine hours might be favoured. Otherwise, direct labour hours might be preferred.

It could appear that one of these bases might be preferred to the other simply because it apportions either a higher or a lower amount of overheads to a particular job. This would normally be irrational, however. Since the total overheads are the same irrespective of the method of charging the total to individual jobs, a method that gives a higher share of overheads to one particular job must give a lower share to the remaining jobs. To illustrate this point, consider Example 10.3.

Example 10.3

A business that provides a service to its customers expects to incur overheads totalling £20,000 next month. The total direct labour time worked is expected to be 1,600 hours and machines are expected to operate for a total of 1,000 hours.

During a particular month, the business expects to do just two large jobs, the outlines of which are as follows:

	Job 1	Job 2
Direct labour hours	800	800
Machine hours	700	300

It is necessary to work out how much of the overheads will be charged to each job if overheads are to be charged on (a) a direct-labour-hour basis, and (b) a machine-hour basis.

(a) Direct-labour-hour basis

$$\text{Overhead recovery rate} = \frac{£20,000}{1,600}$$

$$= £12.50 \text{ per direct labour hour}$$

Job 1: £12.50 × 800 = £10,000
Job 2: £12.50 × 800 = £10,000

(b) Machine-hour basis

$$\text{Overhead recovery rate} = \frac{£20,000}{1,000}$$

$$= £20.00 \text{ per machine hour}$$

Job 1: £20.00 × 700 = £14,000
Job 2: £20.00 × 300 = £6,000

It is clear from these calculations that the total overheads charged to jobs is the same whichever method is used. So, whereas the machine-hour basis gives Job 1 a higher share than does the direct-labour-hour method, the opposite is true for Job 2.

It is not possible to charge overheads on one basis to one job and on the other basis to the other job. This is because either total overheads will not be fully charged to the jobs, or the jobs will be overcharged with overheads. For example, the direct-labour-hour method for Job 1 (£10,000) and the machine-hour basis for Job 2 (£6,000) will mean that only £16,000 of a total £20,000 of overheads will be charged to jobs. As a result, the objective of full costing, which is to charge all overheads to jobs done, will not be achieved. In this particular case, if selling prices are based on full costs, the business may not charge prices high enough to cover all of its costs.

Activity 10.7

The point was made above that it would normally be irrational to prefer one basis of charging overheads to jobs simply because it apportions either a higher or a lower amount of overheads to a particular job. This is because the total overheads are the same irrespective of the method of charging the total to individual jobs. Can you think of any circumstances where it would not necessarily be so irrational?

This might apply where a customer has agreed to pay for a particular job a price based on full cost plus an agreed fixed percentage for profit. Here it would be beneficial to the producer for the total cost of the job to be as high as possible. This would be relatively unusual, but sometimes public-sector organisations, particularly central and local government departments, have entered into contracts to have work done, with the price to be deduced, after the work has been completed, on a cost-plus basis. Such contracts are pretty rare these days, probably because they are open to abuse in the way described. Usually, contract prices are agreed in advance, typically in conjunction with competitive tendering.

Exhibit 10.2 provides some information on overhead recovery rates used in practice.

Exhibit 10.2

Overhead recovery rates in practice

In 1993, *A Survey of Management Accounting Practices in UK Manufacturing Companies* was published by the Chartered Association of Certified Accountants (ACCA). Though this evidence is not totally up to date and it was restricted to private-sector manufacturing companies, it does provide us with some impression of management accounting practices in the real world.

The direct-labour-hour basis of charging overheads to cost units is overwhelmingly the most popular, used by 73 per cent of respondents to the ACCA survey. Where the work has a strong labour element, this seems reasonable, but the survey also showed that 68 per cent of businesses use this rate for automated activities. It is surprising that direct labour hours should be used in an environment where machines, and machine-related costs, dominate.

Source: Information taken from Drury, Braund, Osborne and Tayles (see reference (2) at the end of this chapter).

Segmenting the overheads

Though, as we have just seen, charging the same overheads to different jobs on different bases is not possible, it is possible to charge one part of the overheads on one basis and another part, or other parts, on another basis.

Segmenting the overheads in the way shown in Activity 10.8 may well be seen as providing a better basis of charging overheads to jobs. This is quite often found in practice, usually by dividing a business into separate 'areas' for costing purposes, charging overheads differently from one area to the next.

Activity 10.8

Consider the business in Example 10.3. On closer analysis we find that of the overheads totalling £20,000 next month, £8,000 relate to machines (depreciation, maintenance, rental of the space occupied by the machines, and so on) and the remainder to more general overheads. The other information about the business is exactly as it was before.

How much overheads will be charged to each job if the machine-related overheads are to be charged on a machine-hour basis and the remaining overheads are charged on a direct-labour-hour basis?

Direct-labour-hour basis:

$$\text{Overhead recovery rate } = \frac{£12,000}{1,600} = £7.50 \text{ per direct labout hour}$$

Machine-hour basis:

$$\text{Overhead recovery rate } = \frac{£8,000}{1,000} = £8.00 \text{ per machine hour}$$

Overheads charged to jobs:

	Job 1 £	Job 2 £
Direct-labour-hour basis		
£7.50 × 800	6,000	
£7.50 × 800		6,000
Machine-hour basis		
£8.00 × 700	5,600	
£8.00 × 300		2,400
Total	11,600	8,400

We can see from this that the total expected overheads of £20,000 is charged in total.

Remember that there is no 'correct' basis of charging overheads to jobs, and so our frequent reference to the direct-labour-hour and machine-hour bases should not be taken to imply that these are the correct methods. However, it should be said that these two methods do have something to commend them and are popular in practice. As we have already discussed, a sensible method needs to identify something about each job that can be measured and that distinguishes it from other jobs. There is also a lot to be said for methods that are concerned with time, because most overheads are time-related.

Dealing with overheads on a departmental basis

In general, all but the smallest businesses are divided into departments. Normally, each department deals with a separate activity.

The reasons for dividing a business into departments include the following:

● Many businesses are too large and complex to be run as a single unit and it is more practical to run them as a series of relatively independent units with each one having its own manager.

- Each department normally has its own area of specialism and is managed by a specialist.
- Each department can have its own accounting records that enable its performance to be assessed, which can lead to greater motivation among the staff.

Very many businesses deal with charging overheads to cost units on a department-by-department basis. They do this in the expectation that it will give rise to a more fair means of charging overheads. It is probably not an expensive exercise to apply overheads on a departmental basis. Since costs are collected department by department for other purposes (particularly for control), to apply overheads in the same way is a relatively simple matter.

An example of how the departmental approach to deriving full costs works, in a manufacturing context, is depicted in Figure 10.4.

Figure 10.4

A cost unit passing through the production process

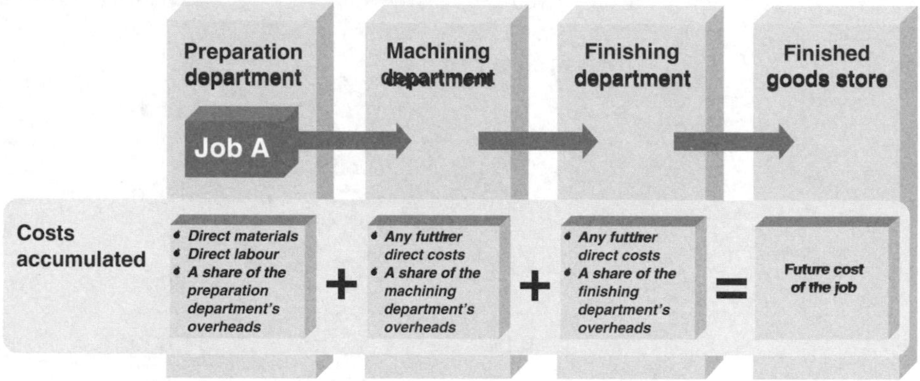

As the particular job passes through the three departments where work is carried out on it, it 'gathers' costs of various types.

The job in Figure 10.4 starts life in the preparation department, when some direct materials are taken from the stores and worked on by a direct worker. Thus, the job will be charged with direct materials, direct labour and with a share of the preparation department's overheads. The job then passes into the machining department, already valued at the costs that it picked up in the preparation department. Further direct labour and, possibly, materials are added in the machining department, plus a share of that department's overheads. The job now passes into the finishing department, valued at the cost of the materials, labour and overheads that it accumulated in the first two departments. In the finishing department, further direct labour and, perhaps, materials are added and the job picks up a share of that department's overheads. The job, now complete, passes into the finished goods store or is despatched to the customer. The basis of charging overheads to jobs (for example, direct labour hours) might be the same for all three departments or it may be different from one department to another.

In the present example, it is quite likely that machine-related costs dominate the machining department, and so overheads might well be charged to jobs on a machine-hour basis. The other two departments may well be labour intensive so that direct labour hours may be seen as being appropriate there. The passage of the job through the departments can be compared to a snowball being rolled across snow; as it rolls, it picks up more and more snow (overheads).

Where costs are dealt with departmentally, each department is known as a **cost centre**. A cost centre can be defined as some physical area or some activity or function for which costs are separately identified.

Charging direct costs to jobs, in a departmental system, is exactly the same as where the whole business is one single cost centre. It is simply a matter of keeping a record of:

- The number of hours of direct labour worked on the particular job and the grade of labour, assuming that there are different grades with different rates of pay.
- The cost of the direct materials taken from stores and applied to the job.
- Any other direct costs – for example, some subcontracted work associated with the job.

This recordkeeping will normally be done departmentally with a departmental system.

It is clearly necessary to identify the production overheads of the entire organisation on a departmental basis. This means that the total overheads of the business must be divided among the departments such that the sum of the departmental overheads equals the overheads for the entire business. By charging all of their overheads to jobs, between them the departments will charge all of the overheads of the business to jobs.

For the present purposes, it is necessary to distinguish between **product cost centres** (or departments) and **service cost centres**. Product cost centres are departments through which the jobs pass and can be charged with a share of their overheads. The preparation, machining and finishing departments, in the example discussed above, are examples of product cost centres.

Activity 10.9	Can you guess what the definition of a service cost centre is? Can you think of an example of a service cost centre?

A service cost centre is one through which jobs do not pass. It renders a service to other cost centres. Examples include:

- General administration
- Accounting
- Stores
- Maintenance
- Personnel
- Catering.

All of these render services to product cost centres.

Service cost centre costs must be charged to product cost centres, and become part of the product cost centres' overheads, so that they can be recharged to jobs.

This must be done so that all of the overheads of the business find their way into the cost of the jobs done. If this is not done, the 'full' cost derived will not really be the full cost of the jobs.

Logically, the costs of a service cost centre should be charged to product cost centres on the basis of the level of service provided to the product cost centre concerned. For example, a production department that has a lot of machine maintenance carried out relative to other production departments should be charged with a larger share of the maintenance department's costs than should those other product cost centres.

The process of dividing overheads between departments is as follows:

1. **Cost allocation**. Allocate costs that are specific to the departments. These are costs that relate to, and are measurable in respect of, individual departments, that is, they are direct costs of running the department. Examples include:

   (a) Salaries of indirect workers whose activities are wholly within the department, for example, the salary of the departmental manager.
   (b) Rent, where the department is housed in its own premises for which rent can be separately identified.
   (c) Electricity, where it is separately metered for each department.

2. **Cost apportionment**. Apportion the more general overheads to the departments. These are overheads that relate to more than one department, and even perhaps to them all. These would include:

   (a) Rent, where more than one department is housed in the same premises.
   (b) Electricity, where it is not separately metered.
   (c) Salaries of cleaning staff who work in a variety of departments.

   These costs would be apportioned to departments on some fair basis, such as by square metres of floor area, in the case of rent, or by level of mechanisation, for electricity used to power machinery. As with charging overheads to individual jobs, fairness is the issue; there is no correct basis of apportioning general overheads to departments.

3. Having totalled, allocated and apportioned costs to all departments, it is now necessary to apportion the total costs of service cost centres to production departments. Logically, the basis of apportionment should be the level of service rendered by the individual service department to the individual production department. With personnel department costs, for example, the basis of apportionment might be the number of staff in each production department, because it could be argued that the higher the number of staff, the more benefit the production department has derived from the personnel department. This is, of course, rather a crude approach. A particular production department may have severe personnel problems and a high staff turnover rate, which may make it a user of the personnel service that is way out of proportion to the number of staff in the production department.

The final total for each product cost centre is that cost centre's overheads. These can be charged to jobs as they pass through. We shall now go on to consider an example dealing with overheads on a departmental basis (Example 10.4).

Example 10.4

A business consists of four departments:

- Preparation department
- Machining department
- Finishing department
- General administration (GA) department.

The first three are product cost centres and the last renders a service to the other three. The level of service rendered is thought to be roughly in proportion to the number of employees in each production department.

Overhead costs, and other data, for next month are expected to be as follows:

	£000
Rent	5,000
Electricity to power machines, etc.	1,500
Electricity for heating and lighting	400
Insurance of premises	100
Cleaning	300
Depreciation of machines	1,000

Salaries of departmental managers, etc.

	£000
Preparation department	1,000
Machining department	1,200
Finishing department	900
General administration department	900

The general administration department has only one employee, the manager. The other departments have a manager and direct workers. Managers never do any 'direct' work.

Each direct worker is expected to work 160 hours next month. The number of direct workers in each department is:

Preparation department	6
Machining department	9
Finishing department	5

Machining department direct workers are paid £5 an hour; other direct workers are paid £4 an hour.

All of the machinery is in the machining department. Machines are expected to operate for 1,200 hours next month.

The floorspace (in square metres) occupied by the departments is as follows:

	m²
Preparation department	800
Machining department	1,000
Finishing department	500
General administration department	100

Deducing the overheads department by department can be done, using a schedule, as follows:

		Total	Prep'n	Mach'g	Fin'g	GA
	£000	£000	£000	£000	£000	£000
Allocated costs:						
Machine power		1,500		1,500		
Machine depreciation		1,000		1,000		
Indirect salaries		4,000	1,000	1,200	900	900
Apportioned costs						
Rent	5,000					
Heating and lighting	400					
Insurance of premises	100					
Cleaning	300					
Apportioned by floor area		5,800	1,933	2,417	1,208	242
Departmental overheads		12,300	2,933	6,117	2,108	1,142
Reapportion GA costs by number of staff (including the manager)			348	496	298	(1,142)
		12,300	3,281	6,613	2,406	zero

Activity 10.10

Assume that the machining department overheads (in Example 10.4) are to be charged to jobs on a machine-hour basis, but that the direct-labour-hour basis is to be used for the other two departments. What will be the full cost of a job with the following characteristics?

	Preparation	Machining	Finishing
Direct labour hours	10	7	5
Machine hours	–	6	–
Direct materials (£)	85	13	6

***Hint*: this should be tackled as if each department were a separate business, then departmental costs added together for the job so as to arrive at the total full cost.**

Firstly, we need to deduce the overhead recovery rates for each department:

Preparation department (direct-labour-hour-based):

$$\frac{£3,281}{6 \times 160} = £3.42$$

Machining department (machine-hour-based):

$$\frac{£6,613}{1,200} = £5.51$$

Finishing department (direct-labour-hour-based):

$$\frac{£2,406}{5 \times 160} = £3.01$$

The cost of the job is as follows:

	£	£
Direct labour:		
Preparation department (10 × £4)	40.00	
Machining department (7 × £5)	35.00	
Finishing department (5 × £4)	20.00	
		95.00
Direct materials:		
Preparation department	85.00	
Machining department	13.00	
Finishing department	6.00	
		104.00
Overheads:		
Preparation department (10 × £3.42)	34.20	
Machining department (6 × £5.51)	33.06	
Finishing department (5 × £3.01)	15.05	
		82.31
Full cost of the job		281.31

Activity 10.11

The manufacturing costs for Buccaneers Ltd for 2002 are expected to be as follows:

	£000
Direct materials:	
Forming department	450
Machining department	100
Finishing department	50
Direct labour:	
Forming department	120
Machining department	80
Finishing department	50
Indirect materials:	
Forming department	40
Machining department	30
Finishing department	10
Administration department	10
Indirect labour:	
Forming department	80
Machining department	70
Finishing department	60
Administration department	60
Maintenance costs	50
Rent and rates	100
Heating and lighting	20
Building insurance	10
Machinery insurance	10
Depreciation of machinery	120
Total manufacturing costs	1,520

The following additional information is available:

(i) All direct labour is paid £4 per hour for all hours worked.

(ii) The administration department renders personnel and general services to the production departments.

(iii) The area of the premises in which the business manufactures amounts to 50,000 square metres, divided as follows:

	Sq m
Forming department	20,000
Machining department	15,000
Finishing department	10,000
Administration department	5,000

(iv) The maintenance staff are expected to divide their time between the production departments as follows:

	%
Forming department	15
Machining department	75
Finishing department	10

(v) Machine hours are expected to be as follows:

	Hours
Forming department	5,000
Machining department	15,000
Finishing department	5,000

On the basis of the foregoing information:

(a) Allocate and apportion overheads to the three production departments.

(b) Deduce overhead recovery rates for each department using two different bases for each department's overheads.

(c) Calculate the full cost of a job with the following characteristics:

Direct labour hours:	
Forming department	4 hours
Machining department	4 hours
Finishing department	1 hour

Machine hours:	
Forming department	1 hour
Machining department	2 hours
Finishing department	1 hour

Direct materials:	
Forming department	£40
Machining department	£9
Finishing department	£4

Use whichever of the two bases of overhead recovery, deduced in (b), that you consider more appropriate.

(d) Explain why you consider the basis used in (c) as the more appropriate.

(a)

Cost	Basis of apport't	Total £000	Forming £000	Machining £000	Finishing £000	Admin. £000
Indirect materials	Specifically allocated	90	40	30	10	10
Indirect labour	Specifically allocated	270	80	70	60	60
Maintenance	Staff time	50	7.5	37.5	5	–
Rent/rates	100					
Heat/light	20					
Buildings insurance	10					
	Area	130	52	39	26	13
Machine insurance	10					
Machine dep'n	120					
	Machine hours	130	26	78	26	–
		670	205.5	254.5	127	83
Admin.	Direct labour		39.84	26.56	16.6	(83)
		670	245.34	281.06	143.6	–

Note that direct costs are not included in the above because they are allocated *directly* to jobs.

(b) Basis 1: direct labour hours

$$\text{Forming} = \frac{£245,340}{120,000/4} = £8.18 \text{ per direct labour hour}$$

$$\text{Machining} = \frac{£281,060}{80,000/4} = £14.05 \text{ per direct labour hour}$$

$$\text{Finishing} = \frac{£143,600}{50,000/4} = £11.49 \text{ per direct labour hour}$$

Basis 2: machine hours

$$\text{Forming} = \frac{£245,340}{5,000} = £49.07 \text{ per machine hour}$$

$$\text{Machining} = \frac{£281,060}{15,000} = £18.74 \text{ per machine hour}$$

$$\text{Finishing} = \frac{£143,600}{5,000} = £28.72 \text{ per machine hour}$$

(c) Cost of job – on direct labour hour basis of overhead recovery

	£	£
Direct labour cost (9 × £4)		36.00
Direct materials (£40 + £9 + £4)		53.00
Overheads:		
Forming (4 × £8.18)	32.72	
Machining (4 × £14.05)	56.20	
Finishing (1 × £11.49)	11.49	100.41
Total		£189.41

(d) The reason for using the direct-labour-hour basis rather than the machine-hour basis was that labour is more important, in terms of the number of hours applied to output, than is machine time. Strong arguments could have been made for the use of the alternative basis; certainly, a machine-hour basis could have been justified for the machining department.

It would be possible, and it may be reasonable, to use one basis in respect of one department's overheads and a different one for those of another department. For example, machine hours could have been used for the machining department and a direct-labour-hours basis for the other two.

Exhibit 10.3 provides some information on 'departmentalisation' of overheads in practice.

Exhibit 10.3

Departmentalisation of overheads in practice

The 1993 ACCA survey of manufacturing businesses revealed that 69 per cent of the businesses that responded use some form of departmental approach to deriving the overhead recovery rate to be charged to cost units. The remainder use some form of company-wide basis. Where overheads are dealt with on a departmental basis, this seems to lead to a number of different rates being applied, presumably as many rates as there are departments. Thirty-seven per cent of the respondents use more than 11 different rates, and 20 per cent use more than 20 different rates.

Where respondents took a departmental approach to charging overheads to cost units, charging service department costs to product departments was done by using some fairly arbitrary factor, such as direct labour hours, in 68 per cent of those respondents who took this approach. Only 32 per cent sought to charge service department costs to product departments on the basis of the level of service provided by the service department.

Source: Information taken from Drury, Braund, Osborne and Tayles (see reference (2) at the end of the chapter).

Batch costing

The production of many types of goods and services (particularly goods) involves producing a batch of identical, or nearly identical, units of output yet where each batch is different from other batches. For example, a theatre may put on a production whose nature (and therefore costs) is very different from those of other productions. On the other hand, ignoring differences in the desirability of the various types of seating, all of the individual units of output (tickets to see the production) are identical.

In these circumstances, we should normally deduce the cost per ticket by using a job-costing approach (taking account of direct and indirect costs and so on) to find the cost of mounting the production, and then we should simply divide this value by the number of tickets expected to be sold, in order to find the cost per ticket. This approach is known as **batch costing**.

Full cost as the break-even price

It may have occurred to you by now that if all goes according to plan (so that direct costs, overheads and the basis of charging overheads, (for example, direct labour hours) prove to be as expected), then selling the output for its full cost should cause the business exactly to break even. Thus, whatever profit (in total) is loaded onto full cost to set selling prices will result in that level of profit being earned for the period.

The forward-looking nature of full costing

Though deducing full costs can be done after the work has been completed, it is often done in advance. In other words, costs are frequently predicted. Where, for example, full costs are needed as a basis on which to set selling prices, it is usually the case that prices need to be set before the customer will enter a contract for the job to be done. Even where no particular customer has been identified, some idea of the ultimate price will need to be known before the manufacturer will be able to make a judgement as to whether potential customers will buy the product and in what quantities.

Full costing in service industries

You should be clear that the concepts of full costing – whether it is through process costing, job costing or batch costing – apply equally to service and manufacturing businesses. The examples and activities in this chapter have reflected this fact.

With service businesses, the full cost of each unit of output is likely to include a relatively low (perhaps zero) proportion of direct material cost.

Self-assessment question 10.1

Hector and Co. Ltd has been invited to tender for a contract to produce 1,000 clothes hangers. The following information relates to the contract.

- *Materials*: The clothes hangers are made of metal wire covered with a padded fabric. Each hanger requires 2 metres of wire and 0.5 square metres of fabric.
- *Direct labour*: Skilled 10 minutes per hanger, unskilled 5 minutes per hanger.

The business already has sufficient stock of each of the materials required to complete the contract. Information on the cost of the stock is as follows:

	Metal wire £/m	Fabric £/m2
Historic cost	2.20	1.00
Current buying-in cost	2.50	1.10
Scrap value	1.70	0.40

The metal wire is in constant use by the business for a range of its products. The fabric has no other use for the business and is scheduled to be scrapped.

Unskilled labour, which is paid at the rate of £5.00 an hour, will need to be taken on specifically to undertake the contract. The business is fairly quiet at the moment, which means that a pool of skilled labour exists that will still be employed at full pay of £7.50 an hour to do nothing if the contract does not proceed. The pool of skilled labour is sufficient to complete the contract.

The business charges jobs with overheads on a direct-labour-hour basis. The production overheads of the entire business for the month in which the contract will be undertaken are estimated at £50,000. The estimated total direct labour hours that will be worked are 12,500. The business tends not to alter the established overhead recovery rate to reflect increases or reductions to estimated total hours arising from new contracts. The total overhead cost is not expected to increase as a result of undertaking the contract.

The business normally adds 12.5 per cent profit loading to the job cost to arrive at a first estimate of the tender price.

Required:
Price this job on a traditional job-costing basis; (a) and (b) indicate the minimum price at which the contract could be undertaken such that the business would be neither better nor worse off as a result of doing it.

Summary

In this chapter we have seen that many – perhaps most – businesses seek to identify the total or full cost of pursuing some objective, typically of a unit of output.

Where all units of goods or service produced by a business are identical, this tends to be a fairly straightforward matter: a case of simply finding the total cost for a period and dividing by the number of units of output for the same period.

Where a business's output is of units that are not similar, we have seen that it is necessary to take a less straightforward approach to the problem. Normally, such businesses identify the direct costs of production – that is, those costs that can be directly measured in respect of a particular unit of output. To these is added a share of the overheads according to some formula, which, of necessity, must be to some extent arbitrary. We saw that survey evidence shows direct labour hours to be the most popular basis of charging overheads to cost units. Costing individual cost units in this way is known as 'job costing'.

Full cost information is widely used by businesses but it is also widely criticised as not providing very helpful and relevant information.

Key terms

Full costing   p. 292
Full cost   p. 292
Cost-plus pricing   p. 293
Process costing   p. 295
Direct costs   p. 296
Indirect costs   p. 296
Overheads   p. 296
Common costs   p. 296
Job costing   p. 296
Cost behaviour   p. 298

Cost unit   p. 299
Overhead absorption (recovery) rate
   p. 300
Cost centre   p. 307
Product cost centre   p. 307
Service cost centre   p. 307
Cost allocation   p. 308
Cost apportionment   p. 308
Batch costing   p. 314

Further reading

If you would like to explore the topics covered in this chapter in more depth, we recommend the following books:

Management Accounting, *Atkinson, A., Banker, R., Kaplan, R. and Mark Young, S.*, 3rd edn, Prentice Hall, 2001, chapter 4.
Management and Cost Accounting, *Drury, C.*, 5th edn, Thompson Learning Business Press, 2000, chapters 3, 4 and 5.
Cost Accounting: A managerial emphasis, *Horngren, C., Foster, G. and Datar, S.*, 10th edn, Prentice Hall International, 2000, chapter 4.
Cost and Management Accounting, *Williamson, D.*, Prentice Hall International, 1996, chapters 6, 8 and 10.

References

1. **Cost Systems Design and Profitability Analysis in UK Companies**, *Drury, C. and Tayles, M.*, CIMA Publishing, 2000.
2. **A Survey of Management Accounting Practices in UK Manufacturing Companies**, *Drury, C., Braund, S., Osborne, P. and Tayles, M.*, Chartered Association of Certified Accountants, 1993.

10.1 What is the problem that the existence of work in progress causes in process costing?

10.2 What is the point of distinguishing direct costs from indirect ones?

10.3 Are direct costs and variable costs the same thing?

10.4 It is sometimes claimed that the full cost of pursuing some objective represents the long-run, break-even selling price. Why is this said and what does it mean?

? EXERCISES

Exercises 10.6–10.8 are more advanced than 10.1–10.5. Those with coloured numbers have answers at the back of the book.

10.1 'In a job costing system it is necessary to divide the business up into departments. Fixed costs (or overheads) will be collected for each department. Where a particular fixed cost relates to the business as a whole, it must be divided between the departments. Usually this is done on the basis of area of floorspace occupied by each department relative to the entire business. When the total fixed costs for each department have been identified, this will be divided by the number of hours that were worked in each department to deduce an overhead recovery rate. Each job that was worked on in a department will have a share of fixed costs allotted to it according to how long it was worked on. The total cost for each job will therefore be the sum of the variable costs of the job and its share of the fixed costs. It is essential that this approach is taken in order to deduce a selling price for the firm's output.'

Required:
Prepare a table of two columns. In the first column you should show any phrases or sentences with which you do not agree in the above statement, and in the second column you should show *briefly* your reason for disagreeing with each one.

10.2 Distinguish between:

- Job costing
- Process costing
- Batch costing.

What tend to be the problems specifically associated with each of these?

10.3 Bodgers Ltd, a business that provides a market research service, operates a job-costing system. Towards the end of each financial year, the overhead absorption rate (the rate at which overheads will be charged to jobs) is established for the forthcoming year.

Required:
(a) Why does the business bother to predetermine the absorption rate in the way outlined?
(b) What steps will be involved in predetermining the rate?
(c) What problems might arise with using a predetermined rate?

10.4 Pieman Products Ltd makes road trailers to the precise specifications of individual customers. The following are predicted to occur during the forthcoming year, which is about to start:

Direct materials cost	£50,000
Direct labour costs	£80,000
Direct labour time	16,000 hours
Indirect labour cost	£25,000
Depreciation (wear and tear) of machinery, etc.	£8,000
Rent and rates	£10,000
Heating, lighting and power	£5,000
Indirect materials	£2,000
Other indirect costs	£1,000
Machine time	3,000 hours

All direct labour is paid at the same hourly rate.

A customer has asked the business to build a trailer for transporting a racing motor cycle to races. It is estimated that this will require materials and components that will cost £1,150. It will take 250 direct labour hours to do the job, of which 50 will involve the use of machinery.

Required:
Deduce a logical cost for the job, and explain the basis of dealing with overheads that you propose.

10.5 Many businesses charge overheads to jobs on a departmental basis.

Required:
(a) What is the advantage that is claimed for charging overheads to jobs on a departmental basis, and why is it claimed?
(b) What circumstances need to exist to make a difference to a particular job whether overheads are charged on a business-wide basis or on a departmental basis. (Note that the answer to this part of the question is not specifically covered in the chapter. You should, nevertheless, be able to deduce the reason from what you know.)

10.6 Promptprint Ltd, a printing business, has received an enquiry from a potential customer for the quotation of a price for a job. The pricing policy of the business is based on the plans for the next financial year shown below.

	£
Sales (billings to customers)	196,000
Materials (direct)	(38,000)
Labour (direct)	(32,000)
Variable overheads	(2,400)
Advertising (for business)	(3,000)
Depreciation	(27,600)
Administration	(36,000)
Interest	(8,000)
Profit (before tax)	49,000

A first estimate of the direct costs for the job are:

	£
Direct materials	4,000
Direct labour	3,600

Required:

Based on the estimated direct costs:

(a) Prepare a recommended price for the job based on the plans, commenting on your method, ignoring the information given in the Appendix (below).

(b) Comment on the validity of using financial plans in pricing, and recommend any improvements you would consider desirable for the pricing policy used in (a).

(c) Incorporate the effects of the information shown in the Appendix (below) into your estimates of direct material costs, explaining any changes you consider it necessary to make to the above direct materials cost of £4,000.

Appendix to Exercise 10.6

Direct material costs were computed as follows based on historic costs:

	£
Paper grade 1	1,200
Paper grade 2	2,000
Card (zenith grade)	500
Inks and other miscellaneous items	300
	4,000

Paper grade 1 is in stock and in regular use. Because it is imported, it is estimated that if it is used for this job, a new stock order will have to be placed shortly. Sterling has depreciated against the foreign currency by 25 per cent since the last purchase.

Paper grade 2 is purchased from the same source as grade 1. However, current stock was bought in for a special order. This order was cancelled, although the defaulting customer was required to pay £500 towards the cost of the paper. The accountant has offset this against the original cost to arrive at the figure of £2,000 shown above. This paper is rarely used, and due to its special chemical coating will be unusable if it is not used on the job in question.

The card is another specialist item currently in stock. There is no use foreseen, and it would cost £750 to replace if required. However, the stock controller had planned to spend £130 on overprinting to use the card as a substitute for other materials costing £640.

Inks and other items are in regular use in the print shop.

10.7 Bookdon plc manufactures three products, X, Y and Z, in two production departments: a machine shop and a fitting section; it also has two service departments: a canteen and a machine maintenance section. Shown below are next year's planned production data and manufacturing costs for the business.

	X	Y	Z
Production	4,200 units	6,900 units	1,700 units
Direct materials	£11/unit	£14/unit	£17/unit
Direct labour			
Machine shop	£6/unit	£4/unit	£2/unit
Fitting section	£12/unit	£3/unit	£21/unit
Machine hours	6 hrs/unit	3 hrs/unit	4 hrs/unit

Planned overheads are as follows:

	Machine shop	Fitting section	Canteen	Machine maintenance section	Total
Allocated overheads	£27,660	£19,470	£16,600	£26,650	£90,380
Rent, rates, heat and light					£17,000
Depreciation and insurance of equipment					£25,000
Additional data:					
Gross book value of equipment	£150,000	£75,000	£30,000	£45,000	
Number of employees	18	14	4	4	
Floorspace occupied	3,600 m²	1,400 m²	1,000 m²	800 m²	

It has been estimated that approximately 70 per cent of the machine maintenance section's costs are incurred servicing the machine shop and the remainder incurred servicing the fitting section.

Required:
(a) Calculate the following planned overhead absorption rates:
   (i)   A machine-hour rate for the machine shop.
   (ii) A rate expressed as a percentage of direct wages for the fitting section.
(b) Calculate the planned full cost per unit of product X.

10.8 Shown below is an extract from next year's plans for a business manuacturing three products, A, B and C, in three production departments.

	A	B	C
Production	4,000 units	3,000 units	6,000 units
Direct material cost	£7 per unit	£4 per unit	£9 per unit
Direct labour requirements:			
Cutting department:			
Skilled operatives	3 hr/unit	5hr/unit	2 hr/unit
Unskilled operatives	6 hr/unit	1 hr/unit	3 hr/unit
Machining department	$\frac{1}{2}$ hr/unit	$\frac{1}{4}$ hr/unit	$\frac{1}{3}$ hr/unit
Pressing department	2 hr/unit	3 hr/unit	4 hr/unit
Machine requirements:			
Machining department	2 hr/unit	$1\frac{1}{2}$ hr/unit	$2\frac{1}{2}$ hr/unit

The skilled operatives employed in the cutting department are paid £8 per hour and the unskilled operatives are paid £5 per hour. All the operatives in the machining and pressing departments are paid £6 per hour.

	Production departments			Service departments	
	Cutting	Machining	Pressing	Engineering	Personnel
Planned total overheads	£154,482	£64,316	£58,452	£56,000	£34,000
Service department costs incurred for the benefit of other departments, as follows:					
Engineering services	20%	45%	35%	–	–
Personnel services	55%	10%	20%	15%	–

The business operates a full absorption costing system.

Required:
Calculate, as equitably as possible, the total planned cost of:

(a) One completed unit of product A.
(b) One incomplete unit of product B, which has been processed by the cutting and machining departments but which has not yet been passed into the pressing department.

11 Managing in a competitive environment

Introduction

In recent years we have witnessed major changes in the business world. Such factors as deregulation, privatisation, the growing expectations of shareholders and the impact of new technology have led to a much more fast-changing and competitive environment that has radically changed the way in which managers should manage. In this chapter we consider some of the financial techniques that are being used to manage in this new era.

We begin by considering the impact of this new, highly competitive environment on the full costing approach that we considered in the previous chapter. We shall see that activity-based costing, which is a development of the traditional full-costing approach, takes a much more enquiring, much less accepting attitude towards overheads. We shall see how, in theory and in practice, a business can use costing information to aid pricing decisions. We shall also examine some recent approaches to costing that can lower costs and, therefore, increase the ability of a business to compete on price.

Finally, we shall consider the increasing importance of non-financial measures in managing a business. We shall examine the Balanced Scorecard approach, which seeks to integrate financial and non-financial measures into a framework for the achievement of business objectives.

Costing and the changed business environment

The traditional approach to costing and pricing output developed when the notion of trying to cost industrial production first emerged, probably around the time of the UK Industrial Revolution. At that time, manufacturing industry was characterised by the following features:

- *Direct-labour-intensive and direct-labour-paced production.* Labour was at the heart of production. To the extent that machinery was used, it was to support the efforts of direct labour, and the speed of production was dictated by direct labour.
- *A low level of overheads relative to direct costs.* Little was spent on power, personnel services, machinery (therefore low depreciation charges) and other areas typical of the overheads of modern businesses.
- *A relatively uncompetitive market.* Transport difficulties, limited industrial production worldwide and a lack of knowledge by customers of competitors' prices meant that businesses could prosper without being too scientific in costing and pricing their output.

Since overheads then represented a pretty small element of total costs, it was acceptable and practical to deal with them in a fairly arbitrary manner. Not too much effort was devoted to trying to control the cost of overheads because the rewards of better control were relatively small – certainly compared with the rewards from controlling direct labour and material costs. It was also reasonable to charge overheads to individual jobs on a direct-labour-hour basis. Most of the overheads were incurred directly in support of direct labour: providing direct workers with a place to work, heating and lighting that workplace, employing people to supervise the direct workers, and so on. At the same time, all production was done by direct workers, perhaps aided by machinery.

By now, the start of this new millennium, the world of much industrial production had fundamentally altered. Most of it is now characterised by:

- *Capital-intensive and machine-paced production.* Machines are at the heart of production. Most labour supports the efforts of machines – for example, technically maintaining them – and the speed of production is dictated by machines.
- *A high level of overheads relative to direct costs.* Depreciation, servicing and power costs are very high. Also, there are costs of a nature scarcely envisaged in the early days of industrial production, such as personnel and staff welfare costs; these, too, are high. At the same time, there are very low (perhaps no) direct labour costs. The proportion of total cost accounted for by direct materials has typically not altered too much, but more efficient production tends to lead to less waste and, therefore, less material cost, again tending to make overheads dominant.
- *A highly competitive international market.* Industrial production, much of it highly sophisticated, is carried out worldwide. Transport, including fast air freight, is relatively cheap. Fax, telephone and the Internet ensure that potential customers can quickly and cheaply find out the prices of a range of suppliers. The market is, therefore, likely to be highly competitive. This means that businesses need to know their costs with a degree of accuracy that historically had been unnecessary. Businesses also need to take a considered and informed approach to pricing their output.

Activity-based costing

In Chapter 10, we considered the traditional approach to job costing (deriving the full cost of output where one unit of output differs from another). This approach is to collect those costs for each job, which can be unequivocally linked to and measured in respect of the particular job (direct costs). All other costs (overheads) are thrown into a pool of costs and charged to individual jobs according to some formula. As we saw in Chapter 10, survey evidence indicates that this formula has usually been on the basis of the number of direct labour hours worked on each individual job.

Whereas the traditional overhead recovery rate (that is, the rate at which overheads are absorbed by jobs) had been much less per direct labour hour than the actual rate paid to direct workers, recently there have been examples of overhead recovery rates five and 10 times the hourly rate of pay. When production is dominated by direct labour paid £5 an hour, it might be reasonable to have a recovery rate of £1 an hour. When, however, direct labour plays a relatively small part in production, to have overhead recovery rates of £50 per direct labour hour is likely to lead to very arbitrary costing. Just a small change in the amount of direct labour worked on a job could massively affect the cost deduced, not because the direct worker is massively well paid, but for no better reason than that this is the way in which it has always been done: overheads, not particularly related to labour, are charged on a direct-labour-hour basis.

The whole question of overheads, what causes them and how they are charged to jobs has been receiving closer attention recently, as a result of changes in the environment in which businesses operate. Historically, businesses have been content to accept that overheads exist and, therefore, they must be dealt with, for costing purposes, in as practical a way as possible.

In recent years there has been an increasing realisation that overheads do not just happen; they must be caused by something. To illustrate this point, let us consider Example 11.1.

Example 11.1

Modern Producers Ltd has, like virtually all manufacturers, a storage area (known as 'the stores') that is set aside for finished goods. The costs of running the stores include a share of the factory rent and other establishment costs, such as heating and lighting. They also include the salaries of staff employed to look after the stock, and the cost of financing the stock held in the stores.

The company has two product lines: A and B. Product A tends to be made in small batches, and low levels of finished stock are held. The company prides itself on its ability to supply product B in relatively large quantities instantly. As a consequence, much of the finished goods store is filled with finished product Bs ready to be despatched soon after an order is received.

Traditionally, the whole cost of operating the stores would have been treated as a general overhead and included in the total of overheads charged to jobs on a direct-labour-hour basis. This means that when assessing the cost of products A and B, the cost of operating the stores has fallen on them according to the number of direct labour hours worked on each one. In fact, most of the stores cost should be charged to product B, since this product causes (and benefits from) the stores cost much more than is true of product A. Failure to account more precisely for

---

the costs of running the stores is masking the fact that product B is not as profitable as it seems to be; it may even be making a loss as a result of the relatively high cost that it causes of operating the stores, but that so far have been charged to product A, without regard to the fact that product A causes little of the cost. In fact, traditionally, the products would absorb stores costs in proportion to the direct-labour-hour content, a factor that has nothing to do with storage.

Cost drivers

Realisation that overheads do not just occur, but that they are caused by activities – like holding products in stores – that 'drive' the costs is at the heart of **activity-based costing (ABC)**. The traditional approach is that direct labour hours are a **cost driver**, which probably used to be true. It is now recognised not to be the case.

There is a basic philosophical difference between the traditional and the ABC approaches. Traditionally we tend to think of overheads as *rendering a service to cost units*, the cost of which must be charged to those units. ABC sees overheads as being *caused by cost units*, and those cost units must be charged with the costs that they cause.

Activity 11.1

Can you think of any other purpose that identification of the cost drivers serves, apart from deriving more accurate costs?

Identification of the activities that cause costs puts management in a position where it may well be able to control them.

The opaque nature of overheads has traditionally rendered them difficult to control, relative to the much more obvious direct labour and material costs. If, however, analysis of overheads can identify the cost drivers, questions can be asked about whether the activity driving certain costs is necessary at all, and whether the cost justifies the benefit. In our example, it may be a good marketing ploy that product B can be supplied immediately from stock, but there is an cost and that cost associated should be recognised and assessed against the benefit.

Advocates of activity-based costing argue that most overheads can be analysed and cost drivers identified. If true, this means that it is possible to gain much clearer insights to the costs that are caused, activity by activity, so that fairer and more accurate product costs can be identified, and costs can be controlled more effectively.

Cost pools

Under ABC, an overhead **cost pool** is established for each type of cost that can be linked to a cost-driving activity. So the business in Example 11.1 would create a cost pool for operating the stores. All costs associated with this activity would be allocated to that cost pool. Costs in that pool would then be allocated to output (goods or services) according to the extent to which each unit of output 'drove' those costs, using the cost driver identified.

<table>
<tr><td>

Example 11.2

</td><td>

The accountant at Modern Producers Ltd (see Example 11.1) has estimated that the costs of running the finished goods stores for next year will be £90,000. This will be the amount allocated to the 'finished goods stores cost pool'.

It is estimated that each product A will spend an average of one week in the stores before being sold. With product B, the equivalent period is four weeks. Both products are of roughly similar size and have very similar storage needs. It is felt, therefore, that the quantity of each product and the period spent in the stores are the cost drivers.

It is estimated that, next year, 50,000 units of Product As and 25,000 units of Product Bs will pass though the stores. The total number of 'product weeks' in store will thus be:

</td></tr>
</table>

Product	A	50,000 × 1 week	=	50,000
	B	25,000 × 4 weeks	=	100,000
				150,000

The stores cost per 'product week' is given by

$$£90,000/150,000 = £0.60.$$

Therefore each product A will be charged with £0.60 for finished stores costs, and each product B with £2.40 (that is, £0.60 × 4).

Allocating overhead costs to cost pools with ABC contrasts with the traditional approach, where the overheads are allocated to production departments, in both cases then to be charged to cost units (products – goods and services). This contrast is illustrated in Figure 11.1.

With the traditional approach, overheads are apportioned to product departments. Each department would then derive an overhead recovery rate, typically overheads per direct labour hour. Overheads would then be applied to units of output according to how many direct labour hours were worked on them.

With ABC, the overheads are analysed into cost pools, with one cost pool for each cost driver. The overheads are then charged to units of output, through activity cost driver rates. These rates are an attempt to represent the extent to which each particular cost unit is believed to cause the particular part of the overheads.

ABC and service industries

Much of our discussion of ABC has concentrated on manufacturing industry, perhaps because early users of ABC were manufacturing businesses. In fact, ABC is possibly even more relevant to service industries because, in the absence of a direct materials element, a service business's total costs are likely to be particularly heavily affected by overheads. There is certainly evidence that ABC has been adopted by businesses that sell services rather than goods.

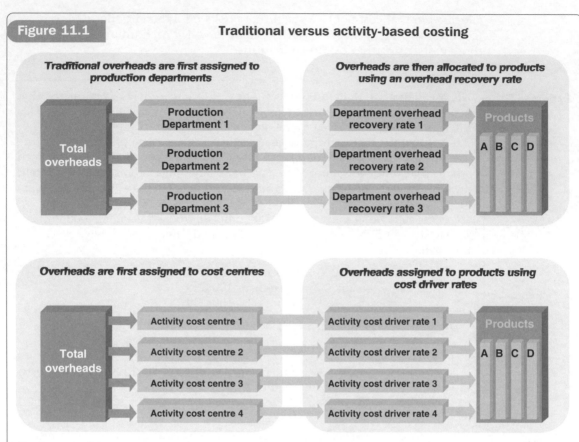

Figure 11.1   **Traditional versus activity-based costing**

Traditional overheads are first assigned to production departments

Overheads are then allocated to products using an overhead recovery rate

Total overheads → Production Department 1 → Department overhead recovery rate 1 → Products A B C D

Total overheads → Production Department 2 → Department overhead recovery rate 2

Total overheads → Production Department 3 → Department overhead recovery rate 3

Overheads are first assigned to cost centres

Overheads assigned to products using cost driver rates

Total overheads → Activity cost centre 1 → Activity cost driver rate 1 → Products A B C D

Total overheads → Activity cost centre 2 → Activity cost driver rate 2

Total overheads → Activity cost centre 3 → Activity cost driver rate 3

Total overheads → Activity cost centre 4 → Activity cost driver rate 4

The figure highlights the main differences in approach between the traditional costing approach and the activity-based costing approach. With the traditional approach, overheads are first assigned to production departments and then overheads are allocated to products based on an overhead recovery rate (based on the direct labour hours worked on the product or some other method of allocation) for each department. With the activity-based costing approach, overheads are assigned to cost centres and then products are charged with overheads to the extent that they drive the costs of the centres.

Source: Adapted from Innes and Mitchell (see reference (1) at the end of the chapter).

Activity 11.2

What is the difference in the way in which direct costs are accounted for when using ABC, relative to their treatment taking a traditional approach to full costing?

....

The answer is no difference at all. ABC is concerned only with the way in which overheads are charged to jobs to derive the full cost.

Criticisms of ABC

Critics of ABC argue that analysis of overheads in order to identify cost drivers is time-consuming and costly, and that the benefit of doing so, in terms of more accurate costing and the potential for cost control, does not justify the cost of carrying out the analysis.

ABC is also criticised for the same reason that full costing generally is criticised: because it does not provide very relevant information for decision making. The point was made in Chapter 10 that full costing tends to use past costs and to ignore opportunity costs. Since past costs are always irrelevant in decision making and opportunity costs can be very significant, full costing information is an expensive irrelevance. In contrast, advocates of full costing claim that it *is* relevant, in that it provides a long-run average cost, whereas 'relevant costing', which we considered in Chapter 8, relates only to the specific circumstances of the short term.

Despite the criticisms that are made of full costing, it is, according to survey evidence, very widely practised. Exhibit 11.1 provides some indication of the extent to which ABC is used in practice.

ABC in practice

A survey of large businesses in 1999 revealed that, on average, 15 per cent of businesses fully use an ABC approach to dealing with full costing. A further 8 per cent use it partially. The remaining 77 per cent do not use ABC at all. Even so, there was a surprising range in the level of usage of ABC from industry to industry (see diagram). It is particularly surprising that so few manufacturing business use ABC.

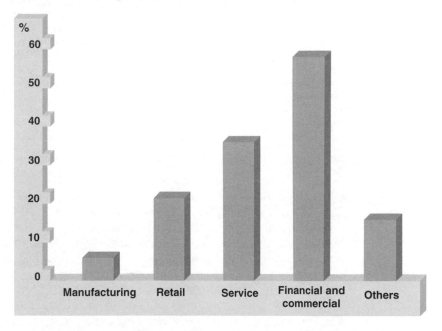

Source: Constructed with data from Drury and Tayles (see reference (2) at the end of the chapter).

There is no real evidence of an increase in the use of ABC, possibly the opposite. A study conducted by Drury, Braund, Osborne and Tayles in 1993 (see reference (3) at the end of the chapter) showed that 13 per cent of manufacturing businesses had adopted ABC at that time.

The Drury and Tayles (reference 2) survey shows that it tends to be larger businessess that adopt ABC.

Psilis Ltd makes a product in two qualities, called 'Basic' and 'Super'. The company had been able to sell these products at a price that gave a standard profit mark-up of 25 per cent of full cost. Management is concerned by the lack of profit.

Full cost per unit is calculated by apportioning overheads to each type of product on the basis of direct labour hours. The costs are as follows:

	Basic	Super
	£	£
Direct labour (all £5/hour)	20	30
Direct material	15	20

The total overheads are £1,000,000.

Based on experience over recent years, for the forthcoming year the company expects to make and sell 40,000 Basics and 10,000 Supers.

Recently, the company's management accountant has undertaken an exercise to try to identify cost drivers in an attempt to be able to deal with the overheads on a more precise basis than had been possible before. This exercise has revealed the following analysis of the annual overheads:

Activity (and cost driver)		Annual number of activities		
	Cost £000	Total	Basic	Super
Number of machine set-ups	280	100	20	80
Number of quality-control inspections	220	2,000	500	1,500
Number of sales orders processed	240	5,000	1,500	3,500
General production (machine hours)	260	500,000	350,000	150,000
Total	1,000			

The management accountant explained the analysis of the £1,000,000 overheads as follows:

- The two products are made in relatively small batches, so that storage of finished stock is negligible. The Supers are made in very small batches because their demand is relatively low. Each time a new batch is produced, the machines have to be reset by skilled staff. Resetting for Basic production occurs about 20 times a year and for Supers about 80 times: about 100 times in total. The costs of employing the machine-setting staff is about £280,000 a year. It is clear that the more set-ups that occur, the higher the total set-up costs; in other words, the number of set-ups is the factor that drives set-up costs.
- All production has to be inspected for quality and this costs about £220,000 a year. The higher specifications of the Supers means that there is more chance that there will be quality problems. Thus the Supers are inspected in total 1,500 times annually, whereas the Basics only need about 500 inspections. The number of inspections is the factor that drives these costs.
- Sales order processing (dealing with customers' orders from receiving the original order to despatching the products) costs about £240,000 a year. Despite the larger amount of Basic production, there are only 1,500 sales orders each year because the Basics are sold to wholesalers in relatively large-sized orders. The

Supers are sold mainly direct to the public by mail order, usually in very small-sized orders. It is believed that the number of orders drives the costs of processing orders.

● The remaining general production overheads, totalling £260,000 a year, are thought to be driven by the number of hours for which the machines operate. The machine time per product is somewhat higher for Supers than for Basics.

Required:

(a) Deduce the full cost of each of the two products on the basis used at present and, from these, deduce the current selling price.
(b) Deduce the full cost of each product, taking account of the management accountant's recent investigations.
(c) What conclusions do you draw? What advice would you offer the management of the company?

Pricing

As we have just seen, full costing can be used as a basis for setting prices for the business's output. We have also seen that it can be criticised in that role. In this section we are going to take a closer look at pricing. We shall begin by considering some theoretical aspects of the subject before going on to look at some more practical issues, particularly the role of management accounting information in pricing decision making.

Figure 11.2

Graph of quantity demanded against price for a commodity

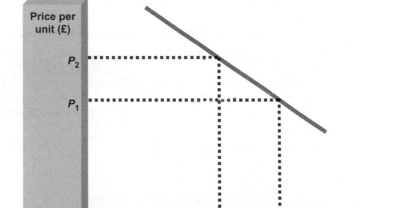

As the price of the commodity under consideration increases from P_1 to P_2, the quantity that the market will buy falls from Q_1 to Q_2.

Economic theory

In most market conditions found in practice, the price charged by a business will determine the number of units sold. This is shown graphically in Figure 11.2.

Figure 11.2 shows the number of units of output that the market would demand at various prices. As price increases, the less willing are people to buy the commodity (call it commodity A). At a relatively low price per unit (P_1), the quantity of units demanded by the market (Q_1) is fairly high. When the price is increased to P_2, the demand decreases to Q_2. The graph shows a linear relationship between price and demand. In practice, the relationship, though broadly similar, may not be quite so straightforward.

Not all commodities show exactly the same slope of line. Figure 11.3 shows the demand/price relationship for commodity B, a different commodity from the one depicted in Figure 11.2.

Though a rise in price of commodity B, from P_1 to P_2, causes a fall in demand, the fall in demand is much smaller than is the case for commodity A with a similar rise in price. As a result, we say that commodity A has a higher **elasticity of demand** than commodity B: demand for A reacts much more dramatically (stretches more) to price changes than demand does for B. Elastic demand tends to be associated with commodities that are not essential, perhaps because there is a ready substitute.

Activity 11.3

Which would be the more elastic of the following commodities?

- A particular brand of chocolate bar
- Mains electricity supply.

....

A branded chocolate bar seems likely to have a fairly *elastic* demand. This is for several reasons, including the following:

- Few buyers of the bar would feel that chocolate bars are essentials.
- Other chocolate bars, probably quite similar to the commodity in question, will be easily available.

    Mains electricity probably has a relatively *inelastic* demand. This is because:

- Many users of electricity would find it very difficult to manage without fuel of some description.
- For neither domestic nor commercial users of electricity is there an immediate, practical substitute. For some uses of electricity – for example, powering machinery – there is probably no substitute. Even for a purpose such as heating, where there are substitutes such as gas and oil, it may be impractical to switch to the substitute because gas and oil heating appliances are not immediately available and are costly to acquire.

It is very helpful for those involved with pricing decisions to have some feel for the elasticity of demand of the commodity that will be the subject of a decision. The sensitivity of the demand to the pricing decision is obviously much greater (and the pricing decision more crucial) with commodities whose demand is elastic than with commodities whose demand is relatively inelastic.

As we saw in Chapter 1, the objective of most businesses is to enhance the wealth of their owners. Broadly speaking, this will be best achieved by seeking to

Figure 11.3

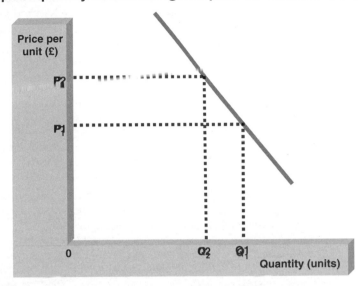

Graph of quantity demanded against price for commodity (B)

As the price of the commodity increases from P_1 to P_2, the quantity that the market will buy falls from Q_1 to Q_2. This fall in demand is less than was the case for commodity A, which has the greater elasticity of demand.

Figure 11.4

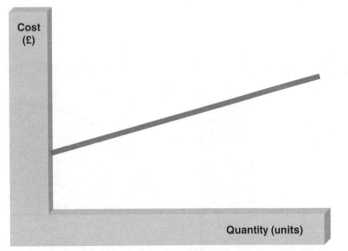

Graph of total cost against quantity (volume) of output of product X

Producing product X will give rise to some costs that are fixed and to some that vary with the level of production.

maximise profits – that is, having the largest possible difference between total costs and total revenues. Thus, prices should be set in a way that is likely to have this effect. To be able to do this, the price decision maker needs to have some insight to the way in which costs and prices relate to volume of output.

Figure 11.4 shows the relationship between cost and volume of output, which we have already met in Chapter 9. The figure shows that the total cost of producing a particular commodity (product X) increases as the quantity of output increases. It is shown here as a straight line; in practice it may be curved, either curving upwards (tending to become closer to the vertical) or flattening out (tending to become closer to the horizontal). The figure assumes that the marginal cost of each unit is constant over the range shown.

Figure 11.5 shows the total sales revenue against quantity of product X sold.

Activity 11.4 What general effect would tend to cause the total cost line in Figure 11.4 to (a) curve towards the vertical, and (b) curve towards the horizontal? (You may recall that we considered this issue in Chapter 9.)

....

(a) Curving towards the vertical would mean that the marginal cost (additional cost of making one more) of each successive unit of output would become greater. This would probably imply that increased activity would be causing a shortage of supply of some factor of production, which had the effect of increasing cost prices. This might be caused by a shortage of labour, meaning that overtime payments would need to be made to encourage people to work the hours necessary for increased production. It might also/alternatively be caused by a shortage of raw materials: perhaps normal supplies were exhausted at lower levels of output and more expensive sources had to be used to expand output.

(b) Curving towards the horizontal might be caused by the business being able to exploit the economies of scale at higher levels of output, making the marginal cost of each successive unit of output cheaper. Perhaps higher volumes of output enable division of labour or more mechanisation. Possibly, suppliers of raw materials offer better deals for larger orders.

Figure 11.5 | **Graph of total sales revenue against quantity (volume) sold of product X**

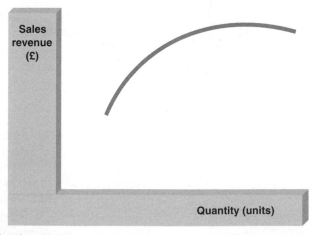

As more units of product X are sold, the total sales revenue initially increases, but at a declining rate. This is because, in order to persuade people to buy increasing quantities, the price must be reduced. Eventually the price will have to be reduced so much, to encourage additional sales, that the total sales revenue will fall as the number of units sold increases.

The total sales revenue increases as the quantity of output increases, up to a certain point.

Activity 11.5

What assumption does Figure 11.5 make about the price per unit of product X at which output can be sold as the number of units sold increases?

....

The graph suggests that, to sell more units, the price must be lowered, meaning that the average price per unit of output reduces as volume sold increases. As we discussed earlier in this section, this is true of most markets found in practice.

Figure 11.5 implies that there will come a point where, to make increased sales, prices will have to be reduced so much that total sales revenue will not increase; it may even reduce.

You may recall from Chapter 9 that, when we considered break-even analysis, we assumed a steady price per unit over the range that we were considering. Now we are saying that, in practice, it does not work like this. How can these two positions be reconciled? The answer is that, when we dealt with break-even analysis, we were only considering a relatively small range of output, namely from zero sales up to the break-even point. It may well be that over a small range, particularly at low levels of output, a constant sales price per unit is a reasonable assumption. That is to say that, to the left of the curve in Figure 11.5, there may be a straight line from zero up to the start of the curve.

There is nothing in break-even analysis that demands that the assumption about steady selling prices is made, but making it does mean that the analysis is very straightforward.

Figure 11.6 combines information about total sales revenue and total cost for product X over a range of output levels. The total sales revenue increases, but at a decreasing rate, and total cost of production increases as the quantity of output increases. The maximum profit is made where the total sales revenue and total cost lines are vertically furthest apart. At the left-hand end of the graph, we are clearly above break-even point because the total-sales-revenue line has already gone above the total-cost line. At the lower levels of volume of sales and output, the total-sales-revenue line is climbing faster than the total cost line. The business will wish to keep expanding output as long as this continues to be the case, because profit is the vertical distance between the two lines. A point will be reached where the total sales line flattens towards the horizontal to such an extent that further expansion will reduce profit.

The point at which profit is maximised is where the two lines stop diverging, that is, the point at which the two lines are climbing at exactly the same rate. Thus we can say that profit is maximised at the point where:

Marginal sales revenue = Marginal cost of production

that is,

$$\begin{bmatrix} \text{Increase in total sales} \\ \text{revenue from selling} \\ \text{one more unit} \end{bmatrix} = \begin{bmatrix} \text{Increase in total costs} \\ \text{that will result from} \\ \text{selling one more unit} \end{bmatrix}$$

Figure 11.6

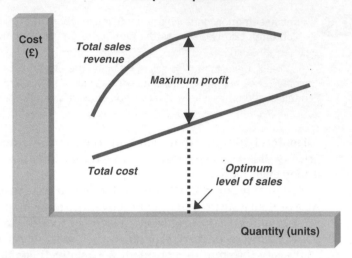

Graph of total sales revenue and total cost against quantity (volume) of output of product X

Profit is the vertical distance between the total-cost and total-sales-revenue lines. For a wealth-maximising business, the optimum level of sales will occur when this is at a maximum.

To see how this approach can be applied, consider Example 11.3.

Example 11.3

A schedule of predicted total sales revenue and total costs at various levels of production for product Y are shown in columns (a) and (c) of the table.

Quantity of output	Total sales revenue	Marginal sales revenue	Total cost	Marginal cost	Profit (loss)
	£	£	£	£	£
	(a)	(b)	(c)	(d)	(e)
0	0		0		0
1	1,000	1,000	2,300	2,300	(1,300)
2	1,900	900	2,600	300	(700)
3	2,700	800	2,900	300	(200)
4	3,400	700	3,200	300	200
5	4,000	600	3,500	300	500
6	4,500	500	3,800	300	700
7	4,900	400	4,100	300	800
8	5,200	300	4,400	300	800
9	5,400	200	4,700	300	700
10	5,500	100	5,000	300	500

Column (b) is deduced by taking the total sales revenue for one less unit sold from the total sales revenue at the sales level under consideration (column (a)). For example, the marginal sales revenue of the fifth unit sold (£600) is deduced by taking the total sales revenue for four units sold (£3,400) away from the total sales revenue for five units sold (£4,000).

Column (d) is deduced similarly, but using total cost figures from column (c). Column (e) is found by deducting column (c) from column (a).

It can be seen by looking at the profit (loss) column that the maximum profit occurs with an output of seven or eight units (£800). Thus the maximum output should be eight units. This is the point where marginal cost and marginal revenue are equal (at £300).

Activity 11.6

Specialist Ltd makes a very specialised machine that is sold to manufacturing businesses. The business is about to commence production of a new model of machine for which facilities exist to produce a maximum of 10 machines each week. To assist management in a decision on the price to charge for the new machine, two pieces of information have been collected:

- *Market demand.* The business's marketing staff believe that at a price of £3,000 per machine, the demand would be zero. Each £100 reduction in unit price below £3,000 would generate one additional sale per week. Thus, for example, at a price of £2,800 each, two machines could be sold each week.
- *Manufacturing costs.* Fixed costs associated with manufacture of the machine are estimated at £3,000 per week. Since the work is highly labour-intensive and labour is short, unit variable costs are expected to be progressive. The manufacture of one machine each week is expected to have a variable cost of £1,100, but each additional machine produced will increase the variable cost for the entire output by £100. For example, if the output were three machines per week, the variable cost per machine (for all three machines) would be £1,300.

It is the policy of the business always to charge the same price for its entire output of a particular model. What is the most profitable level of output of the new machine?

Output	Unit sales revenue £	Total sales revenue £	Marginal sales revenue £	Unit variable cost £	Total variable cost £	Total cost £	Marginal cost £	Profit (loss) £
0	0	0	0	0	0	3,000	3,000	(3,000)
1	2,900	2,900	2,900	1,100	1,100	4,100	1,100	(1,200)
2	2,800	5,600	2,700	1,200	2,400	5,400	1,300	200
3	2,700	8,100	2,500	1,300	3,900	6,900	1,500	1,200
4	2,600	10,400	2,300	1,400	5,600	8,600	1,700	1,800
5	2,500	12,500	2,100	1,500	7,500	10,500	1,900	2,000
6	2,400	14,400	1,900	1,600	9,600	12,600	2,100	1,800
7	2,300	16,100	1,700	1,700	11,900	14,900	2,300	1,200
8	2,200	17,600	1,500	1,800	14,400	17,400	2,500	200
9	2,100	18,900	1,300	1,900	17,100	20,100	2,700	(1,200)
10	2,000	20,000	1,100	2,000	20,000	23,000	2,900	(3,000)

An output of five machines each week will maximise profit at £2,000 per week.

The additional cost of producing the fifth machine compared with the cost of producing the first four (£1,900) is just below the marginal revenue (the amount by which the total revenue from five machines exceeds that from selling four (£2,100)).

The additional cost of producing the sixth machine compared with the cost of producing the first five (£2,100) is just above the marginal revenue (the amount by which the total revenue from six machines exceeds that from selling five (£1,900)).

Some practical considerations

Despite the analysis in Activity 11.6, in practice the answer of five machines a week may prove not to be the best answer. This might be for one or more of several reasons:

- Demand is notoriously difficult to predict, even assuming no changes in the environment.
- The effect of sales of the new machine on the other of the business's products may mean that the machine cannot be considered in isolation. Five machines a week may be the optimum level of output if sales were being taken from a rival firm or a new market is being created, but possibly not in other circumstances.
- Costs are difficult to estimate.
- Since labour is in short supply, the relevant labour cost should probably include an element for opportunity cost.
- The level of sales is calculated on the assumption that short-run profit maximisation is the goal of the business. Unless this is consistent with wealth enhancement in the longer term, it may not be in the company's best interests.

These points highlight some of the weaknesses of the theoretical approaches to pricing, particularly the fact that costs and demands are difficult to predict. It would be wrong, however, to dismiss the theory. The fact that the theory does not work perfectly in practice does not mean that it cannot offer helpful insights to the nature of markets, how profit relates to volume, and the notion of an optimum level of output.

Full cost (cost-plus) pricing

Now that we have considered pricing theory, let us return to the subject of using full cost as the basis for setting prices. We saw in Chapter 10 that one of the reasons why certain businesses deduce full costs is to base selling prices on them. There is a lot of logic in this. If a business charges the full cost of its output as a selling price, the business will, in theory, break even. This is because the sales revenue will exactly cover all of the costs. Charging something above full cost will yield a profit.

If a **full cost (cost-plus) pricing** approach is to be taken, the question that must be addressed is the level of profit that is required from each unit sold. This must logically be based on the total profit that is required for the period. Normally, businesses seek to enhance their wealth through trading. The extent to which they expect to do this is normally related to the amount of wealth that is invested to promote wealth enhancement. Businesses tend to seek to produce a particular percentage increase in wealth. In other words, businesses seek to generate a target return on capital employed. It seems logical, therefore, that the profit loading on full cost should reflect the business's target profit and that the target should itself be based on a target return on capital employed.

A business has just completed a job whose full cost has been calculated at £112. For the current period, the total manufacturing costs (direct and indirect) are estimated at £250,000. The profit target for the period is £100,000.

Suggest a selling price for the job.

If the profit is to be earned by jobs in proportion to their full cost, then the profit per pound of full cost must be £0.40 (£100,000/250,000). Thus, the profit on the job must be:

$$£0.40 \times 112 = £44.80$$

This means that the price for the job must be:

$$£112 + £44.80 = £156.80$$

Other ways could be found for apportioning a share of profit to jobs – for example, direct labour or machine hours. Such bases may be preferred where it is believed that these factors are better representatives of effort and, therefore, profitworthiness. It is clearly a matter of judgement as to how profit is apportioned to units of output.

An obvious problem with cost-plus pricing is that the market may not agree with the price. Put another way, cost-plus pricing takes no account of the market demand function (the relationship between price and quantity demanded, which we considered above). A business may fairly deduce the full cost of some product and then add what might be regarded as a reasonable level of profit, only to find that a rival producer is offering a similar product for a much lower price, or that the market simply will not buy at the cost-plus price.

Most suppliers are not strong enough in the market to dictate pricing. Most are 'price takers' not 'price makers'. They must accept the price offered by the market or they do not sell any of their wares. Cost-plus pricing may be appropriate for price makers, but it has less relevance for price takers.

The cost-plus price is not entirely useless to price takers, however. When contemplating entering a market, knowing the cost-plus price will give useful information. It will tell the price taker whether it can profitably enter the market or not. As has been said already in this chapter, the full cost can be seen as a long-run break-even selling price. If entering a market means that this break-even price, plus an acceptable profit, cannot be achieved, then the business should probably stay out. Having a breakdown of the full cost may put the business in a position to examine where costs might be capable of being cut in order to bring the full cost, plus profit within a figure acceptable to the market.

Being a price maker does not always imply that the business dominates a particular market. Many small businesses are, to some extent, price makers. This tends to be where buyers find it difficult to make clear distinctions between the prices offered by various suppliers. An example of this might be a car repair. Though it may be possible to obtain a series of binding estimates for the work from various garages, most people would not normally do so. As a result, garages normally charge cost-plus prices for car repairs.

Exhibit 11.2 considers the extent to which cost-plus pricing seems to be used in practice.

Relevant/marginal cost pricing

The relevant/marginal-cost approach deduces the minimum price for which the business can offer the product for sale, and which will leave the business better off as a result of making the sale than it would have been if the sale were not made but the next best opportunity pursued instead. We considered the general approach to relevant-cost pricing in Chapter 8. In Chapter 9, we looked at the more restricted case of relevant cost pricing: **marginal cost pricing**. Here it is assumed that fixed costs will not be affected by the decision to produce and, therefore, only the variable-cost element need be considered.

It would normally be the case that a relevant/marginal cost approach would only be used where there is not the opportunity to sell at a price that will cover the full cost. The business can sell at the marginal cost-plus price and still better off, simply because it happens to find itself in the position that certain costs will be incurred in any case.

Activity 11.8

A commercial aircraft is due to take off in one hour's time with 20 seats unsold. What is the minimum price at which these seats could be sold such that the airline company would be no worse off as a result?

> The answer is that any price above the additional cost per passenger, caused by people occupying the previously unsold seats, would represent an acceptable minimum. If there are no such costs, the minimum price is zero.
>
> This is not to say that the airline company will seek to charge the minimum price; it will presumably seek to charge the highest price that the market will bear. The fact that the market will not bear the full cost, plus a profit margin, should not, in principle, be sufficient for the company to refuse to sell seats.

Relevant/marginal pricing must be regarded as a short-term approach that can be adopted because a business finds itself in a particular position, for example, having spare aircraft seats. Ultimately, if the business is to be profitable, all costs must be covered by sales revenue.

Activity 11.9

When we considered marginal costing in Chapter 9, we identified three problems with its use. Can you remember what these problems are?

....

The three problems are as follows:

- The possibility that spare capacity will be 'sold off' cheaply when there is another potential customer who will offer a higher price, but by which time the capacity will be fully committed. It is a matter of commercial judgement as to how likely this will be. With reference to Activity 11.8, would an hour before take-off be sufficiently close to be fairly confident that no 'normal' passenger will come forward to buy a seat?
- The problem that selling the same product but at different prices could lead to a loss of customer goodwill. Would a 'normal' passenger be happy to be told by another passenger that the latter had bought his or her ticket very cheaply, compared with the normal price?
- If the business is going to suffer continually from being unable to sell its full production potential at the 'regular' price, it might be better, in the long run, to reduce capacity and make fixed-cost savings. Using the spare capacity to produce marginal benefits may lead to the business failing to address this issue. Would it be better for the airline company to operate smaller aircraft or to have fewer flights, either of these leading to fixed-cost savings, than to sell off surplus seats at marginal prices?

Pricing strategies

Costs and the market-demand function are not the only determinants of price. Businesses often employ pricing strategies that, in the short term, may not maximise profit. They do this in the expectation that they will gain in the long term. An example of such a strategy is **penetration pricing**. Here, the product is sold relatively cheaply in order to sell in quantity and to gain a large share of the market. This would tend to have the effect of dissuading competitors from entering the market. Subsequently, once the business has established itself as the market leader, prices would be raised to more profitable levels. By its nature, penetration pricing would tend to apply to new products.

Price skimming is almost the opposite of penetration pricing. It seeks to exploit the notion that the market can be stratified according to resistance to price. Here a new product is initially priced highly and sold only to those buyers in the stratum that is fairly unconcerned by high prices. Once this stratum of the market is saturated, the price is lowered to attract the next stratum. The price is gradually lowered as each stratum is saturated. This strategy tends only to be able to be employed where there is some significant barrier to entry for other potential suppliers, such as patent protection.

Mobile telephones are an example of a price-skimming strategy.

Recent developments in pricing and cost management

The increasingly competitive environment in which modern businesses operate is leading to increased effort being applied in trying to manage costs. Businesses need to keep costs to a minimum so that they can supply goods and services at a price that customers will be prepared to pay and, at the same time, generate a level of profit necessary to meet the businesses' objectives of enhancing shareholder wealth. We shall now outline some techniques that have recently emerged in an attempt to meet these goals of competitiveness and profitability.

Firstly, we need to appreciate that the total life-cycle of a product or service has three phases. The first is the period that precedes manufacture of the product for sale: the **preproduction phase**. During this phase, research and development – both of the product and of the market – is conducted. The product is invented/designed and so is the means of production. The phase culminates with acquiring and setting up the necessary production facilities and with advertising and promotion. The second phase is that in which the product is made and sold to the market: the **production phase**. Lastly comes the **post-production phase**; during this phase, any costs necessary to correct faults that arose with products that have been sold (after-sales service) are incurred. There would also be the costs of closing production at the end of the product's life-cycle, such as the cost of decommissioning production facilities. Since after-sales service will tend to arise from as early as the first product being sold and, therefore, well before the last one is sold, this phase would typically overlap the manufacturing phase. The total life-cycle is shown in Figure 11.7.

Total life-cycle costing

In some types of business, particularly those engaged in an advanced manufacturing environment, it is estimated that a very high proportion (as much as 80 per cent) of the total costs that will be incurred over the total life of a particular product are either incurred or committed at the pre-production phase. For example, a motor-car manufacturer, when designing, developing and setting up production of a new model, incurs a high proportion of the total costs that will be incurred on that model during the whole of its life. Not only are pre-production costs specifically incurred during this phase but the need to incur particular costs during the production phase is also established. This is because the design will incorporate features that will lead to particular manufacturing costs. Once the design of the car has been finalised and the manufacturing plant

Figure 11.7

The total life-cycle of a product

Total life-cycle
of a product

Research and
development,
production set-up,
pre-production
marketing costs
→ **Pre-production
phase**

Manufacturing
and
marketing costs
→ **Production
phase**

After-sales service
and production
facility
decommissioning
costs
→ **Post-production
phase**

From the producer's viewpoint, the life of a product can be seen as having three distinct phases. During the first the product is developed and everything is prepared so that production and marketing can start. Next comes production and sales. Lastly, dealing with post-production activities is undertaken.

set up, it may be too late to 'design out' a costly feature without incurring another large cost.

A decision taken at the design stage could well commit the business to costs after the manufacture of the product has taken place. Can you suggest a potential cost that could be built in at the design stage that will show itself after the manufacture of the product?

....

After-sales service costs could be incurred as a result of some design fault. Once the manufacturing facilities have been established, it may not be economic to revise the design but merely to deal with the problem through after-sales service procedures.

Total life-cycle costing seeks to focus management's attention on the fact that it is not just during the production phase that attention needs to be paid to cost management. By the start of the production phase it is too late to try to manage a large element of the product's total life-cycle cost. Efforts need to be made to assess the manufacturing costs of alternative designs.

There needs to be a review of the product over its entire life-cycle, which could be a period of twenty years or more. Traditional management accounting tends to be concerned with assessing performance over periods of just one year or less.

Target costing

With the traditional cost-plus pricing, costs are totalled for a product and a percentage is added for profit to give a selling price. This, for reasons raised earlier in this chapter, is not a very practical basis on which to price output for many businesses – certainly not those operating in a price-competitive market. The cost-plus price may well be totally unacceptable to the market.

Target costing approaches the problem from the other direction. First, with the help of market research or other means, a unit selling price and sales volume are established. From the unit selling price is taken an amount for profit. This unit profit figure must be such as to be acceptable to meet the business's profit objective. The resulting figure is the target cost. Efforts are then made to establish a way of producing the product that will enable the target cost to be met. This may involve revising the design, finding more efficient means of production or requiring raw material suppliers to supply more cheaply.

Target costing is seen as a part of a total life-cycle costing approach, in that cost savings are sought at a very early stage in the life-cycle, during the pre-production phase.

Exhibit 11.3 indicates the level of usage of target costing.

Exhibit 11.3	**Target costing in practice**

The ACCA survey suggests that target costing is not much used by UK businesses. Twenty-two per cent of respondents never use this approach and only 26 per cent use it often or always.

By contrast, survey evidence shows that target costing is very widely used by Japanese manufacturing companies.

Source: Drury, Braund, Osborne and Tayles (see reference (3) at the end of the chapter).

Activity 11.11	Though target costing seems effective and has its enthusiasts, some people feel it has its problems. Can you suggest what these problems might be?

There seem to be three main problem areas:

- It can lead to various conflicts – for example, between the business, its suppliers and its own staff.
- It can cause a great deal of stress for employees who are trying to meet target costs – sometimes ones that are extremely difficult to meet.
- Though, in the end, ways may be found to meet a target cost (through product redesign, negotiating lower prices with suppliers and so on), the whole process can be very expensive.

Kaizen costing

***Kaizen* costing** is linked to total life-cycle costing and focuses on cost saving during the production phase. Since that is at a relatively late stage in the life-cycle (from a cost control point of view), and because major cost savings should already have been effected through target costing, in the production phase only relatively small cost savings can be made. The Japanese word *kaizen* implies 'small changes'.

With *kaizen* costing, efforts are made to reduce the unit manufacturing cost of the particular product under review, if possible taking it below the unit cost in the previous period. Target percentage reductions can be set. Usually, production workers are encouraged to identify ways of reducing costs – something that their 'hands on' experience may enable them to do. Even though the scope to reduce costs is limited at the manufacturing stage, significant savings can still be made.

Benchmarking

Benchmarking is an activity – usually a continuing one – where a business or one of its divisions seeks to emulate a successful business or division and so achieve a similar level of success. The successful business or division provides a benchmark against which the business can measure its own performance, as well as providing examples of approaches that can lead to success. Sometimes the benchmark business will help with the activity, but even where no co-operation is given, observers can still learn quite a lot about what makes that business successful.

Exhibits 11.4 and 11.5 outline the use of benchmarking in practice in the UK.

Exhibit 11.4

Benchmarking in local government

The Audit Commission is a public body that has a statutory right to investigate public-sector organisations and report on the extent to which those organisations provide value for money to the public.

In the context of local government, the Commission sees one way of assessing value for money as benchmarking. It has been doing this since the 1980s, and so while benchmarking may be seen as a recent innovation in the private sector, it has a fairly long history in the public sector.

Since the Commission has statutory powers, it has been able to insist that the various local-government authorities provide information to enable a comprehensive benchmarking operation to take place. Contrast this with the private sector where benchmarking between businesses is difficult because there is no compulsion. Businesses are reluctant to divulge commercially sensitive information to other businesses with which they may be in competition. Often, the best that can be achieved in the private sector is for businesses to benchmark internally, with one division or department comparing itself with another part of the same business.

Exhibit 11.5

Benchmarking on safety issues at Tate & Lyle

Tate & Lyle plc is a large, multinational food business operating through subsidiaries in many parts of the world. The annual report for 2000 describes how the business was able to reduce dramatically the record of injuries at work of its staff. This was achieved by benchmarking the divisions of the business with the best safety records. Other divisions then sought to emulate the benchmark divisions' approaches to safety.

Tate & Lyle, through its size and diversity, provides an example of a private-sector organisation able to use benchmarking successfully.

●●●● Non-financial measures of performance

Financial measures have long held sway as the most important measures for a business. They provide us with a valuable means of summarising and evaluating business achievement, and there is no serious doubt about the continued importance of financial measures in this role. However, in recent years there has been increasing recognition that financial measures alone will not provide managers with the information they require to manage a business effectively. Non-financial measures should also be used to help gain a deeper understanding of the business and to achieve business objectives.

Financial measures portray various aspects of business achievement (for example, sales, profits, return on capital employed and so on) that can help managers determine whether the business is increasing the wealth of its owners. This is vitally important in an increasingly competitive environment, but managers also need to understand what particular things drive the creation of wealth. These **value drivers**, as they are often called, may be such things as employee satisfaction, customer loyalty and the level of product innovation. Often, they do not lend themselves to financial measurement, however, non-financial measures may be used to arrive at some indirect means of assessment.

Activity 11.12

How might we measure the following?

(a) employee satisfaction
(b) customer loyalty
(c) the level of product innovation.

....

(a) *Employee satisfaction* may be measured through the use of an employee survey. This could examine attitudes towards various aspects of the job, the degree of autonomy that is permitted, the level of recognition and reward received, the level of participation in decision making, the degree of support received in carrying out tasks, and so on. Less direct measures of satisfaction may include employee turnover rates and employee productivity, however, other factors may have a significant influence on these measures.

(b) *Customer loyalty* may be measured through the proportion of total sales generated from existing customers, the number of repeat sales made to customers, the percentage of customers renewing subscriptions or other contracts, and so on.

(c) *The level of product innovation* may be measured through the number of innovations during a period compared with those of competitors, the percentage of sales attributable to recent product innovations, the number of innovations that are brought successfully to market, and so on.

It has been argued that financial measures are normally 'lag' indicators, in so far that they tell us about outcomes. In other words, they measure the consequences arising from management decisions that were made earlier. Non-financial measures can be used as lag indicators of course, however, they can also be used as 'lead' indicators by focusing on those things that drive the creation of wealth. It is argued that if we measure changes in these value drivers, we may be able to predict changes in future financial performance. For example, we may find from experience that a 10 per cent fall during a period in levels of product innovation will lead to a 20 per cent fall in sales over the next three periods. In this case, the levels of product innovation can be regarded as a lead indicator that can alert managers to a future decline in sales unless corrective action is taken.

The Balanced Scorecard

One of the most impressive attempts to integrate the use of financial and non-financial measures has been the **Balanced Scorecard** by Robert Kaplan and David Norton. The Balanced Scorecard is really a framework that translates the aims and objectives of business into a series of key performance measures and targets. This framework should make the strategy of the business clearer and more easily communicated to employees; it should also help managers to assess the extent to which the objectives of the business are being fulfilled.

The Balanced Scorecard will involve setting objectives and developing appropriate measures and targets in four main areas:

- *Financial.* This area will specify the financial returns required by shareholders and may involve the use of financial measures such as return on capital employed, net profit margin, percentage sales growth and so on.
- *Customer.* This area will specify the kind of customer and/or markets the business wishes to service and will establish appropriate measures such as customer satisfaction, new customer growth levels and so on.
- *Internal business process.* This area will specify those business processes (for example, innovation, types of operation and after-sales service) that are important to the success of the business and will establish appropriate measures such as percentage of sales from new products, time to market for new products, product cycle times, and speed of response to customer complaints.
- *Learning and growth.* This area will specify the kind of people, the systems and the procedures that are necessary to deliver long-term business growth. This area is often the most difficult for the development of appropriate measures, however, examples of measures may include employee motivation, employee skills profiles, information systems capabilities and so on.

These four areas are shown in Figure 11.8.

The Balanced Scorecard approach does not prescribe the particular objectives, measures or targets that a business should adopt; this is a matter for the individual business to determine. It simply sets out the framework for developing a coherent set of objectives for the business and ensuring that they are then pursued in a systematic manner.

According to Kaplan and Norton, this framework is referred to as a *Balanced* Scorecard because it aims to strike a balance between external measures relating to customers and shareholders, and internal measures relating to internal business process and learning and growth. It also aims to strike a balance between the measures that portray outcomes (lag indicators) and measures that help predict future performance (lead indicators). Finally, the framework aims to strike a balance between 'hard' financial measures and 'soft' non-financial measures.

Figure 11.8

The Balanced Scorecard, for translating a strategy into operational processes

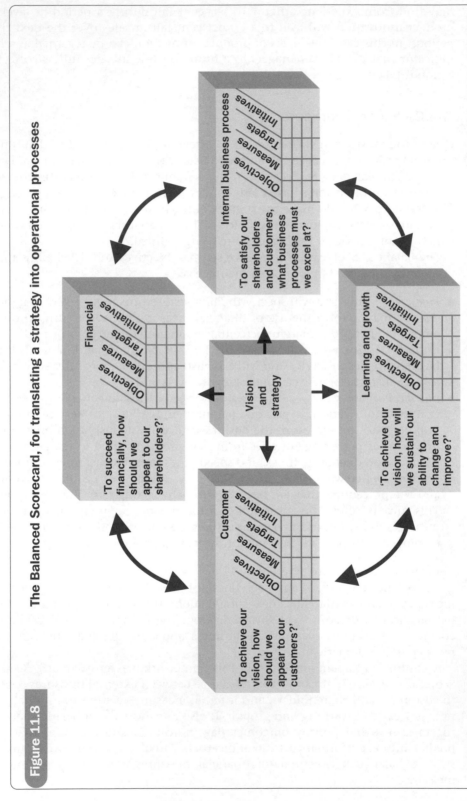

The diagram sets out the four main areas covered by the Balanced Scorecard as described above. Note that, for each area, a fundamental question must be addressed. By answering this question, managers should be able to develop the key objectives of the business. Once this has been done, suitable measures and targets can be developed that are relevant to those objectives. Finally, appropriate management initiatives will be developed to achieve the targets set.

Source: Kaplan and Norton (see reference (4) at end of chapter).

Kaplan and Norton (reference (4)) invite you to imagine the following conversation between yourself and the pilot of a jet aeroplane that you have boarded and whose cockpit you have entered:

Q: I'm surprised to see you operating the plane with only a single instrument. What does it measure?

A: Airspeed. I'm really working on airspeed this flight.

Q: That's good. Airspeed certainly seems important. But what about altitude, wouldn't an altimeter be helpful?

A: I worked on altitude for the last few flights and I've gotten pretty good at it. Now I have to concentrate on proper airspeed.

Q: But I notice you don't even have a fuel gauge. Wouldn't that be useful?

A: You're right; fuel is significant, but I can't concentrate on doing too many things well at the same time. So on this flight I'm focusing on airspeed. Once I get to be excellent at airspeed, as well as altitude, I intend to concentrate on fuel consumption on the next set of flights.

The point they are trying to make (apart from warning you against flying with a pilot like this!) is that to fly a complex machine like an aeroplane a wide range of navigation instruments is required. A business, however, can be even more complex to navigate than an aeroplane and so a wide range of measures, both financial and non-financial, is necessary.

Summary

In this chapter we have seen how modern production methods can mean that traditional approaches to costing and pricing may make a business unable to compete in the modern and increasingly global market. We have seen that the traditional approach of treating all overheads as part of a common pool and charging them to jobs on a direct-labour-hour basis although time honoured, is probably inappropriate in many modern business environments. Activity-based costing (ABC) seeks to identify the activities that are driving overhead costs and to charge jobs with overheads on the basis of the extent to which each job drives costs. Identifying what drives costs is also valuable because it could well enable managers to exercise greater control over those costs.

We have considered the pricing decision in rather more detail, firstly by looking at some theoretical arguments on the subject and then by considering some practical pricing issues. We have seen that cost information, both full and marginal, can have severe limitations as an aid to deciding the best price to be charged for a product.

We then went on to look at some modern approaches to costing that are designed to exert further downward pressure on costs. Total life-cycle costing, target costing and *kaizen* costing have all been developed to help a business survive in today's highly competitive markets.

Finally, we considered the importance of non-financial measures of performance as a means of helping managers to gain a deeper insight to the business. In particular, we examined the Balanced Scorecard, which aims to integrate financial and non-financial measures into a strategic-planning framework. The Balanced Scorecard has attracted much attention in recent years and many large companies now claim to be adopting this approach.

Key terms

Activity-based costing (ABC) p. 326	Price skimming p. 341
Cost driver p. 326	Total life-cycle costing p. 343
Cost pool p. 326	Target costing p. 344
Elasticity of demand p. 332	*Kaisen* costing p. 344
Full cost (cost-plus) pricing p. 338	Benchmarking p. 345
Marginal cost pricing p. 340	Value driver p. 346
Penetration pricing p. 341	Balanced Scorecard p. 347

Further reading

If you would like to explore the topics covered in this chapter in more depth, we recommend the following books:

Management and Cost Accounting, *Drury, C.*, 5th edn, Thompson Learning Business Press, 2000, chapters 10, 11 and 23.

Cost Accounting: A managerial emphasis, *Horngren, C., Foster, G. and Datar, S.*, 10th edn, Prentice Hall International, 2000, chapters 5, 12 and 13.

Cost and Management Accounting, *Williamson, D.*, Prentice Hall International, 1996, chapters 7, 13 and 20.

Management Accounting, *Atkinson, A., Banker, R., Kaplan, R. and Mark Young, S.*, 3rd edn, Prentice Hall, 2001, chapter 5, 7 and 9.

References

1. **Activity Based Costing – A review with case studies**, *Innes, J. and Mitchell, F.*, CIMA Publishing, 1990.
2. **Cost Systems Design and Profitability Analysis in UK Companies**, *Drury, C. and Tayles, M.*, CIMA Publishing, 2000.
3. **A Survey of Management Accounting Practices in UK Manufacturing Companies**, *Drury, C., Braund, S., Osborne, P. and Tayles M.*, Chartered Association of Certified Accounts, 1993.
4. **The Balanced Scorecard**, *Kaplan, R. and Norton, D.*, Harvard Business School, 1996.

REVIEW QUESTIONS

11.1 How does activity-based costing differ from the traditional approach?

11.2 The use of activity-based costing in helping to deduce full costs has been criticised. What has tended to be the basis of this criticism?

11.3 What is meant by elasticity of demand? How does knowledge of the elasticity of demand affect pricing decisions?

11.4 According to economic theory, at what point is profit maximised?

EXERCISES

Exercises 11.6–11.8 are more advanced than 11.1–11.5. Those with coloured numbers have answers at the back of the book.

11.1 Woodner Ltd provides a standard service. It is able to provide a maximum of 100 units of this service each week. Experience shows that at a price of £100, no unit of the service would be sold. For every £5 below this price, the company is able to sell 10 more units. For example, at a price of £95, 10 units would be sold, at £90, 20 units would be sold, and so on. The company's fixed costs total £2,500 a week. Variable costs are £20 per unit over the entire range of possible output. The market is such that it is not feasible to charge different prices to different customers.

Required:
What is the most profitable level of output of the service?

11.2 It appears from research evidence that a cost-plus approach influences pricing decisions in practice. What is meant by cost-plus pricing and what are the problems of using this approach?

11.3 Kaplan plc makes a range of suitcases of various sizes and shapes. There are 10 different models of suitcase produced by the company. In order to keep stocks of finished suitcases to a minimum, each model is made in a small batch. Each batch is costed as a separate job and the cost per suitcase deduced by dividing the batch cost by the number of suitcases in the batch.

At present, the business costs the batches using a traditional job-costing approach. Recently, however, a new management accountant was appointed, who is advocating the use of activity-based costing (ABC) to deduce the cost of the batches. The management accountant claims that ABC leads to much more reliable and relevant costs and that it has other benefits.

Required:
(a) Explain how the business deduces the cost of each suitcase at present.
(b) Discuss the purposes to which the knowledge of the cost per suitcase, deduced on a traditional basis, can be put and how valid the cost is for the purpose concerned.
(c) Explain how ABC could be applied to costing the suitcases, highlighting the differences between ABC and the traditional approach.

(d) Explain what advantages the new management accountant probably believes ABC to have over the traditional approach.

11.4 Comment critically on the following statements that you have overheard:

(a) 'To maximise profit you need to sell your output at the highest price.'
(b) 'Elasticity of demand deals with the extent to which costs increase as demand increases.'
(c) 'Provided that the price is large enough to cover the marginal cost of production, the sale should be made.'
(d) 'According to economic theory, profit is maximised where total cost equals total revenue.'
(e) 'Price skimming is charging low prices for the output until you have a good share of the market, and then putting up your prices.'

Explain clearly all technical terms.

11.5 Comment critically on the following statements that you have overheard:

(a) 'Direct labour hours are the most appropriate basis to use to charge overheads to jobs in the modern manufacturing environment where people are so important.'
(b) 'Activity-based costing is a means of more accurately accounting for direct labour cost.'
(c) 'Activity-based costing cannot really be applied to the service sector because the "activities" that it seeks to analyse tend to be related to manufacturing.'
(d) '*Kaisen* costing is an approach where great efforts are made to reduce the costs of developing a new product and setting up its production processes.'
(e) 'Benchmarking is an approach to job costing where each direct worker keeps a record of the time spent by each job on his or her workbench before it is passed on to the next direct worker or into finished stock stores.'

11.6 The GB Company manufactures a variety of electric motors. The business is currently operating at about 70 per cent of capacity and is earning a satisfactory return on investment.

The management of GB has been approached by International Industries (II) with an offer to buy 120,000 units of an electric motor. II manufactures a motor that is almost identical to GB's motor, but a fire at the II plant has shut down its manufacturing operations. II needs the 120,000 motors over the next four months to meet commitments to its regular customers; II is prepared to pay £19 each for the motors, which it will collect from the GB plant.

GB's product cost, based on current planned cost for the motor is:

	£
Direct materials	5.00
Direct labour (variable)	6.00
Manufacturing overhead	9.00
Total	20.00

Manufacturing overhead is applied to production at the rate of £18.00 per direct labour hour. This overhead rate is made up of the following components:

	£
Variable factory overhead	6.00

Fixed factory overhead	– direct	8.00
	– allocated	4.00
Applied manufacturing overhead rate		18.00

Additional costs usually incurred in connection with sales of electric motors include sales commissions of 5 per cent and freight expense of £1.00 per unit

In determining selling prices, GB adds a 40 per cent mark-up to product costs. This provides a suggested selling price of £28 for the motor. The marketing department however, has set the current selling price at £27.00 to maintain market share. The order would, however, require additional fixed factory overhead of £15,000 per month in the form of supervision and clerical costs. If management accepts the order, 30,000 motors will be manufactured and shipped to II each month for the next four months.

Required:

(a) Prepare a financial evaluation showing the impact of accepting the Industrial Industries order. What is the minimum unit price that the business's management could accept without reducing its operating profit?

(b) State clearly any assumptions contained in the analysis of (a) above and discuss any other organisational or strategic factors that GB should consider.

11.7 Sillycon Ltd is a business engaged in the development of new products in the electronics industry. Subtotals on the spreadsheet of planned overheads reveal:

	Electronics department	Testing department	Service department
Overheads – variable (£000)	1,200	600	700
– fixed (£000)	2,000	500	800
Planned activity: Labour hours ('000)	800	600	–

For the purposes of reallocation of service department overhead, it is agreed that variable overheads accrue in line with the labour hours worked in each department. Fixed overheads of the service department are to be reallocated on the basis of maximum practical capacity of the two departments, which is the same for each.

It has been a long-standing company practice to mark up full manufacturing costs by between 25 and 35 per cent in order to establish selling prices.

One new product, which is in a final development stage, is hoped to offer some improvement over competitors' products, which are currently marketed at between £110 and £130 each. Product development engineers have determined that the direct material content is £7 per unit. The product will take four labour hours in the electronics department and three hours in testing. Hourly labour rates are £10 and £6, respectively.

Management estimates that the fixed costs that would be specifically incurred in relation to the product are: supervision £13,000, depreciation of a recently acquired machine £100,000 and advertising £37,000 per annum. These fixed costs are included in the table given above.

Market research indicates that the business could expect to obtain and hold about 25 per cent of the market or, optimistically, 30 per cent. The total market is estimated at 20,000 units.

Note: it may be assumed that the existing plan has been prepared to cater for a range of products and no single product decision will cause the business to amend it.

Required:

(a) Prepare a summary of information that would help with the pricing decision. Such information should include marginal cost and full cost implications after allocation of service department overheads.

(b) Explain and elaborate on the information prepared.

11.8 A business manufactures refrigerators for domestic use. There are three models: Lo, Mid and Hi. The models, their quality and their price are aimed at different markets.

Product costs are computed on a blanket overhead-rate basis using a labour-hour method. Prices as a general rule are set based on cost plus 20 per cent. The following information is provided:

	Lo	Mid	Hi
Material cost (£/unit)	25	62.5	105
Direct labour hours (per unit)	$\frac{1}{2}$	1	1
Budget production/sales (units)	20,000	1,000	10,000

The budgeted overheads for the business amount to £4,410,000. Direct labour is costed at £8 per hour.

The business is currently facing increasing competition, especially from imported goods. As a result, the selling price of Lo has been reduced to a level that produces very little profit margin. To address this problem, an activity-based costing approach has been suggested. The overheads are examined and these are grouped round main business activities of machining (£2,780,000), logistics (£590,000) and establishment (£1,040,000) costs. It is maintained that these costs could be allocated based respectively on cost drivers of machine hours, material orders and space, to reflect the use of resources in each of these areas. After analysis, the following proportionate statistics are available related to the total volume of products:

| | Lo | Mid | Hi |
	%	%	%
Machine hours	40	15	45
Material orders	47	6	47
Space	42	18	40

Required:

(a) Calculate for each product the full cost and selling price determined by:
   (i) The original costing method.
   (ii) The activity-based costing method.

(b) What are the implications of the two systems of costing in the situation given?

(c) What business/strategic options exist for the business in the light of the new information?

12 Budgeting

Introduction

Budgets are an important tool for management planning and control. In this chapter we consider the role and nature of budgets and we shall also see how budgets are prepared. It is important to recognise that budgets do not exist in a vacuum; they are an integral part of a planning framework that is adopted by well-run businesses. To understand fully the nature of budgets we must, therefore, understand the planning framework within which they are set. The chapter begins with a discussion of this framework and then goes on to consider detailed aspects of the budgeting process.

OBJECTIVES

When you have completed this chapter you should be able to:

- Define a budget and show how budgets, corporate objectives and long-term plans are related.
- Explain the interlinking of the various budgets within the business.
- Discuss the budgeting process.
- Indicate the uses of budgeting and construct various budgets, including the cash budget, from relevant data.

Budgets, long-term plans and corporate objectives

It is vitally important that businesses develop plans for the future. Whatever a business is trying to achieve, it is unlikely to be successful unless its managers are clear what the future direction of the business is going to be.

The development of plans involves five key steps:

1. Setting the aims and objectives of the business.
2. Identifying the options available.
3. Evaluating the options and making a selection.
4. Setting detailed short-term plans or budgets.
5. Collecting information on performance and exercising control.

Step 1: setting the aims and objectives of the business

The aims and objectives set out what the business is basically trying to achieve. It is sometimes useful to make a distinction between aims and objectives. The aims of the business are often couched in broad terms and may be set out in the form of a **mission statement**. This statement is usually brief and will often articulate high standards or ideals for the business. Examples of two mission statements are provided in Exhibit 12.1.

Exhibit 12.1

Railtrack Group plc, the business that owns and manages the UK railway infrastructure, has on the front of its 2000 annual report the following mission statement:

> Our vision is the delivery of a safe, reliable, efficient, modern railway for our customers and the nation, using our railway skills to grow the company to reward our stakeholders and employees.

Cadbury Schweppes plc, the multinational food business, takes a more stark approach. In its 1999 annual report the company states its mission as follows:

> Cadbury Schweppes' objective is growth in shareholder value.

The objectives of a business are more specific than its aims. They will set out more precisely what has to be achieved. The objectives will vary between businesses but may include the following aspects of operations and performance:

- The kind of market the business seeks to serve.
- The share of that market it wishes to achieve.
- The level of operating efficiency (for example, lowest-cost producer).
- The kinds of product and/or service that should be offered.
- The levels of profit and returns to shareholders (for example, return on capital employed or dividends) that are required.
- The levels of growth required (for example, increase in assets, sales).
- Technological leadership (for example, the degree of innovation).

Objectives should be quantifiable and should be consistent with the aims of the business as set out in its mission statement. An example of the objectives of a business are set out in Exhibit 12.2.

Exhibit 12.2

Cadbury Schweppes goes on to say in its 1999 annual report that it intends to achieve its shareholder wealth mission by:

- Focusing on core growth markets of beverages and confectionery.
- Developing robust, sustainable market positions which are built on a platform of strong brands with supported franchises.
- Expanding market share through innovation in products, packaging and route to market, where economically profitable.
- Enhancing market position by acquisitions or disposals where they are in line with strategy, are value-creating and are available.

Step 2: identifying the options available

In order to achieve the objectives set for a business, a number of possible options (strategies) may be available. A creative search for the various strategic options should be undertaken. This will involve collecting information – an activity that can be extremely time-consuming, particularly when the business is considering entering new markets or investing in new technology.

The type of information collected should include an external analysis of the competitive environment and will relate to such matters as:

- Market size and growth prospects
- Level of competition within the industry
- Bargaining power of suppliers and customers
- Threat of new entrants to the market
- Threat of substitute products
- Relative power of trades unions, community interest groups and so on.

Information should also be collected that provides an *internal* analysis of the resources and expertise of the business that are available to pursue each option. Information concerning the capabilities of the business in each of the following areas may be collected:

- Organisation culture
- Marketing and distribution
- Manufacturing and production operations
- Finance and administration
- Research and development
- Information systems
- Human resources.

Any deficiencies or gaps in these areas that could affect the ability of the business to pursue a particular option must be identified.

Step 3: evaluating the options and making a selection

When deciding on the most appropriate option(s) to choose, the managers must examine information relating to each option to see whether the option fits with the objectives that have been set and to assess whether the resources to pursue the option are available. The managers must also consider the effect of pursuing each option on the financial performance and position of the business.

Activity 12.1

The approach described above suggests that decision makers will systematically collect information and then carefully evaluate all the options available. Do you think this is what decision makers really do? Is this how you approach decisions?

In practice, decision makers may not be as rational and capable as implied in the process described. Individuals may find it difficult to handle a wealth of information relating to a wide range of options. As a result, they may restrict their range of possible options and/or discard some information in order to avoid becoming overloaded. They may also adopt rather simple approaches to evaluating the mass of information provided, and these approaches might not fit very well with the outcome they would like to achieve.

Humans have a restricted ability to process information. Too much information can be as bad as too little, as it can overload individuals and create confusion. This, in turn, can lead to poor evaluations and poor decisions. The information provided to managers must be restricted to what is relevant to a particular decision and which is capable of being absorbed. This may mean that, in practice, information is produced in summary form and that only a restricted range of options will be considered.

The option selected will form the basis of the long-term plan for the business. This plan will usually cover a period of five years or more and will specify such things as:

- The market that the business will seek to serve
- The products or services to be offered
- Amounts and sources of finance to be raised by the business
- Capital investments to be made
- Amounts and sources of bought-in goods and services required
- Personnel requirements.

Step 4: setting detailed short-term plans or budgets

A **budget** is a financial plan for the short term – typically one year. It is likely to be expressed mainly in financial terms. Its role is to convert the long-term plans into actionable blueprints for the immediate future. Budgets will define precise targets concerning:

- Cash receipts and payments.
- Sales, broken down into amounts and prices for each of the products or services provided by the business.
- Detailed stock requirements.
- Detailed labour requirements.
- Specific production requirements.

Clearly, the relationship between objectives, long-term plans and budgets is that the objectives, once set, are likely to last for quite a long time – perhaps throughout the life of the business. A series of long-term plans identifies how each objective is to be pursued, and budgets identify how the long-term plan is to be fulfilled.

An analogy might be found in terms of someone enrolling on a course of study. His or her objective might be to embark on a career that will be rewarding in various ways. He or she might have identified the course as the most effective way to work towards this objective. In working towards this, passing a particular stage of the course might be identified as the target for the forthcoming year. Here the intention to complete the entire course is analogous to a long-term plan, and passing each stage is analogous to the budget. Having achieved the 'budget' for the first year, that for the second year becomes passing the second stage.

Step 5: collecting information on performance and exercising control

However well planned the activities of a business might be, they will come to nothing unless steps are taken to try to achieve them in practice. The process of making planned events actually occur is known as **control**.

Control can be defined as compelling events to conform to plan. This definition is valid in any context. For example, when we talk about controlling a motor car, we mean making the car do what we plan that it should do. In a business context, accounting is very useful in the control process. This is because it is possible to state plans in accounting terms (as budgets) and it is also possible to state *actual* outcomes in the same terms, thus making comparison between actual and planned outcomes a relatively easy matter. Where actual outcomes are at variance with budgets, this variance should be highlighted by accounting information. Managers can then take steps to get the business back on track towards the achievement of the budgets.

Figure 12.1 shows the planning and control process in diagrammatic form.

Figure 12.1

The planning and control process

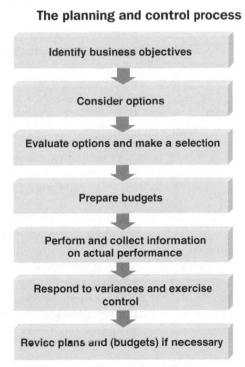

The figure shows the planning and control sequence within a business. Once the objectives of the business have been determined, the various options that can fulfil these objectives must be considered and evaluated in order to derive a long-term plan. The budget is a short-term financial plan for the business that is prepared within the framework of the long-term plan. Control can be exercised through the comparison of budgeted and actual performance. Where a significant divergence emerges, some form of corrective action should be taken. If the budget figures prove to be based on incorrect assumptions about the future, it might be necessary to revise the budget.

It should be emphasised that planning is the role of managers rather than accountants. Traditionally, the role of the management accountant has been simply to provide technical advice and assistance to managers to help them plan.

However, things are changing. Increasingly, the management accountant is seen as a member of the management team and, in this management role, is expected to contribute towards the planning process.

Time horizon of plans and budgets

The setting of plans is typically performed as a major exercise every five years, and budgets are usually set annually. It need not necessarily be the case that long-term plans are set for five years and that budgets are set for 12 months: it is up to the management of the business concerned. Businesses involved in certain industries – say, information technology – may feel that five years is too long a planning period since new developments can, and do, occur virtually overnight. Nor need it be the case that a budget is set for one year. However, this appears to be a widely used time horizon.

Activity 12.2	Can you think of any reason why most businesses prepare detailed budgets for the forthcoming year, rather than for a shorter or longer period?

The reason is probably that a year represents a long enough time for the budget preparation exercise to be worthwhile, yet short enough into the future for detailed plans to be capable of being made. As we shall see later in this chapter, the process of formulating budgets can be a time-consuming exercise, but there are economies of scale – for example, preparing the budget for the next twelve months would not normally take twice as much time and effort as preparing the budget for the next six months.

An annual budget sets targets for the forthcoming year for all levels of the business. It is usually broken down into monthly budgets, which define monthly targets. Indeed, in many instances, the annual budget will be built up from monthly figures. For example, where sales are the key factor determining the level of activity, the sales staff will be required to make sales targets for each month of the budget period. Other budgets will be set, for each month of the budget period, as we shall explain below.

Budgets and forecasts

A budget may be defined as a **financial plan** for a future period of time. *Financial* because the budget is, to a great extent, expressed in financial terms. Note also, particularly, that a budget is a *plan*, not a forecast. To talk of a plan suggests an intention or determination to achieve planned targets; **forecasts** tend to be predictions of the future state of the environment.

Clearly, forecasts are very helpful to the planner/budget-setter. If, for example, a reputable forecaster has forecast the number of new cars to be purchased in the UK during next year, it will be valuable for a manager in a car manufacturing business to obtain and take account of this forecast figure when setting sales budgets. However, a forecast and a budget are distinctly different.

Periodic and continual budgets

Budgeting can be undertaken on a periodic or a continual basis. A **periodic budget** is prepared for a particular period (usually one year). Managers will agree the budget for the year and then allow the budget to run its course. Although it may be necessary to revise the budget on occasions, preparing the budget is in essence a one-off exercise during a financial year. A **continual budget**, as the name suggests, is continually updated. We have seen that an annual budget will normally be broken down into smaller time intervals (usually monthly periods) to help control the activities of a business. A continual budget will add a new month to replace the month that has just passed, thereby ensuring that, at all times, there will be a budget for a full planning period. Continual budgets are also referred to as **rolling budgets**.

Activity 12.3 What do you think are the advantages and disadvantages of each form of budgeting?

Periodic budgeting will usually take less time and effort to prepare and will therefore be less costly. However, as time passes, the budget period shortens and toward the end of the financial year managers will be working to a very short planning period indeed. Continual budgeting, on the other hand, will ensure that managers always have a full year's budget to help them make decisions. It is claimed that continual budgeting ensures that managers plan throughout the year rather than just once each year. However, there is a danger that budgeting will become a mechanical exercise as managers may not have time to step back from their other tasks each month and consider the future carefully.

The interrelationship of various budgets

For a particular business for a particular period, there is more than one budget. Each one will relate to a specific aspect of the business. It is generally considered that the ideal situation is that there should be a separate budget for each person who is in a managerial position, no matter how junior. The contents of all of the individual budgets will be summarised in **master budgets** consisting usually of a budgeted income statement (profit and loss account) and balance sheet. However, the cash flow statement (in summarised form) may also be considered part of the master budget.

Figure 12.2 illustrates the interrelationship and interlinking of individual budgets, in this particular case using a manufacturing business as an example.

Starting at the top of Figure 12.2, the sales budget is usually the first budget to be prepared as this will determine the overall level of activity for the forthcoming period. The finished stock requirement would be dictated largely by the level of sales, although it would also be dictated by the policy of the business on finished stockholding. The requirement for finished stock would define the required production levels, which would, in turn, dictate the requirements of the individual production departments or sections. The demands of manufacturing, in conjunction with the business's policy on raw materials stock, define the raw materials stock budget. The purchases budget will be dictated by the materials stock budget which will, in conjunction with the policy of the business on creditor payment, dictate the trade creditors budget. One of the determinants of the cash budget will

Figure 12.2

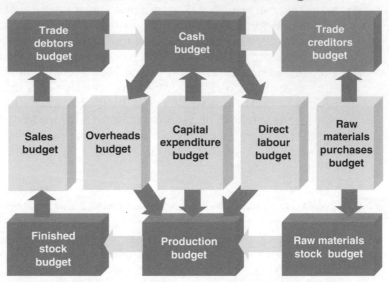

The interrelationship of various budgets

The figure shows the interrelationship of budgets for a manufacturing business. The starting point is usually the sales budget. The expected level of sales normally defines the overall level of activity for the business, and the other budgets will be drawn up in accordance with this. Thus, the sales budget will largely define the finished stock requirements, and from this we can define the production requirements and so on.

be the trade creditors budget; another will be the trade debtors budget, which itself derives, through the debtor policy of the business, from the sales budget. Cash will also be affected by overheads and direct labour costs (themselves linked to production) and by capital expenditure. The factors that affect policies on matters such as stockholding and debtor and creditor collection periods will discussed in some detail in Chapter 16.

Assuming that the budgeting process takes the order just described, it might be found in practice that there is some constraint to achieving the sales target. For example, the production capacity of the business may be incapable of meeting the necessary levels of output to match the sales budget for one or more months. In this case, it might be reasonable to look at the ways of overcoming the problem. As a last resort, it might be necessary to revise the sales budget to a lower level to enable production to meet the target.

Activity 12.4

Can you think of any ways in which a short-term shortage of production facilities might be overcome?

We thought of the following:

- Higher production in previous months and stockpiling to meet the higher demand period(s).
- Increasing production capacity, perhaps by working overtime and/or acquiring (buying or leasing) additional plant.
- Subcontracting some production.

There will be the horizontal relationships between budgets, which we have just looked at, but there will usually be vertical ones as well. For example, the sales budget may be broken down into a number of subsidiary budgets, perhaps one for each regional sales manager. The overall sales budget will be a summary of the subsidiary ones. The same may be true of virtually all of the other budgets, most particularly the production budget. Figure 12.2 gives a very simplified outline of the budgetary framework of a typical manufacturing business.

All of the operating budgets that we have just reviewed are set within the framework of the master budget (the budgeted profit and loss account and balance sheet).

The uses of budgets

Budgets are generally regarded as having five areas of usefulness, which we shall describe below. Figure 12.3 shows those areas in diagrammatic form.

Figure 12.3

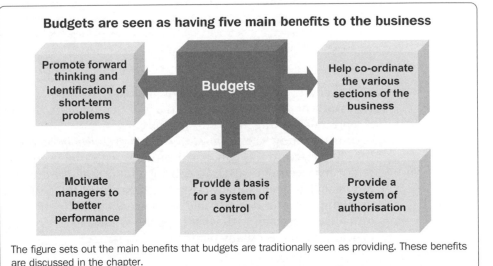

Budgets are seen as having five main benefits to the business

- Promote forward thinking and identification of short-term problems
- Budgets
- Help co-ordinate the various sections of the business
- Motivate managers to better performance
- Provide a basis for a system of control
- Provide a system of authorisation

The figure sets out the main benefits that budgets are traditionally seen as providing. These benefits are discussed in the chapter.

Firstly, they tend to *promote forward thinking and the possible identification of short-term problems*. We saw (above) that a shortage of production capacity might be identified during the budgeting process. Making this discovery in good time could leave a number of means of overcoming the problem open to exploration. Take, for example, the problem of a shortage of production at a particular part of the year. If the potential problem is picked up early enough, all of the suggestions in the answer to Activity 12.4 and, possibly, other ways of overcoming the problem can be explored and considered rationally. Budgeting should help to achieve this.

The second area of usefulness is in their *helping to co-ordinate the various sections of the business*. It is crucially important that the activities of the various departments and sections of the business are linked so that the activities of one are complementary to those of another. For example, the activities of the purchasing/procurement department of a manufacturing business should dovetail with the raw materials needs of the production departments. If this is not the case, production could run out of stock, leading to expensive production stoppages. Alternatively, excessive stocks could be bought, leading to large and unnecessary stockholding costs.

Budgets' third area of usefulness is in their *ability to motivate managers to better performance*. Having a stated task can motivate managers and staff in their performance. It is a well established view that to tell a manager to do his or her best is not very motivating, but to define a required level of achievement is likely to be. It is felt that managers will be better motivated by being able to relate their particular role in the business to the overall objectives of the business. Since budgets are directly derived from corporate objectives, budgeting makes this possible.

Activity 12.5	Do you think there is a danger that requiring managers to work towards predetermined targets will stifle their skill, flair and enthusiasm?

There is this danger if targets are badly set. If, however, the budgets are set in such a way as to offer challenging yet achievable targets, the manager is still required to show skill, flair and enthusiasm.

It is clearly not possible to allow managers to operate in an unconstrained environment. Having to operate in a way that matches the goals of the business is a price of working in an effective business.

Fourthly, budgets can *provide a basis for a system of control*. As stated earlier in the chapter, control is concerned with ensuring that events conform to plans. If senior management wishes to control and to monitor the performance of more junior staff, it needs some yardstick against which the performance can be measured and assessed. It is possible to compare current performance with past performance or perhaps with what happens in another business. However, the most logical yardstick is usually planned performance.

Activity 12.6	What is wrong with comparing actual performance with past performance or the performance of others in an effort to exercise control?

There is no automatic reason to believe that what happened in the past, or is happening elsewhere, represents a sensible target for this year in this business. Considering what happened last year, and in other businesses, may help in the formulation of plans, but past events and the performance of others should not automatically be seen as the target.

If there are data available concerning the actual performance for a period, and this can be compared with the planned performance, then a basis for control will have been established. Such a basis will enable the use of **management by exception**, a technique where senior managers can spend most of their time dealing with those staff or activities that have failed to achieve the budget and not having to spend too much time on those that are performing well. It also allows junior managers to exercise self-control, since by knowing what is expected of them and what they have actually achieved, they can assess how well they are performing and take steps to correct matters where they are failing to achieve.

We shall consider the effect of making plans and being held accountable for their achievement later in this and the next chapter.

The fifth and final recognised area of usefulness lies in the ability of budgets to *provide a system of authorisation* for managers to spend up to a particular limit. A good example of this is where there are certain activities (for example, staff development and research expenditure) that are allocated a fixed amount of funds at the discretion of senior management.

Activity 12.7

Could the five identified uses of budgets conflict with one another on occasions? For example, can you think of a possible conflict:

(a) between the budget as a motivational device and the budget as a means of control?

(b) between the budget as a means of control and the budget as a system of authorisation?

....

It is quite possible for the uses identified to be in conflict with one another.

(a) Where the budget is being used as a motivational device, the budget targets may be set at a more difficult level than is expected to be achieved. This may be valuable as a means of getting managers to strive to reach their targets, however, for control purposes, the budget becomes less meaningful as a benchmark against which to compare actual performance.

(b) Where a budget is being used as a system of authorisation, managers may be motivated to spend to the limit of their budget, even though this may be wasteful. This may occur where the managers are not allowed to carry over unused funds to the next budget period or if they believe that the budget for the next period will be reduced because not all the funds for the current period were spent. The wasting of resources in this way conflicts with the role of budgets as a means of exercising control.

Conflict between the different uses will mean that managers must decide which particular uses for budgets should be given priority; managers must be prepared, if necessary, to trade off the benefits resulting from one particular use for the benefits of another.

●●●● The budget-setting process

Budgeting is such an important area for businesses and other organisations, that it tends to be approached in a fairly methodical and formal way. This usually involves a number of steps, described below and shown in diagrammatic form in Figure 12.4.

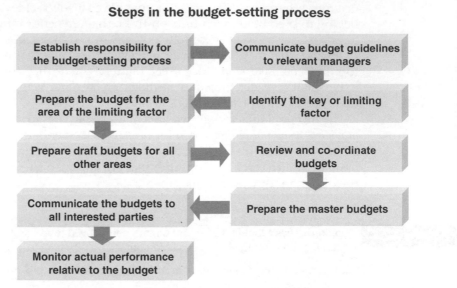

Steps in the budget-setting process

Establish responsibility for the budget-setting process → Communicate budget guidelines to relevant managers

Prepare the budget for the area of the limiting factor ← Identify the key or limiting factor

Prepare draft budgets for all other areas → Review and co-ordinate budgets

Communicate the budgets to all interested parties ← Prepare the master budgets

Monitor actual performance relative to the budget

The figure shows the sequence of events in the preparation of the budgets. Once the budgets are prepared, they are communicated to all interested parties and, over time, actual performance is monitored in relation to the targets set out in the budgets.

Step 1: establish who will take responsibility

It is usually seen as crucial that those responsible for the budget-setting process have real authority within the organisation.

Activity 12.8

Why is it crucial that those responsible for the budget-setting process have real authority in the organisation?

....

One of the crucial aspects of the process is establishing co-ordination between budgets so that the plans of one department match and are complementary to those of other departments. This usually requires compromise where adjustment of initial budgets must be undertaken. This in turn means that someone on the board of directors (or its equivalent) has to be closely involved; only people of this rank are likely to have the necessary moral and, in the final analysis, formal managerial authority to force departmental managers to compromise.

Quite commonly, a **budget committee** is formed to supervise and take resposibility for the budget-setting process. This committee usually comprises a senior representative of most of the functional areas of the business – marketing, production, personnel and so on. Often, a **budget officer** is appointed to carry out, or to take immediate responsibility for others carrying out, the tasks of the committee. Not surprisingly, given their technical expertise in the activity, accountants are often required to take budget officer roles.

Step 2: communicate budget guidelines to relevant managers

Budgets are intended to be the short-term plans that seek to work towards the achievement of long-term plans and to the overall objectives of the business. It is therefore important that, in drawing up budgets, managers are well aware of what the long-term plans are and how the forthcoming budget period is intended to work towards them. Managers also need to be made well aware of the commercial/economic environment in which they will be operating. It is the responsibility of the budget committee to see that managers have all the necessary information.

Step 3: identify the key, or limiting, factor

There will always be some aspect of the business that will stop it achieving its objectives to the maximum extent. This is often a limited ability of the business to sell its products; sometimes, it is some production shortage (labour, materials, plant) that is the **limiting factor**, or, linked to these, a shortage of funds. Often, production shortages can be overcome by an increase in funds – for example, more plant can be bought or leased – but not always, because no amount of money will buy certain labour skills or increase the world supply of some raw material.

As has been pointed out earlier in this chapter, it is sometimes possible to ease an initial limiting factor, for example, a plant capacity problem can be eliminated by subcontracting. This means that some other factor, perhaps sales, will replace the production problem, though at a higher level of output. Ultimately, however, the business will hit a ceiling; some limiting factor will prove impossible to ease.

For entirely practical reasons, it is important that the limiting factor is identified. Ultimately, most, if not all, budgets will be affected by the limiting factor, and so if it can be identified at the outset, all managers can be informed of the restriction early in the process.

Step 4: prepare the budget for the area of the limiting factor

The limiting-factor budget will quite often be the sales budget since the ability to sell is frequently the limiting factor that simply cannot be eased. It is the limiting factor that will determine the overall level of activity for the business. (When discussing the interrelationship of budgets earlier in the chapter, we started with the sales budget for this reason.)

Exhibit 12.3 looks at the methods favoured by businesses of different sizes to determine their sales budgets.

Exhibit 12.3	Determining the future level of sales can be a difficult problem. In practice, a business may rely on the judgements of sales staff, statistical techniques or market surveys (or some combination of these) to arrive at a sales budget. A 1993 survey of UK manufacturing businesses provides the following insights concerning the use of such techniques and methods.

	All respondents	Small businesses	Large businesses
Number of respondents	281	47	46
	%	%	%
Technique			
Statistical forecasting	31	19	29
Market research	36	13	54
Subjective estimates based on sales staff experience	85	97	80

We can see that the most popular approach by far is the opinion of sales staff. We can also see that there are differences between large and small businesses, particularly concerning the use of market surveys.

Source: Drury, Braund, Osborne and Tayles (see reference (1) at the end of the chapter).

Step 5: prepare draft budgets for all other areas

The other budgets are prepared, complementing the budget for the area of the limiting factor. In all budget preparation, the computer has become an almost indispensable tool. Much of the work of preparing budgets is repetitive and tedious, yet the resultant budget has to represent reliably the actual plans made. Computers are ideally suited to such tasks and human beings are not. It is often the case that budgets have to be redrafted several times because of some minor alteration and, again, computers do this without complaint.

There are two broad approaches to setting individual budgets. The **top-down approach** is where the senior management of each budget area originates the budget targets, perhaps discussing them with lower levels of management and, as a result, refining them before the final version is produced. With the **bottom-up approach**, the targets are fed upwards from the lowest level. For example, junior sales managers will be asked to set their own sales targets, which then become incorporated into the budgets of higher levels of management until the overall sales budget emerges.

Where the bottom-up approach is adopted, it is usually necessary to haggle and negotiate at different levels of authority to achieve agreement. This may be because the plans of some departments do not fit in with those of others or because the targets set by junior managers are not acceptable to their superiors. This approach is rarely found in practice.

Activity 12.9	What are the advantages and disadvantages of each type of budgeting approach?

The bottom-up approach allows greater involvement among managers in the budgeting process and this, in turn, may increase the level of commitment to the targets set. It also allows the business to draw more fully on the local knowledge and expertise of its managers. However, this approach can be time-consuming and may result in some managers setting undemanding targets for themselves in order to have an easy life.

The top-down approach enables senior management to communicate plans to employees and to co-ordinate the activities of the business more easily. It may also help in establishing more demanding targets for managers. However, the level of commitment to the budget may be lower as many of those responsible for achieving the budgets will have been excluded from the budget setting process.

There will be a brief discussion of the benefits of participation in target-setting in Chapter 13.

Step 6: review and co-ordinate budgets

A business's budget committee must at this stage review the various budgets and satisfy itself that the budgets complement one another. Where there is a lack of co-ordination, steps must be taken to ensure that the budgets mesh. Since this will require that at least one budget must be revised, this activity normally benefits from a diplomatic approach. Ultimately, however, the committee may be forced to assert its authority and insist that alterations are made.

Step 7: prepare the master budgets

The master budgets are the budgeted profit and loss account and budgeted balance sheet (and perhaps a summarised, budgeted cash flow statement). All of the information required to prepare these statements should be available from the individual budgets that have already been prepared. The task of preparing the master budgets is usually undertaken by the budget committee.

Step 8: communicate the budgets to all interested parties

The formally agreed budgets are now passed to the individual managers who will be responsible for their implementation. This is, in effect, senior management formally communicating to the other managers the targets that they must achieve.

Step 9: monitor performance relative to the budget

Much of the budget-setting activity will have been pointless unless each manager's actual performance is compared with planned performance, which is embodied in the budget. This issue is examined in detail in Chapter 13.

Incremental and zero-base budgeting

Traditionally, much setting of budgets has tended to be on the basis of what happened last year, with some adjustment for any changes in factors that are expected to affect the forthcoming budget period (for example, inflation). This approach is sometimes known as **incremental budgeting**; it is often used for 'discretionary' budgets, such as research and development and staff training, where the **budget holder** (the manager responsible for the budget) is allocated a sum of money to be spent in the area of activity concerned. They are referred to as **discretionary budgets** because the sum allocated is normally at the discretion of senior management. These budgets are very common in local and central government (and in other public bodies) but are also used in commercial businesses to cover certain types of activity.

A feature of the types of activity for which discretionary budgets exist is the lack of a clear relationship between inputs (resources applied) and outputs (benefits). Compare this with, say, a raw materials usage budget in a manufacturing company, where the amount of material used and, therefore, the amount of funds taken by it is clearly related to the level of production and, ultimately, to sales. It is easy for discretionary budgets to eat up funds with no clear benefit being derived. It is often only proposed increases in these budgets that are closely scrutinised.

Zero-base budgeting (ZBB) rests on the philosophy that all spending needs to be justified. Thus, when establishing the training budget each year, it is not automatically accepted that training courses should be financed in the future simply because they were undertaken this year. The training budget will start from a zero base and will only be increased if a good case can be made for the scarce resources of the business to be allocated to this form of activity. Top management will need to be convinced that the proposed activities represent 'value for money'.

ZBB encourages managers to adopt a more questioning approach to their areas of responsibility. To justify the allocation of resources, they are often forced to think carefully about the particular activities and the ways in which they are undertaken. This questioning approach should result in a more efficient use of business resources. With an increasing portion of the total costs of most businesses being in areas where the link between outputs and inputs is not always clear, and where commitment of resources is discretionary rather than demonstrably essential to production, ZBB is increasingly relevant.

| Activity 12.10 | Can you think of any disadvantages of using ZBB? How might any disadvantages be partially overcome? |

The principal problems with ZBB are:

- It is time-consuming and therefore expensive to undertake.
- Managers, whose sphere of responsibility is subjected to ZBB, can feel threatened by it.

The benefits of a ZBB approach can be gained to some extent – perhaps at not too great a cost – by using the approach on a selective basis. For example, a particular budget area could be subjected to a ZBB-type scrutiny only every third or fourth year. If ZBB is used more frequently, there is, in any case, the danger that managers will use the same arguments each year to justify their activities. The process will simply become a mechanical exercise and the benefits will be lost. For a typical business, some areas are likely to benefit from ZBB more than others. ZBB could, in these circumstances, be applied only to those areas that will benefit from it, and not to others. The areas that are most likely to benefit from ZBB are discretionary spending ones, such as training, advertising, and research and development.

If senior management is aware of the potentially threatening nature of this form of budgeting, care can be taken to apply ZBB with sensitivity. However, in the quest for value for money, the application of ZBB can result in some tough decisions being made.

An example of a budget: the cash budget

We shall now look in some detail at one particular budget, the cash budget. We shall use this because:

- It is a key budget; most economic aspects of a business are reflected in cash sooner or later, so that for a typical business the cash budget reflects the whole business more than any other single budget.
- Very small, unsophisticated businesses (for example, a corner shop) may feel that full-scale budgeting is not appropriate to their needs, but almost certainly they should prepare a cash budget as a minimum.

We shall consider other budgets later in the chapter.

Since budgets are documents that are to be used only internally by a business, their style and format is a question of management choice and will therefore vary from one business to the next. However, since managers, irrespective of the business, are likely to be using budgets for similar purposes, there is a tendency for some consistency of approach to exist. We can probably say that, in most businesses, the cash budget would possess the following features:

1. The budget period would be broken down into sub-periods, typically months.
2. The budget would be in columnar form, with one column for each month.
3. Receipts of cash would be identified under various headings and a total for each month's receipts shown.
4. Payments of cash would be identified under various headings and a total for each month's payments shown.
5. The surplus of total cash receipts over payments or of payments over receipts for each month would be identified.
6. The running cash balance would be identified. This would be achieved by taking the balance at the end of the previous month and adjusting it for the surplus or deficit of receipts over payments for the current month.

Typically, all of the pieces of information in (3) to (6) in the above list would be useful to management for one reason or another.

The best way to deal with this topic is through an example (Example 12.1).

Example 12.1

Vierra Popova Ltd is a wholesale business. The budgeted profit and loss account for the next six months is as follows:

	Jan £000	Feb £000	Mar £000	Apr £000	May £000	June £000
Sales	52	55	55	60	55	53
Cost of goods sold	30	31	31	35	31	32

Salaries and wages	10	10	10	10	10	10
Electricity	5	5	4	3	3	3
Depreciation	3	3	3	3	3	3
Other overheads	2	2	2	2	2	2
Total expenses	50	51	50	53	49	50
Net profit	2	4	5	7	6	3

The business allows all of its customers one month's credit (this means, for example, that cash from January sales will be received in February). Sales during December were £60,000.

The business plans to maintain stocks at their existing level until some time in March, when they are to be reduced by £5,000. Stocks will remain at this lower level indefinitely. Stock purchases are made on one month's credit (the December purchases having been £30,000). Salaries, wages and 'other overheads' are paid in the month concerned. Electricity is paid quarterly in arrears in March and June. The business plans to buy and pay for a new delivery van in March. This will cost a total of £15,000, but an existing van will be traded in for £4,000 as part of the deal.

The business expects to have £12,000 in cash at the beginning of January.

Let us show how the cash budget for the six months ending in June will look.

	Jan £000	Feb £000	Mar £000	Apr £000	May £000	June £000
Receipts						
Debtors (note 1)	60	52	55	55	60	55
Payments						
Creditors (note 2)	30	30	31	26	35	31
Salaries and wages	10	10	10	10	10	10
Electricity			14			9
Other overheads	2	2	2	2	2	2
Van purchase			11			
Total payments	42	42	68	38	47	52
Cash surplus	18	10	(13)	17	13	3
Opening balance (note 3)	12	30	40	27	44	57
Closing balance	30	40	27	44	57	60

Notes

1. The cash receipts lag a month behind sales because customers are given a month in which to pay for their purchases.
2. In most months, the purchases of stock will equal the cost of goods sold. This is because the business maintains a constant level of stock. For stock to remain constant at the end of each month, the business must replace exactly the amount which has been used. During March, however, the business plans to reduce its stock by £5,000. This means that stock purchases will be lower than stock usage in that month. The payments for stock purchases lag a month behind purchases because the business expects to be allowed a month to pay for what it buys.

3. Each month's cash balance is the previous month's figure plus the cash surplus (or minus the cash deficit) for the current month. The balance at the start of January is £12,000 according to the information provided earlier.
4. Depreciation does not give rise to a cash payment.

Activity 12.11

Looking at the cash budget of Vierra Popova Ltd, what conclusions do you draw and what possible course of action do you recommend regarding the cash balance over the period concerned?

There appears to be a fairly large cash balance, given the size of the business, and it seems to be increasing. Management might give consideration to putting some of the cash into an income-yielding deposit. Alternatively, it could be used to expand the trading activities of the business by, for example, increasing the investment in fixed assets.

Activity 12.12

Vierra Popova Ltd (see Example 12.1) now wishes to prepare its cash budget for the second six months of the year. The budgeted profit and loss account for the second six months is as follows:

	July £000	Aug £000	Sept £000	Oct £000	Nov £000	Dec £000
Sales	57	59	62	57	53	51
Cost of goods sold	32	33	35	32	30	29
Salaries and wages	10	10	10	10	10	10
Electricity	3	3	4	5	6	6
Depreciation	3	3	3	3	3	3
Other overheads	2	2	2	2	2	2
Total expenses	50	51	54	52	51	50
Net profit	7	8	8	5	2	1

The business will continue to allow all of its customers one month's credit.

The business plans to increase stocks from the 30 June level by £1,000 each month until, and including, September. During the following three months, stock levels will be decreased by £1,000 each month.

Stock purchases, which had been made on one month's credit until the June payment, will, starting with the purchases made in June, be made on two months' credit.

Salaries, wages and 'other overheads' will continue to be paid in the month concerned. Electricity is paid quarterly in arrears in September and December.

At the end of December the business intends to pay off part of a loan. This payment is to be such that it will leave the business with a cash balance of £5,000 with which to start next year.

Required:
Prepare the cash budget for the six months ending in December. (Remember that any information you need that relates to the first six months of the year, including the cash balance that is expected to be brought forward on 1 July, is given in Example 12.1.)

The cash budget for the six months ended 31 December is:

	July £000	Aug £000	Sept £000	Oct £000	Nov £000	Dec £000
Receipts						
Debtors	53	57	59	62	57	53
Payments						
Creditors (note 1)	–	32	33	34	36	31
Salaries and wages	10	10	10	10	10	10
Electricity			10			17
Other overheads	2	2	2	2	2	2
Loan repayment (note 2)	–	–	–	–	–	131
Total payments	12	44	55	46	48	191
Cash surplus	41	13	4	16	9	(138)
Cash balance	60	101	114	118	134	143
Closing balance	101	114	118	134	143	5

Notes:
1. There will be no payment to creditors in July because the June purchases will be made on two months' credit and will therefore be paid in August. The July purchases, which will equal the July cost of sales figure plus the increase in stock made in July, will be paid for in September, and so on.
2. The repayment is simply the amount that will cause the balance at 31 December to be £5,000.

Preparing other budgets

Though each one will have its own idiosyncrasies, other budgets will tend to follow the same sort of pattern as the cash budget. Take the debtors budget for example. This would normally show the planned amount owing from credit sales to the business at the beginning and at the end of each month, the planned total sales for each month and the planned total cash receipts from debtors. The layout would be something like the following:

	Month 1 £	Month 2 £	...
Opening balance	X	X	
Add Sales	X	X	
	X	X	
Less Cash receipts	X	X	
Closing balance	X	X	

A raw materials stock budget (for a manufacturing business) would follow a similar pattern, as follows:

	Month 1 £ (or physical units)	Month 2 £ (or physical units)	...
Opening balance	X	X	
Add Purchases	X	X	
	X	X	
Less Issues to production	X	X	
Closing balance	X	X	

The stock budget will normally be expressed in financial terms, but may well be expressed in physical terms (for example, kilograms or metres) too for individual stock items.

A study of budgeting practice in small and medium-sized enterprises (SMEs) revealed that the most frequently prepared budget is the sales budget, followed by the budgeted profit and loss account and the overheads budget. Relevant data are given in Exhibit 12.4.

Exhibit 12.4

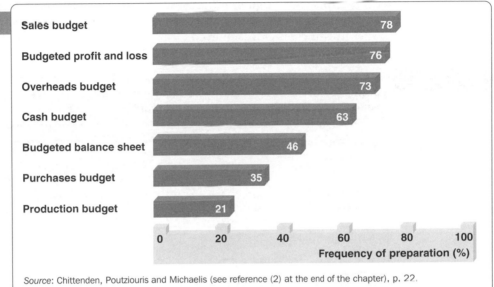

Source: Chittenden, Poutziouris and Michaelis (see reference (2) at the end of the chapter), p. 22.

Activity 12.13

Have a go at preparing the debtors budget for Vierra Popova Ltd for the six months, July to December (see Activity 12.12).

The debtors budget for the six months ended 31 December is:

	July £000	Aug £000	Sept £000	Oct £000	Nov £000	Dec £000
Opening balance (Note 1)	53	57	59	62	57	53
Add Sales (Note 2)	57	59	62	57	53	51
	110	116	121	119	110	104
Less Cash receipts (Note 3)	53	57	59	62	57	53
Closing balance (Note 4)	57	59	62	57	53	51

Notes:
1. The opening debtors figure is the previous month's sales figure (sales are on one month's credit).
2. The sales are the current month's figure.

Note how the debtors budget in Activity 12.13 links to the cash budget: the cash receipts row of figures is the same in both. The debtors budget would link to the sales budget in a similar way. This is how the linking, which was discussed earlier in this chapter, is achieved.

Activity 12.14

Have a go at preparing the creditors budget for Vierra Popova Ltd for the six months of July to December (see Activity 12.12). *Hint*: remember that the creditors' payment period alters from the June purchases onwards.

The creditors budget for the six months ended 31 December is:

	July £000	Aug £000	Sept £000	Oct £000	Nov £000	Dec £000
Opening balance	32	65	67	70	67	60
Add Purchases	33	34	36	31	29	28
	65	99	103	101	96	88
Less Cash payments	–	32	33	34	36	31
Closing balance	65	67	70	67	60	57

This, again, could be set out in any manner that would have given the sort of information that management would require in respect of planned levels of creditors and associated transactions.

Activity-based budgeting

Activity-based budgeting (ABB) applies the philosophy of activity-based costing (ABC), which we discussed in Chapter 11, to planning and control through budgets. You may recall that ABC recognises that it is activities that cause or 'drive' costs. If the cost-driving activities can be identified, ascertaining the cost of the output of a business can be achieved with greater accuracy. Not only this, but costs become easier to control simply because their cause is known.

It is a central feature of budgeting that those who are responsible for meeting a particular budget (budget holders) should have control over the events that affect performance in their area. A typical problem in this regard is illustrated by the manager whose costs are increased beyond the budgeted costs as a result of increased volume of activity, which is outside of that manager's control. In other words, the costs are driven by activities not controlled by the manager who is being held accountable for those costs.

ABB seeks to generate budgets in such a way that the manager who has control over the cost drivers is accountable for the costs that are caused.

Non-financial measures in budgeting

The efficiency of internal operations and customer satisfaction have become of critical importance to businesses striving to survive in an increasingly competitive environment. Non-financial measures have an important role to play in assessing performance in such key areas as customer/supplier delivery times, set-up times, defect levels and customer satisfaction levels. There is no reason why management accounting need be confined to reporting only financial targets and measures. Non-financial measures can also be used as the basis for targets and can be incorporated into the budgeting process and reported alongside the financial targets for the business (see Exhibit 12.5).

Exhibit 12.5

A 1993 survey of manufacturing businesses revealed that non-financial measures are widely used by businesses. The following table is taken from this study.

	Extent to which performance is measured					
	Never/rarely		Sometimes		Often/always	
	Smaller firms %	Larger firms %	Smaller firms %	Larger firms %	Smaller firms %	Larger firms %
Customer satisfaction/ product quality	22	2	11	7	67	91
Customer delivery efficiency	16	2	22	7	62	91
Supplier quality/ delivery	16	4	32	15	52	81
Throughput times	33	6	24	20	43	74
Set-up times	59	32	19	22	22	46

We can see that customer-based measures are the most widely used form of non-financial performance measures. There are also clear differences between the smaller firms and larger firms in the extent to which non-financial measures are used.

Source: Drury, Braund, Osborne and Tayles (see reference (1) at end of chapter).

Budgets and management behaviour

There has been a great deal of literature published on the way in which managers use information generated by the budgeting system and the impact of its use on the attitudes and behaviour of subordinates. A pioneering study by Hopwood (see reference (2) at the end of the chapter) examined the way in which managers working within a manufacturing environment used budget information to evaluate the performance of subordinates. He argued that three distinct styles of management could be observed. These are:

- *Budget-constrained style.* This management style focuses rigidly on the ability of subordinates to meet the budget. Other factors relating to the performance of subordinates are not given serious consideration.

- *Profit-conscious style.* This management style uses budget information in a more flexible way and often in conjunction with other data. The main focus is on the ability of each subordinate to improve the long-term effectiveness of the area for which he/she has responsibility.
- *Non-accounting style.* In this case, budget information plays no significant role in the evaluation of a subordinate's performance.

<table>
<tr><td>Activity 12.15</td><td>How might a manager respond to budget information that indicates a subordinate has not met the budget targets for the period, assuming the manager to operate with:</td></tr>
</table>

(a) A budget-constrained style?
(b) A profit-conscious style?
(c) A non-accounting style?

....

(a) A manager adopting a budget-constrained style is likely to take the budget information very seriously. This may result in criticism of the subordinate and, perhaps, some form of punishment.
(b) A manager adopting a profit-conscious style is likely to take a broader view when examining the budget information and so will take other factors into consideration (for example, factors that could not have been anticipated at the time of preparing the budgets), before deciding whether criticism or punishment is justified.
(c) A manager adopting a non-accounting style will regard the failure to meet the budget as being relatively unimportant and so no action is likely to be taken.

Hopwood found that subordinates working for a manager adopting a budget-constrained style suffered higher levels of job-related stress and had poorer working relationships with both their colleagues and their manager than those subordinates whose manager adopted one of the two other styles. He also found that the subordinates of a budget-constrained style of manager were more likely to manipulate the budget figures or to take undesirable actions to ensure the budgets were met.

Although these findings are interesting, subsequent studies have cast doubt on their universal applicability. Later studies confirm that human attitudes and behaviour are complex and can vary according to the particular situation. For example, it has been found that the impact of different management styles on such factors as job-related stress and the manipulation of budget figures is likely to vary according to such factors as the level of independence enjoyed by the subordinates and the level of uncertainty associated with the tasks to be undertaken.

It seems that where there is a high level of interdependence between business divisions, subordinate managers are more likely to feel that they have less control over their performance. This is because the performance of staff in other divisions could be an important influence on the final outcome. In such a situation, rigid application of the budget could be viewed as being unfair and may lead to undesirable behaviour. However, where managers have a high degree of independence, the application of budgets as a measure of performance is likely to be more acceptable. In this case, the managers are likely to feel that the final outcome is much less dependent on the performance of others.

Later studies have also shown that where a subordinate is undertaking a task that has a high degree of uncertainty concerning the outcome (for example, developing a new product for the market), budget targets are unlikely to be an adequate measure of performance. In such a situation, other factors and measures should be taken into account in order to derive a more complete assessment of performance. However, where a task has a low degree of uncertainty concerning the outcome (for example, producing a standard product using standard equipment and an experienced workforce) budget measures may be regarded as more reliable indicators of performance (see reference (3) at the end of the chapter). Thus, it appears that a budget-constrained style is more likely to work where subordinates enjoy a fair amount of independence and where the tasks set have a low level of uncertainty concerning their outcomes.

Self-assessment question 12.1

Antonio Ltd has planned production and sales for the next nine months as follows:

	Production (units)	Sales (units)
May	350	350
June	400	400
July	500	400
August	600	500
September	600	600
October	700	650
November	750	700
December	750	800
January	750	750

During the period, the business plans to advertise heavily to generate these increases in sales. Payments for advertising of £1,000 and £1,500 will be made in July and October respectively.

The selling price per unit will be £20 throughout the period. Forty per cent of sales are normally made on two months' credit. The other 60 per cent are settled within the month of the sale.

Raw materials will be held in stock for one month before they are taken into production. Purchases of raw materials will be on one month's credit (buy one month, pay the next). The cost of raw materials is £8 per unit of production.

Other direct production expenses, including labour, are £6 per unit of production. These will be paid in the month concerned.

Various production overheads, which during the period to 30 June had run at £1,800 per month, are expected to rise to £2,000 each month from 1 July to 31 October. These are expected to rise again from 1 November to £2,400 per month and to remain at that level for the foreseeable future. These overheads include a steady £400 each month for depreciation. Overheads are planned to be paid 80 per cent in the month of production and 20 per cent in the following month.

To help to meet the planned increased production, a new item of plant will be bought and will be delivered in August. The cost of this item is £6,600; the contract with the supplier will specify that this will be paid in three equal amounts in September, October and November.

Raw materials stock is planned to be 500 units on 1 July. The balance at the bank the same day is planned to be £7,500.

Required:
(a) Draw up the following for the six months ending 31 December:
  (i)   A raw materials budget, showing both physical quantities and financial values.
  (ii) A creditors budget.
  (iii) A cash budget.
(b) The cash budget reveals a potential cash deficiency during October and November. Can you suggest any ways in which a modification of plans could overcome this problem?

● ● ● ● Who needs budgets?

Until recently it would have been a heresy to suggest that budgeting was not of central importance to any business. The benefits of budgeting mentioned earlier in the chapter have been widely recognised and, indeed, the vast majority of businesses still continue to prepare annual budgets. However, there is increasing concern that, in today's highly dynamic and competitive environment, budgets may actually be harmful to the achievement of business objectives. This has led a small but growing number of businesses to abandon budgets as a tool of planning and control.

Various charges have been levelled against the conventional budgeting process (see Exhibit 12.6 for one example). It is claimed that budgets:

- Cannot deal with a fast-changing environment and that budgets are often out of date before the commencement of the budget period.
- Focus too much management attention on the achievement of short-term financial targets. Instead, managers should focus on the things that create value for the business (for example, innovation, building brand loyalty, responding quickly to competitive threats, and so on).
- Reinforce a 'command and control' structure that prevents managers from exercising autonomy. This may be particularly true where a 'top-down' approach that allocates budgets to managers is being used. Where managers feel constrained, attempts to retain and recruit able managers can be difficult.
- Take up an enormous amount of management time that could be better utilised. In practice, budgeting can be a lengthy process that may involve much negotiation, reworking and updating. However, this may add little to the achievement of business objectives.
- Are based around business functions (sales, marketing, production and so on). However, to achieve the business's objectives, the focus should be on business processes that cut across functional boundaries and reflect the needs of the customer.
- Encourage incremental thinking by employing a 'last year plus x per cent'

approach to planning. This can inhibit the development of 'break out' strategies that may be necessary in a fast-changing environment.

Although, some believe that many of the problems identified can be solved by better budgeting systems such as activity-based budgeting and zero-base budgeting, others believe that a more radical solution is required

Those businesses that have abandoned budgets still recognise the need for forward planning. There is still general agreement that there must be appropriate systems in place to steer a business towards its objectives. However, the systems adopted reflect a broader, more integrated approach to planning. The new systems are often based around a 'leaner' financial planning process that is more closely linked to other measurement and reward systems. Emphasis is placed on the use of rolling forecasts, key performance indicators (such as market share, customer satisfaction and innovations) and/or 'scorecards' that identify both monetary and non-monetary targets to be achieved over the long-term and short-term.

It is too early to predict whether or not the trickle of businesses that are now seeking an alternative to budgets will turn into a flood. However, it is clear that in today's highly competitive environment a business must be flexible and responsive to changing conditions. Management systems that in any way hinder these attributes will not survive.

Exhibit 12.6

Jeremy Hope and Robin Fraser are at the forefront of those who argue that budgeting systems have an adverse effect on the ability of businesses to compete effectively. Below we reproduce a short case study of Volvo Cars that they have written.

New steering mechanisms at Volvo Cars

Following losses in 1990–92 and a small profit in 1993, Volvo Cars decided to make a number of important changes, one of which was to adopt a radically different approach to managing the business. But senior managers were quick to realise that such an approach was unlikely to be successful in the longer term unless they tackled the problems of the budgeting and planning process that encouraged the old mindset of compliance and control. As Ole Johannesson, VP finance, explains, 'the budget and long-range planning systems are no longer efficient when the business environment is changing more and more rapidly. Today we need a process that enables us to react not only immediately but even beforehand'. In 1994 there was no budget requested by the Group company, AB Volvo, from operating units for the forthcoming year, 1995. As Johannesson notes, 'we recognised the extent of the cultural change needed. We wanted less and less of order giving, victims of circumstance, administration, checking, reactive positions, functional ties and hierarchical thinking, and more and more of creating opportunities, communication, development, confidence-building, proactive positions, network ties, and process thinking'. Since that time Volvo Cars has built a highly advanced management model that has helped it face the intense competitive pressures that are endemic to the world car market.

Volvo reckoned that its previous planning, budgeting and control processes absorbed around 20% of total management time. By abandoning these processes and managing in a different way, managers have not only saved significant costs but they now have more time to focus on strategy, action planning and beating the competition. This is a battle not tied to an annual cycle, but is waged continuously month by month and quarter by quarter. Strategy and forecasts are reviewed and updated several times a year with four distinct cycles apparent. Each month a 'flash' forecast is prepared covering the next three months; each quarter a two-year rolling forecast is updated; and each year sees a revised four-year and ten-year strategic plan. While targets are broad-brush and comprise a number of key performance indicators, there is more time spent on developing action plans to support them. Monthly reports to the board include financial information (actual month, actual year-to-date, forecast remainder of year, revised forecast for total years, and last year-to-date) and a number of key performance indicators such as market share, order intake, customer satisfaction, product costs, dealer profitability, warranty costs, fault frequency, and total ownership cost (all where possible compared with the competition). Four years after dismantling the budgeting process there is now a strong 'responsibility' and 'no blame' culture at Volvo Cars.

According to Ole Johannesson, 'managers now know that they mustn't come to meetings with problems, but with explanations about what they've done to solve them'. The management accountants now spend more time collecting a whole range of measurement data but, more importantly, they see their role as one of analysing and interpreting the data so that operating managers can take the appropriate action. Indeed the whole emphasis is on 'actions' rather than 'problems'. Volvo has transformed itself into an action orientated company in which decisions are made by people at the appropriate level to meet changing conditions. This has contributed to Volvo's remarkable turnaround. It now ranks as the sixteenth largest motor vehicle manufacturer in the world, but in terms of profitability it is second only to Ford on profits on sales and assets.

Source: Hope and Fraser (see reference (4) at the end of the chapter), p. 17.

● Summary

We began this chapter by considering the relationship between business objectives, long-term plans and budgets. We have seen that budgets are set within the framework of the long-term plans and represent one step towards the realisation of the business objectives. They are concerned with the short term and provide precise targets to be achieved in key business areas. We have considered the potential uses for budgets and have seen that these uses may conflict with one another. Where this occurs, managers must decide which uses are most important for the business and must prepare the budgets accordingly.

We have examined the key steps in the budget-setting process and have seen how budgets for different facets of the business are interlinked. The various budgets of the business are summarised in the form of master budgets, which are the budgeted income statement and balance sheet (and, perhaps, a budgeted cash flow statement in summarised form). We have considered the basic principles of budget preparation and have examined a practical example of how budgets are prepared.

We have examined the impact of budget information on people. We have seen that managers can react to budget information in different ways and that some of these ways could be harmful to the business. There are situations where the inappropriate use of budget information will have an adverse effect on staff attitudes and behaviour.

Finally, we considered the case against budgeting. We saw that some believe that budgets are unable to cope with a fast-changing environment and should be abandoned in favour of more flexible and more integrated methods of planning. However, it would be premature to consign budgets to the dustbin of history. For most businesses, budgets still remain a key tool for planning purposes.

Budgeting is an important topic that requires further consideration. In the next chapter, we discuss in more detail the role of budgets in controlling the business.

Key terms

Mission statement p. 356	Budget officer p. 366
Budget p. 358	Limiting factor p. 367
Forecast p. 360	Incremental budgeting p. 369
Periodic budget p. 361	Budget holder p. 370
Continual budget p. 361	Discretionary budget p. 370
Master budgets p. 361	Zero-base budgeting (ZBB) p. 370
Management by exception p. 365	Activity-based budgeting (ABB) p. 376
Budget committee p. 366	

Further reading

If you would like to explore the topics covered in this chapter in more depth, we recommend the following books:

Management Accounting, *Atkinson, A., Banker, R., Kaplan, R. and Mark Young, S.*, 3rd edn, Prentice Hall International, 2001, chapter 11.

Management and Cost Accounting, *Drury, C.*, 5th edn, Thomson Learning Business Press, 2000, chapter 15.

Accounting for Management Control, *Emmanuel, C. and Otley, D.*, 2nd edn, Chapman and Hall, 1990, chapter 7.

Cost Accounting: A managerial emphasis, *Horngren, C., Foster, G. and Datar, S.*, 10th edn, Prentice Hall International, 2000, chapter 6.

References

1. **A Survey of Management Accounting Practices in UK Manufacturing Companies**, *Drury, C., Braund, S., Osborne, P. and Tayles, M.*, Chartered Association of Certified Accountants, 1993.
2. **Financial Management and Working Capital Practices in UK SMEs**, *Chittenden, F., Poutziouris, P. and Michaelis, N.*, Manchester Business School, 1998.
3. 'An empirical study of the role of accounting data in performance evaluation', *Hopwood, A. G.*, **Empirical Research in Accounting**, a supplement to the Journal of Accounting Research, 1972 pp. 156–82.
4. 'Beyond budgeting', *Hope, J. and Fraser, R.*, **Management Accounting**, January 1999, p. 17.

12.1 Define a budget. How is a budget different from a forecast?

12.2 What were the five uses of budgets which were identified in the chapter?

12.3 What do budgets have to do with control?

12.4 What is a budget committee? What purpose does it serve?

? EXERCISES

Exercises 12.5–12.8 are more advanced than 12.1–12.4. Those with coloured numbers have answers at the back of the book.

12.1 Daniel Chu Ltd, a new business, started production on 1 April. Planned sales for the next nine months are as follows:

	Sales units
May	500
June	600
July	700
August	800
September	900
October	900
November	900
December	800
January	700

The selling price per unit will be a consistent £100, and all sales will be made on one month's credit. It is planned that sufficient finished goods stock for each month's sales should be available at the end of the previous month.

Raw materials purchases will be such that there will be sufficient raw materials stock available at the end of each month precisely to meet the following month's planned production. This planned policy will operate from the end of April. Purchases of raw materials will be on one month's credit. The cost of raw material is £40 per unit of finished product.

The direct labour cost, which is variable with the level of production, is planned to be £20 per unit of finished production. Production overheads are planned to be £20,000 each month, including £3,000 for depreciation. Non-production overheads are planned to be £11,000 per month, of which £1,000 will be depreciation.

Various fixed assets costing £250,000 will be bought and paid for during April.

Except where specified, assume that all payments take place in the same month as the cost is incurred.

The business will raise £300,000 in cash from a share issue in April.

Required:
Draw up the following for the six months ending 30 September:

(a) A finished stock budget, showing just physical quantities.

(b) A raw materials stock budget showing both physical quantities and financial values.

(c) A trade creditors budget.

(d) A trade debtors budget.

(e) A cash budget.

12.2 You have overheard the following statements:

(a) 'A budget is a forecast of what is expected to happen in a business during the next year.'

(b) 'Monthly budgets must be prepared with a column for each month so that you can see the whole year at a glance, month by month.'

(c) 'Budgets are ok but they stifle all initiative. No manager worth employing would work for a business that seeks to control through budgets.'

(d) 'Activity-based budgeting is an approach that takes account of the planned volume of activity in order to deduce the figures to go into the budget.'

(e) 'Any sensible person would start with the sales budget and build up the other budgets from there.'

Required:
Critically discuss these statements, explaining any technical terms.

12.3 A nursing home, which is linked to a large hospital, has been examining its budgetary control procedures, with particular reference to overhead costs.

The level of activity in the facility is measured by the number of patients treated in the budget period. For the current year, the budget stands at 6,000 patients and this is expected to be met.

For months 1 to 6 of this year (assume 12 months of equal length) 2,700 patients were treated. The actual variable overhead costs incurred during this six-month period are as follows:

Expense	£
Staffing	59,400
Power	27,000
Supplies	54,000
Other	8,100
Total	148,500

The hospital accountant believes that the variable overhead costs will be incurred at the same rate during months 7 to 12 of the year.

Fixed overhead costs are budgeted for the whole year as follows:

Expense	£
Supervision	120,000
Depreciation/financing	187,200
Other	64,800
Total	372,000

Required:
(a) Present an overheads budget for months 7 to 12 of the year. You should show each expense, but should not separate individual months. What is the total overhead cost per patient that would be incorporated into any statistics?

(b) The home actually treated 3,800 patients during months 7 to 12, the actual variable overhead was £203,300, and the fixed overhead was £190,000. In summary form, examine how well the home exercised control over its overheads.

(c) Interpret your analysis and point out any limitations or assumptions.

12.4 Linpet is to be incorporated on 1 June. The opening balance sheet of the business will then be as follows:

Assets	£
Cash at bank	60,000
Share capital	
£1 ordinary shares	60,000

During June, the business intends to make payments of £40,000 for a freehold property, £10,000 for equipment and £6,000 for a motor vehicle. The business will also purchase initial trading stock costing £22,000 on credit.

The business has produced the following estimates:

(i) Sales for June will be £8,000 and will increase at the rate of £3,000 per month until September. In October, sales will rise to £22,000 and in subsequent months sales will be maintained at this figure.

(ii) The gross profit percentage on goods sold will be 25 per cent.

(iii) There is a risk that supplies of trading stock will be interrupted towards the end of the accounting year. The business therefore intends to build up its initial level of stock (£22,000) by purchasing £1,000 of stock each month in addition to the monthly purchases necessary to satisfy monthly sales. All purchases of stock (including the initial stock) will be on one month's credit.

(iv) Sales will be divided equally between cash and credit sales. Credit customers are expected to pay two months after the sale is agreed.

(v) Wages and salaries will be £900 per month. Other overheads will be £500 per month for the first four months and £650 thereafter. Both types of expense will be payable when incurred.

(vi) 80 per cent of sales will be generated by salespeople, who will receive 5 per cent commission on sales. The commission is payable one month after the sale is agreed.

(vii) The business intends to purchase further equipment in November for £7,000 cash.

(viii) Depreciation is to be provided at the rate of 5 per cent a year on freehold property and 20 per cent a year on equipment. (Depreciation has not been included in the overheads mentioned in (v) above.)

Required:

(a) State why a cash budget is required for a business.

(b) Prepare a cash budget for Linpet Ltd for the six-month period to 30 November.

12.5 Lewisham Ltd manufactures one product line – the Zenith. Sales of Zeniths over the next few months are planned to be as follows:

1. *Demand*

	Units
July	180,000
August	240,000
September	200,000
October	180,000

Each Zenith sells for £3.

2. *Debtor receipts.* Debtors are expected to pay as follows:

   - 70 per cent during the month of sale
   - 28 per cent during the following month.

   The remainder of debtors are expected to go bad (that is, to be uncollectable). Debtors who pay in the month of sale are entitled to deduct a 2 per cent discount from the invoice price.

3. *Finished goods stocks.* Stocks of finished goods are expected to be 40,000 units at 1 July. The business's policy is that, in future, the stock at the end of each month should equal 20 per cent of the following month's planned sales requirements.

4. *Raw materials stock.* Stocks of raw materials are expected to be 40,000 kg on 1 July. The business's policy is that, in future, the stock at the end of each month should equal 50 per cent of the following month's planned production requirements. Each Zenith requires 0.5 kg of the raw material, which costs £1.50/kg. Raw materials purchases are paid in the month after purchase.

5. *Labour and overheads.* The direct labour cost of each Zenith is £0.50. The variable overhead element of each Zenith is £0.30. Fixed overheads, including depreciation of £25,000, total £47,000 per month. All labour and overheads are paid during the month in which they arose.

6. *Cash in hand.* At 1 August the business plans to have a bank balance (in funds) of £20,000.

Required:
Prepare the following budgets:

(a) Finished stock budget (expressed in units of Zenith) for each of the three months July, August and September.
(b) Raw materials budget (expressed in kilograms of the raw material) for the two months July and August.
(c) Cash budget for August and September.

12.6 Newtake Records Ltd owns a chain of 14 shops selling cassette tapes and compact discs. At the beginning of June the business had an overdraft of £35,000 and the bank had asked for this to be eliminated by the end of November. As a result, the directors have recently decided to review their plans for the next six months in order to comply with this requirement.

The following forecast information was prepared for the business some months earlier:

	May £000	June £000	July £000	August £000	Sept £000	Oct £000	Nov £000
Expected sales	180	230	320	250	140	120	110
Purchases	135	180	142	94	75	66	57
Administration expenses	52	55	56	53	48	46	45
Selling expenses	22	24	28	26	21	19	18
Taxation payment				22			
Finance payments	5	5	5	5	5	5	5
Shop refurbishment	–	–	14	18	6	–	–

Notes:

(i)   Stock held at 1 June was £112,000. The business believes it is preferable to maintain a minimum stock level of £40,000 of goods over the period to 30 November.

(ii)   Suppliers allow one month's credit. The first three months' purchases are subject to a contractual agreement, which must be honoured.

(iii)   The gross profit margin is 40 per cent.

(iv)   All sales income is received in the month of sale. However, 50 per cent of customers pay with a credit card. The charge made by the credit card company to Newtake Records Ltd is 3 per cent of the sales value. These charges are in addition to the selling expenses identified above. The credit card company pays Newtake Records Ltd in the month of sale.

(v)   The business has a bank loan, which it is paying off in monthly instalments of £5,000 per month. The interest element represents 20 per cent of each instalment.

(vi)   Administration expenses are paid when incurred. This item includes a charge of £15,000 each month in respect of depreciation.

(vii)   Selling expenses are payable in the following month.

Required (working to the nearest £1,000):

(a) Prepare a cash budget for the six months ended 30 November which shows the cash balance at the end of each month.

(b) Compute the stock levels at the end of each month for the six months to 30 November.

(c) Prepare a budgeted profit and loss account for the six months ended 30 November. (A monthly breakdown of profit is *not* required.)

(d) What problems is Newtake Records Ltd likely to face in the next six months? Can you suggest how the business might deal with these problems?

12.7 Prolog Ltd is a small wholesaler of personal computers. It has in recent months been selling 50 machines a month at a price of £2,000 each. These machines cost £1,600 each. A new model has just been launched and this is expected to offer greatly enhanced performance. Its selling price and cost will be the same as for the old model. From the beginning of January, sales are expected to increase at a rate of 20 machines each month until the end of June, when sales will amount to 170 units per month. They are expected to continue at that level thereafter. Operating costs including depreciation of £2,000 a month, are forecast as follows:

	January	February	March	April	May	June
Operating costs (£000)	6	8	10	12	12	12

Prolog expects to receive no credit for operating costs. Additional shelving for storage will be bought, installed and paid for in April, costing £12,000. Corporation tax of £25,000 is due at the end of March. Prolog anticipates that debtors will amount to two months' sales. To give their customers a good level of service, Prolog plans to hold enough stock at the end of each period to fulfil anticipated demand from customers in the following month. The computer manufacturer, however, grants one month's credit to Prolog. Prolog Ltd's balance sheet appears below.

Balance sheet at 31 December

	£000	£000
Fixed assets		80
Current assets		
Stock	112	
Debtors	200	
Cash	–	
	312	
Creditors: amounts due within one year		
Trade creditors	112	
Taxation	25	
Overdraft	68	
	205	
Net current assets		107
Total assets less current liabilities		187
Capital and reserves		
Share capital (25p ordinary shares)		10
Profit and loss account		177
		187

Required:

(a) Prepare a cash budget for Prolog Ltd showing the cash balance or required overdraft for the six months ending 30 June.

(b) State briefly what further information a banker would require from Prolog before granting additional overdraft facilities for the anticipated expansion of sales.

12.8 Brown and Jeffreys, a West Midlands business, makes one standard product for use in the motor trade. The product, known as the Fuel Miser, for which the business holds the patent, when fitted to the fuel system of production model cars has the effect of reducing petrol consumption.

Part of the production is sold direct to a local car manufacturer, which fits the Fuel Miser as an optional extra to several of its models and the rest of the production is sold through various retail outlets, garages and so on.

The Fuel Miser is assembled by Brown and Jeffreys but all three components are manufactured by local engineering businesses. The three components are codenamed A, B and C. One Fuel Miser consists of one of each component.

The planned sales for the first seven months of the forthcoming accounting period, by channels of distribution and in terms of Fuel Miser units, are as follows:

	Jan	Feb	Mar	Apr	May	June	July
Manufacturers	4,000	4,000	4,500	4,500	4,500	4,500	4,500
Retail, etc.	2,000	2,700	3,200	3,000	2,700	2,500	2,400
	6,000	6,700	7,700	7,500	7,200	7,000	6,900

The following further information is available:

(i) There will be a stock of finished units at 1 January of 7,000 Fuel Misers.

(ii) The stocks of raw materials at 1 January will be:

A   10,000 units
B   16,500 units
C   7,200 units

(iii) The selling price of Fuel Misers is to be £10 each to the motor manufacturer and £12 each to retail outlets.

(iv) The maximum production capacity of the company is 7,000 units per month. There is no possibility of increasing this output.

(v) Assembly of each Fuel Miser will take 15 minutes of direct labour. Direct labour is paid at the rate of £4.80 per hour during the month of production.

(vi) The components are each expected to cost the following:

A   £2.50
B   £1.30
C   £0.80

(vii) Indirect costs are to be paid at a regular rate of £32,000 each month.

(viii) The cash at the bank at 1 January will be £2,620.

The business plans to follow the following policies for as many months as possible and in a manner consistent with the planned sales:

● Finished stocks at the end of each month are to equal the following month's total sales to retail outlets, and half the total of the following month's sales to the motor manufacturer.

● Raw materials at the end of each month are to be sufficient to cover production requirements for the following month. The production for July will be 6,800 units.

● Creditors for raw materials are to be paid during the month following purchase. The creditors payment for January will be £21,250.

● Debtors will pay in the month of sale in the case of sales to the motor manufacturer and the month after sale in the case of retail sales. Retail sales during December were 2,000 units at £12 each.

Required:

Prepare the following budgets in monthly columnar form, both in terms of money and units (where relevant), for the six months of January to June inclusive:

(a) Sales budget.[†]
(b) Finished stock budget (valued at direct cost).[‡]
(c) Raw materials stock budget.[‡]

(d) Production budget (direct costs only).[†]

(e) Debtors' budget.[‡]

(f) Creditors' budget.[‡]

(g) Cash budget.[‡]

[†] The sales and production budgets should merely state each month's sales or production in units and in money terms.

[‡] The other budgets should all seek to reconcile the opening balance of stocks, debtors, creditors or cash with the closing balance through movements of the relevant factors over the month.

13 Accounting for control

Introduction

This chapter deals with the role of accounting in management control. We shall consider how a budget can be used in helping to control a business. We shall see that, by collecting information on actual performance and comparing it with the revised budget, it is possible to identify fairly precisely which activities are in control and which seem to be out of control.

OBJECTIVES When you have completed this chapter you should be able to:

- Discuss the role and limitations of using budgets to help to exercise control.
- Carry out a complete analysis of variances.
- Explain the nature and role of standard costs.
- Discuss possible reasons for key variances and other practical matters surrounding control through budgets.

Using budgets for control – flexible budgets

In Chapter 12 we saw that budgets can provide a useful basis for exercising control over a business. This is because control is usually seen as making events conform to a plan. Since the budget represents the plan, making events conform to it is the obvious way to try to control the business. Using budgets in this way is popular in practice. As we saw in Chapter 12, for most businesses the routine is as shown in Figure 13.1.

The steps in the control process are fairly easy to understand. The point is that if plans are drawn up sensibly, we have a basis for exercising control over a business. This also requires that we have the means of measuring actual performance in the same terms as those in which the budget is stated. If they are not in the same terms, comparison will not usually be possible.

Taking steps to exercise control means finding out where and why things did not go according to plan and seeking ways to put things right for the future. One of the reasons why things may have gone wrong is that the plans may, in reality, prove to be unachievable. In this case, if budgets are to be a useful basis for

Figure 13.1

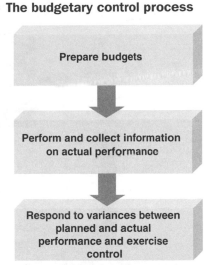

The budgetary control process

Prepare budgets

Perform and collect information on actual performance

Respond to variances between planned and actual performance and exercise control

Budgets, once set, provide the yardstick for assessing whether things are going according to plan. Variances between budgeted and actual performances can be identified and reacted to.

exercising control in the future, it may be necessary to revise them for future periods to bring targets into the realms of achievability.

This last point should not be taken to mean that budget targets can simply be ignored if the going gets tough; rather, they should be flexible. Budgets may prove to be totally unrealistic targets for a variety of reasons, including unexpected changes in the commercial environment (for example, an unexpected collapse in demand for services of the type that the business supplies). In this case, nothing whatsoever will be achieved by pretending that the targets can be met.

By having a system of budgetary control through **flexible budgets**, a position can be established where decision making and responsibility can be delegated to junior management, yet control can still be retained by senior management. This is because senior managers can use the budgetary control system to ascertain which junior managers are meeting targets and, therefore, working towards the objectives of the business. This enables a management-by-exception environment to be created. Here senior management concentrates its energy on areas where things are not going according to plan (the exceptions – it is to be hoped). Junior managers who are performing to budget can be left to get on with their jobs.

Feedback and feedforward controls

The control process that we have just outlined is known as **feedback control**. Its main feature is that steps are taken to get operations back on track as soon as there is a signal that they have gone wrong. This is similar to the thermostatic control that is a feature of most central heating systems. The thermostat senses when the temperature has fallen below a preset level (analogous to the budget), and takes action to correct matters by activating the heating device that restores

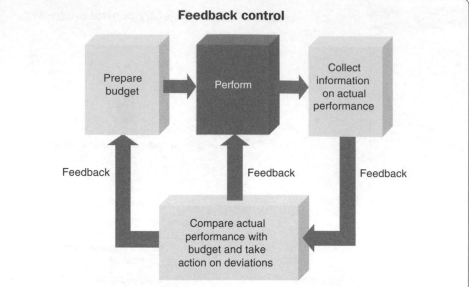

Figure 13.2

Feedback control

Prepare budget → Perform → Collect information on actual performance

Feedback   Feedback   Feedback

Compare actual performance with budget and take action on deviations

When a comparison of actual and budgeted performance shows a divergence, steps can be taken to get performance back to plan. If the plans need revising, this can be done.

the required minimum temperature. Figure 13.2 depicts the stages in a feedback control system using budgets.

There is an alternative type of control, known as **feedforward control**. Here predictions are made as to what can go wrong and steps taken to avoid that outcome. The preparation of budgets, which we discussed in Chapter 12, provides an example of this type of control. When preparing a particular budget it would normally be obvious that a problem will arise unless the business changes its plans. For example, the cash budget may reveal that if the original plans are followed there will be a negative cash balance for some part of the budget period. By recognising this, the plans may be able to be revised so as to eliminate the problem.

Feedforward controls are probably better than feedback controls since, with the former, things should never go wrong because steps are taken to ensure that they cannot go wrong. Feedback controls react to a loss of control. In many situations, however, feedforward controls are not possible to install.

Comparison of actual performance with the budget

Since the principal objective of most private-sector businesses is to enhance their shareholders' wealth, and remembering that profit is the net increase in wealth as a result of trading, the most important budget target to meet is the profit target. In view of this, we shall begin with that aspect in our consideration of making the comparison between actuals and budgets. Example 13.1 shows the budgeted and actual profit and loss account for Baxter Ltd for the month of May.

Example 13.1

Baxter Ltd, Month of May

	Budget 1,000 units		Actual 900 units	
Output (production and sales)				
	£		£	
Sales	100,000		92,000	
Raw materials	(40,000)	(40,000 m)	(36,900)	(37,000 m)
Labour	(20,000)	(5,000 hr)	(17,500)	(4,375 hr)
Fixed overheads	(20,000)		(20,700)	
Operating profit	20,000		16,900	

From Example 13.1 it is clear that the budgeted profit was not achieved. As far as May is concerned, this is a matter of history. However, the business, or at least one aspect of it, is out of control. Senior management must discover where things went wrong and try to ensure that they are not repeated in later months. Thus, it is not enough to know that, overall, things went wrong; we need to know where and why. The approach that is taken is to compare the budgeted and actual figures for the various items (sales, raw materials and so on) in the above statement.

Activity 13.1

Can you see any problems in comparing the various items (sales, raw materials and so on) for the budget and the actual performance of Baxter Ltd in order to draw conclusions as to which aspects were out of control?

The problem is that the actual level of output was not as budgeted. The actual level of output was 900 units, whereas the budgeted level was 1,000. This means that we cannot, for example, say that there was a labour cost saving of £2,500 (£20,000 – £17,500) and conclude that all is well in that area.

Flexing the budget

One practical way to overcome our difficulty is to **'flex' the budget** to what it would have been had the planned level of output been 900 units rather than 1,000 units. Flexing the budget simply means revising it to what it would have been had the planned level of output been some different figure.

In the context of control, the budget is usually flexed to reflect the volume that actually occurred. To be able to do this, we need to know which items are fixed and which are variable, relative to the level of output. Once we have this knowledge, flexing is a simple operation. We shall assume that sales revenue, materials cost and labour cost vary strictly with volume. Fixed overheads, by definition, will not. (Whether, in real life, labour cost really does vary with the level of output is not so certain, but it will serve well enough as an assumption for our purposes).

On the basis of the assumptions regarding the behaviour of costs, the flexed budget would be as follows:

	Flexed budget	
Output (production and sales)	900 units	
	£	
Sales	90,000	
Raw materials	(36,000)	(36,000 m)
Labour	(18,000)	(4,500 hr)
Fixed overheads	(20,000)	
Operating profit	16,000	

Putting the original budget, the flexed budget and the actual for May together, we obtain the following:

	Original budget	Flexed budget		Actual	
Output (production and sales)	1,000 units	900 units		900 units	
	£	£		£	
Sales	100,000	90,000		92,000	
Raw materials	(40,000)	(36,000)	(36,000 m)	(36,900)	(37,000 m)
Labour	(20,000)	(18,000)	(4,500 hr)	(17,500)	(4,375 hr)
Fixed overheads	(20,000)	(20,000)		(20,700)	
Operating profit	20,000	16,000		16,900	

We can now make a more valid comparison between budget (using the flexed figures) and actual. We can now also see that there was a genuine labour-cost saving, even after allowing for the output shortfall.

Sales volume variance

It may occur to you that we seem to be saying that it does not matter if there are volume shortfalls, because we just revise the budget and carry on as if nothing adverse has happened. This must be an invalid approach, because losing sales means losing profit. The first point we must pick up, therefore, is the loss of profit arising from the loss of sales of 100 units of the product.

Activity 13.2

What will be the loss of profit as a result of the sales shortfall, assuming that everything except sales volume was as planned?

....

The answer is simply the difference between the original and flexed budget profit figures. The only difference between these two profit figures is the assumed volume of sales; everything else was the same. Thus, the figure is £4,000 (that is, £20,000 − £16,000).

You will remember from Chapter 9, where we considered the relationship between cost, volume and profit, that selling one unit less will result in one less contribution to profit. The contribution is sales revenue per unit less variable cost per unit. We can see from the original budget that the sales revenue per unit is £100 (that is, £100,000/1,000), raw material cost per unit is £40 (that is,

£40,000/1,000), and labour cost per unit is £20 (that is, £20,000/1,000). Thus the contribution per unit is £40 (that is, £100 – (40 + 20)).

If, therefore, 100 units of sales are lost, £4,000 (that is, $100 \times £40$) of contributions, and, therefore profit, are forgone. This would be an alternative means of finding the sales volume variance, instead of taking the difference between the original and flexed budget profit figures; nevertheless once we have produced the flexed budget, it is generally easier simply to compare the two profit figures.

The difference between the original and flexed budget profit figures is called the **sales volume variance**. It is an **adverse variance** because, taken alone, it has the effect of making the actual profit lower than that which was budgeted. A variance that has the effect of increasing profit above that which was budgeted is known as a **favourable variance**.

We can, therefore, say that a **variance** is the effect of that factor on the budgeted profit. When looking at some particular aspect, such as sales volume we assume that all other factors went according to plan. This is shown in Figure 13.3.

| Activity 13.3 | What else does the senior management of Baxter Ltd need to know about the May sales volume variance? |

It needs to know why the volume of sales fell below the budgeted figure, and so enquiries must be made to find out. Only by discovering this information will management be in any position to try to see that it does not occur again.

Sales volume variance

The difference between the profit as shown in the original budget and the profit as shown in the flexed budget for the period.

Who should be asked about this sales volume variance? The answer would probably be the sales manager. This person should know precisely why the departure from budget has occurred. This is not the same as saying that it was the sales manager's fault. The reason for the problem could easily have been that production was at fault in not having produced the budgeted quantities, meaning that there were not sufficient items to sell. What is not in doubt is that, in the first instance, it is the sales manager who should know the reason for the problem.

The budget and actual figures for Baxter Ltd for June are given in Activity 13.4 below. They will be used as the basis for a series of activities that you should work through as we look at variance analysis. Note that the business had budgeted for a higher level of output for June than it did for May.

Activity 13.4		Budget	Actual
	Output (production and sales)	1,100 units	1,150 units

	£		£	
Sales	110,000		113,500	
Raw materials	(44,000)	(44,000 m)	(46,300)	(46,300 m)
Labour	(22,000)	(5,500 hr)	(23,200)	(5,920 hr)
Fixed overheads	(20,000)		(19,300)	
Operating profit	24,000		24,700	

Try flexing the June budget, comparing it with the original June budget, and so find the sales volume variance.

	Flexed budget	
Output	1,150 units	
(production and sales)		
	£	
Sales	115,000	
Raw materials	(46,000)	(46,000 m)
Labour	(23,000)	(5,750 hr)
Fixed overheads	(20,000)	
Operating profit	26,000	

The sales volume variance is £2,000 (£26,000 – £24,000). This is favourable because the original budget profit was lower than the the flexed budget profit, because more sales were actually made that were budgeted.

   Having dealt with the sales volume variance, we have picked up the profit difference caused by any variation between the budgeted and the actual volumes of sales. This means that, for the remainder of the analysis of the difference between the actual and budgeted profits, we can ignore the original budget and concentrate exclusively on the differences between the figures in the flexed budget and the actual figures.

Figure 13.3

Relationship between the budgeted and the actual profit

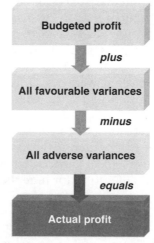

The variances represent the differences between budgeted and actual profit and can be used to reconcile the two profit figures.

Sales price variance

Going back to May, it is now a matter of comparing the actual figures with those in the flexed budget so as to find out the other causes of the £3,100 (£20,000 − £16,900) profit shortfall.

Starting with the sales revenue figure, we can see that there is a difference of £2,000 (favourable) between the flexed budget and the actual figures. This can only arise from higher prices being charged than were envisaged in the original budget, because any variance arising from the volume difference has already been 'stripped out' in the flexing process. This is known as the **sales price variance**. Higher sales prices, all other things being equal, mean more profit, hence a favourable variance.

Sales price variance

The difference between the actual sales figure for the period and the sales figure as shown in the flexed budget.

Activity 13.5

Using the figures in Activity 13.4, what is the sales price variance for June?

The sales price variance for June is £1,500 (adverse) (£115,000 − £113,500). Actual sales prices, on average, must have been lower than those budgeted. The actual price averaged £98.70 (that is, £113,500/1,150) whereas the budgeted price was £100. Selling output at a lower price than budget must tend to reduce profit.

We shall now move on to look at the expenses.

Materials variances

In May there was an overall or **total direct material variance** of £900 adverse (that is, £36,900 − £36,000). It is adverse because the actual material cost was higher that the budgeted one, which has an adverse effect on profit. Who should be held accountable for this variance? The answer depends on whether the difference arises from excess usage of the raw materials, in which case it is the production manager, or whether it is a higher-than-budgeted price per metre being paid, in which case it is the responsibility of the buying manager.

Total direct material variance

The difference between the actual direct material cost and the direct material cost as per the flexed budget (standard usage for the actual output).

Fortunately, we have the means available to go beyond this total variance. We can see from the figures that there was a 1,000-metre excess usage of the raw materials (that is, 37,000 m − 36,000 m). All other things being equal, this alone would have led to a profit shortfall of £1,000, since clearly the budgeted price per metre is £1. The £1,000 (adverse) variance is known as the **direct material usage variance**. Normally, this variance would be the responsibility of the production manager.

> **Direct material usage variance**
>
> The difference between the actual quantity of direct material used and the quantity of direct material as per the flexed budget (standard usage for the actual output). This quantity is multiplied by the standard direct material cost per unit.

Activity 13.6

Using the figures in Activity 13.4, what was the direct materials usage variance for June?

....

The direct materials usage variance for June was £300 (adverse) [(46,300 − 46,000) × £1] It is adverse because more material was used than budgeted for an output of 11,500 units. Excess usage of material will tend to reduce profit.

The other aspect of direct materials is the **direct materials price variance**. Here, we simply take the actual cost of materials used and compare it with the cost that was allowed, given the quantity used. In May, the actual cost of direct materials used was £36,900, whereas the allowed cost of the 37,000 metres was £37,000. Paying less than the budgeted price will tend to increase profit, hence a favourable variance. Thus we have a favourable variance of £100.

> **Direct material price variance**
>
> The difference between the actual cost of the direct material used and the direct material cost allowed (actual quantity of material used at the standard direct material cost).

Activity 13.7

Using the figures in Activity 13.4, what was the direct materials price variance for June?

....

The direct materials price variance for June was zero [(46,300 − 46,300) × £1].

As we have just seen, the total direct materials variance is the sum of the usage variance and the price variance. This is illustrated in Figure 13.4.

Labour variances

Direct labour variances are similar in form to those for raw materials. The **total direct labour variance** for May was £500 favourable (£18,000 − £17,500). It was favourable because £500 less was spent on labour than was budgeted, for the actual level of output achieved. Again, this information is not particularly helpful since the responsibility for the rate of pay lies primarily with the

Figure 13.4

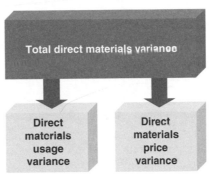

Relationship between the total, usage and price variances of direct materials

Total direct materials variance

Direct materials usage variance

Direct materials price variance

The total direct materials variance is the sum of the direct materials usage variance and the price variance, and can be analysed into those two.

personnel manager, whereas the number of hours taken to complete a particular quantity of output is the responsibility of the production manager.

Total direct labour variance

The difference between the actual direct labour cost and the direct labour cost as per the flexed budget (standard direct labour hours for the actual output).

The **direct labour efficiency variance** compares the number of hours that would be allowed for the level of production achieved with the actual number of hours and then costs the difference at the allowed hourly rate. Thus, for May, it was $(4,500 – 4,375) \times £4 = £500$ (favourable). We know that the budgeted hourly rate is £4 because the original budget shows that 5,000 hours cost £20,000. The variance is favourable because fewer hours were used than would have been allowed for the actual level of output. Working more quickly would tend to lead to higher profit.

Direct labour efficiency variance

The difference between the actual direct labour hours worked and the number of direct labour hours as per the flexed budget (standard direct labour hours for the actual output). This figure is multiplied by the standard direct labour rate per hour.

Using the figures in Activity 13.4, what was the direct labour efficiency variance for June?

The direct labour efficiency variance for June was £680 (adverse) [$(5,920 – 5,750) \times £4$]. It is adverse because the work took longer than the budget allowed. This would tend to lead to less profit.

The **direct labour rate variance** compares the actual cost of the hours worked with the allowed cost. For 4,375 hours worked in May the allowed cost would be

£17,500 (4,375 × £4). Since this is exactly the amount that was paid, there is no rate variance.

> **Direct labour rate variance**
>
> The difference between the actual cost of the direct labour hours worked and the direct labour cost allowed (actual direct labour hours worked at the standard labour rate).

Activity 13.9

Using the figures in Activity 13.4, what was the direct labour rate variance for June?

....

The direct labour rate variance for June was £480 (favourable) [(5,920 × £4) – 23,200]. It is favourable because a lower rate was paid than the budgeted one. Paying a lower wage rate will, of itself, tend to increase profit.

Fixed overheads variance

The remaining area is that of fixed overheads. Here the **fixed overhead spending variance** is simply the difference between the flexed budget and the actual figures. For May, this was £700 (adverse) (that is, £20,700 – £20,000). It is adverse because more overhead cost was actually incurred than was budgeted, which would tend to lead to less profit. In theory, this is the responsibility of whoever controls overheads expenditure. In practice, this tends to be a very slippery area and one which is notoriously difficult to control.

> **Fixed overhead spending variance**
>
> The difference between the actual fixed overhead cost and the fixed overhead cost as per the flexed (and the original) budget.

Activity 13.10

Using the figures in Activity 13.4, what was the fixed overhead spending variance for June?

....

The fixed overhead spending variance for June was £700 (favourable) (£20,000 – £19,300). It was favourable because less was spent on overheads that was budgeted, tending to increase profit.

We are now in a position to reconcile the original May budget profit with the actual one, as follows:

		£	£
	Budgeted profit		20,000
Add	Favourable variances:		
	Sales price variance	2,000	
	Direct materials price	100	
	Direct labour efficiency	500	2,600
			22,600

			£	£
Less	**Adverse variances:**			
	Sales volume		4,000	
	Direct material usage		1,000	
	Fixed overhead spending		700	5,700
	Actual profit			16,900

Activity 13.11 Using the figures in Activity 13.4, try reconciling the original profit figure for June with the actual June figure.

		£	£
	Budgeted profit		24,000
Add	**Favourable variances**		
	Sales volume	2,000	
	Fixed overhead spending	700	
	Direct labour rate	480	
			3,180
			27,180
Less	**Adverse variances**		
	Sales price	1,500	
	Direct material usage	300	
	Direct labour efficiency	680	
			2,480
	Actual profit		24,700

Activity 13.12 The following are the budgeted and actual profit and loss accounts for Baxter Ltd for the month of July:

	Budget		Actual	
Output	1,000 units		1,050 units	
(production and sales)				
	£		£	
Sales	100,000		104,300	
Raw materials	(40,000)	(40,000 m)	(41,200)	(40,500 m)
Labour	(20,000)	(5,000 hr)	(21,300)	(5,200 hr)
Fixed overheads	(20,000)		(19,400)	
Operating profit	20,000		22,400	

Produce a reconciliation of the budgeted and actual operating profit, going into as much detail as possible with the variance analysis.

The original, flexed and actual budgets are as follows:

	Original	Flexed	Actual
Output	1,000 units	1,050 units	1,050 units
(production and sales)			
	£	£	£
Sales	100,000	105,000	104,300
Raw materials	(40,000)	(42,000)	(41,200)
Labour	(20,000)	(21,000)	(21,300)
Fixed overheads	(20,000)	(20,000)	(19,400)
Operating profit	20,000	22,000	22,400

Reconciliation of the budgeted and actual operating profits for June is as follows:

	£	£
Budgeted profit		20,000
Add **Favourable variances**		
Sales volume (22,000 – 20,000)	2,000	
Direct material usage {[(1,050 × 40) – 40,500] × £1}	1,500	
Direct labour efficiency {[(1,050 × 5) – 5,200] × £4}	200	
Fixed overhead spending (20,000 – 19,400)	600	4,300
		24,300
Less **Adverse variances**		
Sales price variance (104,300 – 105,000)	700	
Direct materials price [(40,500 × £1) – 41,200]	700	
Direct labour rate [(5,200 × £4) – 21,300]	500	1,900
Actual profit		22,400

➲ Exhibit 13.1 gives some indication of the extent of use of **variance analysis**, in practice.

<table>
<tr><td>Exhibit 13.1</td><td>

Accounting for control in practice

A 1993 survey of UK manufacturing businesses showed variance analysis to be very widely used: 76 per cent of all the survey respondents used it, with 83 per cent of larger businesses using it. Interestingly, 11 per cent of businesses had abandoned using variance analysis during the 10 years preceding the date of the survey. Does this imply that there is a significant shift away from its use?

The variances that are widely used, and regarded as important, are those that we have looked at in some detail in this chapter.

Source: Taken from information appearing in Drury, Braund, Osborne and Tayles (see reference at the end of the chapter).

</td></tr>
</table>

Standard quantities and costs

The budget is a financial plan for a future period of time. It is built up from stan-
➲ dards. **Standard quantities and costs** (or revenues) are those planned for individual units of input or output. Thus, standards are the building blocks of the budget.

We can say about Baxter Ltd's operations that:

- The standard selling price is £100 per unit of output
- The standard raw material cost is £4 per unit of output
- The standard raw material usage is 4 metres per unit of output
- The standard raw material price is £1 per metre (that is, per unit of input)
- The standard labour cost is £20 per unit of output
- The standard labour time is 5 hours per unit of output
- The standard labour rate is £4 per hour (that is, per unit of input).

The standards, like the budgets to which they are linked, represent targets and, therefore, yardsticks by which actual performance is measured. They are derived from experience of what is a reasonable quantity of input (for labour time and materials usage) and from assessments of the market for the product (standard selling price) and the market for the inputs (labour rate and materials price). These should be subject to frequent review and, where necessary, revision. It is vital, if they are to be used as part of the control process, that they represent realistic targets.

Calculation of most variances is, in effect, based on standards. For example, the materials usage variance is the difference between the standard materials usage for the level of output and the actual usage, costed at the standard materials price.

Standards can have uses other than in the context of budgetary control. The existence of a set of information of costs, usages, selling prices and so on, that are known to be broadly realistic, provides decision makers with a ready set of information for decision making and income-measurement purposes.

Exhibit 13.2 provides some information on the use of standard costs in practice.

Exhibit 13.2

Standard costing in practice

The Drury, Braund, Osborne and Tayles survey from 1993 showed that the respondent businesses found standard costs important to them for the following purposes:

	Percentage of respondents
Cost control and performance evaluation	72
Valuing stock and work in progress	80
Deducing costs for decision-making purposes	62
To help in constructing budgets	69

Thus, standards are seen as very important in the context of the subject of this chapter (cost control and performance evaluation), but they also seem to be widely used for other financial and management accounting purposes.

The conventional wisdom on the level of standards is that they should be demanding but achievable. Thus, if the standard direct labour time for some activity is five minutes, this should be capable of being achieved yet require staff to be working efficiently to achieve it. The survey showed that 44 per cent of respondents deliberately set standards of this type; 46 per cent, however, set standards based on past performance. Perhaps this was because the businesses' managements felt that past performance represents an achievable (obviously) yet demanding level of achievement. Only 5 per cent of respondents set standards at a level that could be achieved if everything went perfectly all of the time. Many people believe that such standards are not helpful because they do not represent a realistic target in a world where things *do* go wrong from time to time.

Standards are formally reviewed annually or more frequently by 91 per cent of the respondent businesses. This would amount to considering whether the existing standards are set at an appropriate level and amending them where necessary.

Source: Drury, Braund, Osborne, and Tayles (see reference at the end of chapter).

Labour cost standards and the learning-curve effect

Where a particular activity undertaken by direct workers has been unchanged in nature for some time, and the workers are experienced at performing it, normally an established standard labour time will be unchanged over time. Where a new activity is introduced, or new people are involved with performing an existing task, a **learning-curve** effect will normally occur. This is shown in Figure 13.5.

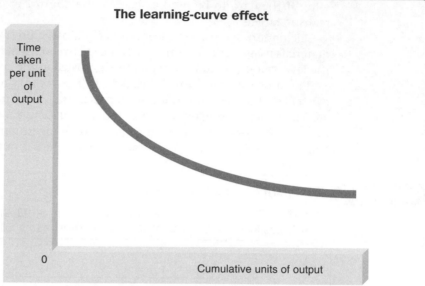

Figure 13.5

The learning-curve effect

Time taken per unit of output

0

Cumulative units of output

Each time a particular task is performed, people become quicker at it. This learning-curve effect becomes less and less significant until, after performing the task a number of times, no further learning occurs.

The first unit of output takes a long time to produce. As experience is gained, the person takes less time to produce each unit of output. The rate of reduction in the time taken will, however, decrease as experience is gained. Thus, for example, the reduction in time taken between the first and second unit produced will be much bigger than the reduction between the ninth and the tenth. Eventually, the rate of reduction in time taken will reduce to zero so that each unit will take as long as the preceding one. At this point, the point where the curve in Figure 13.5 becomes horizontal (the bottom right of the graph), the learning-curve effect will have been eliminated and a steady, long-term standard time for the activity will have been established.

The learning-curve effect seems to have little to do with whether workers are skilled or unskilled; if they are unfamiliar with the task, the learning-curve effect will occur. Practical experience shows that learning curves show remarkable regularity and, therefore, predictability from one activity to the next.

Clearly, the learning-curve effect must be taken into account when setting standards, and when interpreting any adverse labour efficiency variances, where a new process and/or new personnel are involved.

● ● ● ● Reasons for adverse variances

One reason why variances might occur is that the standards against which performance is being measured are not reasonable targets. This is certainly not to say that the immediate reaction to an adverse variance should be that the standard is unreasonably harsh. On the other hand, standards that are not achievable are useless.

The variances that we have considered are:

- Sales volume
- Sales price
- Direct materials usage
- Direct materials price
- Direct labour efficiency
- Direct labour rate
- Fixed overhead spending.

Ignoring the possibility that standards may be unreasonable, jot down any ideas which occur to you as possible practical reasons for adverse variances in each case.

The reasons that we thought of included the following:

Sales volume
- Poor performance by sales personnel.
- Deterioration in market conditions between the selling of the budget and the actual event.
- Lack of stock to sell as a result of some production problem.

Sales price
- Poor performance by sales personnel.
- Deterioration in market conditions between the setting of the budget and the actual event.

Direct materials usage
- Poor performance by production department staff leading to high rates of scrap.
- Substandard materials leading to high rates of scrap.
- Faulty machinery causing high rates of scrap.

Direct materials price
- Poor performance by buying department staff.
- Change in market conditions between setting the standard and the actual event.

Labour efficiency
- Poor supervision.
- A low-skilled grade of worker taking longer to do the work than was envisaged for the correct skill grade.
- Low-grade materials leading to high levels of scrap and wasted labour time.
- Problems with machinery leading to labour time being wasted.
- Dislocation of material supply leading to workers being unable to proceed with production.

Labour rate
- Poor performance by the personnel function.
- Using a higher grade of worker than was planned.
- Change in labour-market conditions between the setting of the standard and the actual event.

Fixed overheads
- Poor supervision of overheads.
- General increase in costs of overheads not taken into account in the budget.

It is possible to calculate a very large number of variances, given the range of operations found in practice. We have considered just the more basic of them. For example, in the Examples and Activities above, we have ignored the possible existence of variable overheads, and we have done this simply to restrict the amount of detailed explantion. All variance analysis is, however, based on similar principles.

Though we have tended to use the example of a manufacturing business to explain variance analysis, this should not be taken to imply that the technique is not equally applicable and useful in a service-sector business.

Non-operating profit variances

There are many areas of business that have a budget but where a failure to meet the budget does not have a direct effect on profit. Frequently, however, it has an indirect effect on profit, and sometimes a profound effect. For example, the cash budget sets out the planned receipts, payments and resultant cash balance for the period. If the person responsible for the cash budget gets things wrong, or is forced to make unplanned expenditures, this could lead to unplanned cash shortages and accompanying costs. These costs might be limited to lost interest on possible investments, which could otherwise have been made, or to the need to pay overdraft interest. If the cash shortage cannot be covered by some form of borrowing, the consequences could be more profound, such as the loss of profits on business that was not able to be undertaken because of the lack of funds.

It is clearly necessary that control is exercised over areas such as cash management as well as over areas such as production and sales in order to avoid adverse **non-operating profit variances**.

Investigating variances

It is unreasonable to expect budget targets to be met precisely each month. Whatever the reason for a variance, finding it will take time, and time is costly. Given that small variances are almost inevitable and that **investigating variances** can be expensive, management needs to establish a policy on which variances to investigate and which to accept. For example, for Baxter Ltd (see Example 13.1) the budgeted usage of materials during May was 40,000 metres at a cost of £1 per metre. Suppose that actual production had been the same as the budgeted quantity of output, but that 40,005 metres of material, costing £1 per metre, had actually been used. Would this adverse variance of £5 be investigated? Probably not. What, though, if the variance were £50 or £500 or £5,000?

| Activity 13.14 | What broad approach do you feel should be taken on whether to spend money investigating a particular variance? |

The general approach to this policy must be concerned with cost and benefit. What benefit there is likely to be from knowing why a variance exists needs to be balanced against the cost of obtaining that knowledge. The issue of balancing the benefit of having information with the cost of having it was discussed in Chapter 1.

Knowing the reason for a variance can only have value when it might provide management with the means to bring things back under control, so that future targets can be met. It should be borne in mind here that variances should normally either be zero or very close to zero. This is to say that achieving targets, give or take small variances, should be normal.

Broadly, we suggest the following:

- Significant adverse variances should be investigated because continuation of the fault that they represent could be very costly. Management must decide what 'significant' means. A certain amount of science (in the form of statistical models) can be brought to bear in making this decision, but ultimately it must be a matter of judgement as to what is significant. Perhaps a variance of 5 per cent from the budgeted figure would be deemed to be significant.
- Significant *favourable* variances should probably also be investigated. Though such variances would not cause such immediate concern as adverse ones, they still represent things not going according to plan. If actual performance is significantly better than target, it may well mean that the target is unrealistically low.
- Insignificant variances, though not triggering immediate investigation, should be kept under review. For each aspect of operations, the cumulative sum of variances over a series of control periods should be zero, with small adverse variances in some periods being compensated for by small favourable ones in others. This should be the case with variances that are caused by chance factors, which will not necessarily repeat themselves.

  Where a variance is caused by a more systematic factor that will repeat itself, the cumulative sum of the periodic variances will not be zero but an increasing figure. Where the increasing figure represents a set of adverse variances, it may well be worth investigating the situation, even though the individual variances might be insignificant. Even where the direction of the cumulative total points to favourable variances, investigation may still be considered to be valuable.

To illustrate this last point, let us consider Example 13.2.

Example 13.2

A business finds that the variances for materials usage for a special plastic, used in the manufacture of a product codenamed XLS 234, since the product was first manufactured at the beginning of the year, are as follows:

	£		£
January	25 (adverse)	July	20 (adverse)
February	15 (favourable)	August	15 (favourable)
March	5 (favourable)	September	23 (adverse)
April	20 (adverse)	October	15 (favourable)
May	22 (adverse)	November	5 (favourable)
June	8 (favourable)	December	26 (adverse)

The average cost of XLS 234 used each month is about £1,200. Management believes that none of these variances, taken alone, is significant given the total cost of plastic used each month. The question is, are they significant when taken together? If we add them together, taking account of the signs, we find that we have

---

a net adverse variance for the year of £73. Of itself this, too, is probably not significant, but we should expect the cumulative total to be close to zero, were the variances random. We might feel that a pattern is developing and, given long enough, a net adverse variance of significant size might build up.

Investigating the plastic usage might be worth doing. (We should note that 12 periods are probably not enough to reach a statistically sound conclusion on whether the variances are random or not, but it provides an illustration of the point.)

Exhibit 13.3 indicates the attitude of businesses to investigating variances in practice.

Exhibit 13.3

Investigating variances in practice

The 1993 survey by Drury, Braund, Osbourne and Tayles showed that a very high proportion of respondent businesses used no formal approach to investigating variances but based a decision as to whether to investigate a particular variance on managerial judgement. Quite a lot of businesses seemed to operate systems where variances were investigated when they exceed a specific monetary amount. Relatively few businesses were found to operate systems where variances exceeding a predetermined percentage of the standard were followed up.

Source: Drury, Braund, Osborne, and Tayles (see reference at the end of the chapter).

●●●● Compensating variances

There is superficial appeal in the idea of **compensating variances**, that is, the act of trading-off linked favourable and adverse variances against each other without further consideration. For example, a sales manager believes that she could sell more of a product if prices were lowered and that this would feed through to increased net operating profit. This would lead to a favourable sales volume variance, but also an adverse sales price variance on the face of it, provided the former is at least equal to the latter, all would be well.

Activity 13.15

What possible reason is there why the sales manager mentioned above should not go ahead with the price reduction?

....

The change in policy will have ramifications for other areas of the business, including the following:

● The need for more goods to be available to sell. Production may not be able to supply them, and it may not be possible to buy the stock in from elsewhere.
● Increased sales will involve an increased need for finance to pay for increased production.

Thus, trading-off variances is not automatically acceptable without a more far-reaching consultation and revision of plans.

Necessary conditions for effective budgetary control

It is obvious from what we have seen of **budgetary control** that if it is to be successful, a system, or a set of routines, must be established to enable the potential benefits to be gained.

Activity 13.16 Jot down the points that you think would need to be included in any system that will enable control through budgets to be effective. (We have not specifically covered these points, but your common sense, and perhaps your background knowledge, should enable you to think of a few points.)

There is no unequivocally correct answer to this activity. However, most businesses that operate successful budgetary control systems tend to show some common factors. These include:

- A serious attitude taken to the system by all levels of management, right from the very top.
- Clear demarcation between areas of managerial responsibility, so that accountability can more easily be ascribed for any area that seems to be going out of control.
- Budget targets being reasonable, so that they represent a rigorous yet achievable target. This may be promoted by managers being involved in setting their own targets. It is argued that this can promote the managers' commitment and motivation.
- Established data collection, analysis and dissemination routines that take the actual results and the budget figures, then go on to calculate and report the variances.
- Reports aimed at individual managers, rather than general-purpose documents. This avoids managers having to wade through reams of reports to find the part that is relevant to them.
- Fairly short reporting periods – typically a month – so that things cannot go too far wrong before they are picked up.
- Variance reports being produced and disseminated shortly after the end of the relevant reporting period.
- Action being taken to get operations back under control if they are shown to be out of control.

Limitations of the traditional approach to control through variances and standards

Budgetary control of the type that we have reviewed in this chapter has obvious appeal. As we have seen through Exhibit 13.1, it is widely used in practice, which suggests that managers believe it has value. It is somewhat limited at times, however. Some of its limitations are:

- Vast areas of most business and commercial activities simply do not have the same direct relationship between inputs and outputs as is the case with, say, level of output and the amount of raw materials used. Many of the expenses of the modern business are in areas such as training and advertising, where the expense is discretionary and not linked to the level of output in a direct way.
- Standards can quickly become out of date as a result of both technological change and price changes. This does not pose insuperable problems, but it

does require that the potential problem is systematically addressed. Standards that are unrealistic are, at best, useless. At worst, they could have adverse effects on performance. A buyer who knows that it is impossible to meet price targets, because of price rises, has a reduced incentive to minimise costs.

- Sometimes factors that are outside the control of the manager concerned can affect the calculation of the variance for which that manager is held accountable. This is likely to have an adverse affect on the manager's performance. The situation can often be overcome by a more considered approach to the calculation of the variance, resulting in the factors that are controllable by the manager being separated from those that are not.
- In practice, creating clear lines of demarcation between the areas of responsibility of various managers may be difficult. Thus, one of the prerequisites of good budgetary control is lost.

Behavioural aspects of budgetary control

Budgets, perhaps more than any other accounting statement, are prepared with the objective of affecting the attitudes and behaviour of managers. The point was made in Chapter 12 that budgets are intended to motivate managers, and research evidence generally shows this to be true. More specifically, the research shows:

- The existence of budgets generally tends to improve performance.
- Demanding, yet achievable, budget targets tend to motivate better than less demanding targets. It seems that setting the most demanding targets that will be accepted by managers is a very effective way to motivate them.
- Unrealistically demanding targets tend to have an adverse effect on managers' performance.
- The participation of managers in setting their targets tends to improve motivation and performance. This is probably because those managers feel a sense of commitment to the targets and a moral obligation to achieve them.

It has been suggested that allowing managers to set their own targets will lead to slack being introduced, so making achievement of the target that much easier. On the other hand, in a effort to impress, a manager may select a target that is not really achievable. These points imply that care must be taken in the extent to which managers have unfettered choice of their own targets. As we saw in Chapter 12, evidence tends to suggest that where managers work in an environment where they are expected to meet the targets represented in the budget, they will, almost irrespective of other factors, tend to try to introduce slack into the budget. Where there is a more relaxed attitude, and other factors (those perhaps less easy to quantify, such as general effectiveness and staff morale) are considered alongside the analysis of variances, managers are less inclined to seek to build in slack.

Where a manager fails to meet a budget, care must be taken by that manager's senior in dealing with the failure. A harsh, critical approach may demotivate the manager. Adverse variances may imply that the manager needs help from the senior.

The existence of budgets gives senior managers a ready means to assess the performance of their subordinates. Where promotion or bonuses depend on the absence of variances, senior management must be very cautious.

Exhibit 13.4 gives some indication of the effects of the **behavioural aspects of budgetary control** in practice.

Self-assessment question 13.1

Toscanini Ltd makes a standard product, which is budgeted to sell at £4.00 per unit, in a competitive market. It is made by taking a budgeted 0.4 kg of material, budgeted to cost £2.40 per kilogram, and working on it by hand by an employee, paid a budgeted £4.00 per hour, for a budgeted 12 minutes. Monthly fixed overheads are budgeted at £4,800. The output for May was budgeted at 4,000 units.

The actual results for May were as follows:

	£
Sales (3,500 units)	13,820
Materials (1,425 kg)	(3,420)
Labour (690 hours)	(2,690)
Fixed overheads	(4,900)
Actual operating profit	2,810

No stocks of any description existed at the beginning and end of the month.

Required:
(a) Deduce the budgeted profit for May and reconcile it with the actual profit in as much detail as the information provided will allow.
(b) State which manager should be held accountable, in the first instance, for each variance calculated.
(c) Assuming that the standards were all well set in terms of labour times and rates and materials usage and prices, suggest at least one feasible reason for each of

the variances which you identified in (a), given what you know about the company's performance for May.

(d) If it were discovered that the actual world-market demand for the company's product was 10 per cent lower than estimated when the May budget was set, state how and why the variances that you identified in (a) could be revised to provide information which would be potentially more useful.

Summary

We began this chapter by reviewing how budgeting itself can be a form of feed-forward control, while budgetary control is a form of feedback control. Next we considered how, by flexing the budget, it is possible to make direct and valid comparisons between budget and actual results and so be in a position to exercise control over operations. We considered how variances reconcile the budgeted profit with the actual profit, because each variance explains any divergence, between budgeted and actual profit, that was caused by the particular factor under review. We considered possible reasons for adverse variances and some general guidelines for the circumstances under which resources should be devoted to finding the precise reason for each adverse variance.

Next we looked at the type of infrastructure that a business needs to enable an effective system of budgetary control to exist. Lastly, we reviewed some of the behavioural issues concerned with trying to exercise control through budgets and variances.

Key terms

Flexible budget   p. 393
Feedback control   p. 393
Feedforward control   p. 394
Flex the budget   p. 395
Sales volume variance   p. 397
Adverse variance   p. 397
Favourable variance   p. 397
Variance   p. 397
Variance analysis   p. 404

Standard quantities and costs   p. 404
Learning curve   p. 406
Non-operating profit variances   p. 408
Investigating variances   p. 408
Compensating variances   p. 410
Budgetary control   p. 411
Behavioural aspects of budgetary control   p. 413

Further reading

If you would like to explore the topics covered in this chapter in more depth, we recommend the following books:

Management Accounting, *Atkinson, A., Banker R., Kaplan, R. and Mark Young, S.*, 3rd edn, Prentice Hall, 2001, chapter 12.

Management and Cost Accounting, *Drury, C.*, 5th edn, Thomson Learning Business Press, 2000, chapters 16, 18 and 19.

Cost Accounting: A managerial emphasis, *Horngren, C., Foster, G. and Datar, S.,* 10th edn, Prentice Hall International, 2000, chapters 7 and 8.

Cost and Management Accounting, *Williamson, D.,* Prentice Hall International, 1996, chapter 15.

● Reference

A Survey of Managment Accounting Practices in UK Manufacturing Companies, *Drury, C., Braund, S., Osborne, P. and Tayles, M.,* Chartered Association of Certified Accountants, 1993.

REVIEW QUESTIONS

13.1 Explain what is meant by feedforward control and distinguish it from feedback control.

13.2 What is meant by a variance?

13.3 What is the point in flexing the budget in the context of variance analysis? Does flexing imply that differences between budget and actual in the volume of output are ignored in variance analysis?

13.4 Should all variances be investigated to find their cause? Explain your answer.

 EXERCISES

Exercises 13.4–13.8 are more advanced than 13.1–13.3. Those with coloured numbers have answers at the back of the book.

13.1 You have recently overhead the following remarks:

(a) 'A favourable direct-labour rate variance can only be caused by staff working more efficiently than budgeted.'
(b) 'Selling more units than budgeted, because the units were sold at less than standard price, automatically leads to a favourable sales volume variance.'
(c) 'Using below-standard materials will tend to lead to adverse materials usage variances but cannot affect labour variances.'
(d) 'Higher-than-budgeted sales could not possibly affect the labour rate variance.'
(e) 'An adverse sales price variance can only arise from selling a product at less than standard price.'

Required:
Critically assess these remarks, explaining any technical terms.

13.2 Pilot Ltd makes a standard product, which is budgeted to sell at £5.00 per unit. It is made by taking a budgeted 0.5 kg of material, budgeted to cost £3.00 per kilogram, and working on it by hand by an employee, paid a budgeted £5.00 per hour, for a budgeted 15 minutes. Monthly fixed overheads are budgeted at £6,000. The output for March was budgeted at 5,000 units.

The actual results for March were as follows:

	£
Sales (5,400 units)	26,460
Materials (2,830 kg)	(8,770)
Labour (1,300 hours)	(6,885)
Fixed overheads	(6,350)
Actual operating profit	4,455

No stocks existed at the start or end of March.

Required:
(a) Deduce the budgeted profit for March and reconcile it with the actual profit in as much detail as the information provided will allow.
(b) State which manager should be held accountable, in the first instance, for each variance calculated.

13.3 Antonio plc makes product X, the standard costs of which are:

	£
Sales revenue	31
Direct labour (2 hours)	(11)
Direct materials (1 kg)	(10)
Fixed overheads	(3)
Standard profit	7

The budgeted output for March was 1,000 units of product X; the actual output was 1,100 units, which was sold for £34,950. There were no stocks at the start or end of March.

The actual production costs were:

	£
Direct labour (2,150 hours)	12,210
Direct materials (1,170 kg)	11,630
Fixed overheads	3,200

Required:
Calculate the variances for March as fully as you are able from the available information, and use them to reconcile the budgeted and actual profit figures.

13.4 You have recently overhead the following remarks:

(a) 'When calculating variances, we in effect ignore differences of volume of output, between original budget and actual, by flexing the budget. If there were a volume difference, it is water under the bridge by the time that the variances come to be calculated.'
(b) 'It is very valuable to calculate variances because they will tell you what went wrong.'
(c) 'All variances should be investigated to find their cause.'
(d) 'Research evidence shows that the more demanding the target, the more movitated the manager.'
(e) 'Most businesses do not have feedforward controls of any type, just feedback controls through budgets.'

Required:
Critically assess these remarks, explaining any technical terms.

13.5 Bradley-Allen Ltd makes one standard product. Its budgeted operating statement for May is as follows:

		£	£
Sales:	800 units		64,000
Direct materials:	Type A	12,000	
	Type B	16,000	
Direct labour:	Skilled	4,000	
	Unskilled	10,000	
Overheads:	(All Fixed)	12,000	
			54,000
Budgeted operating profit			10,000

The standard costs were as follows:

- Direct materials: Type A £50/kg
  - Type B £20/m
- Direct labour: Skilled £5/hour
  - Unskilled £4/hour

During May, the following occurred:

(i)   950 units were sold for a total of £73,000.
(ii)   310 kilos (costing £15,200) of type A material were used in production.
(iii) 920 metres (costing £18,900) of type B material were used in production.
(iv) Skilled workers were paid £4,628 for 890 hours.
(v)   Unskilled workers were paid £11,275 for 2,750 hours.
(vi) Fixed overheads cost £11,960.

There was no stock of finished production or of work in progress at either end of May.

Required:
(a) Prepare a statement that reconciles the budgeted to the actual profit of the company for May. Your statement should analyse the difference between the two profit figures in as much detail as you are able.
(b) Explain how the statement in (a) might be helpful to managers.

13.6 Mowbray Ltd makes and sells one product, the standard costs of which are as follows:

	£
Direct materials (3 kg at £2.50/kg)	7.50
Direct labour: (30 minutes at £4.50/hr)	2.25
Fixed overheads	3.60
	13.35
Selling price	20.00
Standard profit margin	6.65

The monthly production and sales are planned to be 1,200 units.
The actual results for May were as follows:

		£	
	Sales	18,000	
Less	Direct materials	(7,400)	(2,800 kg)
	Direct labour	(2,300)	(510 hr)
	Fixed overheads	(4,100)	
	Operating profit	4,200	

There were no stocks at the start or end of May. As a result of poor sales demand during May, the company reduced the price of all sales by 10 per cent.

Required:
Calculate the budgeted profit for May and reconcile it to the actual profit through - variances, going into as much detail as is possible from the information available.

13.7 Varne Chemprocessors is a business that specialises in plastics. It uses a standard costing system to monitor and report its purchases and usage of materials. During the most recent month, accounting period 6, the purchase and usage of chemical UK 194 were as follows:

Purchases/usage:	28,100 litres
Total price:	£51,704

Because of fire risk and the danger to health, no stocks are held by the business.

UK 194 is used solely in the manufacture of a product called Varnelyne. The standard cost specification shows that, for the production of 5,000 litres of Varnelyne, 200 litres of UK 194 is needed at a total standard cost of £392. During period 6, 637,500 litres of Varnelyne were produced.

Required:
(a) Calculate the purchases price and usage variances for UK 194 for period 6.
(b) The following comment was made by the production manager:

I knew at the beginning of period 6 that UK 194 would be cheaper than the standard cost specification, so I used rather more of it than normal; this saved £4,900 on other chemicals.

What changes do you need to make in your analysis for (a) as a result of this comment?
(c) Calculate, for each material below, the cumulative variances and comment briefly on the results.

Variances: periods 1 to 6		
Period	UK 500	UK 800
	£	£
1	301 F	298 F
2	251 A	203 F
3	102 F	52 A
4	202 A	98 A
5	153 F	150 A
6	103 A	201 A

where F = cost saving and A = cost overrun.

13.8 Brive plc has the following standards for its only product:

Selling price: £110/unit
Direct labour: 2 hours at £5.25/hour
Direct material: 3 kg at £14.00 kg
Fixed overheads: £27.00, based on a budgeted output of 800 units/month

During May, there was an actual output of 850 units and the operating statement for the month was as follows:

	£
Sales	92,930
Direct labour (1,780 hours)	(9,665)
Direct materials (2,410 kg)	(33,258)
Fixed overheads	(21,365)
Operating profit	28,642

There was no stock of any description at the beginning and end of May.

Required:

Prepare the original budget and a budget flexed to the actual volume. Use these to compare the budgeted and actual profits of the company for the month, going into as much detail with your analysis as the information given will allow.

PART 3

Financial management

Part 3 is concerned with the area of accounting and finance usually known as 'business finance' or 'financial management'. Broadly, we shall be looking at decisions concerning the raising and investment of finance. Businesses can be seen, from a purely economic perspective, as organisations that raise money from investors and others (for example, shareholders and lenders) and use those funds to make investments (typically in plant and other assets) that will make the business and its owners more wealthy. Clearly, these are important decision-making areas typically involving large amounts of money and relatively long-term commitments.

Chapter 14 considers how businesses make decisions about what represents a worthwhile investment. We shall be looking particularly at investments in such things as factories and plant, which might enable businesses to provide some product or service for which a profitable market is seen. The decision-making techniques that we shall consider could equally well be applied to making investments in the shares of a company, or any other type of 'financial' investment, which individuals might make using their own money.

Chapter 15 deals with the other side of the investment: where the investment finance comes from. Here we shall be reviewing the various types of funding used by the typical larger business, including raising funds from the owners of the business (the shareholders in the case of limited companies).

Chapter 16 looks at a particular area of fundraising and investment: the management of working capital. Working capital consists of the short-term assets and claims of the business – stock, trade debtors, cash and trade creditors. These items typically involve large amounts of finance and need to be managed carefully. The chapter considers how working capital can be managed effectively.

14 Making capital investment decisions

Introduction

In this chapter we shall look at how businesses can make decisions involving investments in new plant, machinery, buildings and similar long-term assets. The general principles that we shall consider can equally well be applied to investments in any long-term asset, including the shares of companies, irrespective of whether the investment is being considered by a business or by a private individual. We shall also look at the research evidence relating to the use of the various appraisal techniques in practice. We shall see that there are important differences between the theoretical appeal of particular techniques and their popularity in practice. We shall also consider the problems of risk and uncertainty and examine various ways in which risk can be incorporated into capital investment appraisal.

Once a decision has been made to implement a capital investment proposal, proper review and control procedures must be in place. We shall discuss the ways in which managers can oversee capital investment projects and how control may be exercised throughout the life of the project.

OBJECTIVES   When you have completed this chapter you should be able to:

- Explain the nature and importance of investment decision making.
- Identify and discuss the four main investment-appraisal methods used in practice.
- Discuss the strengths and weaknesses of various techniques for dealing with risk in investment appraisal.
- Explain the methods used to review and control capital expenditure projects.

The nature of investment decisions

The essential feature of investment decisions is **time**. Investment involves making an outlay of something of economic value, usually cash, at one point in time that is expected to yield economic benefits to the investor at some other point in time. Usually, the outlay precedes the benefits. Also, the outlay is typically a single large amount and the benefits arrive in a stream of smaller amounts over a fairly protracted period.

Investment decisions tend to be of crucial importance to the business because:

- *Large amounts of resources are often involved.* Many investments made by a business involve committing a significant proportion of its total resources. If the wrong decision is made, the effects on the business could be significant, if not catastrophic.
- *It is often difficult and/or expensive to 'bail-out' of an investment once it has been undertaken.* It is often the case that investments made by a business are specific to its needs. For example, a business may have premises built that are designed to provide its particular service. This may make the premises of much less value to other potential users with different needs. If the business found, after having made the investment, that the service is not selling as well as expected, the only course of action may be to close down the activity and sell the premises at a significant loss.

Activity 14.1 When managers are making decisions involving capital investments, what should their decisions seek to achieve?

Investment decisions must be consistent with the objectives of the business. For a private-sector business, maximising shareholder wealth is usually assumed to be the key objective.

Methods of investment appraisal

Given the importance of investment decisions to investors, it is vital that proper screening of investment proposals takes place. An important part of this screening process is to ensure that the business uses appropriate methods of evaluation. Research shows that there are basically four methods used in practice by businesses throughout the world to evaluate investment opportunities. They are:

- Accounting rate of return (ARR)
- Payback period (PP)
- Net present value (NPV)
- Internal rate of return (IRR).

It is possible to find businesses that use variants of these four methods. It is also possible to find businesses, particularly smaller ones, that do not use *any* formal appraisal method but rely more on the 'gut feeling' of their managers. Most businesses, however, seem to use one (or more) of the four, that we have listed above and that we shall now review in greater depth.

To help us examine each of the four methods, it is useful to see how each would deal with a particular investment opportunity. Consider the following example.

Example 14.1 Billingsgate Battery Company has carried out some market research showing that it is possible to manufacture and sell a product that has recently been developed.

The decision to manufacture would require an investment in a machine costing £100,000, payable immediately. Production and sales of the product would take place throughout the next five years, at the end of which time the machine is expected to be sold for £20,000. Production and sales of the product are expected to occur as follows:

	Number of units
Next year	5,000
Second year	10,000
Third year	15,000
Fourth year	15,000
Fifth year	5,000

It is estimated that the new product can be sold for £12 a unit and that the relevant material and labour costs will total £8 a unit. To simplify matters, we shall assume that cash from sales and payments for production costs are received and paid, respectively, at the end of each year. In practice, these cash flows will tend to occur throughout the year.

Bearing in mind that each product sold will give rise to a net cash inflow of £4 (that is, £12 – £8), the cash flows (receipts and payments) over the life of the product will be as follows:

		£000
Immediately	Cost of machine	(100)
1 year's time	Net profit before depreciation (£4 × 5,000)	20
2 years' time	Net profit before depreciation (£4 × 10,000)	40
3 years' time	Net profit before depreciation (£4 × 15,000)	60
4 years' time	Net profit before depreciation (£4 × 15,000)	60
5 years' time	Net profit before depreciation (£4 × 5,000)	20
5 years' time	Disposal proceeds from the machine	20

Note that, broadly speaking, the net profit before deducting depreciation equals the net amount of cash flowing into the business. Apart from depreciation, all expenses cause cash to flow out of the business, and sales revenues lead to cash flowing in.

We shall now go on to consider how each investment appraisal method works.

●●●● Accounting rate of return (ARR)

➔ The **accounting rate of return (ARR)** method takes the average accounting profit that the investment will generate and expresses it as a percentage of the average investment over the life of the project. Thus:

$$ARR = \frac{\text{Average annual profit}}{\text{Average investment to earn that profit}} \times 100\%$$

We can see from the equation that, to calculate ARR, we need to deduce two pieces of information:

- the annual average profit
- the average investment for the particular project.

In our example, average annual profit *before depreciation* over the five years is £40,000 [(£20,000 + £40,000 + £60,000 + £60,000 + £20,000)/5]. Assuming 'straight-line' depreciation (that is, equal amounts), the annual depreciation charge will be £16,000 [(Cost £100,000 − Disposal value £20,000)/5]. Thus, the average annual profit *after depreciation* is £24,000 (£40,000 − £16,000).

The average investment over the five years can be calculated as follows:

$$\text{Average investment} = \frac{\text{Cost of machine} + \text{disposal value}}{2}$$

$$= \frac{£100,000 + £20,000}{2}$$

$$= £60,000$$

Thus, the ARR of the investment is:

$$\text{ARR} = \frac{£24,000}{£60,000} \times 100\%$$

$$= 40\%$$

In order to decide whether the 40 per cent return is acceptable, we need to compare this percentage return with a minimum required rate set by the business.

Activity 14.2

Chaotic Industries is considering an investment in a fleet of 10 delivery vans to distribute its products to customers. The vans will cost £15,000 each to buy, payable immediately. The annual running costs are expected to total £20,000 for each van (including the driver's salary). The vans are expected to operate successfully for six years, at the end of which they will all have to be scrapped with disposal proceeds expected to be about £3,000 per van. At present, the business uses a commercial carrier for all of its deliveries. It is expected that this carrier will charge a total of £230,000 each year for the next six years to undertake the deliveries.

What is the ARR of buying the vans? (Note that cost savings are as relevant a benefit from an investment as are actual net cash inflows.)

....

The vans will save the business £30,000 a year [£230,000 − (£20,000 × 10)], before depreciation, in total. Thus the inflows and outflows will be:

		£000
Immediately	Cost of vans	(150)
1 year's time	Net saving before depreciation	30
2 years' time	Net saving before depreciation	30
3 years' time	Net saving before depreciation	30
4 years' time	Net saving before depreciation	30
5 years' time	Net saving before depreciation	30
6 years' time	Net saving before depreciation	30
6 years' time	Disposal proceeds from the vans	30

The total annual depreciation expense (assuming a straight-line approach) will be £20,000

[(£150,000 − £30,000)/6] Thus, the average annual saving, after depreciation, is £10,000 (£30,000 − £20,000).

The average investment will be:

$$\text{Average investment} = \frac{£150,000 + £30,000}{2}$$

$$= £90,000$$

Thus, the ARR of the investment is:

$$\text{ARR} = \frac{£10,000}{£90,000} \times 100\%$$

$$= 11.1\%$$

It may have struck you that ARR and the return on capital employed (ROCE) ratio adopt the same approach to performance measurement. We saw in Chapter 7 that ROCE is a popular means of assessing the performance of a business *as a whole*, after the period has passed. In theory, if all investments made by Chaotic Industries (Activity 14.2) actually proved to have an ARR of 11.1 per cent, then the ROCE for that business as a whole should be 11.1 per cent. Many businesses use ROCE as a key performance measure and so, where a preset ROCE is adopted, it may seem logical to use ARR when appraising new investments. We saw earlier that a business using ARR would compare the returns achieved with a minimum required rate of return. This minimum rate may be determined in various ways. For example, it may reflect the rate that previous investments had achieved (as measured by ROCE), or the industry average ROCE. Where there are competing projects that all seem capable of exceeding the minimum rate, the one with the highest ARR would normally be selected.

ARR is said to have a number of advantages as a method of investment appraisal. It was mentioned earlier that ROCE is a widely used measure of business performance and it may, therefore, seem sensible to use a method of investment appraisal that is consistent with this overall approach to measuring business performance. ARR is also a measure of profitability that many believe is the correct way to evaluate investments. Finally, ARR produces a percentage return that managers understand. Percentages are often used when setting targets for a business, and managers seem to feel comfortable with investment appraisal methods that adopt this form of measurement.

Activity 14.3

ARR suffers from a very major defect as a means of assessing investment opportunities. What do you think this is? *Hint*: the defect is not concerned with the ability of the decision maker to forecast future events, though this too can be a problem. Try to remember what was the essential feature of investment decisions that we identified at the beginning of the chapter.

The problem with ARR is that it almost completely ignores the time factor. In the Billingsgate Battery Company example (Example 14.1), exactly the same ARR would have been computed under each of the following three scenarios:

		Original scenario £000	Scenario 2 £000	Scenario 3 £000
Immediately	Cost of machine	(100)	(100)	(100)
1 year's time	Net profit before dep'n	20	10	160
2 years' time	Net profit before dep'n	40	10	10
3 years' time	Net profit before dep'n	60	10	10
4 years' time	Net profit before dep'n	60	10	10
5 years' time	Net profit before dep'n	20	160	10
5 years' time	Disposal proceeds	20	20	20

Since the same total profit *before* depreciation over the five years arises in all three of these cases, (that is, £200,000) the average net profit *after* depreciation must be the same in each case (that is £24,000). This means that each case will give rise to the same ARR of 40 per cent (£24,000/£60,000). We can see, however, that the pattern of profit inflows will vary under each scenario.

Given a financial objective of maximising the wealth of the owners of the business, a manager facing the three possible scenarios set out in Activity 14.3 would strongly prefer scenario 3. This is because most of the benefits from the investment arise within one year of the initial investment. The original scenario would rank second and scenario 2 would come a poor third in the rankings. Any appraisal technique not capable of distinguishing between these three situations is seriously flawed. We shall look in more detail at why time is such an important factor later in the chapter.

There are other defects associated with the ARR method. When measuring performance over the whole life of a project, it is cash flow rather than accounting profit that is important. Cash is the ultimate measure of the economic wealth generated by an investment. This is because it is cash that is used to acquire resources and for distribution to shareholders. Accounting profit, on the other hand, is more appropriate for periodic reporting: it is a useful measure of productive effort for a particular reporting period such as a year or half-year. Thus, it is really a question of 'horses for courses'. Accounting profit is fine for measuring performance over short periods, but cash is the appropriate measure when considering performance over the life of a project.

The ARR method can also create problems when considering competing investments of different size.

Activity 14.4

Joanna Sinclair (Wholesalers) plc is considering opening a new sales outlet in Coventry. Two possible sites have been identified. Site A has a capacity of 30,000 m². It will require an average investment of £6 million and will produce an average profit of £600,000 a year. Site B has a capacity of 20,000 m². It will require an average investment of £4 million and will produce an average profit of £500,000 a year.

What is the ARR of each investment opportunity? Which site would you select and why?

The ARR of site A is:

$$\frac{£600,000}{£6,000,000} = 10\%$$

The ARR of site B is:

$$\frac{£500,000}{£4,000,000} = 12.5\%$$

Thus, site B has the higher ARR. However, in terms of the absolute profit generated, site A is the more attractive. If the ultimate objective is to maximise the wealth of the shareholders, it might be better to choose site A even though the percentage return is lower. It is the absolute size of the return rather than the relative (percentage) size that is important.

Payback period (PP)

The **payback period (PP)** is the length of time it takes for an initial investment to be repaid out of the net cash inflows from a project. Since it takes time into account, the PP method seems to go some way to overcoming the timing problem of ARR – or at least at first glance it does. Let us consider PP in the context of the Billingsgate Battery Company (Example 14.1). You will recall that the project's costs and benefits can be summarised as follows:

		£000
Immediately	Cost of machine	(100)
1 year's time	Net profit before depreciation	20
2 years' time	Net profit before depreciation	40
3 years' time	Net profit before depreciation	60
4 years' time	Net profit before depreciation	60
5 years' time	Net profit before depreciation	20
5 years' time	Disposal proceeds	20

Note that all of these figures are amounts of cash to be paid or received. (We saw earlier that net profit before depreciation is a rough measure of the cash flows from the project.)

Given our earlier assumption that cash flows will arise at year ends, the payback period for this investment project is three years, that is, it will be three years before the £100,000 outlay is covered by the inflows. The payback period can be derived by calculating the cumulative cash flows as follows:

		Net cash flows £000	Cumulative net cash flows £000	
Immediately	Cost of machine	(100)	(100)	
1 year's time	Net profit before depreciation	20	(80)	(−100 + 20)
2 years' time	Net profit before depreciation	40	(40)	(−80 + 40)
3 years' time	Net profit before depreciation	60	20	(−40 + 60)
4 years' time	Net profit before depreciation	60	80	(+20 + 60)
5 years' time	Net profit before depreciation	20	100	(+80 + 20)
5 years' time	Disposal proceeds	20	120	(+100 + 20)

We can see that the cumulative cash flows become positive at the end the third year. Had we assumed that the cash flows arise evenly over the year, the precise payback period would be:

$$2 \text{ years } + \frac{40}{60} = 2\frac{2}{3} \text{ years}$$

(where 40 represents the cash flow still required at the beginning of the third year to pay back the initial outlay and 60 represents the cash flows during the year.) Again, we must ask how to decide whether this measure is acceptable. A manager using PP would need to have a minimum payback period in mind. If, for example, the Billingsgate Battery Company had a minimum PP of three years, the project would be acceptable. If there were two competing projects that both met the minimum PP criterion, the manager should select the project with the shorter payback period.

Activity 14.5

What is the payback period of the Chaotic Industries project from Activity 14.2?

The inflows and outflows are expected to be:

		Net cash flows £000	Cumulative net cash flows £000
Immediately	Cost of vans	(150)	(150)
1 year's time	Net saving before depreciation	30	(120)
2 years' time	Net saving before depreciation	30	(90)
3 years' time	Net saving before depreciation	30	(60)
4 years' time	Net saving before depreciation	30	(30)
5 years' time	Net saving before depreciation	30	0
6 years' time	Net saving before depreciation	30	30
6 years' time	Disposal proceeds from the vans	30	60

The payback period is five years, that is, it is not until the end of the fifth year that the vans will pay for themselves out of the savings that they are expected to generate.

The PP approach has certain advantages. It is quick and easy to calculate and can be easily understood by managers. The logic of PP is that projects that can recoup their cost quickly are economically more attractive than those with longer payback periods. However, this method does not provide us with the *whole* answer to the problem.

Activity 14.6

In what respect is PP not the whole answer as a means of assessing investment opportunities? Consider the cash flows arising from three competing projects:

		Project 1 £000	Project 2 £000	Project 3 £000
Immediately	Cost of machine	(200)	(200)	(200)
1 year's time	Net profit before depreciation	40	10	80
2 years' time	Net profit before depreciation	80	20	100
3 years' time	Net profit before depreciation	80	170	20

4 years' time	Net profit before depreciation	60	20	200
5 years' time	Net profit before depreciation	40	10	500
5 years' time	Disposal proceeds	40	10	20

Hint: once again, the defects are not concerned with the ability of the decision maker to forecast future events. This is a problem whatever approach we take.

The PP for each project is three years and so the PP approach would regard the projects as being equally acceptable. The PP method cannot distinguish between those projects that pay back a significant amount at an early stage and those that do not.

In addition, this method ignores cash flows after the payback period. A decision maker concerned with maximising shareholder wealth would prefer project 3 in the table above because the cash flows come in earlier and they are greater in total. The cumulative cash flows of each project are set out in Figure 14.1.

Figure 14.1

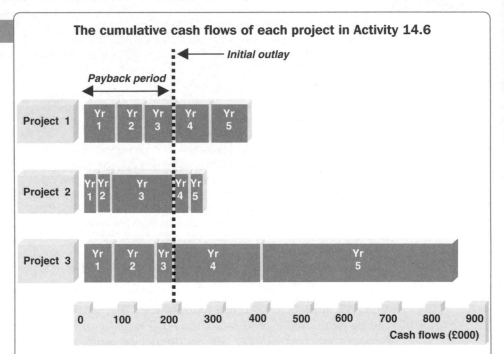

The cumulative cash flows of each project in Activity 14.6

The payback period cannot differentiate between the three projects. They all have the same payback period and are therefore equally acceptable (even though project 3 generated a larger amount of cash at an earlier point within the three-year payback and the cumulative cash flows of project 3 are much greater than those of the other two projects).

We can see that the PP method is not concerned with the profitability of projects; it is concerned simply with their payback periods. Thus, cash flows arising beyond the payback period are ignored. Whilst this neatly avoids the practical problems of forecasting cash flows over a longer period, it means that relevant information will be ignored. You may feel that, by favouring projects with a short payback period, the PP approach does at least provide a means of dealing with the problems of risk and uncertainty. However, this is a fairly crude approach to the problem. We shall see later that there are more systematic approaches to dealing with risk.

Net present value (NPV)

What we really need to help us make sensible investment decisions is a method of appraisal that takes account of *all* of the costs and benefits of each investment opportunity and that also makes a logical allowance for the *timing* of those costs and benefits. The **net present value (NPV)** method provides us with this.

Consider the Billingsgate Battery Company decision of Example 14.1, whose cash flows you will recall can be summarised as follows:

		£000
Immediately	Cost of machine	(100)
1 year's time	Net profit before depreciation	20
2 years' time	Net profit before depreciation	40
3 years' time	Net profit before depreciation	60
4 years' time	Net profit before depreciation	60
5 years' time	Net profit before depreciation	20
5 years' time	Disposal proceeds	20

Given that the principal financial objective of the business is probably to increase wealth, it would be very easy to assess this investment if all the cash inflows and outflows were to occur at the same time. All that we should need to do is to add up the cash inflows (total £220,000) and compare the result with the outflows (£100,000). This would lead us to the conclusion that the project should go ahead, because the business would be better off by £120,000 as a result. Of course, it is not as easy as this because time is involved. The cash outflow (payment) will occur immediately if the project is undertaken. The inflows (receipts) will arise at a range of later times.

The time factor is an important issue because people do not see £100 paid out now as equivalent in value to £100 receivable in a year's time.

<table>
<tr><td>

Activity 14.7

</td><td>

Why would you see £100 to be received in a year's time as unequal in value to £100 to be paid immediately? (There are basically three reasons.)

The three reasons are:

- Interest lost
- Risk
- Effects of inflation.

</td></tr>
</table>

We shall now take a closer look at the three reasons listed in the answer to Activity 14.7.

Interest lost

If you are to be deprived of the opportunity to spend your money for a year, you could equally well be deprived of its use by placing it on deposit in a bank or building society. In this case, at the end of the year you could have your money back and have interest as well. Thus, unless the opportunity to invest offers similar returns, you will be incurring an opportunity cost. An opportunity cost occurs where one course of action deprives you of the opportunity to derive some benefit from an alternative action – for example putting the money in the bank.

Any investment opportunity must, if it is to make you more wealthy, do better than the returns that are available from the next-best opportunity. Thus, if Billingsgate Battery Company sees putting the money in the bank on deposit as the alternative to investment in the machine, the returns from investing in the machine must be better than those from investing in the bank. If the bank offered better returns, the business would become more wealthy by putting the money on deposit.

Risk

Buying a machine to manufacture a product that is to be sold in the market is often a risky venture. Things may not turn out as expected.

Activity 14.8	**Can you suggest why things may not turn out as expected for the Billingsgate Battery Company?**

You may have came up with the following:

- The machine might not work as well as expected; it might break down, leading to loss of production and loss of sales.
- Sales of the product may not be as buoyant as expected.
- The life of the product may be shorter than expected.
- Labour costs may prove to be higher than was expected.
- The sales proceeds of the machine could prove to be less than was estimated.

It is important to remember that the decision whether or not to invest in the machine must be taken *before* any of the potential problems listed in Activity 14.8 are solved. It is only after the machine has been purchased that we may discover that the estimated level of sales is not going to be achieved. We can study reports and analyses of the market. We can commission sophisticated market surveys and these may give us more confidence in the likely outcome. We can advertise strongly and try to promote sales. Ultimately, however, we have to jump into the dark and accept the **risk**, if we want the opportunity to make beneficial investments.

Normally, people expect to receive greater returns where they perceive risk to be a factor. Examples of this in real life are not difficult to find. One is that banks tend to charge higher rates of interest to borrowers whom the bank perceives as more risky, than to those who can offer good security for a loan and can point to a regular source of income.

Going back to Billingsgate Battery Company's investment opportunity, it is not enough to say that we should not advise making the investment unless the returns from it are higher than those from investing in a bank deposit. Clearly, we should want returns *above* the level of bank deposit interest rates because the logical equivalent to investing in the machine is not putting the money on deposit – it is making an alternative investment that seems to have a risk similar to that of the investment in the machine.

We tend to expect a higher rate of return from investment projects where the risk is perceived as being higher. How risky a particular project is, and thus, how large this *risk premium* should be, are matters that are difficult to handle. It is usually necessary to make some judgement on these questions, and we shall consider this point in more detail later in the chapter.

Inflation

If you are to be deprived of £100 for a year, when you come eventually to spend that money it will not buy as much goods and services as it would have done a year earlier. Generally, you will not be able to buy as many loaves of bread, tickets for the cinema or bus tickets for a particular journey for £100, as you could have done a year earlier. This is **inflation**. Clearly, the investor needs to be compensated for this loss of purchasing power if the investment is to be made. This is on top of a return that takes into account the returns that could have been gained from an alternative investment of similar risk.

Actions of a logical investor

To summarise, we can say that the logical investor, who is seeking to increase his or her wealth, will only be prepared to make investments that will compensate for the loss of interest and purchasing power of the money invested and for the fact that the returns expected may not materialise (risk). This is usually assessed by seeing whether the proposed investment will yield a return that is greater than the basic rate of interest (which would include an allowance for inflation) *plus* a risk premium.

The elements of the opportunity finance cost are shown in Figure 14.2. Let us now return to the Billingsgate Battery Company example. Let us assume that, instead of making this investment, the business could make an alternative investment, with similar risk, and obtain a return of 20 per cent a year. We have

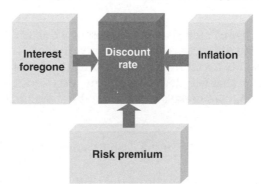

Figure 14.2

The factors influencing the discount rate to be applied to a project

The figure shows the three factors influencing the opportunity cost of finance which were discussed earlier.

already seen that it is not sufficient just to compare the basic cash inflows and outflows for the investment. It would be useful if we could express each of these cash flows in similar terms so that we could make a direct comparison between the sum of the inflows and the immediate £100,000 investment. In fact, we *can* do this.

Activity 14.9

If we know that Billingsgate Battery Company could alternatively invest its money at a rate of 20 per cent a year, how much do you judge the present (immediate) value of the expected first-year receipt of £20,000 to be? In other words, if instead of having to wait a year for the £20,000 and being deprived of the opportunity to invest it at 20 per cent, you could have a sum of money now, what sum would you regard as exactly equivalent to getting £20,000 in a year's time?

We should obviously be happy to accept a lower amount, if we could get it immediately than if we had to wait a year. This is because we could invest it at 20 per cent (in the alternative project) and it would grow to a larger amount in one year's time. Logically, we should be prepared to accept the amount which with a year's income will grow to £20,000. If we call this amount the present value (PV), we can say:

$$PV + (PV \times 20\%) = £20,000$$

that is, the amount plus income from investing the amount for the year equals £20,000. We can restate this equation as:

$$PV \times (1 + 0.2) = £20,000$$

(Note that 0.2 is the same as 20%, but expressed as a decimal.) This equation can be rearranged as:

$$PV = \frac{£20,000}{1 + 0.2}$$

$$= £16,667$$

Thus, rational investors who have the opportunity to invest at 20 per cent a year would not mind whether they have £16,667 now or £20,000 in a year's time. In this sense we can say that, given a 20 per cent investment opportunity, £20,000 to be received in one year's time has a present value of £16,667.

If we could derive the present value (PV) of each of the cash flows associated with Billingsgate's machine investment, we could easily make the direct comparison between the cost of making the investment (£100,000) and the various benefits that will derive from it in years 1 to 5. Fortunately, we can do precisely this.

We can make a more general statement about the PV of a particular cash flow. It is:

$$\text{PV of the cash flow of year } n = \frac{\text{Actual cash flow of year } n}{(1 + r)^n}$$

where n is the year of the cash flow (that is, how many years into the future) and r is the opportunity investing rate expressed as a decimal (instead of as a percentage).

We have already seen how this works for the £20,000 inflow for year 1. For year 2, with a cash inflow of £40,000, the calculation would be:

$$PV = \frac{£40,000}{(1 + 0.2)^2}$$

$$= \frac{£40,000}{(1.2)^2} = \frac{£40,000}{1.44}$$

$$= £27,778$$

Thus, the present value of the £40,000 to be received in two years' time is £27,778.

Activity 14.10 See if you can show that an investor would be indifferent to £27,778 receivable now, or £40,000 receivable in two years' time, assuming that there is a 20 per cent investment opportunity.

The reasoning goes like this:

	£
Amount available for immediate investment	27,778
Add Interest for year 1 (20% × £27,778)	5,556
	33,334
Add Interest for year 2 (20% × £33,334)	6,667
	40,001

(The extra £1 is only a rounding error.)

Thus, because the investor can turn £27,778 into £40,000 in two years, these amounts are equivalent and we can say that £27,778 is the present value of £40,000 receivable after two years (given a 20 per cent rate of return).

Now let us calculate the present values of all of the cash flows associated with the Billingsgate machine project and hence the net present value (NPV) of the project as a whole. The relevant cash flows and calculations are as follows [note that $(1 + 0.2)^0 = 1$]:

	Cash flow £000	Calculation of PV	PV £000
Immediately (time 0)	(100)	$(100)/(1 + 0.2)^0$	(100.00)
1 year's time	20	$20/(1 + 0.2)^1$	16.67
2 years' time	40	$40/(1 + 0.2)^2$	27.78
3 years' time	60	$60/(1 + 0.2)^3$	34.72
4 years' time	60	$60/(1 + 0.2)^4$	28.94
5 years' time	20	$20/(1 + 0.2)^5$	8.04
5 years' time	20	$20/(1 + 0.2)^5$	8.04
Net present value			24.19

Once again, we must ask how we can decide whether the return is acceptable to the business. In fact, the decision rule is simple. If the NPV is positive, we accept the project; if it is negative, we reject the project. In this case, the NPV is positive and so we should accept the project and buy the machine.

The reasoning behind this decision rule is quite straightforward. Given the investment opportunities available to the business, investing in the machine will make the owners of the business £24,190 better off. In other words, the gross benefits from investing in this machine are worth a total of £124,190 today, and since the business can 'buy' these benefits for just £100,000 today, the investment should be made. If, however, the gross benefits were below £100,000, they would be less than the cost of 'buying' these benefits.

Activity 14.11

What is the *maximum* the Billingsgate Battery Company would be prepared to pay for the machine, given the potential benefit of owning it?

....

The company would be prepared to pay up to £124,190 since the wealth of the owners of the business would be increased up to this point, though the company would rather pay less.

Using discount tables

Deducing the present values of the various cash flows was a little laborious using the approach that we have just taken. To deduce each PV we took the relevant cash flow and multiplied it by $1/(1 + r)^n$. Fortunately, there is a quicker way. Tables exist that show values of this **discount factor** for a range of values of r and n. Such a table appears in the Appendix to this chapter. Take a look at it now.

Look at the column for 20 per cent and the row for 1 year. We find that the factor is 0.833. Thus, the PV of a cash flow of £1 receivable in one year is £0.833. So a cash flow of £20,000 receivable in one year's time is £16,667 (that is, $0.833 \times £20,000$) – the same result as we found doing it in longhand.

Activity 14.12

What is the NPV of the Chaotic Industries project from Activity 14.2, assuming a 15 per cent opportunity cost of finance (discount rate)? Remember that the inflows and outflow are expected to be:

		£000
Immediately	Cost of vans	(150)
1 year's time	Net saving before depreciation	30
2 years' time	Net saving before depreciation	30
3 years' time	Net saving before depreciation	30
4 years' time	Net saving before depreciation	30
5 years' time	Net saving before depreciation	30
6 years' time	Net saving before depreciation	30
6 years' time	Disposal proceeds from the vans	30

You should use the discount table in the Appendix to this chapter.

....

The calculation of the NPV of the project is as follows:

	Cash flows £000	Discount factor (from the table)	Present value £000
Immediately	(150)	1.000	(150.00)
1 year's time	30	0.870	26.10
2 years' time	30	0.756	22.68
3 years' time	30	0.658	19.74
4 years' time	30	0.572	17.16
5 years' time	30	0.497	14.91
6 years' time	30	0.432	12.96
6 years' time	30	0.432	12.96
Net present value			(23.49)

Activity 14.13 **How would you interpret your result in Activity 14.12?**

The fact that the project has a negative NPV means that the present value of the benefits from the investment are worth less than the cost of entering into it. Any cost up to £126,510 (the present value of the benefits) would be worth paying, but not £150,000.

The discount tables reveal clearly how the value of £1 diminishes as its receipt goes further into the future. Assuming an opportunity cost of finance of 20 per cent a year, £1 to be received immediately has, obviously, a present value of £1. However, as the time before it is to be received increases, its present value diminishes significantly, as Figure 14.3 illustrates.

Figure 14.3

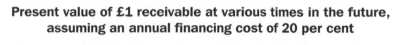

Present value of £1 receivable at various times in the future, assuming an annual financing cost of 20 per cent

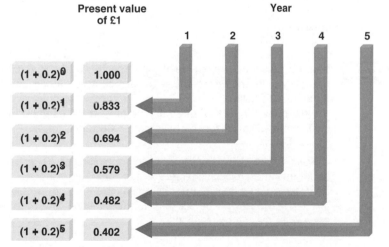

	Present value of £1
$(1 + 0.2)^0$	1.000
$(1 + 0.2)^1$	0.833
$(1 + 0.2)^2$	0.694
$(1 + 0.2)^3$	0.579
$(1 + 0.2)^4$	0.482
$(1 + 0.2)^5$	0.402

The figure shows how the present value of £1 reduces over time. Thus, the further into the future the £1 is received, the lower will be its present value.

Why NPV is superior to ARR and PP

NPV is a better method of appraising investment opportunities than either ARR or PP because it fully addresses each of the following:

- *The timing of the cash flows.* By discounting the various cash flows associated with each project according to when they are expected to arise, NPV takes account of the time value of money. The discount factor is based on the opportunity cost of finance (that is, the return that the next-best alternative opportunity would generate) and so the net benefit after financing costs have been met is identified (as the NPV of the project).
- *The whole of the relevant cash flows.* NPV includes all of the relevant cash flows irrespective of when they are expected to occur. It treats them differently according to their date of occurrence, but they are all taken into account in the NPV and they all have an influence on the decision.
- *The objectives of the business.* The output of the NPV analysis has a direct bearing on the wealth of the shareholders of a business. (Positive NPVs enhance wealth, negative ones reduce it.) Since we assume that private-sector businesses seek to maximise shareholder wealth, NPV is superior to the methods previously discussed.

We saw earlier that a business should take on all projects with positive NPVs, when they are discounted at the opportunity cost of finance. Where a choice has to be made among projects, a business should normally select the one with the largest NPV.

Internal rate of return (IRR)

This is the last of the four major methods of investment appraisal. It is quite closely related to the NPV method as it also involves discounting future cash flows. The **internal rate of return (IRR)** of a particular investment opportunity that is the discount rate that, when applied to its future cash flows, will produce an NPV or precisely zero. In essence, it represents the yield from an investment opportunity.

Activity 14.14

You will recall that when we discounted the cash flows of the Billingsgate Battery Company investment project at 20 per cent, we found that the NPV was a positive figure of £24,190.

What does the NPV of the machine project tell us about the rate of return that the investment will yield for the Billingsgate Battery Company?

....

The fact that the NPV is positive, when discounting at 20 per cent, implies that the rate of return that the project generates is more than 20 per cent. The fact that the NPV is a pretty large figure implies that the actual rate of return is quite a lot above 20 per cent. Increasing the size of the discount rate will reduce NPV because a higher discount rate gives lower discounted cash inflows.

We have seen that the IRR can be defined as the discount rate that equates the discounted cash inflows with the cash outflows. To put it another way, the IRR is the discount rate that will have the effect of producing an NPV of precisely zero. Figure 14.4 illustrates this relation diagrammatically for the Billingsgate company.

It is somewhat laborious to deduce the IRR by hand, since it cannot usually be calculated directly. Iteration (trial and error) is the approach that must usually be adopted. Let us try a higher rate for the Billingsgate Battery Company and see what happens, say, 30 per cent:

	Cash flow £000	Discount factor 30%	PV £000
Immediately (time 0)	(100)	1.000	(100.00)
1 year's time	20	0.769	15.38
2 years' time	40	0.592	23.68
3 years' time	60	0.455	27.30
4 years' time	60	0.350	21.00
5 years' time	20	0.269	5.38
5 years' time	20	0.269	5.38
			(1.88)

In increasing the discount rate from 20 per cent to 30 per cent, we have reduced the NPV from £52,600 (positive) to £1,880 (negative). Since the IRR is the discount rate that will give us an NPV of exactly zero, we can conclude that the IRR of Billingsgate Battery Company's machine project is very slightly under 30 per cent. Further trials could lead us to the exact rate, but there is probably not much point given the likely inaccuracy of the cash flow estimates. It is probably good enough, for practical purposes, to say that the IRR is about 30 per cent.

Figure 14.4

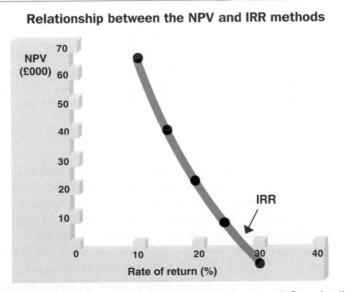

Relationship between the NPV and IRR methods

Where the discount rate is zero, the NPV will be the sum of the net cash flows. In other words, no account is taken of the time value of money. However, as the discount rate increases, there is a corresponding decrease in the NPV of the project. When the NPV line crosses the horizontal axis there will be a zero NPV and that will also represent the IRR.

Activity 14.15

What is the internal rate of return of the Chaotic Industries project from Activity 14.2? You should use the discount table in the Appendix at the end of this chapter.
Hint: remember that you already know the NPV of this project at 15 per cent. Try 10 per cent as your next trial.

Since we know that, at a 15 per cent discount rate, the NPV is a relatively large negative figure, our next trial should use a lower discount rate, say, 10 per cent.

	Cash flows £000	Discount factor (from the table) 10%	Present value £000
Immediately	(150)	1.000	(150.00)
1 year's time	30	0.909	27.27
2 years' time	30	0.826	24.78
3 years' time	30	0.751	22.53
4 years' time	30	0.683	20.49
5 years' time	30	0.621	18.63
6 years' time	30	0.565	16.95
6 years' time	30	0.565	16.95
Net present value			(2.40)

We can see that NPV rose about £21,000 (that is, £23,490 – £2,400) for a 5 per cent drop in the discount rate – that is, about £4,200 for each 1 per cent. We need to know the rate for a zero NPV. (This represents an increase of a further £2,400 in the NPV where the discount rate used is 10 per cent.) As a 1 per cent change in the rate results in a £4,200 change in NPV, the required change in the rate will be roughly 0.6 per cent (£2,400/£4,200). Thus, the IRR is close to 9.4 per cent (10 – 0.6 per cent). However, to say that the IRR is about 9 per cent is near enough for most purposes.

Users of the IRR approach should apply the following decision rules:

- For any project to be acceptable, the project must meet a minimum, IRR requirement. Logically, this minimum should be the opportunity cost of finance.
- Where there are competing projects (for example, the business can choose only one of several viable projects) the one with the highest IRR should be selected.

IRR has certain attributes in common with NPV. All cash flows are taken into account and the timing of them is handled logically. The main disadvantage with IRR is that it does not address the question of wealth generation. It could, therefore, lead to a wrong decision being made. IRR will always see a return of 25 per cent being preferable to a 20 per cent return (assuming an opportunity cost of finance of, say, 15 per cent). Though accepting the project with the higher percentage return will often generate the most wealth, this may not always be the case. This is because the scale of investment has been ignored. With a 15 per cent cost of finance, £1.5 million invested at 20 per cent would make you richer than £0.5 million invested at 25 per cent. IRR does not recognise this.

The problem, nevertheless, tends to be rare; normally, competing projects involve similar-sized investments. Typically, IRR will give the same signal as NPV, but it must be better to use a method (NPV) that is always reliable than to use IRR.

Some practical points

When carrying out an investment appraisal, there are several practical points you should bear in mind:

- *Relevant costs.* We should only take account of cash flows that vary according to the decision in our analysis. Thus, cash flows that will be the same, irrespective of the decision under review, should be ignored. For example, overheads that will be incurred in equal amount whether or not the investment is made should be ignored, despite the fact that the investment could not be made without the infrastructure that the overhead costs create. Similarly, past costs should be ignored as they are not affected by, and do not vary with, a decision on future projects. (See Chapter 8 for a full discussion of these points.)

- *Opportunity costs.* Opportunity costs arising from benefits forgone must be taken into account. Thus, for example, when considering whether to continue to use a machine (already owned by the business) for producing a new product, the realisable value of the machine may be an important opportunity cost.

- *Taxation.* Tax will usually be an important consideration when making an investment decision. The profits from the investment will be taxed and the capital investment may attract tax relief. This means that, in practice, unless tax is formally taken into account, the wrong decision could be made.

- *Cash flow not profit flow.* We have seen that for the NPV, IRR and PP methods, it is cash flows rather than profit flows that are relevant to the evaluation of investment projects. In a problem requiring the application of any of these methods, you may be given details of the profit for the investment period and so will be required to adjust these in order to derive the cash flow. Remember, the net profit *before* depreciation is an approximation to the cash flow for the period, and so you should work back to this figure.

  When the data are expressed in profit rather than cash-flow terms, an adjustment in respect of working capital may also be necessary. Some adjustment to take account of changes in the net cash investment (or disinvestment) in trade debtors, stock and creditors should be made. For example, launching a new product may give rise to an increase in working capital, requiring an immediate outlay of cash. This outlay for additional working capital should be shown in your NPV calculations as part of the initial cost. However, the additional working capital would normally be released at the end of the life of the product, so the resulting inflow of cash at the end of the project should also be taken into account.

- *Year-end assumption.* In the examples above, we have assumed that cash flows arise at the end of the relevant year. This is a simplifying assumption that is used to make the calculations easier. (However, it is perfectly possible to deal more precisely with the cash flows.) The assumption is clearly unrealistic as money will have to be paid to employees on a weekly or a monthly basis, and customers will pay within a month or two of buying a product. It is probably not a serious distortion. Even so, you should be clear that there is nothing about any of the appraisal methods that demands that this assumption is made.

- *Interest payments.* When using discounted cash flow techniques, interest payments should not be taken into account in deriving the cash flow for the period. The discount factor already takes account of the costs of financing, and so to take account of interest charges in deriving cash flow for the period would be double counting.
- *Other factors.* Investment decision making must not be viewed as a mechanical exercise. The results derived from a particular investment appraisal method will be only one input to the decision-making process. There may be broader issues that have to be taken into account but that might be difficult to quantify. For example, a regional bus company may be considering an investment in a new bus to serve a particular route that local residents would like to see operated. Although the NPV calculations may reveal that a loss will be made on the investment, it may be that, by not investing in the new bus and not operating the route, the renewal of the company's licence to operate will be put at risk. In such a situation and before a final decision is made the size of the expected loss, as revealed by the calculations made, must be weighed against the prospect of losing the right to operate. Thus, non-quantifiable factors that may have a significant economic impact must be considered.

The reliability of the forecasts and the validity of the assumptions used in the evaluation will also have a bearing on a final decision. We shall see later in the chapter that various techniques may be applied to the information concerning the proposed investment to take account of risk and to assess sensitivity to any inaccuracies in the figures used.

Activity 14.16

The directors of Manuff (Steel) Ltd have decided to close one of its factories. There has been a reduction in the demand for the products made at the factory in recent years and the directors are not optimistic about the long-term prospects for these products. The factory is situated in the north of England where unemployment is high.

The factory is leased and there are four years of the lease remaining. The directors are uncertain as to whether the factory should be closed immediately or at the end of the period of the lease. Another company has offered to sublease the premises from Manuff at a rental of £40,000 per year for the remainder of the lease period.

The machinery and equipment at the factory cost £1.5 million and have a balance sheet value of £400,000. In the event of immediate closure, the machinery and equipment could be sold for £220,000. The working capital at the factory is £420,000 and could be liquidated for that amount immediately if required. Alternatively, the working capital can be liquidated in full at the end of the lease period. Immediate closure would result in redundancy payments to employees of £180,000 (£150,000 when closure is at the end of the lease period).

If the factory continues in operation until the end of the lease period, the following operating profits (losses) are expected:

Year	1	2	3	4
	£000	£000	£000	£000
Operating profit (loss)	160	(40)	30	20

These figures include a charge of £90,000 per year for depreciation of machinery and equipment. The residual value of the machinery and equipment at the end of the lease period is estimated at £40,000.

The company has a cost of capital of 12 per cent. Ignore taxation.

(a) Calculate the relevant cash flows arising from a decision to continue operations until the end of the lease period rather than to close immediately.
(b) Calculate the net present value of continuing operations until the end of the lease period rather than closing immediately.
(c) What other factors might the directors of the company take into account before making a final decision on the timing of the factory closure?
(d) State, with reasons, whether or not the company should continue to operate the factory until the end of the lease period.

....

(a) Relevant cash flows:

		Year			
	0	1	2	3	4
	£000	£000	£000	£000	£000
Operating cash flows (note 1)		250	50	120	110
Sale of machinery (note 2)	(220)				40
Redundancy costs (note 3)	180				(150)
Sublease rentals (note 4)		(40)	(40)	(40)	(40)
Working capital invested (note 5)	(420)				420
	(460)	210	10	80	380

(b)

Discount rate 12%:	1.000	0.893	0.797	0.712	0.636
Present value	(460)	187.5	8.0	57.0	241.7
Net present value	34.2				

Notes:
1. The operating cash flows are calculated by adding back the depreciation charge for the year to the operating profit for the year. In the case of an operating loss, the depreciation charge is deducted.
2. In the event of closure, machinery could be sold immediately. Thus, an opportunity cost of £220,000 is incurred if operations continue.
3. By continuing operations, there will be a saving in immediate redundancy costs of £180,000. However, redundancy costs of £150,000 will be paid in four years' time.
4. By continuing operations, the opportunity to sublease the factory will be forgone.
5. Immediate closure would mean that working capital could be liquidated. By continuing operations this opportunity is forgone. However, working capital can be liquidated in four years' time.

(c) Other factors that may influence the decision include:
- *The overall strategy of the company.* The company may need to set the decision within a broader context. It may be necessary to manufacture the products made at the factory because they are an integral part of the company's product range. The company may wish to avoid redundancies in an area of high unemployment for as long as possible.
- *Flexibility.* A decision to close the factory is probably irreversible. If the factory continues, however, there may be a chance that the prospects for the factory will brighten in the future.

- *Creditworthiness of sublessee.* The company should investigate the creditworthiness of the sublessee. Failing to receive the expected sublease payments would make the closure option far less attractive.
- *Accuracy of forecasts.* The forecasts made by the company should be examined carefully. Inaccuracies in the forecasts or any underlying assumptions may change the expected outcomes.

(d) The NPV of the decision to continue operations rather than close immediately is positive. Hence, shareholders would be better off if the directors took this course of action. The factory should, therefore, continue in operation rather than close down. This decision is likely to be welcomed by employees as unemployment is high in the area.

●●●● Investment decision making in practice

As a footnote to our examination of investment appraisal techniques, it is interesting to consider their practical significance. In recent years, there has been a number of studies concerning the use of investment appraisal techniques by businesses.

These studies have shown a trend over the past 25 years towards increasing use of the 'discounting' methods: NPV and IRR. Surprisingly, both PP and ARR remain as popular as ever. Exhibit 14.1 shows the results of one of the most recent of these studies, a survey of large UK businesses conducted in 1997.

| Exhibit 14.1 | **Use of different investment appraisal methods by large UK businesses** |

	% of businesses using the technique
Net present value	80
Internal rate of return	81
Payback period	70
Accounting rate of return	56
	287

Note: the percentages sum to more than 100% because the business in the survey used more than one technique (see text following)

Source: Arnold and Hatzopoulos (see reference (1) at the end of this chapter).

Exhibit 14.1 shows that the two discounting methods are clearly each more popular than either PP or ARR. This is a relatively recent development; earlier studies suggest that it was only in the 1990s that the discounting methods overtook PP.

Activity 14.17

How do you explain the popularity of the PP, given the several theoretical limitations discussed earlier in this chapter?

....

A number of possible reasons may explain this finding:

- PP is easy to understand and use.
- It can avoid the problems of forecasting far into the future.
- It gives emphasis to the early cash flows, when there is greater certainty concerning their accuracy.
- It emphasises the importance of liquidity. Where a business has liquidity problems, a short payback period for a project is likely to appear attractive.

The importance of payback may suggest a lack of sophistication among managers concerning investment appraisal. This criticism is most often made against managers of smaller businesses. In fact, survey evidence tends to show that smaller businesses are much less likely to use discounted cash flow methods than larger ones.

The sum of percentage usage for each appraisal method is 287 per cent (see Exhibit 14.1), which indicates that many businesses use more than one method to appraise investments. Indeed, it seems that few businesses use any one method alone. It is, therefore, possible that payback is used by some businesses as an initial screening device and that projects passing successfully through this stage are then subject to a more sophisticated discounted cash flow analysis. Exhibit 14.1 suggests that most businesses use one or both of the two discounted cash flow methods.

IRR may be as popular as NPV, despite its shortcomings, because it expresses outcomes in percentage terms rather than absolute terms. This form of expression appears to be more acceptable to managers. This may be because managers are used to using percentage figures as targets (for example, return on capital employed).

Self-assessment question 14.1

Beacon Chemicals plc is considering buying some new equipment to produce a chemical named X14. The new equipment's capital cost is estimated at £100,000 and if its purchase is approved now, the equipment can be bought and commence production by the begining of year 1. The company has already spent £50,000 on research and development work. Estimates of revenues and costs arising from the operation of the new plant are as follows:

	Year 1	Year 2	Year 3	Year 4	Year 5
Sales price (£/unit)	100	120	120	100	80
Sales volume (units)	800	1,000	1,200	1,000	800
Variable costs (£/unit)	50	50	40	30	40
Fixed costs (£000s)	30	30	30	30	30

If the equipment is bought, sales of some existing products will be lost, resulting in a loss of contribution of £15,000 a year over its life.

The accountant has informed you that the fixed costs include depreciation of £20,000 a year on new equipment. They also include an allocation of £10,000 for fixed overheads. A separate study has indicated that if the new equipment is bought, additional overheads, excluding depreciation, arising from its use will be £8,000 a year.

The equipment would require additional working capital of £30,000. For the purposes of your initial calculations ignore taxation.

Required:
(a) Deduce the relevant annual cash flows associated with buying the equipment.
(b) Deduce the payback period.
(c) Calculate the net present value using a discount rate of 8 per cent.

Hint: you should deal with the investment in working capital by treating it as a cash outflow at the start of the project and an inflow at the end.

Dealing with risk in investment appraisal

We have already considered the fact that risk – the likelihood that what is projected to occur will not actually happen – is an important aspect of financial decision-making. It is a particularly important issue in the context of investment decisions. This is because of (1) the relatively long timescales involved (there is more time for things to go wrong between the decision being made and the end of the project), and (2) the size of the investment. If things go wrong, the impact can be both significant and lasting.

Various approaches to dealing with risk have been proposed. These fall into two categories: assessing the level of risk and reacting to the level of risk. We now consider formal methods of dealing with risk that fall within each category.

Assessing the level of risk

One popular way of attempting to assess the level of risk is to carry out a **sensitivity analysis** on the proposed project. This involves an examination of the key input values affecting the project to see how changes in each input might influence the viability of the project.

If the result of the investment appraisal, using the best estimates, is positive, each input value is then examined to see how far the estimated figure could be changed before the project becomes unviable for that reason alone. Let us suppose that the NPV for an investment in a machine, to produce a particular product, is a positive value of £50,000. If we were to carry out a sensitivity analysis on this project, we should consider in turn each of the key input factors – cost of the machine, sales volume and price, individual manufacturing costs, length of the project, and discount rate. We should seek to find the value that each of them could have before the NPV figure would become negative (that is, the value for the factor at which NPV would be zero). The difference between the value for that factor at which the NPV would equal zero and the estimated value represents the margin of safety for that particular input. The process is set out in Figure 14.5.

Figure 14.5

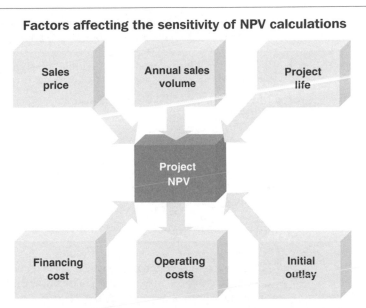

Factors affecting the sensitivity of NPV calculations

Sensitivity analysis involves identifying the key factors that affect the project. In the figure, six factors have been identified for the particular project. (In practice, the key factors are likely to vary between projects.) Once identified, each factor will be examined in turn to find the value it should have for the project to have a zero NPV.

A spreadsheet model of the project can be extremely valuable for this exercise because it then becomes a very simple matter to try various values for the input data and see the effect of each. As a result of carrying out a sensitivity analysis, the decision maker is able to get a 'feel' for the project, which otherwise might not be possible. The following activity can be undertaken without recourse to a spreadsheet.

Activity 14.18

S. Saluja (Property Developers) Ltd intends to bid at an auction, to be held today, for a manor house that has fallen into disrepair. The auctioneer believes that the house will be sold for about £450,000. The company wishes to renovate the property and to divide it into luxury flats to be sold for £150,000 each. The renovation will be in two stages and will cover a two-year period. Stage 1 will cover the first year of the project. It will cost £500,000 and the six flats completed during this stage are expected to be sold for a total of £900,000 at the end of the first year. Stage 2 will cover the second year of the project. It will cost £300,000 and the three remaining flats are expected to be be sold at the end of the second year for a total of £450,000. The cost of renovation is subject to an agreed figure with local builders; however, there is some uncertainty over the remaining input values. The company has a cost of capital of 12 per cent.

(a) What is the NPV of the proposed project?
(b) Assuming none of the other inputs deviates from the best estimates provided:
   (i)   What auction price would have to be paid for the manor house to cause the project to have a zero NPV?
   (ii) What cost of capital would cause the project to have a zero NPV?

(iii) What is the sale price of each of the flats that would cause the project to have a zero NPV? (Each flat will be sold for the same price.)

(c) Is the level of risk associated with the project high or low? Discuss your findings.

....

(a) The NPV of the proposed project is as follows:

	Cash flows £	Discount factor 12%	Present value £
Year 1 (£900,000 – £500,000)	400,000	0.893	357,200
Year 2 (£450,000 – £300,000)	150,000	0.797	119,550
Less Initial outlay			(450,000)
Net present value			26,750

(b)

(i) To obtain a zero NPV, the auction price would have to be £26,750 higher than the current estimate, that is, a total price of £476,750. This is about 6 per cent above the current estimated price.

(ii) As there is a positive NPV, the cost of capital that would cause the project to have a zero NPV must be higher than 12 per cent. Let us try 20 per cent.

	Cash flows £	Discount factor 20%	Present value £
Year 1 (£900,000 – £500,000)	400,000	0.833	333,200
Year 2 (£450,000 – £300,000)	150,000	0.694	104,100
Less Initial outlay			(450,000)
Net present value			(12,700)

The cost of capital lies somewhere between 12 per cent and 20 per cent. Increasing the discount rate by 8 percentage points (from 12% to 20%) causes the NPV to reduce by £39,450 (from £26,750 (positive) to £12,700 (negative)). This means £4,931 (that is, £39,450/8) per 1-percentage-point shift in the discount rate. At 12 % the NPV is £26,750 (above zero), so a discount rate of 12% + [(26,750/4,931) × 1% = 17.4%] applies.

This approach is, of course, the same as that used when calculating the IRR of the project; in other words, 17.4 per cent is the IRR of the project.

(iii) To obtain a zero NPV, the sale price of each flat must be reduced so that the NPV is reduced by £26,750. In year 1, six flats are sold (and in year 2, three flats are sold). The discount factor at the 12% rate for year 1 is 0.893 and for year 2 is 0.797. We can derive the fall in value per flat (Y) to give a zero NPV by using the equation:

$$(6Y \times 0.893) + (3Y \times 0.797) = £26,750$$

$$Y = £3,452$$

The sale price of each flat necessary to obtain a zero NPV is therefore:

$$£150,000 - £3,452 = £146,548$$

This represents a fall in the estimated price of 2.3 per cent.

(c) These calculations indicate that the auction price would have to be about 6 per cent above the estimated price before a zero NPV is obtained. The margin of safety is, therefore, not very high for this factor. The calculations also reveal that the price of the flats would only have to fall by 2.3 per cent from the estimated price before the NPV is reduced to zero. Hence, the margin of safety for this factor is even smaller. However, the cost of capital is less sensitive to changes and there would have to be an increase from 12 per cent to 17.4 per cent before the project produced a zero NPV. It seems from the calculations that the sale price of the flats is the most sensitive factor to consider. A careful re-examination of the market value of the flats seems appropriate before a final decision is made.

There are two major drawbacks with the use of sensitivity analysis:

- It does not give managers clear decision rules concerning acceptance or rejection of the project and so they must rely on their own judgement.
- It is a static form of analysis. Only one input is considered at a time, while the rest are held constant. In practice, however, it is likely that more than one input value will differ from the best estimates provided. Even so it would be possible to deal with changes in various inputs simultaneously, were the project data put on to a spreadsheet model.

Another means of assessing risk is through the use of statistical probabilities. It may be possible to identify a range of feasible values for each of the items of input data and to assign a probability of occurrence to each of these values. Using this information, we can derive an **expected net present value (ENPV)** that is, in effect, a weighted average of the possible outcomes where the probabilities are used as weights. To illustrate this method, let us consider Example 14.2.

Example 14.2

C. Piperis (Properties) Ltd has the opportunity to acquire a lease on a block of flats that has only two years remaining before it expires. The cost of the lease would be £100,000. The occupancy rate of the block of flats is currently around 70 per cent and the flats are let almost exclusively to naval personnel. There is a large naval base located nearby, and there is little other demand for the flats. The occupancy rate of the flats will change in the remaining two years of the lease, depending on the outcome of a defence review. The navy is currently considering three options for the naval base. These are:

- *Option 1.*   Increase the size of the base by closing down a base in another region and transferring the personnel to the one located near the flats.
- *Option 2.*   Close down the base near the flats and leave only a skeleton staff there for maintenance purposes. The personnel would be moved to a base in another region.
- *Option 3.*   Leave the base open but reduce staffing levels by 20 per cent.

The directors of Piperis have estimated the following net cash flows for each of the two years under each option and the probability of their occurrence:

	£	Probability
Option 1	80,000	0.6
Option 2	12,000	0.1
Option 3	40,000	0.3
		1.0

(Note that the sum of the probabilities is 1.0, in other words, it is certain that one of the possible options will arise.) The company has a cost of capital of 10 per cent.
   Should the company purchase the lease on the block of flats?

To calculate the expected NPV of the proposed investment, we must first calculate the weighted average of the expected outcomes for each year where the probabilities are used as weights, by multiplying each cash flow by its probability of occurrence. Thus, the expected annual net cash flows will be:

	Cash flows £ (a)	Probability (b)	Expected cash flows £ (a × b)
Option 1	80,000	0.6	48,000
Option 2	12,000	0.1	1,200
Option 3	40,000	0.3	12,000
Expected cash flows in each year			61,200

Having derived the expected annual cash flows, we can now discount these using a rate of 10 per cent to reflect the cost of capital:

Year	Expected cash flows £	Discount rate 10%	Expected present value £
1	61,200	0.909	55,631
2	61,200	0.826	50,551
			106,182
Less initial investment			100,000
Expected NPV			6,182

We can see that the expected NPV is positive. Hence, the wealth of shareholders is expected to increase by purchasing the lease.

The expected NPV approach has the advantage of producing a single numerical outcome and of having a clear decision rule to apply, namely, if the expected NPV is positive, we should invest; if it is negative, we should not.
   However, the approach produces an average figure that may not be capable of occurring. This point was illustrated in the example above where the expected NPV does not correspond to any of the stated options. Using an average figure can also obscure the underlying risk associated with the project. This point is illustrated in Activity 14.19.

Qingdao Manufacturing Ltd is considering two competing projects. Details are as follows:

- Project A has a 0.9 probability of producing a negative NPV of £200,000 and a 0.1 probability of producing a positive NPV of £3.8 million.
- Project B has a 0.6 probability of producing a positive NPV of £100,000 and a 0.4 probability of producing a positive NPV of £350,000.

What is the expected net present value of each project?

The expected NPV of project A is:

$$(0.1 \times £3.8 \text{ m}) - (0.9 \times £200,000) = £200,000$$

The expected NPV of project B is:

$$(0.6 \times £100,000) + (0.4 \times £350,000) = £200,000$$

Although the expected NPV of each project in Activity 14.19 is identical, this does not mean that the business will be indifferent about which project to undertake. We can see from the information provided that project A has a high probability of making a loss whereas project B is not expected to make a loss under either possible outcome. If we assume that the shareholders of the company dislike risk – which is usually the case – they will prefer the managers of the company to take on project B as this provides the same level of expected return as project A but for a lower level of risk.

It can be argued that the problem identified above may not be significant where the business is engaged in several similar projects as it will be lost in the averaging process. However, in practice, investment projects may be unique events and this argument will not then apply. Also, where the project is large in relation to other projects undertaken, the argument loses its force.

Where the expected NPV approach is being used, it is probably a good idea to make known to managers the different possible outcomes and the probability attached to each outcome. By so doing, the managers will be able to gain an insight to the **downside risk** attached to the project. The information relating to each outcome can be presented in the form of a diagram if required. The construction of such a diagram is illustrated in Example 14.3.

Example 14.3

Zeta Computing Services Ltd has recently produced some software for a client organisation. The software has a life of two years and will then become obsolete. The cost of producing the software was £10,000. The client has agreed to pay a licence fee of £8,000 per year for the software if it is used in only one of its two divisions, and £12,000 per year if it is used in both of its divisions. The client may use the software for either one or two years in either division but will definitely use it in at least one division in each of the two years.

Zeta Computing Services believes there is a 0.6 chance that the licence fee received in any one year will be £8,000 and a 0.4 chance that it will be £12,000. There are four possible outcomes attached to this project (where p denotes probability):

- *Outcome 1.* Year 1 cash flow £8,000 ($p = 0.6$) and year 2 cash flow £8,000 ($p = 0.6$). The probability of both years having cash flows of £8,000 will be:

$$0.6 \times 0.6 = 0.36$$

- *Outcome 2.* Year 1 cash flow £12,000 ($p = 0.4$) and year 2 cash flow £12,000 ($p = 0.4$). The probability of both years having cash flows of £12,000 will be:

$$0.4 \times 0.4 = 0.16$$

- *Outcome 3.* Year 1 cash flow £12,000 ($p = 0.4$) and year 2 cash flow £8,000 ($p = 0.6$).The probability of this sequence of cash flows occurring will be:

$$0.4 \times 0.6 = 0.24$$

- *Outcome 4.* Year 1 cash flow £8,000 ($p = 0.6$) and year 2 cash flow £12,000 ($p = 0.4$). The probability of this sequence of cash flows occurring will be:

$$0.6 \times 0.4 = 0.24$$

The information in Example 14.3 can be displayed in the form of a diagram (Figure 14.6).

Figure 14.6

The different possible project outcomes for Example 14.3

	Cash flow £	Probability
Outcome 1 Year 1 (0.6)	8,000	0.6 x 0.6 = 0.36
Year 2 (0.6)	8,000	
Outcome 2 Year 1 (0.4)	12,000	0.4 x 0.4 = 0.16
Year 2 (0.4)	12,000	
Outcome 3 Year 1 (0.4)	12,000	0.4 x 0.6 = 0.24
Year 2 (0.6)	8,000	
Outcome 4 Year 1 (0.6)	8,000	0.6 x 0.4 = 0.24
Year 2 (0.4)	12,000	Total 1.00

A decision tree sets out the different possible outcomes associated with a particular project and the probability of each outcome. The sum of the probabilities attached to each outcome must equal 1.00, in other words, it is certain that one of the possible outcomes will occur. For example, outcome 1 would occur where only one division uses the software in each year.

As you might expect, assigning probabilities to possible outcomes can often be a problem. There may be many possible outcomes arising from a particular investment project, and to identify each outcome and then assign a probability to it may prove to be an impossible task. When assigning probabilities to possible outcomes, either an objective or a subjective approach may be used. **Objective probabilities** are based on information gathered from past experience. Thus, for example, the transport manager of a company operating a fleet of motor vans may be able to provide information concerning the possible life of a new motor van purchased based on the record of similar vans acquired in the past. From the information available, probabilities may be developed for different possible life-spans. However, the past may not always be a reliable guide to the future, particularly during a period of rapid change. In the case of the motor vans, for example, changes in design and technology or changes in the purpose for which the vans are being used may undermine the validity of past data. **Subjective probabilities** are based on opinion and will be used where past data are either inappropriate or unavailable. The opinions of independent experts may provide a useful basis for developing subjective probabilities, although even these may contain bias, which will affect the reliability of the judgements made.

Despite these problems, we should not be dismissive of the use of probabilities. Assigning probabilities can help to make explicit some of the risks associated with a project and should help decision makers to appreciate the uncertainties that have to be faced.

Activity 14.20

Devonia (Laboratories) Ltd has recently carried out successful clinical trials on a new type of skin cream that has been developed to reduce the effects of ageing. Research and development costs incurred by the company in relation to the new product amount to £160,000. In order to gauge the market potential of the new product, independent market research consultants were hired at a cost of £15,000. The market research report submitted by the consultants indicates that the skin cream is likely to have a product life of four years and could be sold to retail chemists and large department stores at a price of £20 per 100 ml container. For each of the four years of the new product's life, sales demand has been estimated as follows:

Number of 100 ml containers sold	Probability of occurrence
11,000	0.3
14,000	0.6
16,000	0.1

If the company decides to launch the new product, it is possible for production to begin at once. The equipment necessary to produce the skin cream is already owned by the company and originally cost £150,000. At the end of the new product's life, it is estimated that the equipment could be sold for £35,000. If the company decides against launching the new product, the equipment will be sold immediately for £85,000 as it will be of no further use to the company.

The new skin cream will require two hours' labour for each 100 ml container produced. The cost of labour for the new product is £4.00 per hour. Additional workers will have to be recruited to produce the new product. At the end of the product's life, the workers are unlikely to be offered further work with the company and redundancy costs of £10,000 are expected. The cost of the ingredients for each 100 ml container is £6.00. Additional overheads arising from production of the new product are expected to be £15,000 per year.

The new skin cream has attracted the interest of the company's competitors. If the company decides not to produce and sell the skin cream, it can sell the patent rights to a major competitor immediately for £125,000.

Devonia has a cost of capital of 12 per cent. Ignore taxation.

(a) Calculate the expected net present value (ENPV) of the new product.
(b) State, with reasons, whether or not Devonia should launch the new product.

....

Your answer should be as follows:

(a) Expected sales volume per year $= (11,000 \times 0.3) + (14,000 \times 0.6)$
$\qquad + (16,000 \times 0.1)$
$\qquad = 13,300$ units

Expected annual sales revenue $= 13,300 \times £20$
$\qquad = £266,000$

Annual labour $= 13,300 \times £8$
$\qquad = £106,400$

Annual ingredient costs $= 13,300 \times £6$
$\qquad = £79,800$

Incremental cash flows:

| | Years | | | | |
| | 0 | 1 | 2 | 3 | 4 |
	£000	£000	£000	£000	£000
Sale of patent rights	(125.0)				
Sale of equipment	(85.0)				35.0
Sales		266.0	266.0	266.0	266.0
Cost of ingredients		(79.8)	(79.8)	(79.8)	(79.8)
Labour costs		(106.4)	(106.4)	(106.4)	(106.4)
Redundancy					(10.0)
Additional overheads		(15.0)	(15.0)	(15.0)	(15.0)
	(210.0)	64.8	64.8	64.8	89.8
Discount factor (12%)	1.0	0.893	0.797	0.712	0.636
	(210.0)	57.9	51.6	46.1	57.1
ENPV	2.7				

(b) As the ENPV of the project is positive, the wealth of shareholders would be increased by accepting the project. However, the ENPV is very low in relation to the size of the project and careful checking of the key estimates and assumptions would be advisable. A relatively small downward revision of sales or upward revision of costs could make the project ENPV negative.

Reacting to the level of risk

The logical reaction to a risky project is to demand a higher rate of return. Both theory and observable evidence show that there is a relationship between risk and the return required by investors. It was mentioned earlier, for example, that a bank would normally ask for a higher rate of interest on a loan where it perceives the lender to be less likely to be able to repay the amount borrowed.

When evaluating investment projects, it is normal to increase the NPV discount rate in the face of increased risk – that is, to demand a risk premium. The higher the level of risk, therefore, the higher the risk premium that will be demanded. The risk premium is usually added to a 'risk-free' rate of return to derive the total return required. The risk-free rate is normally taken to be equivalent to the rate of return from government loan stock. In practice, a business may divide projects into low-, medium- and high-risk categories and then assign a risk premium to each category. The cash flows from a particular project will then be discounted using a rate based on the risk-free rate plus the appropriate risk premium. This relationship between risk and return is illustrated in Figure 14.7.

Figure 14.7

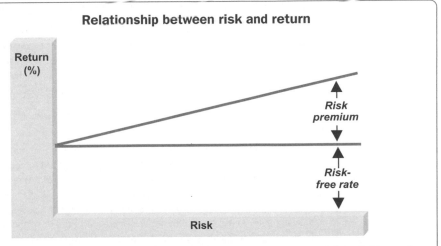

Relationship between risk and return

It is possible to take account of the riskiness of projects by changing the discount rate. A risk premium is added to the risk-free rate to derive the appropriate discount rate. A higher return will normally be expected from projects where the risks are higher. Thus, the more risky the project, the higher the risk premium.

The use of a **risk-adjusted discount rate** provides managers with a single numerical outcome, which can be used when making a decision either to accept or reject a project. Moreover, managers are likely to have an intuitive grasp of the relationship between risk and return and may well feel comfortable with this technique. However, there are practical difficulties with implementing this approach.

Activity 14.21   Can you think of any practical problems with the use of risk-adjusted discount rates?

Subjective judgement is required when assigning an investment project to a particular risk category and then in assigning a risk premium to each category. The choices made will reflect the personal views of the managers responsible and this may differ from the views of the shareholders they represent. The choices made can, nevertheless, make the difference between accepting or rejecting a particular project.

As we saw with Exhibit 14.1, it seems that most larger UK businesses use NPV as a technique for assessing investments. Some businesses mention their approach to using the technique, in their annual report. Exhibit 14.2 gives some examples.

Exhibit 14.2

The use of NPV in practice

In its 2000 annual report, the high-street retailer Marks & Spencer plc said:

> All investment decisions are made using discounted cashflow analysis, applying a hurdle rate determined by assessing the business risk appropriate to the specific operating divison.

The report also said that the business's average financing cost is 10 per cent a year.

The Boots Company plc, the high-street pharmacy that also owns the Halfords chain of motoring requisites shops, said in its 2000 annual report:

> We determine the level of investment in our businesses not by sales growth or operating profits but by 'economic profit'. This is the present value return we expect to make for shareholders after charging an appropriate amount for the capital invested. Currently, this cost of capital for most of the group is 8.5%, after tax and after discounting for specific risk.

In its 1999 annual report, Rolls-Royce plc, the builder of aircraft and other engines, said the following:

> The Group looks to create shareholder value in all activities undertaken. A feature of the company's business is very long product life-cycles. Typically, a gas turbine engine family will sell for over 20 years, followed by long-term aftermarket support. This provides long-term predictability of sales and hence requires extended business plans.
>
> Potential new products, acquisitions and investments are subjected to rigorous examination of risks and future cash flows. The net present value of the opportunity is calculated using a 10 per cent cost of capital to establish its value to the Group. All major investments require Board approval.
>
> The Group has a portfolio of projects at different stages of their life-cycles. Discounted cash flow analysis of the remaining life of projects is performed on a regular basis to compute the value which underlies the Group's market capitalisation.

The three businesses in Exhibit 14.2 seem broadly consistent in using a discount rate around 10 per cent (Boots' 8.5 per cent rate is after having reduced the cash flows to take account of risk, so its effective discount rate is above that value). Ten per cent seems to be the rate that is currently popular in practice, according to research and to comments that appear in the financial press.

Note that all three of the businesses refer specifically to risk in the context of investment appraisal.

Rolls-Royce says that it not only assesses new projects but also re-assesses existing projects. This must be a sensible commercial approach. Businesses should not continue with existing projects unless those projects have a positive

NPV based on future cash flows. Just because a project seemed to have a positive NPV before it started does not mean that this will persist, in the light of changing circumstances.

Management of the investment project

So far, we have been concerned with the process of carrying out the necessary calculations that enable managers to select between already identified investment opportunities. This topic is given a great deal of emphasis in the literature on investment appraisal. Although the evaluation of projects is undoubtedly important, we must bear in mind that it is only *part* of the process of investment decision making. There are other important aspects that managers must also consider.

It is possible to see the investment process as a sequence of five stages, each of which managers must consider. The five stages are set out in Figure 14.8 and described below.

Figure 14.8

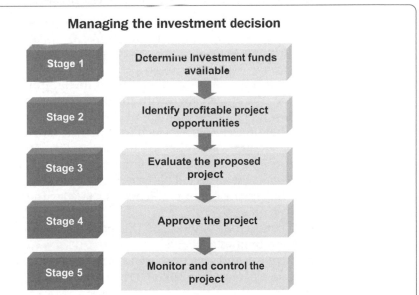

Managing the investment decision

Stage 1 — Determine Investment funds available

Stage 2 — Identify profitable project opportunities

Stage 3 — Evaluate the proposed project

Stage 4 — Approve the project

Stage 5 — Monitor and control the project

The management of an investment project involves a sequence of five key stages. The evaluation of projects using the appraisal techniques discussed earlier represents only one of these stages.

Stage 1: determine investment funds available

The amount of funds available for investment may be determined by the external market for funds or by internal management. In practice, it is often the latter that has the greater influence on the amount available. In either case, it may be that the funds will not be sufficient to finance the profitable investment opportunities available. When this occurs, some form of **capital rationing** has to be undertaken. This means that managers are faced with the task of deciding on the most profitable use of the investment funds available. Various approaches may be used, however, these are beyond the scope of this book.

Stage 2: identify profitable project opportunities

A vitally important part of the investment process is the search for profitable investment opportunities. A business should carry out methodical routines for identifying feasible projects. This may be done through a research and development department or by some other means. Failure to do so will inevitably lead to the business losing its competitive position regarding product development, production methods or market penetration. To help identify good investment opportunities, some businesses provide financial incentives to staff who have good ideas. The search process will, however, usually involve looking outside the business to identify changes in technology, customer demand, market conditions and so on. Information will need to be gathered and this may take some time, particularly for unusual or non-routine investment opportunities.

Stage 3: evaluate the proposed project

If management is to agree to the investment of funds in a project, there must be a proper screening of each proposal. For projects of any size, this will involve providing answers to a number of questions, including:

● What is the nature and purpose of the project?
● Does the project align with the overall objectives of the business?
● How much finance is required?
● What other resources (such as expertise, factory space and so on) are required for successful completion of the project?
● How long will the project last and what are its key stages?
● What is the expected pattern of cash flows?
● What are the major problems associated with the project and how can they be overcome?
● What is the NPV/IRR of the project? How does this compare with other opportunities available?
● Have risk and inflation been taken into account in the appraisal process and, if so, what are the results?

It is important to appreciate that the ability and commitment of those responsible for proposing and managing the project will be vital to the success of the investment. Hence, when evaluating a new project, those proposing it will be judged by its success. In some cases, senior managers may decide not to support a project that appears profitable on paper if they lack confidence in the ability of key managers to see it through to completion.

Stage 4: approve the project

Once the managers responsible for investment decision making are satisfied that the project should be undertaken, formal approval can be given. However, a decision on a project may be postponed if senior managers need more information from those proposing the project, or if revisions are required to the proposal. In some cases, the project proposal may be rejected if it is considered unprofitable or likely to fail. Before rejecting a proposal, however, the implications of not pursuing the project for such areas as market share, staff morale and existing business operations must be carefully considered.

Stage 5: monitor and control the project

Making a decision to invest, say, in the plant needed to go into production of a new product does not automatically cause the investment to be made and production to go smoothly ahead. Managers will need to manage the project actively through to completion. This, in turn, will require further information-gathering exercises.

Management should receive progress reports at regular intervals concerning the project. These reports should provide information relating to the actual cash flows for each stage of the project, which can then be compared against the forecast figures provided when the proposal was submitted for approval. The reasons for significant variations should be ascertained and corrective action taken where possible. Any changes in the expected completion date of the project or any expected variations in future cash flows from budget should be reported immediately; in extreme cases, managers may even abandon the project if circumstances appear to have changed dramatically for the worse. We saw in Exhibit 14.2 that Rolls-Royce undertakes this kind of re-assessment of existing projects. No doubt most other well-managed businesses do this too.

Project management techniques (for example, critical path analysis) should be employed wherever possible and their effectiveness reported to senior management.

An important part of the control process is a **post-completion audit** of the project. This is, in essence, a review of the project performance in order to see whether it lived up to expectations and whether any lessons can be learned from the way that the investment process was carried out. In addition to an evaluation of financial costs and benefits, non-financial measures of performance such as the ability to meet deadlines and levels of quality achieved should also be reported. (See Chapter 11 for a discussion of total life-cycle costing, which is based on similar principles.)

The fact that a post-completion audit is an integral part of the management of the project should also encourage those who submit projects to use realistic estimates. Where over-optimistic estimates are used in an attempt to secure project approval, the managers responsible will find themselves accountable at the post-completion audit stage. Such audits, however, can be difficult and time-consuming to carry out, and so the likely benefits must be weighed against the costs involved. Senior management may feel, therefore, that only projects above a certain size should be subject to a post-completion audit.

Extending the NPV concept: shareholder value analysis

In recent years, there has been increasing recognition that the net present value approach can play an important role in setting financial goals for the business as a whole and for strategic decision making. To explain the role of net present value (NPV) in this context, we must begin by recalling from our discussions in Chapter 1 that the primary goal of a business is to maximise the wealth of its shareholders. The problem for businesses, however, is that conventional measures of performance, such as earnings per share, growth in profits and return on shareholders' funds, do not capture the essence of this objective.

The conventional measures can be criticised for this emphasis on the short-term performance of the business. In practice, it is possible to take decisions that will lead to an improvement in these measures over the short term but that will adversely effect the long-term wealth of shareholders. For example, profits may be increased in the short term by cutting back on staff training and research expenditure, however, this type of expenditure may be vital to long-term survival. NPV analysis, which we use for measuring the wealth created from an investment, does not suffer from these kinds of problems.

We know from our earlier study of NPV that, when evaluating an investment project, shareholder wealth will be maximised by maximising the net present value of the cash flows generated from the project. As a corollary to this point, it is possible that the business as a whole can be viewed as simply a portfolio of investment projects, and so to maximise the wealth of shareholders the same principles should apply. **Shareholder value analysis (SVA)** is founded on this basic idea.

The SVA approach involves evaluating strategic decisions (that is, long-term decisions affecting the business as a whole) according to their ability to maximise value, or wealth, for shareholders. To undertake this evaluation, conventional measures are discarded and replaced by discounted cash flows. We have seen that the net present value of a project represents the value of that particular project. Given that the business can be viewed as a portfolio of projects, the value of the business as a whole can therefore be viewed as the net present value of the cash flows generated by the business as a whole. SVA seeks to measure the discounted cash flows of the business as a whole and then seeks to identify the part that is available to the shareholders.

Activity 14.22	If the net present value of future cash flows generated by the business represents the value of the business as a whole, how can we derive that part of the value of the business that is available to shareholders?

A business will normally be financed by a combination of loan capital and ordinary shareholders' funds. Thus, holders of loan capital will also have a claim on the total value of the business. That part of the total business value that is available to ordinary shareholders can therefore be derived by deducting from the total value of the business (total NPV) the market value of any loans outstanding. Hence:

Shareholder value = Total business value – Market value of outstanding loans

Supporters of SVA believe that this measure should replace the traditional accounting measures of value creation such as earnings per share and return on ordinary shareholders' funds. Thus, only if shareholder value (as defined above) increases over time can we say that there has been an increase in shareholder wealth. SVA takes a long-term view and is not concerned with reported annual profit numbers. Rather, it is concerned with measuring and managing cash flows over time. These cash flows are not affected by accounting policies and have the advantage that they take account of risk and the time value of money (through the discount rate). See Figure 14.9.

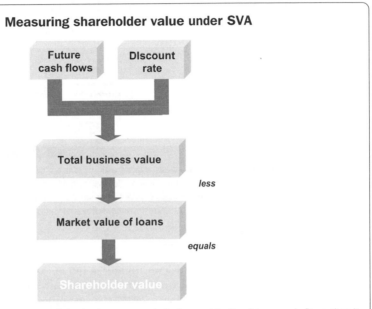

Measuring shareholder value under SVA

The figure shows that the value of the business as a whole is equal to the future cash flows that it generates, suitably discounted to take account of the time value of money. By deducting from this figure the market value of the claims from outside lenders, we are left with the value of the shareholders' wealth invested in the business.

Two US management consultants (see reference (2) at the end of the chapter) have summed up the importance of cash flows to shareholders as follows:

> The stock market sends a clear message that earnings per share is not the most important measure. Nor is it growth for growth's sake. What matters is long-term cash generation. That's what drives long-term stock (share) performance, and that's how we should manage.

Recognising the importance of cash flows on the way in which we should manage a business is a key feature of the SVA approach.

The SVA approach requires that the creation of shareholder value is clearly identified as the key objective of the business. Once this has been done, managers must manage in a way that maximises the long-term cash flows of the business. This will require an understanding of the factors that 'drive' the cash flows and the setting of targets should be based around these 'value drivers'. To encourage a high degree of commitment towards the SVA approach, management rewards should be given on the basis of the contribution made to the generation of long-term cash flows. There will have to be periodic reporting of shareholder value to enable managers to check whether they have succeeded in increasing shareholder wealth. See Figure 14.10.

Figure 14.10

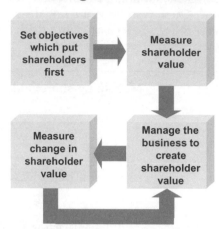

Creating shareholder value

The diagram shows that the starting point for the SVA approach is to establish clearly that the creation of shareholder wealth is the primary purpose of the business and to ensure that this is enshrined in the objectives of the business. The managers should then manage the business in a way that maximises the long-term cash flows of the business. It will be necessary to measure the amount of shareholder value created over a period on a regular basis and to report these results to managers.

We can see that SVA is really a radical departure from the conventional approach to managing a business. It will require different performance indicators, reporting systems, and incentive methods. It may also require a change of culture within the business to accommodate the shareholder value philosophy.

Activity 14.23

What are the practical problems do you think of adopting an SVA approach?

....

Two practical problems spring to mind:

- Forecasting future cash flows lies at the heart of the SVA approach. In practice, forecasting can be difficult and simplifying assumptions will usually have to be made.
- SVA requires more comprehensive information (for example, information concerning the value drivers) than the traditional measures discussed earlier.

● Summary

In this chapter we have considered how managers might approach the problem of assessing investment opportunities. We have seen that there are basically four methods that are used to any significant extent in practice. These are:

- Accounting rate of return
- Payback period
- Net present value
- Internal rate of return.

The first two of these are seriously flawed by their failure to take full account of the time dimension of investments. Assuming that the objective of making investments is to maximise the wealth of shareholders, the NPV method is, theoretically, far superior to the other three methods in that it rationally and fully takes account of all relevant information. Since IRR is similar to NPV, it tends to give similar signals to those provided by NPV. However, IRR suffers from a fundamental theoretical flaw that can lead to it giving misleading signals on some occasions.

We have also looked at evidence concerning the use of appraisal techniques in practice. The discounting methods (NPV and IRR) are now the most popular, among large businesses at least. Despite its theoretical limitations, the payback method remains popular.

We went on to consider the problem of risk in investment appraisal and examined various techniques for incorporating risk into the decision-making process. We saw that none of the techniques discussed was perfect, but that this does not mean they should be dismissed. Any attempt to take account of risk is probably preferable to relying on intuition.

We then went on to consider the procedures for managing the investment process. We saw that investment appraisal techniques are only one aspect of the investment process and that other aspects such as the search for suitable projects and the monitoring and control of projects, are important for successful investment.

Finally, we examined an extension of the NPV concept that has, in recent years, captured the imagination of many managers and commentators in the United States and Europe. Shareholder value analysis (SVA) uses discounted future cash flows as a basis for measuring the performance of a business as a whole and for deciding between different strategic choices. It replaces traditional forms or performance measurement, which emphasise the short term, and offers a new and long-term approach to managing the business.

Key terms

Accounting rate of return (ARR)   p. 426
Payback period (PP)   p. 430
Net present value (NPV)   p. 433
Risk   p. 434
Inflation   p. 435
Discount factor   p. 438
Internal rate of return (IRR)   p. 440
Sensitivity analysis   p. 448
Expected net present value (ENPV)
   p. 451
Objective probabilities   p. 455
Subjective probabilities   p. 455
Risk-adjusted discount rate   p. 457
Post-completion audit   p. 461
Shareholder value analysis (SVA)
   p. 462

● Further reading

If you would like to explore the topics covered in this chapter in more depth, we recommend the following books:

Corporate Financial Management, *Arnold, G.*, Financial Times Prentice Hall, 1998, chapters 2, 3 and 4.

Investment Appraisal and Financial Decisions, *Lumby, S. and Jones, C.*, 6th edn, International Thompson Business Press, 1999, chapters 3, 5 and 6.

Business Finance: Theory and Practice, *McLaney, E.*, 5th edn, Financial Times Prentice Hall, 2000, chapters 4–6.

Corporate Finance and Investment, *Pike, R. and Neale, B.*, 3rd edn, Prentice Hall International, 1999, chapters 5 and 7.

● References

1. 'Investment and finance decision making in large, medium and small UK companies', *Arnold, G. C. and Hatzopoulos, P.*, unpublished but cited in Arnold, G. C. **Corporate Financial Management**, FT Pearson, 1998.
2. 'Managing for shareholders value: from top to bottom', *Wenner, D. and le Ber, R.*, **Harvard Business Review**, 1991, pp. 33–9.

14.1 Why is the net present value method of investment appraisal considered to be theoretically superior to other methods found in the literature?

14.2 The payback method has been criticised for not taking into account the time value of money. Could this limitation be overcome? If so, would this method then be preferable to the NPV method?

14.3 Research indicates that the IRR method is a more popular method of investment appraisal than the NPV method. Why might this be?

14.4 Why are cash flows rather than profit flows used in the IRR, NPV and PP methods of investment appraisal?

? **EXERCISES**

Exercises 14.5–14.8 are more advanced than 14.1–14.4. Those with coloured numbers have answers at the back of the book.

14.1 The directors of Mylo Ltd are currently considering two mutually exclusive investment projects. Both projects are concerned with the purchase of new plant. The following data are available for the projects:

	Project 1 £	Project 2 £
Cost (immediate outlay)	100,000	60,000
Expected annual net profit (loss):		
Year 1	29,000	18,000
Year 2	(1,000)	(2,000)
Year 3	2,000	4,000
Estimated residual value	7,000	6,000

The company has an estimated cost of capital of 10 per cent and uses the straight-line method of depreciation for all fixed assets when calculating net profit. Neither project would increase the working capital of the company. The company has sufficient funds to meet all capital expenditure requirements.

Required:
(a) Calculate for each project:
   (i)   The net present value
   (ii) The approximate internal rate of return
   (iii) The payback period.
(b) State which, if any, of the two investment projects the directors of Mylo Ltd should accept, and why.
(c) State, in general terms, which method of investment appraisal you consider to be most appropriate for evaluating investment projects, and why.

14.2 Myers Software plc is a major distributor of computer software to small and medium-sized businesses. Although the company develops some software products itself, most are purchased from various software houses. The board of directors is currently considering the investment potential of three new tax-accounting software products that have been developed by different software houses and offered for sale to the company. The financial director of Myers Software plc has prepared the following financial estimates concerning the products:

Software name	Initial outlay	Cash flows		
		Year 1	Year 2	Year 3
	£	£	£	£
Taxmate	(60,000)	25,000	30,000	32,000
Easytax	(120,000)	50,000	70,000	40,000
Supertax	(180,000)	95,000	80,000	58,000

The company has a cost of capital of 10 per cent. Ignore taxation.

Required:

(a) Using each of the following appraisal methods, rank the products in order of investment potential:
  (i)   Net present value (NPV)
  (ii) Approximate internal rate of return (IRR)
  (iii) Payback.
(b) If the products were mutually exclusive, which product, if any, would you select and why?

14.3 Haverhill Engineers Limited manufactures components for the car industry. It is considering automating its line for producing crankshaft bearings. The automated equipment will cost £700,000. It will replace equipment with a scrap value of £50,000 and a balance-sheet value of £180,000.

At present, the existing ('old') line has a capacity of 1.25 million units a year but typically it has only been run at 80 per cent of capacity because of the lack of demand for its output. The new line has a capacity of 1.4 million units a year. Its life is expected to be five years and its scrap value at that time £100,000.

The accountant has prepared the following cost estimates based on output of 1,000,000 units a year:

	Old line (per unit)	New line (per unit)
	£	£
Materials	0.40	0.36
Labour	0.22	0.10
Variable overheads	0.14	0.14
Fixed overheads	0.44	0.20
	1.20	0.80
Selling price	1.50	1.50
Profit per unit	0.30	0.70

Fixed overheads include depreciation on the old machine of £40,000 a year and £120,000 for the new machine. It is considered that, for the company overall, fixed overheads are unlikely to change.

The introduction of the new machine will enable stocks to be reduced by £160,000. The company uses 10 per cent as its cost of capital. You should ignore taxation.

Required:
(a) Prepare a statement of the incremental cash flows arising from the project.
(b) Calculate the project's net present value.
(c) Calculate the project's approximate internal rate of return.
(d) Explain the terms 'net present value' and 'internal rate of return'. State which method you consider to be preferable, giving reasons for your choice.

14.4 Lansdown Engineers Limited is considering replacing its existing heating system. A firm of heating engineers has recommended two schemes, each of which will give a similar heating performance. Details of these and of the cost of the existing system appear below:

	Year	Existing system £000	System A £000	System B £000
Capital cost	0		70	150
Annual running cost	1–10	145	140	120
Scrap value	10	10	14	30

The existing heating system at present has a balance sheet value of £50,000 and a scrap value of £5,000. To keep the existing system working, an overhaul costing £20,000 would be required immediately. For your calculations you should ignore inflation and taxation. The company has a 12 per cent cost of capital.

Required:
(a) Calculate the net present value (to the nearest £1,000) of each of the two new schemes. You should consider each in isolation and ignore the existing system.
(b) Calculate the incremental cash flows (to the nearest £1,000) of system B over the existing system.
(c) Estimate the internal rate of return on the cash flow calculated in part (b).
(d) On the basis of your answers to (a), (b) and (c), give briefly your recommendations with reasons.

14.5 Chesterfield Wanderers is a professional football club that has enjoyed considerable success in both national and European competitions in recent years. As a result, the club has accumulated £1 million to spend on its further development. The board of directors is currently considering two mutually exclusive options for spending the funds available.

The first option is to acquire another player. The team manager has expressed a keen interest in acquiring Basil ('Bazza') Ramsey, a central defender, who currently plays for a rival club. The rival club has agreed to release the player immediately for £1 million if required. A decision to acquire 'Bazza' Ramsey would mean that the existing central defender, Vinnie Smith, could be sold to another club. Chesterfield Wanderers has recently received an offer of £220,000 for this player. This offer is still open but will only be accepted if 'Bazza' Ramsey joins Chesterfield Wanderers. If this does not happen,

Vinnie Smith will be expected to stay on with the club until the end of his playing career in five years' time. During this period, Vinnie will receive an annual salary of £40,000 and a loyalty bonus of £20,000 at the end of his five-year period with the club.

Assuming 'Bazza' Ramsey is acquired, the team manager estimates that gate receipts will increase by £250,000 in the first year and £130,000 in each of the four following years. There will also be an increase in advertising and sponsorship revenues of £120,000 for each of the next five years if the player is acquired. At the end of five years, the player can be sold to a club in a lower division and Chesterfield Wanderers will expect to receive £100,000 as a transfer fee. During his period at the club, 'Bazza' will receive an annual salary of £80,000 and a loyalty bonus of £40,000 after five years.

The second option is for the club to improve its ground facilities. The west stand could be converted into an all-seater area and executive boxes could be built for businesses wishing to offer corporate hospitality to clients. These improvements would also cost £1 million and would take one year to complete. During this period, the west stand would be closed, resulting in a reduction of gate receipts of £180,000. However, gate receipts for each of the following four years would be £440,000 higher than current receipts. In five years' time, the club has plans to sell the existing grounds and to move to a new stadium nearby. Payment for the improvements will be made when the work has been completed at the end of the first year. Whichever option is chosen, the board of directors has decided to take on additional ground staff. The additional wages bill is expected to be £35,000 a year over the next five years.

The club has a cost of capital of 10 per cent. Ignore taxation.

Required:
(a) Calculate the incremental cash flows arising from each of the options available to the club.
(b) Calculate the net present value of each of the options.
(c) On the basis of the calculations made in (b) above, which of the two options would you choose and why?
(d) Discuss the validity of using the net present value method in making investment decisions for a professional football club.

14.6 Newton Electronics Ltd has incurred expenditure of £5 million over the past three years researching and developing a miniature hearing aid. The hearing aid is now fully developed and the directors are considering which of three mutually exclusive options should be taken to exploit the potential of the new product. The options are as follows:

1. The business could manufacture the hearing aid itself. This would be a new departure for the business, which has so far concentrated on research and development projects only. However, it has manufacturing space available that it currently rents to another business for £100,000 a year. The business would have to purchase plant and equipment costing £9 million and invest £3 million in working capital immediately for production to begin.

   A market research report, for which the business paid £50,000, indicates that the new product has an expected life of five years. Sales of the product during this period are predicted as follows:

	Predicted sales for the year ended 30 November				
	Year 1	Year 2	Year 3	Year 4	Year 5
Number of units ('000)	800	1,400	1,800	1,200	500

The selling price per unit will be £30 in the first year but will fall to £22 in the following three years. In the final year of the product's life, the selling price will fall to £20. Variable production costs are predicted to be £14 per unit and fixed production costs (including depreciation) will be £2.4 million a year. Marketing costs will be £2 million a year.

The business intends to depreciate the plant and equipment using the straight-line method based on an estimated residual value at the end of the five years of £1 million. The business has a cost of capital of 10 per cent.

2. Newton Electronics Ltd could agree to another business manufacturing and marketing the product under licence. A multinational, Faraday Electricals plc, has offered to undertake the manufacture and marketing of the product and, in return, will make a royalty payment to Newton Electronics of £5 per unit. It has been estimated that the annual number of sales of the hearing aid will be 10 per cent higher if the multinational, rather than Newton Electronics, manufactures and markets the product.

3. Newton Electronics could sell the patent rights to Faraday Electricals for £24 million, payable in two equal instalments. The first instalment would be payable immediately and the second at the end of two years. This option would give Faraday Electricals the exclusive right to manufacture and market the new product.

Ignore taxation.

Required:
(a) Calculate the net present value of each of the options available to Newton Electronics Ltd.
(b) Identify and discuss any other factors that Newton Electronics Ltd should consider before arriving at a decision.
(c) What do you consider to be the most suitable option, and why?

14.7 Simtex Ltd has invested £120,000 to date in developing a new type of shaving foam. The shaving foam is now ready for production and it has been estimated that the new product will sell 160,000 bottles per year over the next four years. At the end of four years, the product will be discontinued and replaced by a new product.

The shaving foam is expected to sell at £6 per can and variable costs are estimated at £4 per can. Fixed costs (excluding depreciation) are expected to be £300,000 per year. (This figure includes £130,000 in fixed costs incurred by the existing business which will be apportioned to this new product.)

To manufacture and package the new product, equipment costing £480,000 must be acquired immediately. The estimated value of this equipment in four years' time is £100,000. The business calculates depreciation using the straight-line method, and has an estimated cost of capital of 12 per cent.

Required:
(a) Deduce the net present value of the new product.
(b) Calculate by how much each of the following must change before the new product is no longer profitable:
    (i)   The discount rate
    (ii) The initial outlay on new equipment
    (iii) The net operating cash flows
    (iv) The residual value of the equipment.
(c) Should the business produce the new product?

14.8 Kernow Cleaning Services Ltd provides street-cleaning services for local councils in the far south west of England. The work is currently labour intensive and few machines are employed. However, the business has recently been considering the purchase of a fleet of street-cleaning vehicles at a total cost of £540,000. The vehicles have a life of four years and are likely to result in a considerable saving of labour costs. Estimates of the likely labour savings and their probability of occurrence are set out below:

	Estimated savings £	Probability of occurrence
Year 1	80,000	0.3
	160,000	0.5
	200,000	0.2
Year 2	140,000	0.4
	220,000	0.4
	250,000	0.2
Year 3	140,000	0.4
	200,000	0.3
	230,000	0.3
Year 4	100,000	0.3
	170,000	0.6
	200,000	0.1

Estimates for each year are independent of other years. The business has a cost of capital of 10 per cent.

Required:
(a) Calculate the expected net present value (ENPV) of the street-cleaning machines.
(b) Calculate the net present value (NPV) of the worst possible outcome and the probability of its occurrence.

Present value table

Present value of 1, that is, $1/(1 + r)^n$ where r = discount rate and n = number of periods until the cash flow occurs.

	Discount rate (r)										
Period (n)	1%	2%	3%	4%	5%	6%	7%	8%	9%	10%	
1	0.990	0.980	0.971	0.962	0.952	0.943	0.935	0.926	0.917	0.909	1
2	0.980	0.961	0.943	0.925	0.907	0.890	0.873	0.857	0.842	0.826	2
3	0.971	0.942	0.915	0.889	0.864	0.840	0.816	0.794	0.772	0.751	3
4	0.961	0.924	0.888	0.855	0.823	0.792	0.763	0.735	0.708	0.683	4
5	0.951	0.906	0.863	0.822	0.784	0.747	0.713	0.681	0.650	0.621	5
6	0.942	0.888	0.837	0.790	0.746	0.705	0.666	0.630	0.596	0.565	6
7	0.933	0.871	0.813	0.760	0.711	0.665	0.623	0.583	0.547	0.513	7
8	0.923	0.853	0.789	0.731	0.677	0.627	0.582	0.540	0.502	0.467	8
9	0.914	0.837	0.766	0.703	0.645	0.592	0.544	0.500	0.460	0.424	9
10	0.905	0.820	0.744	0.676	0.614	0.558	0.508	0.463	0.422	0.386	10
11	0.896	0.804	0.722	0.650	0.585	0.527	0.475	0.429	0.388	0.350	11
12	0.887	0.788	0.701	0.625	0.557	0.497	0.444	0.397	0.356	0.319	12
13	0.879	0.773	0.681	0.601	0.530	0.469	0.415	0.368	0.326	0.290	13
14	0.870	0.758	0.661	0.577	0.505	0.442	0.388	0.340	0.299	0.263	14
15	0.861	0.743	0.642	0.555	0.481	0.417	0.362	0.315	0.275	0.239	15

	11%	12%	13%	14%	15%	16%	17%	18%	19%	20%	
1	0.901	0.893	0.885	0.877	0.870	0.862	0.855	0.847	0.840	0.833	1
2	0.812	0.797	0.783	0.769	0.756	0.743	0.731	0.718	0.706	0.694	2
3	0.731	0.712	0.693	0.675	0.658	0.641	0.624	0.609	0.593	0.579	3
4	0.659	0.636	0.613	0.592	0.572	0.552	0.534	0.516	0.499	0.482	4
5	0.593	0.567	0.543	0.519	0.497	0.476	0.456	0.437	0.419	0.402	5
6	0.535	0.507	0.480	0.456	0.432	0.410	0.390	0.370	0.352	0.335	6
7	0.482	0.452	0.425	0.400	0.376	0.354	0.333	0.314	0.296	0.279	7
8	0.434	0.404	0.376	0.351	0.327	0.305	0.285	0.266	0.249	0.233	8
9	0.391	0.361	0.333	0.308	0.284	0.263	0.243	0.225	0.209	0.194	9
10	0.352	0.322	0.295	0.270	0.247	0.227	0.208	0.191	0.176	0.162	10
11	0.317	0.287	0.261	0.237	0.215	0.195	0.178	0.162	0.148	0.135	11
12	0.286	0.257	0.231	0.208	0.187	0.168	0.152	0.137	0.124	0.112	12
13	0.258	0.229	0.204	0.182	0.163	0.145	0.130	0.116	0.104	0.093	13
14	0.232	0.205	0.181	0.160	0.141	0.125	0.111	0.099	0.088	0.078	14
15	0.209	0.183	0.160	0.140	0.123	0.108	0.095	0.084	0.074	0.065	15

15 Financing a business

Introduction

In this chapter we examine various aspects of financing a business. We begin by considering the sources of finance available to a business and the factors to be considered in choosing an appropriate source of finance. We then go on to consider capital markets, including the role of the Stock Exchange, the role of venture-capital organisations, and the ways in which share capital may be issued.

Sources of finance

When considering the various sources of finance for a business, it is useful to distinguish between external and internal sources; and when considering the various external sources, it is probably helpful to distinguish between long-term and short-term sources. In the sections that follow, we consider the various sources of external finance under each of the above headings. We then go on to consider the various sources of internal finance available.

Figure 15.1 summarises the main sources of long-term and short-term external finance. By external sources we mean sources that require the agreement of someone beyond the directors and managers of the business. Thus, finance from an issue of new shares is an external source because it requires the compliance of potential shareholders. Retained profit, on the other hand, is considered an internal source because the directors of the business have power to retain profits without the agreement of the shareholders (whose profits they are!).

Figure 15.1

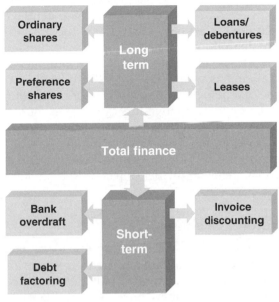

Major external sources of finance

The figure shows that external sources of finance can be divided between long-term and short-term sources. The long-term sources are made up of equity (ordinary shares and preference shares) and borrowing (loans/debentures and leases). The short-term sources are bank overdraft, debt factoring and invoice discounting. These last two are provided by specialist financial institutions.

Long-term sources of external finance

For the purpose of this chapter, long-term sources of finance are defined as those that are not due for repayment within one year. As Figure 15.1 shows, the major forms of long-term external finance are:

● Ordinary shares
● Preference shares
● Loans
● Leases, that is, finance leases and sale-and-leaseback arrangements.

When deciding on the most appropriate form of external finance, we must be clear about the advantages and disadvantages of each.

Ordinary shares

Ordinary shares form the backbone of the financial structure of a business. Ordinary share capital represents the risk finance. There is no fixed rate of dividend, and ordinary shareholders will receive a dividend only if profits available for distribution still remain after other investors (preference shareholders and lenders) have received their interest or dividend payments. If the business is closed down, the ordinary shareholders will receive any proceeds from asset disposals only after lenders and creditors and, in some cases, after preference shareholders have received their entitlements. Because of the high risks associated with this form of investment, ordinary shareholders will normally require the business to provide a comparatively high rate of return.

Although ordinary shareholders have limited loss liability, based on the amount that they have agreed to invest, the potential returns from their investment are unlimited. They have control over the business. They have voting rights, which give them the power to elect the directors and to remove the directors from office.

From the business's perspective, ordinary shares can be a valuable form of financing as, at times, it is useful to be able to avoid paying a dividend. In the case of a new expanding business or one in difficulties, the requirement to make a cash payment to investors can be a real burden. Where the business is financed totally by ordinary shares, this problem need not occur.

However, the costs of financing ordinary shares may be high over the longer term, for the reasons mentioned earlier. Moreover, the business does not obtain any tax relief on dividends paid to shareholders, whereas interest on borrowings is tax deductible.

Preference shares

Preference shares offer investors a lower level of risk than ordinary shares. Provided that there are sufficient profits available, preference shares will normally be given a fixed rate of dividend each year, and preference dividends will be paid before ordinary ones. Where a business is closed down, preference shareholders may be given priority over the claims of ordinary shareholders. (The documents of incorporation will determine the precise rights of preference shareholders in this respect.) Because of the lower level of risk associated with this form of investment, investors will be offered a lower level of return than that normally expected by ordinary shareholders.

There are various types of preference shares that may be issued. **Cumulative preference shares** give investors the right to receive arrears of dividends that have arisen as a result of there being insufficient profits in previous periods. The unpaid amounts will accumulate and will be paid when sufficient profits have been generated. **Non-cumulative preference shares** do not give investors this right. Thus, if a business is not in a position to pay the preference dividend due for a particular period, the preference shareholder loses the right to receive the dividend. **Participating preference shares** give investors the right to a further share in the profits available for dividend after they have been paid their fixed rate and after ordinary shareholders have been awarded a dividend. **Redeemable preference shares** allow the company to buy back the shares from shareholders at some agreed future date. Redeemable preference shares are seen as a lower-risk investment than non-redeemable shares, and so tend to carry a lower dividend. A business can also issue redeemable ordinary shares, but these are rare in practice.

Activity 15.1

Would you expect the market price of ordinary shares or preference shares to be the more volatile? Why?

....

The dividends of preference shares tend to be fairly stable over time, and there is usually an upper limit on the returns that can be received. As a result, the share price, which reflects the expected future returns from the share, will normally be less volatile than for ordinary shares.

Preference shares are no longer an important source of new finance. A major reason for this is that dividends paid to preference shareholders are not allowable against taxable profits, whereas interest on loan capital is an allowable expense. From the business's point of view, preference shares and loans are quite similar, and so the tax deductibility of loan interest is an important issue.

Later in this chapter we shall look at the role of the Stock Exchange in equity financing and the techniques used by larger businesses to make share issues.

Loans

Many businesses rely on loan capital, as well as share capital, to finance operations. Lenders will enter into a contract with the company in which the rate of interest, dates of interest payments and capital repayments, and security for the loan are clearly stated. In the event that the interest payments or capital repayments are not made on the due dates, the lender will usually have the right, under the terms of the contract, to seize the assets on which the loan is secured and sell them to repay the amount outstanding. Security for a loan may take the form of a fixed charge on particular assets of the business (freehold land and premises are often favoured by lenders) or a 'floating charge' on the whole of the company's assets. A floating charge will 'crystallise' and fix on particular assets in the event that the business defaults on its obligations.

Activity 15.2

What do you think is the advantage for the business of having a floating charge rather than a fixed charge on its assets?

A floating charge on assets will allow the managers of the company greater flexibility in their day-to-day operations than a fixed charge. Assets can be traded without reference to the lenders.

It is possible for a business to issue loan capital that is 'subordinated' to (ranked below) other loan capital already in issue. This means that, in the event of the business being closed down, the subordinated lenders will only receive their money back after the other lenders that have a higher ranked claim have been repaid. This increases the risks associated with the loan and, therefore, the level of return required by investors.

Investors will normally view loans as being less risky than preference shares or ordinary shares. Lenders have priority over any claims from shareholders, and will usually have security for their loans. As a result of the lower level of risk associated with this form of investment, investors are usually prepared to accept a lower rate of return.

Activity 15.3

Ken Wong Ltd has approached a financial institution for a long-term loan. What do you think would be the main factors that the financial institution will take into account when considering the loan application?

The main factors would be:

● The period of the loan and the nature of the security which is offered.

- The nature of the business.
- The purpose for which the loan will be used and the quality of the case to support the loan application.
- Security for the loan.
- The financial position of the business.
- The integrity and quality of the management of the business.
- The financial track record of the business.

There is a number of types of financing based on loans. These are described next.

Debentures

➡ One form of long-term loan is the **debenture**. This is simply a loan that is evidenced by a trust deed. The debenture loan is frequently divided into units (rather like share capital), and investors are invited to purchase the number of units they require. The debenture loan may be redeemable or irredeemable. Debentures of public limited companies are often traded on the Stock Exchange, and their listed value will fluctuate according to the fortunes of the business, movements in interest rates, and so on.

Eurobonds

➡ Another form of long-term loan finance is the **eurobond**. Eurobonds are issued by businesses (and other large organisations) in various countries, and the finance is raised on an international basis. They are bearer bonds, which are often issued in US dollars but which may also be issued in other major currencies. Interest is normally paid on an annual basis.

Eurobonds are part of an emerging international capital market, and they are not subject to regulations imposed by authorities in particular countries. There is a market for eurobonds that has been created by a number of financial institutions throughout the world. Here holders of eurobonds are able to sell them to would-be holders. The issue of eurobonds is usually made by placing them with large banks and other financial institutions, who may either retain them as an investment or sell them to the clients.

The extent of borrowing by UK businesses in currencies other than sterling, has expanded massively in recent years. In 1991 only 7 per cent of borrowings by the UK Stock Exchange listed companies was in non-sterling currencies. This increased at a fairly steady rate, such that in both 1997 and 1998 the proportion was over 50 per cent.

Activity 15.4

Why might a business prefer to issue eurobonds in preference to more conventional forms of loan capital?

Businesses are often attracted to eurobonds because of the size of the international capital market. Access to a large number of international investors is likely to increase the chances of a successful issue. In addition, the lack of regulation in the eurobond market means that national restrictions regarding loan issues may be overcome.

Interest rates and deep discount bonds

Interest rates on loan finance may be either 'floating' or fixed. A floating rate means that the required rate of return from lenders will rise and fall with market rates of interest. However, the market value of the lender's investment in the business is likely to remain fairly stable over time. The converse will normally be true for fixed-interest loans and debentures. The interest payments will remain unchanged with rises and falls in market rates of interest, but the value of the loan investment will fall when interest rates rise and will rise when interest rates fall.

A business may issue redeemable loan capital that offers a rate of interest below the market rate. In some cases, the loan capital may have a zero rate of interest. Such loans are issued at a discount to their redeemable value and are referred to as **deep discount bonds**. Thus loan capital may be issued at, say, £80 for every £100 of nominal value. Although lenders will receive little or no interest during the period of the loan, they will receive a gain when the loan is finally redeemed. The **redemption yield**, as it is referred to, is often quite high and, when calculated on an annual basis, may compare favourably with returns from other forms of loan capital with the same level of risk.

Deep discount bonds may have particular appeal to businesses with short-term cash-flow problems. They receive an immediate injection of cash, and there are no significant cash outflows associated with the loan until the maturity date. From an investment perspective, the situation is reversed. Deep discount bonds are likely to appeal to investors who do not have short-term cash flow needs, since they must wait for the loan to mature before receiving a significant return.

Convertible loan stocks

Convertible loan stocks give investors the right to convert a loan into ordinary shares at a given future date and at a specified price. The investor remains a lender to the business, and will receive interest on the amount of the loan until such time as the conversion takes place. The investor is not obliged to convert the loan (or debenture) to ordinary shares; this will be done only if the market price of the shares at the conversion date exceeds the agreed conversion price.

An investor may find **convertibles** a useful hedge against risk. This may be particularly useful when investment in a new business is being considered. Initially the investment is in the form of a loan, and regular interest payments will be made. If the business is successful the investor can then decide to convert the investment into ordinary shares. This form of security is an example of a **financial derivative**. This is any form of financial instrument, based on share or loan capital, that can be used by investors to increase their returns or reduce risk.

A business may also find this form of financing useful. If it is successful, the loan becomes self-liquidating as investors exercise their option to convert. The business may also be able to offer a lower rate of interest to investors because they expect future benefits arising from conversion. There will, however, be some dilution of both control and earnings for existing shareholders if holders of convertible loans exercise their option to convert.

Warrants

Holders of **warrants** have the right, but not the obligation, to acquire ordinary shares in a company at a given price. In the case of both convertible loan capital and warrants, the price at which shares may be acquired is usually higher than the market price prevailing at the time of issue. The warrant will usually state the number of shares that the holder may purchase and the time limit within which the option to buy shares can be exercised. Occasionally, perpetual warrants are issued that have no set time limits. Warrants do not confer voting rights or entitle the holders to make any claims on the assets of the business. They represent another form of financial derivative.

Share warrants are often provided as a 'sweetener' to accompany the issue of loan capital or debentures. The issue of warrants in this way may enable the business to offer lower rates of interest on the loan or to negotiate less restrictive loan conditions. The issue of warrants enables the lenders to benefit from future success of the business, provided that the option to purchase is exercised. However, an investor will exercise this right only if the market price exceeds the option price within the time limit specified. Share warrants may be 'detachable', which means that they can be sold separately from the loan capital.

| **Activity 15.5** | What will be the difference in status between holders of convertible loan capital and holders of loans with share warrants attached when they exercise their right to convert? |

The main difference will be that when holders of convertible loan capital exercise their option to convert, they become ordinary shareholders and are no longer lenders of the company. However, when lenders with warrants exercise their option to convert, they become ordinary shareholders, but remain lenders to the company.

When convertible loan capital holders exercise their option to convert, they swap their loan for shares. When warrant holders exercise their right to buy shares, they pay cash for those shares.

Mortgages

A **mortgage** is a form of loan that is secured on freehold property. Financial institutions such as banks, insurance companies and pension funds are often prepared to lend to businesses on this basis. The mortgage may be over a long period (20 years or more).

Loan covenants

When drawing up a loan agreement, the lender may impose certain obligations and restrictions in order to protect the investment in the business. **Loan covenants** (as they are called) often form part of a loan agreement, and may deal with such matters as:

- *Accounts.* The lender may require access to the financial accounts of the business on a regular basis.
- *Other loans.* The lender may require the business to ask the lender's permission before taking on further loans from other sources.
- *Dividend payments.* The lender may require dividends to be limited during the period of the loan.

● *Liquidity.* The lender may require the business to maintain a certain level of liquidity during the period of the loan. This would typically be a requirement that the borrower business's current ratio was maintained at, or above, a specified level.

Any breach of these restrictive covenants can have serious consequences for the business. The lender may require immediate repayment of the loan in the event of a material breach.

Ordinary shares, preference shares and loans compared

Figure 15.2 plots the issues of capital made by UK-listed businesses. The chart reveals that loan capital and ordinary shares are the major sources of long-term external finance. Preference shares are a much less important source of new finance.`

Figure 15.2

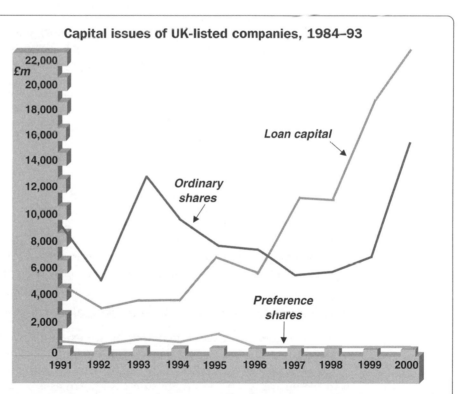

At times, the popularity of ordinary shares and that of loan capital seems broadly to move counter to one another: when ordinary shares are popular, loan capital is unpopular, and vice versa. This tends to reflect the level of interest rates and business confidence. However, in recent years, ordinary share issues and loan capital issues have both moved in the same direction. Preference share issues have dwindled to almost nothing.

The chart shown is not, of course, the whole story. Most equity comes from profit retentions rather than share issues.

Source: Office for National Statistics (see reference (1) at the end of the chapter).

| Activity 15.6 | Both preference shares and loan capital are forms of finance that require a business to provide a particular rate of return to investors. What are the factors that may be taken into account by a business when deciding between these two sources of finance?

The main factors are as follows:

- Preference shares have a higher rate of return than loan capital. From the investor's point of view, preference shares are more risky. The amount invested cannot be secured, and the return is paid after the returns paid to lenders.
- A business has a legal obligation to pay interest and make capital repayments on loans at the agreed dates. It will usually make every effort to meet its obligations, because failure to do so can have serious consequences. (These consequences have been mentioned earlier.) Failure to pay a preference dividend, on the other hand, is less important. There is no legal obligation to pay if profits are not available for distribution. Though failure to pay a preference dividend may, prove an embarrassment for the business, and may make it difficult for it to persuade investors to take up future preference share issues, the preference shareholders will have no redress if there are insufficient profits to pay the dividend due.
- It was mentioned above that the taxation system in the UK permits interest on loans to be allowable against profits for taxation, whereas preference dividends are not. As a result, the cost of servicing loan capital is usually much less for a business than the cost of servicing preference shares.
- The issue of loan capital may result in the management of a business having to accept some restrictions on freedom of action. We saw above that loan agreements often contain covenants that can be onerous. However, no such restrictions can be imposed by preference shareholders.

A further point that has not been dealt with so far is that preference shares issued form part of the permanent capital base of the company. If they are redeemed, the law requires that they are replaced, either by a new issue of shares or by a transfer from reserves, to ensure that the capital base of the company stays intact. Loan capital, however, is not viewed, in law, as part of the permanent capital base of the company, and therefore there is no legal requirement to replace any loan capital that has been redeemed by the company.

Finance leases and sale-and-leaseback arrangements

When a business needs a particular asset (for example, an item of plant), instead of buying it direct from a supplier, the business may decide to arrange for another business (typically a financial institution such as a bank) to buy it and then lease it to the business. The leasing business is known as a 'lessor'.

A **finance lease**, as such an arrangement is known, is in essence a form of lending. Though legal ownership of the asset rests with the lessor, a finance lease agreement transfers to the user (the lessee) virtually all the rewards and risks that are associated with the item being leased. The finance lease agreement covers a significant part of the life of the item being leased, and often cannot be cancelled.

A finance lease can be contrasted to an **operating lease**, where the rewards and risks of ownership stay with the owner and where the lease is short-term in nature. An example of an operating lease is where a builder hires some earth-moving equipment for a week to carry out a particular job.

In recent years, some important benefits associated with finance leasing have disappeared. Changes in UK tax law no longer make it such a tax-efficient form of financing, and changes in accounting disclosure requirements make it no longer possible to conceal this form of 'borrowing' from investors. Nevertheless, the popularity of finance leases has continued to increase. Other reasons must therefore exist for businesses to adopt this form of financing. These reasons are said to include the following:

- *Ease of borrowing.* Leasing may be obtained more easily than other forms of long-term finance. Lenders normally require some form of security and a profitable track record before making advances to a business. However, a lessor may be prepared to lease assets to a new business without a track record, and to use the leased assets as security for the amounts owing.
- *Cost.* Leasing agreements may be offered at reasonable cost. As the asset leased is used as security, standard lease arrangements can be applied and detailed credit checking of lessees may be unnecessary. This can reduce administrative costs for the lessor and thereby help in providing competitive lease rentals.
- *Flexibility.* Leasing can help provide flexibility where there are rapid changes in technology. If an option to cancel can be incorporated into the lease, the business may be able to exercise this option and invest in new technology as it becomes available. This will help the business to avoid the risk of obsolescence.
- *Cash flows.* Leasing, rather than purchasing an asset outright, means that large cash outflows can be avoided. The leasing option allows cash outflows to be smoothed out over the asset's life. In some cases, it is possible to arrange for low lease payments to be made in the early years of the asset's life, when cash inflows may be low, and for these to increase over time as the asset generates positive cash flows.

Exhibit 15.1 provides an example of two businesses, one that acts as a financial lessor and the other as a lessee.

Exhibit 15.1

Both sides of leasing in the aviation industry

British Airways plc (BA) uses finance leasing to fund some of its assets, according to its 2000 annual report. Of the net increase of 31 in the business's fleet of aircraft during the year ended 31 March 2000, 10 were acquired through finance leasing. Moreover, 17.3 per cent of BA's tangible assets at 31 March 2000 were financed through finance leases.

Though, typically, finance lessors tend to be financial institutions, according to Rolls-Royce plc's 1999 annual report, 6.2 per cent of the balance sheet value of the business's tangible assets at 31 December 1999 were aircraft engines leased to other businesses.

A **sale and leaseback** arrangement involves a business selling an asset to a financial institution in order to raise finance. The sale is accompanied by an agreement to lease the asset back to the business to allow it to continue to use the asset. The payment under the lease arrangement is allowable against profits for taxation purposes.

Freehold property is often the asset that is the subject of such an arrangement. When that is the case, there are usually rent reviews at regular intervals through-out the period of the lease, and the amounts payable in future years may be difficult to predict. At the end of the lease agreement, the business must either try to renew the lease or find an alternative asset. Although the sale of the premises will result in an immediate injection of cash for the business, it will lose benefits from any future capital appreciation on the asset. Where a capital gain arises on the sale of the asset to the financial institution, a liability for taxation may also arise.

Exhibit 15.2 gives an example of a well-known business that uses sale and leaseback as a source of finance.

Exhibit 15.2

Sale and leaseback at Sainsbury's

During the year to 1 April 2000, J. Sainsbury plc, the supermarket business, sold, with leaseback arrangements, 16 stores for a total of £325 million, according to its 2000 annual report. To put this into perspective, it represented an amount equivalent to 5.4 per cent of the business's investment in properties, at balance sheet value, at 1 April 2000.

●●●● Gearing and the long-term financing decision

In Chapter 7 we saw that gearing occurs when a business is financed, at least in part, by contributions from fixed-charge capital such as loans, debentures and preference shares. We also saw that the level of gearing associated with a business is often an important factor in assessing the risk and returns to ordinary share-holders. In the example that follows, we consider the implications of making a choice between a geared and an ungeared form of raising long-term finance.

Example 15.1

The following are the summarised accounts of Woodhall Engineers plc:

Woodhall Engineers plc
Profit and loss account year ended 31 December

	2000	2001
	£m	£m
Turnover	47	50
Operating costs	(41)	(47)
Operating profit	6	3
Interest payable	(2)	(2)
Profit on ordinary activities before tax	4	1
Taxation on profit on ordinary activities	–	–
Profit on ordinary activities after tax	4	1
Dividends	(1)	(1)
Profit retained for the financial year	3	–

Balance sheet at 31 December

	2000 £m	2001 £m
Fixed assets (less depreciation)	21	20
Current assets		
Stocks	10	18
Debtors	16	17
Cash at bank	3	1
	29	36
Creditors: amounts falling due within one year		
Short-term debt	(5)	(11)
Trade creditors	(10)	(10)
	(15)	(21)
Total assets less current liabilities	35	35
Less Long-term loans (secured)	15	15
	20	20
Capital and reserves		
Called-up share capital 25p ordinary shares	16	16
Profit and loss account	4	4
	20	20

The business is making plans to expand its premises. New plant will cost £8 million, and an expansion in output will increase working capital by £4 million. Over the 15 years' life of the project, incremental profits arising from the expansion will be £2 million per year before interest and tax. In addition, 2002's profits before interest and tax from its existing activities are expected to return to 2000 levels.

Two possible methods of financing the expansion have been discussed by Woodhall's directors. The first is the issue of £12 million 15-per-cent debt repayable in year 2012. The second is a rights issue of 40 million 25p ordinary shares, which will give the business 30p per share after expenses.

The business has substantial tax losses, which can be offset against future profits, so you can ignore taxation in your calculations. The 2002 dividend per share is expected to be the same as that for 2001.

Prepare a forecast of Woodhall's profit and loss account (excluding turnover and operating costs) for the year ended 31 December 2002, and of its capital and reserves, long-term loans and number of shares outstanding at that date, assuming (a) the business issues debt and (b) the business issues ordinary shares. The forecast profit and loss account will be as follows:

Forecast profit and loss account for the year ended 31 December 2002

	(a) Debt issue £m	(b) Equity issue £m
Profit before interest and taxation (6.0 + 2.0)	8.0	8.0
Loan interest	(3.8)	(2.0)
Profit before tax	4.2	6.0
Taxation	–	–
Profit after tax	4.2	6.0
Dividends (net)	(1.0)	(1.6)
Retained profit for the year	3.2	4.4

The capital structure of the business under each option will be as follows:

	(a) Debt issue £m	(b) Equity issue £m
Capital and reserves		
Share capital 25p ordinary shares	16.0	26.0
Share premium account[a]	–	2.0
Retained profit	7.2	8.4
	23.2	36.4
Number of shares in issue (25p shares)	64 million	104 million

[a]This represents the amount received from the issue of shares that is above the nominal value of the shares. The amount is calculated as follows:

$$40 \text{ million shares} \times (30p - 25p) = £2 \text{ million.}$$

Activity 15.7

Compute the interest cover and earnings per share for Woodhall (see Example 15.1) for the year ended 31 December 2002 and its gearing on that date, assuming:

(a) The business issues debt,
(b) The business issues ordinary shares.

....

	(a) Debt issue	(b) Equity issue
Interest cover ratio		
$\dfrac{\text{Profit before interest and tax}}{\text{Interest payable}}$	$\dfrac{(4.2+3.8)}{3.8}$	$\dfrac{(6.0+2.0)}{2.0}$
	= 2.1 times	= 4.0 times
Earnings per share		
$\dfrac{\text{Earnings available to equity}}{\text{Number of ordinary shares}}$	$\dfrac{£4.2m}{64m}$	$\dfrac{£6.0m}{104m}$
	= 6.6p	= 5.8p
Gearing ratio		
$\dfrac{\text{Long-term liabilities}}{\text{Share capital + Reserves + Long-term liabilities}}$	$\dfrac{£27m}{£23.2m + £27m}$	$\dfrac{£15m}{£36.4m + £15m}$
	= 53.8%	= 29.2%

Activity 15.8

What would your views of the proposed schemes be in each of the following circumstances?

(a) If you were a banker and you were approached for a loan.
(b) If you were an equity investor in Woodhall and you were asked to subscribe to a rights issue.

....

A banker may be unenthusiastic about lending the business funds. The gearing ratio of 53.8 per cent (see Activity 15.7) is rather high and would leave the bank in an exposed position. The existing loan is already secured on assets held by the business, and it is not clear whether the business is in a position to offer an attractive form of security for the new loan. The interest cover ratio of 2.1 (see Activity 15.7 again) is also rather low. If the business is unable to achieve the expected returns from the new project, or if it is unable to restore profits from the remainder of its operations to 2000 levels, this ratio would be even lower.

Equity investors might need some convincing that it would be worthwhile to make further investments in the business. The return to equity for shareholders in 2000 was 20 per cent. The incremental profit from the new project is £2 million and the investment required is £12 million, which represents a return of 16.7 per cent. Thus, the returns from the project are expected to be lower than for existing operations. In making their decision, investors should discover whether the new investment is of a similar level of risk to their existing investment and how the returns from the investment compare with those available from other opportunities with similar levels of risk.

Short-term sources of finance

A short-term source of borrowing is one that is available for a short time period. Although there is no agreed definition of what 'short term' means, we shall define it as being up to one year. The major sources of short-term borrowing are:

- Basic overdrafts
- Debt factoring
- Invoice discounting.

Each is discussed further below.

Bank overdrafts

Bank overdrafts represent a very flexible form of borrowing. The size of an overdraft can (subject to bank approval) be increased or decreased according to the financing requirements of the business. It is relatively inexpensive to arrange, and interest rates are often very competitive. The rate of interest charged on an overdraft will vary, however, according to how creditworthy the customer is perceived to be by the bank. It is also fairly easy to arrange – sometimes an overdraft can be agreed by a telephone call to the bank. In view of these advantages, it is not surprising that this is an extremely popular form of short-term financing.

Banks prefer to grant overdrafts that are self-liquidating: that is, the funds applied will result in cash inflows that will extinguish the overdraft balance. The banks may ask for forecast cash-flow statements from the business to see when the overdraft will be repaid and how much finance is required. The bank may also require some form of security on amounts advanced.

One potential drawback with this form of finance is that it is repayable on demand. This may pose problems for a business that is illiquid. However, many businesses operate using an overdraft, and this form of borrowing, although in theory regarded as short term, can often become a long-term source of finance.

Debt factoring

Debt factoring is a service offered by a financial institution (known as a **factor**).

Many of the large factors are subsidiaries of commercial banks. Debt factoring involves the factor taking over the debt collection for a business. In addition to operating normal credit-control procedures, a factor may offer to undertake credit investigations and to provide protection for approved credit sales. The factor is usually prepared to make an advance to the business of a maximum of 85 per cent of approved trade debtors. The charge made for the factoring service is based on total turnover, and is often 2–3 per cent of turnover. Any advances made to the business by the factor will attract a rate of interest similar to the rate charged on bank overdrafts.

A business may find a factoring arrangement very convenient. It can result in savings in credit management and can create more certain cash flows. It can also release the time of key personnel for more profitable ends. This may be extremely important for smaller businesses that rely on the talent and skills of a few key individuals. However, there is a possibility that some will see a factoring arrangement as an indication that the business is experiencing financial difficulties. This may have an adverse effect on confidence in the business. For this reason, some businesses try to conceal the factoring arrangement by collecting debts on behalf of the factor.

When considering a factoring agreement, the costs and likely benefits arising must be identified and carefully weighed.

Example 15.2

Mayo Computers Ltd has an annual turnover of £20 million before taking into account bad debts of £0.1 million. All sales made by the business are on credit and, at present, credit terms are negotiable by the customer. On average, the settlement period for trade debtors is 60 days. The business is currently reviewing its credit policies to see whether more efficient and profitable methods could be used.

The business is considering whether it should factor its trade debts. The accounts department has recently approached a factoring business, which has agreed to provide an advance equivalent to 80 per cent of trade debtors (where the trade debtors figure is based on an average settlement period of 40 days) at an interest rate of 12 per cent. The factoring business will undertake collection of the trade debts and will charge a fee of 2 per cent of sales turnover for this service. The factoring service is also expected to eliminate bad debts and will lead to credit administration savings of £90,000. The settlement period for trade debtors will be reduced to an average of 40 days, which is equivalent to that of the company's major competitors.

The business currently has an overdraft of £4.8 million at an interest rate of 14 per cent a year. The bank has recently written to the business stating that it would like to see a reduction in this overdraft.

In any evaluation of the factoring arrangement, it is useful to begin by considering the cost of the existing arrangements:

Existing arrangements

	£000
Bad debts written off each year	100
Interest cost of average debtors outstanding [(£20m × 60/365) × 14%]	460
Total cost	560

The cost of the factoring arrangement can now be compared with the above:

Factoring arrangement

	£000
Factoring fee (£20m × 2%)	400
Interest on factor loan (assuming 80% advance and reduction in average credit period) [(£16m × 40/365) × 12%]	210
Interest on overdraft (remaining 20% of debtors financed in this way) [(£4m × 40/365) × 14%]	61
	671
Less Savings in credit administration	90
Cost of factoring	581

The above calculations show that the net additional cost of factoring for the business would be £21,000 (£581,000 − £560,000).

Invoice discounting

➡ **Invoice discounting** involves a business approaching a factor or other financial institution for a loan based on a proportion of the face value of credit sales outstanding. If the institution agrees, the amount advanced is usually 75–80 per cent of the value of the approved sales invoices outstanding. The business must agree to repay the advance within a relatively short period, perhaps 60 or 90 days. The responsibility for collection of the trade debts outstanding remains with the business, and repayment of the advance is not dependent on the trade debt being collected. Invoice discounting will not result in such a close relationship developing between the client and the financial institution as factoring. It may be a one-off arrangement whereas debt factoring usually involves a longer-term relationship between the customer and the financial institution.

Invoice discounting is a much more important source of funds than factoring. There are various reasons why invoice discounting is a more attractive source of raising finance. Firstly, it is a confidential form of financing that the client's customers will know nothing about. Secondly, the service charge for invoice discounting is generally only 0.2 to 0.3 per cent of turnover, compared with 2.0 to 3.0 per cent for factoring. Finally, many companies are unwilling to relinquish control of their customer records; customers are an important resource of the business, and many businesses wish to retain control over all aspects of their relationship with their customers.

● ● ● ● Long-term versus short-term borrowing

Having decided that some form of borrowing is required to finance the business, managers must then decide whether it should be long-term or short-term in form. There are many issues that should be taken into account when making this decision, including:

- *Matching.* The business may attempt to match the type of borrowing with the nature of the assets held. Thus, assets that form part of the permanent operating base of the business, including fixed assets and a certain level of current assets, will be financed by long-term borrowing. Assets held for a short period, such as current assets held to meet seasonal increases in demand, will be financed by short-term borrowing. (See Figure 15.3).

A business may wish to match the asset life exactly with the period of the related loan, however, this may not be possible because of the difficulty of predicting the life of many assets.

Figure 15.3

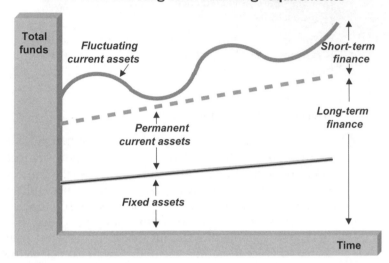

Short-term and long-term financing requirements

The broad consensus on financing seems to be that all of the permanent financial needs of the business should come from long-term sources. Only that part of current assets that fluctuates on a short-term, probably seasonal, basis should be financed from short-term sources.

Activity 15.9

Some businesses may take up a less cautious financing position than shown in Figure 15.3, and others may take up a more cautious one. How would the diagram differ under each of these options?

....

A less cautious position would mean relying on short-term finance to help fund part of the permanent capital base. A more cautious position would mean relying on long-term finance to help finance the fluctuating assets of the business.

● *Flexibility.* Short-term borrowing may be a useful means of postponing a commitment to taking on a long-term loan. This may be seen as desirable if interest rates are high and it is forecast that they will fall in the future. Short-term borrowing does not usually incur penalties if there is early repayment of the amount outstanding, whereas some form of financial penalty may arise if long-term debt is repaid early.
● *Refunding risk.* Short-term borrowing has to be renewed more frequently than long-term borrowing. This may create problems for the business if it is already in financial difficulties, or if there is a shortage of funds available for lending.

- *Interest rates.* Interest payable on long-term debt is often higher than for short-term debt. (This is because lenders require a higher return where their funds are locked up for a long period.) This fact may make short-term borrowing a more attractive source of finance for a business. However, there may be other costs associated with borrowing (arrangement fees, for example) to be taken into account. The more frequently borrowings must be renewed, the higher these costs will be.

Internal sources of finance

In addition to external sources of finance, there are certain internal sources that a business may use to generate funds for particular activities. These sources usually have the advantage that they are flexible. They may also be obtained quickly – particularly from working capital sources – and need not require the permission of other parties. The main sources of internal funds are described below, and are summarised in Figure 15.4.

Figure 15.4

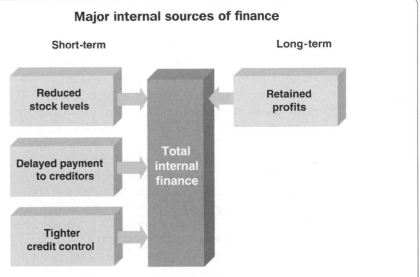

Major internal sources of finance

The figure shows that the major long-term source of internal finance is the profits which are retained rather than distributed to shareholders. The major short-term sources of internal finance involve reducing the levels of debtors and stocks and increasing the level of creditors.

Retained profits

Retained profits are the major source of finance for most businesses. By retaining profits rather than distributing them to shareholders in the form of dividends, the funds of the business are increased.

Are retained profits a free source of finance to the business?

It is tempting to think that retained profits are a 'cost-free' source of funds. However, this is not the case. If profits are reinvested rather than distributed to shareholders, this means that the shareholders cannot invest the profits made, in other forms of investment. They will therefore expect a rate of return from the profits reinvested that is equivalent to what they would have received had the funds been invested in another opportunity with the same level of risk.

The reinvestment of profits rather than the issue of new ordinary shares can be a useful way of raising equity capital. There are no issue costs associated with retaining profits, and the amount raised is certain, once the profit has been made. When issuing new shares, the issue costs may be substantial, and there may be uncertainty over the success of the issue. Retaining profits will have no effect on the control of the business by existing shareholders, whereas new shares are issued to outside investors, and there will be some dilution of control.

The retention of profits is something that is determined by the directors of a business. They may find it easier simply to retain profits rather than ask investors to subscribe to a new share issue. Retained profits are already held by the business, and so it does not have to wait to receive the funds. Moreover, there is often less scrutiny when profits are being retained for reinvestment purposes than when new shares are being issued. Investors and their advisers will examine closely the reasons for any new share issue.

A problem with the use of profits as a source of finance, however, is that the timing and level of profits in the future cannot always be reliably determined.

Some shareholders may prefer profits to be retained by the business, rather than be distributed in the form of dividends. By ploughing back profits, it may be expected that the company will expand, and that share values will increase as a result. In the UK, not all capital gains are liable for taxation. (For the fiscal year 2001/2002, an individual with capital gains totalling less than £7,500 would not be taxed on those gains.) A further advantage of capital gains over dividends is that the shareholder has a choice as to when the gain is realised. Research indicates that investors are often attracted to particular businesses according to the dividend/retention policies that they adopt.

Tighter credit control

If a business has a proportion of its assets in the form of debtors, there is an opportunity cost because the funds are tied up and cannot be used for more profitable opportunities. By exerting tighter control over trade debtors it may be possible for a business to reduce the proportion of assets held in this form and thereby to release funds for other purposes. It is important, however, to weigh the benefits of tighter credit control against the likely costs in the form of lost customer goodwill and lost sales. To remain competitive, a business must take account of the needs of its customers and the credit policies adopted by rival companies within the industry.

H. Rusli Ltd produces a single product which is used in a variety of electronic devices. Details of the product are as follows:

	per unit	
	£	£
Selling price		20
Less Variable costs	14	
Fixed costs	4	(18)
Net profit		2

Sales are £10 million a year and are all on credit. The average credit period taken by customers is 45 days, although the terms of credit require payment within 30 days. Bad debts are currently £100,000 a year. Debtors are financed by a bank overdraft costing 15 per cent a year.

The credit control department believes it can eliminate bad debts and can reduce the average credit period to 30 days if new control procedures are implemented. These will cost £50,000 per year and are likely to result in a reduction in sales of 5 per cent per year.

Should the company implement the new credit control procedures? *Hint*: in order to answer this activity, it is useful to compare the current cost of trade credit with the costs under the proposed approach.

The current annual cost of trade credit is:

	£
Bad debts	100,000
Overdraft [(£10m × 45/365) × 15%]	184,931
	284,931

The annual cost of trade credit under the new policy will be:

	£
Overdraft [((95% × 10m) × (30/365)) × 15%]	117,123
Cost of control procedures	50,000
Net cost of lost sales [((£10m/£20) × 5%) × (20 − 14[a])]	150,000
	317,123

The above figures reveal that the business will be worse off if the new procedures are adopted.

[a] The loss will be the contribution per unit – that is, the difference between the selling price and the variable costs.

Reducing stock levels

This is an internal source of funds that may prove attractive to a business. As with debtors, holding stocks imposes an opportunity cost on a business. By the holding of less stock, funds become available for other purposes. However, a business must ensure that there are sufficient stocks available to meet likely future sales demand. Failure to do so will likely result in lost customer goodwill and lost sales.

The nature and condition of the stock held will determine whether it is possible to exploit this form of finance. A business may be overstocked as a result of poor buying decisions in the past. This may mean that a significant proportion of stocks held are slow-moving or obsolete, and cannot therefore be reduced easily.

Delaying payment to creditors

By delaying payment to creditors, funds are retained within the business for other purposes. This may be a cheap form of finance for a business. However, there may be significant costs associated with it. For example, the business may find it difficult to buy on credit where it is a slow payer.

Self-assessment question 15.1

Helsim Ltd is a wholesaler and distributor of electrical components. The most recent financial statements of the company revealed the following:

Profit and loss account for the year ended 31 May

	£m	£m
Sales		14.2
Opening stock	3.2	
Purchases	8.4	
	11.6	
Closing stock	(3.8)	(7.8)
Gross profit		6.4
Administration expenses	(3.0)	
Selling and distribution expenses	(2.1)	
Finance charges	(0.8)	(5.9)
Net profit before taxation		0.5
Corporation tax		(0.2)
Net profit after taxation		0.3

Balance sheet as at 31 May

	£m	£m	£m
Fixed assets			
Land and buildings			3.8
Equipment			0.9
Motor vehicles			0.5
			5.2
Current assets			
Stock		3.8	
Trade debtors		3.6	
Cash at bank		0.1	
		7.5	
Less **Creditors: amounts falling due within one year**			
Trade creditors	1.8		
Bank overdraft	3.6	5.4	2.1
			7.3

Creditors: amounts falling due after one year	
Debentures (secured on freehold land)	(3.5)
	3.8
Capital and reserves	
Ordinary £1 shares	2.0
Profit and loss account	1.8
	3.8

Notes:

1 Land and buildings are shown at their current market value. Equipment and motor vehicles are shown at their written-down values.
2 No dividends have been paid to ordinary shareholders for the past three years.

In recent months, trade creditors have been pressing for payment. The managing director has therefore decided to reduce the level of trade creditors to an average of 40 days outstanding. To achieve this, he has decided to approach the bank with a view to increasing the business's overdraft. The business is currently paying 12 per cent interest on the overdraft.

Required:
(a) Comment on the liquidity position of the business.
(b) Calculate the amount of finance required in order to reduce trade creditors as shown on the balance sheet, to an average of 40 days outstanding.
(c) State, with reasons, how you consider the bank would react to the proposal to grant an additional overdraft facility.
(d) Evaluate four sources of finance (internal or external, but excluding a bank overdraft) that may be used to finance the reduction in trade creditors, and state, with reasons, which of these you consider the most appropriate.

The role of the Stock Exchange

Earlier we considered the various forms of long-term capital that are available to a business. In this section, we examine the role that the **Stock Exchange** plays in the provision of finance for business. The Stock Exchange acts as an important primary and secondary market in capital for businesses. As a primary market, its function is to enable businesses to raise new capital; as a secondary market, its function is to enable investors to sell their securities (that is, shares and loan capital) with ease. Thus, it provides a 'second-hand' market where shares and loan capital already in issue may be bought and sold.

In order to issue shares or loan capital through the Stock Exchange, a business must be 'listed' with it. This means that it must meet fairly stringent Stock-Exchange requirements concerning size, profit history, disclosure, and so on. Some share issues on the Stock Exchange arise from the initial listing of the business. Other share issues are undertaken by businesses that have already made a share issue and that are seeking additional finance from investors.

The secondary-market role of the Stock Exchange means that shares and other financial claims are easily transferable. This can bring real benefits to a business, because investors may be more prepared to invest if they know their investment can be easily liquidated whenever required. It is important to recognise, however, that investors are not obliged to use the Stock Exchange as the means of transferring shares in a listed business. Nevertheless, it is usually the most convenient way of buying or selling shares. Prices of shares and other financial claims are usually determined by the market in an efficient manner, which should also give investors greater confidence to purchase shares. The business may benefit from this greater investor confidence by finding it easier to raise long-term finance and by obtaining this finance at a lower cost, as investors will view their investment as being less risky.

A Stock Exchange listing can, however, have certain disadvantages for a business. The Stock Exchange imposes strict rules on listed businesses, including requiring additional levels of financial disclosure to those already imposed by law and by the accounting profession – for example, half-yearly financial reports must be published. The activities of listed businesses are closely monitored by financial analysts, financial journalists and others, and such scrutiny may not be welcome, particularly if the business is dealing with sensitive issues or is experiencing operational problems.

It is often suggested that listed businesses are under pressure to perform well over the short term. This pressure may detract from undertaking projects that will only yield benefits in the longer term. If the market becomes disenchanted with the business, and the price of its shares falls, this may make it vulnerable to a takeover bid from another business.

Venture capital and long-term financing

Venture capital is long-term capital provided by certain institutions to help businesses exploit profitable opportunities. The businesses of interest to the venture capitalist will have higher levels of risk than would normally be acceptable to traditional providers of finance, such as the major clearing banks. Venture capital providers may be interested in a variety of businesses, including:

- Business start-ups
- Acquisitions of existing businesses by a group of managers
- Providing additional capital to young, expanding businesses
- The buy-out of one of the owners from an existing business.

The risks associated with the business can vary in practice, but they are often due to the nature of the products or the fact that it is a new business that either lacks a trading record or has new management. Although the risks are higher, the businesses also have potentially higher levels of return – hence their attraction to the venture capitalist. The types of business helped by venture capitalists are normally small or medium-sized, rather than large companies listed on the Stock Exchange.

The venture capitalist will often make a substantial investment in the business, and this will normally take the form of ordinary shares. In order to keep an eye on the sum invested, the venture capitalist will usually require a representative on the board of directors as a condition of the investment. The venture capitalist may not be looking for a quick return, and may well be prepared to invest in a business for five years or more. The return may take the form of a capital gain on the realisation of the investment.

Exhibit 15.3 gives some impression of the importance of venture capital in the UK in recent years.

Activity 15.12

When assessing prospective investment opportunities, what kind of non-financial matters do you think a venture capitalist will be concerned with?

The venture capitalist will be concerned with such matters as the quality of management, the personal stake or commitment made by the owners to the business, the quality and nature of the product, and the plans made to exploit the business opportunities, as well as financial matters.

When examining prospective investment opportunities, the venture capitalist will consider not only all financial aspects and the non-financial aspects listed in Activity 15.12, but also the identification of a clear exit route when the time comes to liquidate the investment.

● ● ● ● Share issues

A business may issues shares in a number of different ways. These may involve direct appeals to investors, or the use of financial intermediaries. The most common methods of share issues are as follows:

- Rights issues
- Bonus issues
- Offers for sale
- Public issues
- Private placings.

Each of these is considered in turn below.

Rights issues

A business may offer existing shareholders the right to acquire new shares in exchange for cash. The new shares will be allocated to shareholders in proportion to their existing shareholdings. To make the issue appear attractive to shareholders, the new shares are often offered at a price significantly below the market value of existing shares.

→ **Rights issues** are now the most common form of share issue. It is a relatively cheap and straightforward way of issuing shares. Expenses are quite low, and procedures are simple. The fact that those offered new shares already have an investment in the business, which presumably suits their risk/return requirements, is likely to increase the chance of the issue being successful.

The law requires that shares to be issued for cash are offered first to existing shareholders. The advantage of this requirement is that control of the business by existing shareholders will not be diluted, provided that they take up the rights offer. A rights offer allows existing shareholders to acquire shares at a price below the current market price. This does not mean that entitlement to participate in a rights offer is a source of value to existing shareholders, however. Provided that shareholders either take up their rights and buy the new shares or sell the rights to someone else who will, they will be neither better nor worse off as a result of the rights issue. Calculating the value of the rights offer received by shareholders is quite straightforward, as shown by Example 15.3.

Example 15.3

Shaw plc has 20 million ordinary shares of 50p in issue. These shares are currently valued on the Stock Exchange at £1.60 per share. The directors of Shaw believe the business requires additional long-term capital, and they have decided to make a one-for-four issue (that is, one new share for every four shares held) at £1.30 per share.

The first step in the valuation process is to calculate the price of a share following the rights issue. This is known as the **ex-rights price** and is simply a weighted average of the price of shares before the issue of rights and the price of the rights shares. In the above example, we have a one-for-four rights issue. The theoretical ex-rights price is therefore calculated as follows:

	£
Price of four shares before the rights issue (4 × £1.60)	6.40
Price of taking up one rights share	1.30
	7.70

$$\text{Theoretical ex-rights price} = \frac{7.70}{5}$$
$$= \underline{£1.54}$$

As the price of each share, in theory, should be £1.54 following the rights issue and the price of a rights share is £1.30, the value of the rights offer will be the difference between the two:

$$£1.54 - £1.30 = £0.24 \text{ per share}$$

Market forces will usually ensure that the actual and theoretical prices of rights issues will be fairly close.

Activity 15.13

An investor with 2,000 shares in Shaw plc (see Example 15.3) has contacted you for investment advice. She is undecided whether to take up the rights issue, sell the rights, or allow the rights offer to lapse.

When considering a rights issue, the directors must first consider the amount of funds that it needs to raise. This will depend on the future plans and commitments of the company. The directors must then decide on the issue price of the rights shares. Generally speaking, this decision is not of critical importance. In Example 15.3, the business made a one-for-four issue with the price of the rights shares set at £1.30. However, it could have raised the same amount by making a one-for-two issue and setting the rights price at £0.65, a one-for-one issue and setting the price at £0.325, and so on. The issue price that is finally decided upon will not affect the value of the underlying assets of the business or the proportion of its underlying assets and earnings to which the shareholder is entitled. The directors must, however, ensure that the issue price is not *above* the current market price of the shares, or the issue will be unsuccessful.

Activity 15.14

Why will a rights issue fail if the issue price of the shares is above the current market price of the shares?

⋯⋯⋯

If the issue price is above the current market price, it would be cheaper for the investor to purchase shares in the open market (ignoring transaction costs) than to acquire the shares by taking up the rights offer.

Despite the attractions of rights issues, it can be argued that the rights given to existing shareholders will prevent greater competition for new shares in the business. This may, in turn, increase the costs of raising finance for the business, because other forms of share issue may raise the required amount of finance more cheaply.

Bonus issues

➡️ A **bonus issue** should not be confused with a rights issue of shares. A bonus, or **scrip**, issue also involves the issue of new shares to existing shareholders in proportion to their existing shareholdings. However, shareholders do not have to pay for the new shares issued. The bonus issue is achieved by transferring a sum from the reserves to the paid-up share capital of the business and then issuing shares, equivalent in value to the amount transferred, to existing shareholders. As the reserves are already owned by the shareholders, they do not have to pay for the shares issued. In effect, a bonus issue will simply convert reserves into paid-up capital. To understand this conversion process, and its effect on the financial position of the company, let us consider Example 15.4.

Example 15.4

Wickham plc has the following abbreviated balance sheet as at 31 March 2001:

	£m
Net assets	20
Financed by	
Share capital (£1 ordinary shares)	10
Reserves	10
	20

The directors decide to convert £5 million of the reserves to paid-up capital. As a result, a one-for-two bonus issue must be made. Following the bonus issue, the balance sheet of Wickham plc will be as follows:

	£m
Net assets	20
Financed by	
Share capital (£1 ordinary shares)	15
Reserves	5
	20

Activity 15.15

Are the shareholders in Wickham plc (see Example 15.4) better off as a result of receiving bonus shares?

We can see that the share capital of the business has increased, and there has been a corresponding decrease in the reserves. The net assets remain unchanged by the bonus issue.

Although each shareholder will own more shares following the bonus issue, the proportion held of the total number of shares in issue will remain unchanged, and so the stake in the net assets will remain unchanged. Thus bonus issues do not, of themselves, result in an increase in shareholder wealth. They will simply switch part of the owners' claim from reserves to share capital.

Assume that the market price per share in Wickham plc (see Example 15.4) before the bonus issue was £2.10. What will be the market price per share following the share issue?

The business has made a one-for-two issue. A holder of two shares would therefore be in the following position before the bonus issue:

Two shares held at £2.10 market price   £4.20

Since the wealth of the shareholder has not increased as a result of the issue, the total value of the shareholding will remain the same. This means that, as the shareholder holds one more share following the issue, the market value per share will now be:

$$\frac{£4.20}{3} = £1.40$$

You may wonder, from the calculations above, why bonus issues are made, particularly as the effect of a bonus issue may be to reduce the reserves available for dividend payments. A number of reasons has been put forward to explain this type of share issue:

- *Share price.* The share price of a company may be very high, and, as a result, its share may become more difficult to trade on the Stock Exchange. It seems that shares that trade within a certain price range generate more interest and activity in the market. By increasing the number of shares in issue, the market value of each share will be reduced, which may have the effect of making the shares more marketable.
- *Lender confidence.* The effect of making a transfer from distributable reserves to paid-up share capital will be to increase the permanent capital base of the business. This move may increase confidence among lenders. In effect, a bonus issue will reduce the risk of the business reducing its equity capital through dividend distributions, thereby leaving lenders in an exposed position.
- *Market signals.* The directors may use a bonus issue as an opportunity to signal to investors their confidence in the future prospects of the business. The issue may be accompanied by the announcement of good news concerning the business (for example, securing a large contract or achieving an increase in profits). Under these circumstances, the share price may rise in the expectation that earnings/dividends per share will be maintained. Shareholders would therefore be better off following the issue. However, it is the *information content* of the bonus issue, rather than the issue itself, that will create this increase in wealth.

Offers for sale

An **offer for sale** involves a business, trading in the form of a public limited company, selling a new issue of shares to a financial institution known as an issuing house. However, shares that are already in issue may also be sold to an issuing house. In this case, existing shareholders agree to sell their shares to the issuing house. The issuing house will, in turn, sell the shares purchased from either the business or its shareholders to the public. The issuing house will publish a prospectus that sets out details of the business and the type of shares to be sold, and investors will be invited to apply for shares.

The advantage of this type of issue, from the business viewpoint, is that the sale proceeds of the shares are certain. The issuing house will take on the risk of selling the shares to investors. This type of issue is often used when a business seeks a listing on the Stock Exchange and wishes to raise a large amount of funds.

Public issue

➡ A **public issue** involves a business making a direct invitation to the public to purchase its shares. Typically, this is done through a newspaper advertisement. The shares may, once again, be a new issue or shares already in issue. An issuing house may be asked to help administer the issue of the shares to the public and to offer advice concerning an appropriate selling price. However, the business rather than the issuing house will take on the risk of selling the shares. An offer for sale and a public issue will both result in a widening of share ownership in the business.

When making an issue of shares, the business or the issuing house will usually set a price for the shares. However, establishing this price may not be an easy task, particularly where the market is volatile or where the business has unique characteristics. If the share price is set too high, the issue will be undersubscribed and the business (or issuing house) will not receive the amount expected. If the share price is set too low, the issue will be oversubscribed and less will be received than could have been achieved.

One way of dealing with the problem is to make a **tender issue** of shares. This involves the investors determining the price at which the shares are issued. Although the business (or issuing house) may publish a reserve price to help guide investors, it will be up to the individual investor to determine the number of shares to be purchased and the price the investor wishes to pay. Once the offers from investors have been received, a price at which all the shares can be sold will be established (known as the **striking price**). Investors who have made offers at, or above, the striking price will be issued shares at the striking price; offers received below the striking price will be rejected. Although this form of issue is adopted occasionally, it is not popular with investors and is therefore not in widespread use.

Private placings

➡ A **placing** does not involve an invitation to the public to subscribe to shares. Instead, the shares are 'placed' with selected investors, such as large financial institutions. This can be a quick and relatively cheap form of raising funds, because savings can be made in advertising and legal costs. However, it can result in the ownership of the business being concentrated in a few hands. Usually, unlisted businesses seeking relatively small amounts of cash will employ this form of issue.

● Summary

In this chapter, we have examined the major sources of long-term and short-term finance available to businesses. We have seen that there are various factors to be taken into account when deciding which source of finance is appropriate to a particular business or a particular set of circumstances. We have also considered the main forms of share issue and explored some of the key factors relating to each form.

We have examined the role of venture capital and the role of the stock market. We saw that venture capital is usually concerned with providing capital for newer and smaller businesses, whereas stock markets are concerned with the needs of larger businesses. Stock markets have a primary role in raising finance for businesses and a secondary role in ensuring that investors can buy and sell securities with ease.

Key terms

Debenture   p. 478
Eurobond   p. 478
Deep discount bond   p. 479
Convertible loan stock   p. 479
Financial derivative   p. 479
Warrant   p. 479
Mortgage   p. 480
Loan covenant   p. 480
Finance lease   p. 482
Operating lease   p. 482
Sale and leaseback   p. 483

Bank overdraft   p. 487
Debt factoring   p. 487
Invoice discounting   p. 489
Stock Exchange   p. 495
Venture capital   p. 496
Rights issues   p. 498
Bonus issue   p. 500
Offer for sale   p. 501
Public issue   p. 502
Placing   p. 502

Further reading

If you would like to explore the topics covered in this chapter in more depth, we recommend the following books:

Business Finance: Theory and Practice, *McLaney, E.*, 5th edn, Financial Times Prentice Hall, 2000, chapter 8.

Corporate Finance and Investment, *Pike, R. and Neale, B.*, 3rd edn, Prentice Hall International, 1999, chapters 16 and 18.

Corporate Financial Management, *Arnold, G.*, Financial Times Prentice Hall, 1998, chapters 11 and 12.

Financial Management and Decision Making, *Samuels, J., Wilkes, F. and Brayshaw, R.*, International Thomson Business Press, 1999, chapters 7, 9 and 19.

References

1. **Financial Statistics**, Office for National Statistics, February 2001.
2. 'Rise of venture capitalism', *Thorpe, D.*, **Accountancy Age**, 12 October 2000.

REVIEW QUESTIONS

15.1 What are the benefits of issuing share warrants for a business?

15.2 Why might a public company that has a Stock Exchange listing revert to being an unlisted company?

15.3 Distinguish between an offer for sale and a public issue of shares.

15.4 Distinguish between invoice discounting and factoring.

EXERCISES

Exercises 15.5–15.8 are more advanced than 15.1–15.4. Those with coloured numbers have answers in the back of the book.

15.1 H. Brown (Portsmouth) Ltd produces a range of central heating systems for sale to builders' merchants. As a result of increasing demand for its products, the directors have decided to expand production. The cost of acquiring new plant and machinery and the increase in working capital requirements are planned to be financed by a mixture of long-term and short-term debt.

Required:
(a) Discuss the major factors that should be taken into account when deciding on the appropriate mix of long-term and short-term debt necessary to finance the expansion programme.
(b) Discuss the major factors that a lender should take into account when deciding whether to grant a long-term loan to the company.
(c) Identify three conditions that might be included in a long-term loan agreement and state the purpose of each.

15.2 'Venture capital may represent an important source of finance for a business.'

Required:
(a) What is meant by the term 'venture capital'? What are the distinguishing features of this form of finance?
(b) What types of business venture may be of interest to a venture capitalist seeking to make an investment?
(c) When considering a possible investment in a business, discuss the main factors a venture capitalist would take into account.

15.3 Answer all three questions below:

(a) Discuss the main factors that should be taken into account when choosing between long-term debt and share capital (equity) finance.
(b) Explain the term 'convertible loan stock'. Discuss the advantages and disadvantages of this form of finance from the viewpoint of both the business and investors.
(c) Explain the term 'debt factoring'. Discuss the advantages and disadvantages of this form of finance.

15.4 Brocmar plc has 10 million ordinary £0.50 shares in issue. The market price of the shares is £1.80. The board of the company wishes to finance a major project at a cost of £2.88 million. Forecasts suggest that the implementation of the project will add £0.4 million to after-tax earnings available to ordinary shareholders in the coming year. After-tax earnings for the year just completed were £2 million, but this figure is expected to decline to £1.8 million in the coming year if the project proposed is not undertaken. A rights issue at a 20 per cent discount on the existing market price is proposed. Issue expenses can be ignored.

Required:
(a) To assist the board in coming to a final decision, you are required to present information in the following format:

- Project not undertaken
    (i) earnings per share for the coming year.

- Project undertaken and financed by a rights issue
    (ii) rights issue price per share
    (iii) number of shares to be issued
    (iv) earnings per share for the coming year
    (v) the theoretical ex-rights price per share.

    All workings should be shown separately.
(b) What information, other than that provided in the question, is needed before the board can make the investment decision?

15.5 Raphael Ltd is a small engineering business that has annual credit sales of £2.4 million. In recent years, the company has experienced credit-control problems. The average collection period for sales has risen to 50 days even though the stated policy of the business is for payment to be made within 30 days. In addition, 1.5 per cent of sales are written off as bad debts each year.

The company has recently been in talks with a factor who is prepared to make an advance to the company equivalent to 80 per cent of debtors, based on the assumption that customers will, in future, adhere to a 30-day payment period. The interest rate for the advance will be 11 per cent a year. The trade debtors are currently financed through a bank overdraft, which has an interest rate of 12 per cent a year. The factor will take over the credit-control procedures of the business and this will result in a saving to the business of £18,000 a year, however, the factor will make a charge of 2 per cent of sales for this service. The use of the factoring service is expected to eliminate the bad debts incurred by the business.

Required:
Calculate the net cost of the factor agreement to the company and state whether or not the company should take advantage of the opportunity to factor its trade debts.

15.6 Carpets Direct plc wishes to increase its number of retail outlets in the south of England. The board of directors has decided to finance this expansion programme by raising the funds from existing shareholders through a one-for-four rights issue. The most recent profit and loss account of the company is as follows:

Profit and loss account for the year ended 30 April

	£m
Sales turnover	164.5
Profit before interest and taxation	12.6
Interest	(6.2)
Profit before taxation	6.4
Corporation tax	(1.9)
Profit after taxation	4.5
Ordinary dividends	(2.0)
Retained profit for the year	2.5

The share capital of the company consists of 120 million ordinary shares with a par value of £0.50 per share. The shares of the company are currently being traded on the Stock Exchange at a price/earnings ratio of 22 times, and the board of directors has decided to issue the new shares at a discount of 20 per cent on the current market value.

Required:

(a) Calculate the theoretical ex-rights price of an ordinary share in Carpets Direct plc.
(b) Calculate the price at which the rights in Carpets Direct plc are likely to be traded.
(c) Identify and evaluate, at the time of the rights issue, each of the options (that is, (i) taking up the rights, (ii) selling the rights and (iii) doing nothing) arising from the rights issue to an investor who holds 4,000 ordinary shares before the rights announcement.

15.7 Gainsborough Fashions Ltd operates a small chain of fashion shops in North Wales. In recent months the business has been under pressure from its trade creditors to reduce the average credit period taken from three months to one month. As a result, the directors have approached the bank to ask for an increase in the existing overdraft for one year to be able to comply with the creditors' demands. The most recent accounts of the business are as follows:

Balance sheet as at 31 May

	£	£	£
Fixed assets			
Fixtures and fittings at cost		90,000	
Less Accumulated depreciation		23,000	67,000
Motor vehicles at cost		34,000	
Less Accumulated depreciation		27,000	7,000
			74,000
Current assets			
Stock at cost		198,000	
Trade debtors		3,000	
		201,000	
Creditors: amounts falling due within one year			
Trade creditors	(162,000)		
Accrued expenses	(5,000)		
Bank overdraft	(7,000)		
Taxation	(10,000)		
Dividends	(10,000)	(194,000)	7,000
			81,000

Creditors: amounts falling due after one year

12% debentures (repayable in just over one year's time)	(40,000)
	41,000

Capital and reserves

£1 ordinary shares	20,000
General reserve	4,000
Retained profit	17,000
	41,000

Abbreviated profit and loss account for the year ended 31 May

	£
Sales	740,000
Net profit before interest and taxation	38,000
Interest charges	(5,000)
Net profit before taxation	33,000
Taxation	(10,000)
Net profit after taxation	23,000
Dividend proposed	(10,000)
Retained profit for the year	13,000

Notes:
1. The debentures are secured by personal guarantees from the directors.
2. The current overdraft bears an interest rate of 12 per cent a year.

Required:
(a) Identify and discuss the major factors that a bank would take into account before deciding whether or not to grant an increase in the overdraft of a business.
(b) State whether, in your opinion, the bank should grant the required increase in the overdraft for Gainsborough Fashions Ltd. You should provide reasoned arguments and supporting calculations where necessary.

15.8 Telford Engineers plc, a medium-sized Midlands manufacturer of automobile components, has decided to modernise its factory by introducing a number of robots. These will cost £20 million and will reduce operating costs by £6 million per year for their estimated useful life of 10 years. To finance this scheme the business can either:

(i) raise £20 million by the issue of 20 million ordinary shares at 100p, or
(ii) raise £20 million debt at 14 per cent interest per year, capital repayments of £3 million per year commencing at the end of 2004.

Extracts from Telford Engineers' accounts appear below:

Summary of balance sheet at 31 December

	1998	1999	2000	2001
	£m	£m	£m	£m
Fixed assets	48	51	65	64
Current assets	55	67	57	55
Less Amounts due in under one year				
Creditors	(20)	(27)	(25)	(18)
Overdraft	(5)		(6)	(8)
	78	91	91	93
Share capital and reserves	48	61	61	63
Loans	30	30	30	30
	78	91	91	93

	80 m	80 m	80 m	80 m
Number of issued 25p shares	80 m	80 m	80 m	80 m
Share price	150p	200p	100p	145p

Summary of profit and loss accounts for years ended 31 December

	1998	1999	2000	2001
	£m	£m	£m	£m
Sales	152	170	110	145
Profit before interest and taxation	28	40	7	15
Interest payable	(4)	(3)	(4)	(5)
Profit before taxation	24	37	3	10
Taxation	(12)	(16)	0	(4)
Profit after taxation	12	21	3	6
Dividends	(6)	(8)	(3)	(4)
Retained profit	6	13	0	2

For your answer, you should assume that the corporate tax rate for 2002 will be 30 per cent, that sales and operating profit will be unchanged except for the £6 million cost saving arising from the introduction of the robots, and that Telford Engineers will pay the same dividend per share in 2002 as in 2001.

Required:
(a) Prepare, for each financing arrangement ((i) and (ii) above), Telford Engineers' profit and loss account for the year ended 31 December 2002 and a statement of its share capital, reserves and loans on that date.
(b) Calculate Telford's earnings per share for 2002 for both schemes.
(c) Which scheme would you advise the company to adopt? You should give your reasons and state what additional information you would require.

16 Managing working capital

Introduction

In this chapter we consider the factors that must be taken into account when managing the working capital of a business. Each element of working capital will be identified, and the major issues surrounding the elements will be discussed.

OBJECTIVES

When you have completed this chapter you should be able to:

- Identify the main elements of working capital.
- Discuss the purpose of working capital and the nature of the working capital cycle.
- Explain the importance of establishing policies for the control of working capital.
- Explain the factors that have to be taken into account when managing each element of working capital.

The nature and purpose of working capital

➔ **Working capital** is usually defined as:

Current assets *less* Current liabilities (that is, creditors due within one year)

The major elements of current assets are:

- Stocks
- Trade debtors
- Cash (in hand and at bank).

The major elements of current liabilities are:

- Trade creditors
- Bank overdrafts.

The size and composition of working capital can vary between industries. For some types of business, the investment in working capital can be substantial. For example, a manufacturing company will typically invest heavily in raw materials, work in progress, and finished goods, and it will often sell its goods on credit thereby generating trade debtors. A retailer, on the other hand, will hold only one form of stock (finished goods) and will usually sell goods for cash.

Working capital represents a net investment in short-term assets. These assets are continually flowing into and out of a business and are essential for day-to-day operations. The various elements of working capital are interrelated and can be seen as part of a short-term cycle. Figure 16.1 depicts the working capital cycle for a manufacturing business.

Figure 16.1

The working-capital cycle

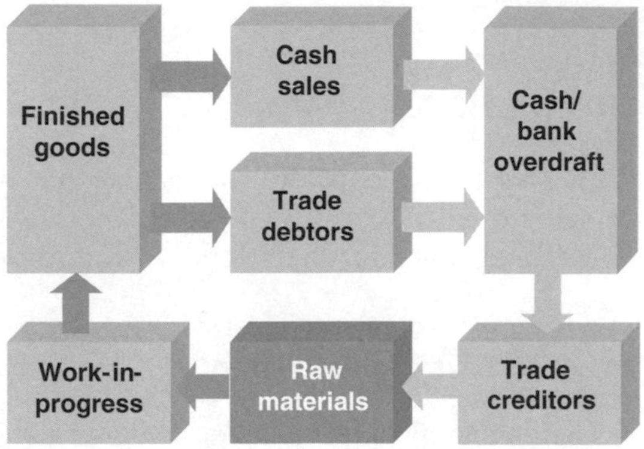

The diagram shows the working-capital cycle for a manufacturing business. Raw materials are acquired and converted into work in progress and, finally, into finished goods. The finished goods are sold to customers for either cash or credit. In the case of credit customers, there will be a delay before the cash is received from the sales. Cash generated from sales can then be used to pay suppliers, who will normally supply goods on credit.

The management of working capital is an essential part of a business's short-term planning process. It is necessary for management to decide how much of each element should be held. As we shall see later, there are costs associated with holding both too much and too little of each element. Management must be aware of these costs in order to manage effectively. Management must also be aware that there may be other, more profitable, uses for the funds of the business. Hence, the potential benefits must be weighed against the likely costs in order to achieve the optimum investment.

The working-capital needs of a particular business are likely to change over time, as a result of changes in the commercial environment. This means that working-capital decisions are rarely one-off decisions. Managers must try to identify changes, in an attempt to ensure that the level of investment in working capital is appropriate.

Activity 16.1

What kinds of change in the commercial environment might lead to a decision to change the level of investment in working capital? Try to identify four possible changes.

In answering this activity, you may have thought of the following:

● Changes in interest rates

- Changes in market demand
- Changes in the seasons
- Changes in the state of the economy.

You may have thought of others.

In addition to changes in the external environment, changes arising within the business – such as changes in production methods (resulting, perhaps, in a need to hold less stock) and changes in the level of risk that managers are prepared to take – could alter the required level of investment in working capital.

The scale of working capital

It is tempting to form the impression that, compared with the scale of investment in fixed assets by a typical business, the amounts involved with working capital are pretty trivial. This would be a false assessment of reality – the scale of working capital for most businesses is vast. Exhibit 16.1 gives some impression of the working capital involvement for five UK businesses that are either very well known by name or whose products are everyday commodities for most of us.

Exhibit 16.1

A summary of the balance sheets of five UK businesses					
Business	The Boots Company plc	Rolls-Royce plc	The Go-Ahead Group plc	Fuller Smith and Turner plc	Anglia Water plc
Balance sheet date	31.3.00	31.12.99	1.7.00	25.3.00	31.3.00
	%	%	%	%	%
Fixed assets	84	73	114	96	99
Current assets					
Stock	29	33	2	3	–
Trade debtors	12	23	14	4	4
Other debtors	6	21	23	3	2
Cash and near cash	18	25	26	8	4
	65	102	65	18	10
Current liabilities					
Trade creditors	15	17	17	5	3
Tax and dividends	14	8	13	5	–
Other short-term liabilities	11	39	46	4	4
Overdrafts and short-term loans	9	11	3	–	2
	49	75	79	14	9
Working capital	16	27	(14)	4	1
Total long-term investment	100	100	100	100	100

The fixed assets, current assets and current liabilities (the last being creditors: amounts falling due within one year) expressed as a percentage of the total net investment of the business concerned. The businesses were randomly selected, except that they were deliberately taken from different industries. Boots (the high-street chemist) is a manufacturer and retailer of health and personal-care products. Rolls-Royce manufactures engines and electrical generating equipment. Go-Ahead provides urban public train and bus services, including Thames trains. Fuller Smith and Turner manages pubs and hotels in and around London, also brewing (perhaps most famously) London Pride bitter. Anglia Water supplies water and collects and treats waste water.

The totals for current assets are generally pretty large when compared with the total long-term investment. The amounts vary considerably from one type of business to the next. Rolls-Royce is the only one of the five businesses that is solely a manufacturer. Boots is the only other one that holds a significant amount of stock. Go-Ahead and Anglia provide a service and so hold little or no stock. Most of Anglia's sales are paid for in advance (water rates), so it has low trade debtors. Rolls-Royce makes most of its sales on credit and so has relatively high trade debtors.

These types of variation in the amounts and types of working capital elements are typical of other businesses.

In the sections that follow, we shall consider each element of working capital separately, examining the factors that must be considered to ensure their proper management.

●●●● Management of stocks

A business may hold stocks for various reasons, the most common of which is to meet the immediate day-to-day requirements of customers and production. However, a business may hold more than is necessary for this purpose if it believes that future supplies may be interrupted or scarce. Similarly, if the business believes that the cost of stocks will rise in the future, it may decide to stockpile.

For some types of business, the stock held may represent a substantial proportion of the total assets held. For example, a car dealership that rents its premises may have nearly all of its total assets in the form of stock. As we have seen, manufacturing businesses' stock levels tend to be higher than in many other types of business. For some types, such as firework manufacturers, the level of stock held may vary substantially over the year owing to the seasonal nature of the industry, whereas, for other businesses, stock levels may remain fairly stable throughout the year.

Where a business holds stock simply to meet the day-to-day requirements of its customers and production, it will normally seek to minimise the amount of stock held. This is because there are significant costs associated with holding stocks. These include storage and handling costs, financing costs, the risks of pilferage and obsolescence, and the opportunities forgone in tying up funds in this form of asset. However, a business must also recognise that, if the levels of stocks held are too low, there will also be associated costs.

Activity 16.2

What costs might a business incur as a result of holding too low a level of stocks? Try to identify at least three types of cost.

....

You may have thought of the following costs:

- Loss of sales, from being unable to provide the goods required immediately.
- Loss of goodwill from customers, for being unable to satisfy customer demand.
- High transport costs incurred to ensure stocks are replenished quickly.
- Lost production owing to shortage of raw materials.
- Inefficient production scheduling due to shortages of raw materials.
- Purchasing stocks at a higher price than might otherwise have been necessary in order to replenish stocks quickly.

In order to try to ensure that the stocks are properly managed, a number of procedures and techniques can be used. These are reviewed below.

Budgets of future demand

One of the best means of a business trying to ensure that there is stock available to meet future sales is to produce appropriate budgets. These budgets should deal with each product that the business sells. It is important that every attempt is made to ensure the accuracy of these budgets as they will determine future ordering and production levels.

The budgets may be derived in various ways. They may be developed using statistical techniques such as time-series analysis, or may be based on the judgement of the sales and marketing staff. We considered stock budgets in Chapter 12.

Financial ratios

One ratio that can be used to help monitor stock levels is the average stock turnover period, which we examined in Chapter 7. As you may recall, this ratio is calculated as follows:

$$\text{Stock turnover period} = \frac{\text{Average stock held}}{\text{Cost of sales}} \times 365 \text{ days}$$

This will provide a picture of the average period for which stocks are held and can be useful as a basis for comparison. It is possible to calculate the stock turnover period for individual product lines as well as for stocks as a whole.

Recording and reordering systems

The management of stocks in a business of any size requires a sound system of recording stock movements. There must be proper procedures for recording stock purchases and sales. Periodic stock checks may be required to ensure that the amount of physical stocks held is consistent with what the stock records indicate is held.

There should also be clear procedures for the reordering of stocks. Authorisation for both the purchase and issue of stocks should be confined to a few senior staff if problems of duplication and lack of co-ordination are to be avoided. To determine the point at which stock should be reordered, information concerning the lead time (the time between the placing of an order and the receipt of the goods) and the likely level of demand will be required.

Activity 16.3

P. Marinov Ltd is an electrical retailer that keeps a particular type of light switch in stock. The annual demand for the light switch is 10,400 units and the lead time for orders is four weeks. Demand for the stock is steady throughout the year. At what level of stock should the business reorder, assuming that it is confident of the figures mentioned above?

The average weekly demand for the stock item is:

$$\frac{10,400}{52} = 200 \text{ units}$$

During the time between ordering the stock and receiving the goods, the stock sold will be:

$$4 \times 200 = 800 \text{ units}$$

So the business should reorder no later than when the stock level reaches 800 units in order to avoid a 'stockout'.

In most businesses, there will be some uncertainty surrounding the above factors and so a buffer or safety stock level may be maintained in case problems occur. The amount of safety stock to be held is a matter of judgement and will depend on the degree of uncertainty concerning the factors. However, the likely costs of running out of stock must also be taken into account.

Levels of control

Management must make a commitment to the management of stocks. However, the cost of controlling stocks must be weighed against the potential benefits. It may be possible to have different levels of control according to the nature of the stocks held. The **ABC system of stock control** (see Figure 16.2) is based on the idea of selective levels of control.

A business may find that it is possible to divide its stock into three broad categories: A, B and C (see Figure 16.2). Each category will be based on the value of stock held. Category A stocks will represent the high-value items. It may be the case, however, that although the items are high in *value* and represent a high proportion of the total value of stocks held, they are a relatively small proportion of the total *volume* of stocks held. For example, 10 per cent of the physical stocks held may account for 65 per cent of the total value. For these stocks, management may decide to implement sophisticated recording procedures, exert tight control over stock movements and have a high level of security at the stock's location. Category B stocks will represent less valuable items held. Perhaps 30 per cent of the total volume of stocks may account for 25 per cent of the total value of stocks held. For these stocks, a lower level of recording and management control would be appropriate. Category C stocks will represent the least valuable items. Say, 60 per cent of the volume of stocks may account for 10 per cent of the

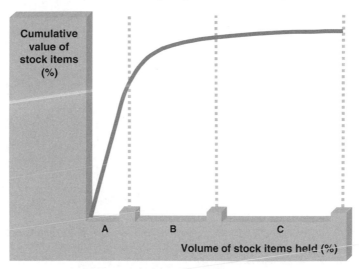

Figure 16.2

ABC method of analysing and controlling stocks

Cumulative value of stock items (%)

A   B   C

Volume of stock items held (%)

The graph shows that it is possible to divide stocks into three broad categories. Category A stocks are high-value items representing a high proportion of the total value of stocks held. However, they are a relatively low proportion of the total volume of stocks held. Category B stocks represent less in terms of total value but account for a higher proportion of the total volume of stocks held. Category C stocks represent an even smaller proportion in terms of total value of stocks held but account for an even higher proportion of the total volume of stocks held.

total value of stocks held. For these stocks, the level of recording and management control would be lower still.

Categorising stocks in this way can help to ensure that management effort is directed to the most important areas and that the costs of controlling stocks are appropriate to their importance.

Stock management models

It is possible to use decision models to help manage stocks. The **economic order quantity (EOQ)** model is concerned with answering the question: how much stock should be ordered? In its simplest form, the EOQ model assumes that demand is constant, so that stocks will be depleted evenly over time and will be replenished just at the point that the stock runs out. These assumptions lead to the 'saw-tooth' representation of stock movements within a business, as shown in Figure 16.3.

The EOQ model assumes that the key costs associated with stock are the costs of holding it and ordering it. The model can be used to calculate the optimum size of a purchase order by taking account of both of these cost elements. The cost of holding stock can be substantial and so management may try to minimise the average amount of stock held. However, by reducing the level of stock held, and therefore the holding costs, there will be a need to increase the number of orders during the period and so ordering costs will rise.

Figure 16.3

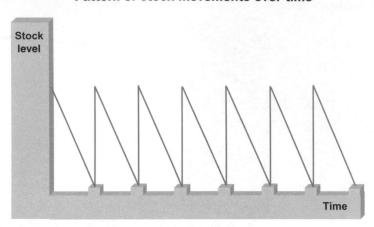

Pattern of stock movements over time

The figure depicts a 'saw-tooth' pattern for stock movements over time. The pattern is based on the assumption that stocks are depleted evenly over time and will be replenished just at the point when the existing stocks run out.

Figure 16.4

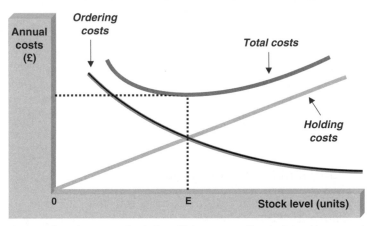

Stockholding and stock order costs

The graph shows how the costs of ordering will decrease as the stock level increases because fewer orders are placed. However, the costs of holding stocks will increase as the stock levels increase. The total costs are made up of the holding costs and ordering costs. Point E represents the point at which total costs are minimised.

Figure 16.4 shows how, as the level of stock and the size of stock orders increase, the annual costs of placing orders will decrease because fewer orders will be placed. However, the cost of holding stock will increase as there will be higher stock levels. The total costs curve, which represents the sum of the holding costs and ordering costs, will fall until the point E, which represents the minimum total cost, is reached. Thereafter, total costs begin to rise. The EOQ model seeks to identify the point E at which total costs are minimised.

This will represent half the optimum amount that should be ordered on each occasion. Assuming – as we are doing – that stock is used evenly over time and that stock falls to zero before being replaced, the average stock level equals half of the order size.

The EOQ model, which can be used to derive the most economic order quantity, is given by:

$$EOQ = \sqrt{\frac{2DC}{H}}$$

where D is the annual demand for the item of stock, C is the cost of placing an order, and H is the cost of holding one unit of stock for one year.

Activity 16.4 Louise Simon Ltd sells 2,000 units of product X each year. It has been estimated that the cost of holding one unit of the product for a year is £4. The cost of placing an order for stock is estimated at £25. Calculate the EOQ for the product.

Your answer should be as follows:

$$EOQ = \sqrt{\frac{2 \times 2,000 \times 25}{4}}$$

$$= 158 \text{ units (to the nearest whole number)}$$

This will mean that the business will have to order product X about 13 times (2,000/158) each year in order to meet sales demand.

The basic EOQ model has a number of limiting assumptions. It assumes that demand for the product can be predicted with accuracy and that this demand is even over the period. It also assumes that no 'buffer' stock is required and that the amount can be purchased in single units that correspond exactly to the economic order quantity – for example, 158 units – and not in multiples of 50 or 100 units. Finally, it assumes that no discounts are available for bulk purchases. However, these limiting assumptions do not mean we should dismiss the model as being of little value. The model can be refined to accommodate the problems of uncertainty and uneven demand. Many businesses use this model (or a development of it) to help in the management of stocks.

Materials requirements planning (MRP) system

A **materials requirement planning (MRP) system** takes forecasts of sales demand as its starting point. It then uses computer technology to help schedule the timing of deliveries of bought-in parts and materials to coincide with production requirements. MRP is a co-ordinated approach that links material and parts deliveries to their scheduled input to the production process. By ordering only those items that are necessary to ensure the flow of production, stock levels may be reduced. MRP is a 'top-down' approach to stock management that recognises that stock-ordering decisions cannot be viewed as being independent from production decisions. In recent years, this approach has been extended to provide a fully integrated approach to production planning. This approach also takes into account other manufacturing resources such as labour and machine capacity.

Just-in-time (JIT) stock management

In recent years, some manufacturing businesses have tried to eliminate the need to hold stocks by adopting **just-in-time (JIT) stock management**. This method was first used in the US defence industry during World War II and, in more recent times, it has been widely used by Japanese businesses. The essence of JIT is, as the name suggests, to have supplies delivered to a business just in time for them to be used in the production process. By adopting this approach, the stockholding problem rests with the suppliers rather than the business itself.

For this approach to be successful, it is important that the business informs suppliers of its production plans and requirements in advance, and that the suppliers in their turn deliver materials of the right quality at the agreed times. Failure to do so could lead to a dislocation of production and could be very costly. Thus, a close relationship between a business and its suppliers is required.

Though a business will not have to hold stocks, there may be certain costs associated with a JIT approach. As the suppliers will be required to hold stocks for the business, they may try to recoup this additional cost through increased prices. The price of stocks purchased may also be increased if JIT requires a large number of small deliveries to be made. Finally, the close relationship necessary between the business and its suppliers may prevent the business from taking advantage of cheaper sources of supply if they become available.

Many people view JIT as more than simply a stock control system. The philosophy underpinning this method is concerned with eliminating waste and striving for excellence. There is an expectation that suppliers will always deliver parts on time and that there will be no defects in the parts supplied. There is also an expectation that the production process will operate at maximum efficiency. This means that there will be no production breakdowns and the queueing and storage times of products manufactured will be eliminated as only that time spent directly on processing the products is seen as adding value. Whilst these expectations may be impossible to achieve, they do help to create a management culture that is dedicated to quality and to the pursuit of excellence (see Exhibit 16.2).

Exhibit 16.2

Tesco plc is one of the leading supermarket chains in the UK. To gain an advantage in this intensely competitive market, the company invested heavily in technology to support its JIT system and other stock-management systems. Laser technology is used to improve its distribution flow and to replenish stocks quickly. As a result, Tesco plc now holds less than two weeks' stock, and almost half of the goods received from suppliers are sent immediately to the stores rather than to the warehouse.

The improvement in distribution procedures has allowed stores to reduce the amount of each line of stock held, which in turn has made it possible to increase the number of lines of stock held by each store. It has also made it possible to convert storage space at the supermarkets into selling space.

Source: Information taken from an article appearing in **The Economist**, 1995.

Management of debtors

Selling goods or services on credit results in costs being incurred by a business. These costs include credit administration costs, bad debts and opportunities forgone in using the funds for more profitable purposes. However, the costs must be weighed against the benefits of increased sales resulting from the opportunity for customers to delay payment.

Selling on credit is very widespread and appears to be the norm outside the retail trade. When a business offers to sell its goods or services on credit, it must have clear policies concerning:

- Which customers it is prepared to offer credit to.
- What length of credit it is prepared to offer.
- Whether discounts will be offered for prompt payment.
- What collection policies should be adopted.

Each of these considerations is discussed further below.

Which customers should receive credit?

A business offering credit runs the risk of not receiving payment for goods or services supplied. Thus, care must be taken over the type of customer to whom credit facilities are offered. When considering a proposal from a customer for the supply of goods or services on credit, the business must take a number of factors into account.

The following '**five Cs of credit**' provide a useful checklist when considering a request from a customer for credit:

- *Capital.* The customer must appear to be financially sound before any credit is extended. Where the customer is a business, its accounts should be examined. Particular attention should be taken of the profitability and liquidity of the customer. In addition, any major financial commitments (for example, capital expenditure, contracts with suppliers) must be taken into account.
- *Capacity.* The customer must appear to have the capacity to pay amounts owing. Where possible, the payment record of the customer should be examined. If the customer is a business, the type of business operated and the physical resources of the business will be relevant. The value of goods that the customer wishes to buy on credit must be related to the total financial resources of the customer.
- *Collateral.* On occasions, it may be necessary to ask for some kind of security for goods supplied on credit. When this occurs, the business must be convinced that the customer is able to offer a satisfactory form of security.
- *Conditions.* The state of the industry in which the customer operates and the general economic conditions of the particular region or country may have an important influence on the ability of a customer to pay the amounts outstanding on the due date.
- *Character.* It is important for a business to make some assessment of the character of the customer. The willingness to pay will depend on the honesty and integrity of the individual with whom the business is dealing. Where the customer is a limited company, this will mean assessing the characters of its

directors. The business must feel satisfied that the customer will make every effort to pay any amounts owing.

Once a customer is considered creditworthy, credit limits for the customer should be established and procedures laid down to ensure that these limits are adhered to.

| Activity 16.5 | Assume that you are the credit manager of a business and that a limited company approached you with a view to buying goods on credit. What sources of information might you decide to use to help assess the financial health of the potential customer? |

There are various possibilities; you may have thought of some of the following:

- *Trade references.* Some businesses ask for a potential customer to supply references from other businesses that have made sales on credit to the customer. This may be extremely useful, provided that the references are truly representative of the opinions of the customer's suppliers. There is a danger that a potential customer will attempt to be highly selective when giving details of other suppliers in order to gain a more favourable impression than is deserved.
- *Bank references.* It is possible to ask the potential customer for a bank reference. Although banks are usually prepared to supply references, the contents of a reference are not always very informative. If customers are in financial difficulties, the bank will usually be unwilling to add to their problems by supplying poor references.
- *Published accounts.* A limited company is obliged by law to file a copy of its annual accounts with the Registrar of Companies. The accounts are available for public inspection and provide a useful source of information.
- *The customer.* You may wish to interview the directors of the company and visit its premises in an attempt to gain some impression of the way that the company conducts its business. Where a significant amount of credit is required, you may ask the company for access to internal budgets and other unpublished financial information to help assess the level of risk involved.
- *Credit agencies.* Specialist agencies exist to provide information that can be used to assess the creditworthiness of a potential customer. The information that a credit agency supplies may be gleaned from various sources, including the accounts of the customer, court judgments and news items relating to the customer from both published and unpublished sources.

Length of credit period

A business must determine what credit terms it is prepared to offer its customers. The length of credit offered can vary significantly between businesses and is influenced by such factors as:

- The typical credit terms operating within the industry.
- The degree of competition within the industry.
- The bargaining power of particular customers.
- The risk of non-payment.
- The capacity of the business to offer credit.
- The marketing strategy of the business.

The last point may require some explanation. The marketing strategy of a business may have an important influence on the length of credit allowed. For example, if a business wishes to increase its market share it may decide to liberalise its credit policy so as to try to stimulate sales. Potential customers may be attracted by the offer of a longer credit period. However, any such change in policy must take account of the likely costs and benefits arising. To illustrate this point, consider Example 16.1.

Example 16.1

Torrance Ltd produces a new type of golf putter. The business sells the putter to wholesalers and retailers and has an annual turnover of £600,000. The following data relate to each putter produced:

	£	£
Selling price		36
Variable costs	18	
Fixed cost apportionment	6	(24)
Net profit		12

The cost of capital of Torrance Ltd is estimated at 15 per cent.

The business wishes to expand sales of this new putter and believes that this can be done by offering a longer period in which to pay. The average collection period of the business is currently 30 days. The business is considering three options, in an attempt to increase sales. These are as follows:

	Option		
	1	2	3
Increase in average collection period	10 days	20 days	30 days
Increase in sales	£30,000	£45,000	£50,000

To enable the business to decide on the best option, it must weigh the benefits of the options against their respective costs. The benefits arising will be represented by the increase in profit from the sale of additional putters. From the cost data supplied, we can see that the contribution (sales less variable costs) is £18 per putter. This represents 50 per cent of the selling price. The fixed costs can be ignored as they will remain the same whichever option is chosen.

The increase in contribution under each option will therefore be:

	Option		
	1	2	3
50% of increase in sales	£15,000	£22,500	£25,000

The increase in debtors under each option will be as follows:

	Option		
	1	2	3
	£	£	£
Planned level of debtors			
630,000 × 40/365	69,041		
645,000 × 50/365		88,356	
650,000 × 60/365			106,849
Less Current level of debtors			
600,000 × 30/365	(49,315)	(49,315)	(49,315)
Increase in debtors	19,726	39,041	57,534

The increase in debtors that results from each option will mean an additional cost to the company. We are told that the company has an estimated cost of capital of 15 per cent. Thus, the increase in the additional investment in debtors will be:

	Option		
	1	2	3
Cost of additional investment (15% of increase in debtors)	£(2,959)	£(5,856)	£(8,630)

The net increase in profits will be:

	Option		
	1	2	3
	£	£	£
Cost of additional investment (15% of increase in debtors)	(2,959)	(5,856)	(8,630)
Increase in contribution (see above)	15,000	22,500	25,000
Net increase in profits	12,041	16,644	16,370

The calculations show that option 2 will be the most profitable for the company. However, there is little to choose between options 2 and 3.

Example 16.1 illustrates the way in which a business should assess changes in credit terms. However, if there is a risk that, by extending the length of credit, there will be an increase in bad debts, this should also be taken into account in the calculations, as should any additional collection costs that will be incurred.

Cash discounts and interest on overdue debts

A business may decide to offer a **cash discount** as a means of encouraging prompt payment from its credit customers. The size of any discount will be an important influence on whether a customer decides to pay promptly.

From the business's viewpoint, the cost of offering discounts must be weighed against the likely benefits in the form of a reduction in both the cost of financing debtors and the amount of bad debts.

In practice, there is always the danger that a customer may be slow to pay and yet may still take the discount offered. Where the customer is important to the business, it may be difficult to insist on full payment. Some businesses may charge interest on overdue accounts as a means of encouraging prompt payment. However, this is only possible if the business is in a strong bargaining position with its customers. For example, the business may be the only supplier of a particular product in the area.

Surveys indicate that small businesses have a much greater proportion of overdue debts than large businesses. In the UK, the government has intervened to help deal with this problem and the law now permits small businesses to charge interest on overdue accounts.

In addition, large companies are now required to disclose in their published accounts the payment policy adopted towards suppliers. There are some signs that these changes in the law have led to a speeding-up of payment to small businesses.

Self-assessment question 16.1

Williams Wholesalers Ltd at present requires payment from its customers by the end of the month after the month of delivery. On average, it takes customers 70 days to pay. Sales amount to £4 million a year and bad debts to £20,000 a year.

It is planned to offer customers a cash discount of 2 per cent for payment within 30 days. Williams estimates that 50 per cent of customers will accept this facility but that the remaining customers, who tend to be slow payers, will not pay until 80 days after the sale. At present the business has an overdraft facility at an interest rate of 13 per cent a year. If the plan goes ahead, bad debts will be reduced to £10,000 a year and there will be savings in credit administration expenses of £6,000 a year.

Required:
Should Williams Wholesalers Ltd offer the new credit terms to customers? You should support your answer with any calculations and explanations that you consider necessary.

Collection policies

A business offering credit must ensure that amounts owing are collected as quickly as possible. An efficient collection policy requires an efficient accounting system. Invoices must be sent out promptly along with regular monthly statements. Reminders must also be despatched promptly where necessary.

When a business is faced with customers who do not pay, there should be agreed procedures for dealing with those customers. However, the cost of any action to be taken against delinquent debtors must be weighed against the likely returns. For example, there is little point in taking legal action against a customer and incurring large legal expenses if there is evidence that the customer does not have the necessary resources to pay. Where possible, the cost of bad debts should be taken into account when setting prices for products or services.

Management can monitor the effectiveness of collection policies in a number of ways. One method is to calculate the **average settlement period for debtors** (see Chapter 7). This ratio is calculated as follows:

$$\text{Average settlement period for debtors} = \frac{\text{Trade debtors}}{\text{Credit sales}} \times 365 \text{ days}$$

Although this ratio can be useful, it is important to remember that it produces an *average* figure for the number of days that debts are outstanding. This average may be badly distorted by a few large customers who are also very slow payers.

A more detailed and informative approach to monitoring debtors is to produce an **ageing schedule of debtors**. Debts are divided into categories according to the length of time the debt has been outstanding. An ageing schedule can be produced for managers on a regular basis in order to help them see the pattern of outstanding debts. An example of an ageing schedule is set out in Example 16.2.

Example 16.2

Ageing schedule of debtors at 31 December 2001

	Days outstanding				
Customer	1–30 days	31–60 days	61–90 days	More than 90 days	Total
	£	£	£	£	£
A Ltd	20,000	10,000	–	–	30,000
B Ltd	–	24,000	–	–	24,000
C Ltd	12,000	13,000	14,000	18,000	57,000
Total	32,000	47,000	14,000	18,000	111,000

This example shows a business's trade debtors figure at 31 December 2001, which totals £111,000. Each customer's balance is analysed according to how long the debt has been outstanding. We can see that A Ltd has £20,000 of debt that is less than 30 days old (that is, arising from sales during December 2001) and £10,000 that is between 31 and 60 days old (arising from November 2001 sales). This information can be very useful for credit-control purposes.

Many accounting software packages now include this ageing schedule as one of the routine reports available. Such packages often have the facility to put customers 'on hold' when they reach their credit limit.

A slightly different approach to exercising control over debtors is to identify the pattern of receipts from credit sales on a monthly basis. This involves monitoring the percentage of trade debtors that pays (and the percentage of debts that remain unpaid) in the month of sale and the percentage that pays in subsequent months. To do this, credit sales for each month must be examined separately. To illustrate how a pattern of credit sales receipts is produced, consider a business that made credit sales of £250,000 in June and received 30 per cent of the amount owing in the same month, 40 per cent in July, 20 per cent in August and 10 per cent in September. The pattern of credit sales receipts and amounts owing is shown in Example 16.3.

Example 16.3

Pattern of credit sales receipts

Month	Receipts from June credit sales	Received	Amount outstanding from June sales at month end	Outstanding
	£	%	£	%
June	75,000	30	175,000	70
July	100,000	40	75,000	30
August	50,000	20	25,000	10
September	25,000	10	–	–

Example 16.3 shows how sales made in June were received over time. This information can be used as a basis for control. The actual pattern of receipts can be compared with the expected (budgeted) pattern of receipts in order to see if there was any significant deviation (see Figure 16.5). If this comparison shows that debtors are paying more slowly than expected, management may decide to take corrective action.

Activity 16.6

What kinds of corrective action might the managers decide to take if they found that debtors were paying more slowly than anticipated?

Managers might decide to do one or more of the following:

- Offer cash discounts to encourage prompt payment.
- Change the collection period.
- Improve the accounting system to ensure that customers are billed more promptly, reminders are sent out promptly, and so on.
- Change the eligibility criteria for customers who receive credit.

Figure 16.5

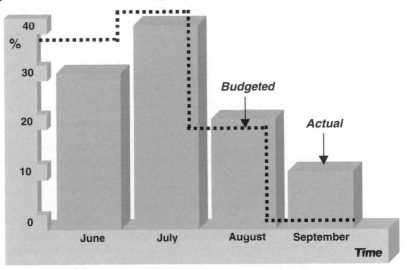

Comparison of actual and budgeted receipts over time for Example 16.3

The graph shows the actual pattern of cash receipts from credit sales made in June. It can be seen that 30 per cent of the sales income for June is received in that month, and the remainder is received in the three following months. The assumed budget pattern of cash receipts for June sales is also depicted. By comparing the actual and budgeted pattern of receipts, it is possible to see whether credit sales are being properly controlled and to decide whether corrective action is required.

Credit management and the small business

Credit management may be a particular problem for small businesses. Often, these businesses lack the resources to manage their trade debtors effectively.

Sometimes, a small business will not have a separate credit-control department, which will mean that both the expertise and the information required to make sound judgements concerning terms of sale and so on may not be available. A small business may also lack proper debt-collection procedures, such as prompt invoicing and the sending out of regular statements. This will increase the risks of late payment and defaulting debtors.

These risks may also increase through an excessive concern for growth. In order to increase sales, small businesses may be too willing to extend credit to customers that are poor credit risks. Whilst this kind of problem can occur in businesses of all sizes, small businesses seem particularly susceptible.

Another problem faced by small businesses is their lack of market power. They will often find themselves in a weak position when negotiating credit terms with larger businesses. Moreover, when a large customer exceeds the terms of credit, the small supplier may feel inhibited from pressing the customer for payment in case future sales are lost.

●●●● Management of cash

Why hold cash?

Most businesses will hold a certain amount of cash. However, the amount of cash held varies considerably between businesses.

Activity 16.7	Why do you think a business may decide to hold at least some of its assets in the form of cash?

According to economic theory, there are three motives for holding cash. They are:

- *Transactionary motive.* To meet day-to-day commitments, a business requires a certain amount of cash. Payments for wages, overheads, goods purchased and so on must be made at the due dates. Cash has been described as the life-blood of a business; unless it circulates through the business and is available for the payment of maturing obligations, the survival of the business will be put at risk. We saw earlier in the book, including in Chapter 5, that profitability alone is not enough: a business must have sufficient cash to pay its debts when they fall due.
- *Precautionary motive.* If future cash flows are uncertain for any reason, it would be prudent to hold a balance of cash. For example, a major customer that owes a large sum to the business may be in financial difficulties. Given this situation, the business can retain its capacity to meet its obligations by holding a cash balance. Similarly, if there is some uncertainty concerning future outlays, a cash balance will be required.
- *Speculative motive.* A business may decide to hold cash in order to be in a position to exploit profitable opportunities as and when they arise. For example, by holding cash, a business may be able to acquire a competitor business that suddenly becomes available at an attractive price. Holding cash has an opportunity cost for the business that must be taken into account. Thus, when evaluating the potential returns from holding cash for speculative purposes, the cost of forgone investment opportunities must be considered.

How much cash should be held?

Although cash can be held for each of the reasons identified in Activity 16.7, this may not always be necessary. If a business is able to borrow quickly at a favourable rate, then the amount of cash it needs to hold can be reduced. Similarly, if the business holds assets that can easily be converted to cash (for example, marketable securities such as shares in Stock Exchange listed companies, government bonds) the amount of cash held can be reduced.

The decision as to how much cash a particular business should hold is a difficult one. Different businesses will have different views on the subject.

Activity 16.8 **What do you think are the major factors that influence how much cash a business will hold? See if you can think of five possible factors.**

You may have thought of some of the following:

- *The nature of the business.* Some businesses, such as utilities (water, electricity and gas suppliers) may have cash flows that are both predictable and reasonably certain. This will enable them to hold lower cash balances. For some businesses, cash balances vary greatly according to the time of year. A seasonal business may accumulate cash during the high season to enable it to meet commitments during the low season.
- *The opportunity cost of holding cash.* Where there are profitable opportunities, it may be wiser to invest in those opportunities than to hold a large cash balance.
- *The level of inflation.* Holding cash during a period of rising prices will lead to a loss of purchasing power. The higher the level of inflation, the greater will be this loss.
- *The availability of near-liquid assets.* If a business has marketable securities or stocks that may easily be liquidated, the amount of cash held may be reduced.
- *The availability of borrowing.* If a business can borrow easily (and quickly), there is less need to hold cash.
- *The cost of borrowing.* When interest rates are high, the option of borrowing becomes less attractive.
- *Economic conditions.* When the economy is in recession, businesses may prefer to hold cash in order to be well-placed to invest when the economy improves. In addition, during a recession, businesses may experience difficulties in collecting debts. They may, therefore, hold higher cash balances than usual in order to meet commitments.
- *Relationships with suppliers.* Too little cash may hinder the ability of a business to pay suppliers promptly. This can lead to a loss of goodwill. It might also mean that cash discounts will not be claimable.

Controlling the cash balance

Several models have been proposed to help control the cash balance of a business. One such model proposes the use of upper and lower control limits for cash balances and the use of a target cash balance. The model assumes that the business will invest in marketable investments that can easily be liquidated. These investments will be purchased or sold, as necessary, to keep the cash balance within the control limits.

The model proposes two upper and two lower control limits (see Figure 16.6). If the business exceeds an *outer* limit, the managers must decide whether or not the cash balance is likely to return, over the following few days, to a point within the *inner* control limits set. If this seems likely, then no action is required. If, on the other hand, this seems unlikely, management must change the cash position of the business by buying or selling marketable securities, or simply by borrowing or lending.

Figure 16.6

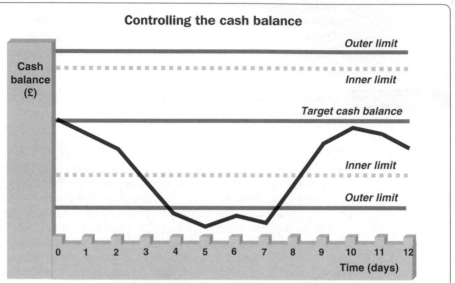

Controlling the cash balance

The graph depicts a model, for controlling the cash balance, that relies on the use of inner and outer control limits. Where outer control limits are breached, and there is no prospect of an early return to a point within these limits, management must take action. A breach of the higher limit will involve buying marketable securities (to ensure cash is not lying idle) and a breach of the lower limit will involve selling marketable securities (to ensure there is sufficient cash available to meet obligations).

In Figure 16.6 we can see that the lower outer-control limit has been breached for four days (days 4 to 7 inclusive). If a four-day period is unacceptable, managers must sell marketable securities to replenish the cash balance.

The model relies heavily on management judgement to determine where the control limits are set and the time period within which breaches of the limits are acceptable. Past experience may be useful in helping managers decide on these issues. There are other models, however, that do not rely on management judgement and, instead, use quantitative techniques to determine an optimal cash policy. One model proposed, for example, is the cash equivalent of the stock economic order quantity model discussed earlier.

Cash budgets and the management of cash

In managing cash effectively, it is useful for a business to prepare a cash budget. This is a very important tool for both planning and control purposes. Cash budgets were considered in Chapter 12 and so we shall not consider them in detail again here. However, it is worth repeating the point that budgets enable managers to see the expected outcome of planned events on the cash balance. The cash budgets will identify periods when cash surpluses and deficits are expected.

When a cash surplus is expected to arise, managers must decide on the best use of the surplus funds. When a cash deficit is expected, they must make adequate provision by borrowing, liquidating assets or rescheduling cash payments/receipts to deal with this. Planning borrowing requirements beforehand can allow the business to use a cheap source of finance; such sources may not be available at the time a deficit arises when decisions have to be made quickly. Cash budgets are also useful in helping to control the cash held. The actual cash flows can be compared with the projected cash flows for the period. If there is a significant divergence between the projected cash flows and the actual cash flows, explanations must be sought and corrective action taken where necessary.

To refresh your memory, an example of a cash budget is given in Example 16.4. Remember, there is no set format for this statement. Managers can determine how best the information should be presented. However, the format set out in the example appears to be in widespread use. Cash budgets covering the short term are usually broken down into monthly (and in some cases, weekly) periods to enable close monitoring of cash movements. Cash inflows are usually shown above cash outflows, and the difference between them (the net cash flow) for a month is identified separately along with the closing cash balance.

Example 16.4

Cash budget for the six months to 30 November

	June £	July £	August £	September £	October £	November £
Cash inflows						
Credit sales	–	–	4,000	5,500	7,000	8,500
Cash sales	4,000	5,500	7,000	8,500	11,000	11,000
	4,000	5,500	11,000	14,000	18,000	19,500
Cash outflows						
Motor vehicles	6,000					
Equipment	10,000					7,200
Freehold premises	40,000					
Purchases	–	29,000	9,250	11,500	13,750	17,500
Wages/salaries	900	900	900	900	900	900
Commission	–	320	440	560	680	680
Overheads	500	500	500	500	650	650
	57,400	30,720	11,090	13,460	15,980	26,930
Net cash flow	(53,400)	(25,220)	(90)	540	2,020	(7,430)
Opening balance	60,000	6,600	(18,620)	(18,710)	(18,170)	(16,150)
Closing balance	6,600	(18,620)	(18,710)	(18,170)	(16,150)	(23,580)

Although cash budgets are prepared primarily for internal management purposes, they are sometimes required by prospective lenders when a loan to a business is being considered.

Operating cash cycle

➲ When managing cash, it is important to be aware of the **operating cash cycle** of the business. This may be defined as the time period between the outlay of cash necessary for the purchase of stocks and the ultimate receipt of cash from the sale of the goods. The operating cash cycle of a business that purchases goods on credit, for subsequent resale on credit, is shown diagrammatically in Figure 16.7.

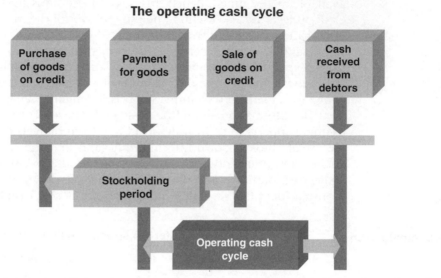

Figure 16.7

The operating cash cycle

The diagram shows that goods purchased on credit will be paid for at a later date and so no immediate cash outflow will occur. Similarly, credit sales will not lead to an immediate inflow of cash. The operating cash cycle is the time period between the payment made to the supplier and the cash received from the customer.

The diagram shows that payment for goods acquired on credit occurs some time after the goods have been purchased and, therefore, no immediate cash outflow arises from the purchase. Similarly, cash receipts from debtors will occur some time after the sale is made and so there will be no immediate cash inflow as a result of the sale. The operating cash cycle is the time period between the payment made to the creditor for goods supplied, and the receipt of cash from the debtor.

The operating cash cycle is important because it has a significant influence on the financing requirements of the business. The longer the cash cycle, the greater the financing requirements of the business and the greater the financial risks. For this reason, a business is likely to want to reduce the operating cash cycle to the minimum possible period.

For the type of business, mentioned above, that buys and sells on credit, the operating cash cycle can be calculated from the financial statements by the use of certain ratios, as follows:

Average stockholding period

+

Average settlement period for debtors

−

Average payment period for creditors

=

Operating cash cycle

The accounts of Freezeqwik Ltd, a distributor of frozen foods, is set out below for the year ended 31 December last year.

Profit and loss account for the year ended 31 December

	£000	£000
Sales		820
Less Cost of sales		
Opening stock	142	
Purchases	568	
	710	
Less Closing stock	166	544
Gross profit		276
Administration expenses	(120)	
Selling and distribution expenses	(95)	
Financial expenses	(32)	(247)
Net profit		29
Corporation tax		(7)
Retained profit for the year		22

Balance sheet as at 31 December

	£000	£000	£000
Fixed assets at written down value			
Freehold premises			180
Fixtures and fittings			82
Motor vans			102
			364
Current assets			
Stock		166	
Trade debtors		264	
Cash		24	
		454	
Less Creditors: amounts falling due within one year			
Trade creditors	159		
Corporation tax	7	166	288
			652
Capital and reserves			
Ordinary share capital			300
Preference share capital			200
Retained profit			152
			652

All purchases and sales are on credit.

Calculate the operating cash cycle for the business and go on to suggest how the business may seek to reduce the cash cycle.

....

The operating cash cycle may be calculated as follows:

Average stockholding period:

$$\frac{(\text{Opening stock} + \text{closing stock})/2}{\text{Cost of sales}} \times 365 = \frac{(142 + 166)/2}{544} \times 365 = 103$$

Add Average settlement period for debtors:

$$\frac{\text{Trade debtors}}{\text{Credit sales}} \times 365 = \frac{264}{820} \times 365 = 118$$

Less Average settlement period for creditors

$$\frac{\text{Trade creditors}}{\text{Credit purchases}} \times 365 = \frac{159}{568} \times 365 = \underline{(102)}$$

Operating cash cycle: $\underline{\underline{119}}$

The company can reduce the operating cash cycle in a number of ways. The average stockholding period seems quite long. At present, average stocks held represent more than three months' sales. This may be reduced by reducing the level of stocks held. Similarly, the average settlement period for debtors seems long at nearly four months' sales. This may be reduced by imposing tighter credit control, offering discounts or charging interest on overdue accounts. However, any policy decisions concerning stocks and debtors must take account of current trading conditions.

The operating cash cycle could also be reduced by edtending the period of credit taken to pay suppliers. However, for reasons that will be explained later, this option must be given careful consideration.

Cash transmission

A business will normally wish to benefit from receipts from customers at the earliest opportunity. The benefit is immediate where payment is made in cash; when payment is by cheque, there is normally a delay of three to four working days before the cheque is cleared through the banking system, and the business must therefore wait for this period before it can benefit from the amount paid in. In the case of a business that receives large amounts in the form of cheques, the opportunity cost of this delay can be very significant.

To avoid this delay, a business could require payments to be made in cash. This is not usually practical for a number of reasons. Another option is to ask for payment to be made by standing order or by direct debit from the customer's bank account. This should ensure that the amount owing is always transferred on the day that has been agreed.

It is also possible for funds to be directly transferred to a business bank account. As a result of developments in computer technology, customers can pay for items by using debit cards which results in the appropriate accounts being instantly debited and sellers' bank accounts being instantly credited with the specified amounts. This method of payment is widely used by large retail businesses and may well extend to other types of business.

●●●● Management of trade creditors

Trade credit is regarded as an important source of finance by many businesses. It has been described as a 'spontaneous' source as it tends to increase in line with the level of sales achieved by a business. Trade credit is widely regarded as a 'free' source of finance and, therefore, a good thing for a business to use. There may be real costs associated with taking trade credit, however.

Firstly, customers who take credit may not be as well-favoured as those who pay immediately. For example, when goods are in short supply, credit customers may receive lower priority when allocating the stock available. In addition, credit customers may be less favoured in terms of delivery dates or the provision of technical support services. Sometimes, the goods or services provided may be more costly if credit is required. However, in most industries, trade credit is the norm and, as a result, the costs listed above will not apply unless, perhaps, the credit facilities are abused by the customer. A business purchasing supplies on credit may also have to incur additional administration and accounting costs in dealing with the scrutiny and payment of invoices, maintaining and updating creditors' accounts, and so on.

Where a supplier offers discount for prompt payment, a buyer should give careful consideration to paying within the discount period. Example 16.5 usefully illustrates the cost of forgoing possible discounts.

Example 16.5

A. Hassam Ltd takes 70 days to pay for goods supplied by its supplier. To encourage prompt payment, the supplier has offered the company a 2 per cent discount if payment for goods is made within 30 days. Hassam is not sure whether it is worth taking the discount offered. The annual percentage cost to the company of forgoing the discount can be deduced as follows.

If the discount is taken, payment could be made on the last day of the period (the 30th day). However, if it is not taken, payment will be made after 70 days. This means that by not taking the discount the business will receive an extra 40 (that is, 70 − 30) days' credit. The cost of this extra credit to the company will be the 2 per cent discount forgone. If we annualise the cost of this discount forgone, we have:

$$\frac{365}{40} \times 2\% = 18.3\%$$

We can see the annual cost of forgoing the discount is very high and it may be profitable for the business to pay the supplier within the discount period even if it means that the company will have to borrow to enable it to do so.

(*Note*: this is an approximate annual rate. For the more mathematically minded, the precise rate is $[((1 + (2/98)^{9.125}) - 1) \times 100\%] = 20.2\%$.)

The above points are not meant to imply that taking credit is a burden to a business. There are, of course, real benefits that can accrue. Provided that trade credit is not abused, it can represent a form of interest-free loan. It can be a much more convenient method of paying for goods and services than paying by cash and, during a period of inflation, there will be an economic gain by paying later rather than sooner for goods and services purchased. For most businesses, these benefits will exceed the costs involved.

Controlling trade creditors

To help monitor the level of trade credit taken, management can calculate the **average settlement period for creditors** which, as we have already seen, is as follows:

$$\text{Average settlement period for creditors} = \frac{\text{Trade creditors}}{\text{Credit purchases}} \times 365 \text{ days}$$

Once again, this provides an average figure, which could be misleading. A more informative approach would be to produce an ageing schedule for creditors. This would look much the same as the ageing schedule for debtors described earlier.

Management of bank overdrafts

We saw in Chapter 15 that a bank overdraft is a flexible form of borrowing and is cheap relative to other sources of finance. For this reason, the majority of UK businesses use bank overdrafts, to a greater or lesser extent, for finance. Although, in theory, bank overdrafts are a short-term source of finance, in practice they can extend over a long period of time as many businesses continually renew their overdraft facility with their bank. Though renewal may not usually be a problem, there is always a danger that the bank will demand repayment at short notice, as it has the right to do. If the business is highly dependent on borrowing and alternative sources of borrowing are difficult to find, this could raise severe problems.

When considering whether or not to have a bank overdraft, the business should first consider the purpose of the borrowing. Overdrafts are most suitable for overcoming short-term funding problems (for example, increases in stock-holding requirements owing to seasonal fluctuations) and should be self-liquidating, as explained in Chapter 15. For longer-term funding problems, or borrowings that are not self-liquidating, other sources of finance might be suitable.

It is important to agree the correct facility with the bank as borrowings in excess of the overdraft limit may incur high charges. To determine the amount of the overdraft facility, the business should produce cash budgets. There should also be regular reporting of cash flows over time to try to ensure that the overdraft limit is not exceeded.

Summary

In this chapter we have identified and examined the main elements of working capital. We have seen that the management of working capital requires an evaluation of both the costs and benefits associated with each element. Some of these costs and benefits may be hard to quantify in practice. Nevertheless, an assessment must be made in order to try to optimise the use of funds within a business. We have examined various techniques for the management of working capital. These techniques vary in their level of sophistication: some rely heavily on management judgement whilst others adopt a more objective, quantitative approach.

Key terms

Working capital   p. 509
ABC system of stock control   p. 514
Economic order quantity (EOQ)   p. 515
Materials requirement planning (MRP) system   p. 517
Just-in-time (JIT) stock management p. 518
Five Cs of credit   p. 519

Cash discount   p. 522
Average settlement period for debtors p. 523
Ageing schedule of debtors   p. 524
Operating cash cycle   p. 529
Average settlement period for creditors p. 534

● Further reading

If you would like to explore the topics covered in this chapter in more depth, we recommend the following books:

Business Finance: Theory and Practice, *McLaney, E.*, 5th edn, Financial Times Prentice Hall, 2000, chapter 13.
Corporate Finance and Investment, *Pike, R. and Neale, B.*, 3rd edn, Prentice Hall International, 1999, chapters 14 and 15.
Financial Management and Decision Making, *Samuels, J., Wilkes, F. and Brayshaw, R.*, International Thomson Business Press, 1999, chapter 18.
Corporate Financial Management, *Arnold, G.*, Financial Times Prentice Hall, 1998, chapter 13.

16.1 Tariq is the credit manager of Heltex plc. He is concerned that the pattern of monthly sales receipts shows that credit collection is poor compared with budget. The sales director believes that Tariq is to blame for this situation but Tariq insists that he is not. Why might Tariq *not* be to blame for the deterioration in the credit collection period?

16.2 How might each of the following affect the level of stocks held by a business?

(a) An increase in the number of production bottlenecks experienced by the business.
(b) A rise in the level of interest rates.
(c) A decision to offer customers a narrower range of products in the future.
(d) A switch of suppliers from an overseas business to a local one.
(e) A deterioration in the quality and reliability of bought-in components.

16.3 What are the reasons for holding stocks? Are these reasons different from the reasons for holding cash?

16.4 Identify the costs of holding: (a) too little cash, and (b) too much cash?

? **EXERCISES**

Exercises 16.5–16.8 are more advanced than 16.1–16.4. Those with coloured numbers have answers at the back of the book.

 16.1 Hercules Wholesalers Ltd has been particularly concerned with its liquidity position in recent months. The most recent profit and loss account and balance sheet of the company are as follows:

Profit and loss account for the year ended 31 May last year

	£000	£000
Sales		452
Less Cost of sales		
Opening stock	125	
Add purchases	341	
	466	
Less Closing stock	143	323
Gross profit		129
Expenses		(132)
Net loss for the period		(3)

Balance sheet as at 31 May last year

	£000	£000	£000
Fixed assets			
Freehold premises at valuation			280
Fixtures and fittings at cost less depreciation			25
Motor vehicles at cost less depreciation			52
			357

Current assets

Stock			143
Debtors			163
			306

Less **Creditors due within one year**

Trade creditors	145		
Bank overdraft	140	285	21
			378

Less **Creditors due after more than one year**

Loans		120
		258

Capital and reserves

Ordinary share capital		100
Retained profit		158
		258

The debtors and creditors were maintained at a constant level throughout the year.

Required:
(a) Explain why Hercules is concerned about its liquidity position.
(b) Calculate the operating cash cycle for Hercules based on the information above. (Assume a 360-day year.)
(c) State what steps may be taken to improve the operating cash cycle of the company.

16.2 International Electric plc at present offers its customers 30 days' credit. Half the customers, by value, pay on time. The other half take an average of 70 days to pay. It is considering offering a cash discount of 2 per cent to its customers for payment within 30 days.

It anticipates that half of the customers who now take an average of 70 days to pay (that is, a quarter of all customers) will pay in 30 days. The other half (the final quarter) will still take an average of 70 days to pay. The scheme will also reduce bad debts by £300,000 per year.

Annual sales of £365 million are made evenly throughout the year. At present the company has a large overdraft (£60 million) with its bank at 12 per cent a year.

Required:
(a) Calculate the approximate equivalent annual percentage cost of a discount of 2 per cent that reduces the time taken by debtors to pay from 70 days to 30 days. *Hint:* this part can be answered without reference to the narrative above.
(b) Calculate debtors outstanding under both the old and new schemes.
(c) How much will the scheme cost the company in discounts?
(d) Should the company go ahead with the scheme? State what other factors, if any, should be taken into account.
(e) Outline the controls and procedures that a company should adopt to manage the level of its debtors.

16.3 The managing director of Sparkrite Ltd, a trading company, has just received summary sets of accounts for last year and this year, as follows.

Profit and loss accounts for years ended 30 September

	last year		this year	
	£000	£000	£000	£000
Sales		1,800		1,920
Less Cost of sales				
Opening stock	160		200	
Purchases	1,120		1,175	
	1,280		1,375	
Less Closing stocks	200		250	
		1,080		1,125
Gross profit		720		795
Less Expenses		680		750
Net profit		40		45

Balance sheets as at 30 September

	last year		this year	
	£000	£000	£000	£000
Fixed assets		950		930
Current assets:				
Stock	200		250	
Debtors	375		480	
Bank	4		2	
	579		732	
Less Creditors due within one year	195		225	
		384		507
		1,334		1,437
Financed by:				
Fully paid £1 ordinary shares		825		883
Reserves		509		554
		1,334		1,437

The finance director has expressed concern at the deterioration in stock and debtors levels.

Required:
(a) Show by using the data given how you would calculate ratios that could be used to measure stock and debtor levels for both years.
(b) Discuss the ways in which the management of Sparkrite Ltd could exercise control over (i) stock levels and (ii) debtor levels.

16.4 Dylan Ltd operates an advertising agency. It has an annual turnover of £20 million before taking into account bad debts of £0.1 million. All sales are on credit and, on average, the settlement period for trade debtors is 60 days. The company is currently reviewing its credit policies.

To encourage prompt payment, the credit control department has proposed that customers should be given a 2½ per cent discount if they pay within 30 days; for those who do not pay within this period, a maximum of 50 days' credit should be given. The credit department believes that 60 per cent of customers will take advantage of the discount by paying at the end of the discount period and the remainder will pay at the end of 50 days.

The credit department believes that bad debts can be effectively eliminated by adopting the above policies and by employing stricter credit investigation procedures, which will cost an additional £20,000 a year. The credit department is confident that these new policies will not result in any reduction in sales.

The business has a £6 million overdraft on which it pays annual interest of 14 per cent.

Required:

Calculate the net annual cost (savings) to the company of abandoning its existing credit policies and adopting the proposals of the credit control department.

16.5 Your superior, the general manager of Plastics Manufacturers Limited, has recently been talking to the chief buyer of Plastic Toys Limited, which manufactures a wide range of toys for young children. At present, Plastic Toys is considering changing its supplier of plastic granules and has offered to buy its entire requirement of 2,000 kilograms a month from you at the going market rate, providing that you will grant it three months' credit on its purchases. The following information is available:

(i) Plastic granules sell for £10 per kilogram, variable costs are £7 per kilogram and fixed costs £2 per kilogram.

(ii) Your own company is financially strong and has sales of £15 million a year. For the foreseeable future it will have surplus capacity and it is actively looking for new outlets.

(iii) Extracts from Plastic Toys' accounts:

	1999 £000	2000 £000	2001 £000
Sales	800	980	640
Profit before interest and tax	100	110	(150)
Capital employed	600	650	575
Current assets			
Stocks	200	220	320
Debtors	140	160	160
	340	380	480
Creditors due within one year			
Creditors	(180)	(190)	(220)
Overdraft	(100)	(150)	(310)
	(280)	(340)	(530)
Net current assets	60	40	(50)

Required:

(a) Write some short notes suggesting sources of information you would use to assess the creditworthiness of potential customers who are unknown to you. You should critically evaluate each source of information.

(b) Describe the accounting controls you would use to monitor the level of your company's trade debtors.

(c) Advise your general manager on the acceptability of the proposal. You should give your reasons and do any calculations you consider necessary.

Hint: to answer this question you must weigh the costs of administration and cash discounts against the savings in bad debts and interest charges.

16.6 Boswell Enterprises Ltd is reviewing its trade credit policy. The business, which sells all of its goods on credit, has estimated that sales for the forthcoming year will be £3 million under the existing policy. 30 per cent of trade debtors are expected to pay one month after being invoiced and 70 per cent are expected to pay two months after being invoiced. These estimates are in line with previous years' figures.

At present, no cash discounts are offered to customers. However, to encourage prompt payment the company is considering giving a 2½ per cent cash discount to debtors who pay in one month or less. Given this incentive, the company expects 60 per cent of trade debtors to pay one month after being invoiced and 40 per cent of debtors to pay two months after being invoiced. The business believes that the introduction of a cash discount policy will prove attractive to some customers and will lead to a 5 per cent increase in total sales.

Irrespective of the trade credit policy adopted, the gross profit margin of the business will be 20 per cent for the forthcoming year and three months' stock will be held. Fixed monthly expenses of £15,000 and variable expenses (excluding discounts), equivalent to 10 per cent of sales, will be incurred and will be paid one month in arrears. Trade creditors will be paid in arrears and will be equal to two months' cost of sales. The company will hold a fixed cash balance of £140,000 throughout the year, whichever trade credit policy is adopted. No dividends will be proposed or paid during the year. Ignore taxation.

Required:
(a) Calculate the investment in working capital at the end of the forthcoming year under:
  - The existing policy
  - The proposed policy.
(b) Calculate the expected net profit for the forthcoming year under:
  - The existing policy
  - The proposed policy.
(c) Advise the business as to whether it should implement the proposed policy.

Hint: the investment in working capital will be made up of stock, debtors and cash, *less* trade creditors and any unpaid expenses at the year end.

16.7 Delphi plc has recently decided to enter the expanding market for minidisc players. The business will manufacture the players and sell them to small TV and hi-fi specialists, medium-sized music stores and large retail chain stores. The new product will be launched next February and predicted sales for the product from each customer group for February and the expected rate of growth for subsequent months are as follows:

Customer type	February sales £000	Monthly compound % sales growth	Credit sales (months)
TV and hi-fi specialists	20	4	1
Music stores	30	6	2
Retail chain stores	40	8	3

The business is concerned about the financing implications of launching the new product as it is already experiencing liquidity problems. In addition, it is concerned that the credit control department will find it difficult to cope. This is a new market for the company and there are likely to be many new customers who will have to be investigated for creditworthiness.

Workings should be in £000 and calculations made to one decimal point only.

Required:

(a) Prepare an ageing schedule of the monthly debtors balance relating to the new product for each of the first four months of the new product's life, and comment on the results. The schedule should analyse the debts outstanding according to customer type. It should also indicate, for each customer type, the relevant percentage outstanding in relation to the total amount outstanding for each month.

(b) Identify and discuss the factors that should be taken into account when evaluating the creditworthiness of the new business customers.

(c) Identify and discuss a method of raising finance for the business, which is based on the use of its trade debtors and which may help deal with the liquidity problems referred to above.

16.8 | Goliath plc is a retail business operating in Ireland. The most recent accounts of the business are as follows:

Profit and loss account for the year to 31 May

	£000	£000
Sales		2,400.0
Less Cost of sales		
Opening stock	550.0	
Add Purchases	1,450.0	
	2,000.0	
Less Closing stock	560.0	1,440.0
Gross profit		960.0
Administration expenses	(300.0)	
Selling expenses	(436.0)	
Interest payable	(40.0)	(776.0)
Net profit before taxation		184.0
Less Corporation tax (25%)		46.0
Net profit after taxation		138.0

Balance sheet as at 31 May

	£000	£000	£000
Fixed assets			
Machinery and equipment at cost		424.4	
Less Accumulated depreciation		140.8	283.6
Motor vehicles at cost		308.4	
Less Accumulated depreciation		135.6	172.8
			456.4
Current assets			
Stock at cost		560.0	
Trade debtors		565.0	
Cash at bank		36.4	
		1,161.4	

Creditors: amounts falling due within one year

Trade creditors	(451.0)		
Corporation tax due	(46.0)	(497.0)	664.4
			1,120.8

Creditors: amounts falling due after one year

Loan capital	(400.0)
	720.8

Capital and reserves

£1 ordinary shares	200.0
Retained profit	520.8
	720.8

All sales and purchases are made on credit.

The business is considering whether to grant extended credit facilities to its customers. It has been estimated that increasing the settlement period for debtors by a further 20 days will increase the turnover of the business by 10 per cent. However, stocks will have to be increased by 15 per cent to cope with the increased demand. It is estimated that purchases will have to rise to £1,668,000 during the next year as a result of these changes. To finance the increase in stocks and debtors, the business will increase the settlement period taken for suppliers by 15 days and utilise a loan facility bearing a 10 per cent rate of interest for the remaining balance.

If the policy is implemented, bad debts are likely to increase by £120,000 and administration costs will rise by 15 per cent.

Required:
(a) Calculate the increase or decrease to each of the following that will occur in the forthcoming year if the proposed policy is implemented:
   (i)   operating cash cycle (based on year-end figures)
   (ii) net investment in stock, debtors and creditors
   (iii) net profit after taxation.
(b) Should the company implement the proposed policy? Give reasons for your conclusion.

PART 4

Supplementary information

Part 4 provides information that is supplementary to the main text of the book.

Appendix A takes the format of a normal textual chapter and describes the way in which financial transactions are recorded in books of account. Generally, this is by means of the 'double entry' system, described in basic terms in the Appendix.

Appendix B gives definitions of the key terms highlighted throughout the main text and summarised at the end of each chapter. The aim of the Appendix is to provide a singular location to check on the meanings of the major accounting terms used in this book and in the world of finance.

Appendices C and D give answers to some of the questions set in the course of the main text. Appendix C gives answers to the self-assessment questions, and Appendix D to those of the exercises that are marked as having their answers provided in the book.

Appendix A
Recording financial transactions

● Introduction

In Chapters 2 and 3, we saw how the accounting transactions of a business may be recorded by making a series of entries on the balance sheet and/or profit and loss account. Each of these entries had its corresponding 'double' such that, after both sides of the transaction had been recorded, the balance sheet continued to justify its name and to balance. Adjusting the balance sheet, by hand for each transaction could be very messy and confusing. With a reasonably large number of transactions it is pretty certain to result in mistakes.

For businesses whose accounting systems are on a computer, this problem is overcome because suitable software can deal with a series of 'plus' and 'minus' entries very reliably. Where the accounting system is not computerised, it would be helpful to have some more practical way of keeping accounting records. Such a system not only exists but, before the advent of the computer, was the routine way of keeping accounts. It is this system that is explained in this Appendix. You should be clear that the system we are going to consider follows exactly the same rules as those that you have already met. Its distinguishing feature is its ability to give those keeping accounting records by hand, a methodical approach to follow, where errors should be minimised.

OBJECTIVES When you have completed this Appendix you should be able to:

- Explain the basic principles of double-entry bookkeeping.
- Write up a series of business transactions and balance the accounts.
- Extract a trial balance and explain its purpose.
- Prepare a set of final accounts from the underlying double-entry accounts.

●●●● The basics of double-entry bookkeeping

➔ In **double-entry bookkeeping**, instead of having a balance sheet where plus and minus entries are made in various areas according to the aspects (for example, cash) that are concerned with a particular transaction, each aspect has its own ➔ 'mini balance sheet', known as an **account**, which, for cash, would appear as follows:

Cash

	£		£

As with the balance sheet, an increase in cash appears on the left-hand side of this account.

Suppose that the entries are for a new business with no cash, but it is started by the owner putting £5,000 in the new business's bank account as initial capital. This entry would appear in the cash account as follows:

Cash

	£		£
1 January Capital	5,000		

The corresponding entry would be made in the capital account as follows:

Capital

	£		£
		1 January Cash	5,000

In the same way as an increase in capital goes on the right-hand side of the balance sheet, we show an increase in capital on the right-hand side of the capital account. It is usual to show, in each account, where the other side of the entry will be found. Thus someone looking at the capital account will know that the £5,000 arose from a receipt of cash. This not only provides potentially useful information, but enables a 'trail' to be followed when checking for errors. Including the date of the transaction provides additional information to the reader of the accounts.

Let us now suppose that £600 of the cash is used to buy some stock. This would affect the cash account as follows:

Cash

	£		£
1 January Capital	5,000	2 January Stock	600

Now we have seen one of the crucial differences between the use of accounts (double-entry bookkeeping) and adjusting the balance sheet: when you reduce an asset or a claim, you do not put an entry in the same column with a minus sign against it but, instead, you put it on the opposite side of the account. This cash account in effect shows 'positive' cash of £5,000 and 'negative' cash of £600, a net amount of £4,400.

Activity A.1

As you know, we must somehow record the other side of the transaction involving the acquisition of the stock for £600. See if you can work out what to do in respect of the stock.

....

We must open an account for stock. Since stock is an asset, an increase in it will appear on the left-hand side of the account, as follows:

Stock				
	£			£
2 January Cash	600			

What we have seen so far highlights the key rule of double-entry bookkeeping: each left-hand entry must have a right-hand entry of equal size. Using the jargon we can say *every* **debit** *must have a* **credit**. ('Debit' simply means the left-hand side of an account, and 'credit' means the right-hand side.)

The rules of double entry also extend to 'trading' transactions – that is, making revenues (sales and so on) and incurring expenses. Thus, when on 3 January the business paid £300 to rent business premises (to include heat and light) for the month, we should normally open a 'rent account' and make the following entries in this account and in the cash account:

Rent				
	£			£
3 January Cash	300			

Cash				
	£			£
1 January Capital	5,000		2 January Stock	600
			3 January Rent	300

The treatment of the rent illustrates an important point: it is not just assets that appear on the debit side of accounts; expenses do as well. This is not altogether surprising since assets and expenses are closely linked. Assets actually transform into expenses as they are 'used up'. Rent, which, as here, is usually paid in advance, is an asset when it is first paid. It represents the value to the business of being entitled to occupy the premises for the forthcoming period (until the end of January in this case). As January progresses, this asset becomes an expense; it is 'used up'. This does not require that we make any adjustment to the rent account, but we need to remember that the debit entry in the rent account does not necessarily represent an asset nor an expense; it could be a mixture of the two. Strictly, by the end of the day on which it was paid (3 January), £29.03 would have represented an expense for the three days, the remaining £270.97 would have been an asset. As each day passes, £9.68 (that is, £300/31) more will transform from an asset into an expense. As we have already seen, it is not necessary for us to make any adjustment to the rent account as the days pass.

Assume, now, that on 5 January the business sold stock costing £200 for £300 on credit. As usual, when we are able to identify the cost of the goods sold at the time of sale, we need to deal with the sale and the cost of the stock sold as two separate issues, each having its own set of debits and credits.

Firstly, let us deal with the sale. We now need to open accounts for both 'sales' and 'trade debtors' – which do not, as yet, exist. The sale is an increase in a revenue, hence the credit entry, which creates an asset, and hence the debit entry in trade debtors:

Sales

	£			£
		5 January	Trade debtors	300

Trade debtors

	£		£
5 January Sales	300		

Let us now deal with the stock sold. Since the stock sold has become the expense 'cost of sales', we need to reduce the figure on the stock account by making a credit entry and make the corresponding debit in a 'cost of sales' account, opened for the purpose:

Stock

	£			£
2 January Cash	600	5 January	Cost of sales	200

Cost of sales

	£		£
5 January Stock	200		

Following the example of sales, we can make the general points that:

- **Debits (left-hand entries) represent increases in assets and expenses and decreases in claims and revenues.**
- **Credits (right-hand entries) represent increases in claims and revenues and decreases in assets and expenses.**

We shall now look at the other transactions for our hypothetical business for the remainder of January. These can be taken to be as follows:

January 8	Bought some stock on credit costing £800
January 11	Bought some office furniture for £400
January 15	Sold stock costing £600 for £900, on credit
January 18	Received £800 from trade debtors
January 21	Paid trade creditors £500
January 24	Paid wages for the month £400
January 27	Bought stock on credit for £800
January 31	Borrowed £2,000 from the Commercial Finance Company

Naturally, we shall have to open several additional accounts to enable us to record all of these transactions in any meaningful way. By the end of January, the set of accounts would appear as follows:

Cash

		£			£
1 January	Capital	5,000	2 January	Stock	600
18 January	Trade debtors	800	3 January	Rent	300
31 January	Comm. Fin Co	2,000	11 January	Office furniture	400
			21 January	Trade creditors	500
			24 January	Wages	400

Capital

		£			£
			1 January	Cash	5,000

Stock

		£			£
2 January	Cash	600	5 January	Cost of sales	200
8 January	Trade creditors	800	15 January	Cost of sales	600
27 January	Trade creditors	800			

Rent

		£		£
3 January	Cash	300		

Sales

	£			£
		5 January	Trade debtors	300
		15 January	Trade debtors	900

Trade debtors

		£			£
5 January	Sales	300	18 January	Cash	800
15 January	Sales	900			

Cost of sales

		£		£
5 January	Stock	200		
15 January	Stock	600		

Trade creditors

		£			£
21 January	Cash	500	8 January	Stock	800
			27 January	Stock	800

Office furniture

		£		£
11 January	Cash	400		

Wages

		£		£
24 January	Cash	400		

Loan creditor – Commercial Finance Company

	£			£
		31 January	Cash	2,000

All of the transactions from 8 January onwards are quite similar in nature to those up to that date, which we discussed in detail, and so you should be able to follow them using the date references as a guide.

Balancing accounts and the trial balance

Businesses keeping their accounts in the way shown would find it helpful to summarise their individual accounts periodically – perhaps weekly or monthly – for two reasons:

- To be able to see at a glance how much is in each account (for example, to see how much cash the business has left).
- To help to check the accuracy of the bookkeeping so far.

Let us look at the cash account again:

Cash

		£			£
1 January	Capital	5,000	2 January	Stock	600
18 January	Trade debtors	800	3 January	Rent	300
31 January	Comm. Fin. Co.	2,000	11 January	Office furniture	400
			21 January	Trade creditors	500
			24 January	Wages	400

Does this account tell us how much cash the business has at 31 January? The answer is partly yes and partly no!

We can fairly easily deduce the amount of cash simply by adding up the debit (receipts) column and deducting the sum of the credit (payments) column, but it would be easier if this were done for us.

To summarise or **balance** this account, we add up the larger column (the debit side) and put this total on both sides of the account. We then put in, on the credit side, the figure that will make that side add up to the same figure. We cannot put in this balancing figure only once or the double-entry rule will have been broken, and so we also put it in on the other side below the totals, as follows:

Cash

		£			£
1 January	Capital	5,000	2 January	Stock	600
18 January	Trade debtors	800	3 January	Rent	300
31 January	Comm. Fin Co	2,000	11 January	Trade creditors	400
			21 January	Trade creditors	500
			24 January	Wages	400
			31 January		
				Balance carried down	5,600
		7,800			7,800
1 February					
	Balance brought down	5,600			

Note that the balance carried down (usually abbreviated to 'c/d') at the end of one period becomes the balance brought down ('b/d') at the beginning of the next. Now we can see at a glance what the present situation is, without having to do any mental arithmetic.

<table>
<tr><td>**Activity A.2**</td><td colspan="5">Have a try at balancing the stock account and then say what we know about the stock situation at the end of January.</td></tr>
</table>

Stock

		£			£
2 January	Cash	600	5 January	Cost of sales	200
8 January	Trade creditors	800 ·	15 January	Cost of sales	600
27 January	Trade creditors	800	31 January	Balance c/d	1,400
		2,200			2,200
1 February	Balance b/d	1,400 ·			

We can see at a glance that the business held stock that had cost £1,400 at the end of January. We can also see quite easily how this situation arose.

We can balance all of the other accounts in similar fashion. There is no point in formally balancing accounts that have only one entry at the moment (for example, the capital account) because we cannot summarise one figure; it is already in as summarised a form as it can be. After balancing, the other accounts will be as follows:

Capital

	£			£
		1 January	Cash	5,000

Rent

		£		£
3 January	Cash	300		

Sales

		£			£
31 January	Balance c/d	1,200	5 January	Trade debtors	300
			15 January	Trade debtors	900
		1,200			1,200
			1 February	Balance b/d	1,200

Trade debtors

		£			£
5 January	Sales	300	18 January	Cash	800
15 January	Sales	900	31 January	Balance c/d	400
		1,200			1,200
1 February	Balance b/d	400			

Cost of sales

		£			£
5 January	Stock	200	31 January	Balance c/d	800
15 January	Stock	600			
		800			800
1 February	Balance b/d	800			

Trade creditors

		£			£
21 January	Cash	500	8 January	Stock	800
31 January	Balance c/d	1,100	27 January	Stock	800
		1,600			1,600
			1 February	Balance b/d	1,100

Office furniture

		£		£
11 January	Cash	400		

Wages

		£		£
24 January	Cash	400		

Loan creditor – Commercial Finance Company

	£			£
		31 January	Cash	2,000

Activity A.3

If we now separately total the debit balances and the credit ones, what should we expect to find?

....

We should expect to find that these two totals are equal. This must, in theory be true since every debit entry was matched by an equally-sized credit entry.

Let us see if our expectation in Activity A.3 works in our example, by listing the debit and credit balances as follows:

	Debits £	Credits £
Cash	5,600	
Stock	1,400	
Capital		5,000
Rent	300	
Sales		1,200
Trade debtors	400	
Cost of sales	800	
Trade creditors		1,100
Office furniture	400	
Wages	400	
Loan creditor		2,000
	9,300	9,300

This statement is known as a **trial balance**. The fact that it agrees gives us some indication that we have not made any bookkeeping errors.

This situation, does not, however, give us total confidence that no error could have occurred. Consider the transaction that took place on 3 January (paid rent for the month of £300). In each of the following cases, all of which would be wrong, the trial balance would still have agreed:

- The transaction was completely omitted from the accounts; that is, no entries were made at all.
- The amount was misread as £3,000 but then (correctly) debited to the rent account and credited to cash.
- The correct amount was (incorrectly) debited to cash and credited to rent.

Nevertheless, a trial balance that agrees does give some confidence that accounts have been correctly written up.

| Activity A.4 | Why do you think the words 'debtor' and 'creditor' are used to describe those who owe money or are owed money by a business? |

The answer simply is that debtors have a debit balance in the books of the business, whereas creditors have a credit balance.

Preparing final accounts

The next stage in the process is to prepare the profit and loss account and balance sheet. Preparing the profit and loss account is simply a matter of going through the individual accounts, identifying those balances that represent revenues and expenses of the period, and transferring them to a profit and loss account, which is part of the double-entry system.

We shall now do this for the example we have been using. To simplify matters, we shall assume that there is no depreciation on the office furniture, nor any interest due on the loan, nor any other prepaid or accrued expenses. You should be clear, however, that end-of-period adjustments of this type can very easily be dealt with in double-entry accounts.

The balances on the following accounts represent expenses or revenues for the month of January:

- Rent
- Sales
- Cost of sales
- Wages.

The balances on these accounts will be transferred to a profit and loss account. The remaining balances represent assets and claims that continue to exist at the end of January.

The four accounts whose balances represent revenues or expenses, and the profit and loss account, are dealt with next. To transfer balances to the profit and loss account, we simply debit or credit the account concerned, such that any balance amount is eliminated, and make the corresponding credit or debit in the profit and loss account. Take rent, for example. This has a debit balance (because the balance represents an expense). We must credit the rent account with £300 and debit profit and loss account with the same amount. So a debit balance on the rent account becomes a debit entry in the profit and loss account which is then, along with the other expenses, compared with the sales For the four accounts, then, we have the following:

Rent

		£			£
3 January	Cash	300	31 January	Profit and loss	300

Sales

		£			£
31 January	Balance c/d	1,200	5 January	Trade debtors	300
			15 January	Trade debtors	900
		1,200			1,200
31 January	Profit and loss	1,200	1 February	Balance b/d	1,200

Cost of sales

		£			£
5 January	Stock	200	31 January	Balance c/d	800
15 January	Stock	600			
		800			800
1 February	Balance b/d	800	31 January	Profit and loss	800

Wages

		£			£
24 January	Cash	400	31 January	Profit and loss	400

Profit and loss account

		£			£
31 January	Cost of sales	800	31 January	Sales	1,200
31 January	Rent	300			
31 January	Wages	400			

We must now transfer the balance on the profit and loss account (a debit balance of £300).

Activity A.5

What does the balance on the profit and loss account represent, and where should it be transferred to?

....

The balance is either the profit or the loss (loss in this case) for the period. This loss must be borne by the owner, and it must therefore be transferred to the capital account.

The two accounts would now appear as follows:

Profit and loss account

	£		£
31 January Cost of sales	800	31 January Sales	1,200
31 January Rent	300		
31 January Wages	400	31 January Capital (net loss)	300
	1,500		1,500

Capital

	£		£
31 January Profit and loss	300	1 January Cash	5,000
(net loss)			
31 January Balance c/d	4,700		
	5,000		5,000
		1 February Balance b/d	4,700

The last thing done was to balance the capital account.

Now all of the balances remaining on accounts represent either assets or claims as at 31 January. These balances can now be used to produce a balance sheet, as follows:

Balance sheet as at 31 January

	£	£
Fixed assets		
Office furniture		400
Current assets		
Stock	1,400	
Trade debtors	400	
Cash	5,600	
	7,400	
Current liabilities		
Trade creditors	1,100	
		6,300
		6,700
Less Loan creditor		2,000
		4,700
Capital		4,700

The profit and loss account could be written in a more stylish manner, for reporting to users, as follows:

Profit and loss account for the month ended 31 January

	£	£
Sales		1,200
Cost of sales		800
Gross profit		400
Less Rent	300	
Wages	400	
		700
Net loss for the month		(300)

Summary

In this Appendix we have reviewed a system for keeping accounting records by hand, such that a relatively large volume of transactions can be handled effectively and accurately. In this system, known as double-entry bookkeeping, there is a separate account for each asset, claim, expense and liability that needs to be separately identified. Each account looks like a letter T. On the left-hand (debit) side of the account we record increases in assets and expenses and decreases in revenues and claims. On the right-hand (credit) side we record increases in revenues and claims and decreases in assets and expenses. This means that there is an equal credit entry in one account for a debit entry in another.

We saw that not only can double-entry bookkeeping be used to record the day-to-day transactions of the organisation, but it can also follow through to generate the profit and loss account. The balance sheet is then simply a list of the net figure (the 'balance') on each of the accounts after appropriate transfers have been made to the profit and loss account.

Key terms

Double-entry bookkeeping p. 546
Account p. 546
Debit p. 548

Credit p. 548
Balance p. 551
Trial balance p. 554

Further reading

If you would like to explore the topics covered in this chapter in more depth, we recommend the following books:

Foundations of Business Accounting, *Dodge, R.,* 2nd edn, Thompson Business Press, 1997, chapter 3.

An Introduction to Financial Accounting, *Thomas, A.,* 2nd edn, McGraw-Hill, 1996, chapters 4 and 5.

Practical Accounting, *Benedict, A. and Elliott, B.,* Financial Times Prentice Hall, 2001, chapters 2 5.

Financial Accounting, *Bebbington, J., Gray, R. and Laughlin, R.,* 3rd edn, Thomson Learning, 2001, chapters 2–7.

Both of these exercises have answers at the back of the book.

A.1 In respect of each of the following transactions, state in which two accounts must an entry be made and whether the entry is a debit or a credit. (For example, if the transaction were purchase of stock for cash, the answer would be debit the stock account and credit the cash account.)

(a) Purchased stock on credit.
(b) Owner made cash drawings.
(c) Paid interest on a business loan.
(d) Purchased stock for cash.
(e) Received cash from a credit customer.
(f) Paid wages to employees.
(g) The owner received some cash from a credit customer, which was taken as drawings rather than being paid into the business's bank account.
(h) Paid a credit supplier.
(i) Paid electricity bill.
(j) Made cash sales.

A.2 (a) Record the following transactions in a set of double-entry accounts:

1 February	Lee (the owner) put £6,000 into a newly opened business bank account to start a new business
3 February	Purchased stock for £2,600 for cash
5 February	Purchased some equipment (fixed asset) for cash for £800
6 February	Purchased stock costing £3,000 on credit
9 February	Paid rent for the month of £250
10 February	Paid fuel and electricity for the month of £240
11 February	Paid general expenses of £200
15 February	Sold stock for £4,000 in cash; the stock had cost £2,400
19 February	Sold stock for £3,800 on credit; the stock had cost £2,300
21 February	Lee withdrew £1,000 in cash for personal use
25 February	Paid £2,000 to trade creditors
28 February	Received £2,500 from trade debtors

(b) Balance the relevant accounts and prepare a trial balance (making sure that it agrees).
(c) Prepare a profit and loss account for the month and a balance sheet at the month end. Assume that there are no prepaid or accrued expenses at the end of the month and ignore any possible depreciation.

Appendix B
Glossary of key terms

ABC system of stock control   A method of applying different levels of stock control, based on the value of each category of stock. *p. 514*

Account   A section of a double-entry bookkeeping system that deals with one particular asset, claim, expense or revenue. *p. 546*

Accounting   The process of identifying, measuring and communicating information to permit informed judgements and decisions by users of the information. *p. 1*

Accounting conventions   Accounting rules that have evolved over time in order to deal with practical problems rather than to reflect some theoretical ideal.

Accounting information system   The system used within a business to identify, record, analyse and report accounting information. *p. 10*

Accounting rate of return (ARR)   The average profit from an investment, expressed as a percentage of the average investment made. *p. 426*

Accounting (financial reporting) standards   Rules established by the UK accounting profession, which should be followed by preparers of the annual accounts of companies. *p. 140*

Accrued expense   An expense that is outstanding at the end of an accounting period. *p. 65*

Acid test ratio   A liquidity ratio that relates the current assets (less stocks) to the current liabilities. *p. 211*

Activity-based budgeting (ABB)   A system of budgeting based on the philosophy of activity-based costing (ABC). *p. 376*

Activity-based costing (ABC)   A technique for more accurately relating overheads to specific production or provision of a service. It is based on acceptance of the fact that overheads do not just occur but are caused by activities, such as holding products in stores, which 'drive' the costs. *p. 326*

Adverse variance   A difference between planned and actual performance, where the difference will cause the actual profit to be lower than the budgeted one. *p. 397*

Ageing schedule of debtors   A report analysing debtors into categories, depending on the length of time outstanding. *p. 524*

Allotted share capital   *See* Issued share capital.

Asset   A resource held by a business, that has certain characteristics. *pp. 29, 31*

Auditor   A professional whose main duty is to make a report as to whether, in his or her opinion, the accounting statements of a company do that which they are supposed to do, namely show a true and fair view and comply with statutory, and accounting standard, requirements. *p. 145*

Authorised share capital   The maximum amount of share capital that directors are authorised by the shareholders to issue. *p. 111*

Average settlement period for debtors/creditors   The average time taken for debtors to pay the amounts owing, or for a business to pay its creditors. *pp. 206, 523 and 534*

Average stock turnover period   The average period for which stocks are held by a business. *p. 205*

Bad debt   An amount owed to the business that is considered to be irrecoverable. *p. 84*

Balance   The net of the debit and credit totals in an account in a double-entry bookkeeping system. *p. 551*

Balance sheet   A statement of financial position that shows the assets of a business and the claim on those assets. *p. 24*

Balanced Scorecard   A framework for translating the aims and objectives of a business into a series of key performance measures and targets. *p. 347*

Bank overdraft   A flexible form of borrowing that allows an individual or business to have a negative bank current-account balance. *p. 487*

Batch costing   A technique for identifying full cost, where the production of many types of goods and services – particularly goods – involves producing in a batch of identical or nearly identical units of output, but where each batch is distinctly different from other batches. *p. 314*

Behavioural aspects of budgetary control   The effect on people's attitudes and behaviour of the various aspects of using budgets as the basis of exercising control over performance. *p. 413*

Benchmarking   Identifying a successful business, or part of a business, and measuring the effectiveness of one's own business by comparison with this standard. *p. 345*

Bonus issue   Reserves that are converted into shares and given 'free' to shareholders. *p. 500*

Bonus shares   *See* Bonus issue. *p. 109*

Break-even analysis   The activity of deducing the break-even point of some activity through analysing costs and revenues. *p. 269*

Break-even chart   A graphical representation of the costs and revenues of some activity, at various levels, that enables the break-even point to be identified. *p. 270*

Break-even point   A level of activity where revenue will exactly equal total cost, so there is neither profit nor loss. *p. 270*

Budget   A financial plan for the short term, typically one year. *p. 358*

Budget committee   A group of managers formed to supervise and take responsibility for the budget-setting process. *p. 366*

Budget holder   An individual responsible for a particular budget. *p. 370*

Budget officer   An individual, often an accountant, appointed to carry out, or take immediate responsibility for having carried out, the tasks of the budget committee. *p. 366*

Budgetary control   Using the budget as a yardstick against which the effectiveness of actual performance may be assessed. *p. 411*

Business entity convention The convention that holds that, for accounting purposes, the business and its owner(s) are treated as quite separate and distinct. *p. 45*

Called-up share capital That part of a company's share capital for which the shareholders have been asked to pay the agreed amount. Part of the claim of the owners against the business. *p. 111*

Capital The owner's claim on the assets of the business. *p. 31*

Capital expenditure The outlay of funds on fixed assets. *p. 172*

Capital reserve A reserve that arises from a 'capital' profit or gain rather than from normal trading activities. *p. 107*

Cash discount A reduction in the amount due for goods or services sold on credit in return for prompt payment. *p. 522*

Cash flow The movement of cash. *p. 167*

Cash flow statement A statement that shows the sources and uses of cash for a period. *p. 24*

Claim An obligation on the part of a business to provide cash or some other benefit to an outside party. *pp. 29, 31*

Combined Code A code of practice for companies listed on the London Stock Exchange that deals with corporate governance matters. *p. 102*

Committed cost A cost that has not yet been incurred but that must, under some existing contract or obligation, be incurred. *p. 253*

Common costs Costs that relate to more than one business segment. *pp. 155, 296*

Comparability The requirement that items that are basically the same should be treated in the same manner for measurement and reporting purposes. Lack of comparability will limit the usefulness of accounting information. *p. 6*

Compensating variances The situation that exists when two variances, both caused by the same factor, one adverse the other favourable, are of equal size and therefore cancel each other out. *p. 410*

Consistency convention The accounting convention that holds that, when a particular method of accounting is selected to deal with a transaction, this method should be applied consistently over time. *p. 83*

Consolidating Reducing the number of shares by increasing their nominal value. *p. 108*

Continual (or rolling) budget A budgeting system that continually updates budgets so that there is always a budget for a full planning period. *p. 361*

Contribution (per unit) Sales revenue per unit less variable costs per unit. *p. 273*

Convertible loan stocks Loan capital that can be converted into equity share capital at the option of the holders. *p. 479*

Corporate governance Systems for directing and controlling a company. *p. 101*

Corporation tax Taxation that a limited company is liable to pay on its profits. *pp. 100, 120*

Cost The amount of resources, usually measured in monetary terms, sacrificed to achieve a particular objective. *p. 248*

Cost allocation Dividing costs between cost centres according to the amount of cost that has been incurred in them. *p. 308*

Cost apportionment The dividing of costs between cost centres according to the amount of cost that is seen as being fair. *p. 308*

Cost behaviour The manner in which costs alter with changes in the level of activity. *p. 298*

Cost centre Some area, object, person or activity for which costs are separately collected. *p. 307*

Cost driver An activity that causes costs. *p. 326*

Cost of sales The cost of the goods sold during a period. Cost of sales can be derived by adding the opening stock held to the stock purchases for the period and then deducting the closing stocks held. *p. 61*

Cost pool The sum of the overhead costs that are seen as being caused by the same cost driver. *p. 326*

Cost-plus pricing An approach to pricing output that is based on full cost, plus a percentage profit loading. *p. 293*

Cost unit The objective for which the cost is being deduced, usually a product or service. *p. 299*

Creative accounting Adopting accounting polices to achieve a particular view of performance and position that preparers would like users to see rather than what is a true and fair view. *p. 233*

Credit An entry made in the right-hand side of an account in double-entry bookkeeping. *p. 548*

Current asset An asset that is not held on a continuing basis. Current assets include cash itself and other assets that are expected to be converted to cash at some point in the future. *p. 36*

Current liabilities Amounts due for repayment to outside parties within 12 months of the balance sheet date. *p. 38*

Current ratio A liquidity ratio that relates the current assets of the business to the current liabilities. *p. 210*

Debenture A long-term loan, usually made to a company, evidenced by a trust deed. *pp. 112, 478*

Debit An entry made in the left-hand side of an account in double-entry bookkeeping. *p. 548*

Debt factoring A service offered by a financial institution (a factor) that involves the factor taking over the management of the trade debtors of the business. The factor is often prepared to make an advance to the business, based on the amount of trade debtors outstanding. *p. 487*

Deep discount bond Redeemable loan capital offering a rate of interest. below the market rate and issued at a discount to its redeemable value. *p. 479*

Depreciation A measure of that portion of the cost (less residual value) of a fixed asset that has been consumed during an accounting period. *p. 68*

Direct costs Costs that can be identified with specific cost units, to the extent that the effect of the cost can be measured in respect of each particular unit of output. *p. 296*

Direct method An approach to deducing the cash flows from trading operations, in a cash flow statement, by analysing the business's cash records. *p. 175*

Director An individual who is elected to act as the most senior level of management of a company. *p. 101*

Directors' report A report containing information of a financial and non-financial nature that the directors must produce as part of the annual financial report to shareholders. *p. 138*

Discount factor The rate applied to future cash flows to derive the present value of those cash flows. *p. 438*

Discretionary budget A budget based on a sum allocated at the discretion of top management. *p. 370*

Dividend The transfer of assets (usually cash) made by a company to its shareholders. *p. 106*

Divided cover ratio An investment ratio that relates the earnings available for dividends to the dividend announced, to indicate how many times the former covers the latter. *p. 219*

Dividend payout ratio An investment ratio that relates the dividends announced for the period to the earnings available for dividends that were generated in that period. *p. 219*

Dividend per share An investment ratio that relates the dividends announced for a period to the number of shares in issue. *p. 218*

Dividend yield ratio An investment ratio that relates the cash return from a share to its current market value. *p. 220*

Double-entry bookkeeping A system for recording financial transactions where each transaction is recorded twice, once as a debit and once as a credit. *p. 546*

Dual aspect convention The accounting convention that holds that each transaction has two aspects and that each aspect must be recorded in the financial statements. *p. 45*

Earnings per share An investment ratio that relates the earnings generated by the business during a period, and available to shareholders, to the number of shares in issue. *p. 220*

Economic order quantity (EOQ) The quantity of stock that should be purchased in order to minimise total stock costs. *p. 515*

Elasticity of demand The manner in which the level of demand alters with changes in price. *p. 332*

Equity Ordinary shares and reserves of a company. *p. 106*

Equity dividends paid A section of the cash flow statement that deals with the cash flows arising from ordinary share dividends paid. *p. 172*

Eurobond A bond issued by a listed company where the finance is raised on an international basis. The bond is issued in a currency that is different from the currency in which the company raising the finance is based. *p. 478*

Expected net present value (ENPV) A weighted average of the possible present value outcomes, where the probabilities associated with each outcome are used as weights. *p. 451*

Expense A measure of the outflow of assets (or increase in liabilities) incurred as a result of generating revenues. *p. 58*

Favourable variance A difference between planned and actual performance, where the difference will cause the actual profit to be higher than the budgeted one. *p. 397*

Feedback control A control device where actual performance is compared with planned and where action is taken to deal with future divergences between these. *p. 393*

Feedforward control A control device where forecast future performance is compared with planned and where action is taken to deal with divergences between these. *p. 394*

Final accounts   The profit and loss account, cash flow statement and balance sheet taken together. *p. 28*

Finance   The study of how businesses raise funds and select appropriate investments. *p. 2*

Finance lease   A financial arrangement where the asset title remains with the owner (the lessor) but the lease agreement transfers virtually all the rewards and risks to the business (the lessee). *p. 482*

Financial accounting   The measuring and reporting of accounting information for external users (those users other than the managers of the business). *p. 10*

Financial derivative   Any form of financial instrument, based on share or loan capital, that can be used by investors either to increase their returns or to decrease their exposure to risk. *p. 479*

Financial gearing   The existence of fixed payment-bearing securities (for example, loans) in the capital structure of a business. *p. 214*

Financial management   A subject area concerned with the financing and investing decisions of businesses. *p. 14*

Financing   A section of the cash flow statement that deals with the cash flows arising from raising and repaying long-term finance. *p. 172*

First in, first out (FIFO)   A method of stock valuation that assumes that the earlier stocks are to be sold first. *p. 79*

Five Cs of credit   A checklist of factors to be taken into account when assessing the creditworthiness of a customer. *p. 519*

Fixed asset   An asset held with the intention of being used to generate wealth rather than being held for resale. Fixed assets can be seen as the tools of the business and are held on a continuing basis. *p. 36*

Fixed cost   A cost that stays the same when changes occur to the volume of activity. *p. 264*

Flexible budget   A budget that is adjusted to reflect the actual level of output achieved. *p. 393*

Flexing (the budget)   Revising the budget to what it would have been had the planned level of output been different. *p. 395*

Forecast   A prediction of future outcomes or of the future state of the environment. *p. 360*

Full cost   The total amount of resources, usually measured in monetary terms, sacrificed to achieve a particular objective. *p. 292*

Full cost (cost-plus) pricing   Pricing output on the basis of its full cost, normally with a loading for profit. *p. 338*

Full costing   Deducing the total direct and indirect (overhead) costs of pursuing some activity or objective. *p. 292*

Fully paid shares   Shares on which the shareholders have paid the full issue price. *p. 111*

Gearing ratio   A ratio that relates the contribution of long-term lenders to the total long-term capital of the business. *p. 215*

Going concern convention   The accounting convention that holds that the business will continue operations for the foreseeable future. In other words, there is no intention, or need, to liquidate the business. *p. 45*

Gross profit   The amount remaining (if positive) after trading expenses (for example, cost of sales) have been deducted from trading revenues (for example, sales). *p. 60*

Gross profit margin A profitability ratio relating the gross profit for the period to the sales for the period. *p. 204*

Group accounts Sets of financial accounting statements that combine the performance and position of a group of companies that are under common control. *p. 121*

Historic cost What an asset cost when it was originally acquired. *p. 249*

Historic cost convention The accounting convention that holds that assets should be recorded at their historic (acquisition) cost. *p. 44*

Incremental budgeting Constructing budgets on the basis of what happened in the previous period, with some adjustment for expected changes in the forthcoming budget period. *p. 369*

Indirect costs (or overheads) All costs except direct costs; that is, those that cannot be directly measured in respect of each particular unit of output. *p. 296*

Indirect method An approach to deducing the cash flows from trading operations, in a cash flow statement, by analysing the business's final accounts. *p. 175*

Inflation The increase in money prices, causing erosion of the value of money. *p. 435*

Intangible assets Assets that do not have a physical substance (for example, patents, goodwill and debtors). *p. 31*

Interest cover ratio A gearing ratio that divides the net profit before interest and taxation by the interest payable for a period. *p. 217*

Internal rate of return (IRR) The discount rate for a project that will have the effect of producing a zero NPV. *p. 440*

Investigating variances The act of looking into the practical causes of budget variances, once those variances have been identified. *p. 408*

Invoice discounting A loan provided by a financial institution based on a proportion of the face value of credit sales outstanding. *p. 489*

Irrelevant cost A cost that is not relevant to a particular decision. *p. 249*

Issued share capital That part of the authorised share capital which has been issued to shareholders. Also known as allotted share capital. *p. 111*

Job costing A technique for identifying the full cost per unit of output, where that output is not similar to other units of output. *p. 296*

Just-in-time (JIT) stock management A system of stock management that aims to have supplies delivered to production just in time for their required use. *p. 518*

Kaizen **costing** An approach to cost control where an attempt is made to control costs by trying continually to make cost savings, often only small ones, from one time period to the next. *p. 344*

Last in, first out (LIFO) A method of stock valuation that assumes that the latest stocks are the first to be sold. *p. 79*

Learning curve The tendency for people to carry out tasks more quickly as they become more experienced in doing so. *p. 406*

Liabilities Claims of individuals and organisations, apart from the owner, that have arisen from past transactions or events such as supplying goods or lending money to the business. *p. 31*

Limited company An artificial legal person that has an identity separate from that of those who own and manage it. *p. 15*

Limited liability The restriction of the legal obligation of shareholders to meet all of the company's debts. *p. 99*

Limiting factor Some aspect of the business (for example, lack of sales demand) that will prevent it achieving its objectives to the maximum extent. *p. 367*

Loan convenant A condition contained within a loan agreement that is designed to help protect the lenders. *p. 480*

Long-term liabilities Those amounts due to other parties that are not liable for repayment within the next 12 months after the balance sheet date. *p. 38*

Management accounting The measuring and reporting of accounting information for the managers of a business. *p. 10*

Management by exception A system of control, based on a comparison of planned and actual performance, that allows managers to focus on areas of poor performance rather than dealing with areas where performance is satisfactory. *p. 365*

Management of liquid resources A section of the cash flow statement that deals with the cash flows arising from movements in short-term liquid resources. *p. 172*

Margin of safety The extent to which the planned level of output or sales lies above the break-even point. *p. 273*

Marginal analysis The activity of decision making through analysing variable costs and revenues, ignoring fixed costs. *p. 279*

Marginal cost The addition to total cost that will be incurred by making/providing one more unit of output. *p. 273*

Marginal cost pricing Pricing output on the basis of its marginal cost, normally with a loading for profit. *p. 340*

Master budgets A summary of the individual budgets, usually consisting of a budgeted profit and loss account, a budgeted balance sheet and a budgeted cash flow statement. *p. 361*

Matching convention The accounting convention that holds that, in measuring income, expenses should be matched to revenues, which they helped generate in the same accounting period as those revenues were realised. *p. 64*

Materials requirement planning (MRP) system A computer-based system of stock control that schedules the timing of deliveries of bought-in parts and materials to coincide with production requirements to meet demand. *p. 517*

Materiality The requirement that material information should be disclosed to users of financial reports. *p. 7*

Materiality convention The accounting convention that states that, where the amounts involved are immaterial, only what is expedient should be considered. *p. 67*

Mission statement A brief statement setting out the aims of the business. *p. 356*

Money measurement convention The accounting convention that holds that accounting should deal only with those items which are capable of being expressed in monetary terms. *p. 43*

Mortgage A loan secured on property. *p. 480*

Net cash flow from operating activities A section of the cash flow statement that deals with the cash flows from trading operations. *p. 170*

Net present value (NPV) A method of investment appraisal based on the present value of all relevant cash flows associated with the project. *p. 433*

Net profit The amount remaining (if positive) after the total expenses for a period have been deducted from total revenues. *p. 60*

Net profit margin A profitability ratio relating the net profit for the period to the sales for the period. *p. 203*

Nominal value The face value of a share in a company. *p. 105*

Non-operating profit variances Differences between budgeted and actual performance that do not lead directly to differences between budgeted and actual operating profit. *p. 408*

Objective probabilities Probabilities based on information gathered from past experience. *p. 455*

Objectivity convention The convention that holds that, in so far as is possible, the financial statements prepared should be based on objective verifiable evidence rather than matters of opinion. *p. 47*

Offer for sale An issue of shares that involves a public limited company (or its shareholders) selling the shares to a financial institution which will, in turn, sell the shares to the public. *p. 501*

Operating and financial review A narrative report that helps users to understand the operating and financial results of a business for a period. *p. 156*

Operating cash cycle The period between the outlay of cash to purchase supplies and the ultimate receipt of cash from the sale of goods. *p. 529*

Operating cash flow per ordinary share An investment ratio that relates the operating cash flows available to ordinary shareholders to the number of ordinary shares. *p. 221*

Operating cash flows to maturing obligations ratio A liquidity ratio that compares the operating cash flows to the current liabilities of the business. *p. 213*

Operating gearing The relationship between the total fixed and the total variable costs for some activity. *p. 275*

Opportunity cost The cost incurred when one course of action prevents an opportunity to derive some benefit from another course of action. *p. 249*

Ordinary shares Shares of a company owned by those who are due the benefits of the company's activities after all other stakeholders have been satisfied. *p. 106*

Outlay cost A cost that involves the spending of money or some other transfer of assets. *p. 249*

Overheads (or indirect costs) Any cost except a direct cost; a cost which cannot be directly measured in respect of each particular unit of output. *p. 296*

Overhead absorption (recovery) rate The rate at which overheads are charged to cost units (jobs), usually in a job costing system. *p. 300*

Overtrading The situation arising when a business is operating at a level of activity which cannot be supported by the amount of finance which has been committed. *p. 226*

Paid-up share capital That part of the share capital of a company that has been called and paid. *p. 111*

Partnership A form of business unit where there are at least two individuals, but usually no more than twenty, carrying on a business with the intention of making a profit. *p. 15*

Past cost A cost that has been incurred in the past. *p. 249*

Payback period (PP) The time taken for the initial investment in a project to be repaid from the net cash inflows of the project. *p. 430*

Penetration pricing Setting prices at a level low enough to encourage wide market acceptance of a product or service. *p. 341*

Periodic budget A budget developed on a one-off basis to cover a particular planning period. *p. 361*

Placing An issue of shares that involves the company 'placing' the shares with selected investors such as large financial institutions. *p. 502*

Post-completion audit A review of the performance of an investment project to see whether actual performance matched planned performance and whether any lessons can be drawn from the way in which the investment was carried out. *p. 461*

Preference shares Shares of a company owned by those who are entitled to the first part of any dividend which the company may pay. *p. 106*

Prepaid expenses Expenses that have been paid in advance at the end of the accounting period. *p. 67*

Price/earnings ratio An investment ratio that relates the market value of a share to the earnings per share. *p. 222*

Price skimming Setting prices at a high level to make the maximum profit from the product or service before the price is lowered to attract the next segment of the market. *p. 341*

Private company A limited company for which the directors can restrict the ownership of its shares. *p. 99*

Process costing A technique for deriving the full cost per unit of output, where the units of output are exactly similar or it is reasonable to treat them as being so. *p. 295*

Product cost centre Some area, object, person or activity for which costs are separately collected, in which cost units have costs added. *p. 307*

Profit The increase in wealth attributable to the owners of a business that arises through business operations. *p. 57*

Profit and loss account A financial statement that measures and reports the profit (or loss) the business has generated during a period. It is derived by deducting from total revenues for a period, the total expenses associated with those revenues. *p. 24*

Profit–volume (PV) chart A graphical representation of the contributions (revenues less variable costs) of some activity, at various levels, which enables the break-even point, and the profit at various activity levels, to be identified. *p. 276*

Provision for doubtful debts An amount set aside out of profits to provide for anticipated losses arising from debts that may prove irrecoverable. *p. 84*

Prudence convention The accounting convention that holds that financial statements should err on the side of caution. *p. 46*

Public company A limited company for which the directors cannot restrict the ownership of its shares. *p. 99*

Public issue A method of issuing shares that involves a public limited company (plc) making a direct invitation to the public to purchase shares in the company. *p. 502*

Realisation convention The accounting convention that holds that revenue should be recognised only when it has been realised. *p. 63*

Reducing-balance method A method of calculating depreciation that applies a fixed percentage rate of depreciation to the written-down value of an asset in each period. *p. 71*

Relevance The ability of accounting information to influence decisions; regarded as a key characteristic of useful accounting information. *p. 6*

Relevant cost A cost that is relevant to a particular decision. *p. 249*

Reliability The requirement that accounting should be free from material error or bias. Reliability is regarded as a key characteristic of useful accounting information. *p. 6*

Reserves Part of the owners' claim on a limited company that has arisen from profits and gains, to the extent that these have not been distributed to the shareholders. *p. 107*

Residual value The amount for which a fixed asset is sold when the business has no further use for it. *p. 70*

Return on capital employed (ROCE) A profitability ratio expressing the relationship between the net profit (before interest and taxation) and the long-term capital invested in the business. *p. 202*

Return on ordinary shareholders' funds (ROSF) A profitability ratio that compares the amount of profit for the period available to the ordinary shareholders with their stake in the business. *p. 201*

Returns from investment and servicing of finance A section of the cash flow statement that deals with the cash flows arising from interest and dividends received and from interest paid. *p. 170*

Revenue A measure of the inflow of assets (for example, cash or amounts owed to a business by debtors), or a reduction in liabilities, that arise as a result of trading operations. *p. 57*

Revenue reserve Part of the owners' claim on a company that arises from realised profits and gains, including after-tax trading profits and gains from disposals of fixed assets. These profits and gains have been reinvested in the company rather than distributed to the owners. *p. 106*

Rights issue An issue of shares for cash to existing shareholders on the basis of the number of shares already held. *pp. 110, 498*

Risk The likelihood that what is estimated to occur will not actually occur. *p. 434*

Risk-adjusted discount rate A discount rate applied to investment projects that is increased (decreased) in the face of increased (decreased) risk. *p. 457*

Rolling (or continual) budget A budgeting system that continually updates budgets so that there is always a budget for a full planning period.

Sale and leaseback An agreement to sell an asset (usually property) to another party and simultaneously to lease the asset back in order to continue using the asset. *p. 483*

Sales per employee An efficiency ratio that relates the sales generated during a period to the average number of employees of the business. *p. 208*

Sales to capital employed An efficiency ratio that relates the sales generated during a period to the capital employed. *p. 207*

Sales volume variance The difference between the profit as shown in the original budget and the profit as shown in the flexed budget to the period. *p. 397*

Segmental financial reports Reports that break down the operating results of a business according to its business or geographical segments. *p. 153*

Semi-fixed (semi-variable) cost A cost that has an element of both fixed and variable cost. *p. 268*

Sensitivity analysis An examination of the key variables affecting a project, to see how changes in each input might influence the outcome. *p. 448*

Service cost centre Some area, object, person or activity for which costs are collected separately, in which cost units do not have cost added, because service cost centres only render services to product cost services and to other service cost centres. *p. 307*

Share A portion of the ownership, or equity, of a company. *p. 5*

Share premium account A capital reserve reflecting any amount, above the nominal value of shares, that is paid for those shares when issued by a company. *p. 108*

Shareholder value analysis (SVA) Method of measuring and managing business value based on the long-term cash flows generated. *p. 462*

Sole proprietorship An individual in business on his or her own account. *p. 14*

Stable monetary unit convention The accounting convention that holds that money, which is the unit of measurement in accounting, will not change in value over time. *p. 46*

Standard quantities and costs Planned quantities and costs (or revenues) for individual units of input or output. Standards are the building blocks used to produce the budget. *p. 404*

Statement of recognised gains and losses A statement that shows the change in the owners' claim on a limited company from the date of one published balance sheet to the next. *p. 142*

Stepped fixed cost A fixed cost that does not remain fixed over all levels of output but which changes in steps as a threshold level of output is reached. *p. 266*

Stock Exchange A market where 'second-hand' shares may be bought and sold and new capital raised. *p. 495*

Straight-line method A method of accounting for depreciation that allocates the amount to be depreciated evenly over the useful life of the asset. *p. 70*

Subjective probabilities Probabilities based on opinion rather than past data. *p. 455*

Summary financial statement A summarised version of the complete annual financial statements, which shareholders may receive as an alternative to the complete statements. *p. 139*

Sunk cost A cost which has been incurred in the past; the same as a past cost. *p. 253*

Takeover The acquisition of control of one company by another, usually as a result of acquiring a majority of the ordinary shares of the former. *p. 122*

Tangible assets Those assets that have a physical substance (for example, plant and machinery, motor vehicles.) *p. 31*

Target costing Where the business starts with the projected selling price and from it deduces the target cost per unit which must be met to enable the company to meet its profit objectives. *p. 344*

Taxation A section of the cash flow statement that deals with the cash flows arising from taxes paid and refunded. *p. 172*

Total cost The sum of the variable and fixed costs of pursuing some activity. *p. 270*

Total life-cycle costing   Paying attention to all of the costs that will be incurred during the entire life of a product or service. *p. 343*

Trading and P and L account   A type of profit and loss account prepared by merchandising businesses (for example, retailers and wholesalers) that measures and reports the gross profit (loss) from trading and then deducts overhead expenses to derive the net profit (loss) for the period. *p. 60*

Transfer price   The price at which goods or services are sold, or transferred, between divisions of the same business. *p. 155*

Trial balance   A totalled list of the of the balances on each of the accounts in a double-entry bookkeeping system. *p. 554*

Understandability   The requirement that accounting information should be understood by those for whom the information is primarily compiled. Lack of understandability will limit the usefulness of accounting information. *p. 7*

Variable cost   A cost that varies according to the volume of activity. *p. 264*

Variance   The financial effect, usually on the budgeted profit, of the particular factor under consideration being more or less than budgeted. *p. 397*

Variance analysis   Carrying out calculations to find the area of the business's operations that has caused the budgets not to have been met. *p. 404*

Venture capital   Long-term capital provided by certain institutions to small and medium-sized businesses to exploit relatively high risk opportunities. *p. 496*

Warrant   A document giving the holder the right, but not the obligation, to acquire ordinary shares in a company at an agreed price. *p. 479*

Weighted average cost (AVCO)   A method of valuing stocks that assumes that stocks entering the business lose their separate identity and any issues of stock reflect the weighted average cost of the stocks held. *p. 79*

Working capital   Current assets less current liabilities (creditors due within one year). *p. 509*

Written-down value (WDV)   The difference between the cost (or revalued amount) of a fixed asset and the accumulated depreciation relating to the assets. The written down-value is also referred to as the net book value (NBV). *p. 71*

Zero-base budgeting (ZBB)   An approach to budgeting, based on the philosophy that all spending needs to be justified annually and that each budget should start as a clean sheet. *p. 370*

Appendix C
Solutions to self-assessment questions

2.1 Kunalan Manufacturing Company

The balance sheet provides an insight into the mix of assets held. Thus, it can be seen that, in value terms, approximately 60 per cent of assets held are in the form of fixed assets and that freehold premises comprise more than half of these fixed assets. Current assets held are largely in the form of stock (approximately 46 per cent of current assets) and trade debtors (approximately 42 per cent of current assets).

The balance sheet also provides an insight into the liquidity of the business. The current assets are £104,000 and can be viewed as representing cash or near-cash assets held, compared with £42,000 in current liabilities. In this case, it appears that the business is fairly liquid as the current assets exceed the current liabilities by a large amount. Liquidity is very important in order to maintain the capacity of the business to pay its debts.

The balance sheet gives an indication of the financial structure of the business. It can be seen in this case that the owner is providing £63,000 and long-term lenders are providing £160,000. This means that outsiders contribute, 72 per cent (£160,000/£223,000) of the total long-term finance required and the business is, therefore, heavily reliant on outside sources of finance. The business is under pressure to make profits that are at least sufficient to pay interest and to make capital repayments when they fall due.

3.1 TT Limited

Balance sheet as at 31 December 2000

Assets	£	Claims	£
Delivery van		Capital	
(12,000 − 2,500)	9,500	(50,000 + 26,900)	76,900
Stock in trade (143,000 +			
12,000 − 74,000 − 16,000)	65,000	Trade creditors	
		(143,000 − 121,000)	22,000
Trade debtors (152,000 −			
132,000 − 400)	19,600	Accrued expenses	
		(630 + 620)	1,250
Cash at bank (50,000 − 25,000			
− 500 − 1,200 − 12,000 −			
33,500 − 1,650 − 12,000			
+ 35,000 − 9,400 + 132,000			
− 121,000)	750		

Assets	£	Claims	£
Prepaid expenses (5,000 + 300)	5,300		
	100,150		100,150

Profit and loss account for the year ended 31 December 2000

	£	£
Sales (152,000 + 35,000)		187,000
Less Cost of stock sold		
(74,000 + 16,000)		90,000
Gross profit		97,000
Less		
Rent	20,000	
Rates (500 + 900)	1,400	
Wages (33,500 + 630)	34,130	
Electricity (1,650 + 620)	2,270	
Bad debts	400	
Van depreciation ($\frac{12,000 - 2,000}{4}$)	2,500	
Van expenses	9,400	
		70,100
Net profit for the year		£26,900

The balance sheet could now be rewritten in a more stylish form as follows:

Balance sheet as at 31 December 2000

	£	£	£
Fixed assets			
Motor van			9,500
Current assets			
Stock in trade	65,000		
Trade debtors	19,600		
Prepaid expenses	5,300		
Cash	750		
		90,650	
Less **Current liabilities**			
Trade creditors	22,000		
Accrued expenses	1,250		
		23,250	
			67,400
			76,900
Capital			
Original			50,000
Retained profit			26,900
			76,900

4.1 Dev Ltd

(a) The summarised balance sheet of Dev Ltd, immediately following the rights and bonus issue is as follows:

Balance sheet as at 31 December 2001

	£
Net assets [235 + 40 (cash from the rights issue)]	275,000

	£
Capital and reserves	
Share capital: 100,000 shares @ £1 [(100 + 20) + 60]	180,000
Share premium account (30 + 20 − 50)	–
Revaluation reserve (37 − 10)	27,000
Profit and loss account balance	68,000
	275,000

Note that the bonus issue of £60,000 is taken from capital reserves (reserves unavailable for dividends) as follows:

	£
Share premium account	50,000
Revaluation reserve	10,000
	60,000

More could have been taken from the revaluation reserve and less from the share premium account without making any difference to dividend payment possibilities.

(b) There may be pressure from a potential creditor for the company to limit its ability to pay dividends. This would place creditors is a more secure position because the maximum buffer or safety margin between the value of the assets and the amount owed by the company is maintained. It is not unusual for potential creditors to insist on some measure to lock up shareholders' funds in this way as a condition of granting the loan.

(c) The summarised balance sheet of Dev Ltd, immediately following the rights and bonus issue, assuming a minimum dividend potential objective, is as follows:

Balance sheet as at 31 December 2001

	£
Net assets [235 + 40 (cash from the rights issue)]	275,000
Capital and reserves	
Share capital: 100,000 shares @ £1 ((100 + 20) + 60)	180,000
Share premium account (30 + 20)	50,000
Revaluation reserve	37,000
Profit and loss account balance (68 − 60)	8,000
	275,000

(d) Before the bonus issue, the maximum dividend was £68,000. Now it is £8,000. Thus the bonus issue has had the effect of locking up an additional £60,000 of the assets of the company in terms of the company's ability to pay dividends.

(e) Before the issues, Lee had 100 shares worth £2.35 (£235,000/100,000) each or £235 in total. Lee would be offered 20 shares in the rights issue at £2 each or £40 in total. After the rights issue, Lee would have 120 shares worth £2.2917 (£275,000/120,000) each or £275 in total.

　　The bonus issue would give Lee 60 additional shares. After the bonus issue, Lee would have 180 shares worth £1.5278 (£275,000/180,000) each or £275 in total.

　　None of this affects Lee's wealth. Before the issues, Lee had £235 worth of shares and £40 more in cash. After the issues, Lee has the same total wealth but all £275 is in the value of the shares.

(f) The things that we know about the company are as follows:

(i)　It is a private (as opposed to a public) limited company, for it has 'Ltd' (limited) as part of its name, rather than plc (public limited company).

(ii)　It has made an issue of shares at a premium, almost certainly after it had traded successfully for a period. (There is a share premium account. It would be very unlikely that the original shares, issued when the company was first formed, would have been issued at a premium.)

(iii) Certain of the assets in the balance sheet have been upwardly revalued by at least £37,000. (There is a revaluation reserve of £37,000. This may just be what is left after a previous bonus issue had taken part of the balance.)

(iv) The company has traded at an aggregate profit (though there could have been losses in some years), net of tax and any dividends paid. (There is a positive balance on the profit and loss account.)

5.1 J. Sainsbury plc

The following ratios may be calculated for each of the main business segments:

	2000 %	1999 %
Net profit to sales		
Food retailing – UK	4.1	5.6
Food retailing – USA	3.3	2.8
DIY retailing – UK	4.5	5.6
Banking – UK	2.2	(3.8)
Property development – UK	9.7	28.1
Sales growth		
Food retailing – UK	5.8	
Food retailing – USA	20.6	
DIY retailing – UK	2.5	
Banking – UK	16.2	
Property development – UK	515.6	
Net profit to capital employed (net assets)		
Food retailing – UK	10.7	16.1
Food retailing – USA	9.9	10.9
DIY retailing – UK	10.5	15.4
Banking – UK	2.6	(5.9)
Property development – UK	13.0	6.9

In all segments of the business, sales increased in 2000 compared with the previous year. We do not know from the information provided in the question to what extent this growth came from expanding operations – for example opening new stores. Inflation would be expected to cause a 2–3 per cent increase in turnover. Sainsbury's annual report gives details of each segment's progress.

In all three retailing segments, the net profit to capital employed fell in 2000 relative to 1999. Only in banking and property development did the business improve its performance, but these segments accounted for relatively little of the total turnover and profit of the business.

6.1 Touchstone plc

Cash flow statement for the year ended 31 December 2001

	£m	£m
Net cash inflows from operating activities		66
(see calculation below)		

Returns from investment and servicing of finance

Interest received	2	
Interest paid	(4)	
Net cash outflow from returns on investment and servicing of finance		(2)

Taxation

Corporation tax paid	(12)	
Net cash outflow for taxation		(12)

Capital expenditure

Land and buildings	(22)	
Plant and machinery (see note below)	(19)	
Net cash outflow for capital expenditure		(41)
		11

Equity dividends paid

Dividends paid (see note below)	(16)	
Net cash outflow for equity dividends		(16)
		(5)

Management of liquid resources —

Financing

Issue of debenture stock	20	
Net cash inflow from financing		20

Net increase in cash 15

To see how this relates to the cash of the business at the beginning and end of the year, it is useful to show a reconciliation as follows:

Reconciliation of cash movements during the year ended 31 December 2001

	£m
Balance at 1 January 2001	4
Net cash inflow	15
Balance at 31 December 2001	19

Calculation of net cash inflow from operating activities

	£m	£m
Net operating profit (from the profit and loss account)		62
Add Depreciation		
Land and buildings	6	
Plant and machinery	10	
		16
		78
Less Increase in debtors (26 − 16)	10	
Decrease in creditors (26 − 23)	3	13
		65
Add Decrease in stocks (25 − 24)		1
		66

Notes
Dividends

	£m
Amount owed at the start of the year	12
Dividend for the year	18
	30
Amount owed at the end of the year	(14)
Dividend paid during the year	16

Taxation

	£m
Amount owed at the start of the year	4
Taxation the year	16
	20
Amount owed at the end of the year	(8)
Tax paid during the year	12

Fixed asset acquisitions	Land and buildings £m	Plant and machinery £m
Position at 31 December 2000	94	53
Less 2001 depreciation	6	10
	88	43
Position at 31 December 2001	110	62
Acquisitions	22	19

7.1 Financial ratios

In order to answer this question you may have used the following ratios:

	A plc	B plc
Current ratio	$\dfrac{853.0}{422.4} = 2.0$	$\dfrac{816.5}{293.1} = 2.8$
Acid-test ratio	$\dfrac{(853.0 - 592.0)}{422.4} = 0.6$	$\dfrac{(816.5 - 403.0)}{293.1} = 1.4$
Gearing ratio	$\dfrac{190}{(687.6 + 190)} \times 100 = 21.6\%$	$\dfrac{250}{(874.6 + 250)} \times 100 = 22.2\%$
Interest cover ratio	$\dfrac{(131.9 + 19.4)}{19.4} = 7.8$ times	$\dfrac{(139.4 + 27.5)}{27.5} = 6.1$ times
Dividend payout ratio	$\dfrac{135.0}{99.9} \times 100 = 135\%$	$\dfrac{95.0}{104.6} \times 100 = 91\%$
Price/earnings ratio	$\dfrac{£6.50}{31.2p} = 20.8$ times	$\dfrac{£8.20}{41.8p} = 19.6$ times

A plc has a much lower current ratio and acid test ratio than does B plc. The reasons for this may be partly due to the fact that A plc has a lower average settlement period for debtors. The acid test ratio of A plc is substantially below 1.0: this may suggest a liquidity problem.

The gearing ratio of each company is quite similar. Neither company has excessive borrowing. The interest cover ratio for each company is also similar. The respective ratios indicate that both companies have good profit coverage for their interest charges.

The dividend payout ratio for each company seems very high. In the case of A plc, the dividends announced for the year are considerably higher than the earnings generated during the year that are available for dividend. As a result, part of the dividend was paid out of retained profits from previous years. This is an unusual occurrence; although it is quite legitimate, such action may nevertheless suggest a lack of prudence on the part of the directors.

The P/E ratio for both companies is high, which indicates market confidence in their future prospects.

8.1 JB Limited

(a)

	£	
Material M1		
1,200 @ £5.50	6,600	The original cost is irrelevant since any stock used will need to be replaced
Material P2		
800 @ £2.00 (that is, £3.60 – £1.60)	1,600	The best alternative use of this material is as a substitute for P4 – an effective opportunity cost of £2.00/kg
Part no. 678		
400 @ £50	20,000	
Labour		
Skilled 2,000 @ £6	12,000	The effective cost is £6/hour
Unskilled 2,000 @ £5	10,000	
Overheads	3,200	It is only the additional cost which is relevant, the method of apportioning total overheads is not relevant
Total relevant cost	53,400	
Potential revenue		
400 @ £150	60,000	

Clearly, on the basis of the information available it would be beneficial for the company to undertake the contract.

(b) There is an almost infinite number of possible answers to this part of the question, including:

- If material P2 had not been in stock, it may be that it would not be possible to buy it in and still leave the contract as a beneficial one. In this case the company may be unhappy about accepting a price under the particular conditions that apply, which could not be accepted under other conditions.
- Will the replacement for the skilled worker be able to do the normal work of that person to the necessary standard?
- Is JB Limited confident that the additional unskilled employee can be made redundant at the end of this contract without cost to itself?

9.1 Khan Ltd

(a) The break-even point if only product A were made would be:

$$\frac{\text{Fixed costs}}{\text{Sales revenue per unit} - \text{Variable cost per unit}} =$$

$$\frac{£40,000}{£30 - (15 + 6)} = 4,445 \text{ units (a year)}$$

(Strictly it is 4,444.44 but 4,445 is the smallest number that must be produced to avoid a loss.)

(b)

	A £/unit	B £/unit	C £/unit
Selling price	30	45	20
Variable materials	(15)	(18)	(10)
Variable production costs	(6)	(16)	(5)
Contribution	9	11	5
Time on machines (hr/unit)	2	3	1
Contribution/hour on machines	£4.50	£3.67	£5.00
Order of priority	2nd	3rd	1st

(c)

	Hours		Contribution £
Produce:			
5,000 product C using	5,000	generating (that is, 5,000 × £5 =)	25,000
2,500 product A using	5,000	generating (that is, 2,500 × £9 =)	22,500
	10,000		47,500
		Less Fixed costs	40,000
		Profit	7,500

Leaving a demand for 500 units of product A and 2,000 units of product B unsatisfied.

10.1 Hector and Co. Ltd

Job costing basis

			£
Materials:	Metal wire	1,000 × 2 × £2.20	4,400
	Fabric	1,000 × 0.5 × £1.00	500
Labour:	Skilled	1,000 × (10/60) × £7.50	1,250
	Unskilled	1,000 × (5/60) × £5.00	417
Overheads		1,000 × (15/60) × (50,000/12,500)	1,000
Total cost			7,567
Add Profit loading		12.5% thereof	946
Total tender price			8,513

Minimum contract price (relevant cost basis)

			£
Materials:	Metal wire	1,000 × 2 × £2.50 (replacement cost)	5,000
	Fabric	1,000 × 0.50 × £0.40 (scrap value)	200
Labour:	Skilled	(there is no effective cost of skilled staff)	–
	Unskilled	1,000 × 5/60 × £5.00	417
Minimum tender price			5,617

The difference between the two prices is partly that the relevant costing approach tends to look to the future, partly that it considers opportunity costs, and partly that the job-costing basis total has a profit loading.

11.1 Psilis Ltd

(a) Full cost (present basis)

	Basic £		Super £	
Direct labour (all £5/hour)	20.00	(4 hours)	30.00	(6 hours)
Direct material	15.00		20.00	
Overheads	18.20	(£4.55* × 4)	27.30	(£4.55* × 6)
	53.20		77.30	

* Total direct labour hours worked = (40,000 × 4) + (10,000 × 6) = 220,000 hours. Overhead recovery rate = £1,000,000/220,000 = £4.55.

Thus the selling prices are currently:

Basic:	£53.20 + 25% = £66.50
Super:	£77.30 + 25% = £96.63

(b) Full cost (activity basis)
Here, the cost of each cost-driving activity is apportioned between total production of the two products.

Activity	Cost £000	Basis of apportionment	Basic £000		Super £000	
Machine set-ups	280	Number of set-ups	56	(20/100)	224	(80/100)
Quality inspection	220	Number of inspections	55	(500/2,000)	165	(1,500/2,000)
Sales order processing	240	Number of orders processed	72	(1,500/5,000)	168	(3,500/5,000)
General production	260	Machine hours	182	(350/500)	78	(150/500)
Total	1,000		365		635	

The overheads per unit are:

$$\text{Basic:} \quad \frac{£365,000}{40,000} = £9.13$$

$$\text{Super:} \quad \frac{£635,000}{10,000} = £63.50$$

Thus, on an activity basis the full costs are as follows:

	Basic £		Super £	
Direct labour (all £5/hour)	20.00	(4 hours)	30.00	(6 hours)
Direct material	15.00		20.00	
Overheads	9.13		63.50	
Full cost	44.13		113.50	
Current selling price	£66.50		£96.63	

(c) It seems that the Supers are being sold for less than they cost to produce. If the price cannot be increased, there is a very strong case for abandoning this product. At the same time, the Basics are very profitable to the extent that it may be worth considering lowering the price to attract more sales.

The fact that the overhead costs can be related to activities and, more specifically, to products does not mean that abandoning Super production would lead to immediate overhead cost savings. For example, it may not be possible or desirable to dismiss machine-setting staff overnight. It would certainly rarely be possible to release factory space occupied by machine setters and make immediate cost savings. Nevertheless, in the medium term these costs can be avoided and it may be sensible to do so.

12.1 Antonio Ltd

(a) (i) Raw materials stock budget for the six months ending 31 December (physical quantities):

	July units	Aug units	Sept units	Oct units	Nov units	Dec units
Opening stock (Current month's production)	500	600	600	700	750	750
Purchases (Balancing figure)	600	600	700	750	750	750
	1,100	1,200	1,300	1,450	1,500	1,500
Less Issues to prod'n (From question)	500	600	600	700	750	750
Closing stock (Next month's production)	600	600	700	750	750	750

Raw materials' stock budget for the six months ending 31 December (in financial terms), that is, the physical quantities × £8:

	July £	Aug £	Sept £	Oct £	Nov £	Dec £
Opening stock	4,000	4,800	4,800	5,600	6,000	6,000
Purchases	4,800	4,800	5,600	6,000	6,000	6,000
	8,800	9,600	10,400	11,600	12,000	12,000
Less Issues to prod'n	4,000	4,800	4,800	5,600	6,000	6,000
Closing stock	4,800	4,800	5,600	6,000	6,000	6,000

(ii) Creditors budget for the six months ending 31 December:

	July £	Aug £	Sept £	Oct £	Nov £	Dec £
Opening balance (Current month's payment)	4,000	4,800	4,800	5,600	6,000	6,000
Purchases (From raw materials stock budget)	4,800	4,800	5,600	6,000	6,000	6,000
	8,800	9,600	10,400	11,600	12,000	12,000
Less Payments	4,000	4,800	4,800	5,600	6,000	6,000
Closing balance (Next month's payment)	4,800	4,800	5,600	6,000	6,000	6,000

(iii) Cash budget for the six months ending 31 December:

	July £	Aug £	Sept £	Oct £	Nov £	Dec £
Inflows						
Receipts:						
Debtors (40% of sales of two months previous)	2,800	3,200	3,200	4,000	4,800	5,200
Cash sales (60% of current month's sales)	4,800	6,000	7,200	7,800	8,400	9,600
Total inflows	7,600	9,200	10,400	11,800	13,200	14,800
Outflows						
Creditors (from creditors budget)	(4,000)	(4,800)	(4,800)	(5,600)	(6,000)	(6,000)
Direct costs	(3,000)	(3,600)	(3,600)	(4,200)	(4,500)	(4,500)
Advertising	(1,000)	–	–	(1,500)	–	–
Overheads: 80%	(1,280)	(1,280)	(1,280)	(1,280)	(1,600)	(1,600)
20%	(280)	(320)	(320)	(320)	(320)	(400)
New plant			(2,200)	(2,200)	(2,200)	
Total outflows	(9,560)	(10,000)	(12,200)	(15,100)	(14,620)	(12,500)
Net inflows (outflows)	(1,960)	(800)	(1,800)	(3,300)	(1,420)	2,300
Balance c/f	5,540	4,740	2,940	(360)	(1,780)	520

The balances carried forward are deduced by deducting the deficit (net outflows) for the month from (or adding the surplus for the month to) the previous month's balance.

Note how budgets are linked; in this case the stock budget to the creditors budget and the creditors budget to the cash budget.

(b) The following are possible means of relieving the cash shortages revealed by the budget:

- Make a higher proportion of sales on a cash basis.
- Collect the money from debtors more promptly, for example during the month following the sale.

- Hold lower stocks, both of raw materials and of finished goods.
- Increase the creditor payment period.
- Delay the payments for advertising.
- Obtain more credit for the overhead costs; at present only 20 per cent are on credit.
- Delay the payments for the new plant.

13.1 Toscanini Ltd

(a) and (b)

	Budget			Actual	
	Original	Flexed		Actual	
Output (units) (prod'n and sales)	4,000	3,500		3,500	
	£	£		£	
Sales	16,000	14,000		13,820	
Raw materials	(3,840)	(3,360)	(1,400 kg)	(3,420)	(1,425 kg)
Labour	(3,200)	(2,800)	(700 hr)	(2,690)	(690 hr)
Fixed overheads	(4,800)	(4,800)		(4,900)	
Operating profit	4,160	3,040		2,810	

	£	Manager accountable
Sales volume variance (4,160 − 3,040)	(1,120) (A)	Sales
Sales price variance (14,000 − 13,820)	(180) (A)	Sales
Materials price variance (1,425 × 2.40) − 3,420	0	−
Materials usage variance [(3,500 × 0.4) − 1,425] × £2.40	(60) (A)	Production
Labour rate variance (690 × £4) − 2,690	70 (F)	Personnel
Labour efficiency variance [(3,500 × 0.20) − 690] × £4	40 (F)	Production
Fixed overhead spending (4,800 − 4,900)	(100) (A)	Various depending on the nature of the overheads
Total net variances	(1,350) (A)	
Budgeted profit	4,160	
Less Total net variance	1,350	
Actual profit	2,810	

(c) Feasible explanations include the following:

- Sales volume   Unanticipated fall in world demand would account for 400 × £2.24 = £896 of this variance. The remainder is probably caused by ineffective marketing, though a lack of availability of stock to sell may be a reason.
- Sales price   Ineffective selling seems the only logical reason.

- Materials usage — Inefficient usage of material, perhaps because of poor performance by labour or substandard materials.
- Labour rate — Less overtime worked or lower production bonuses paid as a result of lower volume of activity.
- Labour efficiency — More effective working, perhaps because fewer hours were worked than planned.
- Overheads — Ineffective control of overheads.

(d) Clearly, not all of the sales volume variance can be attributed to poor marketing, given a 10 per cent reduction in demand.

It will probably be useful to distinguish between that part of the variance that arose from the shortfall in general demand (a planning variance) and a volume variance, which is more fairly attributable to the manager concerned. Thus accountability will be more fairly imposed.

	£
Planning variance (10% × 4,000) × £2.24	896
'New' sales volume variance	
[4,000 − (10% × 4,000) − 3,500] × £2.24	224
Original sales volume variance	1,120

14.1 Beacon Chemicals plc

(a) Relevant cash flows are as follows:

	Year 0 £000	Year 1 £000	Year 2 £000	Year 3 £000	Year 4 £000	Year 5 £000
Sales revenue	–	80	120	144	100	64
Loss of contribution		(15)	(15)	(15)	(15)	(15)
Variable costs		(40)	(50)	(48)	(30)	(32)
Fixed costs (Note 1)		(8)	(8)	(8)	(8)	(8)
Operating cash flows		17	47	73	47	9
Working capital	(30)					30
Capital cost	(100)					
Net relevant cash flows	(130)	17	47	73	47	39

Notes:
1. Only the fixed costs that are incremental to the project (only existing because of the project) are relevant. Depreciation is irrelevant because it is not a cash flow.
2. The research and development cost is irrelevant since it has been spent irrespective of the decision on X14 production.

(b) The payback period is as follows:

	Year 0 £000	Year 1 £000	Year 2 £000	Year 3 £000
Cumulative cash flows	(130)	(113)	(66)	7

Thus the equipment will have repaid the initial investment by the end of the third year of operations.

(c) The net present value is as follows:

	Year 0 £000	Year 1 £000	Year 2 £000	Year 3 £000	Year 4 £000	Year 5 £000
Discount factor	1.00	0.926	0.857	0.794	0.735	0.681
Present value	(130)	15.74	40.28	57.96	34.55	26.56
Net present value	45.09	(That is, the sum of the present values for years 0 to 5.)				

15.1 Helsim Ltd

(a) The liquidity position may be assessed by using the liquidity ratios discussed in Chapter 7:

$$\text{Current ratio} = \frac{\text{Current assets}}{\text{Current liabilities (Creditors due within one year)}}$$

$$= \frac{£7.5m}{£5.4m}$$

$$= 1.4$$

$$\text{Acid test ratio} = \frac{\text{Current assets (excluding stock)}}{\text{Current liabilities (Creditors due within one year)}}$$

$$= \frac{£3.7m}{£5.4m}$$

$$= 0.7$$

These ratios reveal a fairly weak liquidity position. The current ratio seems quite low and the acid test ratio very low. This latter ratio suggests that the company does not have sufficient liquid assets to meet its maturing obligations. It would, however, be useful to have details of the liquidity ratios of similar companies in the same industry in order to make a more informed judgement. The bank overdraft represents 67 per cent of the short-term liabilities and 40 per cent of the total liabilities of the company. The continuing support of the bank is therefore important to the ability of the company to meet its commitments.

(b) The finance required to reduce trade creditors to an average of 40 days outstanding is calculated as follows:

	£m
Trade creditors at balance sheet date	1.80
Trade creditors outstanding based on 40 days' credit 40/365 × £8.4 m (that is, credit purchases)	(0.92)
Finance required	0.88 (say £0.9 m)

(c) The bank may not wish to provide further finance to the company. The increase in overdraft will reduce the level of trade creditors but will increase the exposure of the bank. The additional finance invested by the bank will not generate further funds and will not therefore be self-liquidating. The question does not make it clear whether the company has sufficient security to offer the bank for the increase in overdraft facility. The profits of the company will be reduced and the interest cover ratio, based on the profits generated to the year ended 31 May 2001, would reduce to less than 2.0* times if the additional overdraft was granted (based on interest charged at 10 per cent each year). This is very low and means that only a small decline in profits would leave interest charges uncovered.

*Existing bank overdraft (3.6) + extension of overdraft to cover reduction in trade creditors (0.9) + debentures (3.5) = £8.0 m. Assuming a 10 per cent interest rate means a yearly interest payment of £0.8 m. Before interest, the profit was £1.3 m (that is, 6.4 – 3.0 – 2.1). Interest cover would be 1.63 (that is, 1.3/0.8).

(d) A number of possible sources of finance might be considered. Four possible sources are as follows:

- *Issue equity shares.* This option may be unattractive to investors. The return on equity is fairly low at 7.9 per cent (that is, net profit after tax (0.3)/share capital and reserves (3.8)) and there is no evidence that the profitability of the business will improve. If profits remain at their current level the effect of issuing more equity will be to reduce further the returns to equity.

- *Issue loans.* This option may also prove unattractive to investors. The effect of issuing further loans will have a similar effect to that of increasing the overdraft. The profits of the business will be reduced and the interest cover ratio will decrease to a low level. The gearing ratio of the company is already quite high at 48 per cent (that is, debentures (3.5)/(debentures + capital and reserves (3.5 + 3.8)) and it is not clear what security would be available for the loan. The gearing ratio would be much higher if the overdraft were to be included.

- *Chase debtors.* It may be possible to improve cash flows by reducing the level of credit outstanding from debtors. At present, the average settlement period is 93 days (that is, (debtors (3.6)/sales (14.2)) × 365), which seems quite high. A reduction in the average settlement period by approximately one-quarter would generate the funds required. However, it is not clear what effect this would have on sales.

- *Reduce stock.* This appears to be the most attractive of the four options. At present, the average stockholding period is 178 days (that is, (closing stock (3.8)/cost of sales (7.8)) × 365), which seems very high. A reduction in this period by less than one-quarter would generate the funds required. However, if the company holds a large amount of slow-moving and obsolete stock, it may be difficult to reduce stock levels.

16.1 Williams Wholesalers Ltd

	£	£
Existing level of debtors (£4m × 70/365)		767,123
New level of debtors: £2m × 80/365	438,356	
£2m × 30/365	164,384	602,740
Reduction in debtors		164,383 (say £165,000)
Costs and benefits of policy		
Cost of discount (£2m × 2%)		40,000
Less Savings		
Interest payable (£165,000 × 13%)	21,450	
Administration costs	6,000	
Bad debts (20,000 – 10,000)	10,000	37,450
Net cost of policy		2,550

The above calculations reveal that the company will be worse off by offering the discounts.

Appendix D
Solutions to selected exercises

Chapter 2

2.1

Cash flow statement for day 4

	£
Opening balance (from day 3)	49
Cash from sale of wrapping paper	47
	96
Cash paid to purchase wrapping paper	(53)
Closing balance	43

Profit and loss account for day 4

	£
Sales	47
Cost of goods sold	(33)
Profit	14

Balance sheet at the end of day 4

	£
Cash	43
Stock of goods for resale (28 + 53 − 33)	48
Total business wealth	91

2.2

	£
Cash introduced by Paul on day 1	40
Profit of day 1	15
Profit of day 2	13
Profit of day 3	9
Profit of day 4	14
	91

Thus the wealth of the business, all of which belongs to Paul as sole owner, consists of the cash he put in to start the business plus the profit earned each day.

Profit and loss account for day 1

	£
Sales (70 × £0.80)	56
Cost of sales (70 × £0.50)	(35)
Profit	21

Cash flow statement for day 1

	£
Opening balance	40
Add Cash from sales	56
	96
Less Cash for purchases (80 × £0.50)	40
Closing balance	56

Balance sheet as at end of day 1

	£
Cash balance	56
Stock of unsold goods (10 × £0.50)	5
Helen's business wealth	61

Profit and loss account for day 2

	£
Sales (65 × £0.80)	52.0
Cost of sales (65 × £0.50)	(32.5)
Profit	19.5

Cash flow statement for day 2

	£
Opening balance	56.0
Add Cash from sales	52.0
	108.0
Less Cash for purchases (60 × £0.50)	30.0
Closing balance	78.0

Balance sheet as at end of day 2

	£
Cash balance	78.0
Stock of unsold goods (5 × £0.50)	2.5
Helen's business wealth	80.5

Profit and loss account for day 3

	£
Sales (20 × £0.80) + (45 × £0.40)	34.0
Cost of sales (65 × £0.50)	(32.5)
Profit	1.5

Cash flow statement for day 3

	£
Opening balance	78.0
Add Cash from sales	34.0
	112.0
Less Cash for purchases (60 × £0.50)	30.0
Closing balance	82.0

Balance sheet as at end of day 3

	£
Cash balance	82.0
Stock of unsold goods	–
Helen's business wealth	82.0

2.4

Joe Conday
Balance sheet as at 1 March

	£		£
Bank	20,000	Capital	20,000

Balance sheet as at 2 March

	£		£
Bank (20,000 − 6,000)	14,000	Capital	20,000
Fixtures and fittings	6,000	Creditors	8,000
Stock	8,000		
	28,000		28,000

Balance sheet as at 3 March

	£		£
Bank (14,000 + 5,000)	19,000	Capital	20,000
Fixtures and fittings	6,000	Creditors	8,000
Stock	8,000	Loan	5,000
	33,000		33,000

Balance sheet as at 4 March

	£		£
Bank (19,000 − 7,200)	11,800	Capital	19,800
Fixtures and fittings	6,000	Creditors	8,000
Stock	8,000	Loan	5,000
Motor car	7,000		
	32,800		32,800

Balance sheet as at 5 March

	£		£
Bank (11,800 − 2,500)	9,300	Capital	19,300
Fixtures and fittings	6,000	Creditors	8,000
Stock	8,000	Loan	5,000
Motor car	9,000		
	32,300		32,300

Balance sheet as at 6 March

	£		£
Bank (9,300 + 2,000 − 1,000)	10,300	Capital	21,300
Fixtures and fittings	6,000	Creditors	8,000
Stock	8,000	Loan	4,000
Motor car	9,000		
	33,300		33,300

2.5 (a) Crafty Engineering Ltd

Balance sheet as at 30 June last year

	£000	£000	£000
Fixed assets			
Freehold premises			320
Machinery and tools			207
Motor vehicles			38
			565

	£000	£000	£000
Current assets			
Stock in trade		153	
Debtors		185	
		338	
Less **Current liabilities**			
Creditors	86		
Bank overdraft	116	202	
			136
			701
Less **Long-term liabilities**			
Loan from Industrial Finance Co.			260
			441
Capital (missing figure)			441

(b) The balance sheet reveals a high level of investment in fixed assets. In percentage terms, we can say that more than 60 per cent of the total investment in assets has been in fixed assets. The nature of the business may require a heavy investment in fixed assets. The investment in current assets exceeds the current liabilities by a large amount (approximately 1.7 times). As a result, there is no obvious sign of a liquidity problem. However, the balance sheet reveals that the company has no cash balance and is therefore dependent on the continuing support of the bank (in the form of a bank overdraft) in order to meet obligations when they fall due. When considering the long-term financing of the business, we can see that about 37 per cent [260/(260 + 441)] of the total long-term finance for the business has been supplied by loan capital and about 63 per cent [441/(260 + 441)] by the owners. This level of borrowing seems quite high but not excessive. However, we would need to know more about the ability of the company to service the loan capital (that is, make interest payments and loan repayments) before a full assessment could be made.

Chapter 3

3.1 (a) Capital does increase as a result of the owners introducing more cash into the business, but it will also increase as a result of introducing other assets (for example, a motor car) and by the business generating revenues by trading. Similarly, capital decreases not only as a result of withdrawals of cash by owners but also by withdrawals of other assets (for example, stock for the owners' personal use) and through trading expenses being incurred. For the typical business in a typical accounting period, capital will alter much more as a result of trading activities than for any other reason.

(b) An accrued expense is not one that relates to next year. It is one that needs to be matched with the revenues of the accounting period under review, but that has yet to be met in terms of cash payment. As such, it will appear on the balance sheet as a current liability.

(c) The purpose of depreciation is not to provide for asset replacement. Rather, it is an attempt to allocate the cost of the asset (less any residual value) over its useful life. Depreciation is an attempt to provide a measure of the amount of the fixed asset that has been consumed during the period. This amount will then be charged as an expense for the period in order to derive the profit figure. Depreciation is a book entry (the outlay of cash occurs when the asset is purchased) and does not normally entail setting aside a separate amount of cash for asset replacement. Even if this were done, there would be no guarantee that sufficient funds would be available at the end of the asset's life for its replacement. Factors such as inflation and technological change may mean that the replacement cost is higher than the original cost of the asset.

(d) In the short term, it is possible for the current value of a fixed asset to exceed its original cost. However, nearly all fixed assets will wear out over time as a result of being used to generate wealth for the business. This will be the case for freehold buildings. As a result, some measure of depreciation should be calculated to take account of the fact that the asset is being consumed. Some businesses revalue their freehold buildings where the current value is significantly different from the original cost. Where this occurs, the depreciation charged should be based on the revalued amount. This will normally result in higher depreciation charges than if the asset remained at its historic cost.

3.3 The upward movement in profit and downward movement in cash may be for various reasons, which include the following:

- The purchase of assets for cash during the period (for example, motor cars and stock), which were not all consumed during the period and are therefore not having as great an effect on expenses as they are on cash.
- The payment of an outstanding liability (for example, a loan), which will have an effect on cash but not on expenses in the profit and loss account.
- The withdrawal of cash by the owners from the capital invested, which will not have an effect on the expenses in the profit and loss account.
- The generation of revenues on credit where the cash has yet to be received. This will increase the sales for the period but will not have a beneficial effect on the cash balance until a later period.

3.4 (a) **FIFO**

	Purchases			Cost of sales		
	Tonnes	Cost/tonne £	Total £	Tonnes	Cost/tonne £	Total £
1 Sept	20	18	360			
2 Sept	48	20	960			
4 Sept	15	24	360			
6 Sept	10	25	250			
7 Sept				20	18	360
				40	20	800
	93		1,930	60		1,160

Opening stock + purchases	1,930	
Cost of sales	(1,160)	
Closing stock	770	[(8 × £20) + (15 × £24) + (10 × £25)]

(b) LIFO

	Purchases			Cost of sales		
	Tonnes	Cost/tonne £	Total £	Tonnes	Cost/tonne £	Total £
1 Sept	20	18	360			
2 Sept	48	20	960			
4 Sept	15	24	360			
6 Sept	10	25	250			
7 Sept				10	25	250
				15	24	360
				35	20	700
	93		1,930	60		1,310

Opening stock + purchases	1,930
Cost of sales	(1,310)
Closing stock	620 $\quad$ [(20 × £18) + (13 × £20)]

(c) AVCO

	Purchases			Cost of sales		
	Tonnes	Cost/tonne £	Total £	Tonnes	Cost/tonne £	Total £
1 Sept	20	18	360			
2 Sept	48	20	960			
4 Sept	15	24	360			
6 Sept	10	25	250			
	93	20.8	1,930			
7 Sept				60	20.8	1,248

Opening stock + purchases	1,930
Cost of sales	(1,248)
Closing stock	682

3.5

(a) Rent payable – expense for period   £9,000
(b) Rates and insurance – expense for period   £6,000
(c) General expenses – paid in period   £7,000
(d) Loan interest payable – prepaid   £500
(e) Salaries – paid in period   £6,000
(f) Rent receivable – received during period   £3,000

3.8 An examination of the trading and profit and loss accounts for the two years reveals a number of interesting points, which include:

- An increase in sales value and gross profit of 9.9 per cent in 2001.
- The gross profit expressed as a percentage of sales remaining at 70 per cent.
- An increase in salaries of 7.2 per cent.
- An increase in selling and distribution costs of 31.2 per cent.
- An increase in bad debts of 392.5 per cent.

- A decline in net profit of 39.3 per cent.
- A decline in the net profit as a percentage of sales from 13.3 per cent to 7.4 per cent.

Thus, the business has enjoyed an increase in sales and gross profits, but this has failed to translate to an increase in net profit because of the significant rise in overheads. The increase in selling costs during 2001 suggests that the increase in sales was achieved by greater marketing effort, and the huge increase in bad debts suggests that the increase in sales may be attributable to selling to less creditworthy customers or to a weak debt-collection policy. There appears to have been a change of policy in 2001 towards sales, and this has not been successful overall as the net profit has shown a dramatic decline.

Chapter 4

4.1 Limited companies can no more set a limit on the amount of debts they will meet than can human beings. They must meet their debts up to the limit of their assets, just as we as individuals must. In the context of owners' claim, 'reserves' mean part of the owners' claim against the assets of the company. These assets may or may not include cash. The legal ability of the company to pay dividends is not related to the amount of cash that it has.

Preference shares do not carry a guaranteed dividend. They simply guarantee that the preference shareholders have a right to the first slice of any dividend that is paid. Shares of many companies can, in effect, be bought by one investor from another through the Stock Exchange. Such a transaction has no direct effect on the company, however. These are not new shares being offered by the company, but existing shares that are being sold 'second-hand'.

4.2 (a) The first part of the quote is incorrect. Bonus shares should not, of themselves, increase the value of the shareholders' wealth. This is because reserves, belonging to the shareholders, are used to create bonus shares. Thus, each shareholder's stake in the company has not increased.

Share splits should not increase the wealth of the shareholder, and so that part of the quote is correct.

(b) This statement is incorrect. Shares can be issued at any price, provided that it is not below the nominal value of the shares. Once the company has been trading profitably for a period, the shares will not be worth the same as they were (the nominal value) when the company was first formed. In such circumstances, issuing shares at above their nominal value would not only be legal, but essential to preserve the wealth of the existing shareholders relative to any new ones.

(c) This statement is incorrect. From a legal perspective, the company is limited to a maximum dividend of the current extent of its revenue reserves. This amounts to any after-tax profits or gains realised that have not been eroded through, for example, payments of previous dividends. Legally, cash is not an issue; it would be perfectly legal for a company to borrow the funds to pay a dividend – although whether such an action would be commercially prudent is another question.

(d) This statement is partly incorrect. Companies do indeed have to pay tax on their profits. Depending on their circumstances, shareholders might also have to pay tax on their dividends.

4.6 Pear Limited

Balance sheet as at 30 September 2001

	£000	£000
Fixed assets		
Cost (1,570 + 30)	1,600	
Depreciation (690 + 12)	702	
		898
Current assets		
Stock	207	
Debtors (182 + 18 – 4)	196	
Cash at bank	21	
	424	
Less **Creditors: amounts due within one year**		
Trade creditors	88	
Other creditors (20 + 30 + 15 + 2)	67	
Taxation	17	
Dividend proposed	25	
Bank overdraft	105	
	302	
Net current assets		122
Less **Creditors: amounts due after more than one year**		
10% debenture – repayable 2008		(300)
		720
Capital and reserves		
Shares capital		300
Share premium account		300
Retained profit at beginning of year	104	
Retained profit for year	16	120
		720

Profit and loss account for the year ended 30 September 2001

	£000	£000
Turnover (1,456 + 18)		1,474
Cost of sales		(768)
Gross profit		706
Less Salaries	220	
Depreciation (249 + 12)	261	
Other operating costs [131 + (2% × 200) + 2]	137	
		(618)
Operating profit		88
Interest payable (15 + 15)		(30)
Profit before taxation		58
Taxation (58 × 30%)		(17)
Profit after taxation		41
Dividend proposed		(25)
Retained profit for the year		16

4.7 Chips Limited

Balance sheet as at 30 June 2001

	£000	£000	£000
Fixed assets	Cost	Depreciation	
Buildings	800	112	688
Plant and equipment	650	367	283
Motor vehicles (102 − 8); (53 − 5 + 19)	94	67	27
	1,544	546	998
Current assets			
Stock		950	
Debtors (420 − 16)		404	
Cash at bank (16 + 2)		18	
		1,372	
Less **Creditors due within one year**			
Trade creditors (361 + 23)		(384)	
Other creditors (117 + 35)		(152)	
Taxation		(26)	
Dividends proposed		(28)	
		(590)	
Net current assets			782
Less **Creditors due after more than one year**			
Secured 10% loan			(700)
			1,080
Capital and reserves			
Ordinary shares of £1, fully paid			500
6% Preference shares of £1			300
Reserves at 1 July 2000		248	
Retained profit for year		32	280
			1,080

Profit and loss account for the year ended 30 June 2001

	£000	£000
Turnover (1,850 − 16)		1,834
Cost of sales (1,040 + 23)		1,063
Gross profit		771
Less Depreciation [220 − 2 − 5 + 8 + (94 × 20%)]	(240)	
Other operating costs	(375)	
		(615)
Operating profit		156
Interest payable (35 + 35)		(70)
Profit before taxation		86
Taxation (86 × 30%)		(26)
Profit after taxation		60
Dividends proposed: Preference (300 × 6%)	(18)	
Ordinary (500 × 2p)	(10)	(28)
		32

Chapter 5

5.1 Many believe that the annual reports of companies are becoming too long and contain too much information. To illustrate this point, a few examples of the length of the 2000 accounts of large companies are as follows:

Rolls-Royce plc	76 pages
The Boots Company plc	76 pages
Cadbury Schweppes plc	148 pages
National Express Group plc	76 pages

There is a danger that users will suffer from 'information overload' if they are confronted with an excessive amount of information and that they will be unable to cope with it. This may, in turn, lead them to:

- Fail to distinguish between important and less important information.
- Fail to approach the analysis of information in a logical and systematic manner.
- Feel a sense of confusion and avoid the task of analysing the information.

The problem of lengthy annual reports is likely to be a particular problem for the less sophisticated user. This problem, however, has been recognised and many companies publish abridged accounts for private investors, which include only the key points. However, for sophisticated users the problem may be that the annual reports are still not long enough. They often wish to glean as much information as possible from the company in order to make investment decisions.

5.3

I. Ching (Booksellers) plc
Profit and loss account for the year to 31 December

	£m	£m
Turnover		943
Cost of sales		460
Gross profit		483
Distribution costs	110	
Administration expenses	314	424
		59

	£m	£m
Other operating income		86
		145
Income from other fixed asset investments	42	
Other interest receivable and similar income	25	67
		212
Interest payable and similar charges		40
		172
Tax on profit or loss on ordinary activities (25%)		43
Profit on ordinary activities after taxation		129
Retained profit brought forward from last year		285
		414
Transfer to general reserve	100	
Proposed dividend on ordinary shares (30% × £129)	39	139
Retained profit carried forward		275

5.4

G. Stavros and Co plc
Balance sheet as at end of financial period

	£m	£m	£m
Fixed assets:			
Intangible assets:			
Patents and trademarks		170	
Tangible assets:			
Land and buildings	165		
Plant and machinery	143		
Motor vehicles	22	330	500
Current assets:			
Stocks:			
Raw materials and consumables	120		
Work in progress	18		
Finished goods and goods for resale	96	234	
Debtors:			
Trade debtors	86		
Prepayments and accrued income	15	101	
Cash at bank and in hand		12	
		347	
Creditors: amounts falling due within one year			
Trade creditors	75		
Other creditors including taxation and social security	23		
Accruals and deferred income	47	145	
Net current assets			202
Total assets less current liabilities			702
Creditors: amounts falling due after more than one year			
Debenture loans		230	
Provisions for liabilities and charges			
Pensions		54	284
			418

	£m	£m	£m
Capital and reserves			
Called-up share capital (balancing figure)			50
Share premium account			30
Revaluation reserve			100
General reserves			163
Profit and loss account			75
			418

5.5 Some of the arguments that are relevant to this question are already contained within the chapter and so will not be restated here. However, some further points that might be made concerning accounting regulation and accounting measurement are:

For
- It seems reasonable that companies, particularly given their limited liability, should be required to account to their members and to the general public and that the law should prescribe how this should be done – including how particular items should be measured. It also seems sensible that accounting standards should amplify these rules, to try to establish some uniformity of practice. Investors could be misled if the same item appeared in the accounts of two separate companies but had been measured in different ways.
- Companies would find it difficult to attract finance, credit and possibly employees without publishing credible information about themselves. An important measure of performance is profit, and investors often need to make judgements concerning relative performance within an industry sector. Without clear benchmarks by which to judge performance, investors may not invest in a company.

Against
- Some would argue that it is up to the companies to decide whether or not they can survive and prosper without publishing information about themselves. If they can, then so much the better for them since they will have saved large amounts of money by not doing so. If it is necessary for a company to provide financial information in order to be able to attract investment finance and other necessary factors, then the company can make the necessary judgement of how much information is necessary and what form of measurements are required.
- Not all company managements view matters in the same way. Allowing companies to select their own approaches to financial reporting enables them to reflect their personalities. Thus, a conservative management will adopt conservative accounting policies such as writing off research and development expenditure quickly, whereas more adventurous management may adopt less conservative accounting policies such as writing off research and development expenditure over several years. The impact of these different views will have an effect on profit and will give the reader an insight to the approach adopted by the management team.

5.8 Electricity distribution business

(a) The following ratios may be calculated for each of the three main business segments:

	2002 %	2001 %
Net profit to sales		
Distribution	41.1	41.1
Supply	1.3	1.1
Retail	3.8	4.3
Sales growth		
Distribution	7.7	
Supply	0.4	
Retail	34.4	
Net profit to capital employed (net assets)		
Distribution	30.1	30.7
Supply	*	64.9
Retail	5.0	6.8

* As the net assets are negative (liabilities exceed assets), a ratio is not computed.

The above ratios reveal a high net profit to sales ratio for the distribution area which has remained constant over the two-year period. The distribution area also enjoys a high return on capital employed. Although there was a slight dip in this return in 2002, the increase in sales for the period ensured that net profits increased substantially over the period.

The net profit to sales ratio for the supply area is very low and there has been little sales growth over the period. This area contributes the largest part of the company's turnover but a relatively small part of its total profits for each period. However, the level of investment required is much lower than the other areas (indeed, it was negative in 2002). The return on capital employed in 2001 was very high compared with other areas of activity.

The net profit to sales ratio in the retail area was quite low and declined in 2002 to 3.8 per cent. However, the company managed to increase sales dramatically during the period and this led to a significant increase in profits. The growth in retail sales was accompanied by a significant increase in the level of investment in this area. As a result, there was a decline on the ROCE in 2002.

(b) The intersegment adjustments could be presented so as to show the impact on each operating segment. In the annual reports, it is not possible to identify which segments are most affected by the intersegmental transactions.

Chapter 6

6.1

(a) An increase in the level of stock in trade would, ultimately, have an adverse effect on cash.

(b) A rights issue of ordinary shares will give rise to a positive cash flow, which will be included in the 'financing' section of the cash flow statement.

(c) A bonus issue of ordinary shares has no cash flow effect.

(d) Writing off some of the value of the stock has no cash flow effect.

(e) A disposal for cash of a large number of shares by a major shareholder has no cash-flow effect as far as the business is concerned.

(f) Depreciation does not involve cash at all. Using the indirect method of deducing cash flow from operations involves the depreciation expense in the calculation, but this is simply because we are trying to find out from the profit (after depreciation) figure what the profit before depreciation must have been.

6.3

Torrent plc
Cash flow statement for the year ended 31 December 2001

	£m	£m
Net cash inflows from operating activities		247
(see calculation below)		
Returns from investment and servicing of finance		
Interest received	14	
Interest paid	(26)	
Net cash outflow from returns on investment and servicing of finance		(12)
Taxation		
Corporation tax paid (see note below)	(41)	
Net cash outflow for taxation		(41)
Capital expenditure		
Payments to acquire tangible fixed assets	(67)	
Net cash outflow for capital expenditure		(67)
		127
Equity dividends paid		
Dividends paid (see note below)	(50)	
Net cash flow for equity dividends paid		(50)
		77
Management of liquid resources		–
Financing		
Repayments of debenture stock	(100)	
Net cash outflow from financing		(100)
Net increase(decrease) in cash		(23)

Reconciliation of cash movements during the year ended 31 December 2001

	£m
Balance at 1 January 2001	(6)
Net cash outflow	(23)
Balance at 31 December 2001	(29)

Notes

(i) *Dividend.* Since all of the dividend for 2001 was unpaid at the end of 2001, it seems that the business pays just one final dividend each year, some time after the year-end. Thus it is the *2000* dividend that will have led to a cash outflow in 2001.

(ii) *Taxation*

	£m
Amount owed at 1 January 2001	23
Tax charge for the year	36
	59
Amount owed at 31 December 2001	18
Cash paid during the year	41

(iii) *Debentures*. It has been assumed that the debentures were redeemed for their balance sheet value. This is not always the case, however.

(iv) *Shares*. The share issue was effected by converting the share premium account balance and £60 million of the revaluation reserve balance to ordinary share capital. This involved no flow of cash.

Calculation of net cash inflow from operating activities

	£m	£m
Net operating profit (from the profit and loss account)		182
Add Depreciation:		
Plant, etc. (325 + 67 − 314)*		78
		260
Less Increase in debtors (132 − 123)	9	
Decrease in creditors (39 − 30)	9	
Decrease in accruals (15 − 11)	4	22
		238
Add Decrease in stocks (41 − 35)	6	
Decrease in prepayments (16 − 13)	3	9
		247

* Since there were no disposals, the depreciation charges must be the difference between the fixed-asset values at the start and end of the year, adjusted by the cost of any additions.

The following comments can be made about the Torrent plc's cash flow as shown by the cash flow statement for the year ended 31 December 2001:

- There was a positive cash flow from operating activities.
- There was a net cash outflow in respect of financing.
- The outflow of cash to acquire additional tangible fixed assets was very comfortably covered by cash generated by operating activities, even after allowing for the net cash outflows for financing and tax. This is usually interpreted as a 'strong' cash-flow situation.
- There was a fairly major repayment of debenture loan.
- Overall, there was a fairly significant reduction in cash over the year, leading to a negative cash balance at the year-end.

| | 6.4 | Cheng plc |

Cash flow statement for the year ended 31 December 2001

	£m	£m
Net cash inflows from operating activities		48
(see calculation below)		
Returns from investment and servicing of finance		
Interest paid	(4)	
Net cash outflow from returns on investment and servicing of finance		(4)
Taxation		
Corporation tax paid	(11)	
Net cash flow for taxation		(11)
Capital expenditure		
Land and buildings	(30)	
Plant and machinery (see note below)	(6)	
Net cash outflow for capital expenditure		(36)
		(3)
Equity dividends paid		
Dividends paid (see note below)	(18)	
Net cash flow for equity dividends paid		(18)
		(21)
Management of liquid resources		–
Financing		–
		–
Net decrease in cash		(21)

Reconciliation of cash movements during the year ended 31 December 2001

	£m
Balance at 1 January 2001	19
Net cash outflow	(21)
Balance at 31 December 2001	(2)

Calculation of net cash inflow from operating activities

	£m	£m
Net operating profit (from the profit and loss account)		29
Add Depreciation		
Land and buildings	10	
Plant and machinery	12	
		22
		51
Less Increase in stocks (25 – 24)	1	
Decrease in creditors (23 – 20)	3	4
		47
Add Decrease in debtors (26 – 25)		1
		48

Notes

Dividends

	£m
Amount due at 1 January 2001	14
Dividend for the year	10
	32
Amount due at 31 December 2001	(14)
Cash paid during the year	18

Fixed asset acquisitions

	Land and buildings £m	Plant and machinery £m
Position at 1 January 2001	110	62
Less 2001 depreciation	10	12
	100	50
Position at 31 December 2001	130	56
Acquisitions	30	6

Taxation

	£m
Amount due at 1 January 2001	8
Charge for the year	6
	14
Amount due at 31 December 2001	(3)
Cash paid during the year	11

6.5 Nailsea Ltd

Cash flow statement for the year ended 30 June 2002

	£000	£000
Net cash inflows from operating activities (Note 1)		397
Returns from investment and servicing of finance		
Interest paid	(27)	
Net cash outflow from returns on investment and servicing of finance		(27)
Taxation		
Corporation tax paid (Note 2)	(125)	
Net cash outflow for taxation		(125)
Capital expenditure		
Land and buildings	(400)	
Plant and machinery	(250)	
Net cash outflow from capital expenditure		(650)
		(405)
Equity dividends paid (Note 3)		
Dividends paid	(80)	
Net cash outflow for equity dividends paid		(80)
		(485)
Management of liquid resources		–

	£000	£000
Financing		
Additional share capital (200 + 100)	300	
Debentures	300	
Net cash inflow from financing		600
Net increase in cash		115

Reconciliation of cash movements during the year ended 30 June 2002

	£000
Balance at 1 July 2001	(32)
Net cash inflow	115
Balance at 30 June 2002	83

Notes

Note 1: Calculation of net cash inflow from operating activities

	£000	£000
Net operating profit (from the profit and loss account)		342
Add Depreciation		
Plant and machinery		320
		662
Less Increase in stocks (450 – 275)	175	
Increase in debtors (250 – 100)	150	325
		337
Add Increase in creditors (190 – 130)		60
		397

Note 2: Taxation

	£000
Amount due at 1 July 2001	55
Charge for the year	140
	195
Amount due at 30 June 2000	70
Cash paid during the year	125

Note 3: Dividends
It is clear that the dividend declared in one year is paid in the next, and so the 2001 dividend will be paid in 2002.

6.6   Blackstone plc

Cash flow statement for the year ended 31 March 2002

	£m	£m
Net cash inflows from operating activities (Note 1)		2,541
Returns from investment and servicing of finance		
Interest paid	(456)	
Net cash outflow from returns on investment and servicing of finance		(456)
Taxation (Note 2)		
Corporation tax paid	(300)	
Net cash outflow for taxation		(300)

	£m	£m
Capital expenditure		
Proceeds of sales	54	
Goodwill	(700)	
Plant and machinery	(2,970)	
Fixtures and fittings	(1,608)	
Net cash outflow for capital expenditure		(5,224)
		(3,439)
Equity dividends paid (Note 3)		
Dividends paid	(300)	
Net cash outflow for equity dividends paid		(300)
		(3,739)
Management of liquid resources		–
Financing		
Additional bank loan	2,000	
Net cash inflow from financing		2,000
Net decrease in cash		(1,739)

Reconciliation of cash movements during the year ended 31 March 2002

	£m
Balance at 1 April 2001	(77)
Net cash outflow	(1,739)
Balance at 31 March 2002	(1,816)

Notes

Note 1: Calculation of net cash inflow from operating activities

	£m	£m
Net operating profit (from the profit and loss account)		2,309
Add Depreciation		
Land and buildings	225	
Plant and machinery	745	
Fixtures and fittings	281	
Loss on disposals (54 – 581 + 489)	38	1,289
		3,598
Less Increase in stocks (2,410 – 1,209)	1,201	
Increase in debtors (1,573 – 941)	632	1,833
		1,765
Add Increase in creditors (1,507 – 731)		776
		2,541

Note 2: Taxation

	£m
Amount due at 1 April 2001	105
Charge for the year	390
	495
Amount due at 31 March 2002	(195)
Cash paid during the year	300

Note 3: Dividends
It seems that dividends declared by the company in one year are paid in the next, and so the 2002 payment will be the 2001 dividend.

Chapter 7

7.1 I. Jiang (Western) Ltd
The effect of each of the changes on ROCE is not always easy to predict.

(a) An increase in the gross profit margin *may* lead to a decrease in ROCE in particular circumstances. If the increase in the margin resulted from an increase in price, which in turn lead to a decrease in sales, a fall in ROCE can occur. A fall in sales can reduce the net profit (the numerator in ROCE) if the overheads of the business did not decrease correspondingly.

(b) A reduction in sales can reduce ROCE for the reasons mentioned above.

(c) An increase in overhead expenses will reduce the net profit and this in turn will result in a reduction in ROCE.

(d) An increase in stocks held will increase the amount of capital employed by the business (the denominator in ROCE) where long-term funds are employed to finance the stocks. This will, in turn, reduce ROCE.

(e) Repayment of the loan at the year-end will reduce the capital employed and this will increase the ROCE, provided that the loan repayment does not affect the scale of operations.

(f) An increase in the time taken for debtors to pay will result in an increase in capital employed if long-term funds are employed to finance the debtors. This increase in long-term funds will, in turn, reduce ROCE.

7.2 (a) This part of the question has been dealt with in the text of the chapter. Review as necessary.

(b) The ratios for business A and business B reveal that the debtors turnover ratio for business A is 63 days, whereas for business B the ratio is only 21 days. Business B is therefore much quicker in collecting amounts outstanding from customers. Nevertheless, there is not much difference between the two businesses in the time taken to pay trade creditors: business A takes 50 days to pay its creditors whereas Business B takes 45 days. It is interesting to compare the difference in the debtor and creditor collection periods for each business. As business A allows an average of 63 days' credit to its customers, yet pays creditors within 50 days, it will require greater investment in working capital than business B, which allows an average of only 21 days to its debtors but takes 45 days to pay its creditors.

Business A has a much higher gross profit percentage than business B. However, the net profit percentage for the two businesses is identical. This suggests that business A has much higher overheads than business B. The stock turnover period for business A is more than twice that of business B. This may be due to the fact that business A maintains a wider range of goods in stock in order to meet customer requirements. The evidence therefore suggests that business A is the business that prides itself on personal service. The higher average settlement period is consistent with a more relaxed attitude to credit collection (thereby maintaining customer goodwill) and the high overheads are consistent with the incurring of additional costs in order to satisfy customer requirements. The high stock levels of business A are consistent with maintaining a wide range of stock in order to satisfy a range of customer needs.

Business B has the characteristics of a more price-competitive business. Its gross profit percentage is much lower than business A's, indicating a much lower gross profit per £1 of sales. However, overheads are kept low in order to ensure the net profit percentage is the same as business A's. The low stock turnover period and average collection period for debtors are consistent with a business that wishes to minimise investment in current assets, thereby reducing costs.

| 7.4 | Helena Beauty Products Ltd |

	2000	2001
Profitability ratios		
Net profit margin	$\dfrac{80}{3,600} \times 100\% = 2.2\%$	$\dfrac{90}{3,840} \times 100\% = 2.3\%$
Gross profit margin	$\dfrac{1,440}{3,600} \times 100\% = 40\%$	$\dfrac{1,590}{3,840} \times 100\% = 41.4\%$
ROCE	$\dfrac{80}{2,668} \times 100\% = 3.0\%$	$\dfrac{90}{2,874} \times 100\% = 3.1\%$
Efficiency ratios		
Stock turnover period	$\dfrac{(320 + 400)/2}{2,160} \times 365 = 61$ days	$\dfrac{(400 + 500/2)}{2,250} \times 365 - 73$ days
Average collection period	$\dfrac{750}{3,600} \times 365 = 76$ days	$\dfrac{960}{3,840} \times 365 = 91$ days
Sales/capital employed	$\dfrac{3,600}{2,668} = 1.3$	$\dfrac{3,840}{2,874} = 1.3$

The above ratios reveal a low net-profit margin in each year. The gross profit margin, however, is quite high in each year, suggesting that the company has high overheads. There was a slight improvement of 1.4 percentage points in the gross profit margin during 2001, but this appears to have been largely swallowed up by increased overheads. As a result, the net profit margin improved by only 0.1 percentage points in 2001. The low net profit margin is matched by a rather low sales to capital employed ratio in both years. The combined effect of this is a low ROCE in both years. The ROCE for each year is lower than might be expected from investment in risk-free government securities and should be regarded as unsatisfactory.

The stock turnover period and average collection period for debtors have both increased significantly over the period. The average collection period seems to be high and should be a cause for concern. Although both profit (in absolute terms) and sales improved during 2001, the directors should be concerned at the low level of profitability and efficiency of the business. In particular, an investigation should be carried out concerning the high level of overheads and the higher investment in stocks and debtors.

7.7 | Harridges Ltd

(a)

	2001	2002
ROCE	$\dfrac{310}{1,600} = 19.4\%$	$\dfrac{350}{1,700} = 20.6\%$
ROSF	$\dfrac{155}{1,100} = 14.1\%$	$\dfrac{175}{1,200} = 14.6\%$
Gross profit margin	$\dfrac{1,040}{2,600} = 40\%$	$\dfrac{1,150}{3,500} = 32.9\%$
Net profit margin	$\dfrac{310}{2,600} = 11.9\%$	$\dfrac{350}{3,500} = 10\%$
Current ratio	$\dfrac{735}{400} = 1.8$	$\dfrac{660}{485} = 1.4$
Acid test ratio	$\dfrac{485}{400} = 1.2$	$\dfrac{260}{485} = 0.5$
Days debtors	$\dfrac{105}{2,600} \times 365 = 15$ days	$\dfrac{145}{3,500} \times 365 = 15$ days
Days creditors	$\dfrac{235}{1,560} \times 365 = 55$ days	$\dfrac{300}{2,350^*} \times 365 = 47$ days
Stock turnover period	$\dfrac{250}{1,560} \times 365 = 58$ days	$\dfrac{400}{2,350} \times 365 = 62$ days
Gearing ratio	$\dfrac{500}{1,600} = 31.3\%$	$\dfrac{500}{1,700} = 29.4\%$
EPS	$\dfrac{155}{490} = 31.6$p	$\dfrac{175}{490} = 35.7$p

* Used because the credit purchases figure is not available.

(b) There has been a considerable decline in the gross profit margin during 2002. This fact, combined with the increase in sales by more than one-third, suggests that a price-cutting policy has been adopted in order to stimulate sales. The resulting increase in sales, however, has led to only a small improvement in ROCE and returns to equity. Similarly, there has only been a small improvement in EPS.

Despite a large cut in the gross profit margin, the net profit margin has fallen by less than 2 per cent. This suggests that overheads have been tightly controlled during 2002. Certainly, overheads have not risen in proportion to sales.

The current ratio has fallen and the acid test ratio has fallen by more than half. Even though liquidity ratios are lower in retailing than in manufacturing, the liquidity of the company should now be a cause for concern. However, this may be a passing problem. The company is investing heavily in fixed assets and is relying on internal funds to finance this growth. When this investment ends, the liquidity position may improve quickly.

The debtors period has remained unchanged over the two years, and there has been no significant change in the stock turnover period in 2002. The gearing ratio is quite low and provides no cause for concern given the profitability of the company.

Overall, the company appears to be financially sound. Although there has been rapid growth during 2002, there is no real cause for alarm provided that the liquidity of the company can be improved in the near future. In the absence of information concerning share price, it is not possible to say whether or not an investment should be made.

| 7.8 | Genesis Ltd

(a) and (b) These parts have been answered in the text of the chapter and you are referred to it for a discussion on overtrading and its consequences.

(c)

$$\text{Current ratio} = \frac{232}{550} = 0.42$$

$$\text{Acid test ratio} = \frac{104}{550} = 0.19$$

$$\text{Stock turnover period} = \frac{128}{1,248} \times 365 = 37 \text{ days}$$

$$\text{Average settlement period for debtors} = \frac{104}{1,640} \times 365 = 23 \text{ days}$$

$$\text{Average settlement period for creditors} = \frac{184}{1,260} \times 365 = 53 \text{ days}$$

(d) Overtrading must be dealt with either by increasing the level of funding in order to match the level of activity, or by reducing the level activity to match the funds available. The latter option may result in a reduction in profits in the short-term but may be necessary to ensure long-term survival.

Chapter 8

| 8.1 | Lombard Ltd
Relevant costs of undertaking the contract are:

	£
Equipment costs	200,000
Component X (20,000 × 4 × £5)	400,000
Component Y (20,000 × 3 × £8)	480,000
Additional costs (20,000 × £8)	160,000
	1,240,000
Revenue from the contract (20,000 × £80)	1,600,000

Thus, from a purely financial point of view the project is acceptable. (Note that there is no relevant labour cost since the staff concerned will be paid irrespective of whether the contract is undertaken.)

8.2	The local authority

(a) **'Normal' monthly surplus**

Revenues per performance for a full house:

	£
200 @ £6 =	1,200
500 @ £4 =	2,000
300 @ £3 =	900
	4,100

		£	£
Ticket revenues at 50% capacity for			
20 performances (£4,100 × 50% × 20)			41,000
Refreshment sales			3,880
Programme advertising			3,360
			48,240
Less	Full-time staff	4,800	
	Artistes	17,600	
	Costumes	2,800	
	Scenery	1,650	
	Heating and light	5,150	
	Administration costs	8,000	
	Casual staff	1,760	
	Refreshments	1,180	
			42,940
'Normal' surplus			5,300

Touring company surplus

Revenues per performance for a full house:

	£
200 @ £5.50 =	1,100
500 @ £3.50 =	1,750
300 @ £2.50 =	750
	3,600

		£	£
Ticket revenues	(£3,600 × 10 × 50%)		18,000
	(£3,600 × 15 × $\frac{2}{3}$ × 50%)		18,000
Refreshment sales			3,880
Programme advertising			3,360
			43,240
Less	Full-time staff	4,800	
	Artistes	17,600	
	Heating and light	5,150	
	Administration costs	8,000	
	Refreshments	1,180	
			36,730
Touring company surplus			6,510

Thus on financial grounds, the approach by the touring company will be accepted.

(b) (i) With only the 10 full performances, the deficit for the month would be:

$$£18,000 - 6,510 = £11,490$$

(that is, £18,000 less than the expected surplus).

If y is the required occupancy rate, then:

$$£3,600 \times 15 \times y \times 50\% = £11,490$$

$$y = \frac{11,490}{3,600 \times 15 \times 50\%} = 42.56\% \text{ occupancy}$$

Thus, to avoid a deficit there would need to be a 42.56% occupancy rate for the other 15 performances.

(ii) With only the 10 full performances the deficit for the month, relative to a 'normal' month, would be

$$£11,490 + 5,300 = £16,790$$

(that is, a deficit of £11,490 instead of a surplus of £5,300).

If y is the required occupancy rate, then:

$$£3,600 \times 15 \times y \times 50\% = £16,790$$

$$y = \frac{16,790}{3,600 \times 15 \times 50\%} = 62.19\% \text{ occupancy}$$

Thus the occupancy rate for the other 15 performances would need to be 62.19% to generate the same surplus as in a normal month.

(c) Other possible factors to consider include:

- The reliability of the estimations, including the assumption that programme and refreshment sales will not be altered by the level of occupancy.
- A desire to offer theatre-goers the opportunity to see another group of players.
- Dangers of loss of morale of staff not employed, or employed to do other than their usual work.

8.3 Andrews and Co. Ltd
Minimum contract price

			£
Materials	Steel core:	10,000 × £2.10	21,000
	Plastic:	10,000 × 0.10 × 0.10	100
Labour	Skilled:		–
	Unskilled:	10,000 × 5/60 × £5	4,167
Minimum tender price			25,267

8.6 The local education authority

(a) One-off financial net benefits of closing:

	No schools	D only	A and B	A and C
Capacity reduction	0	800	700	800
	£m	£m	£m	£m
Property developer (A)	–	–	14.0	14.0
Shopping complex (B)	–	–	8.0	–
Property developer (D)	–	9.0	–	–
Safety (C)	(3.0)	(3.0)	(3.0)	–
Adapt facilities		(1.8)		
Total	(3.0)	4.2	19.0	14.0
Ranking based on total one-off benefits	4	3	1	2

(Note that all past costs of buying and improving the schools are irrelevant.)

Recurrent financial net benefits of closing:

	No schools £m	D only £m	A and B £m	A and C £m
Rent (C)	–	–	–	0.3
Administrators	–	0.2	0.4	0.4
Total	–	0.2	0.4	0.7
Ranking based on total of recurrent benefits	4	3	2	1

On the basis of the financial figures alone, closure of either A and B or A and C looks best. It is not possible to add the one-off and the recurring costs directly, but the large one-off cost-saving associated with closing schools A and B makes this option look attractive. (In Chapter 14 we shall see that it is possible to add one-off and recurring costs in a way that should lead to sensible conclusions.)

(b) The costs of acquiring and improving the schools in the past are past costs or sunk costs. The costs of employing the chief education officer is a future cost, but irrelevant because it is not differential between outcomes, it is a common cost.

(c) There are many other factors, some of a non-quantifiable nature. These include:

- Accuracy of projections of capacity requirements.
- Locality of existing schools relative to where potential pupils live.
- Political acceptability of selling schools to property developers.
- Importance of purely financial issues in making the final decision.
- The quality of the replacement sporting facilities compared with those at school D.
- Political acceptability of staff redundancies.
- Possible savings/costs of employing fewer teachers, which might be relevant if economies of scale are available by having fewer schools.
- Staff morale.

8.7 Rob Otics Ltd

(a) The minimum price for the proposed contract would be:

	£
Materials	
Component X 2 × 8 × £100	2,880
Component Y	0
Component Z [(75 + 32) × £20] – (75 × £25)	265
Other miscellaneous items	250
Labour	
Assembly (25 + 24 + 23 + 22 + 21 + 20 + 19 + 18) × £48*	8,256
Inspection 8 × 6 × £18	864
Total	12,515

*£60 – £12 = £48.

Labour is an irrelevant cost here because it will be incurred irrespective of which work the staff do. Thus the minimum price is £12,515.

(b) Other factors include:

- Competitive state of the market.
- The fact that the above figure is unique to the particular circumstances at the time – for example, having component Y in stock but having no use for it. Any subsequent order might have to take account of an outlay cost.
- Breaking even (that is, just covering the costs) on a contract will not fulfil the company's objective.
- Charging a low price may cause marketing problems. Other customers may resent the low price for this contract. The current enquirer may expect a similar price in future.

Chapter 9

9.1 Alpha, Beta and Gamma

(a) and (b) Deduce the total contribution per product and deduce the contribution per £1 of labour and hence the relative profitability of the three products, given a shortage of labour. Strictly, we should use the contribution per hour, but we do not know the number of hours involved. Since all labour is paid at the same rate, using labour cost will give us the same order of priority as using hours.

	Alpha	Beta	Gamma
	£	£	£
Variable costs:			
Materials	(6,000)	(4,000)	(5,000)
Labour	(9,000)	(6,000)	(12,000)
Expenses	(3,000)	(2,000)	(2,000)
Total variable cost	(18,000)	(12,000)	(19,000)
Sales	39,000	29,000	33,000
Contribution	21,000	17,000	14,000
Contribution per £ of labour	2.333	2.833	1.167
Order of profitability	2nd	1st	3rd

Since 50 per cent of each budget (and, therefore, £13,500 of labour) is committed, only £6,500 (£20,000 – £13,500) of labour is left uncommitted. The £6,500 should be deployed as:

	£
Beta	3,000
Alpha	3,500
	6,500

Total labour committed to each product and resultant profit are as follows:

	Alpha £	Beta £	Gamma £	Total £
Labour				
50% of budget	4,500	3,000	6,000	
Allocated above	3,500	3,000	–	
Total	8,000	6,000	6,000	20,000
Contribution per £ of labour	2.333	2.833	1.167	
Contribution per product*	18,664	16,998	7,002	42,664
Less Fixed costs				33,000
Maximum profit (after rounding)				9,664

* The contribution per £ of labour × total labour.

(c) Other factors that might be considered include the following:

- Could all of the surplus labour be used to produce Betas (the most efficient user of labour)? In other words, could the business sell more than £29,000 of this product? It might be worth reducing the price of the Beta, though still keeping the contribution per £1 of labour above £2.33, in order to expand sales.
- Could the commitment to 50 per cent of budget on each product be dropped in favour of producing the maximum of the higher-yielding products?
- Could another source of labour be found?
- Could the labour-intensive part of the work be subcontracted?

9.2 (a) Lannion and Co.

	October	November
Sales (units of the service)	200	300
Sales (£)	5,000	7,500
Costs (balancing figure, £)	(4,000)	(5,300)
Operating profit (£)	1,000	2,200

The increase in output of 100 units (300 – 200) gives rise to additional costs of £1,300 (£5,300 – £4,000) or £13 per unit (£1,300/100). This is the variable cost. Since there were no price changes, the £1,300 can only have arisen from additional sales.

We do not know how much of each month's costs figure is fixed and how much is variable, but we can work it out. For October, total variable cost = 200 × £13 = £2,600. Thus, the fixed cost must be £1,400 (£4,000 – £2,600). This can be checked using the November figures: total variable cost $= 300 \times £13 = £3,900$; fixed cost $= £5,300 - £3,900 = £1,400$. Fixed costs, by definition, must be the same each month.

Sales revenue per unit $= £5,000/200$ or $7,500/300 = £25$. Therefore:

$$\text{Break-even point} = \text{Fixed cost/contribution} \quad \frac{£1,400}{£25 - £13}$$

$$= 116.67, \text{ or } 117 \text{ units per month}$$

(b) Knowledge of the break-even point is useful because it enables management to judge how close the planned level of activity is to the point at which no profit will be made. This enables some assessment of riskiness to be made.

9.3 The hotel group

(a) The variable element and, by implication, the fixed element of the hotel's costs can be deduced by comparing any two quarters, for example:

Quarter	Sales £000	Profit(loss) £000	Total cost £000
1	400	(280)	680
2	1,200	360	840
Difference	800		160

Thus the variable element of the sales price is 20 per cent (160/800). Now:

The fixed costs for quarter 1 = Total costs – Variable costs

$$= £680,000 - (20\% \times 400,000) = £600,000$$

To check that this calculation is correct and consistent for all four quarters, we can 'predict' the total costs for the other three quarters and then check the predicted results against those which can be deduced from the question, as follows:

Quarter 2

Total cost = fixed costs + variable costs

$$= £600,000 + (20\% \times 1,200,000)$$

$$= £840,000 \quad \text{Agrees with the question}$$

Quarter 3

Total cost = fixed costs + variable costs

$$= £600,000 + (20\% \times 1,600,000)$$

$$= £920,000 \quad \text{Agrees with the question}$$

Quarter 4

Total cost = fixed costs + variable costs

$$= £600,000 + (20\% \times 800,000)$$

$$= £760,000 \quad \text{Agrees with the question}$$

Had the fixed and variable elements been deduced graphically, the consistency of the fixed and variable cost elements over the four quarters would have been obvious because a straight line would have emerged.

The provisional results for this year are as follows:

	Total	Per visitor (50,000 visitors)
	£000	£
Sales	4,000	80
Variable costs (20% of sales)	(800)	(16)
Contribution	3,200	64
Fixed costs (that is, fixed costs per quarter × 4)	(2,400)	(48)
Profit	800	16

(b) (i) At the same level of occupancy as for this year and incorporating the increase in variable costs of 10 per cent, the sales revenue for next year will need to be:

	£000
Fixed costs	2,400
Variable costs (800,000 × 110%)	880
Total costs	3,280
Target profit	1,000
Sales target	4,280

Hence, the sales revenue per visitor is:

$$\frac{£4,280,000}{50,000} = £85.60$$

(ii) If the sales revenue per visitor remains at the current rate, the contribution per visitor will be:

$$£80 - (£16 \times 110\%) = £62.40$$

To cover the fixed costs and the target profit, would take:

$$\frac{£2,400,000 + 1,000,000}{£62.40} \approx 54,487 \text{ visitors}$$

(c) The major assumptions of profit–volume analysis are that costs can be analysed as those that vary with the volume of activity (and with that factor alone) and those that are totally unaffected by volume changes. A further assumption is that variable costs vary at a steady rate (straight-line relationship) with volume.

These assumptions are unlikely to be strictly valid in reality. Variable costs are unlikely to vary in a truly straight-line manner relative to volumes. For example, at higher levels of output there may be economies of scale in purchasing (for example, bulk discounts) or the opportunity to use materials or labour more effectively. On the other hand, the opposite may be the case. At higher levels of output, cost per unit increases because a shortage may be created by the higher output level.

9.5 Products A, B and C

(a) Total time required on cutting machines is:

$$(2,500 \times 1.0) + (3,400 \times 1.0) + (5,100 \times 0.5) = 8,450 \text{ hours}$$

Total time available on cutting machines is 5,000 hours. Therefore, this is a limiting factor.

Total time required on assembling machines is:

$$(2,500 \times 0.5) + (3,400 \times 1.0) + (5,100 \times 0.5) = 7,200 \text{ hours}$$

Total time available on assembling machines is 8,000 hours. Therefore, this is not a limiting factor.

	A (per unit) £	B (per unit) £	C (per unit) £
Selling price	25	30	18
Variable materials	(12)	(13)	(10)
Variable production costs	(7)	(4)	(3)
Contribution	6	13	5
Time on cutting machines	1.0 hour	1.0 hour	0.5 hour
Contribution per hour on cutting machines	£6	£13	£10
Order of priority	3rd	1st	2nd

Therefore, produce:

3,400 product B using	3,400 hours
3,200 product C using	1,600 hours
	5,000 hours

(b) Assuming that the company would make no saving in variable production costs by subcontracting, it would be worth paying up to the contribution per unit (£5) for product C, which would therefore be £5 × (5,100 − 3,200) = £9,500 in total.

Similarly it would be worth paying up to £6 per unit for product A – that is, £6 × 2,500 = £15,000 in total.

9.6 Darmor Ltd

(a) Contribution per hour of unskilled labour of product A is:

$$\frac{(£30 - 6 - 2 - 12 - 3)}{(6/6)} = £7$$

Given the scarcity of skilled labour, if the management is to be indifferent between the products, the contribution per skilled labour hour must be the same. Thus for product B the selling price must be:

$$(£7 \times (9/6)) + 9 + 4 + 25 + 7 = £55.50$$

(that is, the contribution plus the variable costs)
and for product C the selling price must be:

$$(£7 \times (3/6)) + 3 + 10 + 14 + 7 = £37.50$$

(b) The company could pay up to £13 an hour (£6 + £7) for additional hours of skilled labour. This is the potential contribution per hour, before taking account of the labour rate of £6 per hour.

Chapter 10

Offending phrase	Explanation
'necessary to divide the business up into departments'	This can be done but it will not always be to much benefit to do so. Only in quite restricted circumstances will it give significantly different job costs.
'Fixed costs (or overheads)'	This implies that fixed costs and overheads are the same thing. They are not really connected with one another. 'Fixed' is to do with how costs behave as the level of output is raised or lowered; 'overheads' are to do with the extent to which costs can be directly measured in respect of a particular unit of output. Though it is true that many overheads are fixed, not all are. Also, direct labour is usually a fixed cost. All of the other references to fixed and variable costs are wrong. The person should have referred to indirect and direct costs.
'Usually this is done on the basis of area'	Where overheads are apportioned to departments, they will be apportioned on some logical basis. For certain costs – for example, rent – the floor area may be the most logical; for others, such as machine maintenance costs, the floor area would be totally inappropriate.
'When the total fixed costs for each department have been identified, this will be divided by the number of hours that were worked'	Where overheads are dealt with on a departmental basis, they may be divided by the number of direct labour hours to deduce a recovery rate. However, this is only one basis of applying overheads to jobs. For example, machine hours or some other basis may be more appropriate to the particular circumstances involved.
'It is essential that this approach is taken in order to deduce a selling price'	It is relatively unusual for the 'job cost' to be able to dictate the price at which the manufacturer can price its output. Job costing may have its uses, but setting prices is not usually one of them.

10.2 All three of the costing techniques listed in the question are means of deducing the full cost of some activity. The distinction between them lies essentially with the difference in the style of the production of the goods or services involved. Thus:

- *Job costing* is used where each unit of output, or 'job', differs from others produced by the same business. Because the jobs are not identical, it is not normally acceptable to those who are likely to use the cost information to treat the jobs as if they were identical. This means that costs need to be identified, job by job. For this purpose, costs fall into two categories: direct costs and indirect costs (or overheads).

    Direct costs are those that can be measured directly in respect of the specific job, such as the amount of labour that was directly applied to the job, or the amount of material that has been incorporated in it. To this must be added a share of the indirect costs. This is usually done by taking the total overheads for the period concerned and charging part of them to the job. This, in turn, is usually done according to some measure of the job's size and importance, relative to the other jobs done during the period. The number of direct labour hours worked on the job is the most commonly used measure of size and/or importance.

The main problem with job costing tends to be the method of charging indirect costs to jobs. Indirect costs, by definition, cannot be related directly to jobs and must, if full cost is to be deduced, be charged on a basis that is more or less arbitrary. If indirect costs accounted for a small proportion of the total, the arbitrariness of charging them would probably not matter. Indirect costs, in many cases, however, form the majority of total costs and so arbitrariness is a problem.

- *Process costing* is the approach taken where all output is of identical units. These units can be treated, therefore, as having identical cost. Sometimes a process costing approach is taken even where the units are not strictly identical. This is because process costing is much simpler and cheaper to apply than the only other option, namely job costing. Provided that users of the cost information are satisfied that treating units as identical is acceptable, the additional cost and effort of job costing is not justified.

  In process costing, the cost per unit of output is found by dividing total costs for the period by the total number of units produced in the period.

  The main problem with process costing tends to be that, at the beginning and end of any period, there will probably be partly completed units of output. An adjustment needs to made for this work in progress if the resulting cost unit figures are not to be distorted.

- *Batch costing* is really an extension of job costing. Batch costing tends to be used where production is in batches. A batch consists of more than one identical units of output. The units of output differ from one batch to the next. For example, a clothing manufacturing business may produce 500 identical jackets in one batch, followed by a batch of 300 identical skirts in another batch.

  Each batch is costed as one job, using a job-costing approach. The full cost of each garment is then found by dividing the cost of the batch by the number of garments in the batch.

  The main problem of batch costing is exactly that of job costing, of which it is an extension: that of dealing with overheads.

10.3 Budgers Ltd

(a) The company predetermines the rate at which overheads are to be charged to jobs because, for most of the reasons that full costing information could be useful, costs usually need to be known either before the job is done or very soon afterwards. The two main reasons why businesses identify full costs are for pricing decisions and for income-measurement purposes.

For pricing, usually the customer will want to know the price in advance of placing the order. Thus, it is not possible to wait until all of the costs have been incurred, and are known, before the price can be deduced. Even where production is not for an identified customer, the business still needs to have some idea of whether it can produce the good or service at a price that the market will bear.

In the context of income measurement, valuing work in progress is the purpose for which full costs are required. If managers and other users are to benefit as much as possible from accounting information, that information must speedily follow the end of the period to which it relates. This usually means that waiting to discover actual cost is not practical.

(b) Predetermining the rate at which overheads are charged to jobs requires that three judgements are made:

   (i) Predicting the overheads for the period concerned.

   (ii) Deciding on the basis of charging overheads to jobs (for example, rate per direct labour hour).

   (iii) Predicting the number of units of the basis factor (for example, number of direct labour hours) which are expected to occur during the period concerned.

   Judgements (i) and (iii) are difficult to make, but there will normally be some past experience to provide guidance. Judgement (ii) is purely a matter of opinion.

(c) The problems of using predetermined rates are really linked to the ability to predict (i) and (iii) in (b) above. The desired result is that the total of the overheads, but no more than this, become part of the cost of the various jobs worked on in the period. Only if (i) and (iii) are both accurately predicted will this happen, except by lucky coincidence. There is clearly the danger that jobs will either be undercharged or overcharged with overheads, relative to the total amount of overheads incurred during the period. In fact, it is almost certain that one of these two will happen to some extent simply because perfect prediction is virtually impossible. Minor errors will not matter, but major ones could well lead to bad decisions.

10.6 Promptprint Ltd

(a) The budget may be summarised as:

	£	
Sales revenue	196,000	
Direct materials	(38,000)	
Direct labour	(32,000)	
Total overheads	(77,000)	(2,400 + 3,000 + 27,600 + 36,000 + 8,000)
Profit	49,000	

The job may be priced on the basis that both overheads and profit should be apportioned to it on the basis of direct labour cost, as follows:

	£	
Direct materials	4,000	
Direct labour	3,600	
Overheads	8,663	(£77,000 × 3,600/32,000)
Profit	5,513	(£49,000 × 3,600/32,000)
	21,776	

This answer assumes that variable overheads vary in proportion to direct labour cost.

Various other bases of charging overheads and profit loading the job could have been adopted. For example, materials cost could have been included (with direct labour) as the basis for profit-loading, or even apportioning overheads.

(b) This part of the question is, in effect, asking for comments on the validity of 'full cost-plus' pricing. This approach can be useful as an indicator of the effective long-run cost of doing the job. On the other hand, it fails to take account of relevant opportunity costs as well as the state of the market and other external factors. For example, it ignores the price that a competitor printing business may quote.

(c) Revised estimates of material direct costs for the job:

	£	
Paper grade 1	1,500	(£1,200 × 125%) This stock needs to be replaced
Paper grade 2	0	It has no opportunity cost value
Card	510	(£640 – 130: using the card on another job would save £640, but cost £130 to achieve that saving)
Inks, etc.	300	This stock needs to be replaced
	2,310	

10.7 Bookdon plc

(a) To answer this question, we need first to allocate and apportion the overheads to product cost centres, as follows:

			Department			
Cost	Basis of app't	Total	Machine shop	Fitting section	Canteen	Machine maintance section
		£	£	£	£	£
Allocated items:	Specific Allocated by:	90,380	27,660	19,470	16,600	26,650
Rent, rates, heat, light	Floor area	17,000	9,000 (3,600/ 6,800)	3,500 (1,400/ 6,800)	2,500 (1,000/ 6,800)	2,000 (800/ 6,800)
Dep'n and insurance	Book value	25,000	12,500 (150/ 300)	6,250 (75/ 300)	2,500 (30/ 300)	3,750 (45/ 300)
		132,380	49,160	29,220	21,600	32,400
Canteen	Number of employees	–	10,800 (18/36)	8,400 (14/36)	(21,600)	2,400 (4/36)
		132,380	59,960	37,620	–	34,800
Machine maintenance section	Specified %	–	24,360 (70%)	10,440 (30%)	–	(34,800)
		132,380	84,320	48,060	–	–

Note that the canteen overheads were reapportioned to the other cost centres first because the canteen renders a service to the machine maintenance section but does not receive a service from it.

Calculation of the overhead absorption (recovery) rates can now proceed:

(i)   Total budgeted machine hours are:

	Hours
Product X (4,200 × 6)	25,200
Product Y (6,900 × 3)	20,700
Product Z (1,700 × 4)	6,800
	52,700

Overhead absorption rate for the machine shop is:

$$\frac{£84,320}{52,700} = £1.60/\text{machine hour}$$

(ii) Total budgeted direct labour cost is:

	£
Product X (4,200 × £12)	50,400
Product Y (6,900 × £3)	20,700
Product Z (1,700 × £21)	35,700
	106,800

Overhead absorption rate for the fitting section is:

$$\frac{£48,060}{£106,800} \times 100\% = 45\% \text{ or } £0.45 \text{ per } £ \text{ of direct labour}$$

of direct labour cost.

(b) The cost of one unit of product X is calculated as follows:

	£
Direct materials	11.00
Direct labour	
Machine shop	6.00
Fitting section	12.00
Overheads	
Machine shop (6 × £1.60)	9.60
Fitting section (£12 × 45%)	5.40
	44.00

Therefore, the cost of one unit of product X is £44.00.

Chapter 11

11.1 Woodner Ltd

A Output	B Sales price per unit	C Total sales revenue (A × B)	D Marginal unit sales revenue	E Total variable cost (A × .£20)	F Total cost (variable cost + £2,500)	G Marginal cost per unit	H Profit/ (loss)
units	£	£	£	£	£	£	£
0	0	0	0	0	2,500	–	(2,500)
10	95	950*	95**	200	2,700	20	(1,750)
20	90	1,800	85	400	2,900	20	(1,100)
30	85	2,550	75	600	3,100	20	(550)
40	80	3,200	65	800	3,300	20	(100)
50	75	3,750	55	1,000	3,500	20	250
60	70	4,200	45	1,200	3,700	20	500
70	65	4,550	35	1,400	3,900	20	650
80	60	4,800	25	1,600	4,100	20	700
90	55	4,950	15	1,800	4,300	20	650
100	50	5,000	5	2,000	4,500	20	500

* (10 × £95)
** ((950 – 0)/(10 – 0))

An output of 80 units each week will maximise profit at £700 per week. This is the nearest, given the nature of the input data, to the level of output where marginal cost per unit equals marginal revenue per unit. (For the mathematically minded, this question could have been solved by using calculus to find the point at which slopes of the total sales revenue and total costs lines were equal.)

11.2 Cost-plus pricing means that prices are based on calculations/assessments of how much it costs to produce the good or service, and includes a margin for profit. 'Cost' in this context might mean relevant cost, variable cost, direct cost or full cost. Usually cost-plus prices are based on full costs.

If a business charges the full cost of its output as a selling price, it will in theory break even. This is because the sales revenue will exactly cover all of the costs. Charging something above full cost will yield a profit. Thus, in theory, cost-plus pricing is logical.

If a cost-plus approach to pricing is to be taken, the question that must be addressed is the level of profit required from each unit sold. This must logically be based on the total profit that is required for the period. Normally, businesses seek to enhance their wealth through trading. The extent to which they expect to do this is normally related to the amount of wealth that is invested to promote wealth enhancement. Businesses tend to seek to produce a particular percentage increase in wealth. In other words, they seek to generate a particular return on capital employed. It seems logical, therefore, that the profit loading on full cost should reflect the business's target profit and that the target should itself be based on a target return on capital employed.

An obvious problem with cost-plus pricing is that the market may not agree with the price. Put another way, cost-plus pricing takes no account of the market demand function (the relationship between price and quantity demanded). A business may fairly deduce the full cost of some product and then add what might be regarded as a reasonable level of profit, only to find that a rival producer is offering a similar product for a much lower price, or that the market simply will not buy at the cost-plus price.

Most suppliers are not strong enough in the market to dictate pricing; most are 'price takers', not 'price makers'. They must accept the price offered by the market or they do not sell any of their wares. Cost-plus pricing may be appropriate for price makers, but it has less relevance for price takers.

The cost-plus price is not entirely useless to price takers. When contemplating entering a market, knowing the cost-plus price will tell the price taker whether it can profitably enter the market or not. As has been said above, the full cost can be seen as a long-run break-even selling price. If entering a market means that this break-even price, plus an acceptable profit, cannot be achieved, then the business should probably stay out. Having a breakdown of the full cost may put the business in a position to examine where costs might be capable of being cut in order to bring the full cost-plus profit to within a figure acceptable to the market.

Being a price maker does not always imply that the business dominates a particular market. Many small businesses are, to some extent, price makers. This tends to be where buyers find it difficult to make clear distinctions between the prices offered by various suppliers. An example of this might be a car repair. Though it may be possible to obtain a series of binding estimates for the work from various garages, most people would not normally do so. As a result, garages normally charge cost-plus prices for car repairs.

|11.3| Kaplan plc

(a) At present, the company makes each model of suitcase in a batch. The direct materials and labour costs will be recorded in respect of each batch. To these costs will be added a share of the overheads of the business for the period in which production of the batch takes place. The basis of the batch absorbing overheads is a matter of managerial judgement. Direct labour hours spent working on the batch, relative to total direct labour hours worked during the period, is a popular method. This is not the 'correct' way, however. There is no correct way. If the activity is capital intensive, some machine-hour basis of dealing with overheads might be more appropriate, though still not 'correct'. Overheads might be collected, department by department, and charged to the batch as it passes through each department. Alternatively, all of the overheads for the entire production facility might be totalled and the overheads dealt with more globally. It is only in restricted circumstances that overheads charged to batches will be affected by a decision to deal with them departmentally, rather than globally.

Once the 'full cost' (direct costs plus a share of indirect costs) has been ascertained for the batch, the cost per suitcase can be established by dividing the batch cost by the number in the batch.

(b) The uses to which full cost information can be put have been identified as:

- *For pricing purposes.*   In some industries and circumstances, full costs are used as the basis of pricing. Here the full cost is deduced and a percentage is added on for profit. This is known as cost-plus pricing. A solicitor handling a case for a client probably provides an example of this.

   In many circumstances, however, suppliers are not in a position to deduce prices on a cost-plus basis. Where there is a competitive market, a supplier will probably need to accept the price that the market offers – that is, most suppliers are 'price takers' not 'price makers'.

- *For income-measurement purposes.* To provide a valid means of measuring a business's income, it is necessary to match expenses with the revenues realised in the same accounting period. Where manufactured stock is made or partially made in one period but sold in the next, or where a service is partially rendered in one accounting period but the revenue is realised in the next, the full cost (including an appropriate share of overheads) must be carried from one accounting period to the next. Unless we are able to identify the full cost of work done in one period, which is the subject of a sale in the next, the profit figures of the periods concerned will become meaningless.

  Unless all production costs are charged in the same accounting period as the sale is recognised in the profit and loss account, distortions will occur that will render the profit and loss account much less useful. Thus it is necessary to deduce the full cost of any production undertaken completely or partially in one accounting period but sold in a subsequent one.

(c) Whereas the traditional approach to dealing with overheads is just to accept that they exist and deal with them in a fairly broad manner, ABC takes a much more enquiring approach. ABC takes the view that overheads do not just 'occur', but that they are caused or 'driven' by 'activities'. It is a matter of finding out which activities are driving the costs and how much cost they are driving.

For example, a significant part of the costs of making suitcases of different sizes is resetting machinery to cope with a batch of a different size from its predecessor batch. Where a particular model is made in very small batches, because it has only a small market, ABC would advocate that this model is charged directly with its machine-setting costs. The traditional approach would be to treat machine setting as a general overhead that the individual suitcases (irrespective of the model) might bear equally. ABC, it is claimed, leads to more accurate costing and thus to more accurate assessment of profitability.

(d) The other advantage of pursuing an ABC philosophy and identifying cost drivers is that, once the drivers have been identified, they are likely to become much more susceptible to being controlled. Thus the ability of management to assess the benefit of certain activities against their cost becomes more feasible.

11.6 GB Company – the International Industries (II) enquiry

(a) The minimum acceptable price of 120,000 motors to be supplied over the next four months is:

	£000	
Direct materials	600	(120,000 × £5.00)
Direct labour	720	(120,000 × £6.00)
Variable manufacturing overheads	360	(120,000 × £3.00)
Fixed manufacturing overheads	60	(4 × £15,000)
Total	1,740	

The offer price is:

120,000 × £19.00 = £2,280,000

On this basis, the price of £19 per machine could be accepted, subject to a number of factors identified in (b) below.

(b) The assumptions on which the above analysis and decision in (a) are based include the following:

- That the contract can be accommodated within the 30-per-cent spare capacity of GB. If this is not so, then there will be an opportunity cost relating to lost 'normal' production, which must be taken account of in the decision.
- That sales commission and freight costs will not be affected by the contract.
- It is unlikely that work more remunerative to GB than the contract will be available during the period of the contract.

There are also some strategic issues involved in the decision, including:

- The possibility that the contract could lead to other and better remunerated work from II.
- A problem of selling similar products in the same market at different prices. Other customers, knowing that GB is selling at marginal prices, may make it difficult for the business to resist demand from other customers for similarly priced output.

11.7 Sillycon Ltd

(a)

Overhead analysis

	Electronics £000	Testing £000	Service £000
Variable overheads	1,200	600	700
Apportionment of service dept (800 : 600)	400	300	(700)
	1,600	900	–
Direct labour hours	800	600	
Variable overheads per direct labour hour	£2.00	£1.50	

	Electronics £000	Testing £000	Service £000
Fixed overheads	2,000	500	800
Apportionment of service dept (equally)	400	400	(800)
	2,400	900	–
Direct labour hours	800	600	
Fixed overheads per direct labour hour	£3.00	£1.50	

Product cost (per unit)

		£	
Direct materials		7.00	
Direct labour	electronics	40.00	(4 × £10.00)
	testing	18.00	(3 × £6.00)
Variable overheads	electronics	8.00	(4 × £2.00)
	testing	4.50	(3 × £1.50)
Total variable cost		77.50	(assuming direct labour to be variable)

Fixed overheads	electronics	12.00	(4 × £3.00)
	testing	4.50	(3 × £1.50)
Total 'full' cost		94.00	
Add Mark-up, say 30%		28.20	
		122.20	

On the basis of the above, the business could hope to compete in the market at a price that reflects normal pricing practice.

(b) At this price, and only taking account of incremental fixed overheads, the break-even point (BEP) would be given by:

$$BEP = \frac{\text{Fixed costs}}{\text{Contribution per unit}} = \frac{£150,000^*}{£122.20 - £77.50} = 3,356 \text{ units}$$

*(£13,000 + £100,000 + £37,000) namely the costs specifically incurred.

As the potential market for the business is around 5,000 to 6,000 units a year, the new product looks viable.

Chapter 12

12.1 Daniel Chu Ltd

(a) The finished goods stock budget for the six months ending 30 September (in units of production) is:

	April units	May units	June units	July units	Aug units	Sept units
Opening stock (note 1)	0	500	600	700	800	900
Production (note 2)	500	600	700	800	900	900
	500	1,100	1,300	1,500	1,700	1,800
Less Sales (note 3)	0	500	600	700	800	900
Closing stock	500	600	700	800	900	900

(b) The raw materials stock budget for the six months ending 30 September (in units) is:

	April units	May units	June units	July units	Aug units	Sept units
Opening stock (note 1)	0	600	700	800	900	900
Purchases (note 2)	1,100	700	800	900	900	900
	1,100	1,300	1,500	1,700	1,800	1,800
Less Production (note 4)	500	600	700	800	900	900
Closing stock	600	700	800	900	900	900

The raw materials stock budget for the six months ending 30 September (in financial terms) is:

	April £	May £	June £	July £	Aug £	Sept £
Opening stock (note 1)	0	24,000	28,000	32,000	36,000	36,000
Purchases (note 2)	44,000	28,000	32,000	36,000	36,000	36,000
	44,000	52,000	60,000	68,000	72,000	72,000
Less Production						
(note 4)	20,000	24,000	28,000	32,000	36,000	36,000
Closing stock	24,000	28,000	32,000	36,000	36,000	36,000

(c) The trade creditors budget for the six months ending 30 September is:

	April £	May £	June £	July £	Aug £	Sept £
Opening balance						
(note 1)	0	44,000	28,000	32,000	36,000	36,000
Purchases (note 5)	44,000	28,000	32,000	36,000	36,000	36,000
	44,000	72,000	60,000	68,000	72,000	72,000
Less Cash payment	0	44,000	28,000	32,000	36,000	36,000
Closing balance	44,000	28,000	32,000	36,000	36,000	36,000

(d) The trade debtors budget for the six months ending 30 September is:

	April £	May £	June £	July £	Aug £	Sept £
Opening balance (note 1)	0	0	50,000	60,000	70,000	80,000
Sales (note 3)	0	50,000	60,000	70,000	80,000	90,000
	0	50,000	110,000	130,000	150,000	170,000
Less Cash received	0	0	50,000	60,000	70,000	80,000
Closing balance	0	50,000	60,000	70,000	80,000	90,000

(e) The cash budget for the six months ending 30 September is:

	April £	May £	June £	July £	Aug £	Sept £
Inflows						
Share issue	300,000					
Receipts – debtors						
(note 6)	0	0	50,000	60,000	70,000	80,000
	300,000	0	50,000	60,000	70,000	80,000
Outflows						
Payments to						
creditors						
(note 7)	0	44,000	28,000	32,000	36,000	36,000
Labour (note 3)	10,000	12,000	14,000	16,000	18,000	18,000

	April £	May £	June £	July £	Aug £	Sept £
Overheads:						
Production	17,000	17,000	17,000	17,000	17,000	17,000
Non-production						
(note 8)	10,000	10,000	10,000	10,000	10,000	10,000
Fixed assets	250,000					
Total outflows	287,000	83,000	69,000	75,000	81,000	81,000
Net inflows						
(outflows)	13,000	(83,000)	(19,000)	(15,000)	(11,000)	(1,000)
Balance c/f	13,000	(70,000)	(89,000)	(104,000)	(115,000)	(116,000)

Notes
1. The opening balance is the same as the closing balance from the previous month.
2. This is a balancing figure.
3. This figure is given in the question.
4. This figure derives from the finished stock budget.
5. This figure derives from the raw materials stock budget.
6. This figure derives from the trade debtors budget.
7. This figure derives from the trade creditors budget.
8. This figure is the non-productive overheads less depreciation, which is not a cash expense.

12.2 (a) A budget is a financial plan for a future period. A forecast is an assessment/ estimation of what is expected to happen in the environment. 'Plan' implies an intention to achieve. Thus a budget is a plan of what is intended to be achieved during the period of the budget. Relevant forecasts may well be taken into account when budgets are being prepared, but there is a fundamental difference between budgets and forecasts.

Though a year is a popular period for detailed budgets to be drawn up, there is no strong reason in principle why they have to be of this length.

(b) The layout described is generally regarded as a useful approach. Budgets are documents exclusively for the use of managers within the business. For this reason, those managers can use whatever layout best suits their purpose and tastes. In fact, there is no legal requirement that budgets should be prepared at all, let alone that they are prepared in any particular form.

(c) It is probably true to say that any manager worth employing would not want to work for a business that did not have an effective system of budgeting. Without budgeting, the advantages of:

● Co-ordination
● Motivation
● Focusing on the future, and
● Provision of the basis of a system of control

would all be lost.

Any good system of budgeting would almost certainly have individual managers participating heavily in the preparation of their own budgets and targets. It would also be providing managers with demanding, but rigorous, targets. This would give good managers plenty of scope to show flair and initiative, yet be part of a business that is organised, in control and potentially successful.

(d) All budgeting must take account of the planned volume of activity. ABB takes an ABC approach to the identification of overheads and to trying to ensure that managers who have control over the activities that drive the costs are held accountable for those costs. Similarly, ABB seeks to ensure that managers who have no effective control over particular costs are not held accountable for them.

(e) Any sensible person would probably start with the budget for the area in which lies the limiting factor – that is, that factor that will, in the end, prevent the business from achieving its objectives to the extent that would have been possible were it not for that factor.

It is true that, in practice, sales demand is often the limiting factor. In those cases, the sales budget is the best place to start. The limiting factor could, however, be a shortage of suitable labour or materials. In this case, the labour or materials budget would be the sensible place to start.

The reason why the starting point is important is simply that it is easier to start with the factor that is expected to limit the other factors and for those other factors to fit in.

12.4 Linpet Ltd

(a) Cash budgets are extremely useful for decision-making purposes. They allow managers to see the likely effect on the cash balance of the plans that they have set in place. Cash is an important asset and it is necessary to ensure that it is properly managed. Failure to do so can have disastrous consequences for the business. Where the cash budget indicates a surplus balance, managers must decide whether this balance should be reinvested in the business or distributed to the owners. Where the cash budget indicates a deficit balance, managers must decide how this deficit should be financed or how it might be avoided.

(b) Cash budget to 30 November

	June £	July £	Aug £	Sept £	Oct £	Nov £
Receipts						
Cash sales (note 1)	4,000	5,500	7,000	8,500	11,000	11,000
Credit sales (note 2)	–	–	4,000	5,500	7,000	8,500
	4,000	5,500	11,000	14,000	18,000	19,500
Payments						
Purchases (note 3)	–	29,000	9,250	11,500	13,750	17,500
Overheads	500	500	500	500	650	650
Wages	900	900	900	900	900	900
Commission (note 4)	–	320	440	560	680	880
Equipment	10,000					7,000
Motor vehicle	6,000					
Freehold	40,000					
	57,400	30,720	11,090	13,460	15,980	26,930
Cashflow	(53,400)	(25,220)	(90)	540	2,020	(7,430)
Opening bal.	60,000	6,600	(18,620)	(18,710)	(18,170)	(16,150)
Closing bal.	6,600	(18,620)	(18,710)	(18,170)	(16,150)	(23,580)

Notes:
1. 50 per cent of the current month's sales.
2. 50 per cent of sales of two months' previous.
3. To have sufficient stock to meet each month's sales will require purchases of 75 per cent of the month's sales figures (25 per cent is profit). In addition, each month the business will buy £1,000 more stock than it will sell. In June, the business will also buy its initial stock of £22,000. This will be paid for in the following month. For example, June's purchases will be (75% × £8,000) + £1,000 + £22,000 = £29,000, paid for in July.
4. This is 5 per cent of 80 per cent of the month's sales, paid in the following month. For example, June's commission will be 5% × 80% × £8,000 = £320, payable in July.

| 12.5 | Lewisham Ltd |

(a) The finished goods stock budget for the three months ending 30 September (in units of production) is:

	July '000 units	Aug '000 units	Sept '000 units
Opening stock (note 1)	40	48	40
Production (note 2)	188	232	196
	228	280	236
Less Sales (note 3)	180	240	200
Closing stock	48	40	36

(b) The raw materials stock budget for the two months ending 31 August (in kg) is:

	July '000 kg	Aug '000 kg
Opening stock (note 1)	40	58
Purchases (note 2)	112	107
	152	165
Less Production (note 4)	94	116
Closing stock	58	49

(c) The cash budget for the two months ending 30 September is:

	Aug £	Sept £
Inflows		
Debtors – Current month (note 5)	493,920	411,600
Preceding month (note 6)	151,200	201,600
Total inflows	645,120	613,200
Outflows		
Payments to creditors (note 7)	168,000	160,500
Labour and overheads (note 4)	185,600	156,800
Fixed overheads	22,000	22,000
Total outflows	375,600	339,300
Net inflows/(outflows)	269,520	273,900
Balance c/f	289,520	563,420

Notes
1. The opening balance is the same as the closing balance from the previous month.
2. This is a balancing figure.
3. This figure is given in the question.
4. This figure derives from the finished stock budget.
5. This is 98 per cent of 70 per cent of the current month's sales revenue.
6. This is 28 per cent of the previous month's sales.
7. This figure derives from the raw materials stock budget.

12.6 Newtake records

(a) The cash budget for the period to 30 November is:

	June £000	July £000	Aug £000	Sept £000	Oct £000	Nov £000
Cash receipts						
Sales (note 1)	227	315	246	138	118	108
Cash payments						
Administration (note 2)	(40)	(41)	(38)	(33)	(31)	(30)
Goods purchased	(135)	(180)	(142)	(94)	(75)	(66)
Finance expenses	(5)	(5)	(5)	(5)	(5)	(5)
Selling expenses	(22)	(24)	(28)	(26)	(21)	(19)
Tax paid			(22)			
Shop refurbishment		(14)	(18)	(6)		
	(202)	(264)	(253)	(164)	(132)	(120)
Cash surplus(deficit)	25	51	(7)	(26)	(14)	(12)
Opening balance	(35)	(10)	41	34	8	(6)
Closing balance	(10)	41	34	8	(6)	(18)

Notes:
1. (50% of the current month's sales) + (97% × 50% of those sales). For example, the June cash receipts = (50% × £230,000) + (97% × 50% × £230,000) = £226,550.
2. The administration expenses figure for the month, *less* £15,000 for depreciation (a non-cash expense).

(b) The stock budget for the six months to 30 November is:

	June £000	July £000	Aug £000	Sept £000	Oct £000	Nov £000
Opening balance	112	154	104	48	39	33
Stock purchased	180	142	94	75	66	57
	292	296	198	123	105	90
Cost of stocks sold (60% sales)	(138)	(192)	(150)	(84)	(72)	(66)
Closing balance	154	104	48	39	33	24

(c) The budgeted profit and loss account for the six months ending 30 November is:

	£000	£000
Sales turnover		1,170
Less Cost of goods sold		702
Gross profit		468
Selling expenses	(136)	
Admin. expenses	(303)	
Credit card charges	(18)	
Interest charges	(6)	(463)
Net profit for the period		5

(d) We are told that the company is required to eliminate the bank overdraft by the end of November. However, the cash budget reveals that this will not be achieved. There is a decline in the overdraft of nearly 50 per cent over the period, but this is not enough and ways must be found to comply with the bank's requirements. It may be possible to delay the refurbishment programme that is included in the forecasts or to obtain an injection of funds from the owners or other investors. It may also be possible to stimulate sales in some way. However, there has been a decline in the sales since the end of July and the November sales are approximately one-third of the July sales. The reasons for this decline should be sought.

The stock levels will fall below the preferred minimum level for each of the last three months. However, to rectify this situation it will be necessary to purchase more stock, which will, in turn, exacerbate the cash-flow problems of the business.

The budgeted profit and loss account reveals a very low net profit for the period. For every £1 of sales, the company is only managing to generate 0.4p in profit. The company should look carefully at its pricing policies and its overhead expenses. The administration expenses, for example, absorb more than one-quarter of the total sales turnover. Any reduction in overhead expenses will have a beneficial effect on cash flows.

Chapter 13

13.1 (a) A favourable direct labour rate variance can only be caused by something that leads to the rate per hour paid being less than standard. Normally, this would not be linked to efficient working. Where, however, the standard envisaged some overtime working, at premium rates, the actual labour rate may be below standard if efficiency has removed the need for the overtime.

(b) The statement is true. The action will lead to an adverse sales-price variance and may well lead to problems elsewhere, but the sales volume variance must be favourable.

(c) It is true that below-standard material could lead to adverse materials usage variances because there may be more than a standard amount of scrap. This could also cause adverse labour efficiency variances because labour time would be wasted by working on materials that would not form part of the output.

(d) Higher-than-budgeted sales could well lead to an adverse labour-rate variance because producing the additional work may require overtime working at premium rates.

(e) The statement is true. Nothing else could cause such a variance.

13.2 Pilot Ltd

(a) and (b)

	Budget			Actual	
	Original	Flexed			
Output (units) (production and sales)	5,000	5,400		5,400	
	£	£		£	
Sales	25,000	27,000		26,460	
Raw materials	(7,500)	(8,100)	(2,700 kg)	(8,770)	(2,830 kg)
Labour	(6,250)	(6,750)	(1,350 hr)	(6,885)	(1,300 hr)
Fixed overheads	(6,000)	(6,000)		(6,350)	
Operating profit	5,250	6,150		4,455	

	£		Manager accountable
Sales volume variance (5,250 − 6,150)	900	(F)	Sales
Sales price variance (27,000 − 26,460)	(540)	(A)	Sales
Materials price variance (2,830 × 3) − 8,770	(280)	(A)	Buyer
Materials usage variance [(5,400 × 0.5) − 2,830] × £3	(390)	(A)	Production
Labour rate variance (1,300 × £5) − 6,885	(385)	(A)	Personnel
Labour efficiency variance [(5,400 × 0.25) − 1,300] × £5	250	(F)	Production
Fixed overhead spending (6,000 − 6,350)	(350)	(A)	Various – depends on the nature of the overheads
Total net variances	£795	(A)	

Budgeted profit	£5,250
Less Total net variance	(795)
Actual profit	£4,455

13.4 (a) Flexing the budget identifies what the profit would have been, had the only difference between the the original budget and the actual figures been concerned with the difference in volume of output. Comparing this profit figure with that in the original budget reveals the profit difference (variance) arising solely from the volume difference (sales volume variance). Thus, flexing the budget does not mean at all that volume differences do not matter. Flexing the budget is the means of discovering the effect on profit of the volume difference.

In one sense, all variances are 'water under the bridge', to the extent that the past cannot be undone, and so it is impossible to go back to the last control period and put in a better performance. Identifying variances can, however, be useful in identifying where things went wrong, which should enable management to take steps to ensure that the same things do not to go wrong in the future.

(b) Variances will not tell you what went wrong. They should, however, be a great help in identifying the manager within whose sphere of responsibility things went wrong. That manager should know why it went wrong. In this sense, variances identify relevant questions, but not answers.

(c) Identifying the reason for variances may well cost money, usually in terms of staff time. It is a matter of judgement in any particular situation, of balancing the cost of investigation against the potential benefits. As is usual in such judgements, it is difficult, before undertaking the investigation, to know either the cost or the likely benefit.

In general, significant variances, particularly adverse ones, should be investigated. Persistent (over a period of months) smaller variances should also be investigated. It should not automatically be assumed that favourable variances can be ignored. They indicate that things are not going according to plan, possibly because the plans (budgets) are flawed.

(d) Research evidence does not show this. It seems to show that managers tend to be most motivated by having as a target the most difficult goals that they find acceptable.

(e) Budgets normally provide the basis of feedforward and feedback control. During a budget preparation period, potential problems (for example a potential stock shortage) might be revealed. Steps can then be taken to revise the plans in order to avoid the potential problem. This is an example of a feedforward control: potential problems are anticipated and eliminated before they can occur.

Budgetary control is a very good example of feedback control, where a signal that something is going wrong triggers steps to take corrective action for the future.

13.5 Bradley-Allen Ltd

(a)

	Budget			Actual	
	Original	Flexed		Actual	
Output (units) (production and sales)	800	950		950	
	£	£		£	
Sales	64,000	76,000		73,000	
Raw materials – A	(12,000)	(14,250)	(285 kg)	(15,200)	(310 kg)
– B	(16,000)	(19,000)	(950 m)	(18,900)	(920 m)
Labour – skilled	(4,000)	(4,750)	(950 hr)	(4,628)	(890 hr)
– unskilled	(10,000)	(11,875)	(2,968.75 hr)	(11,275)	(2,750 hr)
Fixed overheads	(12,000)	(12,000)		(11,960)	
Operating profit	10,000	14,125		11,037	

Sales variances

Volume: 10,000 – 14,125 = £4,125   (F)

Price: 76,000 – 73,000 = £3,000   (A)

Direct material A variances

Usage:	$[(950 \times 0.3) - 310] \times £50 = £1,250$	(A)
Price:	$(310 \times £50) - £15,200 = £300$	(F)

Direct material B variances

Usage:	$[(950 \times 1) - 920] \times £20 = £600$	(F)
Price:	$(920 \times £20) - £18,900 = £500$	(A)

Skilled direct labour variances

Efficiency:	$[(950 \times 1) - 890] \times £5 = £300$	(F)
Rate:	$(890 \times £5) - £4,628 = £178$	(A)

Unskilled direct labour variances

Efficiency:	$[(950 \times 3.125) - 2,750] \times £4 = £875$	(F)
Rate:	$(2,750 \times £4) - £11,275 = £275$	(A)

Fixed overhead variances

Spending:	$(12,000 - 11,960) = £40$	(F)

Budgeted profit				£10,000
Sales:	Volume	4,125	(F)	
	Price	(3,000)	(A)	1,125
Direct material A:	Usage	(1,250)	(A)	
	Price	300	(F)	(950)
Direct material B:	Usage	600	(F)	
	Price	(500)	(A)	100
Skilled labour:	Efficiency	300	(F)	
	Rate	(178)	(A)	122
Unskilled labour:	Efficiency	875	(F)	
	Rate	(275)	(A)	600
Fixed overheads:	Expenditure			40
Actual profit				£11,037

(b) The statement in (a) is useful to management because it enables them to see where there have been failures to meet the original budget and to be able to quantify the extent of such failures. This means that junior managers can be held accountable for the performance of their particular area of responsibility.

	Budget			
	Original	Flexed		Actual
Output (units) (production and sales)	1,200	1,000*		1,000*
	£	£		£
Sales	24,000	20,000		18,000
Raw materials	(9,000)	(7,500)	(3,000 kg)	(7,400)	(2,800 kg)
Labour	(2,700)	(2,250)	(500 hr)	(2,300)	(510 hr)
Fixed overheads	(4,320)	(4,320)		(4,100)
Operating profit	7,980	5,930		4,200

*The sales of £18,000 were at 10 per cent below standard price, at £18 each. Sales volume was, therefore, 1,000 units (that is, £18,000/18).

Sales variances

Volume:	(7,980 – 5,930) = £2,050	(A)
Price:	(20,000 – 18,000) = £2,000	(A)

Direct material variances

Usage:	[(1,000 × 3) – 2,800] × £2.50 =	£500	(F)
Price:	(2,800 × £2.50) – £7,400 =	£400	(A)

Direct labour variances

Efficiency:	[(1,000 × 0.5) – 510] × £4.50 =	£45	(A)
Rate:	(510 × £4.50) – £2,300 =	£5	(A)

Fixed overhead variances

Spending:	(4,320 – 4,100) =	£220	(F)

(The budgeted fixed overheads were £3.60 × 1,200 = £4,320)

Budgeted profit (1,200 × £6.65)			= £7,980	
Variances				
Sales:	Volume	(2,050)	(A)	
	Price	(2,000)	(A)	(4,050)
Direct materials:	Usage	500	(F)	
	Price	(400)	(A)	100
Direct labour:	Efficiency	(45)	(A)	
	Rate	(5)	(A)	(50)
Fixed overheads:	Expenditure			220
Actual profit				£4,200

Since the low sales demand, and the reaction to it of dropping sales prices, seems to be caused by factors outside the control of managers of Mowbray Ltd, there are strong grounds for dividing the sales volume and price variances into those that are controllable and those that are not (planning variances).

Chapter 14

14.1 Mylo Ltd

(a) The annual depreciation of the two projects is:

$$\text{Project 1: } \frac{(£100,000 - £7,000)}{3} = £31,000$$

$$\text{Project 2: } \frac{(£60,000 - £6,000)}{3} = £18,000$$

Project 1
(i)

	Year 0 £000	Year 1 £000	Year 2 £000	Year 3 £000
Net profit(loss)		29	(1)	2
Depreciation		31	31	31
Capital cost	(100)			
Residual value				7
Net cash flows	(100)	60	30	40
10% discount factor	1.000	0.909	0.826	0.751
Present value	(100.00)	54.54	24.78	30.04
Net present value	9.36			

(ii) Clearly the IRR lies above 10 per cent; try 15 per cent:

15% discount factor	1.000	0.870	0.756	0.658
Present value	(100.00)	52.20	22.68	26.32
Net present value	1.20			

Thus the IRR lies a little above 15 per cent, perhaps around 16 per cent.
(iii) To find the payback period, the cumulative cash flows are calculated:

Cumulative cash flows	(100)	(40)	(10)	30

Thus the payback will occur after about 2 years 3 months (assuming that the cash flows accrue equally over the year), or 3 years if we assume year-end cash flows.

Project 2
(i)

	Year 0 £000	Year 1 £000	Year 2 £000	Year 3 £000
Net profit(loss)		18	(2)	4
Depreciation		18	18	18

	Year 0 £000	Year 1 £000	Year 2 £000	Year 3 £000
Capital cost	(60)			
Residual value				6
Net cash flows	(60)	36	16	28
10% discount factor	1.000	0.909	0.826	0.751
Present value	(60.00)	32.72	13.22	21.03
Net present value	6.97			

(ii) Clearly the IRR lies above 10 per cent; try 15 per cent:

15% discount factor	1.000	0.870	0.756	0.658
Present value	(60.00)	31.32	12.10	18.42
Net present value	1.84			

Thus the IRR lies a little above 15 per cent; perhaps around 17 per cent.

(iii) The cumulative cash flows are:

Cumulative cash flows	(60)	(24)	(8)	20

Thus, the payback will occur after about 2 years 3 months (assuming that the cash flows accrue equally over the year) or 3 years (assuming year-end cash flows).

(b) Presuming that Mylo Ltd is pursuing a wealth-maximisation objective, project 1 is preferable since it has the higher NPV. The difference between the two NPVs is not significant, however.

(c) NPV is the preferred method of assessing investment opportunities because it fully addresses each of the following:

- *The timing of the cash flows.* Discounting the various cash flows associated with each project, according to when they are expected to arise, takes account of the fact that cash flows do not all occur simultaneously. Associated with this is the fact that by discounting, using the opportunity cost of finance (namely the return that the next-best alternative opportunity would generate), the net benefit, after financing costs have been met, is identified (as the NPV).
- *The whole of the relevant cash flows.* NPV includes all of the relevant cash flows irrespective of when they are expected to occur. It treats them differently according to their date of occurrence, but they are all taken into account in the calculation of the NPV and they all have, or can have, an influence on the decision.
- *The objectives of the business.* NPV is the only method of appraisal where the output of the analysis has a direct bearing on the wealth of the business. (Positive NPVs enhance wealth; negative NPVs reduce it.) Since most private-sector businesses seek to increase their value and wealth, NPV clearly is the best approach to use.

14.3 Haverhill Engineers Ltd

(a) The first step is to calculate the cash savings from the new machine:

	Per-unit cash flow	
	Old line	New line
	p	p
Selling price	150	150
Less Materials	(40)	(36)
Labour	(22)	(10)
Variable overheads	(14)	(14)
Cash contribution	74	90

The cash saving per unit is (90p – 74p) = 16p. Hence, the cash saving for 1,000,000 units a year is:

$$1{,}000{,}000 \times 16p = £160{,}000$$

The incremental cash flows arising from the project are:

	Year 0 £000	Year 1 £000	Year 2 £000	Year 3 £000	Year 4 £000	Year 5 £000
Cash savings		160	160	160	160	160
New machine	(700)					100
Old machine residual value	50					
Working capital	160					(160)
Net cash flows	(490)	160	160	160	160	100

(b)

Discount factor	1.000	0.909	0.826	0.751	0.683	0.621
Present value	(490)	145.4	132.2	120.2	109.3	62.1
NPV	79.2					

Thus the project's NPV is £79,200.

(c)

Discount factor (20%)	1.000	0.833	0.694	0.579	0.482	0.402
Present value	(490.0)	133.3	111.0	92.6	77.1	40.2
NPV	(35.8) (that is, NPV of £35,800 negative)					

We can see that increasing the discount rate from 10 per cent to 20 per cent, an increase of 10 percentage points, decreases the NVP from +79.2 to –35.8, a decrease of 115. This is an average decrease of 11.5 per 1 per cent increase in the discount rate. The rate at which the project would have a zero NPV (the IRR) is therefore about 10% + (79.2/11.5) = 16.9%, that is, about 17 per cent.

(d) NPV is the difference between the future cash inflows and outflows relating to a project after taking account of the time value of money. The time value of money is taken into account by discounting the future cash flows, using the cost of finance as the appropriate discount rate. The decision rule for NPV is that projects with a positive NPV should be accepted, as this will lead to an increase in shareholder wealth.

The internal rate of return is the discount rate that, when applied to the projected cash flows of the project, produces a zero NPV. The IRR is compared with a 'hurdle rate', determined by management, to see whether the project should be undertaken.

The IRR approach is currently as popular as the NPV method among practising managers. Managers appear to like to use percentage figures, as a basis for evaluating projects, rather than absolute figures. However, the IRR method has disadvantages compared with the NPV method, which were discussed in the chapter.

Normally, the two methods will give the same solution concerning acceptance/rejection of a project and will usually give the same solution concerning the ranking of projects. However, where a difference occurs, it is the NPV method that provides the more reliable answer. As a result, the NPV approach is considered to be the more appropriate method to adopt.

14.4 Lansdown Engineers Ltd

(a)

	System A			System B		
	Cash flow	Discount factor at 12%	NPV	Cash flow	Discount factor at 12%	NPV
	£000		£000	£000		£000
Initial outlay (year 0)	(70)	1.000	(70)	(150)	1.000	(150)
Annual cost (years 1 to 10)	(140)	5.651	(791)*	(120)	5.651	(678)
Residual value (year 10)	14	0.322	4	30	0.322	10
			(857)			(818)

(b)

	System B £000	Existing system £000	Incremental cost £000
Initial outlay (year 0)	(150)	0	(150)
Residual value (year 0)	–	5	5
Overhaul (year 0)	–	20	20
			(125)
Annual cost (years 1 to 10)	120	145	25
Residual value (year 10)	30	10	20

We can only find the IRR by trial and error. Let us use 15 per cent for the first try.

(c)

	Cash flow	Discount factor at 15%	NPV
	£000		£000
Year 0	(125)	1.000	(125)
Years 1 to 10	25	5.019**	125
Year 10	20	0.247	5
			5

Since the NPV is only + 5, 15 per cent is fairly close to the IRR but slightly below it. Let us try 16 per cent.

	Cash flow	Discount factor at 16%	NPV
	£000		£000
Year 0	(125)	1.000	(125)
Years 1 to 10	25	4.833***	121
Year 10	20	0.227	5
			1

We can now say that the IRR is very close to 16 per cent (slightly over).

*This calculation is a bit of a short cut. Since each year has the same cash flow (that is, 140), instead of multiplying each of the ten 140s by its appropriate discount rate, depending on which year it occurs, and adding the ten resulting figures together, we can adopt a slight variation. This is to add the discount factors for the years 1 to 10 inclusive, and multiply this total (5.651) by 140. If you look at the present value table in the appendix to this chapter, you will see that the figures in the 12 per cent column are 0.893 for one year, 0.797 for two years and so on until year 10 when it is 0.322. Adding these ten figures together gives 5.651.
**5.019 is the equivalent to 5.651, but for a 15 per cent discount rate.
***4.833 is the equivalent to 5.651 and 5.019, but for a 16 per cent discount rate.

(d) B is cheaper than A. It is also cheaper than the existing system. The company should, therefore, consider installing system B.

14.5

Chesterfield Wanderers

(a) and (b)

	Player option					
	0	1	2	3	4	5
	£000	£000	£000	£000	£000	£000
Sale of player	220					100
Purchase of Bazza	(1,000)					
Sponsorship, etc.		120	120	120	120	120

	0 £000	1 £000	2 £000	3 £000	4 £000	5 £000
Gate receipts		250	130	130	130	130
Salaries paid		(80)	(80)	(80)	(80)	(120)
Salaries saved		40	40	40	40	60
Net cash received(paid)	(780)	330	210	210	210	290
Discount factor 10%	1.000	0.909	0.826	0.751	0.683	0.621
Present values	(780)	300.0	173.5	157.7	143.4	180.1
NPV	174.7					

Ground improvement option

	1 £000	2 £000	3 £000	4 £000	5 £000
Ground improvements	(1,000)				
Increased gate receipts	(180)	440	440	440	440
	(1,180)	440	440	440	440
Discount factor 10%	0.909	0.826	0.751	0.683	0.621
Present values	(1,072.6)	363.4	330.4	300.5	273.2
NPV	194.9				

(c) The ground improvement option provides the higher NPV and is therefore the preferable option, based on the objective of shareholder wealth maximisation.

(d) A professional football club may not wish to pursue an objective of shareholder wealth maximisation. It may prefer to invest in quality players in an attempt to enjoy future sporting success. If this is the case, the NPV approach will be less appropriate because the club is not pursung a strict wealth-maximisation objective.

14.6 Newton Electronics Ltd

(a)

Option 1

	Year 0 £m	Year 1 £m	Year 2 £m	Year 3 £m	Year 4 £m	Year 5 £m
Plant and equipment	(9.0)					1.0
Sales		24.0	30.8	39.6	26.4	10.0
Variable costs		(11.2)	(19.6)	(25.2)	(16.8)	(7.0)
Fixed costs (ex. depr'n)		(0.8)	(0.8)	(0.8)	(0.8)	(0.8)
Working capital	(3.0)					3.0
Marketing costs		(2.0)	(2.0)	(2.0)	(2.0)	(2.0)
Opportunity costs		(0.1)	(0.1)	(0.1)	(0.1)	(0.1)
	(12.0)	9.9	8.3	11.5	6.7	4.1
Discount factor 10%	1.000	0.909	0.826	0.751	0.683	0.621
Present value	(12.0)	9.0	6.9	8.6	4.6	2.5
NPV	19.6					

	Year 0 £m	Year 1 £m	Year 2 £m	Year 3 £m	Year 4 £m	Year 5 £m
Royalties	–	4.4	7.7	9.9	6.6	2.8
Discount factor 10%	1.000	0.909	0.826	0.751	0.683	0.621
Present value	–	4.0	6.4	7.4	4.5	1.7
NPV	24.0					

Option 3

	Year 0	Year 2
Instalments	12.0	12.0
Discount factor 10%	1.000	0.826
Present value	12.0	10.0
NPV	22.0	

(b) Before making a final decision, the board should consider the following factors:

- The long-term competitiveness of the business may be affected by the sale of the patents.
- At present, the company is not involved in manufacturing and marketing products. Would a change in direction be desirable?
- The company will probably have to buy in the skills necessary to produce the product itself. This will involve costs, and problems will be incurred. Has this been taken into account?
- How accurate are the forecasts made and how valid are the assumptions on which they are based?

(c) Option 2 has the highest NPV and is therefore the most attractive to shareholders. However, the accuracy of the forecasts should be checked before a final decision is made.

Chapter 15

15.1 (a) The main factors to take into account are:

- *Risk.* If a business borrows, there is a risk that at the maturity date of the loan the business will not have the funds to repay the amount owing and will be unable to find a suitable form of replacement borrowing. With short-term loans, the maturity dates will arrive more quickly and the type of risk outlined will occur at more frequent intervals.
- *Matching.* A company may wish to match the life of an asset with the maturity date of the borrowing. In other words, long-term assets will be purchased with long-term loan funds. A certain level of current assets, which form part of the long-term asset base of the business, may also be funded by long-term borrowing. Those current assets that fluctuate owing to seasonality and so on will be funded by short-term borrowing. This approach to funding assets will help reduce risks for the company.

- *Cost.* Interest rates for long-term loans may be higher than for short-term loans as investors may seek extra compensation for having their funds locked up for a long period. However, issue costs may be higher for short-term loans as there will be a need to refund at more frequent intervals.
- *Flexibility.* Short-term loans may be more flexible. It may be difficult to repay long-term loans before the maturity period.

(b) When deciding to grant a loan, a lender should consider the following factors:

- Security
- Purpose of the loan
- Ability of the borrower to repay
- Loan period
- Availability of funds
- Character and integrity of the senior managers.

(c) Loan conditions may include:

- The need to obtain permission before issuing further loans
- The need to maintain a certain level of liquidity during the loan period
- A restriction on the level of dividends and directors pay.

15.3 (a) When deciding between long-term debt and equity finance, the following factors should be considered:

- *Cost.* The cost of equity is higher over the longer term than the cost of loans. This is because equity is a riskier form of investment. Moreover, loan interest is tax deductible whereas dividend payments are not. However, when profits are poor, there is no obligation to pay equity shareholders whereas the obligation to pay lenders will continue.
- *Gearing.* The company may wish to take on additional gearing in order to increase the returns to shareholders. This can be achieved providing the returns from the loans invested exceed the cost of servicing the loans.
- *Risk.* Loan capital increases the level of risk to equity shareholders, who will in turn require higher rates of return. If the level of gearing is high in relation to industry norms, the credit standing of the business may be affected. Managers, although strictly concerned with the interests of shareholders, may feel that their own positions are at risk if a high level of gearing is obtained. However, they may be more inclined to take on additional risk if their remuneration is linked to the potential benefits which may flow from higher gearing.

(b) Convertible loan stock provides the investor with the right, but not the obligation, to convert the loan stock into ordinary shares at a specified future date and a specified price. The investor will exercise this option only if the market value of the shares is above the 'exercise price' at the specified date. The investor will change status from that of lender to that of owner when the option to convert is exercised.

If the company is successful, the convertible loan stock will be self-liquidating, which can be convenient for the company. The company may also be able to negotiate lower rates of interest or fewer loan restrictions because of the potential gains on conversion.

Convertible loan stock is often used in takeover deals. The target company shareholders may find this form of finance attractive if they are uncertain as to the future prospects of the combined business. The investors will be guaranteed a fixed rate of return and, if the combined business is successful, they will be able to participate in this success through the conversion process. However, convertible loan stock can be viewed as part-loan and part-equity finance, and some investors may find it difficult to assess the value to be placed on such securities.

(c) Debt factoring is a service provided by a financial institution (the factor) whereby the sales records of a client company are managed, and credit evaluation and credit protection services may also be offered. The factor will also be prepared to advance funds to the client company of up to 85 per cent of approved sales outstanding. The advantage of factoring is that it can provide an efficient debt-collection service and can release management time for other things. This may be of particular value to small and medium-sized businesses. The company also receives an immediate injection of finance and there is greater certainty concerning cash receipts. The level of finance provided through factoring will increase in line with the increase in the level of activity of the business.

In the past, factoring has been viewed as a form of last-resort lending and so customers may interpret factoring as a sign of financial weakness. However, this image is now fast disappearing. Factoring is quite expensive – a service charge of up to 3 per cent of turnover is levied. Setting up the factoring agreement can be time-consuming, and so factoring agreements are not suitable for short-term borrowing requirements.

15.5 Raphael Ltd

The existing credit policies have the following costs:

	£
Cost of investment in trade debtors [(50/365) × £2.4m × 12%]	39,452
Cost of bad debts (1.5% × £2.4m)	36,000
Total cost	75,452

Employing a factor will result in the following costs and savings:

	£
Charges of the factor (2% × £2.4m)	48,000
Interest charges on advance [(30/365) × (80% × £2.4m) × 11%]	17,359
Interest charges on overdraft [(30/365) × (20% × £2.4m) × 12%]	4,734
Total cost	70,093
Less Credit control savings	(18,000)
Net cost	52,093

We can see the net cost of factoring is lower than the existing costs, and so there would be a benefit gained from entering into an agreement with the factor.

15.6 Carpets Direct plc

(a) The earnings per share (P/E) is:

$$\frac{\text{Profit after taxation}}{\text{Number of ordinary shares}} = \frac{£4.5m}{120m} = £0.0375$$

The current market value per share is:

$$\text{Earnings per share} \times \text{P/E} = £0.0375 \times 22 = £0.825$$

The rights issue price will be £0.825, less 20 per cent discount = £0.66.

The theoretical ex-rights price is:

	£
Original shares (4 @ £0.825)	3.30
Rights share (1 @ £0.66)	0.66
Value of five shares following rights issue	3.96

Therefore, the value of one share following the rights issue is:

$$\frac{£3.96}{5} = 79.2p$$

(b)

Value of one share after rights issue	79.2p
Cost of a rights share	(66.0p)
Value of rights to shareholder	13.2p

(c) (i) Taking up rights issue

	£
Shareholding following rights issue [(4,000 + 1,000) × 79.2p]	3,960
Less Cost of rights shares (1,000 × 66p)	(660)
Shareholder wealth	3,300

(ii) Selling the rights

	£
Shareholding following rights issue (4,000 × 79.2p)	3,168
Add Proceeds from sale of rights (1,000 × 13.2p)	132
Shareholder wealth	3,300

(iii) Doing nothing

As the rights are neither purchased nor sold, the shareholder wealth following the rights issue will be:

Shareholding (4,000 × 79.2p)	3,168

We can see that the investor will have the same wealth under the first two options. However, by the investor doing nothing, the rights offer will lapse and so the investor will lose the value of the rights and will be worse off.

15.8 Telford Engineers plc

(a)

	Debt £m		Shares £m
Profit before interest and tax	21.00		21.00
Interest payable	(7.80)	[5 + (20 × 14%)]	(5.00)
Profit before taxation	13.20		16.00
Corporation tax (30%)	(3.96)		(4.80)
Profit after tax	9.24		11.20
Dividends payable	(4.00)		(5.00)
Retained profit	5.24		6.20

	Debt £m	Shares £m	
Capital and reserves			
Share capital 25p shares	20.00	25.00	(20 + (20 × 0.25))
Share premium	–	15.00	(20 × (1.00 – 0.25))
Reserves*	48.24	49.20	
	68.24	89.20	
Loans	50.00	30.00	
	118.24	119.20	

*The reserves figures are the 2001 reserves *plus* the 2002 retained profit. The 2001 figure for share capital and reserves was 63, of which 20 (that is, 80 × 0.25) was share capital, leaving 43 as reserves. Add to that the retained profit for 2002 (that is, 5.24 (debt) or 6.20 (shares)).

(b)

Earnings per share		
Debt (9.24/80)	11.55p	
Shares (11.20/100)		11.20p

(c) The debt alternative will raise the gearing ratio and lower the interest cover of the business. This should not provide any real problems for the business as long as profits reach the expected level for 2001 and remain at that level. However, there is an increased financial risk as a result of higher gearing and the adequacy of the additional returns expected to compensate for this higher risk must be carefully considered by shareholders. The figures above suggest only a marginal increase in EPS compared with the equity alternative at the expected level of profit for 2001.

The share alternative will have the effect of reducing the gearing ratio and is less risky. However, there may be a danger of dilution of control by existing share-holders under this alternative and it may, therefore, prove unacceptable to them. An issue of equity shares may, however, provide greater opportunity for flexibility in financing future projects.

Information concerning current loan repayment terms and the attitude of shareholders and existing lenders towards the alternative financing methods would be useful.

Chapter 16

16.1 Hercules Wholesalers Ltd

(a) The liquidity ratios of the company seem low. The current ratio is only 1.1 (that is, 306/285) and its acid test ratio is 0.6 (that is, 163/285). This latter ratio suggests the company has insufficient liquid assets to pay its short-term obligations. A cash-flow projection for the next period would provide a better insight to the liquidity position of the business. The bank overdraft seems high and it would be useful to know whether the bank is pressing for a reduction and what overdraft limit has been established for the company.

(b) The operating cash cycle can be calculated as follows:

No. of days

Average stockholding period:

$$\frac{[(\text{Opening stock} + \text{Closing stock})/2] \times 360}{\text{Cost of sales}} = \frac{[(125 + 143)/2] \times 360}{323} = 110$$

Add Average settlement period for debtors:

$$\frac{\text{Trade debtors} \times 360}{\text{Credit sales}} = \frac{163}{452} \times 360 = \underline{130}$$

$$= 279$$

Less Average settlement period for creditors:

$$\frac{\text{Trade creditor} \times 360}{\text{Credit purchases}} = \frac{145}{341} \times 360 = \underline{153}$$

$$\underline{126}$$

(c) The company can reduce the operating cash cycle in a number of ways. The average stockholding period seems quite long: at present, average stocks held represent almost five months' sales. This period may be reduced by reducing the level of stocks held. Similarly, the average settlement period for debtors seems long at more than four months' sales. This may be reduced by imposing tighter credit control, offering discounts, charging interest on overdue accounts, and so on. However, any policy decisions concerning stocks and debtors must take account of current trading conditions.

The operating cash cycle could also be reduced by extending the period of credit taken to pay suppliers. However, for the reasons mentioned in the chapter, this option must be given careful consideration.

16.4 Dylan Ltd
New proposals from credit department

	£000	£000
Current level of investment in debtors		
[£20m × (60/365)]		3,288
Proposed level of investment in debtors		
[(£20m × 60%)(30/365)]	(986)	
[(£20m × 40%)(50/365)]	(1,096)	(2,082)
Reduction in level of investment		1,206

The reduction in overdraft interest as a result of the reduction in the level of investment will be:

$$£1,206,000 \times 14\% = £169,000$$

Thus

	£000	£000
Cost of cash discounts offered (£20m × 60% × $2\frac{1}{2}$%)		300
Additional cost of credit administration		20
		320
Bad debt savings	(100)	
Interest charge savings (see above)	(169)	(269)
Net annual cost of new credit policy		51

These calculations show that the company would incur additional annual costs in order to implement this proposal. It would, therefore, be cheaper to stay with the existing credit policy.

16.6 Boswell Enterprises Ltd

(a)

	Current policy		New policy	
	£000	£000	£000	£000
Debtors				
[(£3m × 1/12 × 30%)				
+ (£3m × 2/12 × 70%)]		425.0		
[(£3.15m × 1/12 × 60%) +				
(£3.15m × 2/12 × 40%)]				367.5
Stocks				
[(£3m − (£3m × 20%) × 3/12]		600.0		
{[£3.15m − (£3.15m × 20%)] × 3/12}				630.0
Cash (fixed)		140.0		140.0
		1,165.0		1,137.5
Creditors				
[£3m − (£3m × 20%) × 2/12]	(400.0)			
{[£3.15m − (£3.15m × 20%)] × 2/12}			(420.0)	
Accrued variable expenses				
(£3m × 1/12 × 10%)	(25.0)			
(£3.15m × 1/12 × 10%)			(26.3)	
Accrued fixed expenses	(15.0)	(440.0)	(15.0)	(461.3)
Investment in working capital		725.0		676.2

(b) The forecast net profit for the year

	Current policy		New policy	
	£000	£000	£000	£000
Sales		3,000.0		3,150.0
Cost of goods sold		(2,400.0)		(2,520.0)
Gross profit (20%)		600.0		630.0
Variable expenses (10%)	(300.0)		(315.0)	
Fixed expenses	(180.0)		(180.0)	
Discounts	−	(480.0)	(47.3)	542.3
Net profit		120.0		87.7

(c) Under the proposed policy we can see that the investment in working capital will be slightly lower than under the current policy. However, profits will be substantially lower as a result of offering discounts. The increase in sales resulting from the discounts will not be sufficient to offset the additional costs of making the discounts to customers. It seems that the company should, therefore, stick with its current policy.

16.7 Delphi plc

(a) The debtors ageing schedule is:

	1 month or below £000	%	Number of months outstanding 1 to 2 months £000	%	2 to 3 months £000	%	Total debtors £000	%
February								
TV and hi-fi	20.0	(22.2)					20.0	(22.2)
Music	30.0	(33.3)					30.0	(33.3)
Retail	40.0	(44.5)					40.0	(44.5)
	90.0	(100.0)					90,00	(100.0)
March								
TV and hi-fi	20.8	(12.5)					20.8	(12.5)
Music	31.8	(19.2)	30.0	(18.1)			61.8	(37.3)
Retail	43.2	(26.1)	40.0	(24.1)	____	____	83.2	(50.2)
	95.8	(57.8)	70.0	(42.2)			165.8	(100.0)
April								
TV and hi-fi	21.6	(10.0)					21.6	(10.0)
Music	33.8	(15.6)	31.8	(14.7)			65.6	(30.3)
Retail	46.6	(21.4)	43.2	(19.9)	40.0	(18.4)	129.8	(59.7)
	102.0	(47.0)	75.0	(34.6)	40.0	(18.4)	217.0	(100.0)
May								
TV and hi-fi	22.4	(9.6)					22.4	(9.6)
Music	35.8	(15.4)	33.8	(14.6)			69.6	(30.0)
Retail	50.4	(21.7)	46.6	(20.1)	43.2	(18.6)	140.2	(60.4)
	108.6	(46.7)	80.4	(34.7)	43.2	(18.6)	232.2	(100.0)

We can see that the debtors figure will increase substantially in the first four months. The retail chains will account for about 60 per cent of the total debtors outstanding by May as this group has the fastest rate of growth. There is also a significant decline in the proportion of total debts outstanding from TV and hi-fi shops over this period.

(b) In answering this part of the question, you should refer to the 'five Cs of credit' that were discussed in detail in the chapter.

(c) In answering this part of the question, a discussion of factoring or invoice discounting is appropriate. Both of these methods are discussed in Chapter 15.

16.8 Goliath plc

(a) (i) The existing operating cash cycle can be calculated as follows:

	No. of days

$$\text{Stockholding period} = \frac{\text{Stock at year-end}}{\text{Cost of sales}} \times 365$$

$$= \frac{560}{1,440} \times 365 = \qquad\qquad\qquad 142$$

$$\textit{Add}\ \text{Debtors settlement period} = \frac{\text{Debtors at year-end}}{\text{Sales}} \times 365$$

$$= \frac{565}{2,400} \times 365 = \qquad\qquad\qquad \underline{86}$$

$$228$$

$$\textit{Less}\ \text{Creditors settlement period} = \frac{\text{Creditors at year-end}}{\text{Purchases}} \times 365$$

$$= \frac{451}{1,450} \times 365 = \qquad\qquad\qquad \underline{(114)}$$

Operating cash cycle $\underline{114}$

The new operating cash cycle is:

	No. of days

$$\text{Stockholding period} = \frac{(560 \times 1.15)}{(2,400 \times 1.10) \times 0.60} \times 365 = \qquad 148$$

Debtors settlement period = 86 + 20 $\underline{106}$

                                                         254

Less Creditors settlement period = 114 + 15 $\underline{(129)}$

                                                         125

New operating cash cycle   125

Existing operating cash cycle $\underline{(114)}$
Increase(decrease) in operating cash cycle (days) $\underline{11}$

(ii)

	£000
Increase(decrease) in stock held [(560 × 1.15) − 560]	84.0
Increase(decrease) in debtors {[(2,400 × 1.1) × (106/365)] − 565}	201.7
	285.7
(Increase)decrease in creditors [1,668 × (129/365) − 451]	(138.6)
Increase(decrease) in net investment	147.1

(iii)

	£000	£000
Gross profit increase [(2,400 × 0.1) × 0.40]		96.0
Adjust for		
Admin. expenses increase (15%)	(45.0)	
Bad debts increase	(120.0)	
Interest (10%) on borrowing for increased net investment in working capital (147.1)	(14.7)	(179.7)
Increase(decrease) in net profit before tax		(83.7)
Decrease in tax charge for the period (25% × 83.7)		20.9
Increase (decrease) in net profit after tax		(62.8)

(b) There has been an increase in the operating cash cycle and this will have an adverse effect on liquidity. The existing debtors period and stockholding period already appear to be quite high, and any increase in either of these periods must be justified. The planned increase in the creditors period must also be justified because it may risk the loss of goodwill from suppliers. Although there is an expected increase in turnover of £240,000 from adopting the new policy, the net profit after taxation will decrease by £62,800. This represents a substantial decrease when compared with the previous year. (The increase in bad debts is a major reason why the net profit is adversly affected.) There is also a substantial increase in the net investment in stocks, debtors and creditors, which seem high in relation to the expected increase in sales. The new policy requires a significant increase in investment and is expected to generate lower profits than are currently being enjoyed. It should, therefore, be rejected.

Appendix A

A.1

Account to be debited	Account to be credited
(a) Stock	Trade creditors
(b) Capital (or a separate drawings account)	Cash
(c) Loan interest	Cash
(d) Stock	Cash
(e) Cash	Trade debtors
(f) Wages	Cash
(g) Capital (or a separate drawings account)	Trade debtors
(h) Trade creditors	Cash
(i) Electricity (or heat and light)	Cash
(j) Cash	Sales

Note that the precise name given to an account is not crucial so long as those who are using the information are clear as to what each account deals with.

(a) and (b)

Cash

		£			£
1 Feb	Capital	6,000	3 Feb	Stock	2,600
15 Feb	Sales	4,000	5 Feb	Equipment	800
28 Feb	Trade debtors	2,500	9 Feb	Rent	250
			10 Feb	Fuel and electricity	240
			11 Feb	General expenses	200
			21 Feb	Capital	1,000
			25 Feb	Trade creditors	2,000
			28 Feb	Balance c/d	5,410
		12,500			12,500
1 Mar	Balance b/d	5,410			

Capital

		£			£
21 Feb	Cash	1,000	1 Feb	Cash	6,000
28 Feb	Balance c/d	5,000			
		6,000			6,000
			1 Mar	Balance b/d	5,000
28 Feb	Balance c/d	7,410	28 Feb	Profit and loss	2,410
		7,410			7,410
			1 Mar	Balance b/d	7,410

Stock

		£			£
3 Feb	Cash	2,600	15 Feb	Cost of sales	2,400
6 Feb	Trade creditors	3,000	19 Feb	Cost of sales	2,300
			31 January	Balance c/d	900
		5,600			5,600
1 Mar	Balance b/d	900			

Equipment

		£			£
5 Feb	Cash	800			

Trade creditors

		£			£
25 Feb	Cash	2,000	6 Feb	Stock	3,000
28 Feb	Balance c/d	1,000			
		3,000			3,000
			1 Feb	Balance b/d	1,000

Rent

		£			£
9 Feb	Cash	250	28 Feb	Profit and loss	250

Fuel and electricity

		£			£
10 Feb	Cash	240	28 Feb	Profit and loss	240

General expenses

		£			£
11 Feb	Cash	200	28 Feb	Profit and loss	200

Sales

		£			£
28 February	Balance c/d	7,800	15 Feb	Cash	4,000
			19 Feb	Trade debtors	3,800
		7,800			7,800
28 Feb	Profit and loss	7,800	28 Feb	Balance b/d	7,800

Cost of sales

		£			£
15 Feb	Stock	2,400	28 Feb	Balance c/d	4,700
19 Feb	Stock	2,300			
		4,700			4,700
28 Feb	Balance b/d	4,700	28 Feb	Profit and loss	4,700

Trade debtors

		£			£
19 Feb	Sales	3,800	28 Feb	Cash	2,500
			28 Feb	Balance c/d	1,300
		3,800			3,800
1 Mar	Balance b/d	1,300			

(b) Trial balance as at 28 February

	Debits £	Credits £
Cash	5,410	
Capital		5,000
Stock	900	
Equipment	800	
Trade creditors		1,000
Rent	250	
Fuel and electricity	240	
General expenses	200	
Sales		7,800
Cost of sales	4,700	
Trade debtors	1,300	
	13,800	13,800

(c)

Profit and loss account

		£		£
28 Feb	Cost of sales	4,700	28 February Sales	7,800
28 Feb	Rent	250		
28 Feb	Fuel and electricity	240		
28 Feb	General expenses	200		
28 Feb	Capital (net profit)	2,410		
		7,800		7,800

Balance sheet as at 28 February

	£	£
Fixed assets:		
Equipment		800
Current assets:		
Stock	900	
Trade debtors	1,300	
Cash	5,410	
	7,610	
Current liabilities		
Trade creditors	1,000	
		6,610
		7,410
Capital		7,410

Profit and loss account for the month ended 28 February

	£	£
Sales		7,800
Cost of sales		4,700
Gross profit		3,100
Less Rent	250	
Fuel and electricity	240	
General expenses	200	
		690
Net profit for the month		2,410

Index

Page numbers in **bold** refer to definitions in glossary.